ADDITIONAL COOKBOOKS AVAILABLE FROM THE PUBLISHERS OF COOK'S COUNTRY INCLUDE:

The Side Dish Bible

Bowls

The Perfect Pie

How to Cocktail

Vegetables Illustrated

Spiced

The Ultimate Burger

The New Essentials Cookbook

Dinner Illustrated

Cook's Illustrated Revolutionary Recipes

Tasting Italy: A Culinary Journey

Cooking at Home with Bridget and Julia

The Complete Diabetes Cookbook

The Complete Slow Cooker

The Complete Make-Ahead Cookbook

The Complete Mediterranean Cookbook

The Complete Vegetarian Cookbook

The Complete Cooking for Two Cookbook

The Complete Cooking for Two Cookbook Gift Edition

Just Add Sauce

How to Braise Everything

How to Roast Everything

Nutritious Delicious

What Good Cooks Know

Cook's Science

The Science of Good Cooking

The Perfect Cake

The Perfect Cookie

Bread Illustrated

Master of the Grill

Kitchen Smarts: Questions and Answers to Boost Your Cooking I.Q.

Kitchen Hacks: How Clever Cooks Get Things Done

100 Recipes: The Absolute Best Way to Make the True Essentials

The New Family Cookbook

The *America's Test Kitchen* Cooking School Cookbook

The *Cook's Illustrated* Meat Book

The *Cook's Illustrated* Baking Book

The *Cook's Illustrated* Cookbook

The *America's Test Kitchen* Family Baking Book

The Best of *America's Test Kitchen* (2007–2020 Editions)

The Complete *America's Test Kitchen* TV Show Cookbook (2001–2019)

America's Test Kitchen Twentieth Anniversary TV Show Cookbook

Mediterranean Instant Pot

Instant Pot Ace Blender Cookbook

Cook It in Your Dutch Oven

Sous Vide for Everybody

Air Fryer Perfection

Multicooker Perfection

Food Processor Perfection

Pressure Cooker Perfection

Vegan for Everybody

Naturally Sweet

Foolproof Preserving

Paleo Perfected

The How Can It Be Gluten-Free Cookbook: Volume 2

The How Can It Be Gluten-Free Cookbook

The Best Mexican Recipes

Slow Cooker Revolution 2: The Easy Prep Edition

Slow Cooker Revolution

The Six-Ingredient Solution

The *America's Test Kitchen* Do-It-Yourself Cookbook

1993–2019 *Cook's Illustrated* Master Index

Cook's Illustrated Annual Hardbound Editions from each year of publication (1993–2019)

THE COOK'S ILLUSTRATED ALL-TIME BEST SERIES

All-Time Best Brunch

All-Time Best Dinners for Two

All-Time Best Sunday Suppers

All-Time Best Holiday Entertaining

All-Time Best Appetizers

All-Time Best Soups

COOK'S COUNTRY TITLES

Big Flavors from Italian America

One-Pan Wonders

Cook It in Cast Iron

Cook's Country Eats Local

The Complete *Cook's Country* TV Show Cookbook

Visit our online bookstore at www.CooksCountry.com to order any of our cookbooks listed above. You can also order subscriptions, gift subscriptions, and any of our cookbooks by calling 800-611-0759 inside the U.S., or 515-237-3663 if calling from outside the U.S.

$35.00

Copyright © 2019 by The Editors of *Cook's Country*
All rights reserved, including the right of reproduction in whole or in part in any form.
Published by *America's Test Kitchen*, 21 Drydock Avenue, Boston, MA 02210

Manufactured in the United States of America

ISBN: 978-1-948703-44-4
ISSN: 1552-1990

To get home delivery of *Cook's Country* magazine, call 800-526-8447 inside the U.S., or 515-237-3663 if calling from outside the U.S., or subscribe online at www.CooksCountry.com/Subscribe.

2019 Recipe Index

Q

R

Cook's Country

Popcorn Chicken
Crispy, Crunchy, Full of Flavor

Weeknight Beef Tacos
Ditch the Prefab Spice Mix

German Potato Salad
Bacon and Vinegar Make It

Cajun Stuffed Turkey Wings
Louisiana "Plate Lunch" Tradition

Triple-Chocolate Sticky Buns
We Took Them over the Top

Ultimate Caesar Salad
Step-by-Step Photos

Clementine Cake
Seasonal Glazed Citrus Treat

STICKY RIBS
Our supertender indoor baby
back ribs glisten with a vibrant
sweet-and-sour sauce.
PAGE 7

FEBRUARY/MARCH 2019
$5.95 U.S./$6.95 CANADA

0 74470 02742 3

03>

DISPLAY UNTIL MARCH 4, 2019

LETTER FROM THE EDITOR

COME CLOSER. IT'S just us now. No one's here to listen in.

Between you and me: Cooking can feel like a real pain sometimes, don't you think? Tell the truth.

Not always, of course. We love to cook, right? I think about cooking (and eating) more than I think about anything else. I daydream about it on the bus in the morning. Whenever I have time to spare or creative energy to exhaust, I head to the kitchen, just to tinker around.

But cooking is a relationship—a complicated, multifaceted, challenging relationship—and not every day is the same. Even for enthusiastic home cooks, there are times when cooking a meal is nothing more than a trip to downtown Dullsville. Uninspiring. Rote. Lackluster.

The best response to these moments, I think, is to stay on the horse and chase one more achievement. To remind yourself how good even small victories feel.

Sometimes all it takes is a quick half-hour effort, such as with our tear-out recipe cards in the middle of every issue of *Cook's Country*. Sometimes it means a more involved project, such as Sweet-and-Sour Baby Back Ribs (page 7), perfect for a Sunday afternoon. Sometimes it means exploring a road less traveled, such as savory Stuffed Turkey Wings (page 13), a beloved local specialty from Lafayette, Louisiana.

And every now and then, it's about embracing the unbridled, giddy exuberance of a completely audacious idea, such as my favorite recipe in this issue, Triple-Chocolate Sticky Buns (page 23). Brazen, extravagant, and way over the top in all the right ways, these buns are exciting to create and a joy to share. I recently produced a batch for some neighbors, and their smiles radiated with delight. I couldn't wait to get back into the kitchen.

TUCKER SHAW

Editor in Chief

P.S. *I invite you to sign up for our weekly* **Dinner Tonight** *email newsletter. Each Monday, I'll answer a common cooking question and offer one of our easy 30-minute recipes. To sign up, go to* **CooksCountry.com/dinnertonight**.

Cook's Country

Chief Executive Officer David Nussbaum
Chief Creative Officer Jack Bishop
Editor in Chief Tucker Shaw
Executive Managing Editor Todd Meier
Executive Food Editor Bryan Roof
Deputy Editor Scott Kathan
Senior Editors Morgan Bolling, Ashley Moore
Associate Editor Cecelia Jenkins
Associate Editor, Web Ashley Delma
Photo Team Manager Tim McQuinn
Test Cooks Alli Berkey, Natalie Estrada, Matthew Fairman
Lead Test Cook, Photo Team Jessica Rudolph
Assistant Test Cooks, Photo Team Sarah Ewald, Jacqueline Gochenouer, Eric Haessler

Senior Copy Editor Jill Campbell
Copy Editor Rachel Schowalter
Contributing Editor Eva Katz
Senior Science Research Editor Paul Adams
Hosts & Executive Editors, Television Bridget Lancaster, Julia Collin Davison

Executive Editors, Tastings & Testings Hannah Crowley, Lisa McManus
Senior Editors, Tastings & Testings Lauren Savoie, Kate Sha
Associate Editor, Tastings & Testings Miye Bromberg
Assistant Editors, Tastings & Testings Riddley Gemperlein-S Carolyn Grillo, Emily Phares

Creative Director John Torres
Photography Director Julie Cote
Art Director Susan Levin
Associate Art Director Maggie Edgar
Senior Staff Photographer Daniel J. van Ackere
Staff Photographers Steve Klise, Kevin White
Photography Producer Meredith Mulcahy

Director, Creative Operations Alice Carpenter
Senior Editor, Special Projects Christie Morrison
Senior Manager, Publishing Operations Taylor Argenzio
Imaging Manager Lauren Robbins
Production & Imaging Specialists Dennis Noble, Jessica Voas, Amanda Yong
Test Kitchen Director Erin McMurrer
Assistant Test Kitchen Director Alexxa Benson
Test Kitchen Manager Meridith Lippard
Test Kitchen Facilities Manager Kelly Ryan
Senior Kitchen Assistant Shopper Michelle Miller
Senior Kitchen Assistant Receiver Heather Tolmie
Lead Kitchen Assistant Ena Gudiel
Kitchen Assistants Gladis Campos, Blanca Castanza, Amarilys Merced, Arlene Rosario

Chief Financial Officer Jackie McCauley Ford
Senior Manager, Customer Support Tim Quinn
Customer Support Specialist Mitchell Axelson
Event Coordinator Michaela Hughes

Chief Revenue Officer Sara Domville
Director, Sponsorship Marketing & Client Services Christine Anagnostis

Chief Digital Officer Fran Middleton
VP, Marketing Natalie Vinard
Senior Director, Social Media Marketing Claire Oliverson
Social Media Manager Morgan Mannino
Social Media Coordinators Charlotte Errity, Sarah Sandler

Senior VP, Human Resources & Organizational Development Colleen Zelina
Human Resources Manager Jason Lynott

Director, Public Relations & Communications Brian Franklin
Public Relations Coordinator Madeleine Cohen

Photography Keller + Keller
Food Styling Catrine Kelty, Kendra Smith
Circulation Services ProCirc

On the cover: Sweet-and-Sour Baby Back Ribs

Illustration: Ross MacDonald

AIR FRYER PERFECTION

Air fryers promise hands-off ease, but getting the best results involves slightly more than simply turning on your machine and walking away. In Air Fryer Perfection we share test kitchen secrets that ensure even cooking; coax better browning; create the crispiest, crunchiest coatings; and guarantee juicy meat. You'll also learn how to make complete meals in an air fryer's compact space and which models impressed our tastings and testings team. Order your copy at **AmericasTestKitchen.com/airfryer**.

 Find us on **Facebook**
facebook.com/CooksCountry

 Find us on **Instagram**
instagram.com/CooksCountry

Follow us on **Pinterest**
pinterest.com/TestKitchen

 Follow us on **Twitter**
twitter.com/TestKitchen

AMERICA'S TEST KITCHEN ®

America's Test Kitchen is a real test kitchen located in Boston. It is the home of more than 60 test cooks, editors, and cookware specialists. Our mission is to test recipes until we understand exactly how and why they work and eventually arrive at the very best version. We also test kitchen equipment and supermarket ingredients in search of products that offer the best value and performance. You can watch us work by tuning in to *America's Test Kitchen* (AmericasTestKitchen.com) and *Cook's Country from America's Test Kitchen* (CooksCountry.com) on public television, and you can listen to our weekly segments on *The Splendid Table* on public radio. You can also follow us on Facebook, Twitter, Pinterest, and Instagram.

20

26

14

Cook's Country magazine (ISSN 1552-1990), number 85, is published bimonthly by America's Test Kitchen Limited Partnership, 21 Drydock Avenue, Suite 210E, Boston, MA 02210. Copyright 2019 America's Test Kitchen Limited Partnership. Periodicals postage paid at Boston, MA, and additional mailing offices, USPS #023453. Publications Mail Agreement No. 40020778. Return undeliverable Canadian addresses to P.O. Box 875, Station A, Windsor, ON N9A 6P2. POSTMASTER: Send address changes to *Cook's Country*, P.O. Box 6018, Harlan, IA 51593-1518. For subscription and gift subscription orders, subscription inquiries, or change of address notices, visit AmericasTestKitchen.com/support, call 800-526-8447 in the United States or 515-237-3663 from outside the United States, or write to us at *Cook's Country*, P.O. Box 6018, Harlan, IA 51593-1518. PRINTED IN THE USA.

Compiled by Morgan Bolling and Cecelia Jenkins

Knife Angles

When I got my knives sharpened at my hardware store, they asked me what angles I wanted the blades sharpened to. What does this mean?

–Beth Balter, Somerville, Mass.

Traditionally, there were two styles of chef's knives: European/American and Asian. The blades of Western knives were manufactured with 20-degree angles, while Asian knives were made with narrower 15-degree angles. But in recent years, the trend toward slimmer blade construction has spread west; many European and American knife manufacturers now offer knives with blades sharpened to 15 degrees. In a recent testing, our top three favorite knives were sharpened to 15 degrees, including our winner, the Victorinox Swiss Army Fibrox Pro 8" Chef's Knife. Assuming similar sharpness, a blade with a thinner edge (sharpened to a smaller angle) will slide through food more easily than one with a thicker edge (sharpened to a larger angle).

Unfortunately, there is no easy way to tell what a blade's angle is just by looking at it. If you don't know the angle of your knife's blade, we suggest contacting the manufacturer to find out so you know what angle it should be sharpened to.

THE BOTTOM LINE: The cutting edges of knives are sharpened to a specific angle. It's important to know this angle so the blade can be properly sharpened.

Some knives have 20-degree angles, while other knives have 15-degree angles.

Homemade Seasoned Salt

My family loves Lawry's Seasoned Salt sprinkled on popcorn, baked potatoes, steak—you name it. Can I make a homemade version from ingredients I already have in my pantry?

–Bonny Mix, Augusta, Maine

Lawry's Seasoned Salt is a blend of salt, sugar, paprika, turmeric, onion powder, cornstarch, garlic powder, and sometimes monosodium glutamate (MSG). We ordered the MSG-free version for reference and tinkered with a homemade facsimile, sampling it on white rice and in our Southern-Style Smothered Pork Chops, until we came up with a version that tasters found nearly identical.

THE BOTTOM LINE: It's easy to make a facsimile of Lawry's Seasoned Salt from spice-cabinet staples; it will be lighter in color than the real McCoy.

HOMEMADE SEASONED SALT
Makes 2 tablespoons
Use sweet paprika, not hot or smoked, in this recipe. We found that turmeric, a less common pantry spice, was used just for color, so we omitted it in our version.

- 1 tablespoon salt
- 1 teaspoon granulated garlic
- 1 teaspoon paprika
- ½ teaspoon sugar
- ¼ teaspoon cornstarch
- ¼ teaspoon onion powder

Combine all ingredients in bowl.

Fat Swap

I keep rendered bacon fat in my refrigerator. A friend suggested using it in place of butter when baking biscuits—will this work?

–Annabeth Martins, Winslow, Ariz.

To put your question to the test, we made two batches of our Buttermilk Drop Biscuits and our North Carolina Cheese Biscuits. We made one batch of each as written and the second batch by swapping in cooled bacon fat for the butter.

There were some notable differences. Butter is 15 to 20 percent water, while bacon fat contains essentially no water. The water in the butter converts to steam in the oven, creating pockets of air, which in turn make for flaky biscuits.

The biscuits made with butter were fluffier than their bacon-fat counterparts. In both tests, the bacon-fat biscuits were denser than the butter versions but very tender. They had a notable smoky, savory flavor that some tasters liked but others thought was too out of place in biscuits.

If you'd like to store bacon fat after cooking, pour it through a fine-mesh strainer or cheesecloth into a heatproof container. Once the fat has cooled completely, cover the container and refrigerate it for four to five days. Even if you don't use it for biscuits, you can use it to cook potatoes or in our Southern-Style Skillet Cornbread.

THE BOTTOM LINE: You can substitute chilled bacon fat for butter in biscuits, but you will end up with dense biscuits that have notable pork flavor.

A Grating Question

Is there a difference between grating and shredding cheese?

–Jason Irving, Oak Park, Ill.

In the test kitchen, we consider grated cheese to be the delicate, tiny gratings of a hard cheese such as Parmesan or Pecorino Romano made with a rasp-style grater. The fluffy flecks deliver cheesy flavor while easily incorporating into or dispersing on top of foods.

We consider shredded cheese to be the larger strands of generally semi-soft block cheeses such as mozzarella, Monterey Jack, and cheddar made with the large holes of a box grater. The

PARMESAN CHEESE
Grated versus shredded

large shreds are easy to sprinkle evenly, which promotes even melting.

THE BOTTOM LINE: We consider grated cheese to be the fine gratings of a hard cheese such as Parmesan made with a rasp-style grater. The larger strands of shredded cheese are made on a box grater, often from soft cheese such as cheddar or mozzarella.

Corned Beef

What exactly is corned beef, and how is it made?

–Mary Morrison, Savannah, Ga.

"Corning" is an old English term that refers to the "corns," or kernels of rock salt, used to cure meat for preservation. The cut used for corned beef is brisket, the large slab of muscle from the cow's chest. Although you can make corned beef from either the point or flat cut of brisket, it is most often made from the leaner, more uniformly shaped flat cut (which is easier to find in markets).

There are two ways to "corn," or salt-cure, beef brisket: dry or wet. In dry curing, you rub the meat with salt and seasonings, wrap it in plastic wrap, and weigh it down for a few days. As the meat sits, the salt draws out water, creating a concentrated brine on the meat's surface. In wet curing, you submerge the meat in a seasoned brine for a period of days. Today, both methods use table salt and curing (or "pink") salt, a specialty product dyed pink to distinguish it from conventional salt. It contains sodium nitrite, which prevents bacterial growth and gives cured meats such as corned beef their pink color.

When the brisket is fully cured, it is seasoned and preserved, but it's still raw; this is how you purchase corned beef at the grocery store. Since brisket is a tough cut loaded with connective tissue, it needs low, slow, moist cooking to become tender; thus, corned beef is usually simmered for hours in a covered pot.

In the test kitchen, we prefer to simmer the brisket in the gentle, even heat of the oven. When it is fork-tender, the corned beef is ready to serve, typically with carrots, potatoes, and cabbage, but it can also be thinly sliced and packed into sandwiches, made into hash, or smoked for pastrami. Web members can find recipes for corned beef at CooksCountry.com.

THE BOTTOM LINE: Corned beef is simply salt-cured brisket; the curing was originally a method of preservation.

PINK SALT = PINK MEAT
Curing salt gives corned beef its color.

No Springform, No Problem!
–Maria Sheahan, Biddeford, Maine

Cheesecake recipes often call for a springform pan, but I found an easy way to make cheesecake using a regular cake pan that is the same diameter as the springform pan called for in the recipe. Once the cheesecake is baked, I let it cool to room temperature in the pan and then run the tip of a sharp paring knife between the cake and the sides of the pan. I then cover the pan with plastic wrap and freeze it. As it freezes, the cake pulls away from the pan sides, so I can just bang the pan on the counter and the cake will pop out easily and cleanly. As a bonus, I have a make-ahead dessert ready for impromptu dinner parties. I just thaw the cake at room temperature a few hours before serving.

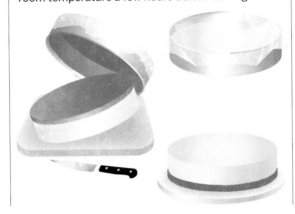

Pepperware
–Ted Bergeron, Aliquippa, Pa.

If you ever find yourself with too many bell peppers, remember this trick. Cut off the tops, remove the seeds and ribs, wrap the peppers individually in foil, and freeze them. The next time you have leftovers—my favorites are beans and rice, macaroni and cheese, and mashed potatoes—stuff them into the peppers, rewrap them, and put them back in the freezer. When you're ready to eat the peppers, simply microwave them for 5 to 10 minutes (or bake them for about 40 minutes at 350 degrees). The steam from the peppers keeps the fillings moist, and as a bonus, you can eat the container. (Web subscribers can find *Cook's Country* stuffed pepper recipes at **CooksCountry.com/stuffedpeppers**.)

French Vanilla French Toast
–Jade French, Cody, Wyo.

Sunday mornings mean French toast in our house. Recently, I sliced the bread and opened the refrigerator to grab the milk and eggs only to find we were out of both. Searching for a solution, I grabbed some vanilla ice cream from the freezer, melted a few scoops in the microwave, and used it as a soaking medium. To my delight, it made such delicious French toast that I may never go back to plain old milk and eggs.

Which Electric Griddle Is Best?

by Riddley Gemperlein-Schirm

ELECTRIC GRIDDLES HAVE a reputation for being, well, retro. But with a good one, you can evenly cook big batches of food without using the stove.

All the models we previously recommended, including our winner by BroilKing, have been discontinued or redesigned, so it was time to retest. We selected six nonstick models, including the updated version of our previous winner, priced from $29.99 to $99.00. We made pancakes, French toast, and hamburgers on each.

Many of the griddles heated unevenly: Some batches of pancakes were both raw and overcooked. We ran a few tests and found that on some griddles, the temperature varied by 80 degrees or more across the cooking surface. The best models' temperatures varied by less than 10 degrees. Why the inconsistency? Our winner had the thickest cooktop of the bunch at about ½ inch. "Something that thick is going to take longer to heat up, and because of this the mass of material is going to stay hot," explained Bridget Smyser, mechanical engineer and associate teaching professor at Northeastern University.

We also preferred griddles that were spacious and easy to clean. In the end, we found two models we liked. Our Best Buy, from Presto, has the roomiest cooking surface. Our new favorite, from BroilKing, is the updated version of our old winner. We loved its removable splash guard and even heating. Web subscribers can read the full testing at **CooksCountry.com/mar19**.

Our favorite model has a roomy surface.

KEY **Good** ★★★ **Fair** ★★ **Poor** ★

HIGHLY RECOMMENDED

CRITERIA

Winner
BroilKing Professional Griddle with Backsplash
Model: PCG-10 **Price:** $99.00
Usable Surface Area: 19.75 x 11.88 in (234.63 sq in)
Thickness of Cooking Surface: 0.44 in
Maximum Temperature Setting: 400°F

Heating ★★★
Capacity ★★★
Ease of Use ★★★
Cleanup ★★★

Comments: Even heating, a roomy cooking surface, and a removable splash guard set this griddle apart.

RECOMMENDED

Best Buy
Presto 19-Inch Electric Tilt-n-Fold Griddle
Model: 07073 **Price:** $43.99
Usable Surface Area: 17.75 x 14.25 in (252.94 sq in)
Thickness of Cooking Surface: 0.10 in
Maximum Temperature Setting: 400°F

Heating ★★
Capacity ★★★
Ease of Use ★★
Cleanup ★★★

Comments: Pros: a huge cooking surface and intuitive controls. Con: a cold spot right in the center.

RECOMMENDED WITH RESERVATIONS

Black+Decker Family-Sized Electric Griddle
Model: GD2051B **Price:** $29.99
Usable Surface Area: 19.75 x 9.63 in (190.19 sq in)
Thickness of Cooking Surface: 0.09 in
Maximum Temperature Setting: 400°F

Heating ★★
Capacity ★★
Ease of Use ★★
Cleanup ★

Comments: This is a decent griddle, but its cooking surface is too small and it was a bit too hard to clean.

NOT RECOMMENDED

Hamilton Beach Reversible Durathon Ceramic Griddle
Price: $39.99

Oster Titanium Infused DuraCeramic Griddle with Warming Tray
Price: $29.99

Elechomes 900W Electric Grill Griddle with LED Touch Control
Price: $73.99

Greek Home Alabama

O N A WARM February afternoon, I join the line that snakes out of Johnny's Restaurant, a second-story lunchroom in a well-dressed strip mall in Homewood, Alabama. Johnny's is what's known as a meat-and-three: a restaurant offering a protein and three side dishes for a fixed price. The menu is built on "Southern ingredients and Greek technique," as chef-owner Timothy Hontzas puts it, a nod to his Greek heritage and Alabama upbringing. A "Greek-and-three," he says.

At Johnny's, items such as souvlaki are listed on the menu next to fried catfish and hamburger steaks. This subtle intermingling of cuisines has long been standard for Greek eateries in the South.

"We laugh and say, if it hadn't been for the Greeks in the '60s and '70s, the people of Birmingham would have starved," Hontzas says. He speaks with a twang and moves with purpose, breaking often from conversation to greet patrons like his cousin Teddy Hontzas, who also runs a restaurant in the area.

"[Greeks] had all the restaurants, but they weren't screaming, 'Hey, look at me—I'm serving *tiropita*, spanakopita, pastitsio, and *keftedes*.'" Instead, Greek restaurants served the Southern-style food of the community, slipping a Greek dish in here and there.

Hontzas points to a framed menu on the wall from Johnny's Restaurant of Distinction, his grandfather's 1950s Jackson, Mississippi, restaurant, which he owned with Hontzas's father and uncle. Among the illustrations of steak and gumbo and a mermaid riding a lobster, one of the only discernible Greek dishes is an Athenian salad. Price: $1.

When the family's ancestors came to the South from the village of Tsitalia in the Peloponnese region of Greece, they tried to create their own new village, bringing saplings from fig and olive trees to plant in their yards, grape vines to grow along their fence lines, clippings of oregano and mint to season their food—little flavors of home. Hontzas has the descendants of some of these plants in his own yard today, and his great uncle still sends him freshly dried oregano from Greece. This generational transfer of food traditions is enough to give him "chill bumps," he says.

But Hontzas is equally enamored by traditional Southern food. He gets as excited about a perfectly fried piece of chicken as he does his Greek spice blend. "Marrying Southern and Greek food together, that's what I love to do. From hospitality to food, the cultures are very much alike." For more photos from our trip to Homewood, visit **CooksCountry.com/mar19**.

Chef Timothy Hontzas (top) on the balcony at Johnny's Restaurant in Homewood, Alabama (middle). He trained under acclaimed chef John Currence before branching out on his own in 2012. Hontzas is not the only restaurateur in the family; his cousin Teddy Hontzas (below, greeting Timothy with a hug and a kiss), runs Niki's West, another local "Greek-and-three."

Greek Baked Chicken

This Alabama favorite features old-world flavors in a wholly American way.

by Bryan Roof

IN HOMEWOOD, ALABAMA, if you say you're going out for "Greek-and-three," folks will assume you're headed to Johnny's Restaurant (see "Greek Home Alabama") for lunch. There, on the menu behind the counter, you'll see Greek baked chicken, a superflavorful dish of tender and juicy marinated and roasted chicken with tons of herbs and lemon. It comes with three sides, hence "Greek-and-three." Once I'd tried it for myself, I knew I wanted to create my own version of this simple yet complex-tasting dish.

Back in the test kitchen, the first order of business was determining which herbs to use in the marinade. After experimenting with fresh herbs, dried herbs, and even dried herb blends such as Italian seasoning and herbes de Provence, I found the best balance with fresh thyme, fresh rosemary, and dried oregano, which packs a more pungent punch than fresh. Rather than finely mince the fresh herbs, I opted to simply chop them; I found that with slightly larger pieces, the bursts of flavor were more pronounced and exciting.

Usually, when adding lemon zest to a recipe like this one, we suggest using a rasp-style grater to grate the zest, but I found that using a vegetable peeler to remove six strips of peel from a lemon and then coarsely chopping the strips gave me pockets of assertive lemon flavor reminiscent of those I'd found in the chicken at Johnny's. It's a more rustic technique for a more rustic profile, and it works beautifully. Some ground coriander and pepper (both red and black) rounded things out. The coriander, with its citrusy notes, helped enhance the lemon and add some complexity to the mix. Salt and olive oil brought it all together.

I cut thin, ½-inch-deep slits in each piece of chicken to maximize its exposure to this marinade and then tossed the chicken with the mixture, making

You're going to want some crusty bread to sop up the savory, herby pan sauce.

sure the marinade got into the slits, before sticking it in the refrigerator.

Once it had marinated for a couple of hours, the chicken was ready for cooking. I nestled the pieces into an ovensafe skillet, poured the excess marinade over the top, and slid the pan into the oven. I chose a 12-inch skillet because I wanted to keep the chicken pieces relatively tightly packed to minimize evaporation of the marinade and the flavorful chicken juices; I was counting on that liquid to transform into a deeply flavorful pan sauce.

But even after roasting the pieces at a relatively high 425 degrees until they were cooked through (about 35 minutes), I wasn't happy with the browning (or, rather, the lack thereof). I tried a few tricks—changing the position of the oven rack and tinkering with the temperature and time—before deciding to hit the chicken with heat from the broiler for a couple of minutes at the end of cooking to give it a lovely brown color.

I served the pieces with the pan sauce spooned over the top—a supersimple yet superflavorful supper of Greek Chicken.

Herbs and Slashing

In addition to lemon zest, we flavor this dish with a mix of herbs to create an incredibly aromatic Greek-inspired flavor profile. We use two fragrant fresh herbs—rosemary and thyme—plus potent dried oregano and ground coriander. To make sure those flavors find their way into the chicken, we slash the raw pieces (above) before combining them with the marinade.

GREEK CHICKEN
Serves 4

Use a vegetable peeler to remove six strips of zest from the lemon. If you have a rasp-style grater and prefer to use it to zest the lemon, you will need about 1 tablespoon of zest. Make sure to use kosher salt here; we developed this recipe using Diamond Crystal Kosher Salt.

- ¼ cup extra-virgin olive oil
- 2 tablespoons chopped fresh rosemary
- 2 tablespoons chopped fresh thyme
- 5 garlic cloves, chopped
- 6 (3-inch) strips lemon zest, chopped, plus 1 tablespoon juice
- 1 tablespoon kosher salt
- 1½ teaspoons dried oregano
- 1 teaspoon ground coriander
- ½ teaspoon red pepper flakes
- ½ teaspoon pepper
- 3 pounds bone-in chicken pieces (2 split breasts, 2 drumsticks, 2 thighs, and 2 wings, wingtips discarded)

1. Combine oil, rosemary, thyme, garlic, lemon zest, salt, oregano, coriander, pepper flakes, and pepper in large bowl. Cut three ½-inch-deep slits in skin side of each chicken breast, two ½-inch-deep slits in skin side of each thigh, and two ½-inch-deep slits in each drumstick; leave wings whole. Transfer chicken to bowl with marinade and turn to thoroughly coat, making sure marinade gets into slits. Cover and refrigerate for at least 30 minutes or up to 2 hours.

2. Adjust oven rack 6 inches from broiler element and heat oven to 425 degrees. Place chicken, skin side up, in 12-inch ovensafe skillet. Using rubber spatula, scrape any remaining marinade from bowl over chicken. Roast until breasts register 160 degrees and drumsticks/thighs register 175 degrees, 30 to 35 minutes.

3. Remove skillet from oven and spoon pan juices over top of chicken to wet skin. Heat broiler. Broil chicken until skin is lightly browned, about 3 minutes, rotating skillet as necessary for even browning. Let chicken rest in skillet for 10 minutes. Transfer chicken to shallow platter. Stir lemon juice into pan juices, then spoon over chicken. Serve.

Sweet-and-Sour Baby Back Ribs

Grab a napkin—these indoor ribs are sticky, flavorful, and impossibly tender.

by Matthew Fairman

GROWING UP IN the South, I always associated ribs with sweet, tangy barbecue sauce. But for a midwinter game-day rib feast in my adopted hometown of Boston, I decided to look for something a little more surprising: something sticky, glossy, and tropical, with sweet and spicy notes of citrus, ginger, and jalapeño.

My first decision was to use baby back ribs. I chose them because they cook relatively quickly and pack tons of pork flavor. A couple of 2-pound racks of baby backs would be plenty for a crew of four to six people, so I started there. Some people get finicky and pre-treat their ribs with a rub, a marinade, or even a brine (I do that sometimes, too). But I wanted to give this a swing without the extra time and effort of those steps.

Instead, I simply spread the racks on a rimmed baking sheet, seasoned them with salt and pepper, brushed on a healthy coating of sauce (more on this later), and popped them into the oven. A few rounds of experimentation showed me that I would have to be precise about the temperature: Too low and the ribs didn't achieve a beautiful burnished color before drying out; too high and they turned black before cooking through.

A 325-degree oven was just right. After 2½ hours, the ribs turned a beautiful, rusty shade of brown. When I tugged at the meat with a pair of tongs, it slipped off in juicy chunks. Perfect. A quick check with the digital thermometer identified this sweet-spot internal temperature: 205 degrees.

As for the sauce, getting the balance right—neither overly sweet nor harshly sour, with just enough heat and salt—took some doing. I relied on a cup of orange juice for a vibrant citrus base. For fresh, aromatic bite and bright, spicy heat, I sautéed garlic and ginger with sliced jalapeños. A half-cup of white sugar and ⅓ cup of tart cider vinegar delivered the sweet and sour portions of the promise.

But I needed some complexity, so I turned to savory ketchup, salty soy sauce, and, surprisingly, fish sauce. This addition was a revelation. The fish sauce (a cousin of Worcestershire) introduced a strong savory background flavor that played well with the other ingredients, and it tasted nothing like fish on the ribs.

Brushing the sauce onto the ribs in two stages—once before roasting and again 10 minutes before they came out of the oven—gave me beautifully lacquered racks. I cut them into individual ribs and then, because I wanted supremely sticky ribs, tossed them in the remainder of the sauce.

With a final gilding of bright green scallions, these ribs were an irresistible sight. But take my advice: Hand out plenty of paper towels when you serve these ribs. They make the most beautiful kind of mess.

Take the Temperature

How do you know when the ribs are te[nder] and ready to be glazed? Use a digital thermometer. Simply insert the tip of t[he] probe into the center of a rib in the mi[ddle] of the rack at an angle that is parallel t[o] the bones. If the temperature registers 205 degrees, the target temperature f[or] tenderness, go ahead and glaze.

We bake some sauce onto the racks, cut them into individual ribs, and then toss 'em with more sauce.

WEET-AND-SOUR BABY BACK RIBS

erves 4 to 6

or a slightly spicier sauce, we leave the eeds in the jalapeños when slicing them to rings. If you're averse to spice, emove the seeds before slicing.

AUCE

1 cup orange juice
½ cup sugar
⅓ cup cider vinegar
2 tablespoons ketchup
2 tablespoons soy sauce
1½ tablespoons cornstarch
1 tablespoon fish sauce
2 tablespoons vegetable oil
2 jalapeño chiles, stemmed and sliced into thin rings
2 garlic cloves, minced
1 teaspoon minced fresh ginger

RIBS

2 (2-pound) racks baby back ribs, trimmed
1 tablespoon kosher salt
1 teaspoon pepper
4 scallions, sliced thin on bias

1. FOR THE SAUCE: Whisk orange uice, sugar, vinegar, ketchup, soy sauce, cornstarch, and fish sauce together in bowl. Heat oil in medium saucepan over medium-high heat until shimmering. Add jalapeños, garlic, and ginger and cook until fragrant, about 30 seconds. Stir in orange juice mixture and bring to boil. Cook, stirring occasionally, until thickened, about 3 minutes. Transfer ½ cup sauce to bowl, leaving jalapeños behind, and set aside.

2. FOR THE RIBS: Adjust oven rack to middle position and heat oven to 325 degrees. Line rimmed baking sheet with aluminum foil and set wire rack in sheet. Sprinkle ribs all over with salt and pepper. Place ribs on prepared wire rack and brush all over with reserved sauce (use all sauce). Arrange ribs meat side up. Roast until tender (fork inserted into meat will meet no resistance) and middle of rib rack registers at least 205 degrees, 2 to 2½ hours.

3. Brush tops of ribs with ¼ cup remaining sauce. Return ribs to oven and roast until sauce sets, about 10 minutes. Let ribs cool for 5 minutes. Reheat remaining sauce over medium heat until hot, about 4 minutes. Cut ribs between bones. Toss ribs, half of scallions, and remaining sauce together in large bowl. Transfer to serving platter and sprinkle with remaining scallions. Serve.

German Potato Salad

Most potato salads are delicious, but this vintage German version had fixer-upper written all over it. **by Alli Berkey**

Bacon fat provides flavor and sheen to this pleasantly sharp potato salad.

WHEN I WAS a kid, every road trip to my grandmother's house resulted in a race to the refrigerator for the first helping of potato salad. Usually served as a side dish but often eaten as a snack, the boiled, dressed-up spuds always hit the spot.

Potato salad is a spectacularly flexible concept. Ask one person to describe the perfect potato salad, and then ask another—you'll get two different answers. I did just that, soliciting ideas from coworkers, but as soon as one described so-called German potato salad, with red potatoes, plenty of bacon, the tangy bite of mustard, and a sharp vinegary finish, I was intrigued. This style of potato salad has a velvety, almost creamy texture, which gives it an extra-comforting profile, especially in cooler months.

All potato salads start with the potatoes, and I needed to figure out how to cut mine for the best ratio of potatoes to dressing and add-ins. I also wanted potatoes that were soft but not mushy. After testing chunks, halves, and slices of red potatoes, I found that ¼-inch-thick slices boiled for about 15 minutes were best.

Following a cue from some old recipes I found, I decided to add salt, sugar, and celery seeds to the boiling water to help flavor the potatoes.

Now I was ready for the dressing. All the research I'd done indicated that a strong vinegar presence was essential here. So I whisked together a few dressings using varying styles and amounts of vinegar. Cider vinegar, with its strong tangy flavor and faint sweetness, won out over distilled white and wine vinegars. And while some dressings called for olive oil or canola oil, the best just called for using the flavorful rendered fat from the bacon.

Tossing the warm potatoes with this dressing and then giving them a 15-minute rest to absorb it created an irresistible salad. A heaping handful of fresh scallions and chopped parsley finished it off. I had the creamy, bacon-enriched, supercomforting salad I'd set out to create.

GERMAN POTATO SALAD

Serves 4 to 6

We developed this recipe with Grey Poupon Harvest Coarse Ground Mustard. Use small red potatoes measuring 1 to 2 inches in diameter.

8 slices bacon, cut into ½-inch pieces
2 pounds small red potatoes, unpeeled, sliced ¼ inch thick
3 cups water
2 tablespoons plus 1 teaspoon sugar
1 teaspoon celery seeds
Salt and pepper
3 tablespoons cider vinegar
2 tablespoons whole-grain mustard
4 scallions, sliced thin
3 tablespoons chopped fresh parsley
3 tablespoons finely chopped sweet green vinegar peppers (optional)

1. Cook bacon in 12-inch nonstick skillet over medium heat until crispy, 5 to 7 minutes. Using slotted spoon, transfer bacon to paper towel–lined plate. Pour bacon fat into liquid measuring cup. (You will need ¼ cup fat for dressing. If you have too much or too little, you can discard excess or add vegetable oil as needed to equal ¼ cup). Set aside.

2. Add potatoes, water, 2 tablespoons sugar, celery seeds, and 1 teaspoon salt to now-empty skillet. Bring to boil over high heat. Cook, stirring occasionally, until potatoes are tender, about 15 minutes. Continue to cook until liquid is syrupy and just coats bottom of skillet, 3 to 5 minutes longer. Transfer potatoes and cooking liquid to large bowl.

3. Stir vinegar, mustard, ¼ teaspoon salt, ¼ teaspoon pepper, and remaining 1 teaspoon sugar into reserved bacon fat until combined. Add dressing to potato mixture and stir to thoroughly combine. Let sit for 15 minutes.

4. Add scallions; parsley; peppers, if using; and bacon to potato mixture. Using rubber spatula, firmly stir to partially break up potatoes and give salad creamy texture, about 20 strokes. Serve warm.

Weeknight Ground Beef Tacos

Our goal: a taco filling flavorful enough to make you want to ditch the prefab spice mix.

by Ashley Moore

I'VE BEEN KNOWN to use a prefab packet of taco seasoning in a pinch, but there's something disappointing about the resulting tacos. There are flavors I like but also a lingering dullness. I challenged myself to do better, to create a quick, weeknight-friendly ground beef taco filling using fresher ingredients but without creating more work.

I knew I wasn't the first person to consider this idea, so my first move was to hit the books and cook through some existing recipes. Some of the resulting tacos were packed with flavor, while others were lackluster. Some were a snap to prepare, others a chore. I wanted simplicity, a list of mostly pantry ingredients, and a high return on minimal effort.

The first idea I latched on to was to mix a bit of fresh Mexican-style chorizo with the ground beef. This superflavorful pork sausage delivers a range of flavors including garlic, chile, and vinegar (see "Use the Right Chorizo").

I added a bit of cumin, for its warming flavors and aromas, and some canned chipotle chile in adobo, which provided a beautiful smoky, spicy backdrop. (This is one of my favorite pantry items; I always keep a few cans on hand.) For a fresh burst of heat and some peppery depth, I added some chopped poblano chile. Garlic and onion contributed their signature pungency to round out the flavors.

We spent a lot of time in the test kitchen debating whether tomatoes belonged in the taco filling, and after much testing, we decided that yes, they add nice acidity and beautiful color. We tried canned tomato products, but when we compared them with cut-up plum tomatoes, the plums delivered better flavor (they're available year-round).

Cooking the mixture was almost absurdly easy: Brown the meats, add the aromatics and spices, cook a bit more, stir in the tomatoes and a little water for sauciness, and simmer while people come to the table. With some fresh cilantro tossed over the top and a pile of warm tortillas, plus fixings such as shredded cheese and lettuce, I had a supereasy, superflavorful, crowd-pleasing supper in about a half-hour.

Rich poblano chile and spicy, smoky canned chipotle chile in adobo sauce make this easy weeknight taco filling sing.

EEKNIGHT GROUND BEEF TACOS

erves 6

or a less spicy filling, reduce the amount
f minced canned chipotle chile to 1 tea-
poon. Serve with your choice of garnishes,
uch as shredded iceberg lettuce, cheddar
heese, and hot sauce.

- 1 pound 90 percent lean ground beef
- 4 ounces Mexican-style chorizo sausage, casings removed
- 1 teaspoon pepper
- ¾ teaspoon salt
- 1 onion, chopped fine
- 1 poblano chile, stemmed, seeded, and chopped fine
- 4 garlic cloves, minced
- 1 tablespoon ground cumin
- 2 teaspoons minced canned chipotle chile in adobo sauce
- 4 plum tomatoes, cored and cut into ¼-inch pieces
- ½ cup water
- ¼ cup chopped fresh cilantro
- 12 (6-inch) corn or flour tortillas, warmed

1. Combine beef, chorizo, pepper, and
alt in 12-inch nonstick skillet. Cook
over medium-high heat until beef is no
onger pink, 6 to 8 minutes, breaking up
meat with wooden spoon. Stir in onion
and poblano and cook until softened, 6 to
8 minutes. Add garlic, cumin, and chipotle
and cook until fragrant, about 30 seconds.
2. Stir in tomatoes and water and bring to
simmer. Reduce heat to medium-low, cover, and continue to cook until tomatoes are
beginning to break down, about 10 minutes longer. Off heat, stir in cilantro.
3. Divide filling evenly among tortillas,
about ¼ cup each. Serve.

Use the Right Chorizo

This recipe calls for Mexican-style chorizo,
which is a fresh sausage and needs to be fully
cooked. Don't substitute Spanish-style
chorizo, which is a cured product
similar to pepperoni.

OUR CHOICE:
Mexican chorizo,
fresh and soft

DON'T USE:
Spanish chorizo,
hard and dry

And if You Can't Find It
Make your own! Substitute 4 ounces of
hot Italian sausage. Add 1 teaspoon of
smoked paprika and ⅛ teaspoon of cayenne pepper to the skillet with the garlic
in step 1; add 1 tablespoon of distilled
white vinegar with the water in step 2.

Mexican Rice

This staple side's beauty lies in its simplicity and a careful balance of fresh flavors.

by Matthew Fairman

AT HEART, MEXICAN rice is no
more than a simple pilaf of white rice
cooked in a mix of chicken broth,
tomatoes, garlic, and chiles. Yet a
well-made version tastes like so much
more than the sum of those parts,
featuring tender rice with a deep
savoriness and refreshing brightness. We wanted our recipe for this
side dish to be delicious while also
allowing ample time and energy for
cooking the rest of the meal. To get
it done, we turned to some simple,
time-tested test kitchen strategies.

Achieving fluffy rice with separate,
intact grains can seem tricky, but it really boils down to remembering a few
simple techniques: rinsing the rice,
toasting the rice in enough oil to coat
the grains, and cooking the rice in just
enough liquid (about a 2:3 ratio of rice
to liquid). Rinsing the rice rids it of
any extra starch that will turn gluey as
the rice cooks. Sautéing the rice not
only deepens its nutty flavor but also
begins to set the remaining starch on
the exterior of the rice, providing extra
insurance against clumping.

For the right tomato presence,
side-by-side tests confirmed that
a mix of pureed fresh tomato and
tomato paste was best. Canned tomato
products resulted in a sweeter, darker
cooked-tomato flavor that came across
as "ketchup-like," whereas fresh
tomatoes imparted bright, savory
flavor without dominating. Tomato
paste added more savoriness and
transformed the color of the rice from
pale pink to the classic bright orange.
A single clove of garlic and a jalapeño
chile added the perfect amount of bite
and subtle permeating heat to help
contrast the mild sweetness of the rice.

As I found out in my testing,
determining the correct amount of
liquid in which to cook the rice can
become tricky when you add solid
ingredients such as tomatoes, chiles,
and garlic to the mix. To streamline
this step, I first whizzed the vegetables in a food processor until they
were smooth and then added enough

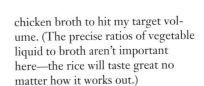

Fresh tomato
and tomato paste
collaborate to bring
this rice a rich hue
and potent flavor.

chicken broth to hit my target volume. (The precise ratios of vegetable
liquid to broth aren't important
here—the rice will taste great no
matter how it works out.)

This Mexican rice is easy, simple,
and delicious.

EASY MEXICAN RICE
Serves 4 to 6
To make this dish spicier, include the
jalapeño seeds.

- 1½ cups long-grain white rice
- 1 tomato, cored and quartered
- 1 jalapeño chile, stemmed, halved, and seeded
  Salt and pepper
- 1 garlic clove, chopped
- 1-1¾ cups chicken broth
- 3 tablespoons extra-virgin olive oil
- 1 tablespoon tomato paste
- ¼ cup chopped fresh cilantro
  Lime wedges

1. Place rice in fine-mesh strainer and
rinse under cold running water for
1½ minutes. Shake strainer vigorously
to remove all excess water; set aside.
2. Process tomato, jalapeño, 1½ teaspoons salt, garlic, and ¼ teaspoon
pepper in food processor until
smooth, about 30 seconds, scraping
down sides of bowl as needed. Transfer mixture to 4-cup liquid measuring
cup. Stir to deflate foam, if necessary, then add enough broth to equal
2½ cups.

3. Heat oil in large saucepan over
medium-high heat until shimmering. Add rice and cook, stirring
frequently, until edges begin to
turn translucent, about 2 minutes.
Add tomato paste and cook, stirring
constantly, until mixture is uniformly
colored, about 1 minute. Add tomato
mixture and bring to boil. Stir rice,
cover, and reduce heat to low. Cook
for 20 minutes.
4. Let stand, covered, off heat for
10 minutes. Stir in cilantro and
season with salt and pepper to taste.
Transfer rice to serving bowl. Serve
with lime wedges.

BACKSTORY

Rice was introduced to Mexico in
the 16th century by the Manila
Galleons, a fleet of trading ships
operated by Spain
that traveled
between the
Philippines and
Acapulco, Mexico,
for more than
200 years. The ships also carried
spices, textiles, lacquerware, and
other goods, which merchants traded for New World silver. Most of this
silver found its way to China, where
it was a common form of currency.
At least two dozen of these ships
were lost at sea over the years;
some of those shipwrecks remain
on the Pacific seafloor to this day.

Steak Marsala

Buttery, sweet, and savory Marsala sauce is perfect when partnered with chicken cutlets. But what about pairing it with steak?

by Heather Tolmie

TO BE HONEST, I'd never heard of steak Marsala until my editor handed me this assignment. But the idea of pairing full-flavored beef with this rich, slightly sweet sauce (based on its namesake fortified wine) sounded appealing, so I was eager to get into the test kitchen and explore the idea.

The recipes I found for steak Marsala followed a similar path: Sear steaks, remove them from the skillet, and then sauté mushrooms and onions in the drippings. Add flour, followed by broth and marsala, and simmer. Slide the steaks back in to warm through, and then finish with a good knob of butter. But there were three big variables I needed to sort through: cut of beef, type of mushroom, and variety of Marsala.

The steak was the natural starting point, so I ordered several different cuts, seared them, and served them with a basic Marsala sauce (I'd perfect the sauce later). Rib eye was delicious, but we didn't think a bold Marsala sauce made much sense on such a flavorful and expensive cut. Flank steak, blade steak, and steak tips lent great beefy flavor to the dish but were all a little too chewy. That left top sirloin; this affordable, relatively tender, and meaty-tasting cut is readily available and was perfect here.

Moving on to the mushrooms. My tasters had preferred the richer flavor of cremini to white mushrooms in my initial tests. But I wanted even more earthy mushroom flavor. I tried ramping up the savoriness by adding soy, fish, and Worcestershire sauces to the mushrooms, but these muddied the mushroom flavor instead of amplifying it. The solution was using dried porcini mushrooms. One benefit of employing these flavor powerhouses is that you need to rehydrate them, and the rehydrating liquid becomes a potent mushroom broth. The porcini and their liquid added a satisfying layer of depth to the sauce.

We like to serve this rich, saucy dish over polenta or buttered noodles.

As for the Marsala, most old-school recipes call for sweet Marsala; it lends a caramel-y richness that beautifully complements the savory flavors of meat and mushrooms. But many newer recipes (including some of ours) have turned to dry Marsala for chicken and veal dishes; the dry type has a lighter, brinier flavor than sweet Marsala. In a side-by-side test pitting sweet Marsala against dry in a sauce over steak, my tasters went old-school and chose sweet, commenting that the dry Marsala was a bit acidic and didn't provide enough sultry richness to stand up to the beef.

With these big issues settled, I could turn my focus to the small details of the dish. I found that starting the cooking by searing the cremini mushrooms—and not the steaks—meant that the seared steaks were still warm when the sauce was ready. After searing the meat, I removed it from the pan and built the sauce by sautéing shallot with rosemary and the rehydrated porcini mushrooms. I added a little flour for thickening and then the Marsala, some broth, the porcini liquid, and the seared cremini mushrooms. Finally, I finished it off with butter, lemon, parsley, and a fresh hit of Marsala to reinforce the flavor. It was very, very tasty.

Move over, chicken and veal. Steak Marsala is here to stay.

STEAK MARSALA
Serves 4 to 6

For a nonalcoholic version of this recipe, substitute an additional ¾ cup of chicken broth for the Marsala in step 4 and omit the 1 tablespoon of Marsala in step 5.

- 1 cup chicken broth
- ½ ounce dried porcini mushrooms, rinsed
- 3 tablespoons extra-virgin olive oil
- 12 ounces cremini mushrooms, trimmed and sliced thin
- Salt and pepper
- 4 (6-ounce) top sirloin steaks, trimmed
- 1 shallot, minced
- 1 tablespoon all-purpose flour
- 3 garlic cloves, minced
- 1 teaspoon minced fresh rosemary
- ¾ cup plus 1 tablespoon sweet Marsala
- 4 tablespoons unsalted butter, cut into 4 pieces and chilled
- 1 tablespoon minced fresh parsley
- 2 teaspoons lemon juice

1. Microwave ½ cup broth and porcini mushrooms in covered bowl until steaming, about 1 minute. Let sit until softened, about 5 minutes. Drain porcini mushrooms in fine-mesh strainer lined with coffee filter, reserve liquid,

Marsala: Sweet or Dry?
The famous fortified wine from Sicily, Marsala, comes in sweet and dry varieties. Some modern recipes for chicken and veal Marsala have turned away from the traditional sweet Marsala in favor of its brinier dry cousin. But we found that the deep, smoky flavor of the sweet variety was a much better match for beef.

and chop porcini mushrooms fine.

2. Heat 1 tablespoon oil in 12-inch nonstick skillet over medium-high heat until shimmering. Add cremini mushrooms, ¼ teaspoon salt, and ¼ teaspoon pepper and cook, covered, until mushrooms release their liquid, about 3 minutes. Uncover and continue to cook, stirring occasionally, until liquid has evaporated and mushrooms are well browned, about 8 minutes longer. Transfer to bowl; cover to keep warm.

3. Pat steaks dry with paper towels and season with salt and pepper. Add 1 tablespoon oil to now-empty skillet and heat over medium heat until just smoking. Add steaks and cook until well browned on first side, about 4 minutes. Flip steaks and cook until well browned on second side and meat registers 125 degrees (for medium-rare), 4 to 6 minutes. Transfer steaks to carving board and tent with aluminum foil.

4. Heat remaining 1 tablespoon oil in now-empty skillet over medium-high heat until shimmering. Add shallot, flour, garlic, rosemary, porcini mushrooms, ¼ teaspoon salt, and ¼ teaspoon pepper and cook until shallot is beginning to soften, about 1 minute. Stir in ¾ cup Marsala, reserved porcini mushroom soaking liquid, and remaining ½ cup broth. Cook until reduced to 1 cup and slightly thickened, 5 to 7 minutes.

5. Reduce heat to low and whisk in butter, 1 piece at a time, until emulsified. Stir in parsley, lemon juice, cremini mushrooms, and remaining 1 tablespoon Marsala. Season with salt and pepper to taste. Slice steaks thin and transfer to warm platter. Spoon sauce over steaks and serve.

Broccoli and Cheese Casserole

Old-school broccoli and cheese casserole is not bad. But with an update, it can be great.

by Morgan Bolling

MY MOTHER USED to make a dump-and-stir broccoli and cheese casserole with frozen broccoli, condensed soup, lots of cheese, and a buttery cracker topping. It was far from fancy, but I loved eating it as a kid. I wanted to serve an adult version of this classic side dish.

To start, I made a few existing recipes for broccoli and cheese casserole from a range of sources: family cookbooks, classics such as *Joy of Cooking*, and more. I learned a few things along the way. Fresh broccoli works much better than frozen, which tasted watery in this context. Casseroles built on flour-thickened white sauces are less gloppy than those made with stir-together sauces using cream cheese or condensed soup. And a crunchy topping is never a bad move.

I made a quick cheese sauce by cooking butter and flour before whisking in half-and-half and grated extra-sharp cheddar cheese, a process similar to the one you might use when making macaroni and cheese. I combined this sauce with 2 pounds of raw broccoli florets, sprinkled on some panko bread crumbs, and baked it. While it smelled delicious, this version featured a curdled cheese sauce and a pool of bubbling fat—a common occurrence when you cook with aged cheeses such as sharp cheddar (the sharper the cheddar, the older it is), which tend to break under prolonged heat. What's more, the broccoli never got fully tender in the time it took to brown the crumbs.

First I dealt with the broccoli. I knew I'd have to precook it to reduce the oven time, which would help prevent the sauce from breaking. I tried blanching and roasting the broccoli but landed on microwaving, which was the easiest, fastest method and gave me consistent results. This step allowed me to reduce the oven time from 45 minutes to 15 minutes while still fully cooking the broccoli. But even with just 15 minutes in the oven, my sauce was breaking into a greasy mess.

I was determined to stick with extra-sharp cheddar for its outsize flavor. A coworker suggested adding a bit of American cheese to the mix to help forestall the breakage I'd been experiencing; because American cheese contains emulsifiers, sauces made with it are more likely to stay together. A 1:3 ratio of American to extra-sharp cheddar gave me a silky, creamy sauce

with plenty of flavor, and additions of garlic, shallot, and dry mustard provided even more.

To take this broccoli and cheese casserole over the top, I mixed some grated Parmesan into the buttery bread-crumb topping before baking. This reinforced the nutty, cheesy flavors and helped the top crust turn extra-golden and crispy. I had a star side dish on my hands.

CRUNCHY BROCCOLI AND CHEESE CASSEROLE
Serves 6 to 8

If you do not have a bowl large enough to hold 2 pounds of broccoli, microwave the broccoli in two batches for 5 to 7 minutes. Make sure your dry mustard is relatively fresh; its flavor starts to fade a few months after it's opened.

- ¾ cup panko bread crumbs
- 1 ounce Parmesan cheese, grated (½ cup)
- 3 tablespoons unsalted butter, melted, plus 3 tablespoons unsalted butter
- Salt and pepper
- 2 pounds broccoli florets, cut into 1-inch pieces
- 1 shallot, minced
- 2 garlic cloves, minced
- 3 tablespoons all-purpose flour
- 3 cups half-and-half
- 6 ounces extra-sharp cheddar cheese, shredded (1½ cups)
- 2 ounces American cheese, chopped (½ cup)
- 2 teaspoons hot sauce
- 1 teaspoon dry mustard

1. Adjust oven rack to upper-middle position and heat oven to 400 degrees. Combine panko, Parmesan, melted butter, and ¼ teaspoon salt in bowl; set aside.
2. Toss broccoli with ½ teaspoon salt in large bowl. Cover and microwave until broccoli is bright green and just tender, 8 to 10 minutes. Drain broccoli in colander, then transfer to 13 by 9-inch baking dish.
3. Melt remaining 3 tablespoons butter in medium saucepan over medium heat. Add shallot and garlic and cook until softened, about 2 minutes. Whisk in flour and cook for 1 minute. Slowly whisk in half-and-half. Increase heat to medium-high and bring mixture to boil. Off heat, quickly whisk in cheddar, American cheese, hot sauce,

mustard, 1½ teaspoons salt, and ¼ teaspoon pepper until smooth.
4. Pour cheese sauce over broccoli in dish and stir to combine. Sprinkle reserved panko mixture over top. Bake, uncovered, until casserole is bubbling around edges and golden brown on top, about 15 minutes. Let cool for 15 minutes. Serve.

TO MAKE AHEAD
Panko mixture and microwaved, drained broccoli can be refrigerated separately for up to 24 hours. To serve, continue with recipe from step 3, increasing baking time by 5 minutes.

How do you turn bread crumbs into a flavorful, crunchy topping? Add butter and Parmesan.

Why Three Cheeses?
We decided to make our supersavory cheese sauce with extra-sharp cheddar because we love this cheese's complex, nutty bite. But a sauce made solely with extra-sharp cheddar will break and become greasy. Instead of switching to another cheese, we added a few ounces of good old American cheese, which contributes subtly milky flavor but does yeoman's work in the texture department. American cheese contains stabilizers that prevent the sauce from separating. So, we use one cheese for flavor and another for texture in the sauce that binds the casserole—plus, we mix a third cheese, Parmesan, with the bread crumbs and butter for the topping.

Text by Bryan Roof; photos by Steve Klise

THE TURKEY WINGS at Laura's II in Lafayette, Louisiana, are an impressive sight: probably close to 2 pounds each, well browned, and served without the gravy that is prevalent on every other dish.

The area along the drumstick of each wing is "stuffed" with a mixture of garlic and spices, of which cayenne is surely one, while the others remain secret. Braised in their own juices, these wings give new identity and life to the otherwise bland turkey dishes most of us non-Louisianians know and, if not love, tolerate.

"This is soul food!" owner Madonna Broussard tells me. This is the cooking she learned from her grandmother and mother.

Madonna's grandmother, Laura Broussard, ran a restaurant out of the back of her house in the 1960s. It was one of Lafayette's first soul food "plate lunch" spots, where working-class residents could find a square meal for a reasonable price.

The restaurant and home were destroyed by a fire in the 1970s, and Laura's relocated to a residential neighborhood. In 2000, the restaurant moved again, to a busy commercial strip on West University Avenue, reopening as Laura's II—a name chosen to acknowledge that the location had changed while reassuring longtime customers that the food had not.

Today the dining room is tight but friendly, with carpeting throughout, a combination of painted and exposed-brick walls, and six skinny windows hung with venetian blinds to let the afternoon sun dribble in.

Customers, who line up early for the lunch rush, are greeted with the sights and smells of the day's entrées, from smothered pork chops to shrimp fricassee. A crew of women scrambles behind the counter, writing down orders, scooping out generous portions, and shouting back to the kitchen for fried chicken and stuffed turkey wings.

All this activity reflects the spirit of Laura's original restaurant. Madonna tells me with a sincere look in her eyes, "When people eat here they are gonna feel like this is a home. And it's a good home." Additional photos from our trip to Lafayette can be found at **CooksCountry.com/mar19**.

A Louisiana "Plate Lunch" Original

Customers pile up in front of the service counter during the weekday lunch rush at Laura's II (top). Owner Madonna Broussard (above) writes down the day's menu on a dry-erase board. The stuffed turkey wings are ready for service (above right). The restaurant has survived despite a devastating fire and more than one relocation. In 2000, it moved to its current location (right).

Cajun Stuffed Turkey Wings

This little-known Cajun classic deserves a bigger audience.

By Bryan Roof

AFTER DOWNING A plate of stuffed turkey wings at Laura's II in Lafayette, Louisiana, I knew I had to bring this idea into the test kitchen. The massive wings—meaty, browned, and braised to tenderness—were served with a scoop of rice but without the Cajun-style gravy that blankets many versions of the dish. This particular "plate lunch" was offered only on Wednesdays until current owner Madonna Broussard took over the restaurant and decided to serve it every day (see "A Louisiana 'Plate Lunch' Original").

These wings are called "stuffed," but if you're imagining Thanksgiving-style stuffing, you're on the wrong track. Instead, the wings, split into flats and drumettes, are slit open and stuffed with cloves of garlic and a powerful mixture of spices.

The spice mix at Laura's II was, and remains, a secret. I knew I'd have to create my own. I started with three spices that were unmistakable in the version I'd eaten: paprika, cayenne, and granulated garlic, which added a savory, less-sharp garlic flavor to the fresh cloves. From there, I tinkered my way to adding onion powder, celery salt, and of course, salt and pepper. I carefully cut slits in both the drumette portions and the flat portions of the wings and then rubbed them inside and out with the spice mix before stuffing halved garlic cloves into the slits.

I set a Dutch oven on the stove and browned my wings on both sides. This step helped render some of the fat from the wings and created a layer of fond in the bottom of the pot. What's more, I found that the searing step helped temper the cayenne's raw heat to create a more complex chile flavor.

Once the wings were browned, I transferred them to a plate so I could make a roux with the fat left behind. Cooking ¼ cup of flour in this fat for just 3 minutes gave me a beautiful caramel-colored roux. This would be the base of my braising liquid (and eventually my gravy, which—with all due respect to the stuffing—is the thing that really makes this dish).

I tossed chopped bell pepper, onion, and celery (aka the "Cajun holy trinity") into the pot to soften with some smashed garlic cloves and fresh thyme plus a bit more of the spice mix. After 5 minutes, I added chicken broth, brought everything to a simmer, and

Don't look for traditional bread stuffing here; these wings are "stuffed" with halved garlic cloves instead.

returned the wings to the pot. I covered the pot, slipped it into a low 300-degree oven, and let it go for an hour.

At this point I was nearly powerless against the gorgeous aromas in the kitchen, but I knew I wasn't there yet. Fortitude! I flipped the wings and returned the pot to the oven for 45 more minutes, at which point the meat was falling off the proverbial (and the literal) bone. While the turkey was finishing I cooked up some rice, whose primary function would be to soak up that gravy.

Once the turkey wings were cooked through, I moved them to a plate and put the pot on the stove for 7 minutes over high heat to further thicken the gravy. I plated up scoops of rice with turkey wings positioned on top and then ladled that impossibly flavorful gravy over it all. The gravy oozed its way into the rice, delivering deep flavor to every open space.

Once I had an all-in-one forkful of tender turkey meat and rice saturated with my Cajun-style gravy, I was straight back in Lafayette.

STUFFED TURKEY WINGS

Serves 4
Serve with rice.

SPICE MIX

- 1¾ teaspoons paprika
- 1 teaspoon granulated garlic
- ¾ teaspoon salt
- ¾ teaspoon pepper
- ½ teaspoon onion powder
- ½ teaspoon celery salt
- ¼ teaspoon cayenne pepper

TURKEY

- 4 (12- to 16-ounce) whole turkey wings, cut at joints into flats and drumettes, wingtips discarded
- 12 garlic cloves, peeled (8 halved lengthwise, 4 smashed)
- ¼ cup vegetable oil
- ¼ cup all-purpose flour
- 1 cup finely chopped green bell pepper
- 1 cup finely chopped onion
- ¼ cup finely chopped celery
- 1 tablespoon chopped fresh thyme
- 3 cups chicken broth
  Salt and pepper

1. FOR THE SPICE MIX: Combine all ingredients in bowl. Measure out 1½ teaspoons spice mix and set aside.

2. FOR THE TURKEY: Adjust oven rack to middle position and heat oven to 300 degrees. Make one 1-inch-long incision, about ½ inch deep, on either side of each drumette bone and one 2-inch-long incision, about ½ inch deep, between bones on underside of each flat. Sprinkle wings inside and out with remaining 4 teaspoons spice mix. Stuff 1 piece halved garlic into each pocket of each drumette and 2 pieces into pocket of each flat.

3. Heat oil in Dutch oven over medium-high heat until shimmering. Add wings and cook until browned on both sides, about 10 minutes. Transfer wings to plate. Reduce heat to medium and add flour to fat left in pot. Cook, stirring often, until roux is caramel-colored, about 3 minutes.

4. Add bell pepper, onion, celery, thyme, smashed garlic, and reserved spice mix and cook, stirring occasionally and scraping up any browned bits, until vegetables are just beginning to soften, about 5 minutes.

5. Stir in broth and bring to simmer. Nestle wings into broth mixture. Cover, transfer pot to oven, and cook for 1 hour. Remove pot from oven and flip wings. Cover, return pot to oven, and continue to cook until tender, about 45 minutes longer.

6. Transfer wings to clean plate. Bring gravy to boil over high heat and cook until slightly thickened, about 7 minutes. Off heat, season with salt and pepper to taste. Return wings to pot and gently turn to coat with gravy. Serve.

Slits for Stuffing

We cut slits in both the flats and the drumettes (below) and then season the wings with our potent spice mix before stuffing the slits with halved garlic cloves.

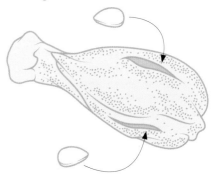

Popcorn Chicken

Bite-size fried chicken is a big seller at fast-food restaurants. Our recipe makes it just as big a hit at home.

by Cecelia Jenkins

The chicken's crispy coating is perfectly seasoned but if you need a little something extra, try dunking the pieces in our sweet-spicy sauce.

FRIED CHICKEN IS a labor of love for me, and it always feels like a special occasion when I make it and eat it. But does it have to be so? What about a more casual fried chicken, one you can eat while lounging on the couch watching a movie or a ballgame?

Enter popcorn chicken, those craggy, crispy, bite-size morsels of fried chicken goodness. The appeal is partly in its crunch and delicious flavor, sure, but also in the sheer fun and immediacy of eating it pretty much hot out of the fryer, when it's at its absolute crunchiest.

But the fun was dampened as I cooked my way through a handful of recipes. A few made crunchy chicken bites but called for fussy breading procedures, which was a lot of work for all those little pieces. Some versions were easier to make but had weak coatings (just a thin layer of fried flour) that flaked off. I wanted juicy meat encased in a thick, savory, crunchy coating, and a method that was easy enough to make any time the craving hit.

First, the chicken. I tried boneless thigh meat, but it didn't seem right here—it was a little too rich and the flesh was a bit too soft—so breast meat was the way to go. While whole boneless, skinless breasts can easily overcook and dry out, the small pieces cooked so quickly that this wasn't an issue; thus, brining was unnecessary. I found that ½-inch pieces were the perfect "popcorn" size, and briefly freezing the raw breasts to firm them up made for easier cutting.

I tried using a batter coating, but the batter's high moisture content made the chicken pieces clump in the oil unless I floated them in one by one, an immediate deal breaker. And my early tests had shown that simply dumping the chicken pieces into seasoned flour made for a dry, scant, unsatisfying coating.

Needing an easy way to get a substantial coating with plenty of cling, I turned to a trusted test kitchen method for fried chicken: After mixing a dredge of flour and cornstarch (the latter added

for extra crispiness), I worked ½ cup of water into the mixture with my hands until it felt like damp sand with tiny craggy bits. To get the flour mixture to stick, I tossed the chicken pieces in beaten eggs before coating them with it. This moist coating clung readily to the chicken, and the craggy bits provided extra mass that fried up supercrunchy. Dredging and frying in two batches helped prevent clumping.

Final refinements: A small amount of sugar added to the dredge helped it brown more quickly while imparting a faint, pleasing sweetness. A little baking powder in the flour mixture

enhanced the crust's crunch, granulated garlic and onion powder provided depth, and a pinch of cayenne put some pop in this popcorn chicken. And finally, augmenting the dredge with a little extra dry flour after breading the first batch kept it from turning too clumpy and made the two batches indistinguishable.

The chicken pieces fried up beautifully golden and crunchy, and my happy tasters quickly gobbled them up—especially once I whipped up a simple honey–hot sauce dip whose flavor was irresistible. Now that's my kind of fast food.

Texture Trick

Adding some water to a mixture of flour and cornstarch and rubbing it together with your hands creates the craggy mixture in which we dredge the chicken pieces. When fried, it transforms into an extra-crunchy coating on every piece.

POPCORN CHICKEN *Serves 6 to 8*

Use a Dutch oven that holds 6 quarts or more. We prefer Frank's RedHot Original Cayenne Pepper Sauce here, but you can substitute your favorite hot sauce, if desired. Freezing the chicken breasts makes them easier to cut.

- 1½ pounds boneless, skinless chicken breasts, trimmed
- 2¾ cups all-purpose flour
- ½ cup cornstarch
- 1½ tablespoons granulated garlic
- 1½ tablespoons sugar
- 1 tablespoon baking powder
  Kosher salt and pepper
- 2 teaspoons onion powder
- 1 teaspoon cayenne pepper
- ½ cup water
- 2 large eggs, lightly beaten
- 1½ quarts peanut or vegetable oil
- 6 tablespoons honey
- 2 tablespoons Frank's RedHot Original Cayenne Pepper Sauce

1. Place chicken on large plate and freeze until firm but still malleable, about 40 minutes.

2. Whisk 2½ cups flour, cornstarch, granulated garlic, sugar, baking powder, 1 tablespoon salt, onion powder, cayenne, and 1 teaspoon pepper together in large bowl. Add water and rub flour mixture between your hands until tiny craggy bits form throughout and mixture holds together like damp sand when squeezed.

3. Cut chicken into ½-inch pieces. Toss chicken, eggs, and 2 teaspoons salt together in second bowl. Transfer half of chicken to flour mixture and toss with your hands, pressing on coating to adhere and breaking up clumps, until chicken is coated on all sides. Pick chicken out of flour mixture and spread in even layer on rimmed baking sheet. Whisk remaining ¼ cup flour into flour mixture until combined, then repeat coating process with remaining chicken.

4. Line second rimmed baking sheet with triple layer of paper towels. Add oil to large Dutch oven until it measures about 1 inch deep and heat over medium-high heat to 400 degrees.

5. Using spider skimmer or slotted spoon, carefully add half of chicken to hot oil in several spoonfuls. Immediately stir to break up clumps. Fry until chicken is evenly golden brown and cooked through, 2 to 3 minutes, stirring occasionally. Using clean spider skimmer or slotted spoon, transfer chicken to paper towel–lined sheet. Return oil to 400 degrees and repeat with remaining chicken. Let cool for 5 minutes.

6. Whisk honey, hot sauce, and pinch salt together in small bowl. Serve chicken with honey sauce.

The Slice Is Right

Slice the chilled breasts lengthwise into ½-inch-wide strips.

Turn the strips on their sides and cut them into ½-inch pieces.

THE AMERICAN TABLE

When Gagliardi Brothers, a family business that sold hamburgers and other meat to restaurant chains in the Philadelphia area, found its sales declining in the mid-1960s, Eugene Gagliardi Jr. got creative. First came his most famous patent: Steak-Umms. To broaden the appeal of making Philly cheesesteaks at home with meat that was easy to chew, he pressed unused meat scraps into a 22-ounce loaf before freezing, slicing, and packaging it. The beef slices, which took only 30 seconds to cook on both sides, flew off grocery store shelves across the country. He eventually sold the product to the Heinz Corporation for $20 million.

He patented several other novel methods of meat preparation—including popcorn chicken, which he sold to Kentucky Fried Chicken for $33 million in 1992. KFC sold 15 million pounds' worth of his invention in the first five weeks after introducing it. While it seems a stretch to patent a way of cutting meat, holding the patent on these products secured Gagliardi's reputation as a small inventor and gave him leverage when selling or licensing his ideas to big food companies.

Are Ready-to-Bake Biscuits Any Good? *by Emily Phares*

PRODUCT TASTING

CENTURIES AGO, BISCUITS closely resembled crackers, which made them easy for travelers, sailors, and soldiers to pack and transport. Modern-day biscuits are fluffier and softer, thanks to leaveners and more fat, but people still care about convenience, as evidenced by the popularity of packaged ready-to-bake biscuits.

Our winning premade refrigerated biscuits were discontinued, so it was time to retest. We tasted four widely available biscuits, and this time we included one product that came frozen in addition to three that were refrigerated.

Biscuits can be broadly categorized as either laminated (created using a process in which buttery pastry dough is folded repeatedly to create defined, flaky layers) or tender (softer and more uniform in consistency). Our lineup included three laminated biscuits and one tender-style offering. The latter was bread-like throughout, with no noticeable distinction between interior and exterior, and tasters lamented the lack of flakiness. Another biscuit was also downgraded because, though it had layers, they weren't well-defined and were chewy, not flaky. We preferred laminated-style biscuits that had great textural contrast, with distinct layers that "pulled apart easily."

Tasters noted flavor differences, too. Our winner had a "neutral butter" flavor, while our runner-up tasted "almost fruity." Both had the same ingredients and nutritional information, so the differences likely were due to each one's natural flavor—lab-created chemical formulations made from natural ingredients such as plants. Tasters also generally preferred biscuits with more sugar and sodium.

Our winner, Immaculate Baking Organic Flaky Biscuits ($3.99 for 16 ounces), had the "best flavor of the bunch." Though we still think homemade biscuits are worth the effort, these are an excellent alternative if you're pressed for time.

HIGHLY RECOMMENDED

Immaculate Baking Organic Flaky Biscuits
Price: $3.99 for 16 oz ($0.50 per biscuit)
Biscuits per Package: 8   **Packaging:** Canned, refrigerated
Sugar: 5 g   **Sodium:** 600 mg
Comments: Our winning biscuit had a "crispy" exterior and was "flaky and tender inside," creating a nice textural contrast. We also liked the well-defined layers that "pulled apart easily." Tasters described these biscuits as "sweet" and "buttery and smooth."

RECOMMENDED

Annie's Organic Flaky Biscuits
Price: $3.99 for 16 oz ($0.50 per biscuit)
Biscuits per Package: 8   **Packaging:** Canned, refrigerated
Sugar: 5 g   **Sodium:** 600 mg
Comments: Our runner-up had a nice "flaky texture," with a "crispy" outside that provided a "good contrast" to the tender interior. Even though these biscuits had the same ingredients as our winner, tasters found them "very sweet" and more "fruity" than buttery, which we surmise is because of differences in the "natural flavor" added.

RECOMMENDED WITH RESERVATIONS

Pillsbury Grands! Buttermilk Biscuits
Price: $2.99 for 25 oz ($0.25 per biscuit)
Biscuits per Package: 12   **Packaging:** Bagged, frozen
Sugar: 2 g   **Sodium:** 531 mg
Comments: This biscuit—the only nonlaminated one in the lineup—had a "golden" exterior and a "soft" interior that "looks and feels more homemade." But some tasters thought it had a "lackluster," "bland" flavor and seemed "more like bread than a biscuit."

NOT RECOMMENDED

Pillsbury Grands! Flaky Layers Butter Tastin' Biscuits
Price: $1.98 for 16 oz ($0.25 per biscuit)
Biscuits per Package: 8   **Packaging:** Canned, refrigerated
Sugar: 5 g   **Sodium:** 442 mg
Comments: The layers in these "sweet and bready" biscuits were "hard to distinguish," and the biscuits lacked textural contrast—the "soft and doughy exterior" was similar to the interior. Testers also noticed an "odd" "fake butter" flavor.

Pasta Aglio e Olio

Would we be able to create a silky, creamy pasta dish without the added cheese?

by Natalie Estrada

AGLIO E OLIO ("garlic and oil" in Italian) are ingredients found in every Italian American home cook's pantry. Pasta *aglio e olio* is a famous pasta dish from Naples composed of these ingredients and not much else, save for perhaps a bit of red chile and some parsley.

The folklore behind this dish ranges from the mythical to the more plausible. It has been said that Ferdinand IV of Bourbon ordered the invention of the fork with four tines so that he could eat more pasta aglio e olio. Additionally, the dish has been referred to as the poor man's *alle vongole fujute* ("spaghetti with clams"—the clams have "escaped").

Despite its simplicity, the dish has evolved over the years, especially in the United States. The pasta aglio e olio many people know today barely resembles its origins—heaping amounts of Parmesan cheese, olive oil, and heavy cream and overwhelming heat from red pepper flakes. I wanted to return this dish to its humble but perfect roots.

It's easy to understand why cooks have introduced cheese and cream to this recipe over the years. Melted cheese is an easy way to create a homogeneous mixture, and the heavy cream helps make a smooth, thick sauce that does not separate. But I was determined to adhere to tradition as much as possible.

My years in restaurant kitchens taught me the importance of paying attention to the details. Treat the ingredients carefully to make them greater than the sum of their parts. Research into aglio e olio confirmed this. I'd have to cook the garlic low and slow in the oil to truly highlight its sweet and nutty notes and avoid the bitterness that comes from burning it. I would need just enough starch from the pasta to help create the silkiness I was after—to get it, I'd need to use the pasta cooking water and some muscle (agitating pasta with sauce ingredients helps create a creamy texture as the pasta starch thickens the sauce).

But my initial tests were disappointing. If I used too little pasta water, the mixture quickly dried out as it sat. Too much oil left an unpalatable glossy sheen. Experimentation led me to the answer: To achieve well-coated strands, the best move was to slightly undercook them in the water and then finish cooking them in a mixture of garlicky oil and reserved pasta water while continuously tossing with tongs to help release more starch and create a smooth sauce.

With so few ingredients (no cream or cheese to hide behind), every measurement mattered and every step had to be strictly controlled. Instead of using our standard pasta cooking ratio (4 quarts water to 1 tablespoon salt), I decided to use 3 quarts to concentrate the amount of starch in the water.

Once the noodles were cooked to slightly al dente in a Dutch oven, drained, and returned to the pot with a measured amount of starchy water, I added that garlicky oil (slowly cooked in a small saucepan) and stirred the lot over medium-high heat for 5 minutes. This finished cooking the pasta, released additional starch to help create the signature silkiness, and ensured that the oil, garlic, and red pepper flakes would be evenly dispersed. A final 2-minute rest and a sprinkling of parsley for color sealed the deal.

Silky, creamy, balanced, and perfectly simple, this was the pasta I'd been dreaming about—and I didn't even have to go grocery shopping.

SPAGHETTI WITH GARLIC AND OLIVE OIL
Serves 4 to 6

Be sure to use the 3 quarts of water specified in the recipe for cooking the pasta. The starch that the pasta releases into the water is essential to achieving the proper consistency in the sauce.

- ⅓ cup extra-virgin olive oil
- 8 garlic cloves, sliced thin
- ½ teaspoon red pepper flakes
- 1 pound spaghetti
  Salt
- 3 tablespoons chopped fresh parsley

1. Heat oil and garlic in small saucepan over medium-low heat until pale golden and fragrant, about 5 minutes. Off heat, stir in pepper flakes. Set aside.

2. Meanwhile, bring 3 quarts water to boil in large Dutch oven. Add pasta and 1 tablespoon salt and cook, stirring often, until strands are flexible but still very firm in center, about 5 minutes. Reserve 3 cups cooking water, then drain pasta.

3. Combine pasta, oil mixture, ½ teaspoon salt, and 2 cups reserved cooking water in now-empty pot and bring to boil over medium-high heat. Cook, stirring often with tongs and folding pasta over itself, until water is mostly absorbed but still pools slightly in bottom of pot, about 5 minutes.

4. Let pasta sit off heat for 2 minutes. Stir in parsley and additional reserved cooking water as needed (approximately ¼ cup) to adjust consistency (noodles should be slightly wet, not oily). Serve.

Pale Gold Garlic
We precook the garlic in olive oil until it's fragrant and pale gold. This removes its harsh edge and infuses the oil with flavor.

To coax the starch out of the pasta and into the sauce, toss like a boss.

Vegetarian Ramen with Shiitakes and Soft Eggs

30-MINUTE SUPPER

Buffalo Chicken Calzones

30-MINUTE SUPPER

Mediterranean Steak and Pita Salad

30-MINUTE SUPPER

Pork Meatball Banh Mi

30-MINUTE SUPPER

Buffalo Chicken Calzones
Serves 4

WHY THIS RECIPE WORKS: Using shredded rotisserie chicken makes this sometimes-complicated dish quick and easy.

- 2 tablespoons extra-virgin olive oil
- 2 cups shredded rotisserie chicken
- 8 ounces mozzarella cheese, shredded (2 cups)
- 3 ounces blue cheese, crumbled (¾ cup)
- ⅓ cup Frank's Original RedHot Cayenne Pepper Sauce
- ½ teaspoon pepper
- 1 pound pizza dough

1. Adjust oven rack to middle position and heat oven to 475 degrees. Line baking sheet with foil and brush foil with 1 tablespoon oil. Combine chicken, mozzarella, blue cheese, hot sauce, and pepper in bowl.
2. Divide pizza dough into 4 equal pieces. Roll and stretch each piece of dough into 8-inch circle on lightly floured counter. Spread 1 cup chicken mixture on bottom half of each dough round, leaving 1-inch border around edges. Fold top half of dough over filling and crimp edges to seal. Cut two 1-inch slits on tops of calzones and transfer to prepared sheet.
3. Brush tops of calzones with remaining 1 tablespoon oil. Bake until crust is golden brown, about 15 minutes. Transfer sheet to wire rack and let calzones cool for 5 minutes. Serve.

TEST KITCHEN NOTE: We used rotisserie chicken for this recipe, but it also works well with any kind of leftover chicken.

Vegetarian Ramen with Shiitakes and Soft Eggs *Serves 4*

WHY THIS RECIPE WORKS: Adding miso to lightly browned vegetables provides a punch of flavor to fortify the vegetable broth.

- 3 tablespoons toasted sesame oil
- 8 ounces shiitake mushrooms, stemmed and sliced thin
- 6 scallions, cut into 1-inch pieces
- 1 (2-inch) piece ginger, peeled and cut into matchsticks
- 2 tablespoons white miso
- 8 cups vegetable broth
- 3 (3-ounce) packages ramen noodles, seasoning packets discarded
- 2 ounces (2 cups) baby spinach
- 4 soft-cooked large eggs, halved
  Asian chili-garlic sauce

1. Heat oil in large Dutch oven over medium-high heat until just smoking. Add mushrooms and scallions and cook until lightly browned and tender, about 5 minutes. Stir in ginger and miso and cook until fragrant, about 30 seconds. Whisk in broth and bring to boil.
2. Add ramen and cook, stirring occasionally to break up noodles, until tender, about 3 minutes. Off heat, stir in spinach.
3. Divide broth, noodles, and vegetables evenly among 4 bowls. Top each portion with 1 egg. Serve with chili-garlic sauce.

TEST KITCHEN NOTE: For soft-cooked eggs with set whites and fluid yolks, boil the eggs for 6 minutes.

Pork Meatball Banh Mi
Serves 4

WHY THIS RECIPE WORKS: Letting the vegetables sit together while making the meatballs pickles them slightly.

- 3 carrots, peeled and cut into 2-inch matchsticks
- ½ English cucumber, cut into 2-inch matchsticks
- ½ cup chopped fresh cilantro
- 4 scallions, white and green parts separated and sliced thin
- 2 tablespoons rice vinegar
- 5 teaspoons fish sauce
  Salt and pepper
- 1½ pounds ground pork
- ½ cup mayonnaise
- 2 (12-inch) baguettes, ends trimmed, halved crosswise, and split lengthwise

1. Combine carrots, cucumber, ¼ cup cilantro, scallion greens, vinegar, 2 teaspoons fish sauce, ¼ teaspoon salt, and ¼ teaspoon pepper in bowl; set aside. Using your hands, combine pork, scallion whites, ½ teaspoon salt, ½ teaspoon pepper, remaining ¼ cup cilantro, and remaining 1 tablespoon fish sauce in separate bowl. Divide pork mixture into 16 equal meatballs.
2. Arrange meatballs in 12-inch nonstick skillet. Cook over medium-high heat until browned on all sides, about 10 minutes. Cover and continue to cook until meatballs register 160 degrees, about 4 minutes longer.
3. Spread mayonnaise evenly on cut sides of each baguette. Divide vegetable mixture and meatballs evenly among sandwiches. Serve.

TEST KITCHEN NOTE: We developed this recipe with Red Boat 40°N Fish Sauce.

Mediterranean Steak and Pita Salad
Serves 4

WHY THIS RECIPE WORKS: Rich, beefy skirt steak contrasts perfectly with a lemony salad of crisp pita, romaine, tomatoes, and mint.

- ½ cup extra-virgin olive oil
- 1 teaspoon grated lemon zest plus 3 tablespoons juice
- 1 garlic clove, minced
  Salt and pepper
- 10 ounces cherry tomatoes, quartered
- 3 (8-inch) pita breads, torn into 1½-inch pieces
- 2 teaspoons ground cumin
- 1 (1-pound) skirt steak, trimmed and cut into 4 equal pieces
- 2 romaine lettuce hearts (12 ounces), cut into 1-inch pieces
- ½ cup chopped fresh mint

1. Whisk 3 tablespoons oil, lemon zest and juice, garlic, ½ teaspoon salt, and ¼ teaspoon pepper together in large bowl. Add tomatoes and set aside. Adjust oven rack to middle position and heat oven to 400 degrees. Toss pita with ¼ cup oil, ½ teaspoon salt, and ¼ teaspoon pepper in bowl. Transfer pita to rimmed baking sheet and bake until browned and crisp, 9 to 13 minutes, stirring halfway through baking. Let cool completely.
2. Combine cumin, 1 teaspoon salt, and ½ teaspoon pepper in bowl. Pat steaks dry with paper towels and sprinkle with cumin mixture. Heat remaining 1 tablespoon oil in 12-inch nonstick skillet over medium-high heat until just smoking. Cook steaks until well browned and registering 135 degrees (for medium), 2 to 4 minutes per side. Transfer to cutting board, tent with foil, and let rest for 5 minutes.
3. Add lettuce, mint, and pita to bowl with tomato mixture and toss to combine. Slice steaks thin against grain and serve over salad.

TEST KITCHEN NOTE: We cook the skirt steak to medium so that it's less chewy than it would be at medium-rare.

Pan-Seared Chicken Breasts with Braised Fennel, Olives, and Orange

30-MINUTE SUPPER

Plantain-Crusted Pork Chops with Black Bean and Avocado Salad

30-MINUTE SUPPER

Filets Mignons with Rosemary Potatoes and Bourbon Cream Sauce

30-MINUTE SUPPER

Orecchiette with Shrimp, Pepperoncini, and Basil

30-MINUTE SUPPER

Plantain-Crusted Pork Chops with Black Bean and Avocado Salad *Serves 4*

WHY THIS RECIPE WORKS: Crushed plantain chips make an easy, crispy coating for these weeknight-friendly pan-fried pork chops.

- 2 (15-ounce) cans black beans, rinsed
- 1 avocado, halved, pitted, and cut into ½-inch pieces
- ½ cup extra-virgin olive oil
- ⅓ cup thinly sliced red onion
- 1½ tablespoons lime juice
  Salt and pepper
- 4 (6- to 8-ounce) bone-in pork rib chops, ½ inch thick, trimmed
- ½ cup all-purpose flour
- 2 large eggs
- 5 ounces plantain chips, crushed fine (1¼ cups)

1. Combine beans, avocado, ¼ cup oil, onion, lime juice, ½ teaspoon salt, and ¼ teaspoon pepper in bowl; set aside.

2. Season chops with salt and pepper. Place flour in shallow dish. Lightly beat eggs in second shallow dish. Place plantain chips in third shallow dish. Working with 1 chop at a time, dredge in flour, shaking off excess; dip in eggs, allowing excess to drip off; and coat with plantain chips, pressing to adhere.

3. Line large plate with paper towels. Heat remaining ¼ cup oil in 12-inch nonstick skillet over medium heat until shimmering. Add 2 chops to skillet and cook until golden brown and meat registers 145 degrees, about 3 minutes per side. Transfer to prepared plate. Repeat with remaining chops. Serve pork chops with salad.

TEST KITCHEN NOTE: Place the plantain chips in a zipper-lock bag and use a rolling pin to crush them.

Pan-Seared Chicken Breasts with Braised Fennel, Olives, and Orange *Serves 4*

WHY THIS RECIPE WORKS: The classic combo of fennel, olives, and orange pairs well with pan-seared, cayenne-spiced chicken breasts.

- 4 (6- to 8-ounce) boneless, skinless chicken breasts, trimmed
  Salt and pepper
- ¼ teaspoon cayenne pepper
- ¼ cup extra-virgin olive oil, plus extra for drizzling
- 3 fennel bulbs, stalks discarded, bulbs halved, cored, and cut into ½-inch-thick wedges
- 4 shallots, sliced into ½-inch-thick rings
- 3 garlic cloves, minced
- 3 (2-inch) strips orange zest plus ¼ cup juice
- ½ cup water
- ⅓ cup pitted kalamata olives, sliced into ¼-inch-thick rounds
- 2 tablespoons chopped fresh parsley

1. Pat chicken dry with paper towels. Sprinkle with 1 teaspoon salt, ¼ teaspoon pepper, and cayenne. Heat 1 tablespoon oil in 12-inch nonstick skillet over medium-high heat until just smoking. Add chicken to skillet, skinned side down, and cook until browned on first side, about 6 minutes. Transfer chicken, browned side up, to large plate; set aside.

2. Heat remaining 3 tablespoons oil in now-empty skillet over medium-high heat until shimmering. Add fennel, shallots, ¼ teaspoon salt, and ¼ teaspoon pepper and cook, covered, until softened and browned, about 8 minutes, stirring occasionally. Add garlic and orange zest and cook until fragrant, about 1 minute. Add water and reduce heat to medium-low. Add chicken, browned side up; cover; and cook until registering 160 degrees, 10 to 14 minutes.

3. Transfer chicken to cutting board and tent with foil. Stir olives and orange juice into fennel mixture in skillet. Slice chicken ½ inch thick. Serve chicken with fennel mixture and pan sauce, sprinkled with parsley and drizzled with extra oil.

Orecchiette with Shrimp, Pepperoncini, and Basil *Serves 4*

WHY THIS RECIPE WORKS: A quick sauce of olive oil, garlic, capers, and *pepperoncini* makes for a bright, briny rendition of weeknight shrimp pasta.

- 1½ pounds extra-large shrimp (21 to 25 per pound), peeled, deveined, tails removed, and cut into ½-inch pieces
  Salt and pepper
- 12 ounces (3⅓ cups) orecchiette
- ⅓ cup extra-virgin olive oil
- 4 garlic cloves, sliced thin
- 1 ounce Parmesan cheese, grated (½ cup), plus extra for serving
- ¼ cup chopped pepperoncini, plus 1 tablespoon brine
- ¼ cup capers, rinsed
- ¼ cup chopped fresh basil
  Lemon wedges

1. Sprinkle shrimp with ¼ teaspoon salt and ¼ teaspoon pepper and refrigerate until ready to use. Bring 4 quarts water to boil in large Dutch oven. Add pasta and 1 tablespoon salt and cook, stirring frequently, until al dente. Reserve ½ cup cooking water, then drain pasta.

2. Heat oil in now-empty pot over medium heat until shimmering. Add garlic and cook until beginning to brown, about 1 minute. Add shrimp and cook until just opaque, about 4 minutes.

3. Off heat, add pasta, Parmesan, pepperoncini and brine, capers, basil, and reserved cooking water and toss to combine. Serve, passing lemon wedges and extra Parmesan separately.

TEST KITCHEN NOTE: We prefer untreated shrimp—those without added sodium or preservatives such as sodium tripolyphosphate.

Filets Mignons with Rosemary Potatoes and Bourbon Cream Sauce *Serves 4*

WHY THIS RECIPE WORKS: Building a quick bourbon cream sauce in the skillet adds a rich depth of flavor to the steak.

- 1½ pounds Yukon Gold potatoes, unpeeled, cut into 1-inch pieces
- ¼ cup vegetable oil
- 2½ teaspoons minced fresh rosemary
  Salt and pepper
- 4 (6- to 8-ounce) center-cut filets mignons, 2 inches thick, trimmed
- 2 shallots, sliced into thin rings
- 2 garlic cloves, sliced thin
- ¾ cup heavy cream
- ¼ cup bourbon

1. Adjust oven rack to lower-middle position and heat oven to 475 degrees. Toss potatoes, 2 tablespoons oil, 2 teaspoons rosemary, 1 teaspoon salt, and ½ teaspoon pepper together on rimmed baking sheet. Bake until potatoes are well browned and tender, about 25 minutes.

2. Meanwhile, pat steaks dry with paper towels and season with salt and pepper. Heat remaining 2 tablespoons oil in 12-inch skillet over medium-high heat until just smoking. Add steaks and cook until well browned and meat registers 125 degrees (for medium-rare), 4 to 6 minutes per side. Transfer to platter and tent with foil.

3. Reduce heat to medium and add shallot, garlic, and remaining ½ teaspoon rosemary to now-empty skillet. Cook until vegetables are softened and lightly browned, about 3 minutes. Off heat, add cream and bourbon. Return to medium heat, bring to simmer, and cook until sauce is slightly thickened, about 3 minutes. Season with salt and pepper to taste. Serve steaks with sauce and potatoes.

TEST KITCHEN NOTE: You can substitute Red Bliss potatoes for the Yukon Gold potatoes, if desired.

Salt

Our bodies require salt for survival; our dinners require it to taste good. Properly salting food is one of the most important skills in all of cooking. **by Scott Kathan**

Salt from up High
"Raining" salt on foods from a high-held hand serves a practical purpose—the higher the salting point (within reason), the more even coverage you get.

Salty Ingredients

Use a light hand when seasoning recipes that contain salty ingredients such as these: capers, soy sauce, mustard, Worcestershire sauce, oyster sauce, ketchup, hot sauce, fish sauce, and olives.

Two Paths to Deep Seasoning

Brine
Brining means submerging meat (most often poultry or pork) in a salt solution so that the salt penetrates the meat, increasing the meat's ability to hold moisture. This helps lean cuts stay moist and juicy. Sometimes we add sugar or spices to the brine for extra flavor.

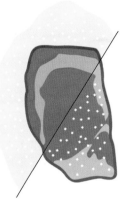

Dry Salt
We often salt large cuts of meat (such as roasts and whole birds) in advance. Given enough time (1 to 24 hours), the salt travels into the meat. In addition to seasoning it, salt helps the meat hold on to moisture to remain juicy throughout cooking and softens and dissolves some meat proteins to result in a more tender texture.

Once one of the world's most valuable traded commodities, salt allowed for the preservation of foods such as fish, meat, and cabbage.

When recipes (including ours) don't specify the type of salt, use table salt.

Salting While Cooking

Salting in stages helps prevent oversalting, as variations in ingredients (how fatty your chicken thighs are, for instance) and burner strength can impact flavor and seasoning. For the most well-rounded seasoning, salt foods early in the cooking process and then taste and add more if needed at the end. If you oversalt a savory dish, you can try adding acid or a sweetener to balance the salt; you can also add more nonsalty ingredients such as more pasta or vegetables.

Cold temperatures dull the salt receptors in our mouths, so season cold foods more assertively.

Which Salt Should I Use?

The three most common types of salt used in cooking are table, kosher, and sea salt. We use table salt in baking because it dissolves into batters and doughs most readily; we usually season meats with kosher salt because its large grains make it easier to feel how much salt we're applying. While large-flaked, crunchy, mineral-y sea salt can be great sprinkled over roasted and grilled meat or vegetables, we don't call for it in recipes because irregularities (in size and flavor) among products make it hard to get consistent results.

Equivalents:

1 teaspoon table salt

1½ teaspoons Morton Kosher Salt

2 teaspoons Diamond Crystal Kosher Salt

Sweet and Savory

Salt's not just for savory foods: Most cakes, cookies, and other confections contain salt to help enhance their flavor. Even most fruit tastes better with a light sprinkling of salt. Skeptical? Try the pineapple challenge: Take two pieces of freshly cut pineapple, lightly sprinkle one of them with salt, and taste them side by side. The salted version should taste sweeter and more complex.

Too Much of a Good Thing?

Be conservative when seasoning stocks and broths that you are going to reduce: The salt will become more prominent as the stock becomes more concentrated. In general, home-cooked dishes contain far less sodium than processed foods such as chips, crackers, and frozen meals do.

Stuffed Pork Tenderloin

To bump up the mild flavor of pork tenderloin, we worked from the inside out. **by Morgan Bolling**

PORK TENDERLOIN—ONE OF America's favorite cuts of pork—is supremely tender and fast-cooking. While I appreciate those attributes, this cut isn't exactly a flavor power-house. The test kitchen has addressed this lack of flavor by creating some great recipes that dress up pork tender-loin with potent crumb crusts, intense spice rubs, or fancy sauces or glazes. But, tasty as they may be, all those solutions are superficial. For maximum impact, I decided to pack the inside of the meat with a bold stuffing.

But before I did, I had two big ques-tions to answer: How, exactly, would I stuff the meat? And what would I stuff it with? For inspiration, I dug up six wildly diverse recipes for stuffed pork tenderloin and prepared them in the test kitchen. The techniques for stuff-ing entailed everything from tying two tenderloins together with filling be-tween them to cutting a pocket in the meat to using the handle of a wooden spoon to bore a hole down the length of the tenderloin.

I found that butterflying held the stuffing in place most reliably. "But-terflying" means slicing the tenderloin almost in half down its length so you can open it up like a book. By doing this, I could lay stuffing on the pork and roll it up like a jelly roll. I found that pounding the butterflied meat to an even thickness made for tidier rolling and more even cooking; it also created a larger surface area that held more

stuffing. Trussing the stuffed tenderloins with kitchen twine ensured that the stuffing stayed secure inside the pork.

Now it was time to nail down the stuffing itself. In my initial test reci-pes, stuffing that used bread or bread crumbs absorbed pork juices and turned gummy. Those based on herb pastes (basically riffs on pesto) tasted good but didn't feel substantial enough to warrant the work. I wanted a knockout stuffing.

Our favorite tenderloin from the initial recipes was stuffed with a simple mix of apple and bacon. For having only two ingredients, it offered a big payoff, hitting both salty and sweet notes. But it lacked depth and cohesion. Soften-ing the chopped apple in bacon fat (left behind after crisping the bacon) added dimension, and sautéing a minced shallot and some fresh thyme added a steady hum of background flavor. As for a binder, grated Gruyère cheese proved perfect; the nutty cheese melted in the oven and united the bacon and apple into a cohesive filling.

For a final test, I butterflied and pounded two tenderloins, loaded on the tasty stuffing, rolled them up and tied them, and then seared the tenderloins in a hot skillet before finishing them in a 350-degree oven. Slicing through their gorgeously browned crusts revealed the soft, cheesy, extremely flavorful stuffing. It smelled amazing—and tasted even better. Finally, pork tenderloin that packed a wallop of intense meaty, savory flavor.

> Our butterflying and stuffing method keeps the filling where you want it: inside the pork.

Key Steps to Stuffing Pork Tenderloin

1. Slice the tenderloins almost in half lengthwise, open the flaps like a book, and then pound them flat.

2. Sprinkle half the stuffing over half the tenderloin, roll the meat into a tight log, and then secure it with twine.

PORK TENDERLOIN ROULADE WITH BACON, APPLE, AND GRUYÈRE
Serves 4 to 6
You will need an ovensafe nonstick skillet for this recipe.

STUFFING
- 3 slices bacon, cut into ½-inch pieces
- 1 Granny Smith apple, peeled, cored, and chopped
- 1 shallot, minced
- 1 teaspoon minced fresh thyme
- 3 ounces Gruyère cheese, shredded (¾ cup)

PORK
- 2 (1- to 1¼-pound) pork tenderloins, trimmed
- 1½ teaspoons kosher salt
- ½ teaspoon pepper
- 1 tablespoon extra-virgin olive oil

1. FOR THE STUFFING: Cook bacon in 12-inch ovensafe nonstick skillet over medium heat until crispy, 5 to 7 minutes. Add apple, shallot, and thyme and cook until apple is softened, 4 to 6 minutes. Transfer to bowl and let cool for 10 minutes. Stir in Gruyère. Wipe skillet clean with paper towels.

2. FOR THE PORK: Adjust oven rack to middle position and heat oven to 350 degrees. Cut tenderloins in half horizontally, stopping ½ inch from

edge so halves remain attached. Open up tenderloins, cover with plastic wrap, and pound to even ¼-inch thickness.

3. Working with 1 tenderloin at a time, trim and discard any ragged edges to create neat rectangle. With long side of tenderloin facing you, sprinkle half of stuffing (scant 1 cup) over bottom half of tenderloin, leaving 1-inch border around edges. Roll tenderloin away from you into tight log.

4. Position tenderloins seam side down and tie crosswise with kitchen twine at 1-inch intervals to secure. (Stuffed tenderloins can be wrapped individu-ally in plastic wrap and refrigerated for up to 24 hours.)

5. Sprinkle each tenderloin with ¾ teaspoon salt and ¼ teaspoon pepper. Heat oil in now-empty skillet over medium-high heat until shimmer-ing. Add tenderloins and brown on all sides, 6 to 8 minutes. Transfer skillet to oven and roast until center of stuffing registers 140 degrees, 16 to 20 minutes. Transfer tenderloins to carving board, tent with aluminum foil, and let rest for 10 minutes. Remove twine, slice into 1-inch-thick medal-lions, and serve.

 Our recipe for Pork Tenderloin Roulade with Pancetta, Pear, and Cheddar is available for free for four months at **CooksCountry.com/mar19**.

Stuffed Portobello Mushrooms

Our easy technique transforms what is typically a tired, squishy vegetarian entrée into a tender, flavor-packed dish anyone would love to eat.

by Ashley Moore

PORTOBELLO MUSHROOM CAPS were made for stuffing. Why? For starters, their hefty size and circular shape make a perfect "dish" to hold stuffing. Plus, they have a brawny, earthy flavor that can stand up to potent stuffing ingredients, making the dish a potential tastebud-rocking powerhouse. I say "potential," though, because most stuffed portobellos I've had have been bland, spongy, and sad.

Determined to break the curse, I set out to create a recipe for truly memorable stuffed portobello mushroom caps. I began by preparing a handful of promising recipes for my tasters. The recipes called for stuffing the caps with various combinations of sautéed vegetables, meats, cheese, and beans. A few literally fell flat, emerging from the oven as thin, deflated disks. But one recipe gave me hope; it called for marinating and roasting the caps before stuffing them, which resulted in moist and tender 'shrooms.

I got busy developing my own version. In addition to stemming the mushrooms, I found that scraping out the dark brown gills from the underside of each cap made them taste much cleaner. Moving on to the marinade, I tested various ingredients and landed on a simple combination of olive oil and red wine vinegar. Letting the mushroom caps soak in the vinaigrette in a zipper-lock bag was efficient and easy; 30 minutes to 1 hour imparted big flavor. A 20-minute stint in a hot oven drove off excess moisture and cooked the mushrooms through, ensuring that they were tender and moist—not spongy or soggy.

I wanted to fill these caps with a vegetarian-friendly mixture, so for a rich, creamy base, I used tangy fresh goat cheese. For bulk and flavor, I tested spinach, kale, and Swiss chard; we preferred the milder flavor and tender texture of sautéed Swiss chard. Toasted Parmesan bread crumbs made for an irresistibly crunchy topping.

Once I'd filled the caps and topped them with the crumbs, they needed only a few more minutes in the oven to heat through. I let the mushrooms cool slightly and called my team to taste. Happy people all around.

STUFFED PORTOBELLO MUSHROOMS *Serves 4*

Use a spoon to remove the gills from the mushroom caps.

- ½ cup plus 1 tablespoon extra-virgin olive oil
- 3 tablespoons red wine vinegar
  Salt and pepper
- 4 portobello mushroom caps (4 to 5 inches in diameter), gills removed
- ½ cup panko bread crumbs
- 1 ounce Parmesan cheese, grated (½ cup)
- 10 ounces Swiss chard, stems and leaves cut into ½-inch pieces
- 3 garlic cloves, minced
- ⅛ teaspoon red pepper flakes
- 4 ounces goat cheese, softened
- ½ cup torn fresh basil leaves
- 1½ teaspoons grated lemon zest

1. Adjust oven racks to upper-middle and lower-middle positions and heat oven to 475 degrees. Combine 6 tablespoons oil, vinegar, ½ teaspoon salt, and ½ teaspoon pepper in 1-gallon zipper-lock bag. Add mushrooms, seal bag, turn to coat, and let sit at room temperature for at least 30 minutes or up to 1 hour.

2. Line rimmed baking sheet with parchment paper. Arrange mushrooms gill side down on prepared sheet. Roast on lower rack until tender, about 20 minutes.

3. Combine panko and 2 tablespoons oil in 12-inch nonstick skillet and cook over medium heat, stirring frequently, until golden brown, about 5 minutes; transfer to bowl and stir in Parmesan. Wipe skillet clean with paper towels.

4. Heat remaining 1 tablespoon oil in now-empty skillet over medium-high heat until shimmering. Add chard and ¼ teaspoon salt and cook until wilted and liquid has evaporated, 5 to 7 minutes. Stir in garlic and pepper flakes and cook until fragrant, about 30 seconds. Off heat, stir in goat cheese, basil, and lemon zest.

5. Flip mushrooms gill side up and distribute filling evenly among mushrooms. Sprinkle panko mixture evenly over top. Bake on upper rack until topping is golden brown, about 4 minutes. Serve.

The caps are filled with Swiss chard, garlic, goat cheese, and basil and topped with a crunchy mixture of Parmesan cheese and panko.

Prepping the Mushrooms

Scrape Out the Gills
Using a spoon to gently scrape the dark gills from the underside of each portobello cap not only makes for cleaner mushroom flavor but also improves the roasted mushrooms' texture.

Roast for 20 Minutes
Roasting the stemmed, gilled, and marinated mushroom caps before stuffing and heating them through not only shrinks them and darkens their color but also helps concentrate their flavor.

Clementine Cake

Oh My Darling

Botanically, a clementine is a variety of mandarin orange. Similar to a tangerine and a satsuma, it is loose-skinned, which makes it easy to peel. Our microwave heating method removes the bitterness from the fruit's peel and pith, so when the clementines are pureed in a food processor and combined with the cake base, there's just a pleasant hint of bitterness—the fruit's aromatic citrus essence shines.

TEST KITCHEN FAVORITE
Swissmar Börner Original
V-Slicer Plus Mandoline

Slicing Tips

Chilling the clementines makes for easier slicing. A mandoline is the best tool to ensure even slices, but if you don't have one, a careful touch with a sharp chef's knife will work fine.

TEST KITCHEN FAVORITE
Victorinox Swiss Army Fibrox
Pro 8" Chef's Knife

THE AMERICAN TABLE

Clementine cake is featured heavily in Ben Stiller's 2013 film *The Secret Life of Walter Mitty*, which was based on a short story of the same name by James Thurber that was first published in *The New Yorker* in 1939. The film bears little resemblance to the original story, but both explore the idea that the wall between a person's inner life and outer life is often porous. While both the film and the story have moments of humor, each also challenges us to consider the role of imagination and fantasy in our own lives and whether the distinction between "real" and "imagined" means anything at all. One thing that's real: this delicious cake.

Ground whole clementines in a cake? When done right, it makes for a bright, delicious, citrus-kissed dessert.

by Ashley Moore

This festive cake is flavored with ground toasted almonds and pulverized whole clementines.

Key Steps to a Cake That Tastes Like Sunshine

Microwave the clementines, covered, so that they steam, soften, release a bit of juice, and become less bitter.

Process the almonds, flour, baking powder, and salt until the almonds are finely ground.

Blitz the cooled softened clementines in a food processor until smooth and add them to the batter.

Adjust the consistency of the glaze with just enough water until it leaves a trail when drizzled from the whisk.

CLEMENTINE CAKES ARE almost always tender single-layer cakes made with ground clementines. They can be upside down or right side up and are typically dusted with confectioners' sugar or covered with a glaze (chocolate or sugar) and decorated with candied slices of their namesake fruit. It seems odd, but the pulverized clementines add just the right amount of sweet, sour, and floral citrus flavor to every bite.

I began by baking five clementine cake recipes. Each one was unique, but they all called for ground almonds as the base of the cake (a few added a bit of flour, too). The clementine flavor in the best of these cakes was surprisingly sweet, with just a hint of pleasant bitterness. But those recipes called for cooking the whole clementines in water for 2 hours (to tame the rind's bitterness and soften the fruit) before pulverizing them in a food processor. Was cooking them for that long really necessary?

Thankfully, through a few days of testing, I discovered that while the clementines did need to be softened before grinding, a long boiling time wasn't necessary. Microwaving the fruit in a covered bowl for just a few minutes did a splendid job of softening it and getting rid of most of the bitterness.

As for the cake itself, my tasters loved the rich flavor provided by the ground almonds (sliced almonds that I had buzzed in a food processor), but using all ground almonds made the texture gritty and dense. Cutting the almonds with some flour made for a sturdier, lighter cake. I also discovered that a well-greased springform pan was necessary to get the best result—it's important that this single-layer cake be tall, and a springform pan has taller sides than a cake pan.

For the top of the cake, we loved the version that called for a thick white glaze draped over the cake, so it was just a matter of finding the ideal ratio of confectioners' sugar to water (plus a pinch of salt). We also fell for the beautiful slices of candied clementines that adorned some versions. To get consistent ¼-inch-thick slices, I found that it helped to chill the fruit and then use a mandoline; from there, all it took was a stint in boiling sugar water to nicely candy the fruit. The candied clementines looked amazing when laid atop the white glaze—they tasted great, too, adding a sweet-tart citrus punch.

Having worked through all the elements, I baked and assembled one last cake. I then listened to my coworkers ooh and aah as I sliced into the finished cake. Let's just say there weren't any leftovers.

CLEMENTINE CAKE
Serves 8

Look for clementines that are about 2 inches in diameter (about 1¾ ounces each). We recommend using a mandoline to get consistent slices of clementine to arrange on top of the cake; you can also use a chef's knife. We found it easier to slice the clementines when they were cold. You will have a few more candied clementine slices than you will need; use the nicest-looking ones for the cake's top.

CAKE
- 9 ounces clementines, unpeeled, stemmed (about 5 clementines)
- 2¼ cups (7½ ounces) sliced blanched almonds, toasted
- 1 cup (5 ounces) all-purpose flour
- 1¼ teaspoons baking powder
- ¼ teaspoon salt
- 10 tablespoons unsalted butter, cut into 10 pieces and softened
- 1½ cups (10½ ounces) granulated sugar
- 5 large eggs

CANDIED CLEMENTINES
- 4 clementines, unpeeled, stemmed
- 1 cup water
- 1 cup (7 ounces) granulated sugar
- ⅛ teaspoon salt

GLAZE
- 2 cups (8 ounces) confectioners' sugar
- 2½ tablespoons water, plus extra as needed
- Pinch salt

1. FOR THE CAKE: Adjust oven rack to middle position and heat oven to 325 degrees. Spray 9-inch springform pan with vegetable oil spray, line bottom with parchment paper, and grease parchment. Microwave clementines in covered bowl until softened and some juice is released, about 3 minutes. Discard juice and let clementines cool for 10 minutes.

2. Process almonds, flour, baking powder, and salt in food processor until almonds are finely ground, about 30 seconds; transfer to second bowl. Add clementines to now-empty processor and process until smooth, about 1 minute, scraping down sides of bowl as needed.

3. Using stand mixer fitted with paddle, beat butter and sugar on medium-high speed until pale and fluffy, about 3 minutes. Add eggs, one at a time, and beat until combined, scraping down bowl as needed. Add clementine puree and beat until incorporated, about 30 seconds.

4. Reduce speed to low and add almond mixture in 3 additions until just combined, scraping down bowl as needed. Using rubber spatula, give batter final stir by hand. Transfer batter to prepared pan and smooth top. Bake until toothpick inserted in center comes out clean, 55 minutes to 1 hour. Let cake cool completely in pan on wire rack, about 2 hours.

5. FOR THE CANDIED CLEMENTINES: Meanwhile, line baking sheet with triple layer of paper towels. Slice clementines ¼ inch thick perpendicular to stem; discard rounded ends. Bring water, sugar, and salt to simmer in small saucepan over medium heat and cook until sugar has dissolved, about 1 minute. Add clementines and cook until softened, about 6 minutes. Using tongs, transfer clementines to prepared sheet and let cool for at least 30 minutes, flipping halfway through cooling to blot away excess moisture.

6. FOR THE GLAZE: Whisk sugar, water, and salt in bowl until smooth. Adjust consistency with extra water as needed, ½ teaspoon at a time, until glaze has consistency of thick craft glue and leaves visible trail in bowl when drizzled from whisk.

7. Carefully run paring knife around cake and remove side of pan. Using thin metal spatula, lift cake from pan bottom; discard parchment and transfer cake to serving platter. Pour glaze over cake and smooth top with offset spatula, allowing some glaze to drip down sides. Let sit for 1 hour to set.

8. Just before serving, select 8 uniform candied clementine slices (you will have more than 8 slices; reserve extra slices for another use) and blot away excess moisture with additional paper towels. Arrange slices around top edge of cake, evenly spaced. Serve. (Cake can be wrapped in plastic wrap and stored at room temperature for up to 2 days.)

Triple-Chocolate Sticky Buns

Naysayers said not to mess with a good thing. We love proving naysayers wrong. **by Cecelia Jenkins**

STICKY BUNS—SOFT, YEASTED spirals of dough dripping with gooey caramel and studded with crunchy nuts—are already a perfect sweet treat. But as far as I'm concerned, perfection is just a starting point. I wanted to take these over the top with chocolate.

First, some context: Like cinnamon rolls, sticky buns start as buttery dough rolled into a log with cinnamon sugar inside; the dough is sliced into buns and allowed to rise before being baked in a rich pool of caramel. Once they're finished, you invert them like an upside-down cake, so the gooeyness drapes over the buns and sinks into their coils.

I'm not the first person to try adding chocolate to the mix; I found a handful of recipes in my research. They ranged from relatively austere (with just chocolate chips rolled up inside) to more daring (melted chocolate in the center, cocoa in the dough). But none had the perfect balance of sweet, gooey caramel and luxurious chocolate over soft, pull-apart dough.

For the dough, I turned to a bread-making technique that some of my coworkers have used for ultratender buns. The method, called *tangzhong*, produces a superhydrated dough, so the buns stay moist. And it's remarkably simple: You just microwave a portion of the flour and milk to form a gel-like paste, which locks in moisture. Once the paste is incorporated, the dough becomes very easy to handle. And it yielded soft, tender buns. Tasted next to buns made the traditional way (which were also delicious), we chose the more foolproof tangzhong route.

On to the chocolate. I assembled every variety: cocoa powder, bar chocolate, and chocolate chips; semisweet, bittersweet, and milk. Then I got to experimenting.

Cocoa powder in the dough was the first casualty; it turned the dough dry and chalky. I moved on to bar chocolate, creating a simple ganache (melted chocolate with cream or butter) in the microwave to spread (once cooled) onto the dough before rolling it up. I loved the complex flavor of bittersweet chocolate for the ganache, but it wasn't sweet enough. After spreading it onto the dough, I sprinkled milk chocolate chips across the surface; once the dough was rolled up, cut, and baked, these made for delightful pockets of sweet, creamy flavor.

I was ready to tackle the chocolate and caramel topping, which starts out, of course, on the bottom of the pan. While caramel traditionally involves cooking sugar on the stovetop—a notoriously fussy affair—I knew I could

There's no need to fret, caramel lovers: There is still plenty of sticky, sweet goo adorning the tops of these buns—it's just infused with chocolate flavor, too.

sidestep this process by simply stirring together the caramel ingredients (brown sugar, corn syrup, butter, and a bit of water and salt) and pouring this mixture into a 13 by 9-inch metal baking pan before adding the buns on top. In the oven, the mixture transformed into a sweet, sticky caramel sauce; the moisture from brown sugar and corn syrup (a liquid sugar) kept it soft and pliable even after the buns cooled. To really seal the deal on the chocolate flavor, I returned to my can of cocoa powder, adding a tablespoon to the stir-together caramel.

When I inverted this final batch out of the pan, the buns glistened with drippy, dark caramel. A sweet bakery aroma saturated the air, drawing coworkers from the farthest corners of the kitchen. Once in a while, there is a recipe in the test kitchen that leaves our entire company begging for leftovers. This was it.

TRIPLE-CHOCOLATE STICKY BUNS

Serves 12

These buns take about 4 hours to make. One packet of rapid-rise or instant yeast contains 2¼ teaspoons of yeast. Be sure to use a metal, not glass or ceramic, baking pan. The tackiness of the dough aids in flattening and stretching it in step 7, so resist the urge to use a lot of dusting flour. Rolling the dough cylinder too tightly in step 7 will result in misshapen rolls. Buns baked according to the make-ahead instructions will be shorter than buns baked after the second proofing.

FLOUR PASTE
- ⅔ cup whole milk
- ¼ cup (1¼ ounces) all-purpose flour

DOUGH
- ⅔ cup whole milk
- 1 large egg plus 1 large yolk
- 3¼ cups (16¼ ounces) all-purpose flour
- 2¼ teaspoons instant or rapid-rise yeast
- 3 tablespoons granulated sugar
- 1½ teaspoons salt
- 6 tablespoons unsalted butter, cut into 6 pieces and softened

TOPPING
- ¾ cup packed (5¼ ounces) brown sugar
- 6 tablespoons unsalted butter, melted
- ¼ cup dark corn syrup
- 2 tablespoons water
- 1 tablespoon unsweetened cocoa powder
- ¼ teaspoon salt

FILLING
- 4 ounces bittersweet chocolate, chopped fine
- 4 tablespoons unsalted butter
- 1 cup (6 ounces) milk chocolate chips

1. FOR THE FLOUR PASTE: Whisk milk and flour in small bowl until no lumps remain. Microwave, whisking every 25 seconds, until mixture thickens to stiff paste, 50 to 75 seconds. Whisk until smooth.

2. FOR THE DOUGH: In bowl of stand mixer, whisk flour paste and milk until smooth. Add egg and yolk and whisk until incorporated. Add flour and yeast. Fit mixer with dough hook and mix on low speed until mass of dough forms and all flour is moistened, 1 to 2 minutes. Turn off mixer, cover bowl with dish towel or plastic wrap, and let dough stand for 15 minutes.

3. Add sugar and salt to dough. Knead on medium-low speed for 5 minutes. Add butter and continue to knead until incorporated, scraping down dough hook and bowl as needed (dough will be sticky), about 5 minutes longer.

4. Transfer dough to lightly floured counter and knead briefly to form ball. Transfer, seam side down, to greased large bowl, cover tightly with plastic, and let rise at room temperature until doubled in size, about 1 hour.

5. FOR THE TOPPING: Meanwhile, whisk all ingredients in bowl until combined. Spray 13 by 9-inch metal baking pan with vegetable oil spray. Pour topping into prepared pan and use rubber spatula to spread to edges of pan; set aside.

6. FOR THE FILLING: About 30 minutes before dough is done rising, microwave bittersweet chocolate and butter in bowl at 50 percent power, stirring occasionally, until melted and combined, about 2 minutes. Refrigerate until matte and firm, 30 to 40 minutes.

7. Transfer dough to lightly floured counter and lightly flour top of dough. Roll and stretch dough to form 18 by 15-inch rectangle with long side parallel to counter's edge. Stir bittersweet chocolate mixture with rubber spatula until smooth and spreadable (mixture should have similar texture to frosting). Using offset spatula, spread mixture over entire surface of dough, leaving 1-inch border along top edge. Sprinkle evenly with chocolate chips.

8. Beginning with long edge nearest you, loosely roll dough away from you into even log, pushing in ends to create even thickness. Pinch seam to seal. Roll log seam side down and slice into 12 equal portions. Place buns, cut side down, in prepared pan in 3 rows of four, lightly reshaping buns into circles as needed. Cover tightly with plastic and let rise until buns are puffy and touching one another, about 1 hour.

9. Adjust oven racks to lowest and lower-middle positions and heat oven to 375 degrees. Place rimmed baking sheet on lower rack to catch any drips. Discard plastic and bake buns on upper rack until golden brown on top, about 20 minutes. Cover loosely with aluminum foil and continue to bake until center buns register at least 200 degrees, about 15 minutes longer.

10. Carefully remove foil from pan (steam may escape) and immediately run paring knife around edge of pan. Place large platter or second rimmed baking sheet over pan and carefully invert pan and sheet. Remove pan and let buns cool for 15 minutes. Serve.

TO MAKE AHEAD

Follow recipe through step 8, then refrigerate buns for at least 8 hours or up to 24 hours. When ready to bake, let buns sit on counter for 30 minutes before proceeding with step 9. Increase uncovered baking time by 10 minutes.

Key Steps to the Best Buns

1. Microwave mixture of flour and milk to make stiff paste.

2. Add paste to more milk, egg, yeast, and flour in mixer. When dough forms, wait 15 minutes, then add sugar and salt.

3. Roll dough into 18 by 15-inch rectangle. Spread bittersweet chocolate filling over top. Sprinkle with milk chocolate chips.

Good Things Come in Threes, Including Chocolate

Could we have simply added some cocoa powder to the dough or drizzled some melted chocolate over the top of these buns and called it a day? Sure—if we didn't care about making a knockout recipe. After testing every kind of chocolate in each component, we ended up keeping the bun dough chocolate-free, but we added **cocoa powder** to the caramel topping, based the filling on **bittersweet chocolate**, and then sprinkled **milk chocolate chips** on top of that. The result is a multifaceted, complex chocolate flavor that contributes to these buns' status as a mind-blowing treat. Chocolate lovers will certainly not be disappointed.

4. Carefully roll dough into even log, then pinch seam to seal. Position log seam side down on counter.

5. Cut log into 12 equal portions and place buns, cut side down, on top of caramel topping in pan. Let rise.

6. Bake buns. Run knife around edge of pan, cover with rimmed baking sheet, and carefully invert. Let cool and serve.

Caesar Salad

Our foolproof method—and a good bit of whisking—produces a bold, bright Caesar salad that just may be the best you've ever had. **by Matthew Fairman**

ULTIMATE CAESAR SALAD
Serves 4

Use a rasp-style grater or the fine holes of a box grater to grate the Parmesan. To shred it, use the large holes of a box grater. The size of the lettuce is important here. To cut the lettuce into 1-inch pieces, first cut off the core and then cut each romaine heart in half lengthwise. Cut the halves in half lengthwise. Finally, cut crosswise into 1-inch pieces.

- ¾ cup extra-virgin olive oil
- 2 garlic cloves, minced
  Salt and pepper
- 4 ounces ciabatta, cut into ½-inch cubes (4 cups)
- 1 large egg yolk
- 1 tablespoon lemon juice
- 2 teaspoons Worcestershire sauce
- 2 teaspoons Dijon mustard
- 2 anchovy fillets, rinsed and minced, plus extra fillets for serving (optional)
- ¼ cup grated Parmesan cheese, plus 1½ ounces shredded (½ cup)
- 2 romaine lettuce hearts (12 ounces), cut into 1-inch pieces

1. Adjust oven rack to middle position and heat oven to 350 degrees. Stir ¼ cup oil, half of garlic, ¼ teaspoon salt, and ¼ teaspoon pepper together in large bowl. Add bread and toss to combine. Transfer bread to rimmed baking sheet and bake until light golden, about 18 minutes, stirring halfway through baking. Let cool completely. Wipe bowl clean with paper towels.

2. Form damp dish towel into ring shape on counter. Set now-empty bowl on towel to stabilize. Whisk egg yolk, lemon juice, Worcestershire, mustard, anchovies, ¼ teaspoon salt, ¼ teaspoon pepper, and remaining garlic together in bowl. Whisking constantly, slowly drizzle in remaining ½ cup oil until emulsified. Whisk in grated Parmesan.

3. Add lettuce, croutons, and shredded Parmesan to bowl with dressing and toss to combine. Season with salt and pepper to taste. Serve, garnished with extra anchovies, if using.

Conquering Caesar

This salad has its origins in Italy, right? Clearly, it must be named after Julius Caesar or maybe his nephew Augustus? Not even close. The famed salad is said to have been invented on July 4, 1924, by celebrity restaurateur Caesar Cardini at his popular Caesar's Bar and Grill in Tijuana, Mexico (a young Julia Child famously ate there with her parents). The story goes that the kitchen was low on ingredients and that Cardini whipped up the salad—using Worcestershire sauce and no anchovies—on the spot.

The salad's popularity over the years has not only endured but increased, and it is said to be a big driver of the growth of farms specializing in romaine lettuce.

Step by Step

1. Cube crusty bread
Use a serrated knife to cut 4 ounces of ciabatta into ½-inch cubes.
Why? Huge croutons are hard to eat; tiny ones disappear. Half-inch cubes are just right.

2. Toss bread with seasoned oil
Combine the olive oil, minced garlic, salt, and pepper in a bowl. Add the bread cubes and toss.
Why? Oil, garlic, salt, and pepper give the croutons plenty of savory flavor.

3. Bake croutons
Spread the seasoned bread cubes into a single layer on a rimmed baking sheet and bake in a 350-degree oven until light golden.
Why? The oven is more efficient than the stovetop for making a big batch of croutons.

4. Prep Parmesan
Grate ¼ cup of Parmesan on a rasp-style grater and shred ½ cup on the large holes of a box or paddle grater.
Why? The finely grated Parmesan will enrich the dressing; the larger shreds will provide pops of salty savor to the salad.

5. Mince anchovies
Finely mince two anchovy fillets; a chef's knife is the most efficient tool for this job.
Why? Pulverizing the anchovy fillets by hand is the best way to get cleanly minced fillets that will blend into the dressing.

Test Kitchen Tips for Caesar Dressing

Choose the Right Whisk

There are specialty whisks such as flat whisks and dough whisks, but most home cooks can get by with just a good all-purpose whisk. In our testing of all-purpose whisks, the **OXO Good Grips 11" Balloon Whisk ($9.99)** came out on top. We love its ergonomic rubber handle and balanced, lightweight feel. It aced our tests in whipping both cream and egg whites and shone when used to emulsify pan sauces. It works great for Caesar dressing, too.

Whisk Correctly

Whisking is whisking, right? Wrong. Our tests have shown that the best, most efficient motion for emulsifying a vinaigrette (such as the one for Caesar Salad) is a basic, vigorous side-to-side motion; it works better than circular stirring or looping beating. Why does the side-to-side motion work best? First, it's simply an easier motion to execute quickly and aggressively, allowing you to make more firm strokes per minute. Second, the reversal in direction creates more of what scientists call "shear force," which most efficiently breaks the oil into tiny droplets that stay suspended in the vinegar, helping keep the dressing emulsified longer. So save circular beating for egg whites: Dressings are best whisked side to side.

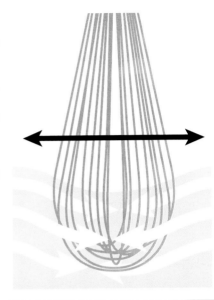

Build a Strong Emulsion

Caesar dressing is based on an emulsion of oil and vinegar. Constant whisking breaks down the oil into tiny droplets that get suspended in the vinegar, forming the creamy emulsion. Add the oil slowly or the ingredients won't come together and the dressing will be greasy.

WEAK
Oil and vinegar separate

STRONG
Oil and vinegar combine

Key Ingredients

Anchovies

Anchovies are a secret ingredient of the savvy cook; even when you can't taste them outright, these potent little fillets add deep savory flavor to myriad dishes. But what to do with the rest of the tin when a recipe calls for only a few? We recommend transferring them to a nonreactive container (an empty jam jar or a small Mason jar is great) along with their oil, topping them off with extra olive oil if necessary to keep them fully covered. Stored this way in the refrigerator, anchovies should last for up to one month.

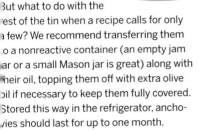

Romaine Lettuce

You simply cannot call a salad a Caesar salad unless it is made with crunchy, lightly sweet romaine lettuce. To store romaine, we recommend wrapping each heart in moist paper towels, placing the hearts in a zipper-lock bag, and stashing them in the crisper drawer of your refrigerator with the bag left slightly open.

Bread for Croutons

While any crusty bread with a soft interior will work, we especially like the texture of croutons made with open-crumbed ciabatta. *Ciabatta* means "slipper" in Italian; the bread has a similarly long, wide shape.

6. Get ready to whisk
Form a damp dish towel into a ring shape on the counter and place a bowl in the center.
Why? Whisking—and lots of it—is key to this recipe, and you'll need both hands. The towel helps stabilize the mixing bowl on the counter while you work.

7. Combine dressing ingredients
Whisk the egg yolk, lemon juice, Worcestershire sauce, Dijon mustard, anchovies, salt, pepper, and garlic together in the bowl.
Why? It's important that the ingredients are well combined and smooth before you add the oil.

8. Slowly add oil
Whisking constantly, very slowly drizzle in ½ cup of olive oil until the dressing is emulsified.
Why? If you add the oil too fast, the dressing will never emulsify and become cohesive.

9. Add grated Parmesan
Whisk the grated Parmesan into the emulsified dressing.
Why? Adding the cheese earlier could prevent the dressing from emulsifying.

10. Put it all together
Add the romaine, croutons, and shredded Parmesan to the dressing and toss thoroughly.
Why? Adding the salad's larger components to the bowl with the dressing is the best way to guarantee that none of it is wasted.

Candied Bacons

The goal: equal parts sweet, savory, salty, smoky, and satisfying. **by Heather Tolmie**

Halving the strips before sugaring and baking them makes for easier eating.

IT'S HARD TO imagine improving on bacon. But over the past few months, more than one of my colleagues has come into the office with a story of a cocktail party where they had been served a surprising twist: candied bacon (bacon cooked with sugar).

At their best, these crispy strips offer a new sweet-savory way of looking at bacon. But when things go south, you find yourself with a fatty, soggy, or even syrupy piece of bacon that sags under the weight of its coating, drooping and dripping dangerously close to your best party clothes. I wanted to create a recipe for crispy bacon strips with surprising flavor and satisfying crunch.

After a few initial tests with existing recipes, I knew for sure that the oven was my best bet for consistent cooking. And while liquid sugars (including simple syrup, maple syrup, and corn syrup) were easy to brush onto the strips, they gave me soggy, droopy bacon. Solid sugar was the way to go. But which one?

A test of granulated sugar, confectioners' sugar, dark brown sugar, and light brown sugar proved that light brown sugar was the way forward. It's easy to sprinkle over the strips and contributes a lovely caramel-toffee background flavor along with its sweetness. And unlike dark brown sugar, it didn't turn the strips too dark.

These tests also revealed that center-cut bacon worked better than thick-cut (which didn't cook through before the sugar burned) and regular cut (the uneven ends made equal coverage difficult). What's more, I learned I'd need two baking sheets for 12 ounces of bacon. Cramming them all onto one sheet left some bits underrendered and flabby.

From there, the process was simple. I just sprinkled sugar (and a bit of black pepper for punch) over strips of bacon and baked them on a foil-lined rimmed baking sheet at 350 degrees for 20 minutes or so—no flipping necessary. Once cooled, the strips crisped up with no hint of syrupiness.

Emboldened, I created four variations: rosemary, chipotle, jerk, and five-spice and sesame. Each is as simple as adding a few ingredients to the sugar and pepper and delivers the same crunch, only with added dimension. Bacon lovers should try all five.

CANDIED BACON
Serves 4 to 6
Do not use dark brown sugar here. We call for center-cut bacon because we found the strips to be of more even thickness than regular bacon. The bacon on one baking sheet may cook more quickly; if this happens, it's OK to remove this sheet from the oven before the other. Lining the sheets with aluminum foil eases cleanup.

- 12 ounces center-cut bacon
- ¼ cup packed light brown sugar
- 1 teaspoon pepper

1. Adjust oven racks to upper-middle and lower-middle positions and heat oven to 350 degrees. Line 2 rimmed baking sheets with aluminum foil. Cut bacon in half crosswise. Arrange bacon on prepared sheets.
2. Combine sugar and pepper in bowl. Sprinkle sugar mixture evenly over bacon (do not flip and sprinkle on second side). Use your fingers to spread sugar mixture evenly over each piece.
3. Bake until bacon is dark brown and sugar is bubbling, 20 to 25 minutes, switching and rotating sheets halfway through baking (if bacon on 1 sheet finishes cooking sooner, it's OK to remove this sheet from oven first). Transfer bacon to wire rack and let cool for 5 minutes. Serve.

ROSEMARY CANDIED BACON
Add 1 tablespoon minced fresh rosemary to sugar mixture.

CHIPOTLE CANDIED BACON
Add ½ teaspoon chipotle chile powder, ½ teaspoon ground cumin, and ¼ teaspoon granulated garlic to sugar mixture.

JERK CANDIED BACON
Add 1 tablespoon minced fresh thyme, 1½ teaspoons ground allspice, ¾ teaspoon granulated garlic, ½ teaspoon dry mustard, and ⅛ teaspoon cayenne pepper to sugar mixture.

FIVE-SPICE AND SESAME CANDIED BACON
Add 1 teaspoon five-spice powder to sugar mixture. After spreading sugar mixture over bacon, sprinkle 1 tablespoon sesame seeds evenly over top.

Huevos Rancheros

We wanted a hearty breakfast that was fast and easy enough to throw together while the coffee was brewing. **by Morgan Bolling**

HUEVOS RANCHEROS, OR "rancher-style eggs," are a happy mess of slightly runny eggs snuggled in spicy tomato sauce and draped with melted cheese. The dish is typically served with tortillas to mop up all the saucy, silky goodness, and it packs enough of a wallop to jump-start even the foggiest of mornings.

The test kitchen has a handful of recipes for huevos rancheros, but they all take a bit of labor to build layers of flavor. I hoped I could create a streamlined version to serve two that avoided the hard work (such as charring tomatoes and onions and making salsa) but still paid off in flavor.

You can certainly cook the eggs and sauce separately and combine them on the plate—many restaurants do it this way. But the flavors meld and the dish tastes better when you cook the eggs directly in the sauce. Plus, cleanup is easier. So to start, I chopped an onion and a jalapeño chile and sautéed them in a little oil. Then I stirred in chopped fresh tomatoes and let the mixture simmer until thickened, which took about 10 minutes. I sprinkled pepper Jack cheese over the top and then used a spoon to make four wells in the tomato mixture before cracking an egg into each well. Finally, I covered the skillet and continued to cook until the egg whites were set.

While this version had good flavor, it took nearly 30 minutes to soften the vegetables, thicken the tomatoes, and poach the eggs—plus, the eggs didn't all cook at the same rate. A few tests proved that rotating the skillet halfway through the eggs' cooking time and reducing the heat to medium-low while poaching made the eggs cook more gently and evenly so I could get soft yolks and set whites in all four eggs at the same time.

I tested a variety of canned tomato products to see if any helped cut back on time, but at best they shaved off a few minutes. Instead, a coworker suggested trying store-bought salsa. While I think of salsa as a condiment, using it as an ingredient sounded smart here; I could omit the onion and jalapeño since most jarred salsas already contain them. Plus, as long as I used jarred salsa, it was thick enough that I could easily make wells for the eggs without

having to simmer and reduce it. (Fresh salsa, such as pico de gallo, was too chunky and would not work here.)

To boost the salsa's flavor, I added sliced garlic, scallions, and a tablespoon of smoky, spicy chipotle chile in adobo sauce. A little bit of brown sugar called out the tomatoes' natural sweetness.

Served straight from the skillet with a fresh sprinkling of cilantro and warmed tortillas for scooping, this savory, filling breakfast is hard to beat. And it's so simple that I can make it while still half-asleep.

HUEVOS RANCHEROS FOR TWO
We developed this recipe using Chi-Chi's Mild Thick & Chunky Salsa. Serve with lime wedges and diced avocado.

- 1 tablespoon extra-virgin olive oil
- 2 scallions, white and green parts separated and sliced thin
- 2 garlic cloves, sliced thin
- 1 (16-ounce) jar mild salsa
- 1 tablespoon minced canned chipotle chile in adobo sauce
- 1½ teaspoons packed brown sugar
- 4 ounces pepper Jack cheese, shredded (1 cup)
- 4 large eggs
  Salt and pepper
- 1 tablespoon chopped fresh cilantro
- 4 (6-inch) corn tortillas, warmed

1. Heat oil in 10-inch nonstick skillet over medium-high heat until shimmering. Add scallion whites and garlic and cook until softened, about 3 minutes.

2. Off heat, stir in salsa, chipotle, and sugar. Sprinkle pepper Jack evenly over salsa mixture. Using rubber spatula, make four 2-inch-diameter wells in salsa mixture evenly around perimeter of skillet. (Skillet bottom should be visible in each well.) Crack 1 egg into each well and season with salt and pepper.

3. Return skillet to medium-high heat and bring to boil. Cover, reduce heat to medium-low, and cook until egg whites are set and no watery patches remain, 4 to 6 minutes for runny yolks or 6 to 8 minutes for set yolks, rotating skillet occasionally for even cooking. Sprinkle with cilantro and scallion greens. Serve with tortillas.

The secret to our easy, flavorful sauce? Enhancing store-bought salsa with scallions, garlic, and smoky chipotle chile in adobo sauce.

Make the Wells
Use a rubber spatula to make room in the salsa mixture for the eggs; you should be able to see the skillet bottom. Crack the eggs into the wells, cover the skillet, and cook until the eggs are done.

TOO CHUNKY
Not saucy enough

TOO WATERY
Won't hold wells

JUST RIGHT
Our favorite

Salsa Consistency
Our favorite salsa, Chi-Chi's Mild Thick & Chunky Salsa, is thick enough to hold wells for the eggs; a watery salsa won't hold the wells, and pico de gallo is too chunky to feel like part of the finished dish.

Meatloaf Dinner

There's something nostalgic about a classic meatloaf supper, but there's no nostalgia for doing lots of dishes. **by Cecelia Jenkins**

MY MOM USED to make a classic, comforting supper of meatloaf, potatoes, and green beans on Sunday nights. For a modern spin on this old favorite, I wanted a version with all the components made on a single baking sheet, so I could slide the whole thing into the oven on a busy weeknight without another thought.

Starting with the meatloaf, I drew on test kitchen expertise and chose straightforward ingredients that didn't need precooking. For the meat, I used beef—as straightforward as it gets—and added a panade (or paste) of crushed saltines and milk, which would help the meatloaf stay moist and tender. For extra depth, I stirred in a little soy sauce and grated Parmesan cheese. Fresh thyme, granulated garlic, and red pepper flakes added pep, and a couple of eggs helped hold it all together. I tried different glazes but ended up using the simplest of all: ketchup, the perfect sweet, savory, and tangy condiment. Delicious.

After a bit of experimenting with different types and cuts of potatoes, I landed on small red potatoes. When halved, they roasted to perfection on the sheet—creamy inside and crisp and browned on the bottoms—and were ready at the same time as the meatloaf (about 45 minutes at 400 degrees).

If only the green beans were as easy to fit into the puzzle. I tried for a week to get them to work, but no matter when I added them, they cooked unevenly on the crowded baking sheet. And no one likes a drab, mushy green bean in one bite and an almost raw, crunchy one in the next. Frozen peas, those fickle little orbs, fared poorly, too.

I landed on an unlikely hero: Brussels sprouts. When roasted, these little cabbages turn tender and sweet. I trimmed and halved 12 ounces of sprouts; snuggled them, cut side down, among the potatoes on the sheet; and roasted them along with the meatloaf. Sure enough, they turned out perfect—browned and crispy outside and tender inside—and they shrank significantly enough that I found I could bump up the amount to a full pound to make more substantial servings.

One last tweak was in order. To brighten up the deep roasted flavor of the vegetables, I gave them a quick toss in a lemon-parsley oil just before serving. This was my easiest one-pan supper yet: no fussing with the different components and no adding ingredients in stages. Here's to hands-off comfort food with just one pan to clean!

For a finishing touch, we toss the roasted potatoes and perfectly cooked Brussels sprouts in a lemon and parsley oil before serving them with the meatloaf.

Cooking: The Cure for Crowding

The raw ingredients make a tight fit.

Cooking = shrinkage = room to brown.

ONE-PAN MEATLOAF WITH POTATOES AND BRUSSELS SPROUTS *Serves 4*

There are about 35 saltines in one sleeve of crackers. Be sure to use small red potatoes measuring 1 to 2 inches in diameter here. Look for Brussels sprouts with small, tight heads that are no more than 1½ inches in diameter, as they're likely to be sweeter and more tender than larger sprouts.

- 35 square saltines
- 2 ounces Parmesan cheese, grated (1 cup)
- 2 large eggs
- ¼ cup milk
- ¼ cup soy sauce
- 1½ tablespoons minced fresh thyme
- 1½ teaspoons granulated garlic
- ¼ teaspoon red pepper flakes
  Salt and pepper
- 2 pounds 85 percent lean ground beef
- ½ cup ketchup
- 1 pound small red potatoes, unpeeled, halved
- 1 pound Brussels sprouts, trimmed and halved
- 3 tablespoons extra-virgin olive oil
- 1 tablespoon chopped fresh parsley
- ½ teaspoon grated lemon zest

1. Adjust oven rack to lower-middle position and heat oven to 400 degrees.

Spray rimmed baking sheet with vegetable oil spray.

2. Transfer saltines to large zipper-lock bag, seal bag, and crush fine with rolling pin. Combine Parmesan, eggs, milk, soy sauce, thyme, granulated garlic, pepper flakes, ¼ teaspoon salt, ¼ teaspoon pepper, and saltine crumbs in large bowl. Mix until all crumbs are moistened and mixture forms paste. Add beef and mix with your hands to thoroughly combine.

3. Transfer meatloaf mixture to center of prepared sheet. Using your wet hands, shape into 9 by 5-inch rectangle; top should be flat and meatloaf should be an even 1½ inches thick. Brush top and sides of meatloaf with ketchup.

4. Toss potatoes, Brussels sprouts, 2 tablespoons oil, ½ teaspoon salt, and ¼ teaspoon pepper together in bowl. Place potatoes and Brussels sprouts on sheet, cut side down, around meatloaf. Bake until meatloaf registers 160 degrees and vegetables are tender and browned on bottoms, 40 to 45 minutes.

5. Remove sheet from oven. Transfer meatloaf to cutting board; let rest for 10 minutes. Stir parsley, lemon zest, and remaining 1 tablespoon oil in medium bowl until combined. Transfer vegetables to parsley mixture and toss until evenly coated. Slice meatloaf and serve with vegetables.

Herbed Pork Roast with White Beans and Kale

We set out to keep this dish's rustic appeal with a lot less work. **by Matthew Fairman**

THE CLASSIC TUSCAN combination of rich pork, creamy white beans, and kale perfumed with garlic, rosemary, sage, and fennel tastes amazing, but recipes for this dish often take more than a day to make. They call for soaking dried beans, making stock, sautéing vegetables, and using all manner of pots and pans in the process. I hoped to find a simpler, more direct path using the slow cooker.

To start, I chose canned white beans rather than dried for a couple of reasons. First, canned beans are already fully hydrated and need almost no added liquid for cooking. To achieve creamy rather than soupy beans, I wanted very little extra liquid (I knew that both the pork and the kale would give up a good deal of moisture in the cooker). Second, surprisingly, canned beans often retain their structure better than dried in long-cooked dishes because, like most canned vegetables, they're processed with a firming agent (see "Canned versus Dried Beans").

For the pork, I chose a boneless pork butt roast. A few tests proved that leaving the roast whole, rather than cutting it into chunks, was not only less work but also made for a sliceable, more attractive final presentation. Many recipes call for searing the pork in a skillet on all sides to build flavor and browning before sautéing onion, carrot, celery, and garlic in the drippings and then moving it all to a Dutch oven. But I was hoping to skip these steps and just put everything in the cooker and hit "on."

I stirred the raw aromatics and beans together in the slow cooker along with a trio of flavorings: rosemary, sage, and fennel seeds. I nestled my seasoned roast atop the whole mix, covered the cooker, and turned it on (the kale would come later; it needed only about a half-hour at the end to soften).

Several hours later, when the roast was tender, I pulled it out to rest, stirred the chopped kale into the beans, and cooked for another 30 minutes. Surprisingly, this dump-and-stir version was darn close to everything I wanted. The creamy beans had soaked up the rich, complex flavor of the pork and herbs, and the kale provided a strong vegetable counterpoint. My only complaint was that the pork cooked a little sad and gray. Instead of searing the roast on the front end to solve this problem, I tried coating my roast with the garlic and herbs that I'd hitherto been stirring into the beans.

This turned out to be an inspired strategy. The beans were just right, and the finished roast now had an alluring garlic-herb crust that made it easier on the eyes and totally delicious. This dish had it all: looks, flavor, and ease.

SLOW-COOKER HERBED PORK WITH WHITE BEANS AND KALE
Serves 6
We prefer the color and texture of Lacinato kale here, but you can substitute curly kale. Note that we use the liquid from one can of beans, so don't drain them all up front. Pork butt is often labeled Boston butt in the supermarket.

- 3 **(15-ounce) cans cannellini beans (2 cans drained and rinsed, 1 can left undrained)**
- 1 **onion, chopped**
- 2 **carrots, peeled and chopped**
- 2 **celery ribs, chopped**
- 8 **garlic cloves (4 sliced thin, 4 minced)**
- 1 **tablespoon extra-virgin olive oil, plus extra for drizzling**
- 1 **tablespoon minced fresh rosemary**
- 1 **tablespoon minced fresh sage**
- 2 **teaspoons ground fennel seeds Salt and pepper**
- 1 **(2½- to 3-pound) boneless pork butt roast, trimmed**
- 12 **ounces kale, stemmed and cut into 1-inch pieces Lemon wedges**

1. Add 2 cans drained beans, 1 can beans and their liquid, onion, carrots, celery, and sliced garlic to slow cooker. Stir to combine.

2. Combine oil, rosemary, sage, fennel seeds, 1½ teaspoons salt, 1 teaspoon pepper, and minced garlic in bowl. Rub paste all over pork. Nestle pork into bean mixture in slow cooker. Cover and cook until pork is tender, 8 to 9 hours on low or 6 to 7 hours on high.

3. Transfer pork to carving board and tent with aluminum foil. Add kale to bean mixture in slow cooker; cover and cook on high until kale is tender, about 30 minutes. Season vegetables with salt and pepper to taste. Slice pork ½ inch thick. Serve pork with vegetables, drizzling individual portions with extra oil and passing lemon wedges separately.

The comforting flavors of this satisfying dish will take the chill off any winter night.

Canned versus Dried Beans

When we first started working on this recipe, we assumed we'd be using dried beans—sure, they take a long time to cook, but this is a slow-cooker recipe. So we were surprised to find that we preferred canned beans, specifically our taste test winner from Goya, to dried in this recipe.

Canned beans have added salt, so they taste well seasoned. The salt in the can has another benefit: It mixes with the bean liquid to form a sort of brine, which helps tenderize the beans' skins. Canned beans also typically contain calcium chloride, which helps maintain firmness and prevent the skins from splitting, even in a long-cooking recipe like this one. When we tried using dried beans, we found that over the long cooking time, they ruptured, turned mushy, or both.

Does this mean we're done with dried beans? Absolutely not. The best dried beans, especially those from specialty producers such as Rancho Gordo, have a rich, earthy flavor that canned beans simply can't equal. But dried beans take time and attention in the kitchen, and—as we found out—can split and get unappealingly mushy if cooked too long.

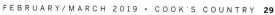

OUR FAVORITE
Stayed firm over the long cooking time

Stainless-Steel Skillets

A versatile stainless-steel frying pan is the backbone of most kitchens.
But can you get a great 12-inch pan for less than $100?

by Lisa McManus

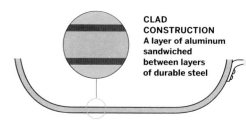

CLAD CONSTRUCTION
A layer of aluminum sandwiched between layers of durable steel

KEY **Good** ★★★ **Fair** ★★ **Poor**

9 Pans 16 Tests

- Measure bottom thickness, cooking surface diameter, height of sides (noting shape), and length of handle
- If no lid, check for fit with favorite lids
- Check levelness of interior surface
- Pan-sear steaks and make pan sauce
- Pan-roast chicken and make pan sauce
- Pan-roast asparagus, using lid
- Pan-roast green beans
- Sauté diced onions
- Wash by hand after each test
- Wash once in dishwasher
- Check interior for warping, using level
- Heat pan to 500°F on stovetop, plunge into ice water, and check for warping
- Whack 3 times on concrete ledge

A 12-INCH STAINLESS-STEEL skillet is the definition of a kitchen workhorse. With its all-metal construction, this pan goes from stovetop to oven effortlessly, so it's perfect for cooking thicker cuts of meat and fish, baking skillet pies, and pan-roasting whole chickens. Our long-time favorite, the All-Clad d3 Stainless Steel 12" Fry Pan with Lid, sells for $119.99, but we wondered if we could get a comparable pan for less money.

To find out, we bought eight skillets, priced from $47.99 to $99.99, and tested them against our favorite. All share its fully clad construction, meaning that the entire pan is built of layers of different metals bonded together. The All-Clad, for example, is made from a layer of aluminum sandwiched between layers of stainless steel, so you get aluminum's speedy heat conduction modulated by heat-retaining, durable steel.

In each pan, we seared four strip steaks, and pan-roasted chicken parts and made a pan sauce. We also sautéed diced onions and green beans and pan-roasted asparagus. We washed each pan by hand and in the dishwasher. Finally, we knocked the pans around to simulate years of use.

While all the pans look similar, our cooking results varied. About half of the pans gave steaks a deep sear on the first side and then struggled to recover their heat, so the second side was paler and created sparse fond (and a weak pan sauce). Why? The cooking surface of some pans was about 8 inches, which

was too small. This effect worsened if the sides were high and trapped condensation. We liked pans with cooking surfaces that measured at least 8½ inches across. On the flip side, bigger pans were often too heavy. Our highest-rated less-expensive pans weighed about 3 pounds; none felt as light and balanced as the All-Clad at 2.8 pounds.

Another factor that mattered: handles that were easy to grab securely (even with potholders), stayed cool on the stovetop, and didn't splay our fingers or twist in our grip. We didn't like helper handles; they added weight and threw the pans off balance.

During our cooking tests, five of the eight pans priced below $100.00 warped with routine use. All became dented in our abuse testing, and three developed wobbly handles. That left just one under-$100.00 pan with a strong handle, only minor dents, and no warping.

To understand why our pans dented and warped, we consulted Mike Tarkanian, senior lecturer and metallurgy expert in the Materials Science and Engineering department at MIT. He explained that thicker pans are less prone to warping and denting and tend to cook better, too. When we measured the thickness of the pans' cooking surfaces, all but one were thinner than the All-Clad, which is 3.0 mm thick.

Tarkanian also cut into the pans to reveal the layered construction. A few of the lowest-ranked pans contained both thick and thin layers of steel, which could contribute to warping as different material thicknesses are prone to expand and contract at different rates when heated or cooled. By contrast, the All-Clad pan appeared to have top and bottom steel layers of equal thickness sandwiching a thicker aluminum layer.

Bottom line: None of the truly cheap pans met our standards. A few of the pans closer to the $100.00 mark were OK, but none was as good as our longtime favorite, which also comes with a useful lid. If you can spend a bit more, we highly recommend the original fully clad skillet, which our tests proved is still the best: the All-Clad d3 Stainless Steel 12" Fry Pan with Lid ($119.99). It's an investment, but it will last a lifetime. Web subscribers can read the complete testing at **CooksCountry.com/mar19**.

HIGHLY RECOMMENDED

All-Clad d3 Stainless Steel 12" Fry Pan with Lid
Model: 41126   **Price:** $119.99
Weight: 2.8 lb
Bottom Thickness: 3.0 mm
Cooking Surface: 9.5 in
Height of Sides: 2 in
Comments: Our longtime favorite still beats the cheaper competition with its broad cooking surface; low, flaring sides; stay-cool handle; perfect balance; and durability.

CRITERIA
Performance ★★
Ease of Use ★★
Cleanup/Durability ★★

RECOMMENDED WITH RESERVATIONS

Made In 12" Fry Pan
Model: COOK-12-FRY-SS
Price: $85.00   **Weight:** 3 lb
Bottom Thickness: 2.8 mm
Cooking Surface: 8.75 in
Height of Sides: 2 in

Performance ★★★
Ease of Use ★★½
Cleanup/Durability ★★
Comments: Didn't sit flat out of the box and warped during testing. Otherwise good.

Tramontina Gourmet Tri-Ply Clad 12-Inch Fry Pan with Helper Handle
Model: 80116/057DS   **Price:** $69.95
Weight: 3.2 lb
Bottom Thickness: 2.8 mm
Cooking Surface: 8.38 in
Height of Sides: 2 in

Performance ★★
Ease of Use ★★½
Cleanup/Durability ★★½
Comments: A narrow cooking surface limited the amount of food we could fit in this sturdy, heavy pan.

Cuisinart Multiclad Pro 12" Skillet with Helper Handle & Cover
Model: MCP22-30HCN   **Price:** $69.95
Weight: 3.75 lb
Bottom Thickness: 2.8 mm
Cooking Surface: 10 in
Height of Sides: 2.13 in

Performance ★★½
Ease of Use ★★½
Cleanup/Durability ★★
Comments: The large cooking surface warped early in routine testing and wobbled noticeably. It browned well.

Calphalon Tri-Ply Stainless Steel 12-In Omelette Pan
Model: 1767730   **Price:** $69.95
Weight: 3 lb
Bottom Thickness: 2.4 mm
Cooking Surface: 9.75 in
Height of Sides: 2.25 in

Performance ★★½
Ease of Use ★★½
Cleanup/Durability ★½
Comments: Steaks browned well on the first side but less well on the second. It warped and dented badly.

OXO Good Grips Stainless Steel Pro 12" Open Frypan
Model: CW000974-003   **Price:** $79.99
Weight: 3.2 lb
Bottom Thickness: 2.7 mm
Cooking Surface: 9.5 in
Height of Sides: 2.13 in

Performance ★★
Ease of Use ★★½
Cleanup/Durability ★★
Comments: This pan felt balanced, but it didn't brown perfectly. Its handle felt short and fat. It was harder to clean.

Winco Tri-Gen 12" Tri-ply Stainless Steel Fry Pan, Natural Finish
Model: TGFP-12   **Price:** $47.99
Weight: 3.4 lb
Bottom Thickness: 2.7 mm
Cooking Surface: 9.25 in
Height of Sides: 2.25 in

Performance ★★
Ease of Use ★½
Cleanup/Durability ★★½
Comments: It felt heavy, and testers disliked the feel of its "bubble-shaped" handle. Its sides were too tall.

American Provolone

This mild-mannered Italian-style cheese finally gets its chance to shine.

Lauren Savoie

PROVOLONE IS UNFAIRLY regarded as the middle child of Italian cheeses: neither as punchy and popular as Parmigiano-Reggiano nor as mild and widely used as mozzarella. Yet iconic sandwiches such as the Philadelphia cheesesteak and the New Orleans muffuletta would be incomplete without slices of this aged cow's-milk cheese; it's also at home in pasta salads, stromboli, cheese bread, and even quesadillas.

Most of us know provolone as a young, slightly soft cheese that is very mild in flavor, but aged provolone can be sharp, almost bitter, and have a crumbly, semihard texture. In Italy, the former is known as *provolone dolce* ("sweet" provolone) and is aged for less than four months, while the latter is called *provolone piccante* ("spicy" provolone) and is aged for up to three years. What makes all provolone similar, however, is the way it's produced. Cow's milk is heated with cultures and enzymes until the curds separate from the whey. The curds are strained, salted, and then plunged into hot water to make them flexible. Once removed from the water, they are stretched until they become smooth and elastic. If the method sounds similar to the way mozzarella is made, that's because it is. However, unlike mozzarella, provolone contains enzymes (added for flavor), is aged, and is almost always made from cow's milk (traditional mozzarella is made from buffalo's milk).

Venture into a specialty cheese shop or an Italian deli and you may see provolone cheeses being aged in the traditional way: hung by ropes from the ceiling, similar to the way prosciutto and other cured meats are hung for aging. The ropes used to secure the cheeses eventually give some of them a characteristic bell-like shape. However, the provolone cheese sold at most supermarkets rarely resembles its traditional counterpart: You can buy it in shrink-wrapped wedges, presliced in packages, or sliced to order at the deli counter.

For our tasting, we focused on sliced domestic provolone, since we call for slices more often than wedges in our recipes. We chose five products from top-selling, nationally available cheese brands—four packaged presliced cheeses and one cheese that we had sliced to order at the deli—priced from $0.38 to $1.15 per ounce. We tasted the cheeses plain and in stromboli.

Tasters were able to identify clear differences when they tried the cheeses plain, but those differences were hard to notice when the cheeses were melted in stromboli. To home in on how the provolones behaved when melted, we added a third tasting, in which we tasted them all in simple cheese quesadillas.

Ultimately, we can recommend every cheese in our lineup; they were all smooth and pliable in texture—perfect for layering onto sandwiches—

and melted easily. While they varied a bit in flavor, none tasted bad. Our favorite cheeses balanced mellow, milky flavor with just a hint of sharpness and had subtle nutty, earthy, and savory notes that added complexity.

We looked at the cheeses' ingredient labels to see if we could identify what set some products apart. All the cheeses had the same amount of fat (5 grams per serving) and similar ingredients. Two of the cheeses had "natural smoke flavor" added—presumably for complexity—but it was so subtle that many tasters didn't even pick up on it. Those who did were split—some liked the slight smokiness, while others preferred a more neutral-tasting provolone.

Instead, we found that good flavor is a function of age and salt. Not all the manufacturers would tell us how long they age their provolones, but among

those that did, it ranged from two weeks to longer than two months. The product that was aged for only two weeks ended up at the bottom of our rankings; tasters thought it was very mild, bordering on bland. Provolones that were aged longer ranked higher.

Our favorite cheeses also had more sodium, which helped amp up their flavor. Sodium ranged from 105 to 190 milligrams per 21-gram serving. The cheese with the least sodium was overly mild despite having been aged for two months. Our top-ranked cheese had the most salt of all.

Though any of the cheeses in our lineup will work just fine, our favorite was Organic Valley Provolone Cheese Slices ($6.89 for 6 ounces). This provolone had a balanced, mild flavor that adapted well to recipes, plus a hint of savory saltiness for added complexity.

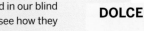

American Provolone versus Italian: What's the Difference?

Tasters noted that the American-made provolones we tried in our blind taste test were "mild" and "mellow" with a soft texture. To see how they compared to imported Italian provolones, we purchased a *provolone piccante* aged for more than a year and a *provolone dolce* aged for four months and tasted them against our winning American provolone, which was aged for just two months. The flavors, textures, and colors of the three cheeses were very different. The darker yellow provolone piccante was hard and crumbly and tartly sharp. The creamy yellow Italian dolce was softer and mellower but still "funky" and "sharp." Tasters noted that the two Italian cheeses would be "a good choice for a cheese board."

PICCANTE   AMERICAN

DOLCE

RECOMMENDED

Our Favorite				
Organic Valley Provolone Cheese Slices	**Kraft** Sliced Provolone Cheese	**Applegate Naturals** Provolone Cheese	**Sargento** Sliced Provolone Cheese	**Galbani** Provolone Cheese
Price: $6.89 for 6 oz ($1.15 per oz)	**Price:** $4.00 for 8 oz ($0.50 per oz)	**Price:** $4.99 for 8 oz ($0.62 per oz)	**Price:** $3.49 for 8 oz ($0.44 per oz)	**Price:** $3.00 for 8 oz ($0.38 per oz)
Aged: 2 months	**Aged:** Proprietary	**Aged:** 2 months	**Aged:** 2 weeks	**Aged:** Proprietary
Packaging: Presliced	**Packaging:** Presliced	**Packaging:** Presliced	**Packaging:** Presliced	**Packaging:** Sliced to order at deli
Sodium: 190 mg	**Sodium:** 166 mg	**Sodium:** 177 mg	**Sodium:** 149 mg	**Sodium:** 105 mg
Comments: Our winning provolone was "pleasantly tangy," with "subtle sharpness" and "nutty," "grassy" notes. Its high salt content intensified the flavor.	**Comments:** This cheese contains natural smoke flavor, which tasters said gave it a "meaty," "smoky" flavor and an "unexpected" aroma. A few thought it tasted more like gouda than provolone.	**Comments:** Tasters found this cheese "creamy" and "a bit sharp," "a little like Swiss cheese." Many picked up on a slightly "bitter" minerality. Overall, it was "great for both snacking and melting."	**Comments:** It was no surprise that this "subtly smoky" cheese also contained natural smoke flavor. A few tasters thought it was "a little too mild."	**Comments:** This provolone, which is available sliced from the deli, has a "mild," "sweet," and "buttery" flavor. Because of its low salt content, some tasters thought it was a bit "dull."

Orange Chocolate Mousse

This dessert was a favorite of my grandmother's, who spiked it with a slosh of liqueur and served it with a wink.

—TUCKER SHAW,
Editor in Chief

ORANGE CHOCOLATE MOUSSE
Serves 6
For a nonalcoholic version of this dessert, substitute orange juice for the Grand Marnier. Garnish the mousse with whipped cream and chocolate shavings or orange zest, if desired.

- 8 ounces bittersweet chocolate, chopped fine
- 2 large eggs plus 2 large yolks
- ¼ cup packed (1¾ ounces) light brown sugar
- ½ teaspoon grated orange zest
- 1 cup heavy cream
- 3 tablespoons Grand Marnier

1. Microwave chocolate in bowl at 50 percent power, stirring occasionally, until melted, 1 to 2 minutes. Let cool for 5 minutes.
2. Process eggs and yolks, sugar, and orange zest in blender until foamy and lightened in color, 30 to 60 seconds. Add cream, Grand Marnier, and chocolate and process until completely combined and slightly thickened, 30 to 60 seconds.
3. Divide mixture evenly among 6 ramekins or serving glasses (scant ½ cup each). Cover with plastic wrap and refrigerate until cold and set, at least 3 hours or up to 2 days. Uncover and let sit at room temperature for 10 minutes before serving.

We're looking for recipes that you treasure—the ones that have been handed down in your family for a generation or more, that always come out for the holidays, and that have earned a place at your table and in your heart through many years of meals. Send us the recipes that spell home to you. Visit CooksCountry.com/recipe_submission (or write to Heirloom Recipes, Cook's Country, 21 Drydock Avenue, Suite 210E, Boston, MA 02210) and tell us a little about the recipe. Include your name and mailing address. If we print your recipe, you'll receive a free one-year subscription to Cook's Country.

COMING NEXT ISSUE

*Spring is coming to Cook's Country. In our April/May issue, we'll show you the secrets to homemade **English Muffins**, pave the way for a showstopping **Grilled Leg of Lamb**, and deliver a recipe for a deeply flavorful **Chicken in Adobo** that's perfect for those cool spring nights. And due to popular demand, we developed a foolproof recipe for **Thin and Crispy Chocolate Chip Cookies**, great for sharing—or keeping to yourself.*

FIND THE ROOSTER!

A tiny version of this rooster has been hidden in a photo in the pages of this issue. Write to us with its location, and we'll enter you in a random drawing. The first correct entry drawn will win our favorite inexpensive stainless-steel skillet, and each of the next five will receive a free one-year subscription to Cook's Country. To enter, visit CooksCountry.com/rooster by March 31, 2019, or write to Rooster FM19, Cook's Country, 21 Drydock Avenue, Suite 210E, Boston, MA 02210. Include your name and mailing address. Francis Riley of Seattle, Wash., found the rooster in the October/November 2018 issue on page 1, and won our favorite 8-inch nonstick skillet.

WEB EXTRAS

Free for four months online at
CooksCountry.com/mar19

Chocolate Layer Cake Rounds
Pork Tenderloin Roulade with Pancetta, Pear, and Cheddar

READ US ON IPAD

Download the Cook's Country app for iPad and start a free trial subscription or purchase a single issue of the magazine. issues are enhanced with full-color Cook's Mode slide shows that provide step-by-step instructions for completing recipes, plus expanded reviews and ratings. Go to CooksCountry.com/iPad to download our app through iTunes.

Chocolate Strawberry Cake

or Valentine's
ay, we made a
ecadent chocolate
ake and frosted
with strawberry
uttercream. Fresh
trawberries,
lazed with jam, sit
n top and make
his cake truly
hine. **by Katie Leaird**

O MAKE THIS CAKE, YOU WILL NEED:

- 20 fresh strawberries, hulled
- ¼ cup strawberry jam
- 1 teaspoon water
- 2 (9-inch) chocolate layer cake rounds*
- 1 recipe Strawberry Frosting

OR THE GLAZED STRAWBERRIES:

eserve 1 whole strawberry. Halve remain-
g 19 strawberries. Place jam and water in
rge bowl and microwave until bubbling,
bout 2 minutes. Add whole and halved
trawberries to jam mixture and toss until
venly coated. Transfer strawberries to
archment paper–lined baking sheet and
pread into single layer. Set aside.

O ASSEMBLE:

lace 1 cake layer on plate or pedestal.
pread 1½ cups frosting evenly over top,
ght to edge of cake. Top with second
ake layer, pressing lightly to adhere.
pread remaining frosting evenly over
op and sides of cake.

O DECORATE:

lace whole glazed strawberry in center
f cake. Arrange 5 glazed strawberry
halves, stem end down and cut side fac-
g in, around whole strawberry. Repeat
n concentric circular pattern 2 times,
ngling tips of strawberries outward at
5 degrees and alternating orientation of
ut side and round side of strawberries.
rrange remaining strawberry halves in
ircle, cut side down, at base of subsequent rings of strawberries, with points
acing outward. Serve.

STRAWBERRY FROSTING

Makes 4¾ cups
Let the frozen strawberries thaw in the
refrigerator overnight.

- 9 ounces frozen strawberries (2 cups),
  thawed
- 1¼ pounds (5 sticks) unsalted butter,
  softened
- 5 cups (20 ounces) confectioners'
  sugar
- 1 tablespoon vanilla extract
- ⅛ teaspoon salt

1. Strain strawberries through fine-mesh
strainer, pressing firmly on fruit with
rubber spatula (discard juice). Transfer
strawberry solids to food processor and
process until smooth, about 1 minute.
2. Using stand mixer fitted with whisk attachment, whip butter on medium-high
speed until smooth, about 20 seconds.
Add sugar and whip on medium-low
speed until most of sugar is moistened,
about 45 seconds. Scrape down bowl.
Add vanilla, salt, and strawberry puree
and whip on medium-high speed until
light and fluffy, about 4 minutes, scraping down bowl as needed.

*The full recipe, including a recipe for Chocolate
Layer Cake Rounds, is available for free for four months
at CooksCountry.com/chocolatestrawberrycake.

INSIDE THIS ISSUE

Cook's Country

CHICKEN IN ADOBO

This comforting braise delivers moist, tender chicken in a complex, lively sauce.

PAGE 12

Crunchy, Spicy Pork Chops
Juicy Inside, Crispy Outside

Easy English Muffins
Fresh, Hot, Ready for Butter

Strawberry Shortcake Trifle
Showstopper Springtime Dessert

Philly Tomato Pie
Chewy-Soft Crust, Flavorful Sauce

Bourbon Praline Cake
A Bit of Booze Brings It to Life

Equipment Test: Toasters
Which Machine Performed Best?

Grilled Leg of Lamb
Get a Jump on the Season

APRIL/MAY 2019
$6.95 U.S./$7.95 CANADA

0 71486 02742 3

05>

DISPLAY UNTIL MAY 6, 2019

LETTER FROM THE EDITOR

HOW DO YOU like your chocolate chip cookies? Are you a fan of the soft, chewy, ooey-gooey style? Or do you fly your flag for the more delicate thin and crispy style?

I can't tell you how many hours we've spent debating this topic in the *Cook's Country* office. It's a good-natured, wholesome, passionate debate, one that inspires remarkably well-articulated arguments on both sides. And in the end, everyone gets a glass of milk. If only every debate were so civil.

Me, I've never met a chocolate chip cookie that I wouldn't eat (except maybe one with nuts—I have a strict no-nuts policy when it comes to cookies). But if pressed for a desert-island decision, I'll choose thin and crispy. I just love the buttery flavor and satisfying snap, with little pockets of chocolate revealing themselves as you crunch your way through. Plus, when a cookie is this thin, you can eat a bunch of them, right?

Lucky for me, our talented test cook Alli Berkey created an excellent recipe for this thinner style, which you can find on page 16. I hope you try it. But if thick and chewy is more your speed, visit **CooksCountry.com**—you'll find a recipe there.

TUCKER SHAW

Editor in Chief

Illustration: Ross MacDonald

Cook's Country

Chief Executive Officer David Nussbaum
Chief Creative Officer Jack Bishop
Editor in Chief Tucker Shaw
Executive Managing Editor Todd Meier
Executive Food Editor Bryan Roof
Deputy Editor Scott Kathan
Senior Editors Morgan Bolling, Ashley Moore
Associate Editor Cecelia Jenkins
Associate Editor, Web Ashley Delma
Photo Team Manager Tim McQuinn
Test Cooks Alli Berkey, Natalie Estrada, Matthew Fairman
Lead Test Cook, Photo Team Jessica Rudolph
Assistant Test Cooks, Photo Team Sarah Ewald,
    Jacqueline Gochenouer, Eric Haessler
Senior Copy Editor Jill Campbell
Copy Editors Christine Campbell, Rachel Schowalter
Contributing Editor Eva Katz
Senior Science Research Editor Paul Adams
Hosts & Executive Editors, Television Bridget Lancaster,
    Julia Collin Davison

Executive Editors, Tastings & Testings Hannah Crowley,
    Lisa McManus
Senior Editors, Tastings & Testings Lauren Savoie, Kate Sh...
Associate Editor, Tastings & Testings Miye Bromberg
Assistant Editors, Tastings & Testings
    Riddley Gemperlein-Schirm, Carolyn Grillo, Emily Phares

Creative Director John Torres
Photography Director Julie Cote
Art Director Susan Levin
Associate Art Director Maggie Edgar
Senior Staff Photographer Daniel J. van Ackere
Staff Photographers Steve Klise, Kevin White
Photography Producer Meredith Mulcahy

Director, Creative Operations Alice Carpenter
Senior Editor, Special Projects Christie Morrison
Senior Manager, Publishing Operations Taylor Argenzio
Imaging Manager Lauren Robbins
Production & Imaging Specialists Dennis Noble,
    Jessica Voas, Amanda Yong
Test Kitchen Director Erin McMurrer
Assistant Test Kitchen Director Alexxa Benson
Test Kitchen Manager Meridith Lippard
Test Kitchen Facilities Manager Kelly Ryan
Senior Kitchen Assistant Shopper Michelle Miller
Senior Kitchen Assistant Receiver Heather Tolmie
Lead Kitchen Assistant Ena Gudiel
Kitchen Assistants Gladis Campos, Blanca Castanza,
    Amarilys Merced, Arlene Rosario

Chief Financial Officer Jackie McCauley Ford
Senior Manager, Customer Support Tim Quinn
Customer Support Specialist Mitchell Axelson
Event Coordinator Michaela Hughes

Chief Revenue Officer Sara Domville
Director, Sponsorship Marketing & Client Services
    Christine Anagnostis

Chief Digital Officer Fran Middleton
VP, Marketing Natalie Vinard
Director, Audience Acquisition & Partnerships Evan Steine...
Social Media Manager Morgan Mannino
Social Media Coordinators Charlotte Errity, Sarah Sandler

Senior VP, Human Resources & Organizational
    Development Colleen Zelina
Human Resources Manager Jason Lynott

Director, Public Relations & Communications Brian Frankli...
Public Relations Coordinator Madeleine Cohen

Photography Keller + Keller
Food Styling Tara Busa, Catrine Kelty, Chantel Lambeth,
    Sean Widman

Circulation Services ProCirc

On the cover: Chicken in Adobo

70+ VEGETABLES, 700+ RECIPES
Vegetables Illustrated

Welcome to a whole new way with vegetables. With this fresh, modern guide as your kitchen companion, you can turn any vegetable into a culinary superstar, shining a spotlight on it in dishes ranging from apps to sides to main courses. Order your copy at **AmericasTestKitchen.com/vegetables.**

 Find us on **Facebook**
facebook.com/CooksCountry

 Find us on **Instagram**
instagram.com/CooksCountry

 Follow us on **Pinterest**
pinterest.com/TestKitchen

 Follow us on **Twitter**
twitter.com/TestKitchen

![America's Test Kitchen]

America's Test Kitchen is a real test kitchen located in Boston. It is the home of more than 60 test cooks, editors, and cookware specialists. Our mission is to test recipes until we understand exactly how and why they work and eventually arrive at the very best version. We also test kitchen equipment and supermarket ingredients in search of products that offer the best value and performance. You can watch us work by tuning in to **America's Test Kitchen** (AmericasTestKitchen.com) and **Cook's Country from America's Test Kitchen** (CooksCountry.com) on public television, and you can listen to our weekly segments on The Splendid Table on public radio. You can also follow us on Facebook, Twitter, Pinterest, and Instagram.

Cook's Country magazine (ISSN 1552-1990), number 86, is published bimonthly by America's Test Kitchen Limited Partnership, 21 Drydock Avenue, Suite 210E, Boston, MA 02210. Copyright 2019 America's Test Kitchen Limited Partnership. Periodicals postage paid at Boston, MA, and additional mailing offices. USPS #023453. Publications Mail Agreement No. 40020778. Return undeliverable Canadian addresses to P.O. Box 875, Station A, Windsor, ON N9A 6P2. POSTMASTER: Send address changes to Cook's Country, P.O. Box 6018, Harlan, IA 51593-1518. For subscription and gift subscription orders, subscription inquiries, or change of address notices, visit AmericasTestKitchen.com/support, call 800-526-8447 in the United States or 515-237-3663 from outside the United States, or write to us at Cook's Country, P.O. Box 6018, Harlan, IA 51593-1518. PRINTED IN THE USA.

by Cecelia Jenkins

Fond of Flavor

When it comes to using fond, I'm confused. Won't the dark bits make my pan sauce taste burnt?

–*Edward Merrell, Olympia, Wash.*

The browned bits that stick to the bottom of the pan when you sear meat are called fond—and they are packed with savory flavor. We understand that the degree to which the fond in the pan has browned can be worrisome, and it can be a problem if it gets too dark.

Fond is the direct result of the Maillard reaction, during which proteins and natural sugars in a food are transformed by heat to create new complex flavor compounds. The flavorful browning on a pan-fried steak is a common example of this reaction, and so is the browning that occurs on a loaf of bread.

The fond left behind in a cooking vessel is a gold mine of flavor. The classic way to harvest fond is to add liquid (usually water, wine, or broth) to the pan and stir. The moisture and stirring motion release the stuck-on bits, which then dissolve into the liquid; this process is called deglazing. The darker the fond, the more pronounced that caramelized flavor will be. But your sauce will taste bitter if the fond has blackened. Fond should be caramel-colored to dark brown; if the fond is getting too dark, add a little water to the pan and reduce the heat slightly.

THE BOTTOM LINE: Fond equals flavor as long as it is dark brown, not black. But a few black bits of fond here and there generally won't ruin a pan sauce.

A TALE OF TWO FONDS
Above: perfect
Below: taken a smidge too far

Colorful Eggs

At my local grocery store, I recently saw eggs that had blue shells. Do these eggs taste different from regular white or brown eggs?

–*Ross Julian, Haverhill, Mass.*

To see if blue-shelled eggs tasted different, we made three batches of scrambled eggs—one with only blue-shelled eggs, one with only brown-shelled eggs, and one with only white-shelled eggs—and tasted them side by side.

Overall, tasters didn't notice flavor differences among the scrambled egg samples. The only notable differences were visual: The blue-shelled eggs had yolks that were smaller and more orange, so they produced yellower scrambled eggs. The blue-shelled eggs we bought cost about three times as much as regular brown- or white-shelled eggs.

THE BOTTOM LINE: The color of an egg's shell is not indicative of the egg's flavor; the flavor of eggs is mostly dependent on freshness and the chicken's diet, while shell color is typically determined by the bird's breed.

GENTLY MIXED
Dense and yellow

FULLY AERATED IN MIXER
Fluffy and pale

Aerating Butter

Why do cake or cookie recipes often call for butter and sugar to be creamed to a light and fluffy texture, not just combined?

–*Gus Sheehan, Auburn, Miss.*

Creaming butter and sugar is a mixing technique that does more than just combine the two ingredients. It also aerates (or forces air into) them; this is known as mechanical leavening. As the sugar granules are forced into the fat, they leave millions of microscopic air bubbles in their wake that lighten the dense, paste-like mixture's color to a pale yellow and transform its texture. When heated in the oven, the air bubbles expand to create volume that gives baked goods height. Skipping this step would result in the butter melting, leading to a more tightly packed, flatter, denser baked good.

THE BOTTOM LINE: Creaming butter and sugar adds air to the mixture, which results in taller baked goods. If you skip the creaming step, your cakes and cookies will likely turn out squatter and more dense.

Suca-what?

I saw a product called Sucanat in the sugar aisle of the grocery store. What is it?

–*Terry Bevard, Storrs, Conn.*

As its name, which is short for *sucre de canne naturel*, suggests, Sucanat is an unrefined, natural cane sugar made from minimally processed sugar cane juice. It has a deep molasses-like flavor and a tannish-brown color. Since it is less processed than granulated or brown sugar, it retains additional vitamins and minerals and its granules are irregular in size and shape.

With more flavor and color than granulated sugar, it can take some getting used to when used in baked goods, especially in ones where neutral granulated sugar is the star (e.g., sugar cookies). Additionally, it is slow to dissolve, giving some baked goods an odd speckled appearance and a gritty texture. We found that it is necessary to grind Sucanat into a fine powder using a spice grinder prior to baking with it to ensure that it incorporates into doughs or batters and to eliminate any grittiness.

Sucanat is a registered trademark, so it is a fairly reliable, consistent product across brands. You can find it in many well-stocked supermarkets and natural foods stores or online.

THE BOTTOM LINE: Sucanat is a minimally processed sugar made from sugar cane juice; it has an assertive molasses-like flavor and a dark brown color. It retains some of the nutritional value that is processed out of granulated sugar. Because Sucanat granules are irregularly shaped and slow to dissolve, we recommend grinding it before using it in baking recipes.

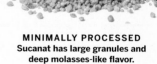

MINIMALLY PROCESSED
Sucanat has large granules and deep molasses-like flavor.

Crushing It

Scott Flaherty, Somerville, Mass.

I like to make stir-fry for a quick supper, but I'm not great at slicing beef or chicken really thin. If I end up with a few slices that are thicker than ideal, I lay them (individually) on my cutting board and, similar to crushing garlic cloves, use the flat side of my knife to flatten and thin the meat with just a quick whack with my hand (you can use a meat pounder, too).

Do Put All Your Eggs in One Basket

—Donna Leach, Nipomo, Calif.

When I was making a big batch of egg salad, it occurred to me that there was a faster way to cut up all those hard-cooked eggs. Instead of using my chef's knife as usual, I put the eggs in a mixing bowl and chopped them up quickly with a pastry cutter. Since it has five blades, it's incredibly fast. Not only that, but it prevents me from getting eggs all over a cutting board.

Proof Positive

—Amy Elizabeth, Sarasota, Fla.

Bread recipes often call for letting dough rise until it's roughly doubled in size, but I have trouble judging the difference. A baker friend taught me a handy trick: I place the dough in a transparent bowl, cover the bowl with plastic wrap, and then trace the outline of the dough on the plastic on the outside of the side of the bowl with a permanent marker. This way, it's easy to tell how big the dough was when I placed it in the bowl.

Upping the Ante with Artisanal Bacon

by Miye Bromberg

PRODUCT TASTING

ALL BACON IS special, but some small-batch artisanal bacon is extra-special—and priced accordingly. Since we last tasted artisanal bacons, more bacons made by smaller-scale producers have become available online. We were curious how our previous favorite, Vande Rose Applewood Smoked Artisan Dry Cured Bacon ($29.07 per pound, including shipping), stacked up against the competition, so we tasted it alongside six other high-end dry-cured bacons, all available online and priced from $8.00 to $14.75 per pound (shipping not included). We tried them plain, in our Southern-Style Green Beans, and in BLTs. What did we find out?

We liked all the bacons we tried, but often in different applications. Some were great in green beans but too intense when eaten plain; others were good plain but got lost in a BLT. As it turned out, a lot hinged on just how long—and how extensively—the bacons had been cured and smoked. In general, we liked complex, meaty-tasting bacons with moderate smoke flavor and relatively low sodium. While we can recommend every product, Vande Rose came out on top once again. We've given some information on where each bacon shined brightest in the comments below. Web members can find a more in-depth version at **CooksCountry.com/may19**.

RECOMMENDED

Vande Rose Applewood Smoked Artisan Dry Cured Bacon
Price: $29.07 per lb (including shipping)
Comments: Balanced smoke, salt, and sugar. Thick and substantial. Great in all applications.

Burgers' Smokehouse Original Country Bacon
Price: $12.49 per lb (plus shipping)
Comments: Salty, mildly smoky. Thin and crispy. Good in all applications.

Tender Belly Signature Blend Dry Cured Maple Bacon
Price: $14.75 per lb (plus shipping)
Comments: Sweet, spiced. Thick and tender. Good in BLTs.

Broadbent Hickory Smoked Bacon
Price: $9.69 per lb (plus shipping)
Comments: Salty, funky. Thick but crispy. Great in BLTs.

Col. Bill Newsom's Hickory Smoked Bacon
Price: $14.49 per lb (plus shipping)
Comments: Smoky, salty, mineral-y. Thin and crispy. Fantastic in green beans.

Benton's Hickory Smoked Country Bacon
Price: $8.00 per lb (plus shipping)
Comments: Smoky, funky, porky. Thick and substantial. Best plain and in green beans.

Bill E's Small Batch Bacon
Price: $12.99 per lb (plus shipping)
Comments: Big porky flavor, very mild smokiness. Thick and meaty. Best plain.

Beauty in the Basics

Text by Bryan Roof; photos by Steve Klise

IN 1953, SAMUEL Cacia purchased a turnkey bakery in South Philadelphia. At first, he offered tomato pie only on Fridays. Today, tomato pie is a permanent fixture. When the elder Cacia passed away in 1964, his grandson, Sam Cacia, and Sam's uncle, Raymond Cacia, took over the business. Although they've expanded to multiple locations, Sam says, "There's always a Cacia family member in each location."

In the crowded front space of the South Philly branch, a glass partition separates customers from the giant rectangular pizzas. "Most people from the neighborhood buy it by the slice; most full-size pies are ordered by out-of-towners," Sam says.

In the kitchen, the true scale of Cacia's reveals itself. There's a light dusting of flour on every surface, emitted from a 50,000-pound-capacity flour silo. Sam grins at a large bubbling pot of tomato sauce. "I make the gravy every day myself. I'm the only one who knows how."

A massive brick oven anchors one wall, faced with subway tile and darkened grout lines, a weathered cast-iron door, and an antique dial thermometer. It's an "80-pan oven," Sam tells me, meaning it can hold 80 full-size sheet pans. (One pan yields two boxes of pizza.) The oven is heated for 90 minutes each morning until it hits 600 degrees. Then it's shut off; the bricks inside retain enough heat to keep cooking through the day. Sam slides pans of pizza deep into the oven with a pizza peel as long as a jousting lance.

But the massive oven isn't just for bread and pizza. Every Thanksgiving, Cacia offers it up to neighbors whose own kitchens are overburdened. Last year, they cooked 125 turkeys. Sam has a hard time pinning down the exact number of pies he makes on most days, but he tells me, "The turkeys, we like to keep track of that."

ON THE ROAD

Sam Cacia (top) mans the main oven, which can hold 80 full-size sheet pans, enough for 160 boxes of pizza. While plain tomato pie (middle) remains a top seller, Cacia's also offers slabs of pie with other toppings, such as pesto and fresh tomato, plus breads, rolls, stromboli, and cannoli. A bakery staffer, below, fills a to-go order.

Philly Tomato Pie

Dough, sauce, and no cheese? Philly tomato pie challenges the pizza equation. **by Cecelia Jenkins**

AS A LOVER of all things topped with gooey melted cheese, I found Philly tomato pie puzzling at first. It has a thick crust similar to that of Sicilian-style pizza. It's sold by the rectangular slice like Sicilian-style pizza. And like all pizza, it has tomato sauce. But this Philly pie features no cheese.

Though I initially wondered where the fun was in that, I've also never met a pizza I didn't like. Philly tomato pie's crust is thick and chewy-soft. The sauce is invigorating—sweet-tart and herby. This pie is generally eaten at room temperature. Cheese or no cheese, I was smitten at first bite and eager for a home version that would be no different.

A South Philadelphia specialty (see "Beauty in the Basics"), Philly tomato pie evolved as a frugal way for the area's Italian American family-owned bakeries to use up leftover bread dough.

The recipes I tried missed the chewy-crust mark, instead ranging from superlight to dense-yet-pliable (read: cardboard-y). The sauces were one-note, with sweetness that trampled the tomato flavor, and most overcooked on the pies, leaving thin, raisiny spots of dried-out sauce. Many recipes caved to outsider expectations of cheese (albeit not the gooey kind) grated on top. I intended to stick to the script: chewy-soft crust, bright sauce, and no cheese.

To get the texture of the crust right, I needed to know how water affected the dough. Generally speaking, the higher the ratio of water to flour in a dough, the more "open" or airy the crumb. Experimentation helped me find the best amounts for small, fine holes and a pleasantly spongy chew.

Once I'd mixed a dough of flour, yeast, water, and oil in my stand mixer, I let it sit for 10 minutes to hydrate before adding salt—if added sooner, it would draw moisture away from the flour (see "Wait on the Salt"). I then turned on the mixer and let it do the remaining kneading. When the dough was satiny and sticky, I scooped

it directly into a greased baking pan to relax and rise. Once the dough had doubled in size, I could easily shape it to fit the pan using my hands. Side-by-side tests of a dough that had risen only once, before shaping, and a dough that had risen a second time after shaping illustrated that more rising time meant more flavor development.

For an assertive sauce, I started by sautéing a bit of onion in olive oil and then flavored it with a moderate amount of minced garlic, a hefty amount of herby dried oregano, and, for kick, ¼ teaspoon of red pepper flakes. For just the right tomato flavor and texture, I added one 15-ounce can of tomato sauce, and for the sauce's signature sweetness, 1 tablespoon of sugar. Simmering it for 10 minutes allowed the flavors to meld and yielded enough sauce to cover the pie in a thin layer that wouldn't overevaporate in the oven. Letting the sauce cool before spreading it and baking the pie made even coverage easier to achieve.

In typical tomato-pie fashion, I let my version cool to room temperature before serving it, and as with pieces scooped up in a South Philly family bakery, no one—myself included—missed the cheese.

Wait on the Salt

To produce a chewy pizza crust, we use a technique called autolyse; this simply entails mixing the flour, yeast, and liquid but withholding the salt for a short period (10 minutes in this case). Salt slows flour's absorption of water, so delaying the addition of salt allows the flour to soak up liquid and become more thoroughly hydrated. More hydration means more gluten formation, which leads to a chewier finished crust—exactly what we were after here.

and oil and mix until dough forms and no dry flour remains, about 30 seconds, scraping down bowl as needed. Turn off mixer, cover bowl with plastic wrap, and let dough stand for 10 minutes.

2. Add salt to dough and knead on medium speed until dough is satiny and sticky and clears sides of bowl but still sticks to bottom, 6 to 8 minutes. Transfer dough to prepared pan, cover pan tightly with plastic, and let dough rise at room temperature until doubled in size, about 1½ hours.

3. FOR THE SAUCE: While dough rises, heat oil in small saucepan over medium heat until shimmering. Add onion and cook, stirring occasionally, until softened and lightly browned, 3 to 5 minutes. Add garlic, oregano, and pepper flakes and cook until fragrant, about 30 seconds. Add tomato sauce and sugar and bring to boil. Reduce heat to medium-low and simmer until sauce is slightly thickened and measures about 1¼ cups, about 10 minutes. Let sauce cool completely.

4. Using your well-oiled hands, press dough into corners of pan. (If dough resists stretching, let it rest for 10 minutes before trying to stretch again.) Cover pan tightly with plastic and let dough rise at room temperature until doubled in size, about 1½ hours. Adjust oven rack to upper-middle position and heat oven to 450 degrees.

5. Spread sauce evenly over dough, leaving ½- to ¼-inch border. Bake until edges are light golden brown and sauce has reduced in spots, about 20 minutes. Let tomato pie cool in pan on wire rack for 5 minutes. Run knife around edge of pan to loosen pie. Using spatula, slide pie onto cutting board. Cut into 8 pieces and serve.

PHILADELPHIA TOMATO PIE *Serves 4*
When kneading the dough on medium speed, the mixer may wobble and shimmy. To keep it in place, position a dish towel or shelf liner beneath the mixer and keep a close watch on it. You will need a nonstick metal baking pan for this recipe.

DOUGH
- 2½ cups (12½ ounces) all-purpose flour
- ¾ teaspoon instant or rapid-rise yeast
- 1 cup water, room temperature
- 1½ tablespoons extra-virgin olive oil
- 1½ teaspoons table salt

SAUCE
- 2 tablespoons extra-virgin olive oil
- ¼ cup finely chopped onion
- 2 garlic cloves, minced
- 2 teaspoons dried oregano
- ¼ teaspoon red pepper flakes
- 1 (15-ounce) can tomato sauce
- 1 tablespoon sugar

1. FOR THE DOUGH: Spray 13 by 9-inch nonstick baking pan with vegetable oil spray. Using stand mixer fitted with dough hook, mix flour and yeast on medium speed until combined, about 10 seconds. With mixer running, slowly add room-temperature water

Pasta with Pancetta and Asparagus

Our goal: a restaurant-quality dish with a weeknight-friendly cooking process. **by Natalie Estrada**

WE'VE ALL HAD the experience of not knowing what to order in a restaurant and settling on that velvety, creamy pasta that just sounds so good. You order it, you like it, and you go home satisfied. Also satisfied? The restaurant owner, because you've just helped the establishment's bottom line more than you know.

Restaurants make a killing on pasta. The food costs are low, and in most cases the preparation is relatively uncomplicated. Before service, a cook will have prepped all the add-ins and perhaps parcooked the pasta. Once an order comes in, all they have to do is finish cooking the pasta, toss it with the other ingredients in a hot pan, and then pile it all on a plate—simple.

I wanted a foolproof recipe for a restaurant-quality pasta dish that was just as easy to make at home. And I wanted to base it on my favorite spring vegetable, asparagus.

Depending on how you cook asparagus, it can reveal itself as grassy, bitter, earthy, or even nutty. It was the nutty side of asparagus that I was after; once the vegetable was tossed with crispy bits of salty pancetta (similar to bacon but without the smokiness) and a creamy sauce, its nuttiness would have a soft place to land.

Browning asparagus is the key to unlocking its nutty notes. Rather than use the dry heat of the oven, I chose a skillet on the stovetop. There, I was able to slowly render the pancetta into crispy, browned bits; after transferring them to some paper towels to drain and crisp further, I had plenty of flavorful fat in which to cook the asparagus. In just 5 minutes, the asparagus took on lovely brown spots, and because

We use mascarpone for creamy texture and pancetta for meaty flavor.

pancetta is cured with black pepper, the fat added a faint peppery flavor to the asparagus. A bit of garlic provided another savory note.

Next up: creating a creamy sauce. Heavy cream worked fine, but I chose mascarpone, a soft cheese that, when heated gently and tossed with the pasta, melts into a beautiful creamy sauce and adds a faintly sweet tanginess. Some salty, savory grated Pecorino; a squeeze of bright lemon juice; and chopped fresh basil rounded out the dish.

By choosing powerhouse ingredients such as mascarpone and pancetta and by coaxing nutty, sweet, and complex flavors out of my asparagus, I had made a restaurant-quality supper that was easy to produce in any home kitchen.

PENNE WITH PANCETTA AND ASPARAGUS

Serves 4 to 6

Buy asparagus spears that are between ¼ inch and ½ inch in diameter. To trim the asparagus, hold a spear with one hand about halfway down the stalk; with the thumb and index finger of your other hand, grasp the spear about 1 inch from the bottom. Bend the stalk until it snaps, discard the bottom portion, and use the stalk as a guide for cutting the rest of the asparagus with your knife. Buy a hunk of pancetta from the deli counter rather than pre-sliced pancetta.

- 4 ounces pancetta, cut into ½-inch pieces
- 1 pound asparagus, trimmed and cut on bias into 2-inch lengths
- ⅛ teaspoon table salt, plus salt for cooking pasta
- 1 garlic clove, minced
- 1 pound penne
- 8 ounces (1 cup) mascarpone cheese
- 1 ounce Pecorino Romano cheese, grated (½ cup), plus extra for serving
- 1 tablespoon lemon juice
- 1 teaspoon pepper
- ⅓ cup chopped fresh basil

1. Cook pancetta in 12-inch nonstick skillet over medium heat until lightly browned and crispy, about 10 minutes. Using slotted spoon, transfer pancetta to paper towel–lined plate, leaving fat in skillet.

2. Heat fat over high heat until just smoking. Add asparagus and salt and cook, without stirring, until just starting to brown, about 3 minutes. Stir and continue to cook until asparagus is browned and tender, about 2 minutes longer. Off heat, stir in garlic.

3. Meanwhile, bring 4 quarts water to boil in large pot. Add pasta and 1 tablespoon salt and cook, stirring often, until al dente. Reserve 1½ cups cooking water, then drain pasta and return it to pot over low heat.

4. Add mascarpone, Pecorino, lemon juice, pepper, pancetta, asparagus, and 1 cup reserved cooking water to pot and toss and stir vigorously to thoroughly combine, about 1 minute. Let pasta rest off heat for 3 minutes. Stir in basil. Adjust consistency with remaining reserved cooking water as needed. Season with salt and pepper to taste. Serve, passing extra Pecorino separately.

California-Style Chicken Salad

or the juiciest, most tender meat for chicken salad, turn on your oven. **by Cecelia Jenkins**

HICKEN SALAD IS one of the orld's most versatile—and to me, ost perfect—foods. While there are enty of lousy versions out there (I'm oking at you, convenience-store ndwiches), the best versions are tisfying yet light, featuring plenty of nder chicken, a creamy and cool-g mayonnaise-based dressing, and unchy bursts of crisp, refreshing lery—just right for lunch on a warm ay. A bonus is that chicken salad is dlessly customizable with ingredi-ts such as herbs, pickles, spices, and ot sauce.

My favorite kind of chicken salad is ten called California-style: It features bed—not shredded—chicken breast athed in a creamy, herby dress-g. Most recipes call for poaching e chicken in a covered pan on the ovetop to cook it gently and letting it ool before chopping and dressing it. ut the problem with poached chicken that it's hard to get consistent results; veryone's burners are different, and us it can be a challenge to explain ow to keep the water at a proper mmer. Could I use the oven—which erforms more consistently—to gently ook the chicken?

There was only one way to find ut. I started with boneless, skinless hicken breasts because they cook ster and are easier to chop up than he bone-in variety. We've learned from ast recipes that chicken cooked in lots f water can lose flavor, so I wanted o minimize the liquid here. I placed our seasoned breasts in a 13 by 9-inch aking dish, poured in ½ cup of water, overed the dish with foil, and baked he chicken in a moderate 350-degree ven until it registered 160 degrees on n instant-read thermometer.

The results were decent but not as good as when I cooked the chicken with no added water; the chicken released enough liquid to create a steamy, moist cooking environment hat resulted in tender, juicy meat. Pounding the breasts to an even thick-ness before cooking ensured that they ll came up to temperature at the same rate. The results were just as good as perfectly poached chicken but much more foolproof.

Once the chicken had cooled, I mixed several versions of creamy dress-ings for my tasters to try. Though sour cream was a common addition, we

Chopped chives, tarragon, and dill provide a range of fresh, herby flavors.

landed on the simple, classic flavor of mayonnaise brightened up with lemon juice. A handful of crunchy chopped celery was a must, and a trio of fresh herbs—chives, tarragon, and dill—brought a wealth of fresh flavor that practically screamed springtime.

This salad was so good that I made a more adventurous version featur-ing tart dried apricots, warm curry powder, scallions, and toasted slivered almonds. In another variation inspired by Waldorf salad, I used tangy Dijon mustard in place of the lemon juice for more complexity and added toasted walnuts, refreshing parsley, and crisp red grapes for bursts of sweetness and textural pop.

CHICKEN SALAD
WITH FRESH HERBS *Serves 6*

We pound the chicken breasts to an even thickness to ensure that they all cook at the same rate. This salad can be served in a sandwich or over lettuce.

- 2 **pounds boneless, skinless chicken breasts, trimmed**
- 1 **tablespoon extra-virgin olive oil**
- ¾ **teaspoon table salt, divided**
- ½ **teaspoon pepper, divided**
- ⅔ **cup mayonnaise**
- ¼ **cup finely chopped celery**
- 3 **tablespoons chopped fresh chives**
- 4 **teaspoons chopped fresh tarragon**
- 1 **tablespoon chopped fresh dill**
- 1 **tablespoon lemon juice**

An Easy Way to Poach

Toss lightly pounded chicken breasts with oil, salt, and pepper and arrange them in a single layer in a baking dish. Cover the dish with aluminum foil and cook for about 30 minutes; the foil traps steam to create a moist cooking environment that helps the chicken stay juicy.

1. Adjust oven rack to middle position and heat oven to 350 degrees. Cover chicken with plastic wrap. Using meat pounder, gently pound thickest part of each breast to ¾-inch thickness.
2. Toss chicken, oil, ¼ teaspoon salt, and ¼ teaspoon pepper together in 13 by 9-inch baking dish. Arrange chicken in single layer in dish and cover tightly with aluminum foil. Bake until chicken registers 160 degrees, 28 to 32 minutes. (When checking tem-perature, carefully open foil so that steam escapes away from you.) Transfer chicken to large plate and let cool for 15 minutes; discard any accumulated juices. Refrigerate chicken until com-pletely cooled, about 30 minutes.
3. Cut chicken into ½-inch pieces. Combine chicken, mayonnaise, celery, chives, tarragon, dill, lemon juice, re-maining ½ teaspoon salt, and remaining ¼ teaspoon pepper in bowl. Cover with plastic and refrigerate for at least 2 hours to allow flavors to meld. Serve. (Salad can be refrigerated for up to 2 days.)

CHICKEN SALAD
WITH CURRY AND DRIED APRICOTS

Omit chives, tarragon, and dill. Add ½ cup finely chopped dried apricots, 6 tablespoons toasted slivered almonds, 4 thinly sliced scallions, and 2 teaspoons curry powder to bowl in step 3.

CHICKEN SALAD
WITH GRAPES AND WALNUTS

Omit tarragon and dill. Add 1 cup halved seedless red grapes; 6 table-spoons walnuts, toasted and chopped; and 3 tablespoons chopped fresh pars-ley to bowl in step 3. Substitute Dijon mustard for lemon juice.

A deeply seasoned panko coating provides big flavor and satisfying crunch.

Spiced Pork Chops

Boring chops can make weeknight dinners a drag. We set out to create an easy recipe for juicy chops with serious punch—and crunch. **by Ashley Moore**

WE'VE ALL SEEN the Shake 'n Bake box at the grocery store—the one that promises an extra-crispy, crunchy pork chop coating in just two simple steps. I grew up eating chops prepared with this product (just seasoned crumbs and a bag), and some in my extended family still enjoy it in their weeknight rotation. I recently revisited it and was disappointed to find that the coating tasted stale and baked up a little soggy.

The truth is that it's difficult to get ultracrunchy chops in the oven because the baking sheet never gets ripping hot and doesn't hold as much fat as a skillet does. The stovetop was the only way to go. I gathered a handful of recipes for pan-fried spiced chops and got to work in the test kitchen. As it turned out, none delivered juicy chops and a potently spiced, crunchy coating. I'd have to start from scratch.

I began with the pork, choosing four good-size bone-in rib chops. I could have used boneless chops here, but the bone makes for a classic presentation and helps keep the meat moist. Chops that measured ½ inch thick were substantial yet thin enough to cook quickly so the crumbs wouldn't burn. I figured a standard three-part bound breading of flour, beaten egg, and seasoned bread crumbs was the way to go, and my tests confirmed it. Panko crumbs won out over fresh and store-bought bread crumbs by virtue of their big crunch.

After playing around with different pans and amounts of oil, I found that cooking two chops at a time in a 12-inch nonstick skillet in 1 cup of vegetable oil was the best path to success; the ample oil and lack of crowding ensured that the chops picked up plenty of flavorful browning and stayed crisp on the plate. (With any less oil, the chops didn't brown on the sides.)

But what about the spices? I tried adding every spice under the sun to the flour, egg, and panko and landed on a simple combination of fragrant ground coriander, kicky cayenne, and bold dry mustard stirred into just the panko. This mix of spices provided deep flavor and a pleasant jolt of heat.

These crunchy, juicy, perfectly spiced pork chops were so good that I know I'll never reach for that boxed stuff again.

SPICED CRUNCHY PORK CHOPS
Serves 4

Use pork chops that measure no more than ½ inch thick in this recipe to ensure that the meat cooks through before the breading begins to burn. If you can find only chops that are slightly thicker than ½ inch, gently pound the meat thin with a meat pounder, taking care not to crush the bones. Using two spatulas rather than tongs to flip the chops helps the coating stay intact.

- 4 (5- to 7-ounce) bone-in pork rib chops, ½ inch thick, trimmed
- ¾ cup all-purpose flour
- 3 large eggs
- 1 cup panko bread crumbs
- 1 tablespoon kosher salt
- 1 tablespoon pepper
- 1 tablespoon ground coriander
- 1 tablespoon dry mustard
- 1 teaspoon cayenne pepper
- 1 cup vegetable oil, for frying
  Lemon wedges

1. Set wire rack in rimmed baking sheet and line half of rack with triple layer of paper towels. Pat chops dry with separate paper towels.
2. Place flour in shallow dish. Lightly beat eggs in second shallow dish. Combine panko, salt, pepper, coriander, mustard, and cayenne in third shallow dish.
3. Working with 1 chop at a time, dredge chops in flour, shaking off excess; dip in eggs, allowing excess to drip off; then coat with panko mixture, pressing gently to adhere. Transfer chops to large plate.
4. Heat oil in 12-inch nonstick skillet over medium-high heat to 350 degrees. Add 2 chops and cook until golden brown on first side, 2 to 3 minutes. (Adjust burner, if necessary, to maintain oil temperature between 325 and 350 degrees.) Using 2 spatulas, gently flip chops; continue to cook until golden brown on second side and meat registers 140 degrees, 2 to 3 minutes longer.
5. Transfer chops to paper towel–lined side of prepared wire rack and let drain for 15 seconds on each side, then move to unlined side of rack. Return oil to 350 degrees and repeat with remaining 2 chops. Serve with lemon wedges.

THE AMERICAN TABLE

Shake 'n Bake seasoned coating mixes were originally introduced in 1965 by the General Foods Corporation as an easier alternative to fried chicken or fried pork chops. The original advertisements were staples during daytime television programs such as *The Price Is Right* and *General Hospital*; they featured child actors delivering the line, "And I helped!" Starting in the 1980s, the Shake 'n Bake spokesperson was Ann B. Davis, who played Alice on *The Brady Bunch*, perhaps the most well-known fictional home cook in pop culture at the time.

Potato, Green Bean, and Tomato Salad

You say tomato, I say potato. And green beans.

by Ashley Moore

salad, simplified: the green beans cook the same saucepan as the potatoes.

An easy vinaigrette and loads of fresh parsley and dill tie this hearty salad together.

AFTER A FULL day of cooking and tasting food at work, I usually have just a salad for dinner. But since greens and vinaigrette can take you only so far, lately I've been looking to broaden my horizons by trying various salads that are still heavy on the vegetables but a bit more substantial. Why not create a hearty salad in the test kitchen that I'd be happy to eat for dinner at home?

Vegetables don't get much heartier than potatoes, so I knew I'd use spuds for my salad. I got to thinking about other ingredients that I don't usually add to my leafy greens and decided to give green beans a shot. And for a fresh, uncooked component that would add substance and sass, I chose halved grape tomatoes. Now, how to bring it all together?

While cooking my way through a few salads made with these ingredients, I figured out an easy, efficient way to cook the potatoes and beans. I started by boiling the potatoes in salted water until they were just tender and then added 1-inch lengths of

green beans to the same water. By the time the beans were done cooking, the potatoes were, too.

For a straightforward dressing, I whisked together the classic, simple combo of extra-virgin olive oil, white wine vinegar, salt, and pepper. Briny capers added punch, a sliced shallot contributed sweetness, and minced anchovies lent depth and salty complexity. Briefly marinating the halved tomatoes in the dressing while the potatoes and beans cooked improved their flavor tremendously.

Fresh herbs added some pizzazz: After testing what seemed like an entire garden's worth, I landed on whole parsley leaves—their big size translated into more potent flavor—and chopped fresh dill. The final touch was to pour some of the dressing (just the seasoned oil and vinegar, without the tomatoes) over the potatoes and green beans immediately after draining them; the hot vegetables greedily soaked up the vinaigrette and tasted deeply seasoned in the finished salad.

POTATO, GREEN BEAN, AND TOMATO SALAD
Serves 4

Make sure to scrub the potatoes well. High-quality extra-virgin olive oil makes a big difference here. You can substitute cherry tomatoes for the grape tomatoes, if desired. For the best results, use a rubber spatula to combine the ingredients in steps 3 and 4.

- 1½ **pounds Yukon Gold potatoes, unpeeled, cut into ¾-inch chunks**
- ¾ **teaspoon table salt, plus salt for cooking vegetables**
- 1 **pound green beans, trimmed and cut into 1-inch pieces**
- ½ **cup extra-virgin olive oil**
- ¼ **cup white wine vinegar**
- ¾ **teaspoon pepper**
- 6 **ounces grape tomatoes, halved**
- ¼ **cup capers**
- 1 **shallot, sliced thin**
- 2 **anchovy fillets, rinsed and minced (optional)**
- ½ **cup fresh parsley leaves**
- ¼ **cup chopped fresh dill**

1. Place potatoes and 2 teaspoons salt in large saucepan and cover with water by 1 inch. Bring to boil over high heat. Reduce heat to medium-low and simmer until potatoes are almost tender, about 7 minutes. Add green beans and continue to cook until both vegetables are tender, about 7 minutes longer.

2. Meanwhile, whisk oil, vinegar, pepper, and salt together in large bowl; measure out ¼ cup dressing and set aside. Add tomatoes, capers, shallot, and anchovies, if using, to bowl with remaining dressing and toss to coat; set aside.

3. Drain potatoes and green beans thoroughly in colander, then spread out on rimmed baking sheet. Drizzle reserved dressing over potatoes and green beans and, using rubber spatula, gently toss to combine. Let cool slightly, about 15 minutes.

4. Add parsley, dill, and potato mixture to bowl with tomato mixture and toss to combine. Season with salt and pepper to taste. Serve.

Hamburger Steak with Onion Gravy

This comforting classic needed a reboot. **by Alli Berkey**

THE CLASSIC "HAMBURG steak" first arrived stateside with German immigrants in the 19th century. This beef patty served with a rich gravy was a staple in German American homes for those who could afford meat regularly. For those who couldn't, it was a special-occasion supper.

But hamburger steak has devolved over the years into little more than a dense, dry burger without a bun. It should be laced with flavor throughout and doused with a buttery brown gravy like it is at Aunt B's Soul Food in Tupelo, Mississippi (see "Don't Call It a Burger"). Generally, it is not. I set out to restore some glory.

Don't confuse hamburger steak with Salisbury steak. Whereas Salisbury steak's gravy is distinctly peppery and heavy with mushrooms, the gravy served with hamburger steak leans on onions and garlic. These additions contribute just enough flavor for a bold, slightly sweet personality. But this restrained ingredient list can also be a quick trip to Dullsville.

My first experiments with existing recipes were a lesson in disappointment, turning out patties that were dry, tough, and drastically underseasoned.

To tackle the dryness, I introduced a panade, a mixture of bread crumbs and liquid that's often incorporated into meatballs and meatloaf to help them retain moisture. Adding a panade made with fresh bread crumbs did just that, but it also gave my patties a gummy texture. I ditched the panade in favor of straight bread crumbs, in this case crunchy panko. These light, flaky bits didn't need a soak before being added to the beef, and they softened just enough as the beef cooked, soaking up all the liquid the meat released (and keeping it from seeping out).

The patties now had great texture but were lacking in flavor. Instead of cooking fresh garlic and onion, I simply added granulated garlic, onion powder, and seasoned salt. Taking the convenience theme one step further, a colleague suggested replacing those ingredients with something her mom had used to make this dish in the 1980s: onion soup mix. It worked—the potent mix seasoned the meat throughout and added a complex oniony flavor.

Gravy time. A pan gravy, generally made while the meat is resting, requires some fond left in the skillet, so a hard sear was the way to go. Searing the patties for 4 minutes per side gave them great color and created a lovely fond. To that I added sliced onion to cook for about 4 minutes until softened, followed by flour, which took about 1 minute to lightly brown. Finally, I stirred in some beef broth.

The steaks were done, but the gravy was too thin—nothing that a vigorous bubble, about 4 minutes, and a bit of butter couldn't fix. Tender meat, flavorful gravy, and a comforting profile—this hamburger steak now had a place in my regular dinner rotation.

THE AMERICAN TABLE

Hamburger steak, or "Hamburg steak," isn't the only bunless ground beef patty meal in the world. Other branches of the family tree include Salisbury steak (named for James Salisbury, a 19th-century doctor who believed that meat was good for you and vegetables were not) and Swiss steak, which, despite its name, has no connection to Switzerland. Instead, its name refers to "swissing," which is a technique for tenderizing meat via rolling and/or pounding.

HAMBURGER STEAKS WITH ONION GRAVY
Serves 4

We developed this recipe using our favorite beef broth, Better Than Bouillon Roasted Beef Base.

1½	pounds 85 percent lean ground beef
½	cup panko bread crumbs
2	tablespoons Lipton Onion Soup and Dip Mix
½	teaspoon pepper
3	tablespoons unsalted butter, divided
1	onion, halved and sliced thin
1½	tablespoons all-purpose flour
1½	cups beef broth
1	tablespoon minced fresh chives

1. In large bowl, mix beef, panko, soup mix, and pepper with your hands until fully combined. Form mixture into four 4-inch-diameter patties, about ½ inch thick. Using your fingertips, press down center of each patty to create slight indentation.

2. Melt 1 tablespoon butter in 12-inch nonstick skillet over medium-high heat. Add patties and cook until well browned and meat registers 130 degrees, about 4 minutes per side. Transfer to platter and tent with aluminum foil.

3. Reduce heat to medium, add onion to now-empty skillet, and cook until lightly browned and beginning to soften, about 4 minutes. Stir in flour and cook for 1 minute. Whisk in broth and bring to boil. Cook until thickened, about 4 minutes. Off heat, stir in remaining 2 tablespoons butter. Season with salt and pepper to taste. Spoon sauce over steaks and sprinkle with chives. Serve.

Don't Call It a Burger

Text by Bryan Roof;
photos by Steve Klise

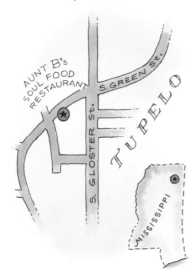

JUST A SHORT drive from Elvis Presley's birthplace in Tupelo, Mississippi, sits Aunt B's Soul Food, a small brick building with a bright yellow awning and a rusted barbecue cooker out front. The service is cafeteria-style, and the menu changes daily.

But there's more at play here than just good food. Tables compete for space with pairs of guitars and amplifiers, a set of conga drums, a keyboard, and more indicators of this town's deep musical roots. Pictures and albums of famous blues and R & B singers cover the walls. Owner Thomas Woods tells me that on Sundays, customers often break into song during lunch. "Go to church, sing a hymn. Come here, sing a hymn. Sometimes they just come up and start singing."

Woods was an electrical engineer with a degree from the University of Southern Mississippi before he turned to food. "I learned [to cook] from watching my mama, beginning on a potbelly stove." Relishing the memory for a moment, he adds, "the prettiest dang piece of cornbread I ever saw came off a potbelly stove."

The restaurant serves mostly regulars, but tourists on the Elvis trail also stop in. "We have a lot of people who just want authentic Mississippi food."

I ask why he named the restaurant for his aunt rather than his mother, Ollie Woods. "Because she was still alive," he says. "There's a thing about giving people their flowers while they're living instead of when they're gone. They can't enjoy them when they're gone."

Woods, his brother, and his sister all surprised Aunt B, whose full name is Lula B. Harris, with the news of the restaurant together. "It was amazing to see an 80-plus-year-old black woman, with everything she's been through here in Mississippi and Alabama, get a restaurant named after her." After a few moments, Aunt B turned to Woods and said, "You better have it right if it's gonna have my name on it." He laughs out loud. "I said, 'Yes, ma'am!'"

ON THE ROAD

Owner Thomas Woods, top, created his menu from childhood favorites. "This is the same food that I grew up on," he says, "the same way my mama used to cook it."

Chicken in Adobo

This fragrant, rich chile sauce isn't fiery, but it will add a spark to your weeknight chicken routine. **by Alli Berkey**

ADOBO, THE POTENT, pleasantly bitter sauce made from dried chiles, plays many roles in the cuisines of Mexico and the American Southwest: marinade, braising sauce, baste, and tableside condiment for all kinds of meats. (In Filipino cuisine, adobo is something else altogether.) Making adobo should be relatively easy: Toast dried chiles to activate their flavor, soak them, and then pulverize them in a blender with vinegar, herbs, and garlic. The best versions are simultaneously complex and deeply comforting. I set out to make a recipe for chicken in adobo that was easy and tasted amazing.

The recipes I found called for different chiles—chipotle, guajillo, ancho, arbol, and pasilla chiles were all in play. My tasters thought that chipotle (smoked-and-dried jalapeño) and arbol chiles brought too much heat to the party and pasilla chiles were a little too rich in this dish; fruity ancho and guajillo chiles, which are available in the Latin American section of most supermarkets, were the best way forward.

Next, I tested various methods to help the chiles reach their fullest potential. Some recipes call for frying the dried chiles in oil to bloom their flavor; this was messy and heightened the chiles' bitterness in an unpleasant way. I found that it was much better and easier to quickly dry-toast the chiles on a baking sheet in the oven; this brought out their multifaceted flavors but not their bitterness.

Once I'd soaked the toasted chiles in hot tap water for 5 minutes, they were soft and pliable and ready to be buzzed in the blender. Some recipes call for adding the soaking water, but again, we found the results unpleasantly bitter. I used a little chicken broth instead; the broth added savoriness and, along with a bit of cider vinegar and orange juice, thinned the blended chiles into a flavorful sauce. A little brown sugar helped deepen the adobo's enchanting flavors.

Once the adobo sauce was ready, marrying it with the chicken was simple. I seared bone-in chicken pieces in a Dutch oven and then transferred the pieces to a plate while I sautéed some chopped onion in the rendered chicken fat. I added garlic, tomato paste, oregano, cumin, cinnamon, and orange zest and then the potent adobo from the blender. I nestled the chicken pieces back into the pot, skin side up, and moved the pot to the oven so the chicken could gently cook through in the flavorful sauce.

By now the kitchen smelled incredible, and my colleagues were starting to hover around my workstation. I plated some chicken for my hungry tasters, spooned the sauce over top, and sprinkled on some chopped cilantro. Some of my coworkers made little tacos with the tortillas I'd warmed, and others ate the saucy chicken with a knife and fork, but they all had one thing in common: They asked for seconds.

Never cooked with dried chiles before? This potent yet comforting sauce is a great starting point.

CHICKEN IN ADOBO *Serves 4*

One ounce of guajillo chiles is about eight chiles; ½ ounce of ancho chiles is approximately one chile. Remove the strips of orange zest with a vegetable peeler. You can use all white-meat or all dark-meat chicken pieces, if desired. Serve with rice or warm flour tortillas.

1	ounce dried guajillo chiles, stemmed and seeded
½	ounce dried ancho chiles, stemmed and seeded
1½	cups chicken broth
¼	cup cider vinegar
2	(3-inch) strips orange zest plus 2 tablespoons juice
1	tablespoon packed brown sugar
1¾	teaspoons table salt, divided
1	teaspoon pepper, divided
3	pounds bone-in chicken pieces (2 split breasts cut in half crosswise, 2 drumsticks, and 2 thighs), trimmed
2	tablespoons vegetable oil
1	onion, chopped fine
5	garlic cloves, minced
1	tablespoon tomato paste
2	teaspoons dried oregano
1	teaspoon ground cumin
½	teaspoon ground cinnamon
3	tablespoons chopped fresh cilantro
	Lime wedges

. Adjust oven rack to lower-middle
osition and heat oven to 300 de-
rees. Place guajillos and anchos
n rimmed baking sheet. Bake until
ragrant and guajillos are deep red
nd have curled edges, about 7 min-
tes. Immediately transfer chiles to
owl and cover with hot water. Let
tand until pliable, about 5 minutes.
. Drain chiles and transfer to
lender. Add broth, vinegar, orange
uice, sugar, 1¼ teaspoons salt, and
½ teaspoon pepper and process un-
il smooth, 1 to 2 minutes, scraping
own sides of blender jar as needed.
et aside adobo.
3. Pat chicken dry with paper towels
nd sprinkle with remaining ½ tea-
poon salt and remaining ½ teaspoon
epper. Heat oil in Dutch oven over
medium-high heat until shimmer-
ng. Add chicken and cook until well
rowned, about 4 minutes per side.
Transfer to plate.
4. Add onion to now-empty pot
nd reduce heat to medium. Cook
until softened, about 4 minutes. Stir
n garlic, tomato paste, oregano,
cumin, cinnamon, and orange zest
nd cook until fragrant, about
30 seconds. Whisk in adobo until
combined. Return chicken, skin
side up, to pot along with any accumulated juices; bring to simmer.
Transfer pot to oven and bake,
uncovered, until chicken is tender
and breasts register 160 degrees and
drumsticks/thighs register 175 degrees, 35 to 40 minutes.
5. Transfer chicken to platter. Stir
sauce to combine and season with
salt and pepper to taste. Pour sauce
over chicken and sprinkle with
cilantro. Serve with lime wedges.

Pepper Primer

Two types of dried chiles combine to create a deep, complex
flavor base for the adobo. Look
for ancho and guajillo chiles in
the Latin American section of
your supermarket.

**ANCHO
CHILE**

**GUAJILLO
CHILE**

Southern-Style Chicken and Rice

*Sometimes the best
thing you can do in the
kitchen is not overthink
things.* **by Morgan Bolling**

ASK A PROFESSIONAL chef
about the foods they crave and
99 percent of the time their answer
will be something surprisingly simple
and comforting. My favorite meal
to make at home is chicken and rice.
The version I grew up eating in
North Carolina featured white rice
that was softened and plumped with
chicken stock and then tossed with
tender pieces of shredded chicken. I
remember it as a supremely savory
dish boasting the clear, unambigu-
ous flavor of chicken and little else.
It's just the kind of thing I want after
spending long hours developing a
recipe for a more complex dish.

Yet this kind of simplicity can be
difficult, but not impossible, to pull off.
To learn how others have mastered it, I
made five different versions of chicken
and rice, each developed by a Southern
cook. After sampling all five, my tasters
and I found that some of them fell flat
on flavor and others were too much
work to produce.

And while none of the five gave
me the exact results I wanted (or
craved), one recipe pointed me in the
right direction. It called for creating
an ultraflavorful stock by simmering chicken pieces in chicken broth
before removing them from the pot
and adding rice to simmer. Once
the rice was cooked, I shredded the
cooked chicken and stirred it into the
rice. Although the result was straightforward and delicious, it was a little
wet—somewhere between a hearty
stew and a risotto.

Unsurprisingly, this recipe was a
hand-me-down from a beloved grandmother. Like many heirloom recipes,
it lacked precise ingredients, such as
the exact amount of liquid I'd need
for the soft, fluffy texture I sought. To
bring this recipe up to our detailed
test kitchen standards and even out the
vagaries, I'd have to be stricter with my
ingredients and technique.

I started with bone-in, skin-on
chicken thighs, a favorite for their juicy
texture and deep flavor. Gently simmering them for 30 minutes coaxed out

some gorgeous flavor. I then removed
them from the pot to cool and turned
to the rice.

I tried toasting the rice in butter
before adding my easy stock to cook
it through, a trick we often use to
add flavor and keep the grains separate when making rice pilaf. But this
batch didn't feel cohesive. Instead,
2 cups of untoasted long-grain rice
added to my stock (made with 4 cups of
store-bought broth and 3 cups of water)
emerged soft and creamy—just right
for this comforting dish.

I conducted a dozen more tests—
adding bay leaves, celery, herbs, and
more—but found that these ingredients interfered with the clarity
of this straightforward dish. Some
chopped onion and a few tablespoons
of unsalted butter proved to be the
only necessary additions, lending just
enough savory richness.

I'm not sure I would have found my
way to this simple recipe without all
the detours. But the journey reminded
me that sometimes the best thing you
can do in the kitchen is trust that your
core ingredients, treated carefully
and nudged along lightly, will deliver
exactly what you're looking for—in
this case, the pure, simple flavors of
chicken and rice.

**SOUTHERN-STYLE STEWED
CHICKEN AND RICE** *Serves 6 to 8*
We developed this recipe using Lund-
berg Organic Long-Grain White Rice.

  - 4 tablespoons unsalted butter, divided
  - 1 onion, chopped fine
  - 1½ teaspoons table salt, divided
  - 2 pounds bone-in chicken thighs, trimmed
  - 4 cups chicken broth
  - 3 cups water
  - 1 teaspoon pepper
  - 2 cups long-grain white rice, rinsed

1. Melt 2 tablespoons butter in Dutch
oven over medium-high heat. Add onion and ½ teaspoon salt and cook until
onion is softened, about 5 minutes.
2. Add chicken, broth, water, pepper, and remaining 1 teaspoon salt
and bring to boil. Reduce heat to low,
cover, and simmer until chicken is tender and registers at least 185 degrees,
about 30 minutes.
3. Remove pot from heat. Transfer
chicken to plate and let cool slightly,
about 15 minutes. Using 2 forks, shred
chicken into bite-size pieces; discard
skin and bones.
4. Return broth to boil over high heat
and stir in rice, chicken, and remaining 2 tablespoons butter. Reduce heat
to medium-low and simmer, uncovered, stirring occasionally, until rice
is tender and liquid level drops just
below surface of rice, 17 to 20 minutes. Season with salt and pepper to
taste. Serve.

**Simple flavors,
such as those of
chicken and rice,
are often the
most satisfying.**

English Muffins

Making English muffins at home is much easier than you think—all you need is a few staple ingredients and a bit of time.

by Ashley Moore

TIME TO BUST a myth: English muffins are not hard to make at home. You don't need special equipment or even much time to turn out English muffins that are fresher and better than any you'd buy at the supermarket.

To develop the best possible recipe, I first had to survey existing recipes for English muffins. The basic process was this: Mix flour, yeast, salt, and milk, and then let the dough rise. Shape it into muffins, dust them with cornmeal, and let them rise again. Next, sear the muffins in a pan before finishing them off in the oven.

But there was a lot of variance in the details among recipes. Some call for letting the dough rise in the refrigerator for two days to develop extra yeasty flavor and big air pockets; others call for complex shaping techniques you'd need to be a pastry chef to understand. I hoped to streamline the process without shortchanging the flavor or texture.

While I wasn't happy with any of the recipes I tried, a few did have elements worth borrowing. One recipe included honey in the usual mix of ingredients; the honey boosted the flavor and gave the muffins a nice

Two rises help create plenty of little pockets to hold melted butter.

Making English Muffins at Home Isn't Hard—Here's How We Do It

Portion the Dough
Using a greased ¼-cup dry measuring cup, make eight dough rounds.

Brown on the Stove
Cook the dough rounds in butter in a skillet until both sides are browned.

Bake in the Oven
Place the browned muffins on a baking sheet and bake in a 350-degree oven.

Check for Doneness
Use a digital thermometer to see if the muffins register 205 to 210 degrees.

olden color. Another employed arm milk to help jump-start the east and thus reduce the rising ime—a great idea. And finally, some ecipes called for bread flour, which as more protein than all-purpose our and thus results in chewier aked goods, a definite bonus here.

In terms of streamlining the rec- pe, I was hoping to avoid two rises one before portioning the dough nd one after), but it turned out that oth rises were necessary for nicely ocketed muffins that were light yet hewy. The good news was that each ise needed to be only 1 hour (al- hough the second one can be longer f you refrigerate the dough).

Another trick I came up with: after he first rise, using a greased ¼-cup neasuring cup to simultaneously coop, portion, and shape the dough nto squat cylinders that rise into the signature English muffin shape.

For searing the muffins to give the outsides the proper brown hue, I landed on using a nonstick skillet (the dough stuck to traditional steel skillets, and it was too hard to regu- late the temperature in cast iron). Once they were browned, I trans- ferred the muffins to a baking sheet and baked them in a 350-degree oven for just 10 minutes, until they were cooked through.

After working out the details over 40 tests, I was finally pleased with my easy method and fantastic results. One word to the wise: For the best interior texture, don't use a knife. Use the tines of a fork to separate the halves before toasting.

Fresh Muffins for Breakfast

Do you want to make the dough rounds ahead so that all you have to do when you wake up is cook and then toast them? Here's how.

THE NIGHT BEFORE:
Make dough, let it rise, portion and shape dough, place on rimmed baking sheet, cover sheet with plastic wrap, and let rounds rise for at least 12 hours in refrigerator.

IN THE MORNING:
Brown both sides of chilled rounds in butter in nonstick skillet, then finish cooking (about 10 minutes) in oven. Let muffins cool before toasting.

ENGLISH MUFFINS *Makes 8 muffins*
For the best texture, use a fork to split the muffins. Don't heat the milk higher than 110 degrees; doing so will kill the yeast and result in squat muffins.

- 2¾ cups (15⅛ ounces) bread flour
- 1 tablespoon instant or rapid-rise yeast
- 1¼ teaspoons table salt
- 1 cup plus 6 tablespoons (11 ounces) warm whole milk (110 degrees)
- 2 tablespoons honey
- 5 tablespoons cornmeal, divided
- 2 tablespoons unsalted butter, cut into 2 pieces, divided

1. Combine flour, yeast, and salt in large bowl. In second bowl, whisk warm milk and honey together. Add milk mixture to flour mixture and stir until no pockets of dry flour remain. Cover bowl with plastic wrap and let dough rise in warm place until doubled in size, about 1 hour.
2. Line rimmed baking sheet with parchment paper and spray with vegetable oil spray. Sprinkle prepared sheet with 4 tablespoons cornmeal. Us- ing greased ¼-cup dry measuring cup, divide dough into 8 heaping ¼-cup por- tions. Using your lightly greased hands, lightly cup each portion of dough and shape into even 2- to 2½-inch-diameter round about 1 inch tall, then place on prepared sheet. Sprinkle tops of rounds with remaining 1 tablespoon cornmeal. Cover sheet loosely with greased plastic and let rounds rise in warm place until puffy and nearly doubled in size, about 1 hour.
3. Adjust oven rack to middle posi- tion and heat oven to 350 degrees. Melt 1 tablespoon butter in 12-inch nonstick skillet over medium heat. Add 4 dough rounds and cook until deep golden brown on first side, about 2 minutes, moving rounds as needed for even browning. Flip muffins and cook until deep golden brown on second side, about 2 minutes, pressing down lightly with spatula if muffins begin to rise unevenly. Transfer muffins to clean baking sheet. Wipe skillet clean with paper towels and repeat with remain- ing 1 tablespoon butter and remaining 4 dough rounds.
4. Bake muffins until centers register 205 to 210 degrees, 10 to 12 minutes. Let muffins cool completely on wire rack. Using fork, split muffins. Toast and serve.

TO MAKE AHEAD
In step 2, let dough rounds rise in refrig- erator for at least 12 hours, until nearly doubled in size (you can refrigerate them for up to 48 hours). When ready to bake, proceed with step 3.

And the Best Blade-Style Coffee Grinder Is … *by Lauren Savoie*

EQUIPMENT REVIEW

FOR THE BEST cup of coffee, we always recommend freshly grinding the beans. Many home brewers use blade grinders, which feature rapidly spinning blades that chop the coffee beans into small fragments.

To find the best blade grinder, we tested six models, priced from $14.96 to $21.95, using each to grind enough beans to make one, four, and 10 cups of coffee. We used the grinders to achieve fine, medium, and coarse grinds with both light-roasted and dark-roasted beans. We then asked six testers to operate each grinder and gauge its user-friendliness.

When using a blade grinder, if you simply hold down the grind button, some beans end up overground, while others never come in contact with the blade. Experts recommend pulsing the grind button and shaking the grinder in between pulses to redistribute the grounds. When we adopted this pattern, half the grinders gave us coffee that was acceptably evenly ground; the other half produced unacceptably uneven grinds.

We wondered if blade height mattered, so we measured the height of the blade in each grinder. We found that the blades of the best-performing mod- els sat low in the grinding chamber. Since the average length of a coffee bean is 10 millimeters, models with less than 9 millimeters between the blade and the base of the grinding chamber gave us an even grind. Our favorite models had blades that sat just over 6 millimeters off the base of the grinder.

We also rated the grinders on capacity (we wanted to be able to fit enough beans to brew a full pot of coffee), ease of use, and cleanup. When we tallied the scores, our previous favorite from Krups came out on top again. Web subscrib- ers can see the full results at **CooksCountry.com/may19.**

KEY **Good ★★★** **Fair ★★** **Poor ★**

HIGHLY RECOMMENDED

Krups Coffee and Spice Grinder
Model: F2034251
Price: $17.99
Capacity: 75 g **Blade Height:** 6.4 mm
Comments: Our former favorite again received top marks for its even grinding and simple, easy-to-use design. The wide, clear lid afforded us a great view of the grinding process. Its grinding chamber was roomy and easy to load and empty. It held plenty of beans, and its low-lying blade ensured that no whole beans were left after grinding.

Grinding	★★★
Ease of Use	★★★
Capacity	★★★
Cleanup	★★★

RECOMMENDED

Bodum Bistro Blade Coffee Grinder
Model: 11160
Price: $21.95
Capacity: 70 g **Blade Height:** 6.1 mm
Comments: Overall, this grinder is compact and intuitive. It made quick work of grinding smaller amounts of beans, but when it was loaded to capacity with enough beans to make 10 cups of coffee, its blade could hardly turn under the compacted beans. Its smaller grinding chamber also made loading and unloading coffee messier.

Grinding	★★½
Ease of Use	★★★
Capacity	★★½
Cleanup	★★½

RECOMMENDED WITH RESERVATIONS

Capresso Cool Grind Blade Grinder, Black
Model: #505.01
Price: $19.99
Capacity: 80 g **Blade Height:** 14.1 mm
Comments: This roomy grinder easily accom- modated 10 cups' worth of coffee beans, but it sometimes left whole beans unprocessed because its blade sat relatively high in the grinding chamber. Despite this, it made quick work of processing the beans. The domed lid made it a bit harder to observe the grinding.

Grinding	★½
Ease of Use	★★
Capacity	★★★
Cleanup	★★★

Thin and Crispy Chocolate Chip Cookies

Thick and chewy chocolate chip cookies are a classic, but their thin, crunchy, butterscotch-y cousins deserve a spot in the cookie jar, too. **by Alli Berkey**

Keys to the Perfect Texture

Mini chocolate chips keep a low profile.

Cake flour makes the batter light.

Plenty of butter helps the cookies spread.

THE GOOD THING about the battle between thick and chewy chocolate chip cookies and thin and crispy chocolate chip cookies is that nobody loses—when done well, both styles are great. So I was excited when my editor handed me the assignment of developing a recipe for the thin and crispy variety.

A good thin and crispy cookie needs to live up to its name. Rather than having a range of textures, these cookies must keep a consistent snap. Just like a good potato chip, the best crispy cookie will be as crispy in the middle as it is at the edge.

In researching existing recipes, I found that there were two common tricks for creating thin, crispy chocolate chip cookies. One option was to simply increase the amount of butter in the recipe. This did make for thin and crispy cookies, as the extra butter melted and helped the cookies spread in the oven, but the cookies spread too much and were greasy from the extra fat. The other trick was to mix the batter entirely by hand—no creaming the butter and sugar using a mixer—so that the cookies held less air and thus had less structure, which also encouraged them to spread wide and thin. But again, these cookies spread too much and ran into each other on the baking sheet. That wouldn't do.

I needed to find a middle ground between domed cookies and super-flat cookies. I started by combining a melted stick of butter with ⅔ cup of sugar; my tasters liked a combination of granulated and brown sugars for that signature butterscotch flavor. I worked with a baseline of 1 cup of all-purpose flour, and I knew the batter needed eggs for structure. Two seemed like the right number, but the eggs were making the cookies rise a little too high. Losing the egg whites and using just two yolks made for lower-profile, crispier cookies. Vanilla extract, salt, and baking soda rounded out the batter ingredients. Mini chocolate chips, rather than full-size ones, also helped these cookies ride low.

I was making good progress, but the cookies weren't quite as crispy as I wanted. I tried fiddling with the oven temperature and rack placement, but in the end the solution was adding just 1½ tablespoons of whole milk. The milk provided extra moisture so that the cookies didn't completely dry out with the extra baking time required to crisp them up; plus, the natural sugars in the milk aided in browning. These cookies were good, but overspreading was still an issue.

The batter needed a bit more flour to hold the cookies together and keep them from spreading too much. Just ¼ cup more did the trick, but the extra flour made the cookies a little too chewy. I was at my wit's end when a colleague suggested switching from all-purpose flour to lighter cake flour, which contains less protein and makes for more-tender baked goods. That solved the problem and was the finishing touch on my new favorite cookie: thin, crispy, studded with chocolate chips, and packed with flavor. Now that's the way these cookies crumble.

THIN AND CRISPY CHOCOLATE CHIP COOKIES
Makes 16 cookies
Note that this recipe calls for cake flour and mini (not full-size) chocolate chips.

- 1¼ cups (5 ounces) cake flour
- ¾ teaspoon table salt
- ¼ teaspoon baking soda
- 8 tablespoons unsalted butter, melted and cooled
- ⅓ cup (2⅓ ounces) granulated sugar
- ⅓ cup packed (2⅓ ounces) dark brown sugar
- 2 large egg yolks
- 1½ tablespoons whole milk
- 2 teaspoons vanilla extract
- ¾ cup (4½ ounces) mini semisweet chocolate chips

1. Adjust oven rack to middle position and heat oven to 350 degrees. Line 2 baking sheets with parchment paper. Whisk flour, salt, and baking soda together in bowl.
2. Using stand mixer fitted with paddle, mix melted butter, granulated sugar, and brown sugar on low speed until fully combined. Increase speed to medium-high and beat until mixture is lightened in color, about 1 minute. Reduce speed to low; add egg yolks, milk, and vanilla; and mix until combined. Slowly add flour mixture and mix until just combined, scraping down bowl as needed. Using rubber spatula, stir in chocolate chips.
3. Using greased 1-tablespoon measure, divide dough into 16 heaping-tablespoon portions on prepared sheets, 8 portions per sheet. Divide any remaining dough evenly among portions. Using your moistened fingers, press dough portions to ½-inch thickness. Bake cookies, 1 sheet at a time, until deep golden brown, 16 to 18 minutes, rotating sheet halfway through baking. Let cookies cool on sheet for 20 minutes. Serve. (Cookies can be stored at room temperature for up to 3 days.)

Glazed Chicken Breasts
with Currant-Pistachio Couscous

30-MINUTE SUPPER

Chicken and Leek Soup
with Parmesan Dumplings

30-MINUTE SUPPER

Grilled Strip Steaks
with Smashed Cucumber Salad

30-MINUTE SUPPER

Crispy Broiled Salmon
with Lemon-Butter Green Beans

30-MINUTE SUPPER

Chicken and Leek Soup
with Parmesan Dumplings *Serves 4*

Sprinkle with chopped parsley before serving, if desired.

1   cup all-purpose flour
1   ounce Parmesan cheese, grated (½ cup)
⅓   cup water
1   large egg, lightly beaten
1   teaspoon table salt, divided
½   teaspoon baking powder
¼   teaspoon pepper
4   tablespoons unsalted butter
1   pound leeks, white and light green parts only, halved lengthwise, sliced ½ inch thick, and washed thoroughly
2   garlic cloves, minced
6   cups chicken broth
1   (2½-pound) rotisserie chicken, skin and bones discarded, meat shredded into bite-size pieces (3 cups)

1. Combine flour, Parmesan, water, egg, ½ teaspoon salt, baking powder, and pepper in bowl; set aside.
2. Melt butter in Dutch oven over medium-high heat. Add leeks and remaining ½ teaspoon salt and cook until softened and beginning to brown, 8 to 10 minutes. Add garlic and cook until fragrant, about 1 minute. Stir in broth and bring to simmer.
3. Reduce heat to medium. Using 2 spoons, scrape rough tablespoon-size dumplings into soup and cook, without stirring, for 2 minutes. Gently stir to break up dumplings and continue to cook 2 minutes longer. Carefully stir in chicken and cook until heated through, about 1 minute. Serve.

Glazed Chicken Breasts
with Currant-Pistachio Couscous *Serves 4*

Harissa, a chile paste, can be found in the international aisle of your supermarket, usually with Middle Eastern or Indian ingredients. Sprinkle with torn fresh mint leaves before serving.

2   tablespoons apricot preserves
1   tablespoon harissa
5   tablespoons extra-virgin olive oil, divided
¼   cup dried currants
1   teaspoon grated lemon zest plus 2 tablespoons juice
1   garlic clove, minced
1½   teaspoons table salt, divided
½   teaspoon pepper, divided
4   (6- to 8-ounce) boneless, skinless chicken breasts, trimmed
1½   cups water
1¼   cups couscous
½   cup shelled pistachios, toasted and chopped

1. Combine apricot preserves, harissa, and 1 tablespoon oil in bowl. Transfer 1 tablespoon harissa mixture to second bowl and stir in currants, lemon zest and juice, garlic, ½ teaspoon salt, ¼ teaspoon pepper, and 3 tablespoons oil.
2. Pat chicken dry with paper towels and sprinkle with remaining 1 teaspoon salt and remaining ¼ teaspoon pepper. Heat remaining 1 tablespoon oil in 12-inch nonstick skillet over medium-high heat until just smoking. Cook chicken until golden brown and meat registers 160 degrees, about 6 minutes per side. Transfer chicken to cutting board, brush all over with harissa-apricot mixture (without currants), and tent with foil.
3. Bring water to boil in now-empty skillet over high heat. Stir in couscous, cover, and remove from heat. Let stand for 5 minutes. Stir in pistachios and harissa-currant mixture. Slice chicken ½ inch thick and serve over couscous.

Crispy Broiled Salmon
with Lemon-Butter Green Beans *Serves 4*

To ensure uniform cooking, we prefer to buy a whole 1½- to 2-pound center-cut salmon fillet and cut it into four equal pieces.

⅓   cup sour cream
2   tablespoons dill pickle relish
3   (2-inch) strips lemon zest, plus 2 tablespoons juice, divided
1   tablespoon chopped fresh parsley
¾   teaspoon table salt, divided
½   teaspoon pepper, divided
1   tablespoon Old Bay seasoning
1   tablespoon sugar
4   (6- to 8-ounce) skin-on salmon fillets, 1 to 1½ inches thick
1½   pounds green beans, trimmed and cut into 2-inch lengths
3   tablespoons unsalted butter, divided

1. Combine sour cream, relish, 1 tablespoon lemon juice, parsley, ¼ teaspoon salt, and ¼ teaspoon pepper in bowl; set aside sauce. Combine Old Bay and sugar in second bowl.
2. Adjust oven rack 8 inches from broiler element and heat broiler. Line rimmed baking sheet with foil and set wire rack in sheet. Place salmon, skin side down, on prepared wire rack. Sprinkle Old Bay–sugar mixture evenly over salmon. Broil salmon until deeply browned and centers of fillets register 125 degrees (for medium-rare), 8 to 12 minutes.
3. Combine green beans, ¼ cup water, 1 tablespoon butter, lemon zest, remaining ½ teaspoon salt, and remaining ¼ teaspoon pepper in 12-inch nonstick skillet and bring to simmer over medium-high heat. Cover and cook until green beans are just tender, about 5 minutes. Uncover and continue to cook until green beans are slightly browned, about 4 minutes longer. Off heat, stir in remaining 1 tablespoon lemon juice and remaining 2 tablespoons butter. Serve salmon with green beans and sauce.

Grilled Strip Steaks with
Smashed Cucumber Salad *Serves 4*

We like to sprinkle the cucumber salad with toasted sesame seeds before serving.

2   English cucumbers, quartered lengthwise and cut into 2-inch lengths
3½   teaspoons kosher salt, divided
2   (1-pound) strip steaks, 1 inch thick, trimmed
½   teaspoon pepper
4   teaspoons seasoned rice vinegar
2   tablespoons soy sauce, divided
2   teaspoons toasted sesame oil
1   garlic clove, minced
½   teaspoon red pepper flakes
3   tablespoons chopped fresh basil
4   tablespoons unsalted butter, melted and cooled

1. Combine cucumbers and 1½ teaspoons salt in 1-gallon zipper-lock bag, seal bag, and turn to distribute salt. Using rolling pin or small skillet, gently smash cucumbers in bag; set aside.
2. Pat steaks dry with paper towels and sprinkle with pepper and remaining 2 teaspoons salt. Grill over hot fire until meat registers 125 degrees (for medium-rare), 4 to 8 minutes per side. Transfer steaks to cutting board, tent with foil, and let rest for 10 minutes.
3. Drain cucumbers in colander. Whisk vinegar, 1 tablespoon soy sauce, oil, garlic, and pepper flakes together in large bowl. Add cucumbers and basil to vinegar mixture and toss to combine. Whisk melted butter and remaining 1 tablespoon soy sauce together in second bowl. Slice steaks ½ inch thick. Drizzle steaks with soy sauce–butter mixture and serve with cucumber salad.

Sirloin Steak Tips with Charro Beans

30-MINUTE SUPPER

Pan-Roasted Pork Tenderloin with Spring Asparagus Salad

30-MINUTE SUPPER

Linguine with Broccoli, Tomatoes, and Pecorino

30-MINUTE SUPPER

Maple-Bacon Pork Burgers

30-MINUTE SUPPER

Pan-Roasted Pork Tenderloin with Spring Asparagus Salad *Serves 4*

We developed this recipe using Buitoni Pesto with Basil.

- 1 pound asparagus, trimmed and sliced thin on bias
- 1 (15-ounce) can chickpeas, rinsed
- 1 cup pesto
- 3 tablespoons lemon juice
- 3 tablespoons extra-virgin olive oil, divided
- 4 teaspoons kosher salt, divided
- 1½ teaspoons pepper, divided
- 2 (1-pound) pork tenderloins, trimmed
- 1 teaspoon dry mustard
- 4 ounces feta cheese, crumbled (1 cup)
- 2 tablespoons chopped fresh chives

1. Adjust oven rack to middle position and heat oven to 375 degrees. Combine asparagus, chickpeas, pesto, lemon juice, 2 tablespoons oil, 2 teaspoons salt, and ½ teaspoon pepper in large bowl. Transfer to platter and set aside.

2. Pat pork dry with paper towels and sprinkle with mustard, remaining 2 teaspoons salt, and remaining 1 teaspoon pepper. Heat remaining 1 tablespoon oil in 12-inch nonstick skillet over medium-high heat until just smoking. Cook pork until well browned on all sides, about 8 minutes. Transfer pork to rimmed baking sheet. Roast until meat registers 135 degrees, 12 to 15 minutes. Transfer pork to carving board and let rest for 5 minutes.

3. Slice pork on bias ½ inch thick and arrange alongside salad on platter. Sprinkle feta and chives over salad. Serve.

Sirloin Steak Tips with Charro Beans

Serves 4

Sirloin steak tips are often sold as flap meat. We like to garnish this dish with fresh cilantro leaves.

- ½ small red onion, sliced thin
- ¼ cup distilled white vinegar
- 1 small jalapeño chile, stemmed, seeded, and sliced thin
- 2 pounds sirloin steak tips, trimmed and cut into 2-inch chunks
- 3½ teaspoons kosher salt, divided
- 2½ teaspoons ground cumin, divided
- 1½ teaspoons pepper, divided
- 2 tablespoons vegetable oil
- 3 garlic cloves, minced
- 3 (15-ounce) cans pinto beans, rinsed
- 1½ cups chicken broth

1. Combine onion, vinegar, and jalapeño in small bowl. Cover and microwave until hot, about 2 minutes; set aside.

2. Sprinkle beef with 2 teaspoons salt, ½ teaspoon cumin, and 1 teaspoon pepper. Heat oil in 12-inch nonstick skillet over medium-high heat until just smoking. Add beef and cook until browned on all sides and meat registers 120 to 125 degrees (for medium-rare), about 7 minutes. Transfer beef to large plate and tent with foil.

3. Reduce heat to medium, add garlic and remaining 2 teaspoons cumin to now-empty skillet, and cook until fragrant, about 30 seconds. Stir in beans, broth, remaining 1½ teaspoons salt, and remaining ½ teaspoon pepper. Using potato masher, lightly mash beans until about one-quarter of beans are broken down. Bring to simmer and cook until thickened and liquid is fully incorporated into bean mixture, about 4 minutes. Serve steak with beans and pickled onion mixture.

Maple-Bacon Pork Burgers *Serves 4*

Serve with bread-and-butter pickles.

- 1½ pounds ground pork
- 4 teaspoons kosher salt, divided
- 2 teaspoons pepper, divided
- 6 cups (7 ounces) coleslaw mix
- ½ cup mayonnaise
- ¼ cup maple syrup
- 1½ tablespoons cider vinegar
- 2 teaspoons whole-grain mustard
- 4 slices thick-cut bacon
- 4 ounces sharp cheddar cheese, shredded (1 cup)
- 4 brioche hamburger buns, split and toasted

1. Divide pork into 4 equal balls. Flatten balls into even ¾-inch-thick patties. Using your fingertips, press down center of each patty until about ½ inch thick, creating slight divot. Sprinkle patties with 2 teaspoons salt and 1 teaspoon pepper. Combine coleslaw mix, mayonnaise, maple syrup, vinegar, mustard, remaining 2 teaspoons salt, and remaining 1 teaspoon pepper in bowl; set aside.

2. Cook bacon in 12-inch cast-iron skillet over medium-high heat until crispy, about 6 minutes. Transfer bacon to paper towel–lined plate; once cooled, break slices in half. Add patties to now-empty skillet and cook until well browned on both sides and meat registers 160 degrees, about 10 minutes. Top burgers with cheddar, transfer to large plate, and let rest for 3 minutes. Place burgers on bun bottoms and top with slaw and bacon, then add bun tops. Serve.

Linguine with Broccoli, Tomatoes, and Pecorino *Serves 4*

Use a wine you'd be happy drinking for this recipe.

- 10 ounces broccoli florets, cut into 1½-inch pieces
- ¾ teaspoon table salt, plus salt for cooking broccoli
- 1 pound linguine
- ⅓ cup extra-virgin olive oil, plus extra for drizzling
- 4 garlic cloves, sliced thin
- ¼ teaspoon red pepper flakes
- 2 tomatoes, cored and chopped
- ¼ cup dry white wine
- ½ teaspoon pepper
- 1 ounce Pecorino Romano cheese, grated (½ cup), plus extra for serving

1. Bring 4 quarts water to boil in large pot. Add broccoli and 1 tablespoon salt and cook until broccoli is bright green and tender, about 3 minutes. Using slotted spoon, transfer broccoli to paper towel–lined plate. Add pasta to boiling water and cook, stirring often, until al dente. Reserve ½ cup cooking water, then drain pasta and set aside.

2. Heat oil in now-empty pot over medium-high heat until shimmering. Add garlic and pepper flakes and cook until fragrant, about 1 minute. Add tomatoes, wine, pepper, and salt and cook until tomatoes begin to break down and darken slightly, about 5 minutes.

3. Off heat, add Pecorino, broccoli, pasta, and reserved cooking water to pot and stir to combine. Serve, drizzling individual portions with extra oil and passing extra Pecorino separately.

> *"The cow is of the bovine ilk; one end is moo, the other, milk."*
>
> **—Ogden Nash**

Milk

Milk is an indispensable ingredient that finds its way into all kinds of sweet and savory foods. Here's what you need to know to start cooking with it. **by Scott Kathan**

HIDING IN PLAIN SIGHT

BISCUITS
It doesn't have to be buttermilk—regular milk works fine, too.

SCRAMBLED EGGS
Here, milk adds richness and fat to help keep the curds tender.

MEATBALLS
Milk-based panades help keep meatballs moist and tender.

MAC AND CHEESE
Milk makes white sauces that are flavorful but not too rich.

BREAD
Breads made with milk have a gentle sweetness.

Milk Paste

Meatloaf, meatball, and some hamburger recipes call for panades—pastes of bread crumbs (or crackers) mashed with milk—to help keep the meat moist. This works because, when cooked, the starch in the bread absorbs water from the meat and forms a gel that holds on to moisture. Milk is our preferred liquid for panades because it adds richness and most cooks have it on hand, but our tests have shown that you can use broth, tomato juice, water, or other liquids in place of or in addition to milk.

Busting a Milk Myth

Some bread recipes call for scalding milk (bringing it to the verge of a boil, about 180 degrees) before adding it to the dough. The idea is that scalding breaks down the milk proteins that can otherwise thicken and hinder the rise of yeast. To test this, we made loaves of white sandwich bread with scalded and unscalded milk (which was heated to 110 degrees to help activate the yeast, per the recipe). The loaf made with scalded milk did rise slightly higher, but the loaf made with warmed milk was still very good. Since scalding introduces the possibility of killing the yeast if the baker doesn't let the hot milk cool down sufficiently (temperatures higher than 120 degrees will kill most yeast), we don't recommend scalding.

Fat Is Where the Flavor Is

Milk is made up of water, fat, proteins, sugar (lactose), and minerals. The fat in milk gives it both flavor and richness. The percentage of fat in milk varies depending on the cow's diet and breed. But supermarket milk has been standardized to the following fat percentages:

Skim Milk	1% Milk	2% Milk	Whole Milk	Heavy Cream
0% fat	1% fat	2% fat	3.5% fat	35% fat

Nondairy Milks

In experimenting with the myriad alternative milks, we've found that specific products work better in certain dishes. We love oat milk in baked goods because its high natural sugar content translates into good browning—but it can taste out of place in savory dishes. Soy and almond milks are both good, relatively neutral options for savory dishes. Coconut milk can straddle sweet and savory recipes. We don't use rice milk in cooking—it's too watery.

What's in the Can?

Both sweetened condensed milk and evaporated milk consist of milk from which 60 percent of the water has been removed. The only difference between the two is that sweetened condensed milk contains added sugar. Evaporated milk can be substituted for regular milk in recipes by adding an equal amount of water (1 cup of evaporated milk plus 1 cup of water equals 2 cups of whole milk).

Grilled Bone-In Leg of Lamb

A grill-roasted bone-in leg of lamb served with a charred-scallion sauce makes for an impressive holiday centerpiece.

It took 112 pounds of meat, but we finally achieved a leg of lamb that tasted as impressive as it looked.

by Morgan Bolling

THE GRILLING AREA at our Boston test kitchen sits next to a cruise ship terminal. This means that any test cook who grills on a Friday has a crowd of spectators eager to watch while they wait to set sail. It can be fun to have an audience when you're expertly searing a thick-cut steak. Or it can mean that there are hundreds of people to bear witness when a beautiful 8-pound leg of lamb gets enveloped in menacing flames from the grill. I should know. It happened to me.

I'd been thrilled to be assigned the task of developing a recipe for grilled leg of lamb. I love lamb's meaty, mildly gamy flavor, especially the leg. This grand cut has an iconic figure, impressive enough for any celebration, but its tapered shape also means that, over a fire, the meat will cook unevenly, ending up burnt on the narrow end and raw in the middle. My task: to achieve a more even range of doneness, from the charred exterior to a lovely medium-rare in the center, with plenty of flavor. And no major flare-ups.

To get started, I coated an 8-pound bone-in leg of lamb with salt and pepper. I got a charcoal grill ripping hot with smoldering coals spread evenly over its base and placed the lamb on the grate. It wasn't long before the lamb's fat began to render and drip onto the coals. The ensuing flames grew quickly, engulfing the leg and prompting oohs and aahs from my audience. The flames may have looked cool, but they resulted in a sooty flavor. My lamb tasted like a spent cigar.

I needed to contain the flames, so for my next test I built a half-grill fire, with all the coals on one side of the grill. I wanted to sear the lamb over the hotter side and then race to move it to the cooler side before the fat rendered and the flames licked up. I lost the race. I tried trimming the fat more aggressively and cooking the lamb entirely over the cooler side. There were no flare-ups, but the leg was pale and sad-looking.

Here in the test kitchen, we often turn to a technique called reverse searing when cooking big cuts of meat. You cook the meat through at a lower temperature first and then sear it to create a flavorful crust. Using this method, I figured, would allow the fat to gently render long before the meat saw the direct heat, minimizing flare-ups.

I placed the lamb on the cooler side of the grill and let it cook until it reached 120 degrees, which took about 1½ hours. I then moved it to the hotter side, where it seared perfectly, acquiring a gorgeous dark brown crust to go with its nicely medium-rare center. Perfect.

To dress it up, I smeared my next leg of lamb with a paste of fresh thyme, dried oregano, coriander, garlic, lemon zest, and plenty of salt and pepper. I found that leaving this powerful paste on the lamb overnight before grilling helped season the meat and add flavor to the exterior.

A beautiful roast needs a beautiful sauce, so I charred some scallions on the grill before searing the lamb. I then chopped them and stirred them into a mixture of extra-virgin olive oil, parsley, red wine vinegar, and spicy red pepper flakes.

The cruise ship passengers watched wistfully as I took that final leg back into the kitchen. And as I sliced off a bit of that juicy meat with its dark brown, flavor-packed crust and dipped it in some charred-scallion sauce, I started making plans to cook another for an upcoming dinner party. I'd finally mastered the flames.

GRILLED BONE-IN LEG OF LAMB WITH CHARRED-SCALLION SAUCE
Serves 10 to 12

The seasoned meat must be refrigerated for at least 12 hours before cooking. For an accurate temperature reading in step 5, insert your thermometer into the thickest part of the leg until you hit bone, then pull it about ½ inch away from the bone.

LAMB
- 12 garlic cloves, minced
- 2 tablespoons vegetable oil
- 2 tablespoons kosher salt
- 1½ tablespoons pepper
- 1 tablespoon fresh thyme leaves
- 1 tablespoon dried oregano
- 2 teaspoons finely grated lemon zest
- 1 teaspoon ground coriander
- 1 (8-pound) bone-in leg of lamb, trimmed

SCALLION SAUCE
- ¾ cup extra-virgin olive oil
- ¼ cup chopped fresh parsley
- 1 tablespoon red wine vinegar
- 2 garlic cloves, minced
- 1 teaspoon pepper
- ¾ teaspoon kosher salt
- ¼ teaspoon red pepper flakes
- 12 scallions, trimmed

1. FOR THE LAMB: Combine garlic, oil, salt, pepper, thyme, oregano, lemon zest, and coriander in bowl. Place lamb on rimmed baking sheet and rub all over with garlic paste. Cover with plastic wrap and refrigerate for at least 12 hours or up to 24 hours.

2. FOR THE SCALLION SAUCE: Combine oil, parsley, vinegar, garlic, pepper, salt, and pepper flakes in bowl; set aside.

3A. FOR A CHARCOAL GRILL: Open bottom vent completely. Light large chimney starter filled with charcoal briquettes (6 quarts). When top coals are partially covered with ash, pour evenly over half of grill. Set cooking grate in place, cover, and open lid vent completely. Heat grill until hot, about 5 minutes.

3B. FOR A GAS GRILL: Turn all burners to high, cover, and heat grill until hot, about 15 minutes. Leave primary burner on high and turn off other burner(s). (Adjust primary burner [or, if using 3-burner grill, primary burner and second burner] as needed to maintain grill temperature between 350 and 400 degrees.)

4. Clean and oil cooking grate. Place scallions on hotter side of grill. Cook (covered if using gas) until lightly charred on both sides, about 3 minutes per side. Transfer scallions to plate.

5. Uncover lamb and place fat side up on cooler side of grill, parallel to fire. (If using gas, it may be necessary to angle thicker end of lamb toward hotter side of grill to fit.) Cover grill (position lid vent directly over lamb if using charcoal) and cook until thickest part of meat (½ inch from bone) registers 120 degrees, 1¼ hours to 1¾ hours.

6. Transfer lamb, fat side down, to hotter side of grill. Cook (covered if using gas) until fat side is well browned, 7 to 9 minutes. Transfer lamb to carving board, fat side up, and tent with aluminum foil. Let rest for 30 minutes.

7. Cut scallions into ½-inch pieces, then stir into reserved oil mixture. Season sauce with salt and pepper to taste. Slice lamb thin and serve with sauce.

The Case for Bone-In
Would a boneless leg of lamb be easier to cook evenly and carve perfectly? Yes. So why go bone-in here? The practical reasons are that boneless roasts come in netting that you have to cut away (it is not grill-safe), necessitating tying with twine. Also, a bone-in leg gives you a range of doneness throughout the roast to please all tastes. But mostly it comes down to the grand, festive look of a whole bone-in leg. The cut is also a nod to earlier times when animals were butchered more simply and large cuts were cooked over a live fire, as in this recipe. Go all out—go for a bone-in leg of lamb.

Four Steps to Juicy Lamb with a Flavorful Crust

1. Rub with Paste
Massage the spice paste into the lamb, cover the lamb with plastic wrap, and refrigerate it for at least 12 hours.

2. Grill Low and Slow
Set up the grill with hotter and cooler zones and grill the lamb, fat side up, over the cooler side until it's almost done.

3. Sear over High Heat
Move the lamb to the hotter side of the grill, fat side down, to create a flavorful seared crust.

4. Carve into Thin Slices
Starting at the widest part of the lamb, thinly slice at a 45-degree angle toward the exposed bone end.

Cauliflower Salad

Cauliflower's delicate flavor makes it an ideal canvas for a springtime salad—as long as you treat it right.

by Morgan Bolling

FOR DECADES, MOST Americans regarded cauliflower as an afterthought—a fine (if bland) choice for crudités or for a side dish when steamed with carrots and broccoli, but that was about it. But with this vegetable's recent surge in popularity, our eyes have been opened to newfound—and delicious—possibilities, most of them based on the enhanced appeal of roasted cauliflower. When it's roasted, the sugars in this vegetable caramelize, turning the flavor nutty and sweet. I wanted to do my part in service of this once-neglected vegetable and literally dress it up in a compelling salad.

I collected and prepared a handful of recipes for roasted cauliflower salads. Our favorite of the bunch, from acclaimed London-based chef and author Yotam Ottolenghi, was an herb-heavy salad that called for roasting two-thirds of a head of cauliflower until browned, soft, and sweet and then grating the remaining third on the large holes of a box grater and adding it to the salad raw. The contrasting flavors and textures of one vegetable treated two different ways were very appealing.

Inspired by this success, I cut the florets into bite-size pieces and roasted them in a rimmed baking sheet on the lowest rack of a hot 475-degree oven. This oven rack position ensured that the bottoms of the florets caramelized while the tops retained a slightly firm texture. Rather than use one-third of the head, I roasted all the florets and blitzed just the raw core in the food processor until it was finely chopped. It took on an almost grain-like texture with a pleasant crunch. I whisked lemon juice and olive oil together for a quick vinaigrette and tossed in both types of cauliflower.

As for the herbs, parsley and mint added a cooling brightness that highlighted the subtle cauliflower flavor. Since I already had my food processor out, I used it to do the work of chopping the fresh herbs (about five pulses did the trick). This salad had a pleasing mix of sweet, roasted flavors balanced

with freshness from the uncooked cauliflower and herbs.

Now, for the finishing touches. To play up the cauliflower's natural sweetness, I stirred in a minced shallot and some concentrated, fruity golden raisins, which I let soften in the vinaigrette while assembling the salad. A little bit of coriander added a citrusy perfume and flavor. For a light crunch, I sprinkled on some toasted sliced almonds.

This salad was so good—savory, sweet, and complex—that I developed two additional versions: one with potent smoked paprika, apricots, and hazelnuts and a second with ground fennel, tart dried cranberries, and toasted pistachios. I'm sorry, cauliflower; I'll never call you boring again.

ROASTED CAULIFLOWER SALAD WITH GOLDEN RAISINS AND ALMONDS

Serves 4

When shopping, look for cauliflower with no leaves attached to the base of the head. Alternatively, if you can find only cauliflower with many leaves still attached, buy a slightly larger head (about 2¼ pounds). Kitchen shears make easy work of cutting the cauliflower florets away from the core, but you can use a paring knife if you prefer. For the best results, be sure to use a high-quality extra-virgin olive oil here. Toast the sliced almonds in a dry skillet over medium heat, stirring often, until browned and fragrant, 3 to 5 minutes.

1	head cauliflower (2 pounds)
5	tablespoons extra-virgin olive oil, divided
1¼	teaspoons table salt, divided
1	teaspoon pepper, divided
⅓	cup golden raisins
1	shallot, minced
1	teaspoon grated lemon zest plus 1 tablespoon juice
1	teaspoon ground coriander
1	cup fresh parsley leaves
½	cup fresh mint leaves
¼	cup sliced almonds, toasted

1. Adjust oven rack to lowest position and heat oven to 475 degrees. Trim outer leaves from cauliflower and cut stem flush with bottom of head. Flip cauliflower stem side up. Using kitchen shears, cut around stem and core to remove large florets. Chop core coarse and set aside. Cut florets through stems into 1-inch pieces (you should have about 6 cups florets).

2. Toss florets, 1 tablespoon oil, 1 teaspoon salt, and ½ teaspoon pepper together in bowl. Transfer to rimmed baking sheet and roast until florets are tender and browned on bottoms, 12 to 15 minutes. Let cool for 15 minutes.

3. While florets are roasting, combine raisins, shallot, lemon zest and juice, coriander, remaining ¼ cup oil, remaining ¼ teaspoon salt, and remaining ½ teaspoon pepper in large bowl; set aside.

4. Transfer core to food processor and process until finely chopped, 10 to 20 seconds, scraping down sides of bowl as needed; transfer to bowl with dressing. Add parsley and mint to now-empty processor and pulse until coarsely chopped, 5 to 7 pulses, scraping down sides of bowl as needed; transfer to bowl with dressing.

5. Add florets and almonds to bowl with dressing mixture and toss to combine. Season with salt and pepper to taste. Transfer to platter and serve.

ROASTED CAULIFLOWER SALAD WITH APRICOTS AND HAZELNUTS

Substitute chopped dried apricots for golden raisins, ½ teaspoon smoked paprika for coriander, and hazelnuts, toasted, skinned, and chopped, for almonds.

ROASTED CAULIFLOWER SALAD WITH CRANBERRIES AND PISTACHIOS

Substitute dried cranberries for golden raisins, ground fennel for coriander, and shelled pistachios, toasted and chopped, for almonds.

Greek Spinach and Chickpeas

This light, lively vegetable side dish comes together in minutes. **by Morgan Bolling**

WHEN I THINK of chickpeas, my mind usually goes to the spice-rich flavors of curry or hummus. But recently at a neighborhood Greek restaurant, I was served tender chickpeas tossed with garlic and a tangle of wilted spinach in a vibrant, lemony, dill-scented broth. It was light, bright, and punchy.

In an effort to re-create this enticing dish, I started by heating sliced garlic and red pepper flakes in olive oil in a large skillet until the oil was infused with flavor. Next, I added two drained cans of chickpeas before stirring in curly-leaf spinach one handful at a time, waiting for one portion to wilt before adding the next. Before serving, I spritzed the dish with lemon and sprinkled in a hefty ¼ cup of fresh dill.

The dish was OK, but it felt a little awkward to make, and the elements tasted disjointed, not unified. Switching to a Dutch oven provided enough room so that I could add the spinach all at once, which was much more efficient. Baby spinach proved easier to work with than curly-leaf spinach, as it didn't require any stemming or chopping. Cooking the spinach for just 5 minutes kept its flavor fresh.

A little chicken broth provided a savory base that carried all the flavors and tied the dish together. The last trick was not draining one of the cans of chickpeas; the starchy chickpea liquid added body to the broth, giving it a creamy consistency that was perfect for sopping up with a torn piece of crusty bread.

GREEK SPINACH AND CHICKPEAS
Serves 4 to 6
Vegetable broth can be substituted for the chicken broth, if desired.

- 2 tablespoons extra-virgin olive oil, plus extra for drizzling
- 3 garlic cloves, sliced thin
- ¼ teaspoon red pepper flakes
- 2 (15-ounce) cans chickpeas (1 can drained and rinsed, 1 can left undrained)
- 10 ounces (10 cups) baby spinach
- ½ cup chicken broth
- ¼ teaspoon table salt
- ¼ cup chopped fresh dill
- 1 tablespoon lemon juice

1. Combine oil, garlic, and pepper flakes in Dutch oven and cook over medium heat until garlic is golden brown, 3 to 5 minutes.
2. Stir in 1 can drained chickpeas, 1 can chickpeas and their liquid, spinach, broth, and salt. Increase heat to medium-high and cook, stirring occasionally, until spinach is wilted and liquid is slightly thickened, about 5 minutes. Off heat, stir in dill and lemon juice. Season with salt and pepper to taste. Transfer to shallow platter and drizzle with extra oil. Serve.

Rustic Mashed Potatoes

No peeling, no fancy ingredients, no fuss— just perfect mashed potatoes. **by Matthew Fairman**

WE'VE ALL SAMPLED "fancy" restaurant versions of mashed potatoes made with ingredients such as goat cheese or prosciutto. But sometimes you want simpler, rustic mashed potatoes. That kind of basic, comforting mash was my goal here, with the added aim of making it easy.

With that in mind, my first move was to leave the potatoes unpeeled and simply slice them before boiling. While many modern recipes call for Yukon Gold potatoes to create a creamy mash, I grew up eating a version made with russets, which are starchier and create a fluffier mash; russets it would be. Once the spuds were tender, I drained them and returned them to the same pot (to save on cleanup) before mashing.

Butter was a must, as was some sort of dairy. My tasters preferred the rich (but not too rich) flavor and silky texture of half-and-half. Combining the butter and half-and-half and microwaving them until warm made them easier to incorporate into the mashed potatoes. With that, I had an easy, delicious, and simple rustic mash.

RUSTIC MASHED POTATOES
Serves 4
Don't be tempted to use another kind of potato here; your mash won't be as fluffy. Scrub the potatoes well.

- 2 pounds russet potatoes, unpeeled, sliced ½ inch thick
- ¾ teaspoon table salt, plus salt for cooking potatoes
- 1 cup half-and-half
- 10 tablespoons unsalted butter, cut into 10 pieces
- ½ teaspoon pepper

1. Place potatoes and 1 tablespoon salt in large saucepan, add water to cover by 1 inch, and bring to boil over high heat. Reduce heat to medium and simmer until potatoes are tender and paring knife can be easily slipped into and out of potatoes, 18 to 22 minutes.
2. Meanwhile, combine half-and-half and butter in 2-cup liquid measuring cup and microwave, covered, until butter is melted and mixture is warm to touch, about 2 minutes.
3. Drain potatoes and return them to saucepan. Using potato masher, mash potatoes until smooth and no lumps remain. Stir in half-and-half mixture, pepper, and salt until fully combined. Season with salt and pepper to taste. Serve.

LOADED RUSTIC MASHED POTATOES
Decrease half-and-half to ¾ cup and butter to 8 tablespoons. Stir 4 slices bacon, cut into ½-inch pieces and cooked; ½ cup shredded cheddar; ¼ cup sour cream; and ¼ cup minced fresh chives into potatoes after half-and-half mixture is incorporated.

RESPLENDENT IN APPEARANCE but made up of humble parts, a sweet fruit trifle is equally comfortable as a casual weekend dessert or a showstopping holiday centerpiece.

A trifle's architecture usually goes like this: A layer of sponge cake or ladyfingers doused in sweet wine such as sherry or Marsala forms the base; it's followed by a layer of fruit (often jam), a layer of rich chilled pastry cream, and a lathering of whipped cream. The layers repeat one or more times, depending on the depth of the vessel. Each layer sinks slightly into the next as the trifle grows taller, gradually melding the flavors and textures to form a delightful mess.

With strawberry season in full swing, I wanted to create a trifle with strawberries as the star. To get the most out of my berries, I chopped them, tossed them with a bit of sugar, and let them sit for a spell; this resting period intensified their sweetness while leaving behind a slightly sugared syrup. For the booze element, I chose orange liqueur; its subtle citrus flavors lent a festive, grown-up vibe.

My trifle needed a base with enough structure to stand up to the strawberry juice and support the layers above, but the obvious pastry options—angel food cake, pound cake, or chiffon cake cut into cubes—missed the mark. Whether too soft, too dense, or too time-consuming, each cake had its faults.

Inspired by another favorite dessert, strawberry shortcake, I decided to use quick-and-easy shortcake biscuits. Fluffy and tender, they provided just the right texture (soft but not mushy) and a pleasant buttery flavor.

Pastry cream, a vanilla-flavored custard, is an essential component of a trifle. It isn't difficult to make but requires some time and attention. And it must be made first because it needs to be refrigerated for at least 3 hours before you can use it.

Once I'd whipped the cream, I was ready for construction. First, I lined the bottom of my trifle dish with chunks of the biscuits. I then added a bit of that strawberry juice to soak into the biscuits, followed by some of the berries themselves. Next came a healthy dollop of pastry cream and some whipped cream, and then I started all over again. Once I'd completed this process three times, I covered my dish with plastic wrap and stuck it in the fridge to relax.

An hour or so later, I decorated the top with a few sliced strawberries and called my tasters. They were entranced by the bold look of the trifle and delighted by the range of sweet, nuanced flavors. "Only one thing is missing," said a colleague. "Champagne."

Strawberry Shortcake Trifle

A showstopper dessert like this takes work, so every component needs to be perfect. **by Alli Berkey**

STRAWBERRY SHORTCAKE TRIFLE

Serves 12

We call for a 3½-quart trifle dish for this recipe; however, a 4-quart bowl can be used in its place. Individual trifles can also be made in twelve 1-cup bowls or cups.

PASTRY CREAM

- 5 large egg yolks
- ½ cup (3½ ounces) sugar, divided
- 3 tablespoons cornstarch
- 2 cups whole milk
  Pinch table salt
- 4 tablespoons unsalted butter, cut into 4 pieces and chilled
- 1½ teaspoons vanilla extract

BISCUITS

- 2 cups (10 ounces) all-purpose flour
- 2 teaspoons baking powder
- ½ teaspoon baking soda
- 1 teaspoon sugar
- ¾ teaspoon table salt
- ½ cup whole milk, chilled
- ½ cup heavy cream, chilled
- 8 tablespoons unsalted butter, melted

STRAWBERRIES

- 3 pounds strawberries
- ½ cup sugar
- ¼ cup Grand Marnier
  Pinch table salt

WHIPPED CREAM

- 1½ cups heavy cream, chilled
- 2 tablespoons sugar
- ½ teaspoon vanilla extract

FOR THE PASTRY CREAM: Whisk egg yolks, 2 tablespoons sugar, and cornstarch in medium bowl until mixture is pale yellow and thick, about 1 minute; set aside. Combine milk, salt, and remaining 6 tablespoons sugar in medium saucepan and bring to simmer over medium heat, stirring occasionally to dissolve sugar.

2. Gradually whisk half of milk mixture into yolk mixture to temper. Return milk-yolk mixture to saucepan. Return to simmer over medium heat and cook, whisking constantly, until mixture is thickened and 3 or 4 bubbles burst on surface, about 3 minutes. Off heat, whisk in butter and vanilla. Transfer mixture to clean bowl, press parchment paper directly onto surface, and refrigerate until set, at least 3 hours.

3. FOR THE BISCUITS: Meanwhile, adjust oven rack to middle position and heat oven to 450 degrees. Line baking sheet with parchment. Whisk flour, baking powder, baking soda, sugar, and salt together in large bowl. Stir milk, cream, and melted butter together in small bowl (butter will form clumps).

4. Add dairy mixture to flour mixture and stir with rubber spatula until just combined. Using greased ¼-cup dry measuring cup, drop 12 scant scoops of batter 1½ inches apart on prepared sheet. Bake until biscuit tops are golden brown, about 12 minutes, rotating sheet halfway through baking. Transfer biscuits to wire rack and let cool completely, about 20 minutes.

5. FOR THE STRAWBERRIES: Set aside 6 strawberries. Hull remaining strawberries and cut into ½-inch pieces. Combine cut strawberries, sugar, Grand Marnier, and salt in large bowl. Let sit at room temperature for 30 minutes.

6. FOR THE WHIPPED CREAM: Using stand mixer fitted with whisk attachment, whip cream, sugar, and vanilla on low speed until foamy, about 1 minute. Increase speed to high and whip until stiff peaks form, 1 to 3 minutes. Refrigerate until ready to use.

7. Drain strawberries in colander set in bowl, reserving all juice. Whisk chilled pastry cream to recombine. Break 4 biscuits into 1-inch pieces and arrange on bottom of 3½-quart trifle dish. Pour one-third of reserved strawberry juice over biscuits. Top with one-third of strawberries, followed by one-third of pastry cream. Spread 1 cup whipped cream evenly over pastry cream. Repeat layers twice. Cover dish with plastic wrap and refrigerate for at least 1 hour or up to 24 hours. Hull reserved strawberries and slice thin, then shingle in center of trifle. Serve.

Don't want to go big? Make individual trifles in 1-cup dishes.

Soaking It Up

We crumble our easy homemade biscuits and moisten them with the flavorful juice extracted from the macerated strawberries. The amount of liquid you get from the 3 pounds of berries in this recipe will vary; we got anywhere from ½ cup to 1 cup. The juice gets divided in thirds and poured over each layer of biscuits.

Four Steps to Perfect Pastry Cream

1. Whisk yolks, sugar, and cornstarch in bowl until mixture is pale yellow and thick.

2. Bring milk, salt, and remaining sugar to simmer in saucepan, stirring occasionally to dissolve sugar.

3. Gradually whisk half of milk mixture into yolk mixture to temper.

4. Simmer milk-yolk mixture, whisking constantly, until thickened, then whisk in butter and vanilla off heat.

Easy Homemade Mayonnaise

Even the best jarred mayonnaise can't compare with this simple homemade version. **by Matthew Fairman**

THE MAKING OF some condiments, such as ketchup and mustard, is best left to the professionals (that is, the huge manufacturers who spend a lot of money on equipment to guarantee the consistent mass production of their condiments). But that's not the case for mayonnaise: With just 10 minutes of measuring, pouring, and buzzing the ingredients in a food processor at home, you can create a light, creamy, flavorful mayonnaise or aioli that easily outpaces the stuff they're offering at the supermarket. Homemade mayonnaise is an easy way to take your cooking—and your sandwich game—to another level.

EASY HOMEMADE MAYONNAISE

Serves 24 (Makes about 1½ cups)
Do not substitute olive oil for the vegetable oil; the mayonnaise will turn out bitter.

1	large egg
4	teaspoons white wine vinegar
1½	teaspoons Dijon mustard
¾	teaspoon table salt
¼	teaspoon sugar
1½	cups vegetable oil

Process egg, vinegar, mustard, salt, and sugar in food processor until combined, about 5 seconds. With processor running, slowly drizzle in oil until emulsified and mixture is thick, about 2 minutes. Scrape down sides of bowl with rubber spatula and continue to process 5 seconds longer. Transfer to airtight container and refrigerate until ready to use. (Mayonnaise can be refrigerated for up to 1 week.)

Essential Gear

While this recipe should work in any food processor, our top-rated model is the **Cuisinart Custom 14**. This machine is versatile and durable and processes beautifully. Web subscribers can read our review at CooksCountry.com/may19.

Why do you use a whole egg when other recipes call for just yolks?

It's easier and less wasteful (no separating required), and the larger volume allows the processor blades to catch more easily.

Don't Make This Mistake

If you add the oil too quickly, the emulsion will break and look like lumpy, greasy salad dressing—not appealing. Add the oil slowly, especially at first, and your mayo will come together perfectly.

Why not use more-flavorful olive oil instead of vegetable oil in the mayo?

If we made this food processor mayonnaise with only olive oil, it would taste unpalatably bitter. Why? Extra-virgin olive oil contains bitter-tasting compounds that are normally hidden by the fatty acids in the oil. The blades of a food processor break olive oil into tiny droplets, which allows those bitter compounds to break free and disperse into liquids (in this case, the egg and vinegar), causing the emulsion to taste bitter. (This is why we whisk in a small amount of olive oil by hand in our aioli variation on the opposite page.)

What's up with the Dijon mustard?

Many mayonnaise recipes don't contain mustard. We use sharp, tangy Dijon here

to add a pleasant bite to the flavor and enrich the color. Additionally, mustard seeds contain compounds that naturally aid in emulsification, so it helps the mayonnaise come together and stay emulsified longer. Our winning Dijon is **Trois Petits Cochons Moutarde de Dijon**, an expensive French import (you may have to order it online) that's worth every penny.

Step by Step

1. Measure carefully
Crack the egg into a bowl. Measure out the vinegar, mustard, salt, and sugar.
Why? Mayonnaise is an emulsion that could break if the proportions of ingredients are off.

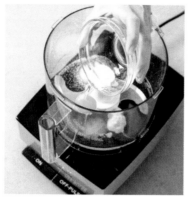

2. Add ingredients to processor
Add everything to the bowl of a food processor.
Why? Making mayonnaise by hand is certainly possible, but it's much easier and faster in the food processor.

3. Mix
Process for 5 seconds to combine the ingredients.
Why? The oil will incorporate most easily into a homogenized mixture of ingredients.

4. Add oil and emulsify
With the processor running, very slowly add the oil in a thin, steady stream until the mayonnaise is emulsified and thick (about 2 minutes).
Why? Adding the oil slowly (especially at first) builds a strong emulsion that stays together.

Stages of Emulsion: *A Closer Look at the Critical Part of This Recipe*

The mix of ingredients starts off as a thin liquid as the first of the oil is blended in.

As more oil is added and the emulsion forms, the mixture thickens and becomes lighter in color; you can hear the processor start to gurgle when this happens, and it's a sign that you can start to add the oil a little faster.

5. Scrape bowl
Use a rubber spatula to scrape down the sides of the processor bowl.
Why? Scraping down the bowl helps ensure that all the ingredients are fully incorporated into the mayonnaise.

6. Buzz again
Process the mixture for an additional 5 seconds.
Why? To make this recipe foolproof, it's important that everything is 100 percent incorporated.

7. Store
Transfer the mayonnaise to an airtight container and refrigerate it.
Why? Refrigerating the mayonnaise in an airtight container will allow it to last for up to one week.

TRADITIONAL AIOLI IS made with just olive oil and garlic—nothing else. But most versions use eggs (commonly just yolks) to make what is essentially a garlic-flavored mayonnaise. Use aioli as a dip for crudités; a topping for lamb, beef, or roasted fish; a garnish for seafood soups; or a condiment for French fries.

EASY HOMEMADE AIOLI
Serves 24 (Makes about 1½ cups)
Do not substitute olive oil for the vegetable oil; the aioli will turn out bitter.

- 1 large egg
- 4 teaspoons lemon juice
- 1½ teaspoons Dijon mustard
- 1 garlic clove, minced
- ¾ teaspoon table salt
- ¼ teaspoon sugar
- Pinch cayenne pepper
- 1½ cups vegetable oil
- 2 tablespoons extra-virgin olive oil

Process egg, lemon juice, mustard, garlic, salt, sugar, and cayenne in food processor until combined, about 5 seconds. With processor running, slowly drizzle in vegetable oil until emulsified and mixture is thick, about 2 minutes. Scrape down sides of bowl with rubber spatula and continue to process 5 seconds longer. Transfer to airtight container and whisk in olive oil. Cover and refrigerate until ready to use. (Aioli can be refrigerated for up to 1 week.)

Cream Cheese Spreads

Your bagel deserves better than a prefab spread. **by Ashley Moore**

IN A BAGEL shop, I'm a bit like a kid in a candy store—wide-eyed and greedy to try everything in sight. And for me, it's not just the bagels but the cream cheese spreads, too. Oddly, even though I cook and develop recipes for a living, I'd never really considered making my own cream cheese spreads. It was time to turn that corner.

I headed into the kitchen, rolled up my sleeves, and got to work on a basic garlic and herb spread (my favorite variety). I quickly found that it helped to let the cream cheese come to room temperature (about 30 minutes on the counter) before adding other ingredients. I auditioned a dozen herbs for the spread before my tasters and I landed on the full-flavored, fresh-tasting combination of parsley and basil. I tried mixing in the herbs and minced garlic by hand, but the results were too chunky, and even distribution was a problem.

A colleague recommended using a food processor to blend everything. I decided to give it a go, adding the softened cream cheese and herbs to the processor bowl with one small clove of garlic and a bit of lemon juice for acidity and brightness. Twenty seconds of whirling later, I had an amazingly fragrant, herby spread. Easy.

I started looking around the kitchen for flavorful, potent ingredients to create more spreads with real personality and flair.

For a take on a bagel with lox, I combined some sliced smoked salmon with fresh chives. Another version starred salty olives and oniony scallions. For a more unusual sweet-savory rendition, I combined honey and piney rosemary (I love this one on a raisin bagel). And finally, a classic combination of cinnamon and sugar rounded out the lineup. Get your toaster ready (see page 30 for the results of our latest toaster testing).

❶ GARLIC AND HERB CREAM CHEESE SPREAD

Serves 8 (Makes 1 cup)
For the smoothest results, let the cream cheese come to room temperature before processing it. A garlic press or a rasp-style grater will make quick work of mincing the garlic. The test kitchen's favorite cream cheese is Philadelphia Cream Cheese Brick Original.

8	ounces cream cheese, softened
½	cup fresh parsley leaves
¼	cup fresh basil leaves
1	teaspoon lemon juice
1	small garlic clove, minced
¼	teaspoon table salt
¼	teaspoon pepper

Process all ingredients in food processor until smooth, about 20 seconds, scraping down sides of bowl as needed. Serve. (Cream cheese spread can be refrigerated in airtight container for up to 1 week.)

❷ CINNAMON AND SUGAR CREAM CHEESE SPREAD

Omit lemon juice, garlic, salt, and pepper. Substitute 2 tablespoons packed brown sugar and 1 teaspoon ground cinnamon for parsley and basil.

❸ SMOKED SALMON AND CHIVE CREAM CHEESE SPREAD

Omit garlic and salt. Substitute 2 ounces sliced smoked salmon, torn into 2-inch pieces, and ¼ cup chopped fresh chives for parsley and basil.

❹ OLIVE AND SCALLION CREAM CHEESE SPREAD

Omit lemon juice, garlic, and salt. Reduce cream cheese to 6 ounces and increase pepper to 1 teaspoon. Substitute ½ cup pitted kalamata olives, patted dry, plus 2 teaspoons brine, and 4 chopped scallions for parsley and basil.

❺ HONEY AND ROSEMARY CREAM CHEESE SPREAD

Omit lemon juice and garlic. Substitute 2 tablespoons honey and 1 tablespoon minced fresh rosemary for parsley and basil.

Peruvian-Style Chicken Dinner

We wanted a weeknight chicken supper with big flavors—without a big pile of dishes to clean.

by Cecelia Jenkins

WEEKNIGHT CHICKEN CAN get pretty boring. My goal was to liven up dinner while keeping it real on a busy weeknight: maximum flavor with minimal work and cleanup. My path to these goals went through South America—specifically, Peru.

One of the test kitchen's all-time favorite chicken marinades is inspired by the flavors of Peruvian roast chicken: mint, chile, lime, smoke, and spice. This complex, concentrated, and vibrant marinade comes together quickly in the blender, which only adds to its appeal.

Here's how it starts: You toss a seeded habanero chile in the blender along with a handful of mint leaves, olive oil, some smoked paprika and cumin for earthy depth, potent dried oregano, six whole garlic cloves, sugar, salt and pepper, and lime juice and zest. Can you almost smell it?

I poured this bold, spicy marinade into a zipper-lock bag and sealed four chicken leg quarters inside, pressing the bag with my fingers to ensure even coverage. Refrigerating the marinating chicken for at least an hour (or up to 12 hours) helped deliver the biggest kick of flavor.

I needed vegetables that made sense with the dish's profile. Chunks of sweet potatoes fit the bill, and red onion

wedges provided a complementary subtle sweetness. Cauliflower florets turned nutty and tender as they cooked, adding another dimension.

But how to cook it all together with the least amount of fuss? The vegetables took longer to cook than the chicken, so roasting everything at once required removing the chicken halfway through; plus, starting everything at the same time meant the vegetables were crowded on the edges and failed to brown.

I found it easier to give the vegetables a 15-minute head start in a 425-degree oven; once the cauliflower started to pick up some nice color on its edges, I pushed all the vegetables to one side of the baking sheet and arranged the chicken legs on the other. Forty minutes later, the legs hit their target internal temperature of 175 degrees and the sweet potatoes, cauliflower, and onion were tender.

With flavorful chicken juices and the vibrant marinade deliciously mingling together on the baking sheet, a colleague suggested tossing the vegetables and juices with peppery arugula to add fresh flavor and a pop of vibrant color while the chicken rested. Boring? No. Inspired and smart? Definitely.

Cooking in Stages

Our two-step process ensures that everything is done at the same time.

1. Start with just the vegetables
They need more time in the oven.

2. Add the spiced chicken legs
Everything finishes cooking together.

ONE-PAN PERUVIAN CHICKEN WITH CAULIFLOWER AND SWEET POTATOES
Serves 4

You can substitute 1 tablespoon of minced serrano chile for the habanero, if desired. Wear gloves when handling the chile.

- 6 tablespoons extra-virgin olive oil, divided
- ¼ cup fresh mint leaves
- 6 garlic cloves, peeled
- 3½ teaspoons pepper, divided
- 1 tablespoon ground cumin
- 1 tablespoon sugar
- 2 teaspoons grated lime zest plus ¼ cup juice (2 limes)
- 2 teaspoons table salt, divided
- 2 teaspoons smoked paprika
- 2 teaspoons dried oregano
- ½ habanero chile, stemmed and seeded
- 4 (10-ounce) chicken leg quarters, trimmed
- 1 small head cauliflower (1½ pounds), cored and cut into 1½-inch florets
- 1 pound sweet potatoes, peeled and cut into 1-inch pieces
- 1 small red onion, halved and sliced through root end into ½-inch-thick wedges
- 3 cups (3 ounces) baby arugula

1. Process 3 tablespoons oil, mint, garlic, 1 tablespoon pepper, cumin, sugar, lime zest and juice, 1½ teaspoons salt, paprika, oregano, and habanero in blender until smooth, 10 to 20 seconds. Transfer marinade to 1-gallon zipper-lock bag. Add chicken, seal bag, and turn to coat chicken with marinade. Refrigerate for at least 1 hour or up to 12 hours.

2. Adjust oven rack to middle position and heat oven to 425 degrees. Toss cauliflower, potatoes, onion, remaining 3 tablespoons oil, remaining ½ teaspoon pepper, and remaining ½ teaspoon salt together on rimmed baking sheet and spread into even layer. Bake until top edges of cauliflower and potatoes are lightly browned, about 15 minutes.

3. Remove sheet from oven. Using spatula, push vegetables to 1 side of sheet (they will no longer be in single layer). Place chicken, skin side up, on now-empty side of sheet. Roast until chicken registers 175 degrees and vegetables are tender, about 40 minutes, rotating sheet halfway through roasting.

4. Transfer chicken to carving board; let rest for 10 minutes. Add arugula to sheet with vegetables and gently toss to combine. Transfer vegetable mixture to platter. Separate leg quarters into thighs and drumsticks, then transfer to platter with vegetable mixture. Serve.

Shrimp Creole

You don't have to go to New Orleans—or spend hours cooking—to taste real-deal Creole cooking.

by Natalie Estrada

Shrimp Prep

Here's how to get shell-on shrimp ready for cooking.

1. Use kitchen shears to snip through convex side of shell.

2. Pull shell from shrimp, taking care to remove small "legs" from concave side.

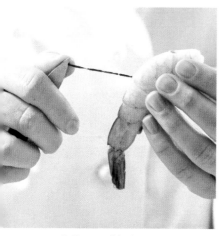

3. Remove black vein before removing tail.

I LOVE BRINY, sweet, tender shrimp. And for me, one of their best uses is the bold, nuanced Louisiana dish called shrimp Creole. I wanted to make a rendition of this jazzy, saucy dish to serve two hungry diners on a busy weeknight.

My research led me to recipes that called for Creole seasoning mixes containing 10 or more ingredients; homemade stocks that required sautéing, simmering, and then straining; and active cooking times measured in hours, not minutes. I was determined to streamline the process without sacrificing the punchy flavor of this classic dish—cooking for two is just as important as cooking for 20. I wanted a rich sauce base, the perfect amount of spice, and delicately cooked shrimp.

I began with the traditional roux of butter and flour, added the "holy trinity" of Louisiana cooking (chopped green bell pepper, onion, and celery), and cooked the vegetables until they were softened and lightly browned before deglazing the pan with wine.

Tomatoes were another essential ingredient. I tested fresh tomatoes against canned crushed tomatoes, canned whole tomatoes, and tomato paste. Fresh tomatoes made for a mealy sauce that required long simmering to thicken, so they were out. Tomato paste was too dense. But canned crushed tomatoes were just right; their consistency and flavor made the most sense. I added a little chicken broth to thin the sauce and a splash of Worcestershire for a bit more savoriness. But I still needed some spice.

Whether it's billed as Cajun or Creole, a Louisiana-style spice mixture can deliver lots of ingredients and flavor in a single spoonful. Instead of a homemade blend, I went with our winning store-bought Louisiana seasoning, Tony Chachere's, which had just about everything I wanted, including plenty of salt (I did add a little extra fresh thyme).

It's no secret that overcooked shrimp can turn rubbery and hard. So I took a gentler approach, slowly poaching them, covered, in the sauce until they were just done—about 5 minutes. Off the heat, I stirred in lemon juice and sliced scallions to bring it all into sharper focus.

With that, I'd hit my target: a flavorful sauce studded with tender, sweet shrimp. And the best part? It's a weeknight-friendly dinner for two that comes together in well under an hour.

This comforting dish features lively Louisiana flavors.

SHRIMP CREOLE FOR TWO
Serve over white rice.

- 1 tablespoon unsalted butter
- 1 tablespoon all-purpose flour
- ½ cup finely chopped onion
- ½ cup finely chopped green bell pepper
- ¼ cup finely chopped celery
- 1 teaspoon chopped fresh thyme
- 1 teaspoon Tony Chachere's Original Creole Seasoning
- ¼ cup dry white wine
- 1 cup canned crushed tomatoes
- ½ cup chicken broth
- ¼ cup water
- 1½ teaspoons Worcestershire sauce
- 12 ounces extra-large shrimp (21 to 25 per pound), peeled, deveined, and tails removed
- ⅛ teaspoon table salt
- ⅛ teaspoon pepper
- 2 scallions, sliced thin
- 1 teaspoon lemon juice

1. Melt butter in large saucepan over medium heat. Add flour and cook, stirring often, until roux is peanut butter–colored, 3 to 5 minutes. Add onion, bell pepper, celery, thyme, and Creole seasoning and cook, stirring often and scraping up any browned bits, until vegetables are softened, about 5 minutes.

2. Add wine and cook until nearly evaporated, about 3 minutes. Add tomatoes, broth, water, and Worcestershire and bring to boil. Reduce heat to medium-low, cover, and simmer until slightly thickened, about 15 minutes, stirring occasionally to prevent scorching.

3. Pat shrimp dry and sprinkle with salt and pepper. Stir shrimp into saucepan and cook, covered, stirring occasionally, until opaque and cooked through, about 5 minutes. Off heat, stir in scallions and lemon juice. Season with salt and pepper to taste. Serve.

The Color of Roux

Recipes call for varying shades of roux, the simple cooked mixture of flour and fat. Roux adds body, sheen, and flavor to many dishes. Here we call for the roux to be cooked to the color of peanut butter to give our version of this dish the proper look, feel, and flavor.

Lentil and Chorizo Soup

One powerhouse ingredient—chorizo—brings smoky, spicy, meaty flavor to this simple lentil soup.

Matthew Fairman

WITH EARTHY LENTILS, smoky Spanish-style chorizo, and a heady mix of garlic and warm spices, lentil and chorizo soup is one of my favorites. But there are days when I can't bring myself to do the hands-on work involved: browning the sausage, sautéing the vegetables, frying the garlic and spices to bloom their flavors, and pulling out the blender to puree a portion of the lentils to thicken the soup. I began to wonder if all the work was necessary. Could I just toss all the ingredients into my slow cooker and come back a few hours later to find the soup I love?

Though my initial attempts at doing held some promise, they yielded soups that were one-dimensional and, for lack of a better word, a little boring. The savory, creamy lentils almost carried the soup on their own—and I was happy to find that they didn't break down into total mush—but they needed some support. I wanted an easy lentil soup with savory depth, complex spice flavor, and brightness to balance the earthy lentils, as well as a colorful, fresh garnish to set off the flavors I'd built into the soup.

To ensure savory depth in my soup, I began with an aromatic base of chopped onion and carrots along with a can of diced tomatoes and some chicken broth. The tomatoes contributed a bright acidity that highlighted the subtle flavors of the lentils. Adjusting the amount of chicken broth so that the soup was neither too watery nor too thick and stew-like proved to be key.

To achieve the complex spice flavor I was after, I began by carefully choosing my chorizo. I looked for cured, ready-to-eat Spanish-style chorizo; it has a texture similar to that of hard salami and offers a complex blend of richness and smoked paprika flavor. From there, I tinkered with the seasonings until I landed on a mixture that would complement the chorizo and lentils: fresh garlic and thyme along with cumin, coriander, cinnamon, a bay leaf, and, for punch, a bit of cayenne pepper.

A healthy glug of dry white wine introduced a pleasant acidity to cut the soup's richness and brighten its flavors. A dollop of cool, slightly tart yogurt and a sprinkling of fresh parsley added

a further contrast of bright color and flavor. Now this was the soup I'd been hoping for. As I stood over my last test batch of stir-together lentil and chorizo soup, I grinned happily, knowing I'd found an easier path to an even better version of the soup I loved so much.

SLOW-COOKER LENTIL AND CHORIZO SOUP

Serves 4 to 6
For the best results, use a dry-cured Spanish-style chorizo in this recipe. If Spanish-style chorizo is unavailable, you can substitute Portuguese linguiça sausage. We like to serve individual portions of this soup drizzled with plain yogurt and sprinkled with chopped fresh parsley.

- 4 cups chicken broth
- 1 (14.5-ounce) can diced tomatoes, drained
- 8 ounces Spanish-style chorizo sausage, sliced ¼ inch thick
- 1 cup dried brown lentils, picked over and rinsed
- 1 onion, chopped fine
- 2 carrots, peeled and chopped fine
- ½ cup dry white wine
- 3 garlic cloves, minced
- 3 sprigs fresh thyme
- 1 teaspoon ground cumin
- 1 teaspoon ground coriander
- ½ teaspoon table salt
- ½ teaspoon ground cinnamon
- ¼ teaspoon cayenne pepper
- 1 bay leaf

Combine all ingredients in slow cooker. Cook until lentils are tender, 5 to 6 hours on high or 7 to 8 hours on low. Discard thyme sprigs and bay leaf. Serve.

Finishing touches of tangy yogurt and fresh parsley bring the other flavors into focus.

All About Lentils

RED LENTILS

Cook and break down more quickly than other kinds

GREEN LENTILS

All-purpose lentils that can be subbed for brown

LENTILLES DU PUY

French imports with an earthy richness

BROWN LENTILS

Delicious, affordable, readily available, and our choice here

Toasters

These toasters accommodate big bagels and oversize artisan breads. But which one should you buy? **by Lisa McManus**

8 Toasters 10+ Tests

- Measure toaster dimensions
- Measure slot dimensions
- Toast sandwich bread at 3 settings
- Time toasting 6 times
- Check exterior temperature while toasting
- Toast large slices of artisan bread
- Toast bagels
- Toast full capacity of bread 5 times
- Evaluate ease of use
- Empty and evaluate crumb trays
- Toast 365 consecutive slices in top 3 models

It took 1,400 pieces of toast to find a winner.

IS YOUR TOASTER stuck in the 1950s, when all bread was white, skinny, and square? Today, Americans are buying bigger loaves of bread, and the slices don't always fit in the average toaster. The last time we tested toasters, our winner, the Magimix Vision Toaster ($249.95), was unique for its one extra-long, extra-wide slot that fit any kind of bread, even bigger slices. It toasted evenly, using responsive quartz heating elements. It also boasted see-through glass walls and a "stop" button to halt toasting at your exact browning preference. The downside? The price.

But there's hope: Recently, a handful of "long-slot" toasters have appeared on the market at a range of prices. We bought eight models, including our previous winner, priced from $36.03 to $249.95; all had one or two long, wide slots. We put them through their paces, toasting all kinds of breads and bagels.

We wanted a toaster that gave us the browning we'd selected, with uniform coloring. But with most of the toasters, getting medium–golden brown toast was a cumbersome process that required retoasting. Some models also failed to toast evenly. Only two gave us one-and-done, reliable browning that corresponded to the settings.

Most toasters work by heating rows of thin metal wires that line both sides of the toasting slot. The best toaster in this style had 15 wires on each side of its toaster slots; lower-rated models had as few as six or eight. Two toasters heated using quartz rods instead of wires on each side of the toasting slot. Quartz heats and cools much more quickly than metal, and we liked the even, golden toast these models produced. But in the end, our top two models were split: One used metal wires, the other quartz rods. We liked another feature they shared, though: Both let you check on browning while toasting—one with a window, the other with a lever to "lift and look" without stopping the cycle.

You use these long-slot toasters not only for giant slabs of artisan toast but also for regular-size sandwich bread by placing two slices side by side in the same slot. The trouble is, some of the long slots were just a little too short for this, so bread sometimes got stuck at the top, crusts got torn, or slices bent and toasted unevenly.

Depth also mattered: Bagels and large bread stuck out of the tops of shorter models, leaving big, white untoasted stripes. Toasting slots ranged from 4.75 to 6.88 inches deep, and anything less than 5 inches was too shallow.

In the end, we found two toasters to recommend at far more affordable prices than our previous winner. The Dash Clear View Toaster ($36.03) toasted beautifully and has many helpful features; the only downside is that its toast sometimes sprang up too forcefully and flew out. Ultimately, the solid performance of the Breville The Bit More Toaster ($79.99) won the day. It produced crisp, uniform, golden toast every time.

KEY **Good** ★★★ **Fair** ★★ **Poo**

HIGHLY RECOMMENDED

CRITERIA

Breville The Bit More Toaster
Model: BTA730XL
Price: $79.99
Toaster Dimensions: 15.8 x 8 x 7.8 in
Slot Dimensions: 10 x 5 in
Heating Element: Wires
Features: "A Bit More" button, "Lift and Look" lever to check browning
Average Speed: 2 min, 8 sec

Performance ★★¹/₂
Speed ★★★
Ease of Use ★★★
Cleanup ★★★
Comments: This solid toast er performed reliably and has helpful features such its "A Bit More" button.

Best Buy
Dash Clear View Toaster
Model: DVTS501   **Price:** $36.03
Toaster Dimensions: 15 x 5 x 8 in
Slot Dimensions: 10.5 x 5 in
Heating Element: Quartz
Features: Window, "cancel" button, reheating
Average Speed: 2 min, 12 sec

Performance ★★¹/₂
Speed ★★★
Ease of Use ★★★
Cleanup ★★★
Comments: This model made pretty toast without any fuss. We loved its window to monitor browning.

RECOMMENDED

Russell Hobbs Glass Accent Long Slot 2-Slice Toaster
Model: TRL9300GYR (stainless steel)
Price: $99.99
Toaster Dimensions: 15 x 5 x 7.1 in
Slot Dimensions: 10.25 x 5 in
Heating Element: Wires
Feature: Bun-warming rack
Average Speed: 1 min, 44 sec

Performance ★★¹/₂
Speed ★★★
Ease of Use ★★¹/₂
Cleanup ★★★
Comments: Produced good toast, but our first one died (the replacement worked fine). Controls not intuitive

Magimix Vision Toaster
Model: 11526 (chrome)
Price: $249.95
Toaster Dimensions: 15.5 x 7 x 9 in
Slot Dimensions: 10.25 x 6.88 in
Heating Element: Quartz
Features: Windows, "stop" button, bread-lift lever
Average Speed: 1 min, 25 sec

Performance ★★
Speed ★★★
Ease of Use ★★★
Cleanup ★★★
Comments: Made gorgeo toast and was a pleasure use, but toast browned too much at higher settings.

Hamilton Beach Keep Warm 4-Slice Long-Slot Toaster
Model: 24810
Price: $36.85
Toaster Dimensions: 15.75 x 7.5 x 7.75 in
Slot Dimensions: 10 x 4.75 in
Heating Element: Wires
Feature: "Keep warm" button
Average Speed: 2 min, 3 sec

Performance ★★
Speed ★★★
Ease of Use ★★
Cleanup ★★★
Comments: This model toasted fast but kept us fid dling with settings to get o desired color. Short slots.

RECOMMENDED WITH RESERVATIONS

Cuisinart Bakery Artisan Bread 2 Slice Toaster
Model: CPT-2400
Price: $49.96
Toaster Dimensions: 15.25 x 6.75 x 8.5 in
Slot Dimensions: 10 x 5.25 in
Heating Element: Wires
Feature: Bread-lift lever
Average Speed: 2 min, 30 sec

Performance ★★
Speed ★★
Ease of Use ★★
Cleanup ★★★
Comments: Slots were too short and shallow for som jobs. We often had to retoa to get good results.

Oster 4-Slice Long-Slot Toaster
Model: TSSTTR6330-NP
Price: $52.89
Toaster Dimensions: 16.75 x 7 x 7.5 in
Slot Dimensions: 10.38 x 4.75 in
Heating Element: Wires
Feature: Bread-lift lever
Average Speed: 2 min, 3 sec

Performance ★★
Speed ★★★
Ease of Use ★★
Cleanup ★★
Comments: Its surface got very hot. It toasted quickly but browning was uneven.

Smeg 4-Slice Toaster
Model: TSF01PGUS (pastel green)
Price: $199.95
Toaster Dimensions: 15 x 8 x 8.5 in
Slot Dimensions: 10.25 x 5.5 in
Heating Element: Wires
Feature: Reheating
Average Speed: 2 min, 58 sec

Performance ★★
Speed ★
Ease of Use ★★
Cleanup ★★★
Comments: Like a sports car: beautiful, expensive, and a bit unreliable. Exteri became quite hot.

Yellow Mustard

Mild but not dull, this ballpark and backyard classic punches up everything from hot dogs to salad dressing. **by Emily Phares**

THE CONDIMENT world, yellow mustard is often considered the Robin to ketchup's Batman, relegated to a supporting role on burgers and hot dogs. But it's much more than a sidekick. Yellow mustard's pungency and relatively low spice level make it highly versatile, ideal for adding tang and flavor to hot dogs, potato salad, barbecue sauce, marinades, salad dressings, and more.

When we heard that our favorite yellow mustard from our last tasting had been reformulated, we decided to retest. We selected seven top-selling, nationally available products, priced from $0.08 to $0.44 per ounce. We included a low-sodium mustard from Boar's Head since it was that brand's only yellow mustard. We tasted each mustard plain and on pigs in a blanket.

Mustard seeds are a cool-weather crop. Canada is the world's largest producer, so most mustard manufacturers use seeds grown in Canada. According to the Canadian Grain Commission, the regulatory agency tasked with grading mustard seeds, three seed types are grown in Canada: brown, oriental, and yellow (sometimes referred to as white). Brown and oriental seeds are used in spicier mustards, and yellow seeds—flavorful but with less heat—are used in yellow mustard. (Of note: This condiment's sunny color doesn't come from the seeds, which are a more muted hue—it's from the addition of turmeric.)

The seeds become prepared mustard through a straightforward mechanical process. The ingredients (typically mustard seeds, water, vinegar, salt, and spices) are stirred together and then milled between two large stones. According to Allen Sass, president of Wisconsin Spice, the largest miller of mustard seeds in the United States, milling serves two purposes: It extracts mucilage (a thick, gelatinous substance) from the seeds, and it combines all the ingredients. Once milled, the mixture is bottled.

Mustard is often paired with fatty meats, as its characteristic tang can help cut the richness. Some products tasted more acidic, while others were more subdued. We examined ingredient labels and noted that some of the mustards added relatively more water and others more vinegar, but this wasn't the full story. Experts told us that vinegar can have different concentrations, so quantity didn't necessarily explain why certain mustards were tangier than others. And while some tasters appreciated the tartness, the majority preferred mustards that were mellower, with a moderate acidity that didn't dominate other flavors.

Our two favorite mustards had sweet notes that nicely balanced their acidity.

But there were no signs of sugar in their ingredient lists or nutritional information. These mustards did include "natural flavor," whereas most others didn't. This is a catchall term used by the U.S. Food and Drug Administration, and food manufacturers don't have to specify which natural flavors they use. These mustards' ingredient lists also included "spices," which don't have to be disclosed either. It's possible that these unspecified ingredients contributed to a mustard's perceived sweetness.

Among the products in our lineup, sodium levels ranged from 25 to 80 milligrams per serving, with the former being the low-sodium option from Boar's Head. While none of the mustards tasted strikingly salty or underseasoned, this low-sodium product fell to the bottom of our rankings, as tasters found it less flavorful, spicier, and sharper than a typical yellow mustard.

Flavor was most important to our tasters, but they considered texture, too. A mustard's texture is determined by the mill's grind settings: the distance between the two stones that crush and grind the mustard seeds. As Sass told us, "The further away the stones are, the less mucilage extracted (and coarser

Hold the ketchup.

product); vice versa when stones are close together."

One product's grainy, thick texture reminded us of whole-grain mustard; water wasn't listed as an ingredient. Sass told us that mustard without water (with only vinegar as the liquid) would be expected to have relatively more solids (mustard seeds), which could make it thicker. On the opposite end of the spectrum, an "ultrasmooth" mustard seemed aerated and foamy to some tasters, which might have been due to processing conditions. According to Sass, yellow mustard seeds contain approximately 30 percent protein, and processing them aggressively can lead to aeration.

The majority of tasters found all mustard textures acceptable, but our favorite products had a moderately creamy texture and enough body to cling nicely to pigs in a blanket. Our winner, Heinz Yellow Mustard ($0.14 per ounce), hit all the right notes for both texture and flavor. It was "smooth in texture and taste," with "some zing" and a "hint of sweetness." Its "good old-fashioned mustard flavor" conjured up images of ballparks. As one taster said, "It tastes like mustard should."

RECOMMENDED

Our Favorite

Heinz
Yellow Mustard
Price: $1.99 for 14 oz
($0.14 per oz)
Sodium: 60 mg
Comments: We liked this mustard's "nice sweetness" and "good acidity," which gave it "some zing," as well as its smooth texture and "old-fashioned," "iconic" flavor. As one taster noted, it "tastes like classic mustard on a ballpark hot dog."

French's Classic
Yellow Mustard
Price: $3.19 for 20 oz
($0.16 per oz)
Sodium: 55 mg
Comments: Our runner-up had many of the characteristics we liked: a "hint of sweet" and "acidic bite" combined with a "creamy texture." Some tasters detected a slightly "earthy," "herby" flavor when tasting the mustard plain, but it was less noticeable on pigs in a blanket.

Koops' Original
Yellow Mustard
Price: $5.95 for 18 oz
($0.33 per oz)
Sodium: 60 mg
Comments: Overall, we liked this product's thicker texture, which was "a little coarser," with a "grainy" consistency. It also had an "acidic" bite that paired nicely with food, though tasters deemed its mustard flavor "neutral" and "nondescript."

Woeber's
Yellow Mustard
Price: $1.30 for 16 oz
($0.08 per oz)
Sodium: 80 mg
Comments: Not everyone liked this mustard's "very vinegary" flavor, but some loved its tartness and thicker consistency. Tasters compared it to both pickles and brined olives, but some thought it was too "sour." It also had a "thick and grainy" consistency.

Gulden's
Yellow Mustard
Price: $2.50 for 12 oz
($0.21 per oz)
Sodium: 55 mg
Comments: Some tasters thought this "punchy" mustard had an "earthy aftertaste." The "herbal taste" was evident even on pigs in a blanket, but overall we liked this product's "sharp and tangy" "dill pickle flavor" and "smooth," "creamy" texture.

Annie's Organic
Yellow Mustard
Price: $3.99 for 9 oz
($0.44 per oz)
Sodium: 50 mg
Comments: Tasters picked up on "funky," "musty" notes, but overall this mustard's flavor was deemed milder and "missing a little complexity." Most tasters also liked the silky texture, but some found it "foamy."

Boar's Head
54% Lower Sodium
Yellow Mustard
Price: $3.39 for 9 oz
($0.38 per oz)
Sodium: 25 mg
Comments: The only yellow mustard available from Boar's Head, this low-sodium product had more heat than flavor and was sharper and thicker than the others. Tasters described it as "sharp" and "more viscous," like whole-grain mustard.

Asparagus Pickles

> "These crunchy asparagus spears are just as fun to eat alongside barbecue as they are to use as a swizzle stick in a bloody Mary on Sunday morning. My mother made several versions and would adjust the herbs and spices based on her intended use."
>
> —VEDA SCARPETTI,
> San Mateo, Calif.

We're looking for recipes that you treasure—the ones that have been handed down in your family for a generation or more, that always come out for the holidays, and that have earned a place at your table and in your heart through many years of meals. Send us the recipes that spell home to you. Visit CooksCountry.com/recipe_submission (or write to Heirloom Recipes, Cook's Country, 21 Drydock Avenue, Suite 210E, Boston, MA 02210) and tell us a little about the recipe. Include your name and address. If we print your recipe, you'll receive a free one-year subscription to Cook's Country.

COMING NEXT ISSUE

*We love every season at Cook's Country, but there's something special about summer. Don't miss our June/July 2019 issue, which features Texas-style **Smoked Beef Ribs**, a step-by-step cooking class on perfect **Mixed Berry Scones**, and a very opinionated tasting of supermarket ketchups. We'll also share **Five Easy Barbecue Sauces**, the simplest **Buttermilk Biscuits**, and **Cheese Enchiladas for Two**. Join us.*

ASPARAGUS PICKLES

Serves 6 to 8 (Makes 1 quart)

Trim the asparagus spears so they are no taller than the jar you're using. Depending on the size of your jar, you may have extra brine; the important thing is to make sure that the asparagus spears are fully submerged in the brine.

- 1 pound thick asparagus
- 6 sprigs fresh dill
- 1 bay leaf
- 1½ cups cider vinegar
- 1½ cups water
- ⅓ cup sugar
- ¼ cup kosher salt
- ½ teaspoon black peppercorns
- ½ teaspoon yellow mustard seeds

1. Trim asparagus spears to fit in wide-mouth 1-quart glass jar with tight-fitting lid. Place spears upright in jar. Add dill sprigs and bay leaf.
2. Combine vinegar, water, sugar, salt, peppercorns, and mustard seeds in small saucepan and bring to boil. Pour brine into jar, making sure spears are fully submerged. Let cool completely, about 1 hour.
3. Affix jar lid and refrigerate for at least 3 hours before serving. (Pickles can be refrigerated for up to 1 week.)

RECIPE INDEX

FIND THE ROOSTER!

A tiny version of this rooster has been hidden in a photo in the pages of this issue. Write to us with its location and we'll enter you in a random drawing. The first correct entry drawn will win our favorite inexpensive blender, and each of the next five will receive a free one-year subscription to Cook's Country. To enter, visit CooksCountry.com/rooster by May 31, 2019, or write to Rooster AM19, Cook's Country, 21 Drydock Avenue, Suite 210E, Boston, MA 02210. Include your name and address. Patrick Frieslander of Nokesville, Virginia, found the rooster in the December/January 2019 issue on page 7 and won our favorite loaf pan.

WEB EXTRAS

Free for four months at
CooksCountry.com/may19

Bourbon–Brown Sugar Cake Layers
Bourbon–Brown Sugar Frosting

READ US ON IPAD

Download the Cook's Country app for iPad and start a free trial subscription or purchase a single issue of the magazine. All issues are enhanced with full-color slide shows that provide step-by-step instructions for completing recipes, plus expanded reviews and ratings. Go to CooksCountry.com/iPad to download our app through iTunes.

Bourbon Praline Cake

Inspired by the Kentucky Derby, this bourbon-laced cake sports a winning combination of bourbon, brown sugar, and pecans. A ring of rosettes adds a finishing touch worthy of the Triple Crown.

by Sarah Ewald

TO MAKE THIS CAKE, YOU WILL NEED:

- 1 cup pecans
- ¼ cup (1¾ ounces) granulated sugar
- ¼ cup plus 1 tablespoon water
- ½ teaspoon table salt
- ⅓ cup packed (2⅓ ounces) light brown sugar
- ¼ cup bourbon
- 1 recipe Bourbon–Brown Sugar Cake Layers*
- 1 recipe Bourbon–Brown Sugar Frosting*

FOR THE CANDIED PECANS:

Line baking sheet with parchment paper. Bring pecans, granulated sugar, ¼ cup water, and salt to boil in medium saucepan over medium heat. Cook, stirring constantly, until water evaporates and sugar appears dry, opaque, and somewhat crystallized and evenly coats pecans, about 5 minutes. Reduce heat to low and continue to stir until sugar turns amber color, about 2 minutes longer. Transfer pecans to prepared sheet and spread into even layer. Let cool completely, about 10 minutes. Chop pecans coarse.

FOR THE BOURBON SYRUP:

Bring brown sugar, bourbon, and remaining 1 tablespoon water to boil in small saucepan over medium heat; cook until sugar dissolves, about 2 minutes.

TO ASSEMBLE:

Using skewer, poke 30 holes in top of each cake layer. Brush bourbon syrup generously over top and sides of each cake layer (use all of syrup). Set aside 1 cup frosting for piping rosettes. Combine 1½ cups remaining frosting with ½ cup chopped candied pecans in bowl. Place 1 cake layer on platter. Spread pecan-frosting mixture evenly over top, right to edge of cake. Top with second cake layer, press lightly to adhere, then spread remaining 2½ cups frosting evenly over top and sides of cake. Refrigerate until frosting is firm, about 30 minutes.

TO DECORATE:

Fill pastry bag fitted with star tip with reserved 1 cup frosting. Pipe rosettes (spiraling from inside out) around edge of cake. Sprinkle remaining candied pecans in even layer inside ring of rosettes, covering all exposed frosting. Serve.

*Our recipes for Bourbon–Brown Sugar Cake Layers and Bourbon–Brown Sugar Frosting are available for free for four months at CooksCountry.com/may19.

INSIDE THIS ISSUE

Cook's Country

BISCUITS EVERY DAY

Our easiest-ever method produces tall, fluffy, flavorful buttermilk biscuits bathed in melted butter in record time.

PAGE 18

Dinner Tonight
New ideas for 30-minute meals

Smoked Chicken Wings
Fire Up the Grill

Spicy Sesame Noodles
Supremely Slurpable

One-Pan Glazed Salmon
Rice and Vegetables, Too

Smoked Beef Ribs
Big Texas Favorite,
Big Texas Flavor

Buckeye Candies
Ohio State Sweet Treat

Cheese Enchiladas for Two
Super Skillet Supper

Peach Dumplings
Perfect Peak-Season Dessert

JUNE/JULY 2019
$6.95 U.S./$7.95 CANADA

0 71486 02742 3

07>

DISPLAY UNTIL JULY 8, 2019

Illustration: Ross MacDonald

HAVE YOU EVER used one of our recipe cards? The ones you find in the middle of every issue? I hope you have. To me, they represent some of our very best work.

Each of the recipes on those tear-out cards is designed with speed and ease in mind. The cooks who develop them are limited to 10 ingredients (not including kitchen staples such as salt and pepper) and 30 minutes of cooking time, and they aim to minimize the dirty dishes.

But these parameters don't mean that the recipes get a pass on the rigorous testing we're known for. The recipe cards have to clear the same gauntlet of diligence and scrutiny that all our recipes do—often dozens of tests, weeks of refinements, and the occasional one-way ticket to the trash can.

We believe that dinner should be good every night of the week, not just when you have the time to go the extra mile. After all, it's on those harried evenings after long and trying days that you need homespun nourishment the most. We want to make that easy.

For more dinner inspiration, we have a weekly email newsletter called **Dinner Tonight**. Every Monday, I choose one of our favorite quick recipes; add a tip, trick, or piece of knowledge to make it even easier; and deliver a shopping list to your inbox. I invite you to sign up for the free Dinner Tonight newsletter at **CooksCountry.com/dinnertonight**.

TUCKER SHAW

_____

Editor in Chief

Cook's Country

Chief Executive Officer David Nussbaum
Chief Creative Officer Jack Bishop
Editor in Chief Tucker Shaw
Executive Managing Editor Todd Meier
Executive Food Editor Bryan Roof
Deputy Editor Scott Kathan
Deputy Food Editor Morgan Bolling
Senior Editor Cecelia Jenkins
Associate Editors Alli Berkey, Matthew Fairman
Associate Editor, Web Ashley Delma
Photo Team Manager Tim McQuinn
Test Cooks Natalie Estrada, Jessica Rudolph
Assistant Test Cooks, Photo Team Sarah Ewald, Jacqueline Gochenouer, Eric Haessler
Senior Copy Editor Jill Campbell
Copy Editors Christine Campbell, Rachel Schowalter
Contributing Editor Eva Katz
Senior Science Research Editor Paul Adams
Hosts & Executive Editors, Television Bridget Lancaster, Julia Collin Davison

Executive Editors, Tastings & Testings Hannah Crowley, Lisa McManus
Senior Editors, Tastings & Testings Lauren Savoie, Kate Sk
Associate Editor, Tastings & Testings Miye Bromberg
Assistant Editors, Tastings & Testings Riddley Gemperlein-Schirm, Carolyn Grillo, Emily Phares

Creative Director John Torres
Photography Director Julie Cote
Art Director Susan Levin
Associate Art Director Maggie Edgar
Senior Staff Photographer Daniel J. van Ackere
Staff Photographers Steve Klise, Kevin White
Photography Producer Meredith Mulcahy

Senior Director, Creative Operations Alice Carpenter
Senior Editor, Special Projects Christie Morrison
Senior Manager, Publishing Operations Taylor Argenzio
Imaging Manager Lauren Robbins
Production & Imaging Specialists Dennis Noble, Jessica Voas, Amanda Yong
Test Kitchen Director Erin McMurrer
Assistant Test Kitchen Director Alexxa Benson
Test Kitchen Manager Meridith Lippard
Test Kitchen Facilities Manager Kelly Ryan
Senior Kitchen Assistant Shopper Michelle Miller
Senior Kitchen Assistant Receiver Heather Tolmie
Lead Kitchen Assistant Ena Gudiel
Kitchen Assistants Gladis Campos, Blanca Castanza, Amarilys Merced, Arlene Rosario

Chief Financial Officer Jackie McCauley Ford
Senior Manager, Customer Support Tim Quinn
Customer Support Specialist Mitchell Axelson
Event Coordinator Michaela Hughes

Chief Digital Officer Fran Middleton
VP, Marketing Natalie Vinard
Director, Audience Acquisition & Partnerships Evan Steine
Director, Social Media Marketing Kathryn Przybyla
Social Media Coordinators Charlotte Errity, Sarah Sandler

Chief Revenue Officer Sara Domville

Senior VP, Human Resources & Organizational Development Colleen Zelina
Human Resources Manager Jason Lynott

Director, Public Relations & Communications Brian Frankl
Public Relations Coordinator Madeleine Cohen

Photography Keller + Keller
Food Styling Catrine Kelty

Circulation Services ProCirc

On the cover: Pat-in-the-Pan Buttermilk Biscuits

THE ULTIMATE BURGER

Plus DIY Condiments, Sides, and Boozy Milkshakes

*What is the ultimate burger? Ask that question and you will ignite an enthusiastic debate about meats, cooking methods, degrees of doneness, bun types, condiments, toppings, and accompaniments. Fortunately, the answer is simple: It is whatever you want it to be. The Ultimate Burger shows you how to get there. Go to **AmericasTestKitchen.com/ultimateburger** to order your copy.*

Find us on **Facebook**
facebook.com/CooksCountry

Find us on **Instagram**
instagram.com/CooksCountry

Follow us on **Pinterest**
pinterest.com/TestKitchen

Follow us on **Twitter**
twitter.com/TestKitchen

AMERICA'S TEST KITCHEN ®

America's Test Kitchen is a real test kitchen located in Boston. It is the home of more than 60 test cooks, editors, and cookware specialists. Our mission is to test recipes until we understand exactly how and why they work and eventually arrive at the very best version. We also test kitchen equipment and supermarket ingredients in search of products that offer the best value and performance. You can watch us work by tuning in to *America's Test Kitchen* (AmericasTestKitchen.com) and *Cook's Country from America's Test Kitchen* (CooksCountry.com) on public television, and you can listen to our weekly segments on *The Splendid Table* on public radio. You can also follow us on Facebook, Twitter, Pinterest, and Instagram.

12

23

16

Cook's Country magazine (ISSN 1552-1990), number 87, is published bimonthly by America's Test Kitchen Limited Partnership, 21 Drydock Avenue, Suite 210E, Boston, MA 02210. Copyright 2019 America's Test Kitchen Limited Partnership. Periodicals postage paid at Boston, MA, and additional mailing offices, USPS #023453. Publications Mail Agreement No. 40020778. Return undeliverable Canadian addresses to P.O. Box 875, Station A, Windsor, ON N9A 6P2. POSTMASTER: Send address changes to Cook's Country, P.O. Box 6018, Harlan, IA 51593-1518. For subscription and gift subscription orders, subscription inquiries, or change of address notices, visit AmericasTestKitchen.com/support, call 800-526-8447 in the U.S. or 515-237-3663 from outside the U.S., or write to us at Cook's Country, P.O. Box 6018, Harlan, IA 51593-1518. PRINTED IN THE USA.

by Cecelia Jenkins

Going Against the Grain

Recipes often call for slicing beef against the grain, but I don't understand what this means or how to do it. Can you please clarify?

–Bridgette Holmes, New York, N.Y.

If you look closely at a piece of beef, you'll notice little lines—bundles of closely packed muscle fibers that run parallel to one another. This pattern of fibers is referred to as the "grain" because it looks similar to the grain on a piece of wood.

When recipes call for slicing meat against (or across) the grain, it means you slice it perpendicular to the fibers instead of parallel to them. If you think of the fibers as a handful of dry spaghetti, you want to cut the bundle of spaghetti into shorter sections.

This is important because shorter lengths of muscle fibers are easier to chew. Luxe cuts such as rib eye or tenderloin are tender no matter how you slice them, but for tougher cuts such as flank steak or skirt steak, cutting against the grain is important to ensure pleasant eating.

To cut against the grain, look for the lines of muscle fibers and orient them so they run north to south on your cutting board. Then, slice east to west, perpendicular to the grain line. Sometimes that means making long cuts across a large piece of meat, such as a long skirt steak. To make slicing more manageable, we recommend first cutting the meat with the grain into smaller sections and then rotating the meat accordingly and proceeding to slice against the grain of the smaller sections.

THE BOTTOM LINE: Slicing against the grain means slicing across the muscle fibers, which makes otherwise tough meat more tender. Tender cuts do not need to be sliced against the grain.

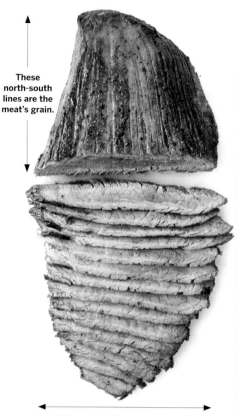

These north-south lines are the meat's grain.

Slice east-west across the grain for the most tender meat.

A Mediterranean Mix

I love your recipe for homemade Italian seasoning. Could you create a recipe for homemade Greek seasoning?

–Cheryl James, Streetsboro, Ohio

Aiming to please, we ordered in several Greek seasoning mixes and were surprised to find how different they were. Some were just mixtures of herbs, others were dominated by onion, and still others included warm spices such as nutmeg and cinnamon. We wanted a lemony, herb-heavy blend that would be great mixed into vinaigrette, added to marinades for chicken or lamb, or simply sprinkled over rice. Here's our version.

HOMEMADE GREEK SEASONING

Makes about ¼ cup
One lemon yields 1 tablespoon of zest. We love this seasoning in salad dressings and on feta cheese, baked potatoes, or grilled chicken.

- 1 tablespoon grated lemon zest
- 2 tablespoons dried oregano
- 1 teaspoon table salt
- 1 teaspoon pepper
- 1 teaspoon garlic powder

1. Spread lemon zest evenly on plate and microwave until dry and zest separates easily when crumbled between your fingers, about 2 minutes, stirring halfway through microwaving.

2. Combine oregano, salt, pepper, garlic powder, and lemon zest in small bowl. (Seasoning can be stored at room temperature for up to 1 week.)

Bye-Bye, Baby (Carrots)

It seems that my bagged baby carrots spoil faster than regular carrots. Why is that?

–Deb Hines, Tiverton, R.I.

Bagged baby carrots are not young carrots harvested when they're small; rather, they are merely processed pieces of large carrots that are typically too blemished to sell whole. The larger, imperfect carrots (usually varieties high in sugar and beta carotene and therefore sweeter and brighter in color) are forced through a machine that peels them and cuts them down to baby carrots' signature small size. Then, like a lot of produce nowadays, the baby carrots are washed in an FDA- and EPA-regulated chlorinated solution to kill off bacteria before they are bagged.

Because baby carrots don't have the natural protective outer layer present on whole, mature carrots (it is peeled off) and have a relatively large amount of surface area exposed to air, they are inclined to spoil faster than regular carrots. Without this protective skin, baby carrots are prone to losing their moisture; when the exterior dries out, it forms a white blush that looks unappetizing (but is generally safe to consume). To combat moisture loss, some manufacturers add extra water to the bagged carrots; this sealed, high-moisture environment means that the baby carrots can turn slimy.

THE BOTTOM LINE: Due to their processing—primarily the removal of their natural protective outer coating—baby carrots do indeed spoil faster than whole carrots. If your baby carrots are dried out, try soaking them in ice water to revive them.

GET YOUR GRAPES HERE!
Fruit that tastes like candy

Next-Generation Grapes

My grocery store carries Cotton Candy grapes. What are they?

–Gus Gendron, Orlando, Fla.

A few of our test cooks are enthusiastic fans of Cotton Candy grapes and were eager to order some for us to taste. The grapes looked like any other green grapes, but true to their name, these juicy specimens had a bubblegum-y sweetness much like that of cotton candy. A few tasters noted a similarity to the artificial "blue raspberry" flavor found in some candies and drinks. First-time tasters were shocked by the grapes' sweetness and perfumy flavor.

We assumed that these were genetically modified Frankengrapes, but in fact, they were developed by a California company called The Grapery using traditional, all-natural crossbreeding methods. Cotton Candy grapes contain about 12 percent more sugar than most other commercial varieties.

THE BOTTOM LINE: Cotton Candy grapes are an all-natural grape hybrid that is sweeter than many other grape varieties. Their availability in late summer is limited, but they can be found at many major grocery store chains.

ompiled by Matthew Fairman

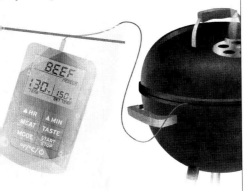

Gloomy Grilling

Amber Nelson, Pensacola, Fla.

s a die-hard griller, I don't let rainy days
op me from cooking outside—especially
hen I'm slow-smoking meat on a covered
ill. The grill lid protects the meat and fire
om the rain but not my probe thermom-
ter/timer. I just throw it in a zipper-lock
ag and snake the probe through the mostly
ealed top. Bad weather is no match for a
ttle ingenuity!

Just Chillin'

–Sharon Norman, Sunbury, Ohio

Your equipment review of ice packs reminded me
of a trick I use to make more efficient use of cooler
space—and to avoid buying ice packs. I fill empty
plastic soda bottles—large
and small—with water, iced
tea, or juice (leaving some
space at the top to allow
the frozen liquid to expand)
and freeze them. The frozen
bottles keep my cooler
contents cool. And once
they thaw, I have
cold drinks at
the ready.

Yeast Test

–Claude Charles, Surfside Beach, S.C.

I'm an occasional bread baker, so I don't buy yeast
that often. When I decided to make your recipe for
bagel bread (CooksCountry.com/bagelbread), I
was sad to see that my yeast was more than two
years old. My friend who's a professional baker
gave me a great tip. To check if yeast is expired,
just add a little bit of sugar to some warm water
(no hotter than 110 degrees) and stir in a teaspoon
of yeast (either instant or active dry yeast). In
about 5 minutes, the mixture should start to foam.
If it does, your yeast is good to use; if it doesn't,
you'll have to pitch it and buy new yeast.

When Tasting Ketchup, Is Familiar Better?

by Carolyn Grillo

HEINZ ORGANIC KETCHUP
Thick, smooth, and glossy

SIR KENSINGTON'S CLASSIC KETCHUP
Pulpy and coarse

RECOMMENDED

Our Favorite
Heinz Organic Tomato Ketchup
"Lively," "familiar,"
and perfectly balanced

RECOMMENDED
WITH RESERVATIONS

THERE'S NO DENYING it: Americans love ketch-
up. Ketchup hits all five basic tastes: salty, sweet, sour,
bitter, and umami. And it's more than just a condiment.
In the test kitchen, we add ketchup not just to meatloaf
glazes and barbecue sauces but also to more surprising
dishes such as tacos and stuffed peppers.

Heinz has dominated the market for decades, but
since our last tasting, two major condiment companies,
Hellmann's and French's, have started manufactur-
ing ketchup. Meanwhile, small companies have gained
traction with American shoppers looking for "artisan"
alternatives. How do these new options stack up to their
more familiar counterparts? To find out, we purchased
eight top-selling ketchups and compared them in two
blind taste tests, plain and with French fries.

Every ketchup was bright and tangy enough for our
tasters. They were all sweet and salty enough, too. But
they weren't all perfect. Some ketchups had assertive and
unusual flavors. Our tasting panel rejected products containing unconventional ingredients such as lime juice,
green bell pepper, and warm spices.

As for texture, two of our lowest-rated products were
noticeably grainy and pulpy—not OK. Our top-rated
ketchups were silky-smooth; according to industry
experts, they were likely pushed through a finer sieve
before being bottled.

In the end, we had reservations about three products,
but the other five earned our approval. Our two favorites
were both from Heinz. Web subscribers can read the full
tasting at **CooksCountry.com/jul19**.

Texas-Style Smoked Beef Ribs

Wanted: a foolproof method for gigantic beef ribs.

by Morgan Bolling

TEXAS-STYLE BEEF RIBS are intimidating—so big they look like they came off a *T. rex*. But fans know that beneath the dark, peppery crust and pink smoke ring is succulently tender beef so flavorful that barbecue sauce is unnecessary (and, in some corners, verboten). You think brisket lovers are committed? Wait till you meet a smoked beef rib enthusiast.

I'm specifically referring to beef plate ribs, the meatiest ribs on the steer. They are marbled with fat and collagen; over low, slow heat, they achieve a tender, juicy texture. They are rarely available prepackaged, so I had to start with a special order at the butcher (see "Buy the Right [Very Big!] Ribs").

There is no universal code for how butchers cut plate ribs, so I gave strict specs to my butcher: "Two sets of beef plate ribs, three ribs per set and 4 to 5 pounds each. I want 1 to 1½ inches of meat on top of the bone." The butcher was happy to have the direction, and I got exactly what I wanted.

Pit masters use commercial-size smokers with lots of controls, but all I had was a humble charcoal grill. Drawing on knowledge I picked up while developing a recent smoked brisket recipe, I turned to a technique called a charcoal snake. This grill setup involves arranging coals in a C shape in the grill and lighting just one end. The coals slowly ignite each other as they burn along the length of the snake, producing hours of heat without requiring reloading. And because the heat moves around the edges of the grill, you don't have to reposition the ribs as they cook.

I set up a charcoal snake and topped it with five evenly spaced wood chunks to smolder for smoke flavor. I placed a pan of water in the middle of the snake to keep the temperature stable and sprinkled a generous amount of salt and pepper over two sets of beef plate ribs (enough to serve about eight people). I lit one end of the snake, closed the grill lid, and waited a nervous 5 hours before opening it again.

When I finally did, the ribs had reached an internal temperature of 200 degrees and they looked—and smelled—like barbecue bliss. But they were chewy when sliced, and one set of ribs was burnt on the bottom.

It turned out that the burnt parts had spent some time directly over the coals. I needed to find a different orientation, one that would allow the ribs to cook through without burning in spots. For my next test, I placed the ribs slightly off-center, with the meat carefully positioned over the gap in the snake between the head and the tail—and no meat sitting directly over the hot coals. This minimized the charring, but the ribs were still a little bit tough.

I reached out to Daniel Vaughn, a Texas barbecue expert. He advised me to cook these ribs to 210 degrees. Cuts that require low, slow cooking, such as these ribs, need to hang out above 180 degrees for a long time so that the collagen melts. I tried another batch, this time keeping the grill covered for 6 hours to allow both sets of ribs to reach 210 degrees. I then let the ribs rest for an hour before slicing into the tender, juicy meat. Perfect.

I served these at a backyard gathering recently and, if I do say so myself, my guests' minds were blown.

Buy the Right (Very Big!) Ribs

Individual beef short ribs (left) are too small to work here. This recipe is specifically engineered for racks of beef plate ribs (right), which you may need to special-order from a butcher.

Whoa! These ribs are big in size and even bigger in smoky, meaty flavor.

TEXAS-STYLE SMOKED BEEF RIBS
Serves 6 to 8

We developed this recipe using a 22-inch Weber Kettle charcoal grill. We call for beef plate ribs here; you may need to special-order these. We recommend reading the entire recipe before starting.

- 3 tablespoons kosher salt
- 3 tablespoons pepper
- 2 (4- to 5-pound) racks beef plate ribs, 1 to 1½ inches of meat on top of bone, trimmed
- 5 (3-inch) wood chunks
- 1 (13 by 9-inch) disposable aluminum pan

1. Combine salt and pepper in bowl, then sprinkle ribs all over with salt-pepper mixture.

2. Open bottom vent completely. Set up charcoal snake: Arrange 60 briquettes, 2 briquettes wide, around perimeter of grill, overlapping slightly so briquettes are touching, leaving 8-inch gap between ends of snake. Place second layer of 60 briquettes, also 2 briquettes wide, on top of first. (Completed snake should be 2 briquettes wide by 2 briquettes high.)

3. Starting 4 inches from 1 end of snake, evenly space wood chunks on top of snake. Place disposable pan in center of grill so short end of pan faces gap in snake. Fill disposable pan with 4 cups water. Light chimney starter filled with 15 briquettes (pile briquettes on 1 side of chimney to make them easier to ignite). When coals are partially covered with ash, pour over 1 end of snake. (Make sure lit coals touch only 1 end of snake.)

4. Set cooking grate in place. Clean and oil cooking grate. Position ribs next to each other on cooking grate, bone side down, crosswise over disposable pan and gap in snake (they will be off-center; this is OK). Cover grill, position lid vent over gap in snake, and open lid vent completely. Cook undisturbed until rack of ribs overhanging gap in snake registers 210 degrees in meatiest portion, 5½ to 6¼ hours.

5. Transfer ribs to carving board, tent with aluminum foil, and let rest for 30 minutes. Cut ribs between bones and serve.

Desert Oak Barbecue proprietor Richard Funk (bottom) smokes beef ribs over oak wood, which he "imports" to El Paso from central Texas.

Text by Bryan Roof; photos by Steve Klise

Bigger in Texas

ON THE ROAD

I ARRIVE AT DESERT Oak Barbecue in El Paso, Texas, promptly at 6:00 a.m., which is when owner Richard Funk says the beef ribs will be ready to come off the cooker. I park around back, a few feet behind a trailer that houses the wood and supplies needed for the custom-built 1,000-gallon cooker a few feet away.

Richard's wife, Suzanne, introduced him to a charcoal grill while the couple was living in Michigan. It was love at first fire. Without a proper mentor, Richard tinkered with recipes and techniques almost nonstop. "It was torture for my family at first because I had no idea what I was doing," he says. "The first brisket I ever made is still by far the worst brisket I've ever eaten."

In 2012, after they had returned to El Paso, Suzanne urged Richard to embrace his passion and try to make a living from it. He thought the idea was ridiculous. "I didn't know if people in El Paso would like [my barbecue], other than our friends and family who were just being nice." He started with a food truck, a relatively low-risk venture. It took off.

Richard pulls the beef ribs off the cooker with gloved hands and sprays each rack with a solution of red wine vinegar and water to keep them moist once they're wrapped in butcher paper. The ribs rest at room temperature for 45 minutes and then go into a warming box to await customers. The ideal serving temperature, Richard says, is comfortable enough for a pit master to touch with bare hands but still hot and juicy, about 140 degrees.

The dining room is a combination of raw wood planks and corrugated tin. Hanging every few feet are snapshots of the Funk family standing in front of the great barbecue landmarks of central Texas. Other families might post pictures of Disney vacations, but the Funks plan their travels around barbecue.

I order a little of everything: two links of sausage made by Richard and his son, Marcelo; half a pound of brisket; a few thin slices of turkey; a scoop of pulled pork; three pork ribs; and a giant beef rib. I ignore the bottle of sauce on the table and dig right in. I switch between the politeness of a fork and knife and the appropriateness of fingers and napkins.

Richard refers to his barbecue as "central Texas–style," which is typically cooked with oak. But oak isn't native to El Paso, so he has it shipped in, which tightens his margins. The beef ribs, sold only on Saturdays, also shrink those margins because of their wholesale cost and the labor involved in cooking them.

"[Beef ribs] are hard to love," Richard says. "But I love cutting them. Take out that first rack, carve into it, slap it on the scale, and everyone's eyes just pop out of their heads. It's awesome. And they pop out even further once they see the price at the register. I just keep my head down and keep going." For more photos of our trip to El Paso, visit **CooksCountry.com/oakbarbecue19.**

A Fresh Take on Grilled Zucchini

Fresh, cheap, plentiful . . . and often boring.
Time for a new you, zucchini. **by Natalie Estrada**

SOMEONE SHOULD MAKE a horror movie about a society overtaken by uncontrollable hordes of summer zucchini. In peak season, this vegetable is everywhere and home gardeners struggle to give it away. Attack of the killer zucchini, indeed. I wanted to write a happier script for this handsome vegetable, set in my favorite place for summer cooking—on the grill.

My early experiments confirmed prior test kitchen findings: Large zucchini tasted dull and were much tougher and more fibrous than their smaller brethren. Medium zucchini (around 8 ounces each) were sweeter and more tender.

Since I wanted to avoid having to move lots of small pieces around the grill grate, I cut the zucchini in half lengthwise (as opposed to into spears or medallions) and began by marinating them in olive oil, salt, and pepper. I hoped the salty marinade would add flavor and help pull out some of the extra moisture before the vegetable hit the cooking grate, thus reducing mushiness. And here was my first scary scene: The oil dripped off the grilling zucchini and caused flare-ups that resulted in a sooty taste. On top of that, the zucchini was bland and still mushy. Thumbs down.

An oily marinade was out. To encourage the zukes to give up their moisture on the grill, I tried cutting a shallow crosshatch pattern into the flesh side of each half. As long as I was gentle enough not to cut through

the skin, this trick worked great and resulted in a firmer, nonmushy texture.

I now had perfectly cooked zucchini, but I still needed to jazz up the flavor. My mind immediately went to romesco sauce, a Spanish staple built on a puree of roasted red peppers, almonds, and olive oil. I threw a red bell pepper onto the grill with the zucchini and, once all the vegetables were cooked, headed inside to figure out the sauce.

After a bit of fiddling, I perfected my streamlined version of a romesco-style sauce. The grilled bell pepper provided a great foundation. Sliced almonds contributed a clean flavor and blended easily into the sauce. I added garlic for bite, red wine vinegar for tang, and basil for an intense herbal punch. The sauce came together in the blender in a flash.

Beautifully charred zucchini paired with a summery sauce makes zucchini a less scary presence during the summer months. Stay tuned for the sequel.

GRILLED ZUCCHINI WITH RED PEPPER SAUCE
Serves 4 to 6

Look for zucchini that are no more than 2 inches in diameter and weigh about 8 ounces each to ensure correct grilling times. Clean and oil the cooking grate thoroughly to prevent the zucchini from sticking. Note that we leave the bell pepper whole (minus the stem and core) and grill only two sides of it.

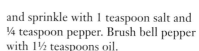

The crosshatching helps the excess liquid cook out of this often-watery vegetable.

Go Small
Larger zucchini can be bland, tough, and full of seeds. For this recipe, we call for medium zucchini that weigh about 8 ounces each.

A medium zucchini should be about as wide as a banana.

- 4 zucchini (8 ounces each), trimmed
- 1 red bell pepper
- 1½ tablespoons plus ⅓ cup extra-virgin olive oil, divided
- 1¼ teaspoons table salt, divided
- ½ teaspoon pepper, divided
- 2 tablespoons sliced almonds, toasted
- 1½ tablespoons red wine vinegar
- 2 small garlic cloves, peeled
- 2 teaspoons chopped fresh basil

1. Cut zucchini in half lengthwise. Using paring knife, cut ½-inch crosshatch pattern, about ¼ inch deep, in flesh of each zucchini half, being careful not to cut through skin. Cut around stem of bell pepper and remove core and seeds. Brush flesh sides of zucchini with 1 tablespoon oil

and sprinkle with 1 teaspoon salt and ¼ teaspoon pepper. Brush bell pepper with 1½ teaspoons oil.

2A. FOR A CHARCOAL GRILL: Open bottom vent completely. Light large chimney starter filled with charcoal briquettes (6 quarts). When top coals are partially covered with ash, pour evenly over grill. Set cooking grate in place, cover, and open lid vent completely. Heat grill until hot, about 5 minutes.

2B. FOR A GAS GRILL: Turn all burners to high, cover, and heat grill until hot, about 15 minutes. Turn all burners to medium-high.

3. Clean and oil cooking grate. Place zucchini, flesh side down, and bell pepper, skin side down, on cooking grate. Cook (covered if using gas) until vegetables are well charred on first side, 7 to 9 minutes, rearranging zucchini as needed to ensure even browning.

4. Flip vegetables and continue to cook

(covered if using gas) until fork inserted into zucchini meets little resistance and bell pepper is charred on second side, 8 to 10 minutes longer. Transfer zucchini to plate, flesh side up, as they finish cooking. Transfer bell pepper to small bowl, cover with plastic wrap, and let sit for 5 minutes.

5. Using spoon, remove skin from bell pepper (it's OK if some small pieces of skin remain; do not rinse bell pepper to remove skin); cut into 1-inch pieces. Process bell pepper, almonds, vinegar, garlic, remaining ⅓ cup oil, remaining ¼ teaspoon salt, and remaining ¼ teaspoon pepper in blender until smooth, 30 to 60 seconds, scraping down sides of blender jar as needed. Transfer sauce to bowl and stir in basil. Season sauce with salt and pepper to taste.

6. Spread half of sauce on platter. Arrange zucchini over sauce, flesh side up. Spoon remaining sauce over zucchini, as desired. Serve.

Cuke and Onion Salad

Is it a pickle? Is it a salad? No matter—this side belongs in your barbecue spread. **by Morgan Bolling**

MY GRANDMOTHER USED to throw together thinly sliced cucumbers and onions in a tangy-sweet dressing to create harmony on our summer table. It's not that the table was in disharmony, but the rich southern main dishes we commonly enjoyed—succulent pulled pork, crunchy fried chicken—needed a bright side dish to balance things out. This simple, refreshing combination of cucumbers and onions was just the ticket.

I'm pretty sure my grandmother didn't follow a recipe for this dish. I've tried to re-create her version many times, but my attempts have never come out exactly right (either too pickled or too sweet). I wanted to develop a formula so I could get it right every time. For inspiration, I made five existing recipes from a mix of Southern sources. Our favorite version combined peeled cucumbers with thinly sliced onion in a pungent dressing of apple cider vinegar and sugar.

The dressing was too assertive and sharp, so I tamed it by adding ¼ cup of water. As for the cukes, I tested regular cucumbers, English cucumbers, and smaller pickling cucumbers. The pickling cucumbers were hard to track down without going to a specialty grocer or farm stand. The English cucumbers worked fine, but our top choice was regular cucumbers; my tasters preferred their ultracrunchy texture. Peeling the cukes eliminated any bitter taste.

I assumed sweet, Georgia-born Vidalia onions would be the right choice here. But in a side-by-side test, tasters couldn't tell the difference between sweet and regular yellow onions once the salad was dressed. Not having to call for a specialty onion was good news.

My grandmother always told me this dish got better as it sat, so I refrigerated a batch for a few hours before serving. As I expected, she was correct; the flavors came together and the vegetables softened just enough. Time to fire up the grill for that pulled pork.

PICKLED CUCUMBER AND ONION SALAD
Serves 4 to 6
This recipe can easily be doubled.

- ½ cup cider vinegar
- ¼ cup water
- 2 tablespoons sugar
- 1½ teaspoons table salt
- ½ teaspoon pepper
- 1 pound cucumbers, peeled, halved lengthwise, and sliced ⅛ inch thick (about 3 cups)
- 1 cup thinly sliced onion

Whisk vinegar, water, sugar, salt, and pepper together in medium bowl. Add cucumbers and onion and toss to combine. Cover with plastic wrap and refrigerate for at least 1 hour to allow flavors to meld. Use slotted spoon to serve. (Salad can be refrigerated in airtight container for up to 3 days.)

Honey Butter Corn

It takes a sweet touch to bring out corn's full potential. **by Cecelia Jenkins**

FRESH CORN ON the cob, shucked, boiled, and buttered, is a summertime treasure. But with enough repetition, even treasures can become a little tired. I wanted to create a simple, easy recipe that added pizzazz to summer corn by enhancing its fresh, sweet flavor.

I started by stripping the kernels from six cobs of freshly husked corn. The best method was to cut the husked cobs in half crosswise and then stand the halves on their stable, flat cut sides before cutting off the kernels with downward strokes of a sharp knife. The six ears gave me about 4½ cups of fresh, sweet kernels to work with.

One simple way to enrich corn's flavor is to brown it, so I dumped the kernels into a stainless-steel skillet with a little vegetable oil. After about 9 minutes over medium-high heat (with a bit of stirring), the corn was tender and had loads of flavorful browning. The bottom of my skillet, however, was hard to clean; I found that it was best to use nonstick (or cast iron) instead.

To highlight the sweet, nutty flavor even more, I melted 3 tablespoons of butter into the hot kernels, which gave each little nub a rich, glistening coating. Some fresh thyme provided its signature fragrance and gave the corn a savory anchor. Finally, just a bit of a surprising ingredient—honey—brought the dish together by gently accentuating the corn's sweetness.

HONEY BUTTER CORN
Serves 4
We prefer fresh corn in this recipe, but you can substitute 4½ cups of thawed frozen corn, if desired.

- 2 tablespoons vegetable oil
- 6 ears corn, kernels cut from cobs (4½ cups)
- ¾ teaspoon table salt
- ½ teaspoon pepper
- 3 tablespoons unsalted butter, cut into 3 pieces
- 2 tablespoons honey
- 1 tablespoon fresh thyme leaves

1. Heat oil in 12-inch nonstick skillet over medium-high heat until shimmering. Add corn, salt, and pepper and cook, stirring occasionally, until tender and spotty brown, 8 to 10 minutes.
2. Off heat, stir in butter, honey, and thyme until butter is melted and mixture is combined, about 30 seconds. Serve.

MISO HONEY BUTTER CORN
Decrease honey to 1 tablespoon. Substitute 2 scallions, sliced thin on bias, for thyme. Add 1 tablespoon white miso and 1 teaspoon soy sauce with butter in step 2.

Proper Browning
To ensure the best flavor, make sure the corn gets good and browned—like this—by the end of step 1.

Tomato Primer

You can use any medium-size round, ripe tomatoes in this recipe (do not use plum tomatoes). Ripe tomatoes should feel heavy for their size and give slightly when pressed. Here are a few good choices.

VINE-RIPENED

KUMATO

YELLOW

Marinating Tomatoes
Laying the zipper-lock bag flat minimizes jostling (and thus breakage) while maximizing marinade contact (and thus flavor).

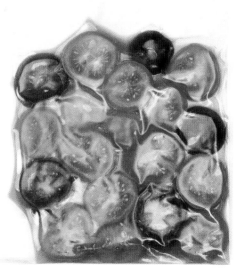

Summer Tomato Sandwiches

This summertime stalwart seems so simple. But it's also particular.

by Natalie Estrada

WHAT IS THE ultimate way to savor summer? Ask any of the Southerners on the *Cook's Country* team (we have a few), and they'll tell you: white sandwich bread, mayonnaise (preferably Duke's, a Southern favorite), slices of perfectly ripe tomato, salt, and pepper. That's it. No fancy artisanal bread, elaborate aioli, Himalayan salt, arugula, or cheese. It's all about simplicity. And yet we found ourselves talking about it for hours.

Although the recipe has few ingredients, so many things can go wrong. The tomatoes may be underripe, the slices too large and unwieldy, or the construction imperfect. And what about those days (let's face it: months) when you don't have access to a perfect tomato? I not only was determined to develop an exceptional tomato sandwich but also wanted to create a recipe that would be equally successful no matter what condition the tomatoes were in: a recipe that could live year-round, from the start of summer, before the best of the harvest, to well beyond the season's end.

To get the most out of my tomatoes, I sliced them and then marinated them in a mixture of extra-virgin olive oil, red wine vinegar, and salt. The olive oil encouraged the complex tomato flavor to come forward, the vinegar enhanced the tomatoes' brightness, and the salt—well, salt amplifies everything. I found that this mixture worked just as well with perfect tomatoes straight off the vine as it did with tough, bland off-season tomatoes.

Marinating extruded some of the liquid and jelly from the tomatoes; rather than discard these intensely flavorful elements (the jelly, in particular, is full of flavor), I reserved some—along with some marinade— to stir into the mayo before spreading it on the bread.

A few side-by-side tests proved that the right tomato slice thickness is crucial to the success of the sandwich. After experimenting with several different measurements, I found that ¼-inch-thick slices were ideal to ensure stable architecture both on the plate and in hand. A serrated knife made for tidy slicing. All the sandwich needed was a hint of ground black pepper to finish.

This was the contemporary makeover of the Southern tomato sandwich that I had been looking for. And for once, I didn't mind using less-than-perfect tomatoes.

THE AMERICAN TABLE

In many corners of the South, a summertime tomato sandwich isn't worth eating unless the mayonnaise is Duke's. This supertangy regional favorite has a devoted following among Southerners; according to *The Washington Post*, one elderly customer even wrote to the company requesting a few old-style glass Duke's mayonnaise jars to hold her eventual cremains.

TOMATO SANDWICHES
Serves 4

Choose tomatoes that measure no more than 2 inches in diameter. The tomatoes should smell fruity and feel heavy for their size. You're more likely to break up the tomatoes if you toss them with the marinade in a bowl; combining them in a zipper-lock bag is gentler.

- 3 tablespoons extra-virgin olive oil
- 1 tablespoon red wine vinegar
- ¾ teaspoon table salt
- 1 pound mixed ripe tomatoes, cored and sliced ¼ inch thick
- ½ cup mayonnaise
- 8 slices hearty white sandwich bread, toasted
  Pepper

1. Whisk oil, vinegar, and salt together in medium bowl; transfer marinade to 1-gallon zipper-lock bag. Add tomatoes to bag, press out air, seal bag, and gently turn to coat tomatoes with marinade. Lay bag flat on counter and let sit for 10 minutes.
2. Transfer tomato slices to now-empty bowl, leaving marinade in bag. Combine 1½ tablespoons marinade with mayonnaise in small bowl. Discard remaining marinade.
3. Place toast on cutting board. Spread 1 tablespoon mayonnaise mixture on 1 side of toast. Shingle tomatoes evenly on 4 slices of toast, covering as much of toast as possible. Season tomatoes with pepper to taste. Top tomatoes with remaining 4 slices of toast, mayonnaise side down. Cut sandwiches in half. Serve.

Roasted Potato Salad
To breathe new life into this classic salad, we turned to the oven.

by Ashley Moore

BOILED POTATOES MAKE a great salad. Roasted potatoes with flavorful browned exteriors make a fantastic side. I wanted to combine the two for a dish that boasted the best of both worlds.

I selected five very different recipes for roasted potato salad and fired up the oven. A few hours later, I presented the finished salads to my colleagues to taste. While some salads had components we liked, none of them fully satisfied us. I had more work ahead of me.

Choosing a potato was easy. I knew from my initial test recipes that russets were too starchy and Red Bliss potatoes were too waxy—I wanted a softer interior here. That left Yukon Golds, which have excellent flavor and come in many sizes. I opted for the small ones (no more than 2 inches in diameter) and cut them in half for bite-size pieces with exposed sides that would pick up lots of flavorful browning in the oven. Roasting the little guys cut side down for 25 minutes at 425 degrees gave me the golden color and creamy texture I was looking for.

While the potatoes cooled, I whipped up a dressing. For this salad, I was committed to mayo; I doctored it up with some white wine vinegar and Dijon mustard for punch. For crunch, I tossed in some chopped celery. A shallot and some garlic cloves (which I roasted with the potatoes), chopped up and stirred into the dressing, added a soft sweet-and-savory note. Chopped roasted red peppers from a jar provided additional sweetness and a bit of color.

I stirred everything together until the potatoes were well coated with the dressing, and then sprinkled a good handful of sliced chives over the top for brightness. Success: My tasters were pleased.

Why Shallot?
Most home cooks have onions at the ready, but fewer regularly buy the onion's smaller, sweeter cousin, the shallot. While it's true that you can usually substitute an equal amount of onion for shallot in recipes, we love shallots' more gentle, refined flavor. Plus, their smaller size means fewer forgotten onion halves in the back of your refrigerator.

Browned potatoes, a punchy dressing, and a little celery crunch make this salad a new favorite.

ROASTED POTATO SALAD
Serves 4 to 6

We prefer to use Yukon Gold potatoes in this recipe; however, small Red Bliss potatoes will work. For the best results, use small Yukon Gold potatoes measuring 1 to 1½ inches in diameter. Be sure to pat the roasted red peppers dry with paper towels before chopping them; any excess moisture will water down the dressing.

- 2 pounds small Yukon Gold potatoes, unpeeled, halved
- 1 shallot, halved through root end
- 2 tablespoons extra-virgin olive oil
- 4 garlic cloves, smashed and peeled
- 1¼ teaspoons table salt, divided
- 1¼ teaspoons pepper, divided
- ½ cup mayonnaise
- 1 tablespoon white wine vinegar
- 1 teaspoon Dijon mustard
- 1 cup jarred roasted red peppers, patted dry and chopped
- 2 celery ribs, chopped fine
- ¼ cup thinly sliced fresh chives

1. Adjust oven rack to lowest position and heat oven to 425 degrees. Toss potatoes, shallot, oil, garlic, ½ teaspoon salt, and ½ teaspoon pepper together in bowl. Arrange potato mixture in single layer on rimmed baking sheet and flip potatoes cut side down. Roast until potatoes are tender and golden brown on bottoms, about 25 minutes.
2. Meanwhile, whisk mayonnaise, vinegar, mustard, remaining ¾ teaspoon salt, and remaining ¾ teaspoon pepper together in large bowl. Stir in red peppers and celery.
3. Transfer sheet to wire rack. Using tongs, transfer shallot and garlic to cutting board; let cool for 5 minutes. Discard root end of shallot; finely chop shallot and garlic and add to bowl with dressing. Let potatoes cool for 30 minutes.
4. Add cooled potatoes to bowl with dressing and toss to combine. Season with salt and pepper to taste. Transfer to serving platter and sprinkle with chives. Serve.

The most flavorful fried chicken you'll ever taste.

Thai-Style Fried Chicken

With so many powerful flavors in play, the challenge was to find a balance. **by Alli Berkey**

LET'S GET ONE thing straight: I would never throw shade on a good piece of classic Southern-style fried chicken. But I do like to dress it up in a funky outfit from time to time.

Fried chicken can be so much more than the Southern standard—there are countless varieties belonging to cuisines around the United States (we have recipes for dozens of regional styles) and the world. And after my editor described the fantastic Thai-style fried chicken that he'd had at a couple of restaurants in Seattle that made him swoon, I knew I had to try to make my own version.

My editor's lowdown on the key components of this rendition? Tender dark-meat chicken (either bone-in or boneless) aggressively seasoned with garlic, chiles, soy sauce, and deeply savory fish sauce, all coated in an ultracrispy, ultracrunchy crust made with lightly sweet rice flour. As if that wasn't enough, the chicken is served with a shower of fresh herbs plus sweet chile sauce to spoon over top. Wow. I was up for the challenge.

For the chicken, I decided off the bat to use boneless thighs: They cook more quickly than bone-in parts, require less oil to fry, and are easier to eat. For the marinade, I knew that haphazard use of potent ingredients such as soy sauce and fish sauce can be dangerous; while these sauces add tons of savory flavor, they can also make your food taste out of whack or too salty if not used judiciously. I found that a balanced combo of the two—3 tablespoons of soy sauce and 2 tablespoons of fish sauce—mixed with a good dose of minced garlic and red pepper flakes was best for 2 pounds of boneless thighs; this formula provided strong but balanced flavor. After just an hour in the marinade, this seasoned chicken was ready to fry.

The coating was more challenging. A basic all-purpose flour coating, the kind used for classic craggy fried chicken, was not in play here; I was after a smoother, crunchier crust. Straight rice flour fried up plenty crunchy but was hard and tough to bite through. After several days of playing around with different flours and ingredients, I landed on a tempura-like batter made with 1 cup each of rice flour, cornstarch, and water, plus a little baking powder for lightness. You can find rice flour with the alternative flours in the supermarket (it is used in many gluten-free recipes); it makes for an incredibly crisp coating.

After weeks of testing, I landed on an easy process. Just marinate the chicken in a zipper-lock bag for convenience, stir together the batter in a bowl, dump the chicken and its marinade into the batter, and toss to coat. From there the chicken went right into the hot oil for about 5 minutes of frying, then onto paper towels set on a wire rack to absorb excess oil, and then straight onto the serving platter.

The chicken was flavorful and supercrunchy, but I hoped to crank up the flavor just one more notch. Eyeing the store-bought sweet chili sauce I had planned to use for dipping, I decided to boost its flavor by stirring in a little of the soy and fish sauces I was already using in the marinade, plus a good glug of mild rice vinegar for extra brightness. Perfect.

Big Crunch, Big Flavor

Three products make all the difference in this dish. White rice flour makes for a supercrunchy fried coating. Fish sauce, an umami powerhouse, combines with sweet chili sauce to create a marinade that adds a ton of flavor (don't worry—the chicken won't taste fishy). Serve the chicken with extra sweet chili sauce for a finishing pop of sweet-and-savory heat.

THAI-STYLE FRIED CHICKEN
Serves 4 to 6

Boneless chicken breasts can be substituted for the chicken thighs; halve the breasts horizontally before slicing them crosswise into 1-inch-thick strips. Use a Dutch oven that holds 6 quarts or more for this recipe. We developed this recipe using Bob's Red Mill Stone Ground White Rice Flour.

- 3½ tablespoons fish sauce, divided
- 3 tablespoons plus 1 teaspoon soy sauce, divided
- 7 garlic cloves, minced, divided
- 2½ teaspoons white pepper, divided
- 1½ teaspoons red pepper flakes, divided
- 2 pounds boneless, skinless chicken thighs, trimmed and sliced crosswise into 1-inch-thick strips
- 5 tablespoons Asian sweet chili sauce, plus extra for serving
- 2 tablespoons rice vinegar
- 1 cup white rice flour
- 1 cup cornstarch
- 1 cup water
- 1 teaspoon baking powder
- 3 quarts peanut or vegetable oil, for frying
- 2 tablespoons chopped fresh cilantro
- 2 tablespoons chopped fresh basil

1. Combine 2 tablespoons fish sauce, 3 tablespoons soy sauce, 6 garlic cloves, 2 teaspoons white pepper, and 1 teaspoon pepper flakes in 1-gallon zipper-lock bag. Add chicken to marinade, seal bag, and turn to distribute marinade. Refrigerate for at least 30 minutes or up to 1 hour.

2. Meanwhile, combine chili sauce, vinegar, remaining 1½ tablespoons fish sauce, remaining 1 teaspoon soy sauce, remaining 1 garlic clove, remaining ½ teaspoon white pepper, and remaining ½ teaspoon pepper flakes in large bowl. Set aside.

3. Whisk flour, cornstarch, water, and baking powder in second large bowl until smooth. Add chicken and marinade to batter and stir to coat.

4. Set wire rack in rimmed baking sheet and line with triple layer of paper towels. Add oil to large Dutch oven until it measures about 2 inches deep and heat over medium-high heat to 375 degrees.

5. Working with one-third of chicken, 1 piece at a time, remove from batter, allowing excess to drip back into bowl, and add to hot oil. Cook until deep golden brown, about 5 minutes, stirring gently as needed to prevent pieces from sticking together. Adjust burner, if necessary, to maintain oil temperature between 350 and 375 degrees. Transfer chicken to prepared rack. Return oil to 375 degrees and repeat with remaining chicken in 2 batches.

6. Add fried chicken, cilantro, and basil to bowl with reserved chili sauce mixture and toss to combine. Transfer chicken to serving platter. Serve with extra chili sauce.

Spicy Sesame Noodles with Pork

We took cues from a Sichuan favorite for our new take on a weeknight noodle dinner.

by Matthew Fairman

WHEN MY EDITORS asked me to develop a recipe for Chinese-style sesame noodles, I knew exactly which dish I wanted to use for inspiration: *dan dan* noodles. The first time I had these noodles (at an unassuming Sichuan restaurant near Boston), they opened up flavor possibilities I didn't even know existed. They were tossed with a lively, bright-red chili oil but had a tempered spiciness that was enhanced and balanced with scallion, toasted sesame oil, meaty soy sauce, tangy vinegar, and pleasantly numbing Sichuan peppercorns. The noodles were also dotted with little bits of supersavory minced pork. I ordered a second bowl before I finished the first.

For a home-cooked version of these noodles, I decided that my goal would not be to create an exact replica of an authentic Sichuan dish. Rather, I would develop a delicious, foolproof recipe that was true to the essential idea of the original but didn't require hard-to-find ingredients or a wok.

Traditional dan dan noodles have four primary components: thin, long, soft noodles; a complex sauce; a topping of salty-sweet-savory minced pork; and a punch of heat. (They usually also include pickled mustard greens, which would be too time-consuming for my weeknight goal.) For a similarly shaped but commonly available noodle, I started with plain old spaghetti cooked beyond al dente until fully tender.

Using ground pork for the topping was a no-brainer, and to enhance its flavor, I knew I'd use hoisin and soy sauces. But many recipes also call for Chinese rice wine, which can be hard to find. Luckily, we've had good results substituting dry sherry for rice wine in other recipes, and it worked great here, too. With a pound of spaghetti setting the baseline, I found that 8 ounces of pork was the right amount; the heavily seasoned pork is an accent here, not the star.

For the heart of my rich sesame sauce, a combination of toasted sesame oil and tahini (sesame paste) worked great. To achieve bold but balanced heat traditionally provided by dried Sichuan chiles, I used a combination of crushed red pepper flakes—sautéed in oil with scallion whites and garlic to bloom their flavor—and Asian chili-garlic sauce. A little rice vinegar added brightness and spark. A sprinkling of ground Sichuan peppercorns, which have a heady citrusy aroma and a mild numbing effect, imparted the signature lip-tingling sensation that's characteristic of much Sichuan cuisine. (Don't worry if you can't find them and don't want to mail-order—the dish is still great without them.)

As I was putting the finishing touches on the recipe, I was happy to see that the noodles were becoming so popular in the test kitchen that I could hardly save any for myself. Luckily, I now had a simple recipe that was fast enough for me to whip up my own batch—no sharing—as soon as I got home.

HOT SESAME NOODLES WITH PORK
Serves 4 to 6

We like to drizzle Sichuan Chili Oil (recipe follows) over the noodles before serving. Tahini is a Middle Eastern paste made from toasted sesame seeds.

- 1 **pound spaghetti**
- ¼ **teaspoon table salt, plus salt for cooking pasta**
- 2 **tablespoons toasted sesame oil**
- 8 **ounces ground pork**
- ¼ **cup soy sauce, divided**
- 5 **teaspoons hoisin sauce, divided**
- 1 **tablespoon dry sherry**
- ¼ **cup tahini**
- 2 **tablespoons rice vinegar**
- 1 **tablespoon Asian chili-garlic sauce**
- 2 **teaspoons sugar**
- ¼ **cup vegetable oil**
- 6 **scallions, white parts sliced thin, green parts sliced thin on bias**
- 3 **garlic cloves, minced**
- 1 **teaspoon red pepper flakes**
- ½ **teaspoon ground Sichuan peppercorns, plus extra for serving (optional)**

1. Bring 4 quarts water to boil in large Dutch oven. Add pasta and 1 tablespoon salt and cook, stirring often, until tender. Drain pasta and return it to pot.

Optional homemade chili oil adds irresistible heat and depth to these knockout noodles.

Add sesame oil and toss to coat; cover to keep warm.

2. Cook pork in 12-inch nonstick skillet over medium-high heat until no longer pink, 3 to 5 minutes, breaking up meat with wooden spoon. Stir in 1 tablespoon soy sauce, 1 tablespoon hoisin, and sherry and cook until all liquid has evaporated and pork is well browned, 3 to 5 minutes. Transfer pork to bowl; set aside.

3. Whisk 1 cup hot water, tahini, vinegar, chili-garlic sauce, sugar, salt, remaining 3 tablespoons soy sauce, and remaining 2 teaspoons hoisin together in bowl; set aside. Combine vegetable oil, scallion whites, garlic, pepper flakes, and peppercorns, if using, in now-empty skillet and cook over medium heat until fragrant, about 2 minutes.

4. Add oil mixture and tahini mixture to pot with pasta and toss to coat. Transfer pasta to platter and top with pork, scallion greens, and extra peppercorns, if using. Adjust consistency with additional hot water as needed. Serve.

SICHUAN CHILI OIL
Makes about ¾ cup

Note that you may need to mail-order the Sichuan peppercorns. There's no need to peel the ginger. Make sure to use toasted sesame oil here.

- ½ **cup peanut or vegetable oil**
- 2 **tablespoons red pepper flakes**
- 1 **tablespoon Sichuan peppercorns**
- 2 **teaspoons smoked paprika**
- 2 **garlic cloves, smashed and peeled**
- 1 **(½-inch) piece ginger, smashed**
- 1 **cinnamon stick**
- 2 **tablespoons toasted sesame oil**

Heat peanut oil in small saucepan over medium heat to 350 degrees. Off heat, add pepper flakes, peppercorns, paprika, garlic, ginger, and cinnamon stick. Let come to room temperature, about 1 hour. Strain oil mixture through fine-mesh strainer into jar; discard solids. Stir in sesame oil. (Oil can be stored at room temperature in airtight container for up to 3 weeks or refrigerated for up to 3 months.)

SMOKED
Chicken
Wings

Don't just wing it—follow our method for perfectly tender, juicy, char-kissed smoked chicken bliss.

by Matthew Fairman

SMOKE
SEAR
SAUCE
AND
TOSS

WHAT'S NOT TO like about cooking chicken wings—one of America's favorite finger foods—on the grill over plumes of aromatic, intensely flavored woodsmoke? Plenty, as I quickly discovered when I made a collection of what I thought were promising recipes. The resulting wings shared a host of disappointing pitfalls such as tough, rubbery skin; an acrid, ashy smokiness; dried-out meat; and overpowering, unbalanced spice rubs and sauces.

I knew I could do better. I set out to make wings that featured fully rendered skin; juicy, tender meat; and a balanced, lip-smacking combination of spice and smoke.

With chicken wings, the key is cooking them just enough to render their copious subcutaneous fat, crisp the skin, and not overcook the meat. To do this, you need the right combination of heat and time. Wings that I cooked over direct heat got too dark before the fat melted out; plus, the chicken didn't have enough time to soak up smoke. But wings that I cooked low and slow with lots of smoke and indirect heat lacked a flavorful char and dried out if I left them on a few minutes too long.

The solution, it turned out, was to combine the two cooking setups. After several days of experimenting, I perfected the method and timing by setting up a hot fire on just half the grill, starting the wings on the cooler side (with plenty of smoke rolling over them) to render and cook through and then finishing them right over the heat for color and char.

With this method, the fat was rendered out and the wings absorbed just the right amount of flavorful smoke. But I wasn't all the way home yet, as some batches were a little dry.

I knew from experience that I had to cook the wings to an internal temperature of 180 to 200 degrees for them to be perfectly tender. But doing so meant cooking out a lot of their moisture. Luckily, brining the wings for 1 hour before they hit the grill allowed them to stay moist and juicy as they cooked to doneness.

These wings were excellent; all that was left for me to do was put on the finishing touches of flavor. A barbecue-inspired spice rub of paprika, chili powder, dried oregano, and cayenne gave the wings a harmonious blend of heat and aromatic complexity. And to make the wings literally shine, I mixed melted butter with cider vinegar and ketchup to create an irresistibly savory sauce that gave the char-kissed wings a beautiful sheen. Not that you'll have much time to stand around and admire them—these wings disappear fast!

oak the wood chips in water, and then nclose them in an aluminum foil packet.

Place the wood chip packet on one side of the bottom grill grate when the charcoal is almost ready.

Pour the lit coals over the packet, keeping them on one side of the grill.

Smoke the wings on the cooler side of the grill, and then finish them directly over the heat to create flavorful char.

MOKED CHICKEN WINGS

erves 4 to 6

Ve prefer to buy whole wings and utcher them ourselves because they end to be larger than wings that come blit. If you can find only split wings, ook for larger ones. Twelve whole ings should ideally equal 3 pounds and ill yield 24 pieces (12 drumettes and 2 flats, tips discarded). Do not brine he chicken for longer than 3 hours in tep 1 or it will become too salty.

VINGS

- ¼ cup table salt, for brining
- ¼ cup sugar, for brining
- 3 pounds chicken wings, cut at joints, wingtips discarded
- 2 teaspoons paprika
- 2 teaspoons chili powder
- 1¼ teaspoons dried oregano
- 1¼ teaspoons pepper
- 1¼ teaspoons garlic powder
- 1 teaspoon sugar
- ¼ teaspoon cayenne pepper
- 2 cups wood chips

SAUCE

- 4 tablespoons unsalted butter
- 2 tablespoons cider vinegar
- 2 tablespoons ketchup
- ¼ teaspoon table salt

1. FOR THE WINGS: Dissolve salt and ¼ cup sugar in 2 quarts cold water in large container. Submerge wings in brine, cover, and refrigerate for at least 1 hour or up to 3 hours. Combine paprika, chili powder, oregano, pepper, garlic powder, 1 teaspoon sugar, and cayenne in bowl. Measure out 1 tablespoon spice mixture and set aside.

2. FOR THE SAUCE: Melt butter in small saucepan over medium-low heat. Add reserved 1 tablespoon spice mixture and cook until fragrant, about 30 seconds. Carefully add vinegar (mixture will bubble up). Bring to quick simmer, then remove from heat. Whisk in ketchup and salt. Cover and set aside.

3. Remove wings from brine and pat dry with paper towels. Sprinkle wings all over with remaining spice mixture.

4. Just before grilling, soak wood chips in water for 15 minutes, then drain. Using large piece of heavy-duty aluminum foil, wrap soaked chips in 8 by 4½-inch foil packet. (Make sure chips do not poke holes in sides or bottom of packet.) Cut 2 evenly spaced 2-inch slits in top of packet.

5A. FOR A CHARCOAL GRILL: Open bottom vent completely. Light large chimney starter mounded with charcoal briquettes (7 quarts). When top coals are partially covered with ash, place wood chip packet on 1 side of grill and pour coals evenly over half of grill, covering wood chip packet. Set cooking grate in place, cover, and open lid vent completely. Heat grill until hot and wood chips are smoking, about 5 minutes.

5B. FOR A GAS GRILL: Remove cooking grate and place wood chip packet directly on primary burner. Turn all burners to high, cover, and heat grill until hot and wood chips are smoking, about 15 minutes. Leave primary burner on high and turn off other burner(s). (Adjust primary burner [or, if using 3-burner grill, primary burner and second burner] as needed to maintain grill temperature of 400 degrees.)

6. Clean and oil cooking grate. Place wings, fatty side up, on cooler side of grill, arranging drumettes closest to coals. Cover and cook until wings are darkened in color and meat registers at least 180 degrees, about 40 minutes, flipping wings halfway through cooking.

7A. FOR A CHARCOAL GRILL: Slide half of wings to hotter side of grill and cook, uncovered, until charred in spots, 1 to 3 minutes per side. Transfer wings to platter and tent with foil. Repeat with remaining wings.

7B. FOR A GAS GRILL: Turn all burners to high and cook, uncovered, until wings are charred in spots, 5 to 7 minutes per side. Transfer wings to platter and tent with foil.

8. Reheat sauce over medium heat, about 2 minutes. Toss wings and sauce together in bowl. Serve.

Only One of the Brushes We Tried Made Cleaning the Grill Easy

y Emily Phares

EQUIPMENT
ESTING

THE CLEANER YOUR grill grate, the less food will stick to it. A good grill brush should allow you to scrub the entire cooking grate, even the hard-to-reach grate ends, and remove debris with minimal effort.

Our previous winner has had some availability issues, so we set out to find a widely available brush for both charcoal and gas grill grates. We bought eight models, priced from about $5 to almost $35 and made from a variety of materials.

Then we got to grilling: chicken thighs coated in barbecue sauce on charcoal grills and hamburgers on gas grills. In the end, every brush got the cooking grates on both types of grill satisfactorily clean, but some required a lot more work than others to get the job done, and some lacked the durability we want.

We generally like brushes with stiff bristles, and we found that shorter bristles (about ½ inch long) worked best. Brushes with triangular heads could get into corners and between grill grate bars better than those with square or rectangular heads. Models with scrapers had limited reach, as the scrapers got in the way. And shorter handles gave us better leverage without putting our hands too close to the heat.

Our new winner, the Weber 12 Inch Grill Brush, has metal bristles and a triangular head that made cleaning gunky grates a breeze. If you're worried about the risk of ingesting a loose bristle, our second-place brush, from Kona, is bristle-free. Web subscribers can read the full story at **CooksCountry.com/grillbrush19**.

Best Bristle-Free Brush

RECOMMENDED — NOT RECOMMENDED

Our Favorite

Weber 12 Inch Grill Brush
Model: 6494
Price: $7.99
Type: Stainless-steel bristle brush
Bristle Length: 0.5 in
Handle Length: 7.5 in

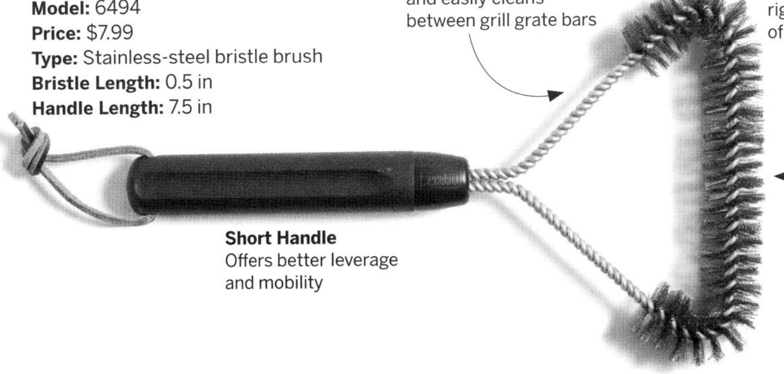

Triangular Head
Has greater versatility and easily cleans between grill grate bars

Design
Lack of scraper allowed us to clean right up to edges of grate

Short Handle
Offers better leverage and mobility

Short Bristles
Easily glide over all areas of grill grate

Text by Bryan Roof;
photos by Steve Klise

I**T'S A WEEK** after Easter and the shelves of Eagle Family Candy Company in Columbus, Ohio, are mostly empty except for the green shredded-plastic grass that lines children's Easter baskets. The chocolate bunnies are all gone. I ring a bell at the counter, and James Peck, co-owner of the company with Dee Dee Eagle, emerges from behind a deep-brown curtain that matches the walls—the shop has a dark-chocolate motif.

The Eagle Family Candy Company was founded in 1912 by George Eagle, Dee Dee's great-grandfather. Over the years, the business thrived, growing to include eight locations throughout Columbus. Today, however, the shop on North High Street is the only one remaining.

At Valentine's Day, Easter, and Christmas, Peck makes up to 100 pounds of candy a day. "The toughest part about [the business] is it's very seasonal. You gotta make your money when you can."

Peck takes me behind the curtain to see how the shop's 20-plus varieties of candy are made. The facility is divided into four adjoining rooms, each with a name. The Packing Room, where the candies are boxed to order, sits closest to the front of the store. Next is The Beater Room. Here, molten sugar is whipped with butter and flavorings in heirloom cream beaters that combine and cool the ingredients for buttercream. All the equipment is from the 1940s and '50s—stand mixers, faded copper kettles, a water-cooled steel table for tempering fudge and toffee. "We're still doing it the same way we used to," Peck says, referring not only to the equipment but also to the techniques, which were handed down by his father-in-law.

Mints are made in The Mint Room, and all the candies are finished in The En-rober Room, where they're loaded onto a conveyor belt and rolled through a curtain of melted chocolate. As the candies exit the enrober, they're marked "C" for chocolate buttercream and "V" for vanilla butter-cream. Finally, the conveyor belt transports the candies through an air-cooled tunnel to The Packing Room.

Peck hands me an Eaglette, their version of a chocolate-covered caramel turtle, one of their best sellers. He motions to another room, way in the back, where he keeps his caramel cutter. I ask what he calls that room. He looks at me sideways and says, "Oh, that room? We just call that The Back Room." For more photos of our trip to Columbus, go to **CooksCountry.com/candycompany19**.

ON THE ROAD

Owner James Peck (left) says the Eagle Family Candy Company produces more than 20 varieties of candy, but buckeyes (below) are the most popular. The vintage equipment and hands-on process make it clear that the old-fashioned way is the best.

One Sweet Century (and Counting)

Buckeye Candies

Our target: a sweet, snappy, and satisfying take on this Ohio favorite.

by Alli Berkey

AMED FOR THE nut of Ohio's state tree, this sweetened peanut butter ball dipped up to its shoulders in melted chocolate is a fan favorite across the state but particularly in Columbus (see "One Sweet Century [and Counting]"). I'm from Ohio and am a fan of buckeyes, but I find that they are often too sweet and are a mess to make. I set out to remedy both of these issues while sticking to the traditional roster of ingredients: peanut butter, butter, chocolate, and confectioners' sugar.

I tackled the peanut butter filling first. Because the combination of butter and peanut butter is naturally sticky and difficult to work with, most recipes call for adding confectioners' sugar to thicken the mixture. This extra-fine sugar incorporates easily into the sticky filling and firms it up so that it's easy to roll into balls that hold their shape. But to achieve a rollable mixture, the recipes I tried called for a lot of sugar. After a series of tests, I found a better way to get the texture I wanted: using soft but still slightly chilled butter. Any cooler and the mixture was too solid to shape; but any warmer, and it went goopy. I had to work quickly.

Next, I started scaling back the sugar, eventually arriving at an amount that gave me the best balance of structure and sweetness. Less sugar and a bit of salt meant more peanut butter flavor. I was satisfied and ready to start dipping.

Chocolate and peanut butter tango together beautifully, but when their textures are too similar they start to lose their stride. I wanted a luscious chocolate coating with a slight firmness and snap that would be a welcome contrast to the soft peanut butter filling. This meant quickly tempering the chocolate—heating and cooling it to help create a snappy texture—which the microwave makes easy. Gently melting most of the chocolate in the microwave and then stirring in a small amount of solid chocolate at the end meant that the chocolate would coat the balls easily and set to just the right snappy texture.

About that dipping: Chilling the balls for 1 hour before dipping them in the melted chocolate made it easier, and chilling the buckeyes after they were dipped ensured that the coating stayed snappy. When my coworkers devoured these sweet treats, I knew I'd done my home state proud.

To achieve the signature look of these irresistible confections, we dip chilled peanut butter balls up to their shoulders in melted chocolate.

BUCKEYE CANDIES
Makes 32 candies

We developed this recipe with Ghirardelli 60% Cacao Bittersweet Chocolate Premium Baking Bars. You can substitute bittersweet chocolate chips for the bar chocolate, but be sure to finely chop the chips. Do not use natural peanut butter here. The butter should be about 67 degrees and give slightly when pressed; it should not be so warm that it loses its shape. The chocolate is divided here, so if you don't have a scale, note that each Ghirardelli bar weighs 4 ounces. You will need 32 toothpicks for this recipe.

- 1 cup creamy peanut butter
- 8 tablespoons unsalted butter, cut into 8 pieces, softened but still cold
- ¼ teaspoon table salt
- 2½ cups (10 ounces) confectioners' sugar
- 12 ounces bittersweet chocolate, chopped fine, divided

1. Using stand mixer fitted with paddle, mix peanut butter, butter, and salt on medium speed until mixture is nearly combined with some visible pieces of butter remaining, about 30 seconds. Reduce speed to low and slowly add sugar. Mix until just combined, scraping down bowl as needed. Refrigerate for 15 minutes.

2. Line 2 large plates with parchment paper. Divide dough into 32 pieces (about 1 tablespoon each). Using your hands, gently roll dough into balls and transfer to prepared plates. Insert 1 toothpick three-quarters of the way into each ball. Freeze balls until firm, about 1 hour.

3. Microwave 10 ounces chocolate in 4-cup liquid measuring cup at 50 percent power, stirring with rubber spatula every 30 seconds, until nearly melted, 2 to 3 minutes (chocolate should still be slightly lumpy). Remove measuring cup from microwave and stir in remaining 2 ounces chocolate until melted and smooth.

4. Tilt measuring cup slightly so chocolate pools on 1 side. Working with 1 plate of balls at a time (keeping second plate in freezer), grasp toothpicks and dip balls in chocolate until covered by two-thirds. Return balls to prepared plate. Refrigerate balls, uncovered, until chocolate is set and dough is no longer frozen, about 30 minutes.

5. Remove toothpicks and serve. (Buckeyes can be refrigerated for up to 1 week.)

It's time for a simple, sweet, summery dessert. **by Morgan Bolling**

Peach Dumplings

Peaches, dough, and sweet syrup: Sometimes simple is the most satisfying.

To form a dumpling, simply roll a peach slice in a triangle of dough.

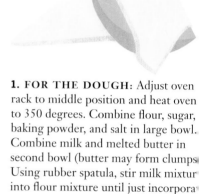

FRUIT DUMPLINGS HAD their heyday in 19th-century America. Back then, peach versions of the dessert were made by wrapping peach slices or halves in tender pastry dough and baking or boiling them, sometimes swaddled in cheesecloth, in a sweetened syrup.

Since then, recipes for peach dumplings have evolved. When I made six existing recipes for my team, we were most drawn to one from Ree Drummond, aka The Pioneer Woman. Her version leans toward the traditional: peaches wrapped in dough and cooked in syrup. Her recipe calls for wrapping frozen peach slices in store-bought crescent roll dough. She then bakes the dumplings in a syrup of sugar, butter, and—wait for it—half a can of lemon-lime soda. It's an innovative idea that produces tender dumplings, jammy fruit, and a thick, sweet syrup. I wanted to hit some of the same notes using homemade dough and no soft drinks.

I started by cutting two large fresh peaches into wedges. I wrapped the wedges in triangles of homemade pie dough and laid them snugly in an 8-inch square baking pan. I then quickly cooked a syrup of butter, sugar, and lemon juice to pour over the dumplings before baking them.

While the general construction was what I wanted, the dough wasn't as tender as I'd hoped and the dish was lacking peach flavor. For my next test, I blended slices from half a peach into the syrup. It helped, but the flavor got even better when I added ½ cup of peach preserves. This concentrated product amplified the peach flavor and helped create a thicker, more luscious sauce.

Cut dough into 12 triangles.

Turning to the dough, I explored the test kitchen archives for options that would produce the light, tender dumplings I wanted. The pie and biscuit doughs I tried were not designed to be used in such a wet application; they baked up dense and doughy. And making a yeasted crescent dough from scratch was just too much work.

One coworker suggested the dough from our Chicken and Pastry recipe. This dough is made by stirring together milk, melted butter, flour, salt, and baking powder. The significant 2 teaspoons of baking powder in the dough helps it puff into tender, fluffy noodles as it cooks. While the dough was from a savory recipe, I was intrigued by the fact that it was designed to cook in liquid. So I added a tablespoon of sugar to the recipe to bring it into dessert territory, rolled it out, assembled my dumplings, and baked. My dumplings had that excellent mix of soft texture, buttery flavor, and bright peachiness. Tasters approved.

While peach season is one of my favorite times of the year, it doesn't last forever. So to find an alternative that could work all year round, I tried frozen peaches. I found that as long as I picked out the thickest slices to wrap in the dumplings and blended the thinner slices into the sauce, the dessert was just as good.

PEACH DUMPLINGS *Serves 6 to 8*
We developed this recipe using a metal baking pan. If using a glass or ceramic baking dish, increase the baking time by 10 minutes in step 6. Serve with vanilla ice cream or whipped cream, if desired.

DOUGH
- 1½ cups (7½ ounces) all-purpose flour
- 1 tablespoon sugar
- 2 teaspoons baking powder
- ¾ teaspoon salt
- ½ cup whole milk
- 2 tablespoons unsalted butter, melted

PEACHES AND SAUCE
- 2 large fresh peaches, peeled, halved, pitted, and each half cut into 4 equal wedges, or 10 ounces frozen sliced peaches, divided
- ¾ cup water
- 6 tablespoons unsalted butter, cut into 6 pieces
- ⅓ cup (2⅓ ounces) plus 1 teaspoon sugar, divided
- Pinch salt
- ½ cup peach preserves
- 1 tablespoon lemon juice
- ¼ teaspoon ground cinnamon

1. FOR THE DOUGH: Adjust oven rack to middle position and heat oven to 350 degrees. Combine flour, sugar, baking powder, and salt in large bowl. Combine milk and melted butter in second bowl (butter may form clumps). Using rubber spatula, stir milk mixture into flour mixture until just incorporated. Turn out dough onto lightly floured counter and knead until no streaks of flour remain, about 1 minute. Return dough to large bowl, cover with plastic wrap, and set aside.

2. FOR THE PEACHES AND SAUCE: Set aside 12 peach slices. (If using frozen peaches, select 12 largest slices and freeze until ready to use.)

3. Combine water, butter, ⅓ cup sugar, salt, and remaining 4 peach slices in medium saucepan. Bring to simmer over medium-high heat and cook, stirring occasionally, until butter is melted and sugar is dissolved (and frozen peaches are thawed). Remove from heat and let cool for 5 minutes. Transfer peach mixture to blender, add peach preserves and lemon juice, and process until smooth, about 30 seconds. Set aside peach sauce.

4. Roll dough into 12-inch square, about ⅛ inch thick. Using pizza cutter or chef's knife, trim away and discard outer ½-inch edges of dough to make neat square. Cut dough in half. Working with 1 dough half at a time, cut crosswise into 3 equal rectangles, then cut each rectangle diagonally to create triangles. Repeat with second dough half. (You should have 12 triangles.)

5. Working with 1 dough triangle at a time, place 1 reserved peach slice on wide end of triangle. Roll dough around peach slice and transfer dumpling, seam side down, to 8-inch square baking pan. Repeat with remaining dough triangles and peach slices, staggering dumplings in 3 rows of 4 (dumplings will touch; this is OK).

6. Pour peach sauce over dumplings in pan. Combine cinnamon and remaining 1 teaspoon sugar in small bowl. Sprinkle dumplings with cinnamon sugar. Bake until dumplings are golden on top and syrup is bubbling in center of pan, about 45 minutes. Let cool for 10 minutes before serving.

Ham and Jack Frittata

30-MINUTE SUPPER

Grilled Swordfish with Potatoes and Salsa Verde

30-MINUTE SUPPER

Mustard Pork Tenderloin with Cauliflower

30-MINUTE SUPPER

Beef, Shiitake, and Carrot Stir-Fry

30-MINUTE SUPPER

Grilled Swordfish with Potatoes and Salsa Verde *Serves 4*

Use small red potatoes measuring 1 to 2 inches in diameter. You will need six 12-inch metal skewers for this recipe.

1½ pounds small red potatoes, halved
⅓ cup extra-virgin olive oil, divided
2⅛ teaspoons table salt, divided
1 teaspoon pepper, divided
2 (1-pound) skinless swordfish steaks, 1 to 1½ inches thick
½ cup minced fresh parsley
2 tablespoons capers, rinsed and minced
2 teaspoons finely grated lemon zest plus 4 teaspoons juice
2 anchovy fillets, rinsed and minced
1 garlic clove, minced

1. Toss potatoes with 1 tablespoon oil, ½ teaspoon salt, and ¼ teaspoon pepper in large bowl. Cover and microwave until tender, 8 to 12 minutes, stirring halfway through microwaving.
2. Cut swordfish steaks in half to make 4 equal pieces. Brush swordfish with 1 tablespoon oil and sprinkle with 1½ teaspoons salt and ½ teaspoon pepper. Thread potatoes onto six 12-inch metal skewers, with all cut sides facing in same direction. Combine parsley, capers, lemon zest and juice, anchovies, garlic, remaining oil, remaining ⅛ teaspoon salt, and remaining ¼ teaspoon pepper in bowl; set aside salsa verde.
3. Grill swordfish over hot fire until browned on both sides and swordfish registers 130 degrees, 8 to 12 minutes. Transfer swordfish to platter and tent with foil. Grill potatoes until hot throughout and charred in spots, about 3 minutes per side. Serve swordfish and potatoes with salsa verde.

Ham and Jack Frittata *Serves 4*

We like to serve this frittata with a mixed green salad.

12 large eggs
¼ cup half-and-half
2 teaspoons Dijon mustard
½ teaspoon table salt
¼ teaspoon pepper
4 ounces Monterey Jack cheese, shredded (1 cup)
2 tablespoons extra-virgin olive oil
1 green bell pepper, stemmed, seeded, and sliced thin
1 large shallot, sliced thin
6 ounces thinly sliced deli ham, cut into ½-inch pieces

1. Adjust oven rack to upper-middle position and heat oven to 400 degrees. Whisk eggs, half-and-half, mustard, salt, and pepper together in large bowl. Stir in Monterey Jack; set aside.
2. Heat oil in 12-inch nonstick skillet over medium heat until shimmering. Add bell pepper and shallot and cook until shallot is softened, about 3 minutes. Add ham and continue to cook until bell pepper is tender, about 2 minutes longer.
3. Stir egg mixture into skillet and cook, using spatula to scrape bottom of skillet, until large curds form but eggs are still very wet, about 3 minutes. Smooth egg mixture into even layer. Transfer skillet to oven and bake until top of frittata is set, 8 to 10 minutes. Let frittata rest in skillet for 5 minutes. Slide frittata onto platter and serve.

Beef, Shiitake, and Carrot Stir-Fry *Serves 4*

Soaking the steak briefly in a mild baking soda solution delivers supertender, restaurant-quality stir-fried beef.

1 (1-pound) flank steak, trimmed
½ cup plus 2 tablespoons water, divided
3 tablespoons oyster sauce, divided
2 tablespoons cornstarch, divided
¼ teaspoon baking soda
1 tablespoon soy sauce
3 tablespoons toasted sesame oil, divided
12 ounces shiitake mushrooms, stemmed and halved
3 medium carrots, peeled and cut into 2-inch matchsticks
5 scallions, white parts sliced thin, green parts cut into 1-inch pieces
3 garlic cloves, sliced thin

1. Cut steak into thirds with grain, then slice each piece thin against grain. Whisk 1 tablespoon water, 1 tablespoon oyster sauce, 1 tablespoon cornstarch, and baking soda together in medium bowl. Add beef and stir to combine. Let sit at room temperature for 15 minutes. Whisk soy sauce, ½ cup water, remaining 2 tablespoons oyster sauce, and remaining 1 tablespoon cornstarch together in second bowl; set aside.
2. Heat 1 tablespoon oil in 12-inch nonstick skillet over high heat until just smoking. Add half of beef, breaking up clumps with tongs. Cook, without stirring, until browned on bottom, about 2 minutes. Stir and continue to cook until spotty brown and no longer pink, about 30 seconds longer. Transfer to large plate. Repeat with 1 tablespoon oil and remaining beef.
3. Heat remaining 1 tablespoon oil in now-empty skillet until just smoking. Add mushrooms, carrots, and remaining 1 tablespoon water. Cover and cook until vegetables are tender, about 3 minutes. Stir in scallion whites and garlic and cook until fragrant, about 1 minute. Whisk soy sauce mixture to recombine, add to skillet, and cook until sauce has thickened. Off heat, stir in scallion greens and beef. Serve.

Mustard Pork Tenderloin with Cauliflower *Serves 4*

The vinaigrette makes a great salad dressing; make a double batch and store the remainder in the refrigerator for up to three weeks.

3 tablespoons cider vinegar
3 tablespoons whole-grain mustard
2 tablespoons maple syrup
1½ teaspoons table salt, divided
¾ teaspoon pepper, divided
5 tablespoons vegetable oil, divided
2 (1-pound) pork tenderloins, trimmed
1 tablespoon dry mustard
1 head cauliflower (2 pounds), cored and cut into 1-inch pieces
1 red bell pepper, stemmed, seeded, and cut in ¼-inch-wide strips
¼ cup fresh parsley leaves

1. Adjust oven rack to middle position and heat oven to 450 degrees. Whisk vinegar, whole-grain mustard, maple syrup, ¼ teaspoon salt, and ¼ teaspoon pepper together in bowl. Gradually whisk in ¼ cup oil. Set aside vinaigrette.
2. Sprinkle pork with dry mustard, ¾ teaspoon salt, and remaining ½ teaspoon pepper. Heat remaining 1 tablespoon oil in 12-inch nonstick skillet over medium-high heat until just smoking. Cook pork until browned on all sides, 5 to 7 minutes. Transfer pork to rimmed baking sheet and roast until meat registers 140 degrees, about 15 minutes.
3. Add cauliflower, bell pepper, and remaining ½ teaspoon salt to now-empty skillet. Cover and cook over medium-high heat, stirring occasionally, until vegetables are just tender, about 6 minutes. Stir in ½ cup vinaigrette and continue to cook until vegetables are well browned, about 6 minutes longer. Off heat, stir in parsley. Slice pork, drizzle with remaining vinaigrette, and serve with vegetables.

Israeli Couscous with Tomatoes and Chickpeas

30-MINUTE SUPPER

Pastrami Rachel Sandwiches

30-MINUTE SUPPER

Grilled Chicken Cobb Salad

30-MINUTE SUPPER

Quick Chicken Jambalaya

30-MINUTE SUPPER

Pastrami Rachel Sandwiches

Serves 4

Buy refrigerated prepared horseradish, not the shelf-stable kind, which contains preservatives and additives.

- ⅓ cup mayonnaise
- ¼ cup sweet pickle relish
- 2 tablespoons cocktail sauce
- 2 tablespoons prepared horseradish
- ½ teaspoon pepper
- 2 cups (5 ounces) coleslaw mix
- ½ teaspoon table salt
- 8 slices hearty rye bread, divided
- 4 ounces Gruyère cheese, shredded (1 cup), divided
- 12 ounces thinly sliced deli pastrami, divided
- 4 tablespoons unsalted butter, divided

1. Adjust oven rack to middle position, place rimmed baking sheet on rack, and heat oven to 200 degrees. Whisk mayonnaise, relish, cocktail sauce, horseradish, and pepper together in bowl. Toss coleslaw mix with salt and ⅓ cup mayonnaise mixture in large bowl; set aside.

2. Spread remaining mayonnaise mixture evenly on 1 side of each slice of bread. Sprinkle ½ cup Gruyère on mayonnaise side of 4 slices of bread, then top with 6 ounces pastrami. Distribute coleslaw evenly on top of pastrami, then top with remaining 6 ounces pastrami and remaining ½ cup Gruyère. Top with remaining bread, mayonnaise side down.

3. Melt 2 tablespoons butter in 12-inch nonstick skillet over medium heat. Place 2 sandwiches in skillet and cook, covered, until golden brown on first side, 2 to 4 minutes. Flip sandwiches and continue to cook, covered, until second side is golden brown and cheese is melted, 2 to 4 minutes longer. Transfer to preheated sheet in oven to keep warm. Repeat with remaining 2 tablespoons butter and remaining 2 sandwiches. Serve.

Israeli Couscous with Tomatoes and Chickpeas   *Serves 4*

Serve with shaved Parmesan or Pecorino Romano cheese.

- 3 tablespoons extra-virgin olive oil, plus extra for drizzling
- 1 small onion, chopped fine
- 3 garlic cloves, minced
- ¾ teaspoon table salt
- ½ teaspoon pepper
- ½ teaspoon red pepper flakes
- 4 cups vegetable broth
- 1 (28-ounce) can crushed tomatoes
- 1½ cups Israeli couscous
- 1 (14-ounce) can chickpeas, rinsed
- 2 tablespoons fresh oregano leaves, chopped coarse

1. Heat oil in large Dutch oven over medium heat until shimmering. Add onion and cook until softened, about 4 minutes. Stir in garlic, salt, pepper, and pepper flakes and cook until fragrant, about 30 seconds.

2. Stir in broth, tomatoes, and couscous and bring to vigorous simmer. Cook, stirring often, until couscous is tender and sauce has thickened, about 15 minutes.

3. Stir in chickpeas. Divide evenly among 4 individual bowls. Sprinkle with oregano, drizzle with extra oil, and serve.

Quick Chicken Jambalaya

Serves 4

We like to serve the jambalaya sprinkled with fresh thyme leaves. Be sure to use fully cooked chicken sausage here.

- 2 tablespoons Worcestershire sauce
- 1 tablespoon tomato paste
- 1 tablespoon ketchup
- 2 teaspoons Louisiana seasoning, divided
- 1½ cups long-grain white rice
- 2 tablespoons extra-virgin olive oil
- 1 pound boneless, skinless chicken thighs, trimmed and cut into 1-inch pieces
- 8 ounces chicken andouille sausage, sliced ¼ inch thick
- 1 green bell pepper, stemmed, seeded, and chopped
- 4 scallions, white and green parts separated and sliced thin

1. Combine Worcestershire, tomato paste, ketchup, and ½ teaspoon Louisiana seasoning in bowl; set aside. Bring 3 quarts water to boil in large saucepan over high heat. Add rice and cook, stirring occasionally, until just tender, about 12 minutes. Drain rice in fine-mesh strainer and rinse.

2. Heat oil in 12-inch nonstick skillet over medium-high heat until just smoking. Add chicken, andouille, bell pepper, scallion whites, and remaining 1½ teaspoons Louisiana seasoning and cook, stirring occasionally, until chicken is cooked through and beginning to brown, 8 to 10 minutes.

3. Add rice and Worcestershire mixture to skillet and cook, stirring frequently, until mixture is heated through and fully combined, about 5 minutes. Stir in scallion greens and serve.

Grilled Chicken Cobb Salad

Serves 4

We like to serve this salad with a sprinkling of chopped fresh chives.

- 2 ounces blue cheese, crumbled (½ cup)
- ¼ cup plus 2 tablespoons extra-virgin olive oil, divided
- 3 tablespoons red wine vinegar
- 2 teaspoons table salt, divided
- 1 teaspoon pepper, divided
- 3 romaine lettuce hearts (6 ounces each), halved lengthwise
- 2 avocados, halved and pitted
- 4 (6- to 8-ounce) boneless, skinless chicken breasts, trimmed
- 8 ounces cherry tomatoes, halved
- 4 hard-cooked large eggs, halved
- 6 slices cooked bacon, crumbled (½ cup)

1. Combine blue cheese, ¼ cup oil, vinegar, ½ teaspoon salt, and ¼ teaspoon pepper in bowl; set aside. Brush remaining 2 tablespoons oil onto cut sides of lettuce and avocados and sprinkle with ½ teaspoon salt and ½ teaspoon pepper. Pat chicken dry with paper towels and sprinkle with remaining 1 teaspoon salt and remaining ¼ teaspoon pepper.

2. Grill chicken over hot fire until browned and meat registers 160 degrees, about 5 minutes per side. Transfer to plate and tent with foil. Grill lettuce and avocados, cut sides down, until charred in spots, about 2 minutes. Using spoon, scoop avocado flesh from skin.

3. Cut lettuce in half lengthwise. Slice chicken ½ inch thick. Arrange lettuce, avocados, chicken, tomatoes, and eggs on serving platter. Top salad with bacon and drizzle with dressing. Serve.

Freezing

by Scott Kathan

Freezing occurs when a liquid is chilled enough to transform into a solid; with water, this happens at 32 degrees Fahrenheit. Most foods contain salt and sugar that lowers their freezing point below 32 degrees.

Some Foods Freeze Better Than Others

How successfully a food can be frozen and defrosted depends on many factors. Dry foods such as breads and pastries freeze really well. Dense, relatively dry carrots freeze well, while wet cucumbers become squishy and slimy when frozen and thawed. Liquid-based foods such as soups and stews freeze beautifully.

Colder Is Better

You want the air in your freezer to be as cold as possible, and you want it to be able to circulate freely around the food. Therefore, always keep your freezer at zero degrees or below, and don't overcrowd it—there should be room for air to circulate around the food on all sides.

Minimize Headroom:
Fill a plastic container to ½ inch from the top and place plastic wrap on the food's surface before adding the lid.

Double Up:
Wrap in plastic wrap or foil, and then seal in zipper-lock freezer bags.

The Best Frozen Vegetables

Broccoli, cauliflower, carrots, and green beans also freeze well.

PEAS

CORN

LIMA BEANS

PEARL ONIONS

SPINACH

The Worst?
Bell peppers, cucumbers, and mushrooms

Most vegetables contain enzymes that can compromise flavor, texture, and color when frozen. To deactivate these enzymes, quickly blanch and shock the raw vegetables before freezing them.

Freeze Your Cheese

Our testing has proven that most cheeses freeze surprisingly well. Wrap the cheese tightly in plastic wrap, and then seal it in a zipper-lock freezer bag, squeezing out as much air as you can. Stored this way, cheese freezes beautifully for up to two months.

TEST KITCHEN TIP:
Use small wire shelving to maximize space and airflow.

Meanwhile, Behind the Refrigerator . . .
Keep the exterior coils and filters on the back of your freezer and refrigerator clean to help maximize cooling efficiency; unplug before vacuuming or dusting. Clean the coils and filters at least twice a year.

FREEZE 'EM
- Butter
- Coffee Beans
- Nuts
- Unfrosted Cakes
- Bacon
- Whole-Wheat Flour
- Oatmeal
- Grated Ginger
- Tomato Paste
- Chipotle in Adobo
- Coconut Milk
- Wine

Want to see what else you can freeze? Web members can visit CooksCountry.com/leftovers19 to learn more.

Wrap Master
Vacuum sealers remove oxygen from customized storage bags, creating a snug seal around food that makes it possible to freeze it longer while avoiding freezer burn. The test kitchen's favorite model is the **Gourmia GVS9945 Handheld Vacuum Sealer Set ($22)**.

Enemies of Frozen Food: Ice and Air

Freezing preserves food by halting (or greatly slowing) the growth of bacteria and by slowing enzymatic reactions that naturally lead to decomposition. All foods contain water; in the freezer, that water freezes and expands. In produce, this ice breaks the cell walls, resulting in fruits or vegetables that are less structurally sound and more watery once defrosted (since the water that was trapped inside the cells is freed). If frozen food isn't wrapped tightly, water from within the food can form ice crystals on its surface and compromise flavor. Before freezing, wrap food tightly in plastic wrap and/or aluminum foil and then seal it in a zipper-lock freezer bag.

ICE CRYSTALS

SOGGY VEG

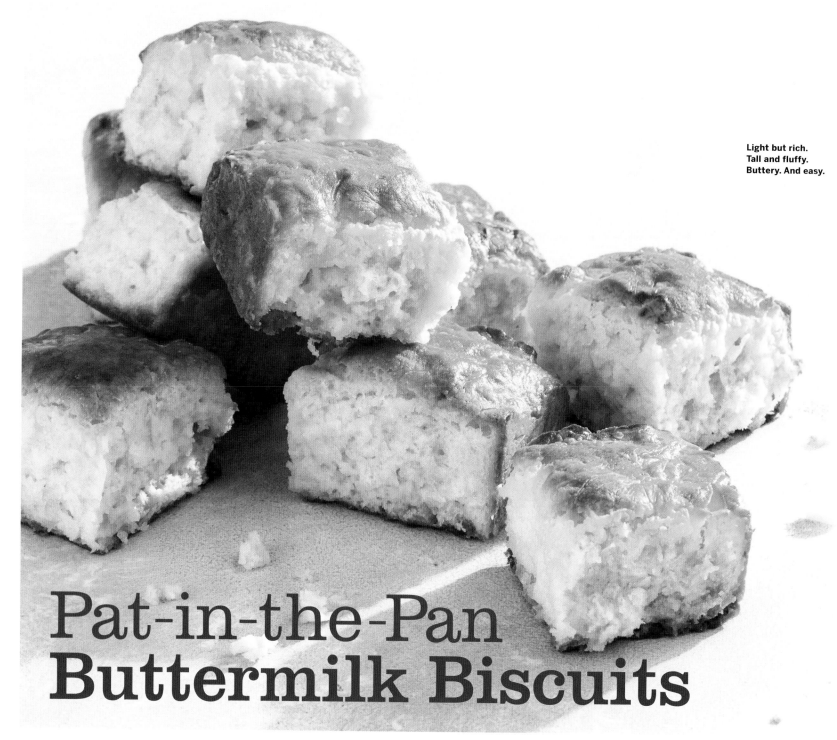

Light but rich.
Tall and fluffy.
Buttery. And easy.

Pat-in-the-Pan
Buttermilk Biscuits

Biscuits belong at every meal. So they need to be easy. **by Cecelia Jenkins**

I DEFY YOU to corral the range of the humble biscuit. Biscuits are as welcome at breakfast as they are at lunch. They're a treat at dinner, and make a rib-sticking afternoon snack. And they take a thousand forms: square, round, large, small, stamped, dropped, flaky, fluffy, cheesy, and so on.

But in my mind, because they are so versatile, biscuits are the kind of thing you want to know how to make by hand—and by heart. I was determined to create a simple buttermilk biscuit recipe with a no-brainer method that yielded buttery biscuits with soft, fluffy interiors and tangy buttermilk flavor.

Biscuit making usually starts with breaking up bits of cold butter into flour. You then add liquid and form biscuits from the resulting dough. In the oven, the cold bits of butter melt and produce steam, creating a fluffy interior. Rather than breaking out the food processor to get my dough to the right consistency, I chose to use my hands— the best tool in the kitchen—for this important task.

I dropped ½-inch pieces of cold butter into my dry ingredients (flour, salt, and leavener) and then pinched the pieces between my fingers to break them into pea-size, flour-coated chunks (larger pieces left craters in the biscuits). I stirred in buttermilk, dumped the shaggy dough out onto a heavily floured counter, and rolled it to an even thickness, adding flour as needed to combat stickiness. I stamped out the biscuits with a round cutter, nestled them into a baking pan, and baked. The biscuits were tasty, but they weren't as tall as I'd hoped. Worse, I was left with a messy counter and lots of dough scraps.

To eliminate scraps, I decided to make square biscuits (no stamping). For a taller result, I would tightly fill an 8-inch square baking pan using all the dough and crowding the biscuits to encourage them to bake upward, not outward. I cut my next batch of dough into squares and squished them into the pan. I was happy to see them bake up fluffy and tall, and each one pulled apart nicely from the group. But I still had an annoying mess of flour on my counter.

That's when a colleague offered a simple yet extraordinary suggestion: Skip the counter and just dump the dough from the bowl directly into the pan. Talk about an aha moment!

This method was a breeze and eliminated the mess. After patting the dough evenly into the pan, I made a few swift cuts with my bench scraper to create nine squares (two cuts in each direction—think tic-tac-toe) and then slid the pan into the oven. Thirty minutes later, I had golden-topped, tangy biscuits with snow-white, fluffy insides—and they were a whopping 3 inches tall.

A few details: I chose cake flour for extra fluffiness, though heavier all-purpose flour is an acceptable substitute. I used a combination of baking powder and baking soda for the most impressive height and least chance of off-flavors (too much baking powder can taste tinny). When pinching the butter into the flour, I found that it was best to move fast and not mush too aggressively; the heat from fingers can compromise the result.

Now, when I need biscuits, my hands know the way. After one round with these beauties, yours will, too.

PAT-IN-THE-PAN BUTTERMILK BISCUITS

Makes 9 biscuits

If you have leftover buttermilk, it can be frozen in ice cube trays, transferred to zipper-lock freezer bags, and frozen for up to a month. Upon thawing, the whey and the milk solids will separate; simply whisk the buttermilk back together before using it. We developed this recipe using Softasilk cake flour. This recipe can easily be doubled to yield 15 biscuits: Use a 13 by 9-inch baking pan and extend the baking time by about 15 minutes. We developed this recipe using a metal baking pan.

- 12 tablespoons unsalted butter, divided
- 4 cups (16 ounces) cake flour, plus extra for sprinkling
- 2 teaspoons baking powder
- ½ teaspoon baking soda
- 2 teaspoons table salt
- 2 cups buttermilk, chilled

1. Adjust oven rack to middle position and heat oven to 450 degrees. Grease 8-inch square baking pan with 1 tablespoon butter. Cut 10 tablespoons butter into ½-inch pieces and freeze until chilled, about 15 minutes. Let remaining 1 tablespoon butter sit at room temperature to soften.

2. Whisk flour, baking powder, baking soda, and salt together in bowl. Add chilled butter to flour mixture and smash butter between your fingertips into pea-size pieces. Gently stir in buttermilk until no dry pockets of flour remain. Using rubber spatula, transfer dough to prepared pan.

3. Lightly sprinkle extra flour evenly over dough to prevent sticking. Using your floured hands, pat dough into even layer and into corners of pan. Using bench scraper sprayed with vegetable oil spray, cut dough into 9 equal squares (2 cuts by 2 cuts), but do not separate. Bake until golden brown on top, about 30 minutes.

4. Let biscuits cool in pan for 5 minutes. Using thin metal spatula, slide biscuits onto wire rack. Brush tops with softened butter. Let cool for 10 minutes. Pull biscuits apart at cuts and serve warm.

FLAKY LAYERS
Lots of work

FLUFFY INTERIOR
Fast and easy

Flaky versus Fluffy

There are many kinds of biscuits—and we're fans of them all. The flaky biscuit shown on the left is made using the careful process of laminating (a technique also used to make croissants), which involves rolling out the dough, folding it up, and repeating several times to create alternating layers of butter and dough. The results are great, but the path is steep. Our Pat-in-the-Pan Buttermilk Biscuits, shown on the right, are much easier to make and bake up soft and fluffy—perfect for mopping up sauce or gravy.

THE AMERICAN TABLE

The Pillsbury Doughboy's real name is Poppin' Fresh.

Refrigerators were still a novelty in many corners of the United States in 1931 when Lively B. Willoughby of Louisville, Kentucky, patented his process for producing refrigerated biscuit dough using a special baking powder developed by Fleischmann's Yeast Company and a cylindrical container originally developed for epsom salts. Willoughby's product was called Ye Old Kentuckie Buttermilk Biscuits and sold well throughout the 1930s and '40s.

After a few corporate twists and turns, the Pillsbury Company entered the picture in 1951, selling refrigerator biscuits made using Willoughby's process with a few improvements. The 1950s saw Pillsbury's national profile explode—the wildly popular Pillsbury Bake-Off was televised in prime time on CBS, and the corporate jingle ("Nothin' says lovin' like somethin' from the oven") became ubiquitous. But it wasn't until 1965 that the stop-motion Pillsbury Doughboy (real name: Poppin' Fresh) burst onto the scene. His signature giggle was originally voiced by Paul Frees, the actor who also provided the voice of Boris in *The Rocky and Bullwinkle Show*.

Pat and Portion

Pat Dough into Greased Pan
No kneading or rolling required—simply stir together the dough, transfer it to the pan, and pat it in to fill.

Make Two Cuts in Each Direction
A greased bench scraper makes easy work of cutting nine biscuits in the pan—no rolling pin or cutter required.

Buttermilk or Bust

For many of our recipes that call for buttermilk, we offer a substitution: clabbered (or acidulated) milk. Curious if that would work here, we tested clabbered whole, low-fat, skim, and soy milks in these biscuits—and none of them worked. Either the dough was too wet to pat into the pan and cut or the flavor of the biscuits wasn't up to snuff. Buy buttermilk—these biscuits are worth it (if you have any left over, you can freeze it).

Chicken with Poblanos and Cream

Sure, you can make a cream sauce by cooking a roux and whisking in milk or cream.
But there's an easier way—just use crema. **by Natalie Estrada**

This rich, creamy sauce is a perfect foil for the smoky charred poblanos.

THE MEXICAN DISH *rajas con crema* ("strips with cream") features strips of charred poblano peppers folded into a rich mixture of cream, onions, and sometimes corn. When I was living in Mexico City, I was always excited to see this dish at taco joints—it never failed to comfort me after a long day of restaurant work.

Dark-emerald poblanos, an American supermarket staple, have a rich chile flavor and an unpredictable punch of mild heat. I set out to create a weeknight-friendly supper of chicken with *rajas* using this approachable, ultratasty pepper.

Poblanos are transformed when charred—their inherent fruity flavor is dramatically enhanced with subtle smokiness. But I quickly found that the peppers were too spicy when I broiled or grilled them whole because so much of a poblano's heat is concentrated in the seeds. I decided to stem, halve, and seed the peppers to tone down the heat before charring them under the broiler. Since I was charring only the skin side of the halved peppers, I didn't have to flip them partway though broiling.

Once the pepper halves were charred, I transferred them to a bowl and covered them so the steam would loosen the skins. When they were cool enough to handle, I peeled off the blackened skins and cut the flesh into rajas. The rest of the dish came together quickly.

I browned chicken breasts in a nonstick skillet (I'd finish cooking them in the sauce), transferred them to a plate, and cooked the onions in the same pan. Traditionally this dish calls for a sauce based on Mexican or Central American crema, which come in two main forms: It can be a shelf-stable table cream (usually canned and called *media crema*), or it can be found in the refrigerated dairy aisle. The refrigerated version is easier to find and thus was my choice here; it's typically a combination of heavy cream, sour cream, cream cheese, and stabilizers. This crema has a rich, tangy flavor and (thanks to the stabilizers) doesn't separate or break when heated.

I stirred the crema into my mixture of onions, poblanos, and garlic; brought it all to a boil; and then nestled the seared chicken back in the skillet and turned down the heat so the chicken could gently cook through in the simmering sauce. Once the chicken was fully cooked, I removed it and reduced the sauce until it was nice and thick. A sprinkling of cilantro added freshness, and a squirt of lime juice brought all the flavors into focus.

Whether you stuff it into warmed tortillas or serve it with some rice, I hope this version of rajas con crema becomes a part of your weeknight dinner routine.

CHICKEN WITH RAJAS
Serves 4
Crema can typically be found in the refrigerated dairy aisle of the supermarket. If you can't find it, you can substitute 1 cup of heavy cream plus 2 tablespoons of cream cheese. Whisk the mixture once it's in the skillet to ensure that the cream cheese dissolves.

Preparing the Poblanos

Remove Stems
Cut around the stem and pull it out.

Halve and Seed Poblanos
Remove the seeds with your gloved hands.

Broil; Then Steam
Cover the poblanos to loosen their skins.

Scrape Off Skins
Use a spoon to remove the charred skins.

Our secret? Toast the rice, and then cook it in a combination of bean liquid and chicken broth.

1 pound poblano chiles, stemmed, halved, and seeded
4 (6- to 8-ounce) boneless, skinless chicken breasts, trimmed
¼ teaspoon pepper
1 teaspoon table salt, divided
2 tablespoons vegetable oil, divided
3 onions, halved and sliced ¼ inch thick (3 cups)
2 garlic cloves, minced
1 cup Mexican crema
2 tablespoons chopped fresh cilantro
2 teaspoons lime juice

. Adjust oven rack 6 inches from roiler element and heat broiler. rrange poblanos skin side up on uminum foil–lined rimmed bak- g sheet. Broil until skins are well harred, 6 to 8 minutes, rotating heet halfway through broiling. ransfer poblanos to bowl, cover ith plastic wrap, and let steam or 5 minutes. Using spoon, scrape harred skin from poblanos (do not nse to remove skin). Slice peppers to ¼-inch-thick strips; set aside.

. Pat chicken dry with paper towels nd sprinkle all over with pepper and ½ teaspoon salt. Heat 1 tablespoon il in 12-inch nonstick skillet over nedium-high heat until shimmering. dd chicken and cook until browned n both sides, 3 to 5 minutes per ide. Transfer chicken to plate.

. Reduce heat to medium. Add emaining 1 tablespoon oil, onions, nd ¼ teaspoon salt to now-empty killet and cook, stirring occasionally, ntil onions are lightly browned nd beginning to soften, about minutes. Add garlic, poblanos, nd remaining ¼ teaspoon salt and ook until fragrant, about 1 minute. dd crema and bring to boil. Nestle hicken into poblano mixture. Re- luce heat to medium-low, cover, nd cook until chicken registers 60 degrees, 10 to 12 minutes.

. Transfer chicken to carving oard, tent with aluminum foil, nd let rest for 5 minutes. Return killet to medium heat and cook ntil spatula leaves distinct trail vhen dragged through pepper mix- ure, 2 to 4 minutes. Off heat, stir n cilantro and lime juice. Season vith salt and pepper to taste. Slice hicken and serve with rajas.

Black Beans and Rice

The goal: a quicker route to ultimate comfort. **by Natalie Estrada**

CUBAN-STYLE BLACK BEANS and rice are a common side dish in Miami. But it can take days to make, from softening and cooking the beans to building the layers of flavor that characterize the dish. I wanted a simpler way.

Many versions of beans and rice are built on *sofrito*, a fragrant, flavorful base of vegetables and herbs. So that's where I started. In many kitchens, green bell peppers, sweet red ají peppers, and onions make the base for a sofrito. Unfortunately, ají peppers are not widely available, but a side-by-side test showed that my tasters liked a sofrito made with only bell peppers just as much here.

Instead of pureeing the mixture, as many sofrito recipes call for, I opted to dice the vegetables and cook them in a nonstick skillet until they just started to brown. I then added garlic, potent oregano, and cumin for warmth.

Traditionally, the rice is cooked in the pot liquor left over from precooking the dried beans, giving it an inky hue and a bit of earthy flavor. Since I was using canned beans, I reserved their liquid after straining them and bolstered it with enough chicken broth to cook the rice. It was a perfect stand-in for the pot liquor.

For the rice, I started by rinsing away its exterior starch so it would cook up fluffy. After cooking the sofrito and setting it aside, I toasted the rinsed rice in the skillet for a few minutes to unlock its nutty flavor. I added the sofrito, along with the beans and liquid, to the toasted rice and covered the skillet. After about 20 minutes, I had lovely rice and beans that had stayed intact.

Cuban-style beans and rice often includes salt pork, a commonly available but frequently overlooked ingredient. Nestling a few cubes of it into the rice just before adding the liquid allowed it to render its fat, delivering porky flavor and silky texture throughout.

As labor-intensive as the original? Not even close. But every bit as comforting and flavorful? You bet.

Add Salt Pork for Depth
This meaty, salty cured pork infuses the beans and rice with savory flavor.

BLACK BEANS AND RICE
Serves 4 to 6
If you can't find salt pork, you can substitute two slices of bacon; the dish will have a smokier flavor. Rinse the rice in a fine-mesh strainer under running water until the water runs almost clear, about 1½ minutes, stirring the rice a few times with your hand.

1 (15-ounce) can black beans
2¼ cups chicken broth, plus extra as needed
2 tablespoons vegetable oil, divided
¾ cup finely chopped onion
¾ cup finely chopped green bell pepper
½ teaspoon table salt
½ teaspoon pepper
3 garlic cloves, minced
1 teaspoon dried oregano
¾ teaspoon ground cumin
1½ cups long-grain white rice, rinsed
4 ounces salt pork, cut into 4 pieces
1 bay leaf

1. Place beans in fine-mesh strainer set over 4-cup liquid measuring cup and let drain for 5 minutes; reserve bean liquid. Add enough broth to bean liquid to equal 2½ cups and stir to combine. Set aside beans and broth mixture.
2. Heat 1 tablespoon oil in 12-inch nonstick skillet over medium-high heat until shimmering. Add onion, bell pepper, salt, and pepper and cook until vegetables are softened and just beginning to brown, about 6 minutes. Stir in garlic, oregano, and cumin and cook until fragrant, about 30 seconds. Transfer vegetable mixture to bowl; set aside.
3. Heat remaining 1 tablespoon oil in now-empty skillet over medium-high heat. Add rice and cook, stirring frequently, until edges begin to turn translucent and rice is fragrant, about 2 minutes. Stir in salt pork, bay leaf, beans, broth mixture, and vegetable mixture and bring to boil (submerge salt pork as best you can). Cover, reduce heat to low, and cook, without stirring, for 20 minutes.
4. Let stand, covered, off heat for 10 minutes. Discard salt pork and bay leaf. Gently fluff rice with fork. Season with salt and pepper to taste. Serve.

Pork GYRO

Could we re-create this Greek American favorite without a live fire and a spit?

by Alli Berkey

Sliced lettuce, cucumber, and red onion add freshness and crunch. The creamy, easy-to-make tzatziki sauce ties it all together.

PICTURE A TOWERING vertical spit packed with layers of marinated pork. Flames lick the meat as the spit turns, slowly rendering the fat in each layer to create juicy, charred pork flavored with plenty of garlic and oregano.

Gyro ("YEE-ro") is a Greek word that loosely translates as "turn," which the spit continues to do as the cook thinly slices the meat into a warm pita. The gyro is then loaded with toppings: onion, tomato, lettuce, tzatziki (yogurt-cucumber sauce) and sometimes even French fries. Sounds good, doesn't it? But could it be made at home?

Many existing recipes are extraordinarily involved, calling for marinating the meat for several days and using convoluted cooking techniques to try to replicate the spit-cooked meat. I cooked my way through a few and then set them aside to start from scratch. I was determined to get the intense, garlicky kick I was looking for with just an hour of marinating. The key: Pack that marinade with extra garlic, oregano, coriander, paprika, and pepper, plus plenty of salt. Once roasted, the pork was full of flavor. But it was just a pork roast. I needed to settle on a cut and devise a new technique to achieve that charred but still juicy meat.

Pork tenderloin was too lean, and country-style ribs were too inconsistent. Pork butt did the job. Taken from the shoulder of the pig, pork butt is marbled with flavorful fat. When the roasted meat is thinly sliced, you get rich, juicy strips with deeply browned edges. After a series of tests, I found that the best way to cook 4 pounds of meat (enough for eight pitas) was a three-part process.

I first cut the meat into four equal pieces and roasted it, covered, on a rack

Turning a Pork Roast into Flavorful, Tender Gyro Filling

Cut the pork butt roast lengthwise into four equal steaks.

Set the pork on a wire rack, cover it, and roast it to render the excess fat.

Roast the pork uncovered to dry the exterior so it will brown better.

Broil the pork on only one side until it develops deep, flavorful char.

set in an aluminum foil–lined rimmed baking sheet; the foil cover trapped steam and jump-started the rendering. After 40 minutes, I removed the cover and roasted the pork for 20 minutes, until it was cooked through. Finally, for flavorful char, I broiled it for 10 minutes.

Once I had let the meat rest (to help its fibers relax and redistribute the juices), I sliced it thin and tossed it with the juices left on the carving board. Piled onto toasted pita bread and topped with a quick stir-together tzatziki sauce, this pork was intensely flavorful and totally satisfying. My coworkers claimed that it was the best lunch of the week.

PORK GYRO *Makes 8 sandwiches*
Pork butt roast is often labeled Boston butt in the supermarket. Buy a boneless pork butt roast from the center of the shoulder that is in one piece. Do not use a picnic roast, which often comes tied in netting or string and unravels into several smaller pieces.

GYRO
- 1 **(4-pound) boneless pork butt roast, trimmed**
- ½ **cup plus 1 tablespoon extra-virgin olive oil, divided**
- 6 **garlic cloves, minced**
- 1½ **tablespoons dried oregano**
- 1½ **tablespoons kosher salt**
- 1 **tablespoon ground coriander**
- 1 **tablespoon paprika**
- 2 **teaspoons pepper**
- 8 **(8-inch) pita breads**
- 1 **romaine lettuce heart (6 ounces), sliced thin**
- 1 **small red onion, halved and sliced thin**
  Lemon wedges

Thinly slice the pork and toss it with the juices on the carving board.

TZATZIKI
- 1 **English cucumber, halved lengthwise and seeded, divided**
- 1½ **cups plain Greek yogurt**
- 2 **tablespoons extra-virgin olive oil**
- 1 **tablespoon lemon juice**
- 1 **tablespoon chopped fresh dill**
- 1½ **teaspoons kosher salt**
- 1 **large garlic clove, minced**
- ½ **teaspoon pepper**

1. FOR THE GYRO: Slice pork lengthwise into 4 equal steaks, about 1 inch thick (if steaks are thicker than 1 inch, press them with your hand to 1-inch thickness). Place pork in 1-gallon zipper-lock bag. Whisk ½ cup oil, garlic, oregano, salt, coriander, paprika, and pepper together in bowl. Add marinade to bag with pork. Seal bag and turn to distribute marinade evenly. Refrigerate for at least 1 hour or up to 24 hours.
2. Adjust oven rack 6 inches from broiler element and heat oven to 350 degrees. Line rimmed baking sheet with aluminum foil and set wire rack in sheet. Remove pork from marinade and place on prepared wire rack; discard marinade.
3. Cover sheet tightly with foil and transfer to oven. Roast until pork registers 100 degrees, about 40 minutes. Remove sheet from oven and carefully remove foil so steam escapes away from you. Return sheet to oven and continue to roast until pork registers 160 degrees, 20 to 25 minutes longer.
4. FOR THE TZATZIKI: While pork roasts, shred half of cucumber on large holes of box grater. Combine shredded cucumber, yogurt, oil, lemon juice, dill, salt, garlic, and pepper in bowl. Refrigerate until ready to serve. Slice remaining cucumber thin and set aside.
5. Leave sheet in oven and turn on broiler. Broil until pork is well browned on top side only, about 10 minutes. Transfer pork to carving board and let rest for 5 minutes.
6. Brush 1 side of pitas with remaining 1 tablespoon oil. Place 4 pitas oiled side up on now-empty wire rack. Broil until pitas are soft and lightly toasted, about 1 minute. Repeat with remaining 4 pitas.
7. Slice pork crosswise very thin. Toss pork with accumulated juices on carving board. Divide pork evenly among pitas and top with lettuce, onion, sliced cucumber, and tzatziki. Serve with lemon wedges.

Greek Tomato Salad

How you handle the tomatoes makes all the difference in this fresh summer salad.

by Ashley Moore

THE IDEA OF a bright, sunny Greek salad—juicy tomatoes, briny feta and olives, crisp greens, and herby dressing—often outpaces the execution. Some sad versions I've had featured pink, hard, and tasteless tomatoes; tired lettuce; and ho-hum dressing. Since amazing peak-season tomatoes are available in the summertime, I thought I could make a better, fresher version.

Ripe tomatoes were a must—otherwise, what's the point? But even ripe tomatoes need salt to reach their full potential, and I found that salting the tomatoes a good half-hour before assembling the salad had the dual benefits of deeply seasoning them and draining off some excess moisture to concentrate their flavor. Sliced cucumber received the same treatment (I salted and drained it with the tomatoes) and benefited similarly. And don't worry—the amounts of salt called for here won't make the salad too salty. Finally, since the vegetables were so great, I decided to forgo the lettuce entirely.

For the vinaigrette, I whisked together some red wine vinegar, lemon juice, and extra-virgin olive oil—a pleasantly sharp and flavorful base. I added some sliced pickled peppers and shallot to the dressing for a little texture and a big pop of flavor. Fresh mint provided a cooling Mediterranean element while fresh oregano anchored the salad in Greece.

I transferred my new Greek salad to a platter and topped it with a sprinkling of feta cheese; the flavors shone as bright as the sun on the Aegean Sea. My colleagues were quick converts and fast fans. No more of that mediocre Greek salad for me, thank you.

TEAR THE MINT
Chopped mint will turn black; torn won't.

GREEK TOMATO SALAD
Serves 4 to 6
Ripe tomatoes are essential to the success of this salad. For a crunchy twist, serve the salad with some crushed pita chips sprinkled over top.

- 1½ **pounds ripe tomatoes, cored**
- ½ **English cucumber, halved lengthwise and sliced crosswise ⅛ inch thick**
- 1½ **teaspoons table salt, divided**
- 5 **tablespoons extra-virgin olive oil**
- 2 **tablespoons red wine vinegar**
- 1 **tablespoon lemon juice**
- ½ **teaspoon pepper**
- ⅓ **cup thinly sliced pepperoncini**
- 1 **shallot, sliced into thin rings**
- ¼ **cup fresh mint leaves, torn**
- 1 **tablespoon chopped fresh oregano**
- 4 **ounces feta cheese, crumbled (1 cup)**

1. Cut tomatoes into ½-inch-thick wedges, then cut wedges in half crosswise. Toss tomatoes, cucumber, and 1 teaspoon salt together in bowl; transfer to colander and let drain for 30 minutes.
2. While vegetables drain, whisk oil, vinegar, lemon juice, pepper, and remaining ½ teaspoon salt together in large bowl. Add pepperoncini and shallot and let sit until slightly softened, about 15 minutes.
3. Add mint, oregano, and drained vegetables to bowl with dressing and toss to combine. Season with salt and pepper to taste. Transfer to platter and sprinkle with feta. Serve.

Mixed Berry Scones

These berry scones, a favorite from our archive, are sweet, buttery, and simple to make.

by Matthew Fairman

MIXED BERRY SCONES
Makes 8 scones

Work the dough just until it comes together; do not overmix. For the best results, work quickly to keep the butter and berries as cold as possible. Note that the butter is divided in this recipe. If your berry mix contains strawberries, cut them in half before tossing them with the confectioners' sugar in step 1. An equal amount of frozen blueberries, raspberries, blackberries, or strawberries (halved) can be used in place of the mixed berries, if desired.

SCONES
- 8¾ ounces (1¾ cups) frozen mixed berries
- 3 tablespoons confectioners' sugar
- 3 cups (15 ounces) all-purpose flour
- 12 tablespoons unsalted butter, cut into ½-inch pieces and chilled, divided
- ⅓ cup (2⅓ ounces) granulated sugar
- 1 tablespoon baking powder
- 1¼ teaspoons table salt
- ¾ cup plus 2 tablespoons whole milk
- 1 large egg plus 1 large yolk

GLAZE
- 2 tablespoons unsalted butter, melted
- 1 tablespoon honey

1. FOR THE SCONES: Adjust oven rack to upper-middle position and heat oven to 425 degrees. Line rimmed baking sheet with parchment paper. Toss berries with confectioners' sugar in bowl until evenly covered; freeze until needed.

2. Process flour, 6 tablespoons butter, granulated sugar, baking powder, and salt in food processor until butter is fully incorporated, about 15 seconds. Add remaining 6 tablespoons butter and pulse until butter is reduced to pea-size pieces, 10 to 12 pulses. Transfer mixture to large bowl. Stir in berries.

3. Beat milk and egg and yolk together in separate bowl. Make well in center of flour mixture and pour in milk mixture. Using rubber spatula, gently stir, scraping from sides of bowl and folding inward until very shaggy dough forms and some bits of flour remain. Do not overmix.

4. Turn out dough onto well-floured counter and, if necessary, knead briefly until dough just comes together, about 3 turns. Using your floured hands and bench scraper, shape dough into 12 by 4-inch rectangle, about 1½ inches thick. Using knife or bench scraper, cut dough crosswise into 4 equal rectangles. Cut each rectangle diagonally into 2 triangles (you should have 8 triangles total). Transfer triangles to prepared sheet. Bake until scones are lightly golden, 16 to 18 minutes, rotating sheet halfway through baking.

5. FOR THE GLAZE: While scones bake, combine melted butter and honey in small bowl.

6. Remove sheet from oven and brush tops of scones evenly with glaze. Return sheet to oven and continue to bake until scones are golden brown, 5 to 8 minutes longer. Transfer scones to wire rack and let cool for at least 10 minutes before serving.

Step by Step

1. Prepare
Heat the oven; prepare the baking sheet; freeze the sugared berries.
Why? Sugaring the berries adds sweetness; plus, the cornstarch in the confectioners' sugar absorbs excess juice. Freezing the berries helps prevent their juice from bleeding into the dough.

2. Process dry ingredients
Process the flour, half the butter, the sugar, the baking powder, and the salt until the butter is fully incorporated.
Why? The key is to coat the flour with the butter so that the flour doesn't form as much gluten and the scones stay tender.

3. Add more butter
Add the remaining butter and pulse until the butter is broken into pea-size pieces.
Why? The larger pieces of butter melt in the oven, creating small pockets of buttery flavor and producing steam that promotes a flaky, tender texture.

4. Add berries
Transfer the flour mixture to a bowl and gently stir in the berries.
Why? Use a light hand when stirring in the berries so they don't break apart and make a juicy mess. It's easier to incorporate the berries before adding the heavy liquids.

5. Mix in wet ingredients
Combine the milk and the egg and yolk. Make a well in the flour mixture and pour in the milk mixture.
Why? Milk and eggs add richness and structure. Pouring them into a well makes it easier to incorporate them into the dry ingredients and keeps the berries intact.

Essential Tools

Bench Scraper

A bench scraper is handy for portioning and cutting doughs and scraping sticky flour residue from counters, but it is also good for scooping up and transporting prepped ingredients such as herbs, vegetables, and pieces of meat for stir-fries. Like a good pair of tongs, a good bench scraper becomes an extension of your hands. Our favorite is the **Dexter-Russell 6" Dough Cutter/Scraper—Sani-Safe Series ($11)**.

Parchment Paper

The winner of our recent testing of parchment paper brought about a revelation: Parchment that lies flat for storage, instead of the more traditional roll, is much more convenient because it eliminates the problem of curling edges. Our new favorite is a mail-order product: **King Arthur Flour Parchment Paper 100 Half-Sheets ($23 plus shipping)**. These precut sheets store flat and are the perfect size to fit in standard rimmed baking sheets.

Silicone Spatula

A heatproof silicone spatula is an essential tool. We use them for stirring sizzling onions, scrambling eggs, folding whipped egg whites into batters, and scraping down bowls, among many other uses. Our favorite all-purpose model is the **Di Oro Living Seamless Silicone Spatula—Large ($13)**. We also like the **Rubbermaid 13.5" High-Heat Scraper ($13).** It has a larger head and longer handle that can reach into deep pots and bowls.

TO MAKE AHEAD

After cutting dough into triangles in step 4, transfer scones to parchment paper–lined baking sheet and freeze. Transfer frozen scones to zipper-lock freezer bag and freeze for up to 2 months. When ready to bake, heat oven to 375 degrees and extend baking time in step 4 to 23 to 26 minutes. (Baking time in step 6 does not change.)

Shaping the Scones

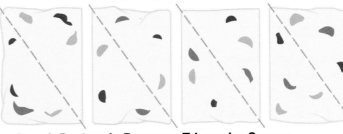

How a Dough Rectangle Becomes Triangular Scones

First, roll the dough into a rectangle that is 12 inches long, 4 inches wide, and 1½ inches thick. Second, cut the rectangle crosswise into 4 equal rectangles. Third, cut each rectangle diagonally into two triangles, for a total of eight scones.

Keys to Tender Scones

Gluten is an elastic protein network that is formed when flour is mixed with liquid; gluten formation is accelerated when the dough (or batter) is manipulated via mixing or kneading. To prevent excess gluten formation (and chewy scones), we did five things.

"Waterproof" the Flour
Mix the flour and half the butter in the food processor so that the butter breaks down and coats the flour. This prevents the flour from absorbing too much liquid.

Stir the Berries into the Flour Mixture
Stir the cold, sugared berries into the dry mixture before liquid is added. This way the berries are stirred in before the liquid hits the flour and starts forming gluten.

Mix Efficiently
Carefully and quickly stir the wet mixture into the dry ingredients to minimize the physical manipulation that encourages gluten formation.

Knead Briefly
Knead the dough just a few times.

Pat Out and Cut
Shape and cut the scones with minimal handling.

6. Turn out and knead briefly
Turn out the dough onto the counter and briefly knead until everything is well incorporated.
Why? The brief kneading is just to make sure all ingredients are fully incorporated; kneading too much would develop more gluten, which would make the scones tough.

7. Shape scones
Gently form the dough into a rectangle, and then make diagonal cuts to form triangular scones.
Why? Shaping the scones this way means there's no need to roll out the dough, stamp out the scones, and reroll the scraps.

8. Bake
Bake the scones in a 425-degree oven until light golden, rotating the sheet 180 degrees halfway through baking.
Why? Rotating the sheet is the best way to guarantee even baking, as hot and cool spots in your oven are balanced out.

9. Glaze
Mix butter and honey to make the glaze. Brush the glaze over the tops of the hot scones and return the sheet to the oven.
Why? A simple glaze of butter and honey adds sweetness and gives the tops of the scones a nice sheen.

10. Bake, let rest, and serve
Bake for 5 to 8 minutes, until the glaze is set and the scones are cooked through. Remove the scones from the oven and let them rest for 10 minutes before serving.
Why? The final bake sets the glaze. The resting time lets the delicate scones set up and cool.

Glazed Salmon with Broccoli and Rice

This easy one-dish salmon supper is bolstered with potent Asian flavors.

by Cecelia Jenkins

DID YOU KNOW that you can cook rice in a casserole dish in the oven? It may sound strange, but we've had success with this technique before, and I wanted to use it to create a one-pan dinner with rice, salmon, and broccoli.

Our testing has shown that the best pretreatment for oven-baked rice is rinsing it in a fine-mesh strainer to get rid of excess surface starch and then combining it with cold water in a 13 by 9-inch baking dish. Tightly covered with aluminum foil and baked in a 400-degree oven, the rice cooks up tender and fluffy in about 40 minutes. I just had to figure out how and when to add salmon and broccoli to the equation—and how to flavor them.

I started by pulling the rice out of the oven after 30 minutes—about 10 minutes short of it being perfectly cooked. After carefully removing the foil (protecting myself from the hot steam), I laid four salmon fillets and ½ pound of broccoli florets on top of the rice and returned the baking dish to the oven. Ten minutes later, the rice was perfectly cooked, but the broccoli was crunchy and the salmon, though cooked through, was pale and boring.

After some experimenting, I found that switching to the broiler to cook the fish and broccoli (and finish the rice) gave me better results. In the 9 to 12 minutes it took to cook the salmon to a perfect 125 degrees, the tops of the fillets picked up a little color and the broccoli turned a lovely deep brown.

My hybrid bake-broil method was set; now I just had to work through some details. Using chicken broth instead of water to cook the rice gave it more flavor. Completely covering the surface of the rice with the fish and vegetables before broiling ensured that there were no hard, crunchy bits of exposed rice that dried up under the broiler's blast. Placing the salmon around the edges of the dish rather than in the middle helped all four fillets cook more evenly. And adding sliced shiitake mushrooms to the broccoli gave the dish more savory oomph.

Finally, I created a flavorful stir-together sauce to brush onto the salmon before broiling. The sauce gave the salmon fillets a sweet, tangy, complex punch of flavor and helped the tops caramelize into beautifully browned, sticky-crisp crusts. Reserving a portion of the sauce before brushing meant that I had a tasty condiment to pass at the table. What made this supper even more appealing? Knowing that cleanup would be easy.

Our stir-together sauce caramelizes under the broiler, becoming an ultraflavorful glaze.

Steam the Rice; Then Broil the Fish and Vegetables

First we bake the rice, covered, in chicken broth.

Then we add the other elements, glaze the fish, and broil.

[...]E-PAN SALMON WITH RICE, [...]OCCOLI, AND SHIITAKE [...]SHROOMS *Serves 4*

[...]u will need a broiler-safe 13 by [...]nch baking dish for this recipe. [...] not use a Pyrex dish; it is not [...]oiler-safe. Rinse the rice in a [...]e-mesh strainer under cold running [...]ter until the water runs almost [...]ear, about 1½ minutes, stirring the [...]e with your hand every so often.

[...]CE, VEGETABLES, AND SALMON

- [...]¼ cups chicken broth
- 1 cup long-grain white rice, rinsed
- 1 teaspoon table salt, divided
- 8 ounces broccoli florets, cut into 1½-inch pieces (4 cups)
- 4 ounces shiitake mushrooms, stemmed and sliced thin
- 3 tablespoons vegetable oil
- 4 (6- to 8-ounce) center-cut skinless salmon fillets, 1 to 1½ inches thick
- 2 scallions, sliced thin on bias

[...]UCE

- 2 tablespoons ketchup
- 2 tablespoons hoisin sauce
- 2 tablespoons rice vinegar
- 2 tablespoons packed light brown sugar
- 1 tablespoon soy sauce
- 1 tablespoon toasted sesame oil
- 2 teaspoons Asian chili-garlic sauce
- 1 teaspoon grated fresh ginger

[...] FOR THE RICE, VEGETABLES, [...]ND SALMON: Adjust oven rack [...] middle position and heat oven to [...]0 degrees. Combine broth, rice, and [...] teaspoon salt in broiler-safe 13 by [...]inch baking dish. Jiggle dish on [...]ounter to even out layer of rice. Cover [...]ghtly with aluminum foil and bake [...]ntil rice is tender, about 30 minutes.

[...] FOR THE SAUCE: Meanwhile, [...]ir all ingredients together in bowl. [...]ransfer ¼ cup sauce to second bowl; [...]t aside both bowls.

[...] Remove dish from oven and heat [...]roiler. Carefully remove foil, allow-[...]g steam to escape away from you; [...]scard foil. Toss broccoli, mushrooms, [...]l, and remaining ½ teaspoon salt [...]gether in bowl. Place 1 salmon fillet, [...]inned side down, along each side of [...]ish. Brush tops and sides of fillets with [...]served ¼ cup sauce. Place vegetables [...] center and corners of dish so no rice [...] exposed (do not cover fillets).

[...] Return dish to oven and broil [...]ntil vegetables are very dark around [...]dges and centers of fillets are still [...]anslucent when checked with tip of [...]aring knife and register 125 degrees [...]or medium-rare), 9 to 12 minutes. [...]prinkle with scallions and serve, pass-[...]g remaining sauce separately.

Homemade Barbecue Sauces

Put down that supermarket bottle: It takes only 10 minutes to make a better breed of barbecue sauce. **by Ashley Moore**

IN A MATTER of minutes, you can make a homemade barbecue sauce that easily outpaces anything you'll pull off the shelves in the supermarket. I'm talking about all-purpose barbecue sauce here: the dark red, sweet-and-tangy elixir that works just as well as a dip for chicken nuggets as it does slathered on sizzling chicken, brisket, or ribs.

Here's how you make it. Start by sautéing a grated onion in a couple of tablespoons of oil; grating the onion (a box or a paddle grater works well here) allows it to melt into the sauce and provide subtle sweetness and savory backbone. Next, add spices to the hot oil so they can bloom and reach their full potential; I found that the best combination was a mix of garlic and onion powders, chili powder, and cayenne pepper. Finally, stir in ketchup, molasses for depth, Worcestershire

sauce for complexity, cider vinegar, sharp Dijon mustard, and a good glug of hot sauce.

After just 5 minutes of simmering the mixture, you will have a tangy, slightly sweet, glistening barbecue sauce that tastes fresher and richer than the bottled stuff. The small effort pays off big time.

Following this easy method, I came up with four variations. I made a sauce with some Asian flavors that is a great match for grilled pork or chicken (try it on wings!). Like bourbon? Then try the bourbon sauce on grilled chicken legs or as a glaze and/or dipping sauce for grilled steak tips. The smoky chipotle barbecue sauce is especially awesome on pork ribs. And the bold, pleasantly bitter espresso sauce pairs perfectly with smoked beef (such as our Texas-Style Smoked Beef Ribs on page 4).

Tangy, thick, glossy—and there's one for every occasion.

page 4

EASY ALL-PURPOSE BARBECUE SAUCE

Serves 6 to 8 (Makes 2½ cups)
This recipe was developed using Frank's RedHot Original Cayenne Pepper Sauce. Grate the onion on the large holes of a box or paddle grater.

- 2 tablespoons vegetable oil
- ½ cup grated onion
- 1 teaspoon garlic powder
- 1 teaspoon chili powder
- ¼ teaspoon cayenne pepper
- 1½ cups ketchup
- ¼ cup molasses
- 3 tablespoons Worcestershire sauce
- 3 tablespoons cider vinegar
- 2 tablespoons Dijon mustard
- 1 teaspoon hot sauce

1. Heat oil in medium saucepan over medium heat until shimmering. Add onion and cook, stirring occasionally, until softened, about 5 minutes. Stir in garlic powder, chili powder, and cayenne and cook until fragrant, about 30 seconds.

2. Stir in ketchup, molasses, Worcestershire, vinegar, mustard, and hot sauce and bring to simmer. Reduce heat to low and cook until flavors meld, about 5 minutes. Let cool completely before serving. (Cooled sauce can be refrigerated for up to 1 week.)

EASY ASIAN BARBECUE SAUCE

Omit hot sauce. Substitute 1 tablespoon grated fresh ginger for chili powder, 3 tablespoons hoisin sauce for molasses, and soy sauce for Worcestershire sauce.

EASY BOURBON BARBECUE SAUCE

Off heat, carefully add ¼ cup bourbon to saucepan after cooking spices in step 1; return saucepan to heat and cook until bourbon is nearly evaporated, 1 to 2 minutes. Proceed with step 2.

EASY CHIPOTLE BARBECUE SAUCE

Substitute 1 tablespoon minced canned chipotle chile in adobo sauce for chili powder.

EASY ESPRESSO BARBECUE SAUCE

Combine 2 tablespoons instant espresso powder and 1 tablespoon hot water in small bowl; let sit for 3 minutes. Add espresso mixture to saucepan with ketchup in step 2.

This thick, meaty ragu is best with a heavy dusting of Parmesan cheese.

Pork Ragu

Sunday sauce on a weekday? We found a way.

by Matthew Fairman

FEW THINGS ARE as satisfying as pasta tossed in a comforting, meaty "Sunday sauce"—one that you've stood over all day, doting on it from morning until evening, adding a touch of this and a touch of that until, after hours of attention, it's just right. But what if you get that hankering on a weekday? It would be a challenge, but I wanted to make a superporky, Sunday-worthy sauce in the slow cooker.

My goal was to create a hearty tomato-based sauce with loads of tender meat, serious pork flavor, and bright acidity that said, "I sweated over this sauce all day—and it was worth it." But I wanted to just put the ingredients in my slow cooker and turn it on.

Spoiler alert: My first attempt flopped. I added a combination of pork butt, which turns tender and juicy during long cooking; canned whole peeled tomatoes; red wine; chopped onion; carrots; and garlic to the slow cooker and wound up with a weak and watery sauce. It was soupy and too acidic, with hardly any pork flavor and an overall flat character.

In an effort to achieve a full-bodied sauce, I rethought my tomato element, trading whole peeled tomatoes for a large can of crushed tomatoes and a big dollop of potent tomato paste, which added sweetness and sheen. To round out the flavor, I added a fistful of earthy, aromatic thyme (whole sprigs to avoid laboriously picking the leaves) and a spoonful of potent, licorice-y fennel seeds. This version was thicker and much more full-flavored, but it was still a little sour and seriously lacking in meaty flavor.

Thinking the intense acidity might be masking the pork flavor, I reduced the amount of red wine and added a good glug of olive oil. The resulting sauce struck a nice balance, with the brightness of the wine and tomatoes now complementing the richness rather than overpowering it. But the sauce still lacked meatiness—what was the best way to add meaty oomph?

Taking a cue from one of the better recipes I'd found during my research, I added a few ounces of chopped pancetta (basically Italian bacon), hoping its concentrated pork flavor would permeate the sauce and amp up the relatively mild sweetness of the pork butt. I also cut the pork into small pieces to ensure even, thorough cooking.

Hours later, when I came back to finish the ragu, I was greeted by an irresistible aroma. Using a potato masher, I made quick work of mashing the pork. I then called my tasters. To my delight, their first bites were accompanied by vigorous nods of approval immediately followed by people packing up quarts of the sauce to take home. I knew I'd achieved the improbable: a fully hands-off slow-cooker sauce for any day of the week.

SLOW-COOKER PORK RAGU

Serves 8 to 10

Pork butt roast is often labeled Boston butt in the supermarket. This recipe yields enough sauce for 2 pounds of pasta (3 cups of ragu per pound of pasta). We like this ragu with rigatoni. If you're using table salt instead of kosher salt, decrease the amount to 1 teaspoon.

- 2 pounds boneless pork butt roast, trimmed and cut into 1½-inch pieces
- 2 teaspoons kosher salt
- 1 teaspoon pepper
- 1 (28-ounce) can crushed tomatoes
- 4 ounces pancetta, cut into ¼-inch pieces
- 1 onion, chopped fine
- 2 carrots, peeled and chopped fine
- ½ cup red wine
- ¼ cup extra-virgin olive oil
- 6 sprigs fresh thyme
- 2 tablespoons tomato paste
- 4 garlic cloves, minced
- 1 teaspoon fennel seeds
- ½ teaspoon red pepper flakes
- ½ cup chopped fresh parsley

- 1–2 pounds cooked pasta
  Grated Parmesan cheese

1. Sprinkle pork with salt and pepper and place in slow cooker. Add tomatoes, pancetta, onion, carrots, wine, oil, thyme sprigs, tomato paste, garlic, fennel seeds, and pepper flakes and stir to combine. Cover and cook until pork is tender, 6 to 7 hours on high or 8 to 10 hours on low.

2. Discard thyme sprigs. Using potato masher, mash pork in slow cooker until broken into bite-size pieces. Stir in parsley. (Cooled sauce can be frozen for up to 2 months.) Toss with desired amount of pasta (3 cups ragu will sauce 1 pound pasta). Serve with Parmesan.

The Easy Way to Shred Pork

Trim the fat from the pork butt, and then cut the meat into ½-inch pieces so it will shred more easily.

At the end of cooking, use a potato masher to break down the tender pork into bite-size pieces.

Tex-Mex Cheese Enchiladas

'e pared down the parts and the process but kept the deep, rich flavor.

Alli Berkey

HEESE ENCHILADAS ARE
mfort food at its finest: earthy
rn tortillas filled with melty cheese
d covered in a deeply flavorful,
ced-but-not-spicy chile sauce.
nple and satisfying.

But enchiladas can be laborious to
ke: Toasting, soaking, and grind-
g dried chile peppers for the sauce
ces some time and effort—and that's
fore you get to filling and rolling the
rtillas. Some recipes even insist on
ing homemade tortillas. I wanted a
npler, more direct path to the same
arty, complex flavor, and I wanted to
ake just enough for two.

For the tortillas, I knew I was going
th the store-bought corn variety.
ur testing has proven that wrapping
tack of tortillas in a clean towel
d microwaving them is a fast way
bloom their flavor and make them
able enough to roll around a cheese
ling. Easy.

Texans love their dark, thick chile
uce (some call it gravy), and many
e it as the quintessential example
Tex-Mex food. Like poultry gravy,
based on broth thickened with a
ux (made with flour and oil or lard).
t instead of getting its flavor from
eat drippings, it's powered by dried
iles—typically anchos—and spices.

Good store-bought chili powder is a
mbination of dried chiles and spices,
d I found that as long as I toasted the
ili powder in oil to fully activate its
vor, it was a great timesaving substi-
te for my streamlined version.

After several days of testing, I nailed
own the method for making the
ile sauce. First I sautéed chopped
ion in a little oil in a 10-inch skillet.
hen I added the chili powder, flour,
me tomato paste for sweetness and
pth, garlic, oregano, and pepper.
nce these ingredients had bloomed
the hot oil (which took only about
minute), I whisked in chicken broth
d cooked the sauce down until it
ickened slightly, which took about
minutes.

From there, all I had to do was roll
the cheese in six tortillas, line up the
chiladas in the skillet, pour on the
uce, top with cheese, and bake until
e cheese melted. Garnished with a
tle more chopped onion and a squirt
lime for freshness, these easy, cheesy
chiladas are fast enough for a week-
ght and sure to please any old time.

TEX-MEX CHEESE ENCHILADAS FOR TWO

If you do not have a 10-inch skillet,
make the sauce in a 12-inch skillet and
transfer the remaining sauce in step 1 to
an 8-inch square baking pan. In step 2,
arrange the enchiladas in the baking pan
before adding the reserved sauce and
the remaining cheese.

SAUCE
- 2 tablespoons vegetable oil
- ½ cup finely chopped onion
- 1½ tablespoons chili powder
- 1½ tablespoons all-purpose flour
- 2 teaspoons tomato paste
- 2 garlic cloves, minced
- 1 teaspoon dried oregano
- ½ teaspoon pepper
- 1½ cups chicken broth

ENCHILADAS
- 6 (6-inch) corn tortillas
- 8 ounces Monterey Jack cheese, shredded (2 cups), divided
- 2 tablespoons finely chopped onion
  Lime wedges

1. FOR THE SAUCE: Adjust oven
rack to middle position and heat oven
to 450 degrees. Heat oil in 10-inch
ovensafe skillet over medium heat until
shimmering. Add onion and cook until
softened, about 3 minutes. Add chili
powder, flour, tomato paste, garlic,
oregano, and pepper and cook until
fragrant, about 1 minute. Gradually
whisk in broth and bring to simmer.
Cook until slightly thickened, about
4 minutes. Remove from heat. Measure
out 1 cup sauce and set aside, leaving
remaining sauce in skillet.

2. FOR THE ENCHILADAS:
Stack tortillas and wrap in damp dish
towel. Microwave until pliable, about
30 seconds. Place ¼ cup Monterey
Jack across center of 1 tortilla, tightly
roll tortilla around cheese, and place
seam side down in sauce in skillet.
Repeat with remaining 5 tortillas and
1¼ cups Monterey Jack, arranging
enchiladas side by side in single row
in skillet.

3. Pour reserved sauce over enchiladas
and sprinkle with remaining ½ cup
Monterey Jack. Bake, covered, until
cheese is melted, about 10 minutes.
Uncover and continue to bake until
sauce is bubbling around edges, about
5 minutes longer. Sprinkle with onion
and serve with lime wedges.

A squeeze of lime adds a burst of energy to this comforting weeknight dish.

A Faster Path to Deep Flavor

We love the rich, deep flavor that dried chiles
impart to Tex-Mex enchilada sauce, which is
also called chile gravy. But for a quick
dinner to serve two, we found
that good store-bought
chili powder—in
combination with
garlic, oregano, and
tomato paste—
made a great, and
easier, substitute.

Can Openers

We tested traditional can openers as well as safety openers. Which style came out on top? **by Emily Phares**

KEY **Good** ★★★ **Fair** ★★ **Poor**

7 Can Openers 7 Tests

- Open 6 cans of black beans
- Open 4 cans of tuna
- Open 4 cans of tomato paste
- Open 4 cans of whole tomatoes
- Have users open 1 can of black beans with each opener
- Wash by hand 5 times
- Winner-only durability test: Open 25 cans of black beans

A CAN OPENER typically has a propeller-like knob called a driving handle that users turn to move a small, circular blade around the top of a can. Traditional models puncture and cut the lid inside the rim of the can so that the lid can be removed. Safety models, however, cut into the side of the can just beneath the rim so that both the lid and its rim can be removed, thereby creating a smoother, safer edge. This also keeps the lid from slipping into the can.

In our most recent testing, we chose a safety opener as our winner for its sleek, comfortable design and easy lid removal. However, we soon started hearing complaints. Our test cooks said that the new opener was confusing because they couldn't always tell when the opener had successfully attached to the can. Unlike a traditional can opener that clamps down tightly as it punctures the lid, this model latches on to the side and doesn't give a clear audible or tactile indication that it's properly attached.

It was time to retest. We chose seven popular models—four traditional openers and three safety openers—priced from about $8 to just under $55. We opened cans of varying sizes, from hefty cans of whole tomatoes to petite cans of tomato paste, to find an easy-to-use model that eliminated any guesswork.

Two of the safety can openers were difficult to use because their handles blocked our view, making it hard to know if the blades were securely attached to the can. We could see the blade of the third safety opener—our previous winner—so we could position it correctly, but the opener was still not intuitive to use.

While our testers appreciated that safety openers prevented lids from sinking into the cans' contents, they didn't like seeing the stringy glue stretching from the can to the lid as the lid was removed. As far as we could tell, no glue got into our food, but it was off-putting. On the whole, the traditional models were much easier and more intuitive to use than the safety openers, which often confused our testers.

The driving handles of two of the safety openers were especially hard to turn. This was because the side of the can is typically a heavier gauge of metal than the lid and therefore requires more force to cut through. The driving handles on the traditional-style openers were much easier to turn.

In the end, our winning can opener was the EZ-DUZ-IT Can Opener, a traditional model. Testers found it intuitive and easy to use, and its long driving handle—the longest of all the models we tested—made it a breeze to turn. As a bonus, it can be used as a safety opener, too (see "One Opener, Two Techniques"). Web subscribers can read the complete testing at **CooksCountry.com/jul19.**

HIGHLY RECOMMENDED

EZ-DUZ-IT Can Opener
Model: 89 **Price:** $10.00
Style: Traditional
Driving Handle Length: 3½ in

CRITERIA

Ease of Use ★★★
Comfort ★★★
Durability ★★★

Comments: Our favorite opener required almost no thought to operate—it was intuitive and easy to use. It had the longer driving handle, which made it easier and more comfortable to rotate. Can opening was effortless.

RECOMMENDED

Swing-A-Way Portable Can Opener
Model: 407BK **Price:** $7.99
Style: Traditional
Driving Handle Length: 3¼ in

Ease of Use ★★★
Comfort ★★½
Durability ★★★

Comments: Though this model was a cinch to use, it was a little less comfortable than our winner, and testers noted that its "turning mechanism is not as smooth." Its slightly shorter driving handle required some force to turn.

OXO Good Grips
Soft-Handled Can Opener
Model: 28081 **Price:** $13.95
Style: Traditional
Driving Handle Length: 3 in

Ease of Use ★★★
Comfort ★★★
Durability ★★

Comments: This model was intuitive, and we liked its comfortable driving handle. Our testers thought it was "lovely," but we docked durability points because one of the handle covers became loose during testing.

RECOMMENDED WITH RESERVATIONS

Zyliss Lock 'n Lift
Can Opener
Model: 20362 **Price:** $13.95
Style: Traditional
Driving Handle Length: 3 in

Ease of Use ★★
Comfort ★★½
Durability ★★★

Comments: This model was fine overall, but its handle had an annoying button that we were forced to press to attach it and to remove it from a can. Once it was attached, testers found it "very smooth" to operate.

Fissler
Magic Can Opener
Model: 020-081-18-000/0
Price: $43.95 **Style:** Safety
Driving Handle Length: 3¼ in

Ease of Use ★½
Comfort ★★
Durability ★★★

Comments: Our previous winner has a sleek design and prevents sinking lids, but we couldn't easily tell when we had successfully attached it to cans, and its driving handle was harder to rotate than those of higher-ranking models.

NOT RECOMMENDED

Rösle Can Opener with Pliers Grip
Model: 12757 **Price:** $54.99
Style: Safety
Driving Handle Length: 2⅞ in

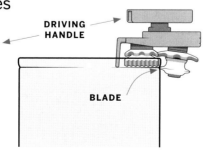

Kuhn Rikon Auto Safety Lid Lifter
Model: 2242 **Price:** $15.00
Style: Safety
Driving Handle Length: 3½ in

One Opener, Two Techniques

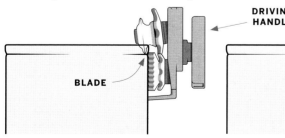

DRIVING HANDLE

BLADE

BLADE

TRADITIONAL METHOD
Our winner can be used like a traditional opener, cutting into the top of the lid.

SAFETY-STYLE
It can also be used like a safety opener, cutting into the side of the can.

Vanilla Ice Cream

Vanilla is America's favorite ice cream flavor, but which product is the cream of the crop? **by Lauren Savoie**

HAVE YOU EVER met anyone who doesn't like vanilla ice cream? Neither have we. Vanilla ice cream is a classic, but it's also the purest expression of ice cream—there's nowhere for inferiority to hide. So which product is best?

We selected eight top-selling nationally available brands (including Blue Bell, which is sold in stores in only about 20 states but can be ordered by phone) and started sorting through all their varieties: "vanilla bean," "original vanilla," "homemade vanilla," "French vanilla," and just plain "vanilla." We tasted 17 different products to find one from each brand to include in our final taste test.

In almost every case, we preferred products labeled "French" or "homemade" vanilla to those labeled "vanilla bean." While the specks of ground vanilla beans in "vanilla bean" ice creams were visually appealing, these products weren't very vanilla-y. Experts told us that the ground beans stirred into ice cream are usually left over from vanilla extract production and have already lost much of their flavor. A lot of "vanilla bean" ice creams have natural or artificial flavors added to amp up the vanilla taste, but we still found them lacking.

As for the differences among "French," "homemade," and just plain "vanilla" ice creams, we didn't see any clear trends. While it's often thought that "French" denotes ice cream that contains eggs, this wasn't always the case for the products in our lineup.

We did see one common thread among products that made it to the second round: They all had slightly less sugar. Every product in our final lineup had 20 grams of sugar or less per ½-cup serving, while the eliminated products ranged from 21 to 24 grams of sugar in the same serving size. Tasters thought that products with more sugar were too sweet and that the vanilla flavor was more pronounced in products with slightly less sugar.

With our eight products selected, we held a final blind tasting. Most of the ice creams earned high enough marks that we can fully recommend all but one of them. And while we noticed that some products in our final lineup had prominent vanilla notes, some also had a slightly "boozy" aftertaste.

The ice creams were made with both imitation vanilla flavoring and real vanilla extracts. We didn't have a preference for one style of vanilla flavoring, which isn't surprising since vanillin—the key compound responsible for vanilla's flavor—is molecularly identical in imitation and real vanilla extracts. But since pure vanilla extract must contain at least 35 percent alcohol, the ice creams made with it were a bit too boozy for some tasters.

Regarding texture, we looked at each product's overrun percentage, (the amount of added air). Manufacturers add air to ice cream because some consumers like ice creams with lighter textures. Producing ice creams with high

overrun percentages is more profitable than making ice creams with low overrun percentages because an ice cream with 100 percent overrun is half air. We sent the ice creams to a lab to have their overrun percentages measured, and they ranged from 21 percent to 117 percent, a huge difference.

Ice creams with low overrun percentages are typically dense and silky premium-style products (such as Ben & Jerry's and Häagen-Dazs). However, our tasters were split on whether they preferred high- or low-overrun ice cream. Our winner had a relatively high overrun percentage (97 percent) but was still praised for its creamy, smooth texture; it compensates for the addition of air by using corn syrup (instead of sugar) as its main sweetener. Since corn syrup is thicker than sugar, it gives this ice cream a smooth, rich texture. Many ice creams, including our winner, also

contain added stabilizers, gelling agents, and thickeners to help keep their textures thick and silky despite having high overrun percentages.

Ice creams also rely on fat and sugar for creamy texture; both substances prevent ice crystals from forming, and without enough of either, the ice cream becomes icy and hard. The amounts of fat and sugar in the ice creams we tried varied widely. Our top-rated ice cream had a relatively moderate 7 grams of fat and 12 grams of sugar, striking the right balance for our tasters.

In the end, we named Turkey Hill Original Vanilla Premium Ice Cream our favorite vanilla ice cream. Its relatively high overrun percentage and use of corn syrup combined to create a perfectly smooth, scoopable, and creamy texture that we loved in both tastings. It also had balanced sweetness and a prominent, rich vanilla flavor.

Is the Halo Top Hype Justified?

"Light" ice creams—especially the Halo Top brand—are having a moment, rising 500 percent in sales in the last two years. So is Halo Top any good? We found that, without the fat and sugar of other products, it was rock-hard straight from the freezer. After about 15 minutes of thawing, we could get an ice cream scoop into it, but its texture was "mushy," not creamy, and still "notably icy." Our tasters picked up on unpleasant flavor notes, likely from the stevia leaf extract used as a sweetener. If you want low-fat ice cream, Edy's Slow Churned, our third-place finisher, is a much better bet.

NOT RECOMMENDED

Halo Top Vanilla Bean
Price: $5.19 per pint
Overrun: 106%
Fat: 2 g
Sugar: 6 g

RECOMMENDED

Turkey Hill
Original Vanilla
Premium Ice Cream
Our Favorite
Price: $2.99 for 1.5 qt
($1.00 per pint)
Overrun: 97%
Fat: 7 g **Sugar:** 12 g
Comments: Tasters loved this "silky" ice cream, which had "rich" vanilla flavor. It was spoonable and "airy," thanks to its relatively high overrun percentage, but still "velvety" due to the use of viscous corn syrup.

Ben & Jerry's
Vanilla Ice Cream
Price: $4.99 per pint
Overrun: 21%
Fat: 16 g **Sugar:** 20 g
Comments: This premium product had the lowest overrun percentage, so its texture was "creamy" and "almost luxurious." While most tasters loved its "rich" flavor and texture, a few found it "dense" and also "boozy" due to the addition of pure vanilla extract.

Edy's Slow Churned
Classic Vanilla
Ice Cream (also sold as Dreyer's)
Price: $5.99 for 1.5 qt
($2.00 per pint)
Overrun: 117%
Fat: 3 g **Sugar:** 14 g
Comments: Marketed as a light ice cream, this product was indistinguishable from full-fat ice cream. Tasters loved its "airy" texture (its overrun percentage is high), but some found it a bit too "whipped."

Häagen-Dazs
Vanilla Ice Cream
Price: $3.99 per pint
Overrun: 38%
Fat: 15 g **Sugar:** 18 g
Comments: This premium product had the shortest ingredient list in our lineup. Tasters liked its "familiar," "sweet" taste. Many noted that it had the "strongest" vanilla flavor, but some disliked the "booziness" from pure vanilla extract. Some also found it "a bit chewy" in texture.

Breyers French Vanilla
Ice Cream
Price: $4.99 for 1.5 qt
($1.66 per pint)
Overrun: 53%
Fat: 7 g **Sugar:** 14 g
Comments: Though this wasn't the only product with added egg yolks, tasters picked up on a "rich," "prominent" eggy flavor that reminded some of "eggnog." We also wished it had a bit more vanilla flavor. Its texture was "thick" and "creamy."

Blue Bell Homemade
Vanilla Ice Cream
Price: $7.89 for 2 qt
($1.97 per pint)
Overrun: 82%
Fat: 9 g **Sugar:** 19 g
Comments: Tasters praised this product's "supercreamy" and "smooth" texture, but some found its sweetness "overpowering." This Texas brand has limited national distribution but can be ordered by phone.

Edy's Vanilla Ice
Cream (also sold as Dreyer's)
Price: $5.99 for 1.5 qt
($2.00 per pint)
Overrun: 99%
Fat: 7 g **Sugar:** 14 g
Comments: This "neutral" ice cream earned satisfactory marks for its "sweet cream" flavor, but it was notably missing any trace of vanilla. Its texture was "thick," "creamy," and "whipped."

and sugar amounts are based on a ½-cup serving size.

Fried Bananas

> "These were a favorite dessert in my town growing up. Some folks served them with a sweet, lemony sauce, but my favorite accompaniment was always a drizzle of chocolate syrup. Don't eat them too quickly or you'll burn your tongue!"
>
> —MARGIE WAKEFIELD,
> *Salinas, Calif.*

FRIED BANANAS *Serves 6 to 8*

Use ripe yellow bananas. Avoid ones that are green or have begun to turn black. Serve with store-bought chocolate sauce, if desired.

4	ripe bananas, sliced 1 inch thick
2	tablespoons all-purpose flour, plus ¾ cup (3¾ ounces), divided
½	cup (3½ ounces) sugar
½	teaspoon baking powder
½	teaspoon finely grated lemon zest
¼	teaspoon table salt
¾	cup whole milk
2	quarts vegetable oil, for frying

1. Toss bananas with 2 tablespoons flour in bowl. Freeze until bananas are firm, about 30 minutes.

2. Whisk sugar, baking powder, lemon zest, salt, and remaining ¾ cup flour together in bowl. Slowly whisk milk into flour mixture until smooth batter forms.

3. Set wire rack in rimmed baking sheet and line rack with triple layer of paper towels. Add oil to large Dutch oven until it measures about 1½ inches deep and heat over medium-high heat to 375 degrees.

4. Transfer half of bananas to batter and stir to coat. Using tongs or fork and working with 1 piece at a time, remove bananas from batter, allowing excess batter to drip back into bowl, then add to hot oil. Cook until golden brown, about 2 minutes, stirring occasionally and flipping bananas as needed. Adjust burner, if necessary, to maintain oil temperature between 350 and 375 degrees.

5. Transfer bananas to prepared rack. Return oil to 375 degrees and repeat with remaining bananas and batter. Serve.

We're looking for recipes that you treasure—the ones that have been handed down in your family for a generation or more, that always come out for the holidays, and that have earned a place at your table and in your heart through many years of meals. Send us the recipes that spell home to you. Visit CooksCountry.com/recipe_submission (or write to Heirloom Recipes, Cook's Country, 21 Drydock Avenue, Suite 210E, Boston, MA 02210) and tell us a little about the recipe. Include your name and address. If we print your recipe, you'll receive a free one-year subscription to Cook's Country.

COMING NEXT ISSUE

Summer in Cook's Country means **Hot Buttered Lobster Rolls**, **Grilled Jerk Chicken**, and the loveliest **Rustic Tomato Tart** you've ever seen. We also visit New Mexico, for a lesson in making **Gorditas**, and Ohio, where an afternoon spent in an Italian American kitchen gave us the secrets to perfect **Eggplant Parmesan**. And to satisfy your sweet tooth, we'll have **No-Churn Ice Cream** and classic **Pineapple Upside-Down Cake**.

FIND THE ROOSTER!

A tiny version of this rooster has been hidden in a photo in the pages of this issue. Write to us with its location, and we'll enter you in a random drawing. The first correct entry drawn will win our favorite ca opener, and each of the next five will recei a free one-year subscription to Cook's Country. To enter, visit CooksCountry. com/rooster by June 30, 2019, or write to Rooster JJ19, Cook's Country, 21 Drydock Avenue, Suite 210E, Boston, MA 02210. Include your name and address. Ann Mola of Bar Harbor, Maine, found the rooster in the February/March 2019 issue on page 14 and won our favorite inexpensive stainless-steel skillet.

WEB EXTRAS

Free for four months online at **CooksCountry.com**

Lime Yellow Cake Layers
Lime Frosting

READ US ON IPAD

Download the Cook's Country app for iPad and start a free trial subscription or purchase a single issue of the magazine. issues are enhanced with Cooking Mode slide shows that provide step-by-step instructions for completing recipes, plus expanded reviews and ratings. Go to CooksCountry.com/iPad to download o app through iTunes.

RC = Recipe Card

Raspberry-Lime Rickey Cake

To enjoy a taste of summertime, we reimagined this New England soda fountain classic as a showstopping cake. **by Sarah Ewald**

TO MAKE THIS CAKE, YOU WILL NEED:

- 1¼ teaspoons unflavored gelatin
- 2 tablespoons water
- 3 large egg yolks
- 2 teaspoons cornstarch
- 1 pound (3¼ cups) thawed frozen raspberries
- ⅔ cup (4⅔ ounces) sugar
- 2 tablespoons unsalted butter
  Pinch table salt
- 1¼ cups heavy cream, chilled
- 1 recipe Lime Yellow Cake Layers*
- ¾ cup (6 ounces) frozen limeade concentrate, thawed
- 1 recipe Lime Frosting*
- 5–7½ ounces (1–1½ cups) fresh raspberries
- 3 thin lime slices

FOR THE RASPBERRY CURD AND MOUSSE:

Sprinkle gelatin over water in large bowl and set aside. Whisk egg yolks and cornstarch in medium bowl until combined. Combine frozen raspberries, sugar, butter, and salt in medium saucepan. Lightly mash with whisk and stir until no dry sugar remains. Cook over medium heat, whisking frequently, until mixture is simmering and raspberries are almost completely broken down, 4 to 6 minutes.

Remove saucepan from heat and, whisking constantly, slowly add ½ cup raspberry mixture to yolk mixture to temper. Whisking constantly, return tempered yolk mixture to raspberry mixture in saucepan. Cook over medium heat, whisking constantly, until mixture thickens and bubbles, about 1 minute. Strain mixture through fine-mesh strainer into bowl with gelatin mixture, pressing on solids with back of ladle or rubber spatula until only seeds remain. Discard seeds and stir raspberry mixture until gelatin is dissolved. Let sit, stirring occasionally, until curd is slightly thickened and completely cooled, about 1 hour. Transfer ½ cup curd to small bowl and set aside.

Using stand mixer fitted with whisk attachment, whip cream on medium-low speed until foamy, about 1 minute. Increase speed to high and whip until soft peaks form, 1 to 2 minutes. Add one-third of whipped cream to remaining curd and gently whisk until mixture is lightened. Using rubber spatula, gently fold in remaining whipped cream until mixture is homogeneous.

TO ASSEMBLE:

Using long serrated knife, cut each cake layer in half horizontally. Place 1 cake layer on cake turntable. Brush about 3 tablespoons limeade concentrate over top and sides of cake. Spread 1½ cups raspberry mousse evenly over top, leaving ¼-inch border around edge. Top with second cake layer, pressing lightly to adhere. Brush with limeade concentrate, then spread with 1½ cups mousse. Top with third cake layer, pressing lightly to adhere. Brush with limeade concentrate, then spread with remaining 1½ cups mousse. Top with fourth cake layer, pressing lightly to adhere, and brush with remaining limeade concentrate.

Frost top and sides of cake with thin layer of frosting, about 1½ cups, taking care to fill in gaps on sides between layers to create smooth sides. Refrigerate until frosting is firm, 30 to 45 minutes. Frost only sides again with thicker layer of remaining frosting. While turning cake turntable, run small offset spatula vertically from bottom to top of cake at 45-degree angle. Arrange fresh raspberries around top edge of cake (set aside 3 raspberries for center of cake). Spread reserved raspberry curd inside ring of raspberries using offset spatula, covering all exposed frosting on top. Shingle lime slices in center of cake; top with reserved raspberries. Serve.

*Our recipes for Lime Yellow Cake Layers and Lime Frosting are available for free for four months at **CooksCountry.com/rickeycake.**

INSIDE THIS ISSUE

Cook's Country

12 EASY ICE CREAMS
You don't need a machine to make these easy ice creams.

PAGE 14

Buttery Lobster Rolls
Summertime Special

Perfect Grilled Corn
Cook It Husk-On

One-Pot Pasta Salad
Dinner in a Dutch Oven

New Mexico Gorditas
Las Cruces Fan Favorite

Rustic Tomato Tart
Easy Showstopper

Three-Way Brioche Dough
Buns, Rolls, or Loaves

Pineapple Upside-Down Cake
Real Pacific Flavor

Get to Know Your Knives
Top Tips for Care and Use

AUGUST/SEPTEMBER 2019
$6.95 U.S./$7.95 CANADA

09>

0 71486 02742 3

DISPLAY UNTIL
SEPTEMBER 9, 2019

LETTER FROM THE EDITOR

IN JUST THE past 12 months, our executive food editor, Bryan Roof, and our staff photographer, Steve Klise, have traveled to New Mexico, Mississippi, the Bronx, Seattle, and Philadelphia looking for great recipes. They've been doing this for years, making trips to Tennessee, Kentucky, North and South Carolina, Florida, Alabama, California, Wisconsin, Chicago, Detroit, Pittsburgh, and Texas.

These journeys take tons of planning: researching regional traditions, telephoning local cooks, and corresponding with journalists on the ground. Bryan and Steve create extensive and detailed itineraries to make the most of their time on the road.

But they're still surprised on every trip. Take, for example, a recent visit to Ohio. At a small strip mall restaurant outside Cleveland, they came across an unexpected take on an otherwise predictable dish—eggplant Parmesan. Flavorful and satisfying but not overburdened with goopy cheese or cloying sauce, it turned the concept of this dish on its head (see page 13).

The food they find is great, but the real gift is the people they meet along the way. I was lucky to tag along for their trip to Las Cruces, New Mexico, and was inspired by the generous and welcoming Guerra family—not just by their fantastic gorditas but also by their commitment to their craft and their community (see page 4). I won't soon forget them.

TUCKER SHAW

Editor in Chief

P.S. Here's something extra-fun: In this issue, instead of our usual "Five Easy" column, we have "12 Easy"—and it's an amazing, supersimple recipe for no-churn ice cream that we dress up with all kinds of stir-ins (see page 15). You really aren't going to believe how easy it is to make ice cream at home, without a machine. Summer!

Illustration: Ross MacDonald

GET THE DOUGH ROLLING

The Perfect Pie

This book is the definitive guide to gorgeous pies and tarts. Maybe you want to master homespun pies that celebrate seasonal produce or get creative with pastry-encased canvases for modern flavor profiles. No matter your interest, this collection will inspire you to bake. We tested our way to the best techniques for building foolproof, bakery-quality pies from the crust up. To order your copy, go to AmericasTestKitchen.com/perfectpie.

 Find us on **Facebook**
facebook.com/CooksCountry

 Find us on **Instagram**
instagram.com/CooksCountry

 Follow us on **Pinterest**
pinterest.com/TestKitchen

 Follow us on **Twitter**
twitter.com/TestKitchen

Cook's Country

Chief Executive Officer David Nussbaum
Chief Creative Officer Jack Bishop
Editor in Chief Tucker Shaw
Executive Managing Editor Todd Meier
Executive Food Editor Bryan Roof
Deputy Editor Scott Kathan
Deputy Food Editor Morgan Bolling
Senior Editor Cecelia Jenkins
Associate Editors Alli Berkey, Matthew Fairman
Associate Editor, Web Ashley Delma
Test Cooks Natalie Estrada, Jessica Rudolph
Photo Team/Special Events Manager Tim McQuinn
Assistant Test Cooks, Photo Team Sarah Ewald, Hannah Jacqueline Gochenouer, Eric Haessler
Senior Copy Editor Jill Campbell
Copy Editors Christine Campbell, Rachel Schowalter
Contributing Editor Eva Katz
Senior Science Research Editor Paul Adams
Hosts & Executive Editors, Television Bridget Lancaster, Julia Collin Davison

Executive Editors, Tastings & Testings Hannah Crowley, Lisa McManus
Senior Editors, Tastings & Testings Lauren Savoie, Kate S
Associate Editor, Tastings & Testings Miye Bromberg
Assistant Editors, Tastings & Testings Riddley Gemperlein-Schirm, Carolyn Grillo, Emily Phares

Creative Director John Torres
Photography Director Julie Cote
Art Director Susan Levin
Associate Art Director Maggie Edgar
Senior Staff Photographer Daniel J. van Ackere
Staff Photographers Steve Klise, Kevin White
Photography Producer Meredith Mulcahy

Senior Director, Creative Operations Alice Carpenter
Senior Editor, Special Projects Christie Morrison
Senior Manager, Publishing Operations Taylor Argenzio
Imaging Manager Lauren Robbins
Production & Imaging Specialists Dennis Noble, Jessica Voas, Amanda Yong
Test Kitchen Director Erin McMurrer
Assistant Test Kitchen Director Alexxa Benson
Test Kitchen Manager Meridith Lippard
Test Kitchen Facilities Manager Kelly Ryan
Senior Kitchen Assistant Shopper Michelle Miller
Senior Kitchen Assistant Receiver Heather Tolmie
Lead Kitchen Assistant Ena Gudiel
Kitchen Assistants Gladis Campos, Blanca Castanza, Amarilys Merced

Chief Financial Officer Jackie McCauley Ford
Senior Manager, Customer Support Tim Quinn
Customer Support Specialist Mitchell Axelson
Event Coordinator Michaela Hughes

Chief Digital Officer Fran Middleton
VP, Marketing Natalie Vinard
Director, Audience Acquisition & Partnerships Evan Steir
Director, Social Media Marketing Kathryn Przybyla
Social Media Coordinators Charlotte Erity, Sarah Sandler

Chief Revenue Officer Sara Domville

Director, Public Relations & Communications Brian Frank
Public Relations Coordinator Madeleine Cohen

Senior VP, Human Resources & Organizational Development Colleen Zelina
Human Resources Manager Jason Lynott

Photography Keller + Keller
Food Styling Catrine Kelty

Circulation Services ProCirc

On the cover: 12 Easy Ice Creams

erica's Test Kitchen is a real test kitchen located
oston. It is the home of more than 60 test cooks,
rs, and cookware specialists. Our mission is to
recipes until we understand exactly how and
they work and eventually arrive at the very
t version. We also test kitchen equipment and
ermarket ingredients in search of products that
r the best value and performance. You can watch
work by tuning in to **America's Test Kitchen**
ericasTestKitchen.com) and **Cook's Country**
oksCountry.com) on public television, and you
listen to our weekly segments on *The Splendid*
le on public radio. You can also follow us on
ebook, Twitter, Pinterest, and Instagram.

24

20

Cook's Country magazine (ISSN 1552-1990), number 88, is published bimonthly by America's Test Kitchen Limited Partnership, 21 Drydock Avenue, Suite 210E, Boston, MA 02210. Copyright 2019
America's Test Kitchen Limited Partnership. Periodicals postage paid at Boston, MA, and additional mailing offices. USPS #023453. Publications Mail Agreement No. 40020778. Return undeliverable Canadian addresses to P.O. Box 875, Station A, Windsor, ON N9A 6P2. POSTMASTER: Send address changes to *Cook's Country*, P.O. Box 6018, Harlan, IA 51593-1518. For subscription and gift
subscription orders, subscription inquiries, or change of address notices, visit AmericasTestKitchen.com/support, call 800-526-8447 in the U.S. or 515-237-3663 from outside the U.S., or write to
us at *Cook's Country*, P.O. Box 6018, Harlan, IA 51593-1518. PRINTED IN THE USA.

by Cecelia Jenkins

SQUAT CAKE
Overwhipped eggs and aggressive folding

TALL CAKE
Properly whipped eggs and gentle folding

Whip Correctly, Fold Gently

When I cut into my round of sponge cake, it was dense and gummy on the bottom half but not on the top half. Why did this happen?
–Ellie Bergeron, Tempe, Ariz.

Delicate sponge and chiffon cakes call for whipped egg whites as a leavener; the air trapped in the whipped whites expands in the oven, giving the cakes lift. However, both the texture of the whipped egg whites and how they're folded into the batter can impact the overall texture and height of a cake.

To illustrate this, we baked several versions of our Lemon Chiffon Layer Cake recipe, which calls for whipping egg whites to soft peaks and then folding them into the batter. At soft peaks, the whites have nearly reached their fullest volume, and since their texture is similar to that of the batter, they incorporate seamlessly with a few folds. But when overwhipped, the foam collapses (so it contains less air) and becomes chunky. This chunky texture requires more aggressive folding to incorporate into the batter, which further deflates the foam. And even with properly whipped whites, you can still deflate the batter if you use too heavy a hand in folding.

A cake made with properly whipped whites that are gently folded in will be tall and fluffy with an even crumb; if you overwhip the whites or fold them into the batter too aggressively, the cake will be squat and dense.

THE BOTTOM LINE: To ensure a tall chiffon cake, whip the egg whites just to the soft peak stage before folding them into the batter, and use a light hand when folding.

PROPER WHIPPING
Soft peaks

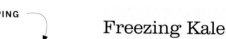

MIX MASTER
Be sure to fold the whites in gently.

Freezing Kale

I always blanch kale to soften it before sautéing it. Since freezing also softens vegetables, can I have the freezer do that softening for me?
–Andrea O'Rourke, Palmer, Mass.

The process of freezing and thawing ruptures vegetables' cell walls and makes them softer; while this is often a bad thing, could it eliminate the need to blanch kale before sautéing it?

To find out, we stemmed, washed, and dried raw curly kale and froze it for a few days. Then we pulled it from the freezer and tried it in our recipe for Simple Sautéed Kale (which calls for the kale to be blanched before sautéing). We made a batch of the regular recipe for comparison.

The frozen-and-thawed raw kale was very wet out of the freezer, and it turned stringy and mushy (even after we squeezed it dry) when sautéed. The kale that we'd blanched, drained, and pressed dry according to the recipe was pleasantly tender and flavorful, not washed-out.

But the frozen-and-thawed kale was perfectly fine when added directly to our Quick Hearty Tuscan Bean Stew and blended into our Kale-Pineapple Smoothies—tasters barely detected a difference between raw and frozen samples.

THE BOTTOM LINE: Freezing and then thawing raw kale does indeed soften it, but it compromises the kale's texture. We don't recommend this technique if you are going to sauté the kale.

Improv Hummus

If I don't have tahini on hand, can I substitute something else and still make tasty hummus?
–Rowan Flanders, Charlotte, N.C.

Tahini, a paste made from ground sesame seeds, gives hummus a smooth texture and complex flavor; we use a full ¼ cup of tahini and one 15-ounce can of chickpeas (plus olive oil, garlic, lemon juice, and water) in our Classic Hummus. To see if we could make hummus without tahini, we simply omitted the tahini and proceeded with our recipe; the result tasted too lean and lacked the richness and depth of the original version.

So we looked for a replacement for the tahini, testing various ingredients in its stead. Simply using more olive oil (which has bitter notes similar to those of tahini) made the mixture too loose and wet. Whole-milk yogurt added body, but its flavor was too tangy and the result just didn't taste like hummus. The best substitute was peanut butter; it provided ample body and creaminess and a toasty, nutty depth reminiscent of tahini. But peanut butter's sweetness was a problem—it was easily identifiable as an outlier in the hummus. Cutting the amount back from ¼ cup to 2 tablespoons and making up the difference with extra olive oil solved the problem. Skippy, our winning creamy peanut butter, worked here, but our tasters preferred natural peanut butter, which isn't as sweet.

THE BOTTOM LINE: You can use smooth peanut butter cut with olive oil in place of tahini in hummus, but the results won't taste exactly like the genuine article.

Go Ahead and Vent

Your grilling recipes specify how the vents should be configured for charcoal grills. Does their placement really matter?
–Craig Campbell, Warwick, R.I.

Unlike the fixed vents that run across the rear walls of gas grills, the vents on charcoal grills, which are located on the top of the grill lid and at the base of the kettle, are adjustable and give the cook the power to control the strength of the charcoal fire as well as the flow of smoke.

Their operation and function are pretty simple: When the grill lid is in place and the top and bottom vents are fully open, air flows through the grill and allows the fire to burn at the maximum heat level. When both vents are fully closed, the air supply is cut off and the fire will eventually die out. You can modulate the strength of the fire by adjusting the vents accordingly.

The position of the top vent on the lid also directs the flow of heat and smoke, which rises from the coals and is drawn out through the lid vent. You can position the vent to minimize or maximize heat and smoke contact with the food you're grilling.

THE BOTTOM LINE: Adjusting the top and bottom vents on a charcoal grill allows the cook to control the heat and the flow of smoke inside the grill.

TOP VENT

BOTTOM VENT

compiled by
Matthew Fairman

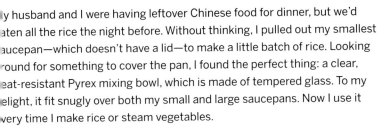

No Lid, No Problem
Pamela Navo, Charlevoix, Mich.

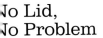

My husband and I were having leftover Chinese food for dinner, but we'd eaten all the rice the night before. Without thinking, I pulled out my smallest saucepan—which doesn't have a lid—to make a little batch of rice. Looking around for something to cover the pan, I found the perfect thing: a clear, heat-resistant Pyrex mixing bowl, which is made of tempered glass. To my delight, it fit snugly over both my small and large saucepans. Now I use it every time I make rice or steam vegetables.

Removing Baked-On Gunk
–Ingrid Haun, Louisville, Tenn.

Lasagna and other baked foods containing cheese or eggs can leave stubborn residue in baking dishes—and this residue ends up embedded in your sponge or brush after washing. So after soaking a glass or ceramic dish, I first use a wire or silicone whisk to remove the majority of the food residue. Then I finish the job with my sponge or brush. The gunk is easily rinsed off the whisk. (If using a wire whisk, make sure your dish can handle metal utensils.)

An Udderly Genius Funnel
–Virginia Hawkins, Bostic, N.C.

To create a handy reusable funnel, I use my kitchen shears to cut an empty plastic half-gallon milk jug across the middle, just below the handle. I can then use it as a funnel to transfer slightly cooled liquids (such as marinara sauce or vegetable soup) from a saucepan to jars, bowls, or plastic storage containers. It's especially practical because it has a handle and a wide mouth.

One Brand of Macaroni Elbowed Its Way to the Top
by Emily Phares

YOU CAN USE elbow macaroni in recipes from pasta salads to casseroles, but its claim to fame is, of course, its use in macaroni and cheese.

To determine which macaroni is best, we selected five widely available products and tasted each one plain (tossed with canola oil) and in our Classic Macaroni and Cheese.

The size of the macaroni was a big factor in our preferences. Once cooked, the macaroni ranged in length from roughly 0.5 inches to almost a full inch long. We liked larger elbows because they were easier to spear with a fork; our favorite macaroni was the longest, averaging 0.88 inches once cooked.

Another deciding factor was the texture of the cooked macaroni. Most of the products in our lineup had a satisfactory springy quality, but our favorite was notable for its "slightly firmer" texture that was tender but not overly so; it had a nice chewiness that tasters liked.

As for flavor, many products were OK, but our favorite macaroni had a "buttery" flavor even when tasted plain.

Our science editor explained that there are buttery-tasting compounds naturally found in wheat flour, primarily diacetyl (also called 2,3-butanedione), the same chemical used to flavor some microwave popcorns. It's possible that our winning elbow macaroni has a greater concentration of diacetyl in its flour than the other products in our lineup.

The texture of our winner, Creamette Elbow Macaroni, was pleasantly firm, and its tubes were long and easy to spear. One note: This macaroni is found primarily in the Midwest, but we were able to purchase it easily online. De Cecco and Barilla also scored well and are more widely available.

Web subscribers can read the complete tasting results at **CooksCountry.com/elbow**.

HIGHLY RECOMMENDED		TASTERS' NOTES
Creamette Elbow Macaroni **Price:** $3.46 for 16 oz ($0.22 per oz) **Noodle Length:** 0.88 in		Our winner had a distinct "buttery" flavor that set it apart from all the others, and the "long tubes" were deemed the "perfect size and shape." As one taster noted, it was "a great size for spearing." We liked its "tender" yet "slightly firmer" texture.
RECOMMENDED		
De Cecco No. 81 Elbows **Price:** $1.67 for 16 oz ($0.10 per oz) **Noodle Length:** 0.75 in		Like our winner, this was a longer noodle. Though its flavor was deemed "mild" and "neutral," the standout factor was its texture. Tasters said that these "pleasantly chewy" noodles were "light and springy."
Barilla Elbows **Price:** $1.67 for 16 oz ($0.10 per oz) **Noodle Length:** 0.63 in		Although the flavor was "not particularly noticeable," tasters said that this pasta was "tender but has structure," with a "great bouncy chew" and a "nice spring."
Ronzoni Smart Taste Elbows **Price:** $1.12 for 12 oz ($0.09 per oz) **Noodle Length:** 0.56 in		These "teeny little elbows" were "fine" in terms of flavor, with a "pleasantly chewy" texture. Some tasters said that these elbows were "too small" and were "overpowered by the cheese" when eaten in macaroni and cheese.
Goya Small Elbows **Price:** $0.50 for 7 oz ($0.07 per oz) **Noodle Length:** 0.56 in		Some tasters liked these tiny elbows for their "pleasant" wheat flavor, but others thought they were "too small." The cheese sauce overwhelmed the "teeny tiny noodles" in macaroni and cheese.

After 20-odd years in the gordita business, the Guerra family is going strong.

Text by Bryan Roof; photos by Steve Klise

FAMILY STYLE

At Saenz Gorditas in L Cruces, New Mexico, it's family affair. Albert Guer (above left); his mother, V ginia Guerra (above cente and his son, Austin Guer (above right) set a welco ing tone. Their gordit are so popular that duri happy hour, drive-throu customers are limited just a few gorditas apiec

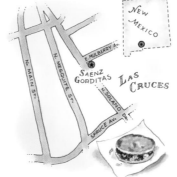

ALBERT GUERRA MAKES the gordita dough in a giant stainless-steel bowl. He eyeballs a good pour of masa harina and follows it up with generous amounts of salt and grated yellow cheddar. Next, he props the bowl precariously on the edge of the sink and adds warm tap water before he aggressively kneads the mixture into a cohesive mass. People ask him for the recipe all the time, but it's all done by feel and sight. "I don't know. I just do it," he says.

Albert and his family operate Saenz Gorditas, a restaurant located in Las Cruces, New Mexico, housed in what used to be a drive-up burger joint. Cars park out front under a corrugated tin awning, and you half expect to see waitresses on roller skates handing off burgers and shakes. A small building houses the kitchen, and the seating is all outdoors. Customers place their orders at one window and pick them up at the next a few minutes later. I take a seat at one of the plastic picnic benches under the awning; others choose to eat in their cars.

Owner Virginia Guerra learned to make gorditas from her mother and has been making them herself for more than 40 years. She and her family used to cook at local events and festivals around Las Cruces; eventually, customers and fans encouraged them to set up something more permanent. A space off North Solano Drive had been vacant for about a year when Virginia inquired about it in 1996. A month later, she was open for business. "I didn't even remodel. I just walked in and cleaned."

The first menu was simple: gorditas and tacos. But 22 years later, both the business and the menu have grown. Albert turns the masa mixture onto a table, and Virginia pulls up a stool. It's a sizable mountain of dough, enough to make about 1,000 gorditas, and it will take Virginia about 3 hours to get through.

Grabbing one handful at a time, she rolls the dough into a ball between her wet hands and then presses the ball into a perfect ½-inch-thick puck using a small Pyrex pie plate (her tool of choice). She's attached to the plate but is still heartbroken since her favorite dough press fell from the counter and broke.

Shaping gorditas takes Virginia to her happy place, and each disk she forms is as perfect as the next. "I love it," she says. "I sit here and just relax . . . and think of everything I need to do tomorrow!" For more photos from our trip to Las Cruces, go to CooksCountry.com/saenz19.

Gorditas

We visited Las Cruces, New Mexico, to learn the secrets to these chubby little snacks. **by Cecelia Jenkins**

WHEN OUR EXECUTIVE food editor, Bryan Roof, returned from a trip to Las Cruces, New Mexico, he spoke enthusiastically about the gorditas he had eaten at Saenz Gorditas (see "Family Style"). There, the gorditas (Spanish for "little fat ones") are plump corn cakes with crisp exteriors and tender interiors that are split open like pitas and stuffed with ground beef picadillo. They bear almost no resemblance to the fast-food item that shares their name.

The dough rounds—made with corn flour (masa harina), water, and sometimes cheese—are often fried in a hot pan (without fat) to form a crust and develop toasted-corn flavor. At Saenz, the cooks skip the pan and the griddle and go straight to the deep-fryer to make gorditas with soft and moist interiors, exteriors with crunch, extra savoriness from the cheese, and a captivating corn flavor. They're perfect for stuffing.

I started with corn flour (masa harina), which is much finer than cornmeal and available in the Latin American section of most supermarkets. When mixed with water, corn flour takes on a soft, pliable texture that is very easy to manipulate. When cooked, this pliable dough (masa) has much less structure than doughs made with wheat flour.

The amount of liquid in the dough was the first code to crack. With too little water, the dough was dry and crumbly and the dough rounds cracked in the oil. With too much water, the dough became an unworkable paste. We found that a combination of 5 cups of masa harina and 3⅔ cups of water created a workable, putty-like dough that was delicate yet sturdy. I had no trouble kneading in a big handful of shredded Colby Jack cheese.

I shaped portions of this dough into rounds streaked with tangy, rich cheese. After some experimenting, I found that at ½ inch thick, the rounds required about 10 minutes of frying in 375-degree oil. What's more, I found that I needed only 6 cups of oil for even, nonsplashy frying.

A version of picadillo the test kitchen developed a few years back—a mixture of ground beef, cubed potato, and plenty of seasoning—was the perfect fit as a filling for our gorditas. Once the golden pockets were split and stuffed, my tasters happily munched away—none more happily than Bryan. That's how I knew I'd nailed it.

GORDITAS Serves 6

We developed this recipe using Maseca Instant Corn Masa Flour. Monterey Jack or cheddar cheese can be substituted for the Colby Jack. Add hot sauce, shredded iceberg lettuce, diced tomatoes, and shredded cheese to your filled gorditas, if desired.

FILLING

- 1 pound 85 percent lean ground beef
- 1 russet potato, peeled and cut into ¼-inch pieces
- 1 teaspoon table salt
- 1 teaspoon pepper
- 1 onion, chopped fine
- 1 tomato, cored and chopped fine
- 3 garlic cloves, minced
- 1½ teaspoons ground cumin
- 2 teaspoons all-purpose flour
- ¾ cup water

DOUGH

- 5 cups (20 ounces) masa harina
- 2 teaspoons table salt
- 3⅔ cups water, room temperature
- 3 ounces Colby Jack cheese, shredded (¾ cup)
- 1½ quarts vegetable oil, for frying

1. FOR THE FILLING: Combine beef, potato, salt, and pepper in 12-inch nonstick skillet. Cook over medium-high heat until beef and potato begin to brown, 6 to 8 minutes, breaking up meat with wooden spoon. Add onion and tomato and cook until softened, 4 to 6 minutes. Add garlic and cumin and cook until fragrant, about 30 seconds.

2. Stir in flour and cook for 1 minute. Stir in water and bring to boil. Cook until slightly thickened, about 1 minute. Off heat, season with salt and pepper to taste. Cover and set aside.

3. FOR THE DOUGH: Line baking sheet with parchment paper. Whisk masa harina and salt together in large bowl. Add room-temperature water and Colby Jack and knead with your hands until mixture is fully combined. (Mixture should have texture of Play-Doh and easily hold fingerprint.)

4. Divide dough into 12 level ½-cup portions and place on large plate; divide any remaining dough evenly among portions. Working with 1 portion at a time (keep remaining dough covered with damp dish towel), roll dough into smooth ball between your wet hands, then return it to plate. Cut

We stuff these crispy fried corn cakes with a spiced beef and potato filling.

sides of 1-quart zipper-lock bag, leaving bottom seam intact.

5. Enclose 1 dough ball in split bag. Using clear plate or dish (so you can see size of dough round), press dough into 4-inch round, about ½ inch thick. Smooth any cracks around edges of

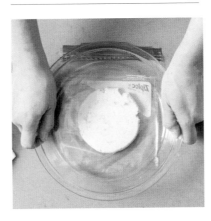

A Pressing Issue

To press the gordita dough, cut the sides of a zipper-lock bag. Then put one dough round in the bag and press it to a ½-inch thickness with a clear plate or dish (we like to use a clear pie plate).

round; transfer to prepared sheet. Repeat with remaining dough balls, placing second sheet of parchment on top once sheet is filled so you can stack dough rounds as needed. Cover with damp dish towel. (Dough rounds can be covered tightly with plastic wrap, without dish towel, and refrigerated for up to 2 hours.)

6. Set wire rack in rimmed baking sheet and line with triple layer of paper towels. Add oil to Dutch oven until it measures about ¾ inch deep and heat over medium-high heat to 375 degrees.

7. Fry 4 dough rounds until golden brown on both sides, 5 minutes per side. Adjust burner, if necessary, to maintain oil temperature between 350 and 375 degrees. Transfer fried rounds to prepared rack to drain. Return oil to 375 degrees and repeat with remaining dough rounds in 2 batches. Let fried rounds cool for 10 minutes. While rounds are cooling, reheat filling.

8. Insert paring knife into side of fried dough rounds and split 180 degrees to create pocket. Stuff each pocket with ⅓ cup filling and serve.

Shashlik

A visit to Brighton Beach in Brooklyn, New York, inspired our take on this flavorful cousin of kebabs.

by Matthew Fairman

A little sugar in the marinade adds a hint of sweetness and encourages charring.

I DIDN'T KNOW I was hungry until I smelled it—that unmistakable aroma of smoke and flame-kissed beef. My wife and I had been walking around the Brighton Beach neighborhood of Brooklyn, New York, when we followed our noses to a street vendor tending a wood-fired grill with a dozen or so sword-like skewers of sizzling beef. It wasn't until we took our place in line that I asked the person next to us what exactly we were waiting for. In a thick accent, the man said, *"Shashlik."* We'd take it.

As I finished off the last bite of the juicy, deeply seasoned, and well-charred beef topped with yogurt sauce, I was determined to figure out what was in the marinade—it had a unique vibrancy rounded out with warm spices that beautifully cut through the richness of the meat.

With some research, I found out that shashlik is a popular street food in Russia, Kazakhstan, the Caucasus, and anywhere in the United States with immigrant communities from these areas. Shashlik marinades vary, but there are three common elements: an acidic liquid such as vinegar, wine, or fruit juice; olive oil or vegetable oil; and a lot of onion.

After cooking through a pile of recipes, none of which produced shashlik as good as what had enchanted me in Brighton Beach, I got to work on my own marinade, which I would use to season 2 pounds of sirloin steak tips, one of our favorite cuts for kebabs because of its juiciness, big beefy flavor, and loose grain that enables it to soak up ample marinade.

Over the course of several days, I tested each element of the marinade. I opted for vegetable oil since its neutral flavor didn't obscure the impact of the marinade's other components. For the acidic component, I tested red wine vinegar, red wine, and pomegranate juice; we liked the assertive tang of the vinegar. And for the onion, I tried both slicing it and pureeing it in a blender; the pureed version won for its deeper onion flavor and smooth texture that clung to the meat. For each test, I grilled the skewered meat over a screaming-hot charcoal fire.

At this point the beef was juicy and flavorful, but my shashlik was far from perfect. With so much wet marinade on the beef, it was hard to get sufficient char, and the tanginess was monotonous and lacked balance.

I achieved the deeper browning I was after by adding a tablespoon of sugar, which caramelizes quickly over high heat. As for the spices, I remembered the kebabs in Brooklyn having cinnamon, just a hint of heat, and the earthy warmth of cumin. A lot of recipes call for citrusy coriander and savory bay leaf, so I added those to the blender as well. The complex smell of the marinade hit me as the blades spun, and my mouth began to water. I was on the right track.

The yogurt sauce I'd had that day contained caramelized onions. I wondered if it had been an ingenious use of the onions left over from the marinade, so I tested the theory while my beef marinated. I sautéed finely chopped onion in a little bit of reserved marinade and then stirred it into a mix of tangy yogurt and fresh cilantro. The familiar taste of the sauce was more proof that I was headed in the right direction.

But when the kebabs hit the grill, I knew for sure: My shashlik had that same unmistakable aroma, and true to the original, it tasted even better than it smelled. That street corner moment was mine to relive, again and again, in my own backyard.

SHASHLIK-STYLE BEEF KEBABS
Serves 4 to 6

Sirloin steak tips are often sold as flap meat; we prefer to buy one large piece and cut it into pieces ourselves. We cook this beef past medium-rare in order to get more charring and to keep it from being too chewy. If you prefer it less cooked, remove it from the grill sooner (125 degrees for medium-rare).

MARINADE
- ½ cup coarsely chopped onion
- ¼ cup vegetable oil
- 2 tablespoons red wine vinegar
- 4 garlic cloves
- 1 tablespoon soy sauce
- 1 tablespoon kosher salt
- 1 tablespoon sugar
- 1 teaspoon ground cumin
- ½ teaspoon pepper
- ½ teaspoon ground coriander
- ¼ teaspoon ground cinnamon
- ¼ teaspoon cayenne pepper
- 1 bay leaf, crumbled

BEEF AND SAUCE
- 2 pounds sirloin steak tips, trimmed and cut into 1-inch pieces
- 1 onion, chopped fine
- ⅓ cup water
- 1 tablespoon vegetable oil
- ½ cup plain whole-milk yogurt
- ⅓ cup chopped fresh cilantro
- 2 teaspoons lemon juice
- 6 (10-inch) wooden skewers, soaked in water for at least 30 minutes

1. FOR THE MARINADE: Process all ingredients in blender until smooth, about 30 seconds. Measure out 2 tablespoons marinade and set aside.

2. FOR THE BEEF AND SAUCE: Combine beef and remaining marinade in 1-gallon zipper-lock bag. Press out air, seal bag, and turn to coat beef in marinade. Refrigerate for 1 to 2 hours.

3. While beef marinates, combine onion, water, oil, and reserved marinade in 10-inch skillet. Cover and cook over medium-high heat until liquid has evaporated and onion is beginning to brown, 5 to 7 minutes, stirring occasionally. Uncover, reduce heat to medium, and continue to cook until onion is well browned, 8 to 10 minutes longer. Transfer onion to bowl and stir in yogurt, cilantro, and lemon juice. Season with salt and pepper to taste.

4. Thread beef tightly onto skewers, leaving ends of skewers slightly exposed.

5A. FOR A CHARCOAL GRILL: Open bottom vent completely. Light large chimney starter mounded with charcoal briquettes (7 quarts). When top coals are partially covered with ash, pour evenly over half of grill. Set cooking grate in place, cover, and open lid vent completely. Heat grill until hot, about 5 minutes.

5B. FOR A GAS GRILL: Turn all burners to high, cover, and heat grill until hot, about 15 minutes. Leave all burners on high.

6. Clean and oil cooking grate. Arrange kebabs on grill (over hotter side if using charcoal) and cook (covered if using gas), turning every 2 to 3 minutes, until beef is well browned, charred around edges, and registering between 135 and 145 degrees, 8 to 12 minutes. Transfer kebabs to platter, tent with aluminum foil, and let rest for 5 minutes. Serve with sauce.

Grilled Jerk Chicken

For a dish that packs such a powerful punch, it took some finesse to bring jerk chicken into balance.

by Cecelia Jenkins

LET ME START by asking three questions: How spicy is too spicy? When does "smoky" cross the line into "campfire"? And finally, when is it considered a compliment to be called "a master of jerk"?

These were all things I needed to consider in my quest to develop a recipe for bold, spicy, and nuanced grilled jerk chicken. Jerk seasoning is Jamaican in origin; the spice paste is based on Scotch bonnet chiles, thyme, warm spices, garlic, and scallions. Variations abound, and most traditional versions are smoked over pimento wood (from the tree that gives us allspice berries).

I selected five promising recipes to try. I made the jerk pastes; slathered them on bone-in, skin-on chicken pieces; fired up the grills; and got cooking. The good: The smell of smoke, chicken, and spices was amazing. The bad: None of the recipes turned out great. Some were overpoweringly spicy, some were bitter and acrid from too much smoke, and some tasted awkwardly out of balance. What's more, the wet jerk pastes made it hard to render the chicken's fat, which resulted in flabby skin. I knew I could do better.

My first step was to perfect my version of jerk paste. Since Scotch bonnet peppers can be hard to find, I decided to use habaneros, their similarly fiery cousins, instead. To the blender I added a couple of habaneros, four scallions, a good handful of fresh thyme leaves, garlic, brown sugar for sweetness and depth, salt, and some vegetable oil and buzzed everything to a paste. This first stab was decent, but the paste definitely needed more seasoning and complexity.

I considered adding more salt until a colleague suggested soy sauce instead; just ¼ cup worked great, contributing salty, savory depth to the paste. A bit of ground allspice, ginger, and cinnamon brought the requisite warm spice profile, and a little vinegar helped balance the brown sugar. In subsequent tests, my tasters kept asking for more thyme, and as I increased the amount, I grew more and more frustrated with the laborious task of pulling the tiny leaves from the stems. On a whim, I tossed a whole bunch of fresh thyme—stems and all—into the blender; my tasters loved the big herby punch and had no idea there were stems in the paste. Win.

Determining the best grilling method took a bit of trial and error, but I finally landed on a foolproof method. After marinating the chicken in the jerk paste, I set up the grill with a cooler side and a hotter side. I grilled the chicken pieces on the cooler side until they were cooked through before brushing them with a little reserved marinade (for a fresh burst of jerk flavor) and searing them on the hotter side of the grill. As for the smoke, my tasters surprisingly preferred the chicken without it. The jerk flavor came through more clearly, and the chicken was picking up plenty of char and grill flavor anyway.

This chicken is bold, but it's balanced. And this recipe will help you, too, become a master of jerk.

GRILLED JERK CHICKEN
Serves 4

Plan ahead: The chicken needs to marinate for at least 1 hour before cooking. Use more or fewer habaneros depending on your desired level of spiciness. You can also remove the seeds and ribs from the habaneros or substitute jalapeños for less heat. We recommend wearing rubber gloves or plastic bags on your hands when handling the chiles. Use thyme sprigs with a generous amount of leaves; there's no need to separate the leaves from the stems. Keep a close eye on the chicken in step 5 since it can char quickly.

4	scallions
¼	cup vegetable oil
¼	cup soy sauce
2	tablespoons cider vinegar
2	tablespoons packed brown sugar
1–2	habanero chiles, stemmed
10	sprigs fresh thyme
5	garlic cloves, peeled
2½	teaspoons ground allspice
1½	teaspoons table salt
½	teaspoon ground cinnamon
½	teaspoon ground ginger
3	pounds bone-in chicken pieces (split breasts cut in half crosswise, drumsticks, and/or thighs), trimmed
	Lime wedges

Herbs, spices, and a touch of brown sugar balance the chile heat.

1. Process scallions, oil, soy sauce, vinegar, sugar, habanero(s), thyme sprigs, garlic, allspice, salt, cinnamon, and ginger in blender until smooth, about 30 seconds, scraping down sides of blender jar as needed. Measure out ¼ cup marinade and refrigerate until ready to use.

2. Place chicken and remaining marinade in 1-gallon zipper-lock bag. Press out air, seal bag, and turn to coat chicken in marinade. Refrigerate for at least 1 hour or up to 24 hours, turning occasionally.

3A. FOR A CHARCOAL GRILL: Open bottom vent completely. Light large chimney starter mounded with charcoal briquettes (7 quarts). When top coals are partially covered with ash, pour evenly over half of grill. Set cooking grate in place, cover, and open lid vent completely. Heat grill until hot, about 5 minutes.

3B. FOR A GAS GRILL: Turn all burners to high, cover, and heat grill until hot, about 15 minutes. Leave primary burner on high and turn off other burner(s). (Adjust primary burner [or, if using 3-burner grill, primary burner and second burner] as needed to maintain grill temperature between 450 and 500 degrees.)

4. Clean and oil cooking grate. Place chicken skin side up on cooler side of grill, with breast pieces farthest away from heat. Cover and cook until breasts register 160 degrees and drumsticks/thighs register 175 degrees, 22 to 30 minutes, transferring pieces to plate, skin side up, as they come to temperature. (Re-cover grill after checking pieces for doneness.)

5. Brush skin side of chicken with half of reserved marinade. Place chicken skin side down on hotter side of grill. (Turn all burners to high if using gas.) Brush with remaining reserved marinade and cook until lightly charred, 1 to 3 minutes per side. Check browning often and move pieces as needed to avoid flare-ups.

6. Transfer chicken to platter, tent with aluminum foil, and let rest for 5 to 10 minutes. Serve with lime wedges.

Rustic Tomato Tart

Slices of ripe tomato nestled into a buttery, flaky crust? Sounds great, until the liquid in the tomatoes rains on your parade. **by Alli Berkey**

THE IDEA OF a rustic tomato tart—aka tomato galette—is simple: Slice tomatoes, season them, pile them onto flaky dough, fold the dough's edges up, and bake until the crust is golden and crisp. A tomato tart is perfect for lunch or as a light supper with a salad, and it's a fantastic way to showcase the sweetness and flavor of ripe tomatoes. But tomatoes contain a lot of water, and water and crisp pastry crust are mortal enemies. The crusts of more than a few tomato galette recipes I made during my research phase were so soggy that I couldn't cut a clean slice. And some attempts were dull in flavor, too. I headed back to the kitchen determined to make the best possible version.

The test kitchen has a recipe for a fantastic, easy, crisp crust that I was confident would work here. But I knew I'd have to do something to extract some liquid from the tomatoes before putting them into that crust. The two obvious paths were roasting and salting. Roasting worked but took too long. Slicing and salting the tomatoes and letting them drain in a colander was a better solution; it was quicker, taking just 30 minutes, and allowed the tomatoes to retain more of their fresh flavor.

Speaking of flavor, I decided to follow the lead of a few recipes I'd tried and add cheese to the mix. I tested several kinds: cheddar, mozzarella, Parmesan, gouda, and Gruyère. My tasters couldn't decide between the Parmesan and the Gruyère, so I used them both. I sprinkled the melty Gruyère right onto the dough before layering the tomato slices on top, and I saved the Parmesan for sprinkling over the assembled galette. The cheeses added welcome richness and also preserved the dough's crisp texture; the Gruyère helped waterproof the dough on the bottom while the wisps of Parmesan soaked up any extra moisture on top.

The galette was really good, but I had a feeling it could be better. Lightning struck when a colleague mentioned that she loved fresh tomato sandwiches not with mayo but with mustard.

Our crisp, buttery crust is the perfect complement to sweet, tangy tomatoes.

Mustard! After a bit of testing, I ~~de~~termined that 2 teaspoons spread ~~on~~to the raw crust (before the grated ~~G~~ruyère) provided the perfect gentle ~~kic~~k and brightness to this showstop~~pin~~g galette. If you like tomatoes, please ~~try~~ this recipe. It's a game changer.

~~FR~~ESH TOMATO GALETTE

~~Se~~rves 4 to 6

~~Sh~~arp cheddar cheese can be used in ~~pl~~ace of the Gruyère, if desired.

- 1½ cups (7½ ounces) all-purpose flour
- 2 teaspoons table salt, divided
- 10 tablespoons unsalted butter, cut into ½-inch pieces and chilled
- ~~6~~–7 tablespoons ice water
- 1½ pounds mixed tomatoes, cored and sliced ¼ inch thick
- 1 shallot, sliced thin
- 2 tablespoons extra-virgin olive oil
- 1 teaspoon minced fresh thyme
- 1 garlic clove, minced
- ¼ teaspoon pepper
- 2 teaspoons Dijon mustard
- 3 ounces Gruyère cheese, shredded (¾ cup)
- 2 tablespoons grated Parmesan cheese
- 1 large egg, lightly beaten
- 1 tablespoon chopped fresh basil

~~1.~~ Process flour and ½ teaspoon salt in ~~fo~~od processor until combined, about ~~3~~ seconds. Scatter butter over top and ~~pu~~lse until mixture resembles coarse ~~cr~~umbs, about 10 pulses. Transfer to

Three Keys to a Savory, Not Soggy, Tart

Drain tomatoes
Slice, salt, and transfer to colander to drain.

"Waterproof" crust
Cover dough with mustard and Gruyère.

Shape tart
Fold dough edges up and crimp to seal.

large bowl. Sprinkle 6 tablespoons ice water over flour mixture. Using rubber spatula, stir and press dough until it sticks together, adding up to 1 tablespoon more ice water if dough doesn't come together.

2. Turn out dough onto lightly floured counter, form into 4-inch disk, wrap tightly in plastic wrap, and refrigerate for 1 hour. (Wrapped dough can be refrigerated for up to 2 days or frozen for up to 1 month.)

3. Toss tomatoes and 1 teaspoon salt together in second large bowl. Transfer tomatoes to colander and set colander in sink. Let tomatoes drain for 30 minutes.

4. Adjust oven rack to lower-middle position and heat oven to 375 degrees. Line rimmed baking sheet with parchment paper. Let chilled dough sit on counter to soften slightly, about 10 minutes, before rolling. Roll dough into 12-inch circle on lightly floured counter, then transfer to prepared sheet (dough may run up lip of sheet slightly; this is OK).

5. Shake colander well to rid tomatoes of excess juice. Combine tomatoes, shallot, oil, thyme, garlic, pepper, and remaining ½ teaspoon salt in now-empty bowl. Spread mustard over dough, leaving 1½-inch border. Sprinkle Gruyère in even layer over mustard. Shingle tomatoes and shallot on top of Gruyère in concentric circles, keeping within 1½-inch border. Sprinkle Parmesan over tomato mixture.

6. Carefully grasp 1 edge of dough and fold up about 1 inch over filling. Repeat around circumference of tart, overlapping dough every 2 inches, gently pinching pleated dough to secure. Brush folded dough with egg (you won't need it all).

7. Bake until crust is golden brown and tomatoes are bubbling, 45 to 50 minutes. Transfer sheet to wire rack and let galette cool for 10 minutes. Using metal spatula, loosen galette from parchment and carefully slide onto wire rack; let cool until just warm, about 20 minutes. Sprinkle with basil. Cut into wedges and serve.

Finding the Best Liquid Measuring Cup *by Kate Shannon*

HIGHLY RECOMMENDED

~~P~~yrex
~~1~~ Cup Measuring Cup
~~P~~rice: $10.05
~~M~~aterial: Glass

Pours Neatly

Easy to Clean

~~O~~XO Good Grips
~~1~~ Cup Angled Measuring Cup
~~P~~rice: $6.99
~~M~~aterial: Plastic

~~C~~omfortable ~~H~~andle

Easy to Read

FOR FLOUR, SUGAR, beans, grains, and other foods that can be scooped up and leveled off, dry measuring cups are best. But using them to measure liquids won't work. It's difficult to see the liquid inside the cups and easy to overfill them. For everything from buttermilk to broth, we use liquid measuring cups.

EQUIPMENT REVIEW

To find the best model, we focused on those with a 1-cup capacity, the smallest size most companies make. It's essential that 1-cup liquid measuring cups have markings for ¼, ⅓, ½, ⅔, ¾, and 1 cup, so we nixed models that lacked any of those increments. We purchased 10 models, priced from about $5 to about $35. Most were glass or plastic, and two were made from silicone. Two cups had innovative measurement markings set on an angled ridge inside them, designed to be read from above. Another model was a nesting set that looked like lab beakers. We put all the cups through a battery of tests to evaluate their accuracy, ease of use (including pouring liquids into and out of them), readability, and durability.

About half the models we tested were accurate or off by just a smidge. But on the worst models, the 1-cup markings were off by a full tablespoon, enough to negatively affect a recipe. As for the readability of the markings, we preferred clear glass cups with bold, clearly marked lines that intuitively corresponded to plainly marked numbers. We also really appreciated that we could just look down into the innovative models with markings inside, no bending required. We found that cups with wide, round openings were easiest to fill; for tidy pouring, a centered, well-defined spout was key.

In the end, the no-frills, durable Pyrex 1 Cup Measuring Cup took top honors. It was accurate, spacious, and microwave-safe; it poured well; and it was easy to read. We also like the OXO Good Grips 1 Cup Angled Measuring Cup, which has a secondary set of measurement markings inside that can be read from above. Web subscribers can read the full story and results chart at **CooksCountry.com/cups**.

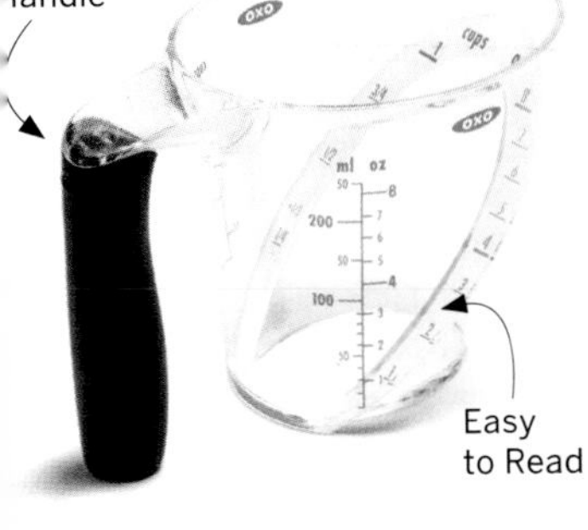

RECOMMENDED WITH RESERVATIONS

NOT RECOMMENDED

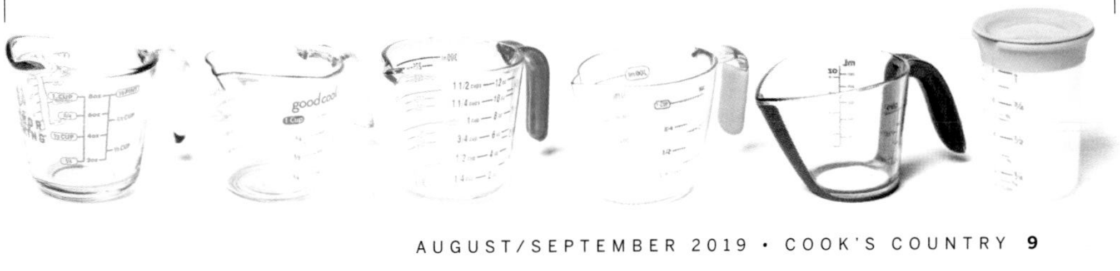

Picnic Sandwich

We wanted equal parts delicious and portable.

by Morgan Bolling

WHETHER IT'S FOR a picnic in the park, a hike in the hills, or a day at the beach, summer provides a lot of opportunities to pack a lunch. Sandwiches are a common choice, but every time I make a sandwich to enjoy later, I'm disappointed when I finally sit down to eat it. It either falls apart or has turned to mush. I wanted to create a flavorful sandwich that I could make several hours in advance and that could survive some travel and jostling without falling apart.

I found a ton of recipes promising "make-ahead" or "picnic" sandwiches. I made six that called for different breads, spreads, meats, and cheeses and let them sit overnight in the refrigerator to really push their limits. The next day, I called in my coworkers and we dug in.

We know that bread stales in the refrigerator, so it was no surprise that most of these sandwiches were really dry. Those made with mayo, aioli, or similar spreads were fused together with soggy layers. None of these sandwiches was great, but one was constructed in a way that intrigued us; it was built using a whole loaf of bread and then cut into portions. The sandwich's considerable heft helped it hold up better than smaller sammies; the big shield of bread on either side protected the contents from getting squished. Plus, a huge sandwich is really fun!

I started to work on my version from the outside in by testing different breads. Soft breads such as Italian or brioche fell apart or got soggy shortly after assembly. The crusts of other breads such as baguettes and *boules* were too tough to easily bite through. Plus, it's hard to know when supermarket breads have been baked; many straddle the line between fresh and stale.

Instead I decided to use (semi) homemade bread. I baked store-bought pizza dough into a puffy bread square, which I split horizontally once it had cooled. This pleasantly chewy bread was sturdy enough to hold up to fillings, and by baking it myself, I could control its freshness and size.

Mayonnaise doesn't travel well (it turns bread gummy), so instead I chose a spread inspired by red pesto, which uses sun-dried tomatoes instead of basil. I processed drained sun-dried tomatoes with briny capers, toasted almonds, parsley, garlic, lemon, and extra-virgin olive oil. This potent condiment not only added flavor but also helped glue the sandwich together.

From there, I let my tasters direct my choices. Deli turkey got the team's thumbs-up. Mild Muenster cheese added pleasant creaminess. Sweet jarred roasted red peppers provided color and flavor; patting them dry kept the bread from going soggy. Rather than lettuce (which can go limp during a walk in the woods), I opted for flavorful parsley leaves, which stayed fresh and bright.

With the basic setup settled, I wrapped a sandwich in plastic wrap and carried it a mile in a reusable grocery bag. When I unwrapped it and went in for a slice, the layers shifted off each other like tectonic plates. For the next round, I pressed the wrapped party-size sandwich under a heavy Dutch oven for an hour. Doing so not only helped fuse the layers together but also compacted the sandwich, making it much easier to bite through.

I plan on spending a lot of time outdoors this summer, so I created two more versions: a spicy sandwich using artichokes, hot cherry peppers, capicola, and provolone cheese and another using an olive spread with ham and creamy mozzarella.

Making Better Bread

1. Press store-bought pizza dough into 7-inch square, then bake and let cool.

2. Using serrated knife, slice baked bread horizontally into 2 even halves.

Pressing the sandwich makes it easier to eat and helps the flavors meld.

Finish by Pressing

After assembling the sandwich, wrap it tightly in plastic wrap and use a Dutch oven (the one shown above is about 14 pounds) to weigh it down for 1 hour. This compresses the sandwich to help it hold together.

TURKEY PICNIC SANDWICH WITH SUN-DRIED TOMATO SPREAD
Serves 4

Letting the pizza dough sit at room temperature for 1 hour makes it easier to shape. Toast the almonds in a dry skillet over medium heat for 5 minutes, until fragrant and golden brown. If you don't have a Dutch oven, you can use a baking sheet or skillet loaded with hefty canned goods to press the sandwich.

SANDWICH

- 1 pound store-bought pizza dough
- 1 teaspoon extra-virgin olive oil
- 4 ounces sliced Muenster cheese
- 8 ounces thinly sliced deli turkey
- ½ cup fresh parsley leaves
- 1¼ cups jarred roasted red peppers, drained and patted dry

SPREAD

- ¾ cup oil-packed sun-dried tomatoes, drained and patted dry
- ¼ cup sliced almonds, toasted
- ¼ cup capers, rinsed
- 1 teaspoon lemon juice
- 1 small garlic clove, minced
- ¼ teaspoon table salt
- ¼ teaspoon red pepper flakes
- 6 tablespoons extra-virgin olive oil

South Carolina Barbecue Hash

This local favorite requires a leap of faith.

by Morgan Bolling

1. FOR THE SANDWICH: Line rimmed baking sheet with parchment paper and grease parchment. Place dough on prepared sheet. Cover loosely with greased plastic wrap and let sit at room temperature for 1 hour.
2. Adjust oven rack to upper-middle position and heat oven to 425 degrees. Keeping dough on sheet, use your hands to shape dough into rough 7-inch square (edges may be rounded; this is OK). Brush top of dough with oil. Bake until light golden brown, 13 to 15 minutes. Let cool completely on sheet, about 1 hour.
3. FOR THE SPREAD: Meanwhile, process tomatoes, almonds, capers, lemon juice, garlic, salt, and pepper flakes in food processor until finely chopped, about 20 seconds, scraping down sides of bowl as needed. Transfer to bowl and stir in oil.
4. Slice bread in half horizontally. Spread tomato mixture on cut sides of bread, about ½ cup per piece (use all of it). Layer Muenster, turkey, parsley, and red peppers on bread bottom. Cap with bread top and wrap sandwich tightly in double layer of plastic.
5. Place Dutch oven on top of sandwich and let sit at room temperature for 1 hour. (Pressed sandwich can be refrigerated for up to 24 hours. Let come to room temperature before serving.) Unwrap sandwich, cut into quarters, and serve. (Sandwich can be kept unrefrigerated for up to 2 hours.)

CAPICOLA PICNIC SANDWICH WITH ARTICHOKE SPREAD

Substitute provolone for Muenster, hot capicola for turkey, and 1 thinly sliced small fennel bulb for roasted red peppers. For spread, substitute 1 (14-ounce) can artichoke hearts, drained and patted dry, for sun-dried tomatoes; chopped jarred hot cherry peppers for almonds; and 1 teaspoon chopped fresh thyme for capers.

HAM PICNIC SANDWICH WITH OLIVE SPREAD

Substitute mozzarella for Muenster, Black Forest ham for turkey, and 1 cup shredded carrots for red peppers. For spread, substitute pitted kalamata olives for sun-dried tomatoes and ½ cup fresh parsley leaves for almonds.

THE TERM "HASH" comes from the English word "haslet," which refers to the entrails (such as the heart, liver, and lungs) and/or the head of a hog. Don't worry. Stay with me.

As Southern food historian Robert Moss explains, "Hash comes out of traditions from probably as far back as the colonial days." When a hog was killed in a time before refrigeration, it was imperative to use as much of the animal as possible. Hams and shoulders were preserved with salt and smoke, fat was rendered into lard for cooking, and any other cuts were pickled and cured. Everything else got thrown into a big cast-iron pot, seasoned heavily, and cooked down for hours. The inedible bits were skimmed off, and the rest was served as hash.

Times have changed: Modern-day hash features ultratender shreds of pork butt, sometimes bolstered with pork livers or other offal, simmered in a tangy barbecue sauce. It falls somewhere between stew and gravy and is served as a side to barbecue.

Many restaurants flavor their hash with a tangy, often mustard-based sauce that is ideal for cutting through the richness of pork. The hash is simmered for hours, making for meat that's more finely shredded than standard pulled pork. It isn't pretty, but it sops into rice really well.

For my version, I cut a 3-pound boneless pork butt into chunks and seasoned it with salt, black pepper, and cayenne. I transferred the meat to a Dutch oven with some water and braised it in a 300-degree oven, which I prefer to the stovetop for its controlled heat. Two hours later the pork was fall-apart tender. I shredded it using two forks and stirred in a favorite mustard-based barbecue sauce.

But this first batch of hash was soupy and bland. Plus, the pork was still in relatively large shreds, not the fine pieces that are typical of this dish, so I returned the pot to the heat and simmered the hash, uncovered, until it thickened and the flavors intensified. This helped break down the meat, but the hash was still missing something.

After some brainstorming and research, I added 8 ounces of chopped chicken livers (which are easier to find than pork livers) to my next batch and switched from water to chicken broth. This hash had the deep, soul-warming flavor I'd envisioned. And it gave a nod to the original version (without my having to use a pig head).

Moss told me, "[Hash] is an essential part of South Carolina barbecue. You really can't go to Midlands or Lowcountry and not get hash. It's just part of the deal." After my final batch, I knew that from then on, hash would be just part of the deal in the test kitchen, too.

ON THE ROAD

Standing in his home kitchen in Columbia, South Carolina, Garland Hudgins pulls eight varieties of barbecue hash from his oven for my personal tasting. He and his wife, Rebecca May, frequently stop at barbecue

joints across the Palmetto State, even at places they've never heard of, just to sample the hash. Garland prefers a beef and liver hash that's heavy on the butter and light on the liver flavor. He presents me with an array of beef and pork versions with varying strengths of liver flavor and ranging from deep, sweet red to bright, mustard-tinged yellow. He tells me, "Hash can go in so many different directions. I won't say one is better than the other; you just like some more than others."

SOUTH CAROLINA BARBECUE HASH
Serves 8 to 10
Instead of chopping the chicken livers by hand, you can use a food processor; it will take about six pulses to get them finely chopped.

- 3 **pounds boneless pork butt roast, trimmed and cut into 1½-inch chunks**
- 4 **cups chicken broth**
- 8 **ounces chicken livers, trimmed and chopped fine**
- 1 **large onion, chopped coarse**
- 6 **scallions, cut into 1-inch pieces**
- 3 **garlic cloves, peeled**
- 1 **tablespoon pepper**
- 2 **teaspoons table salt**
- ½ **teaspoon cayenne pepper**
- 1 **cup yellow mustard**
- ⅓ **cup cider vinegar**
- 3 **tablespoons packed brown sugar**
- 1 **teaspoon hot sauce**
- 1 **teaspoon Worcestershire sauce**
  Cooked white rice

1. Adjust oven rack to lower-middle position and heat oven to 300 degrees. Combine pork, broth, livers, onion, scallions, garlic, pepper, salt, and cayenne in Dutch oven. Bring to boil over high heat. Transfer to oven and cook, uncovered, until fork inserted into pork meets little resistance, 2 to 2½ hours.
2. Transfer pot to stovetop. Using potato masher, mash pork until finely shredded. Stir in mustard, vinegar, sugar, hot sauce, and Worcestershire. Bring to boil over medium-high heat. Reduce heat to medium-low and simmer until slightly thickened, about 10 minutes. Season with salt and pepper to taste. Serve over rice.

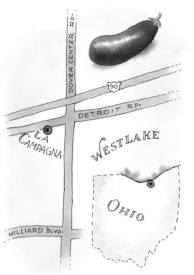

"If you want to find me, you'll find me."

Text by Bryan Roof; photos by Steve Klise

L A CAMPAGNA HAS no sign, so it's easy to miss the restaurant if you're not looking for it in the progression of storefronts in the strip mall. Carmella Fragassi tells me that her sign was 3 inches too big for the town's building code, and rather than redo it, she decided to do without. "If you want to find me, you'll find me," she says.

After 21 years as a narcotics agent, Carmella turned to the restaurant business. Her first restaurant caught fire two years after opening. It was a

At La Campagna, Carmella Fragassi (top) serves dishes inspired by her memories of visiting family in the Puglia region of Italy. Her brother Michael Fragassi (center) helps out in the kitchen.

big, demanding operation, and when it burned down she decided that the next venture would be smaller.

During a trip to Puglia, Italy, where she went to visit family and reflect, Carmella decided to change the way she wrote menus. With her new restaurant she would follow the practical Italian model of an ever-changing menu based on seasonality, availability, and economy.

She reopened La Campagna in a suburban strip mall 25 minutes outside of downtown Cleveland, Ohio. She wasn't looking for this location, and when it came to her it was supposed to be a temporary situation. It's just big enough for 10 tables; you can see into the kitchen from the front door. The peach walls are covered with racks of wine

and Italian imports, some of which Carmella uses in the kitchen and all of which are for sale. There's comfort in all the small details.

Carmella's earliest kitchen memories are of cooking with her grandmothers in Puglia, where she's traveled since she was 14 years old. "If you went to their houses, they never kicked you out of the kitchen. They would teach you how to cook." Now in her own restaurant, she tells me, "The biggest compliment I can receive is when someone tells me they haven't had something like this since their grandma cooked it."

Carmella's niece waits tables, her brother helps out in the kitchen, and her sister and cousin jump in from time to time. We begin discussing a recipe she calls "veal pocket": a rack of veal ribs stuffed with meatball mix and then roasted. Carmella can't remember the name and suddenly breaks from her train of thought to call across the dining room to a couple finishing their dinner. "Hey, Uncle Ralph! What did Grandma call that veal pocket in Italian?" Ralph pinches his fingers and bounces his hand in the air: "A-STUFFED-A-MEAT!" He laughs out loud.

Since she's been in business for 22 years, I ask Carmella how much longer she plans to cook. "I can't imagine that I'd ever retire." And then she adds with all sincerity, "I consider [cooking] a great gift that I can share with people." For more photos from our trip to Cleveland, go to CooksCountry.com/lacampagna19.

Eggplant Pecorino

*n updated take on eggplant Parmesan puts
e focus back where it belongs.* **by Bryan Roof**

EAD THE WORDS "eggplant
armesan" on almost any restaurant
enu and you know what you're in for:
mountain of mozzarella, a loaf's worth
bread crumbs, a swimming pool of
veet red sauce, and, buried deep be-
eath it all, a fat slab of mushy eggplant.
's usually a heavy dish that requires a
p afterward.

But at La Campagna, a small strip
all restaurant in Westlake, Ohio (see
f You Want to Find Me, You'll Find
e"), I was served a version of eggplant
arm that turned the concept on its
ead. A lighter hand produced a dish
at actually showcased the eggplant in
l the right ways: savory, faintly bitter,
uttery, and satisfying. The cheese and
uce added just enough context to
mplify the eggplant but not obscure it.

At La Campagna they slice the
ggplant superthin, which nixes the pos-
bility of a big bite of mush. Following
his approach, I chose eggplants of a
ertain size—1 pound or smaller—and
arefully cut them lengthwise into
-inch-thick slices.

I also decided early on to skip the
read crumbs and instead focus on fry-
g the eggplant in a thin flour and egg
oating. It's a simple process (dredge
ach slice in flour, dip it in beaten egg,
nd then shallow-fry in a skillet), but it
akes a bit of patience because you have
o do it in batches. It's worth the effort:
The process creates a light, fluffy shell
round each eggplant slice rather than
thick, bready coating—a much more
efined result.

At the restaurant, the dish is served
s an individual stack of about five slices
of eggplant layered with cheese and
auce. This is easy to do in a restaurant,
where you can build the stacks to order
vith prefried eggplant and sauce kept
varm on the back of the stove and then
hrow each serving into the oven to
inish. But I wanted a one-and-done
olution to serve six people. So I built
our stacks of eggplant in a 13 by 9-inch
aking dish, with sauce and cheese in
etween the layers.

About that sauce: Since this dish
lready requires a fair amount of work,
I wanted a quick sauce that remained
right, with underpinnings of deep
lavor. I softened onion, garlic, ancho-
ies, red pepper flakes, and oregano in
a couple of tablespoons of butter just
ong enough to extract their flavors,
bout 3 minutes, and then added

a combination of canned crushed
tomatoes and diced tomatoes with
their juice. A quick 10-minute simmer
concentrated the sauce beautifully. I
finished it with a fistful of chopped
basil for a fresh note and a tablespoon
of extra-virgin olive oil for some
Italian-style richness.

And about that cheese: I love
Parmesan (who doesn't?), but at La
Campagna they use Pecorino Romano
instead. Great idea: Pecorino's nutty,
tangy flavor pairs so beautifully with
the soft, mild eggplant that I chose to
follow suit. A final flourish of creamy,
tangy shredded fontina cheese, melted
and browned under the broiler, made
my eggplant Parmesan—I mean, eggplant Pecorino—extra-special.

EGGPLANT PECORINO
Serves 6

Do not use eggplants weighing more
than 1 pound each or the slices won't
fit in the baking dish. Use a rasp-style
grater to grate the Pecorino Romano;
shred the fontina on the large holes of
a box grater. Depending on the size of
your eggplants, you may not need to
use all three to get the 20 slices needed
to assemble the casserole.

SAUCE
- 2 tablespoons unsalted butter
- ¼ cup finely chopped onion
- 3 garlic cloves, minced
- 2 anchovy fillets, rinsed and minced
- ¾ teaspoon table salt
- ¼ teaspoon red pepper flakes
- ¼ teaspoon dried oregano
- 1 (28-ounce) can crushed tomatoes
- 1 (14.5-ounce) can diced tomatoes
- ½ teaspoon sugar
- ¼ cup chopped fresh basil
- 1 tablespoon extra-virgin olive oil

EGGPLANT
- 3 (10- to 16-ounce) eggplants
- ½ cup all-purpose flour
- 4 large eggs
- 1 cup extra-virgin olive oil, for frying
- 4 ounces Pecorino Romano cheese, grated (2 cups)
- 4 ounces fontina cheese, shredded (1 cup)

1. FOR THE SAUCE: Melt butter in
medium saucepan over medium-low
heat. Add onion, garlic, anchovies,
salt, pepper flakes, and oregano and
cook until onion is softened, about

We layer slices of breaded-and-fried eggplant with sauce and cheese to create delicious stacks.

3 minutes. Stir in crushed tomatoes,
diced tomatoes and their juice, and
sugar; increase heat to medium-high;
and bring to simmer. Reduce heat to
medium-low and simmer until slightly
thickened, about 10 minutes. Off
heat, stir in basil and oil. Season with
salt and pepper to taste. Set aside.
(Sauce can be refrigerated for up to
48 hours.)

2. FOR THE EGGPLANT: Cut stem
end off eggplants and discard. Cut
¼-inch-thick slice from 1 long side
of each eggplant and discard. Using
mandoline or slicing knife and starting
on cut side, slice eggplants lengthwise
¼ inch thick until you have 20 slices total (you may not need all 3 eggplants).

3. Place flour in shallow dish. Beat
eggs in second shallow dish. Line
baking sheet with triple layer of paper
towels. Heat oil in 12-inch skillet over
medium heat to 350 degrees (to take
temperature, tilt skillet so oil pools on
1 side). Working with 3 or 4 slices at a
time (depending on size of eggplant),
dredge eggplant in flour, shaking off
excess; dip in egg, allowing excess
to drip off; then place in hot oil. Fry
until lightly browned on both sides,
about 1½ minutes per side. Transfer

to prepared sheet. (As eggplant slices
cool, you can stack them to make
room on sheet.)

4. Adjust oven rack 6 inches from
broiler element and heat oven to
375 degrees. Spread 1 cup sauce in
bottom of broiler-safe 13 by 9-inch
baking dish. Starting with largest
slices of eggplant, place 4 eggplant
slices side by side over sauce in dish.
Spread ½ cup sauce over eggplant,
then sprinkle ½ cup Pecorino over
top. Repeat layering 3 times to make
4 stacks of 4 slices. Place remaining
eggplant slices on top. Spread remaining sauce over top layer of eggplant,
then sprinkle with fontina.

5. Bake until bubbling around edges
and center of casserole is hot, about
30 minutes. Broil until fontina is
lightly browned, 1 to 3 minutes. Let
cool for 20 minutes. Serve.

TO MAKE AHEAD
Casserole can be assembled through
step 4, without fontina, and refrigerated for up to 24 hours. When ready
to serve, cover with aluminum foil
and bake for 20 minutes. Remove foil,
sprinkle with fontina, and continue to
bake as directed in step 5.

No Need to Churn!

12 Easy Ice Creams

by Morgan Bolling

I ONCE MADE BRUSSELS sprout ice cream. Allow me to explain. Instead of going to the movies, my boyfriend and I make ice cream on Friday nights. And over four years, we've found ourselves in some flavor territories better left uncharted.

We've based most of our adventures on a recipe from this magazine's sister publication, *Cook's Illustrated*. It calls for using an ice cream maker to create a delightfully rich and luxurious texture, and it can accommodate all sorts of flavors and mix-ins.

An ice cream maker works by churning a mixture (usually milk, cream, sugar, and egg yolks) as it freezes to keep the ice crystals small as they form and to incorporate air—so that instead of a solid block of frozen milk, you have silky, scoopable ice cream.

But did we really need to use the machine? Last year, I found a recipe for a no-churn orange ice cream tucked in my editor's grandmother's recipe box. It called for whipping heavy cream in a blender to stiff peaks and then blending in sweetened condensed milk, evaporated milk, corn syrup, sugar, and citrus zest and juice—about a minute of work. No ice cream machine, no churning. You just pop the blended mixture in the freezer and wait.

The results rocked my world: velvety, creamy, scoopable ice cream. How could it be? As I read through the ingredient list, one piece of the puzzle was clear. The whipped cream—or, more specifically, the air trapped within it—stood in for the air normally incorporated by an ice cream maker. But in my experiments, I learned that too much air was trouble. When I used a stand mixer instead of a blender to whip the cream, I introduced too much air and ended up with a texture similar to that of frozen whipped topping. Not bad, but it wasn't ice cream. I'd stick with the blender, which produces whipped cream that's not quite as fluffy—a positive here.

The sweetened condensed milk and corn syrup called for in the heirloom recipe, both liquid sweeteners, helped create a smooth texture. I'd keep those. I found that I could replace the evaporated milk with whole milk (which I had on hand) with no negative effects. Two cups cream to 1 cup sweetened condensed milk and ¼ cup whole milk was the best, most consistent ratio.

This basic formula proved very adaptable. A hefty 1 tablespoon of vanilla extract and ¼ teaspoon of salt (to enhance the flavor) produced an intense vanilla ice cream with a texture that could hold a generous scoop of add-ins.

Melted chocolate incorporated beautifully. Soft stir-ins such as jams and caramel took a bit more experimentation, but with some tinkering and a light hand, I found the ratios that worked.

With a blender, some pantry ingredients, and a little know-how, the ice cream world can be your oyster. (But please don't put oysters in your ice cream—or Brussels sprouts. Trust me.)

Freeze It in a Loaf Pan

1 VANILLA NO-CHURN ICE CREAM

Serves 8 to 10 (Makes about 1 quart)

The cream mixture freezes more quickly in a loaf pan than in a taller, narrower container. If you don't have a loaf pan, use an 8-inch square baking pan.

- 2 **cups heavy cream, chilled**
- 1 **cup sweetened condensed milk**
- ¼ **cup whole milk**
- ¼ **cup light corn syrup**
- 2 **tablespoons sugar**
- 1 **tablespoon vanilla extract**
- ¼ **teaspoon table salt**

1. Process cream in blender until soft peaks form, 20 to 30 seconds. Scrape down sides of blender jar and continue to process until stiff peaks form, about 10 seconds longer. Using rubber spatula, stir in condensed milk, whole milk, corn syrup, sugar, vanilla, and salt. Process until thoroughly combined, about 20 seconds, scraping down sides of blender jar as needed.

2. Pour cream mixture into 8½ by 4½-inch loaf pan. Press plastic wrap flush against surface of cream mixture. Freeze until firm, at least 6 hours. Serve.

2 BIRTHDAY CAKE

Decrease vanilla to 2 teaspoons. Add ½ cup store-bought vanilla frosting and ⅛ teaspoon yellow food coloring with condensed milk. After transferring cream mixture to loaf pan, gently stir in 2 tablespoons rainbow sprinkles before freezing.

3 BANANA–WALNUT–CHOCOLATE CHUNK

Omit vanilla. Add 2 very ripe bananas with condensed milk. After transferring cream mixture to loaf pan, gently stir in ¼ cup chopped toasted walnuts and ¼ cup coarsely chopped bittersweet chocolate before freezing.

4 MILK CHOCOLATE

Decrease vanilla to 1 teaspoon. Add 6 ounces melted milk chocolate with condensed milk.

5 PEACH COBBLER

Omit sugar. Substitute bourbon for vanilla. Add ½ cup peach preserves and ¼ teaspoon ground cinnamon with condensed milk in step 1. After transferring cream mixture to loaf pan, gently stir in ½ cup coarsely chopped shortbread cookies before freezing.

6 SALTED CARAMEL–COCONUT

Decrease vanilla to 1 teaspoon. Increase salt to ½ teaspoon. Substitute caramel sauce for corn syrup. After transferring cream mixture to loaf pan, gently stir in ¼ cup toasted sweetened shredded coconut. Dollop additional ⅓ cup caramel sauce over top and swirl into cream mixture using tines of fork before freezing.

7 MINT-COOKIE

Substitute ¾ teaspoon peppermint extract for vanilla. Add ⅛ teaspoon green food coloring with condensed milk. After transferring cream mixture to loaf pan, gently stir in ½ cup coarsely crushed Oreo cookies before freezing.

8 KEY LIME

Omit vanilla. Substitute buttermilk for whole milk. Add ½ cup limeade concentrate with condensed milk. After transferring cream mixture to loaf pan, gently stir in ½ cup coarsely chopped graham crackers before freezing.

9 DARK CHOCOLATE

Decrease vanilla to 1 teaspoon. Add 6 ounces melted bittersweet chocolate and ½ teaspoon instant espresso powder with condensed milk.

10 STRAWBERRY-BUTTERMILK

Substitute ½ cup buttermilk for whole milk and 1 teaspoon lemon juice for vanilla. After transferring cream mixture to loaf pan, dollop ⅓ cup strawberry jam over top. Swirl jam into cream mixture using tines of fork before freezing.

11 PEANUT BUTTER CUP

Omit vanilla. Add ½ cup creamy peanut butter with condensed milk. After transferring cream mixture to loaf pan, gently stir in ½ cup coarsely chopped peanut butter cups before freezing.

12 MALTED MILK CHOCOLATE

Decrease vanilla to 1 teaspoon. Add 6 ounces melted milk chocolate and 6 tablespoons malted milk powder with condensed milk.

Six Hours in the Freezer

Nanaimo Bars

*Canadians have loved this tri-layer bar cookie for ages.
Time to bring it south.* **by Morgan Bolling**

NANAIMO, A SMALL city on Vancouver Island in the Canadian province of British Columbia, is just a few miles from Washington State, yet the city's namesake sweet is virtually unknown in the United States. But Nanaimo ("nuh-NIGH-moe") bars deserve a bigger stage. These three-layer bars, with their coconutty cookie bases, creamy centers, and chocolate ganache tops, have a spectrum of sweet flavors and satisfying textures worthy of international recognition.

To bring the bars stateside, I found five different recipes for Nanaimo bars, including a version from Nanaimo's city government. I spread them out for my tasters, and we assessed, layer by layer.

While some recipes took a no-cook route for the base, our favorite from this initial lineup called for cooking butter, sugar, cocoa powder, and an egg in a double boiler and then stirring in graham cracker crumbs, coconut, and chopped nuts once the mixture had thickened. We loved the fudgy and slightly chewy texture of this crust: sturdy enough to carry around but soft enough to sink our teeth into without destroying the bar. But I wanted to see if I could achieve it in an easier way.

I first ditched the egg, which requires cooking to do its work as a binder and stabilizing agent. Instead I turned to chocolate chips, which I melted in the microwave and stirred into the mixture. Once cooled, the crust was firm—but too firm, almost candy bar–like. In my next test I added some corn syrup and achieved the slightly softer result I was after.

In most recipes, that soft middle layer is made by creaming butter, confectioners' sugar, vanilla, and custard powder, an ingredient common in Canadian kitchens. Though it's hard to find in the United States, we found a supplier and ordered some to see what it was all about. Much like instant pudding mix, it contains cornstarch, salt, vanilla, and coloring. It didn't taste like much on its own, but when used as the base for the custard layer in the bars, it contributed eggy richness and a golden color. I needed to find a work-around for U.S. cooks.

I considered making a homemade custard from scratch, but the ideal thickness and sturdiness (I wanted the filling to hold its shape once sliced) proved elusive. So I experimented with

instant pudding mix, which made the bars too sweet. Next I tried cornstarch, which I mixed with butter, sugar, and heavy cream, but it lacked flavor. Nonfat dry milk powder turned out to be the solution. Combined with the other ingredients, it produced a rich, buttery, vanilla-y, salty-sweet filling with the perfect consistency.

Nearly all the recipes I'd found had included a matching top layer of ganache made by melting chocolate chips and butter. It's hard to improve on that. But adding a tablespoon of corn syrup made the ganache easier to slather over the chilled filling and gave the chocolate a winning shine once it was fully set.

Nanaimo bars, welcome to *Cook's Country*. We are so glad you're here.

A coconut cookie crust and a chocolate topping sandwich a silky, creamy filling.

NANAIMO BARS

Makes 18 bars

For bars with tidy edges, be sure to wipe your knife clean with a dish towel after each cut. We developed this recipe with Ghirardelli 60% Premium Baking Chips.

CRUST

- ½ cup (3 ounces) bittersweet chocolate chips
- 6 whole graham crackers, broken into 1-inch pieces
- ⅔ cup (2 ounces) sweetened shredded coconut
- ½ cup pecans, toasted
- ¼ cup (¾ ounce) unsweetened cocoa powder
- ⅛ teaspoon table salt
- ⅓ cup light corn syrup

FILLING

- 1¼ cups (5 ounces) confectioners' sugar
- 8 tablespoons unsalted butter, softened
- ¼ cup (¾ ounce) nonfat dry milk powder
- ⅛ teaspoon table salt
- ¼ cup heavy cream
- 2 teaspoons vanilla extract

TOPPING

- ⅔ cup (4 ounces) bittersweet chocolate chips
- 2 tablespoons unsalted butter
- 1 tablespoon light corn syrup

1. FOR THE CRUST: Make foil sling for 8-inch square baking pan by folding 2 long sheets of aluminum foil so each is 8 inches wide. Lay sheets of foil in pan perpendicular to each other, with extra foil hanging over edges of pan. Push foil into corners and up sides of pan, smoothing foil flush to pan. Spray foil with vegetable oil spray.

2. Microwave chocolate chips in bowl at 50 percent power, stirring occasionally, until melted, 1 to 2 minutes. Process cracker pieces, coconut, pecans, cocoa, and salt in food processor until cracker pieces are finely ground, about 30 seconds. Add corn syrup and melted chocolate and pulse until combined, 8 to 10 pulses (mixture should hold together when pinched with your fingers). Transfer to prepared pan. Using bottom of greased measuring cup, press crumbs into even layer in bottom of pan. Refrigerate while making filling.

3. FOR THE FILLING: In clean, dry workbowl, process sugar, butter, milk powder, and salt until smooth, about 30 seconds, scraping down sides of bowl as needed. Add cream and vanilla and process until fully combined, about 15 seconds. Spread filling evenly over crust. Cover pan with plastic wrap and refrigerate until filling is set and firm, about 2 hours.

4. FOR THE TOPPING: Microwave chocolate chips, butter, and corn syrup in bowl at 50 percent power, stirring occasionally, until chocolate chips and butter are melted and mixture is smooth, 1 to 2 minutes. Using offset spatula, spread chocolate mixture evenly over set filling. Refrigerate until topping is set, about 30 minutes.

5. Using foil overhang, lift bars out of pan and transfer to cutting board; discard foil. Using chef's knife, trim outer ¼ inch of square to make neat edges (wipe knife clean with dish towel after each cut). Cut square into thirds to create 3 rectangles. Cut each rectangle crosswise into 6 equal pieces. Let bars sit at room temperature for 20 minutes before serving. (Bars can be refrigerated for up to 2 days.)

Chickpea and Poblano Quesadillas

30-MINUTE SUPPER

Strip Steaks with Creamed Kale

30-MINUTE SUPPER

Kielbasa Hash with Potatoes and Fried Eggs

30-MINUTE SUPPER

Sweet and Savory Chicken Stir-Fry

30-MINUTE SUPPER

Strip Steaks with Creamed Kale
Serves 4

Be sure to wash the kale leaves well before cooking, as they can often be full of sand.

- 1½ **pounds curly kale, stemmed, leaves cut into 2-inch pieces**
- ½ **teaspoon table salt, plus salt for cooking kale**
- 2 **tablespoons vegetable oil, divided**
- 1 **shallot, sliced thin**
- 4 **garlic cloves, sliced thin**
- 1½ **cups heavy cream**
- ½ **teaspoon pepper, divided**
- 2 **(1-pound) strip steaks, 1 inch thick, trimmed and halved crosswise**
  Lemon wedges

1. Bring 4 quarts water to boil in Dutch oven over high heat. Add kale and 2 tablespoons salt and cook until wilted, 2 minutes. Drain kale in colander, pressing with rubber spatula to remove excess water; set aside.
2. Heat 1 tablespoon oil in now-empty pot over medium heat until shimmering. Add shallot and garlic and cook until just softened, about 2 minutes. Stir in kale and cook until any remaining water has evaporated, 2 minutes. Add cream and ¼ teaspoon pepper and cook until cream is thickened and clings to kale, about 3 minutes. Remove pot from heat and cover to keep warm.
3. Pat steaks dry with paper towels and sprinkle with salt and remaining ¼ teaspoon pepper. Heat remaining 1 tablespoon oil in 12-inch nonstick skillet over medium-high heat until just smoking. Add steaks and cook, flipping steaks every 2 minutes, until well browned and meat registers 125 degrees (for medium-rare), 10 to 12 minutes. Transfer steaks to platter and let rest for 5 minutes. Serve steaks with kale and lemon wedges.

Chickpea and Poblano Quesadillas
Serves 4

If your avocados are not yet ripe, you may need to add an extra 1 to 2 tablespoons of water to the blender when processing the avocado sauce.

- 2 **ripe avocados, halved and pitted**
- 3 **tablespoons water**
- 1 **tablespoon lime juice**
- ¾ **teaspoon table salt, divided**
- 1 **tablespoon chopped fresh cilantro**
- 1 **(15-ounce) can chickpeas, rinsed**
- 8 **ounces Monterey Jack cheese, shredded (2 cups)**
- 1 **poblano chile, stemmed, seeded, and chopped fine**
- 3 **scallions, sliced thin**
- ¼ **teaspoon pepper**
- 4 **(10-inch) flour tortillas**
- 2 **tablespoons vegetable oil, divided**

1. Process avocados, water, lime juice, and ¼ teaspoon salt in blender until smooth, about 30 seconds. Transfer to bowl and stir in cilantro; set aside.
2. Using potato masher, mash half of chickpeas in second bowl. Stir in Monterey Jack, poblano, scallions, pepper, remaining ½ teaspoon salt, and remaining chickpeas until combined. Spread 1 cup chickpea mixture over half of each tortilla, leaving ½-inch border at edge. Fold tortillas over filling and press firmly to seal.
3. Heat 1 tablespoon oil in 12-inch nonstick skillet over medium heat until shimmering. Place 2 quesadillas in skillet. Set large saucepan on top of quesadillas and cook until browned on both sides and cheese is melted, about 2 minutes per side. Transfer to cutting board. Repeat with remaining 1 tablespoon oil and remaining 2 quesadillas. Cut into wedges and serve with avocado sauce.

Sweet and Savory Chicken Stir-Fry
Serves 4

Serve over rice noodles.

- 1 **cup pineapple juice**
- 3 **tablespoons soy sauce**
- 3 **tablespoons Asian sweet chili sauce**
- 2 **tablespoons cornstarch**
- 3 **garlic cloves, minced**
- 3 **(6- to 8-ounce) boneless, skinless chicken breasts, sliced crosswise ½ inch thick**
- 1 **tablespoon vegetable oil**
- 12 **ounces broccoli florets, cut into 1½-inch pieces**
- 1 **cup 1-inch pineapple chunks**
- ¼ **teaspoon table salt**
- ¼ **cup water**
- ¼ **cup fresh cilantro leaves**

1. Whisk pineapple juice, soy sauce, chili sauce, cornstarch, and garlic in bowl until cornstarch is dissolved. Combine chicken and 3 tablespoons pineapple juice mixture in second bowl and let sit for 15 minutes.
2. Heat oil in 12-inch nonstick skillet over high heat until just smoking. Add chicken and cook, without stirring, until well browned on bottom, about 2 minutes. Stir and continue to cook until chicken is spotty brown and cooked through, about 2 minutes longer. Transfer chicken to large plate.
3. Add broccoli, pineapple, and salt to now-empty skillet. Cover and cook over high heat, shaking skillet occasionally, until broccoli is tender, about 3 minutes. Return chicken to skillet. Add water and remaining pineapple juice mixture and cook until slightly thickened, about 1 minute. Sprinkle with cilantro leaves and serve.

Kielbasa Hash with Potatoes and Fried Eggs
Serves 4

Other types of precooked sausage can be substituted for the kielbasa, if desired.

- 2 **tablespoons unsalted butter, divided**
- 1 **onion, chopped fine**
- 1 **green bell pepper, stemmed, seeded, and cut into ½-inch pieces**
- 1½ **pounds Yukon Gold potatoes, peeled, grated, and patted dry**
- 1 **pound kielbasa sausage, cut into ½-inch chunks**
- ¾ **teaspoon table salt**
- ¼ **teaspoon pepper**
- 5 **teaspoons minced fresh sage, divided**
- 8 **large eggs, divided**

1. Melt 1 tablespoon butter in 12-inch nonstick skillet over medium-high heat. Add onion and bell pepper and cook until softened, about 4 minutes. Stir in potatoes, kielbasa, salt, and pepper and cook, stirring occasionally, until potatoes are lightly browned, about 10 minutes. Stir in 1 tablespoon sage and gently press mixture into even layer. Continue to cook until potatoes are well browned on bottom, 2 to 4 minutes longer.
2. Transfer hash to serving platter. Reduce heat to medium and melt 1½ teaspoons butter in now-empty skillet. Add 4 eggs to skillet and cook, without flipping, until whites are set, 2 to 3 minutes. Divide eggs between 2 plates. Repeat with remaining 1½ teaspoons butter and remaining 4 eggs. Serve eggs with hash, sprinkled with remaining 2 teaspoons sage.

Steak Salad with Carrot-Ginger Vinaigrette

30-MINUTE SUPPER

Pan-Roasted Chicken Thighs with Fennel-Apple Slaw

30-MINUTE SUPPER

Sausage and White Bean Soup

30-MINUTE SUPPER

Shrimp and Orzo Risotto with Saffron and Lemon

30-MINUTE SUPPER

Pan-Roasted Chicken Thighs with Fennel-Apple Slaw

Serves 4

We developed this recipe with Honeycrisp apples.

- 3 tablespoons sour cream
- 2 tablespoons maple syrup
- 1½ tablespoons lemon juice
- 1¼ teaspoons table salt, divided
- ½ teaspoon pepper, divided
- 1 large fennel bulb, 2 tablespoons fronds chopped, stalks discarded, bulb halved, cored, and sliced thin
- 1 large red apple, halved, cored, and sliced thin
- 8 (5- to 7-ounce) bone-in chicken thighs, trimmed
- ½ teaspoon cayenne pepper
- 1 tablespoon vegetable oil
- ¼ cup torn fresh basil leaves

1. Adjust oven rack to middle position and heat oven to 450 degrees. Whisk sour cream, maple syrup, lemon juice, ¾ teaspoon salt, and ¼ teaspoon pepper together in large bowl. Add fennel bulb and apple and toss to combine; set aside.

2. Pat chicken dry with paper towels and sprinkle with cayenne, remaining ½ teaspoon salt, and remaining ¼ teaspoon pepper. Heat oil in 12-inch nonstick skillet over medium-high heat. Add chicken, skin side down, and cook until browned on both sides, about 5 minutes per side. Transfer chicken, skin side up, to rimmed baking sheet and roast until chicken registers 175 degrees, about 15 minutes.

3. Transfer salad to serving platter and sprinkle with basil and fennel fronds. Serve salad with chicken.

Steak Salad with Carrot-Ginger Vinaigrette

Serves 4

The vinaigrette can be refrigerated for up to 1 week; whisk before serving.

- 4 carrots (2 peeled and chopped, 2 peeled and cut into 2-inch matchsticks)
- ¼ cup seasoned rice vinegar
- 2 tablespoons water
- 1 (1½-inch) piece ginger, peeled and chopped coarse
- 1 teaspoon toasted sesame oil
- 1 teaspoon table salt, divided
- ¼ cup plus 2 tablespoons vegetable oil, divided
- 1½ pounds skirt steak, trimmed and cut with grain into approximate 4-inch lengths (about 8 pieces)
- ¼ teaspoon pepper
- 3 romaine lettuce hearts (18 ounces), quartered and sliced thin
- ½ English cucumber, halved lengthwise and sliced thin
- 4 radishes, trimmed and sliced thin

1. Process chopped carrots, vinegar, water, ginger, sesame oil, and ½ teaspoon salt in blender until finely ground, about 30 seconds. With blender running, slowly add ¼ cup vegetable oil and process until smooth, about 30 seconds; set aside vinaigrette.

2. Pat steak dry with paper towels and sprinkle with pepper and remaining ½ teaspoon salt. Heat 1 tablespoon vegetable oil in 12-inch nonstick skillet over medium-high heat until just smoking. Add half of steak and cook until well browned and meat registers 125 degrees (for medium-rare), about 2 minutes per side. Transfer to carving board. Repeat with remaining 1 tablespoon vegetable oil and remaining steak. Let rest for 5 minutes.

3. Toss lettuce, cucumber, radishes, carrot matchsticks, and ½ cup vinaigrette together in bowl. Divide salad among 4 plates. Slice steak thin against grain. Top salads with steak. Serve, passing remaining vinaigrette separately.

Shrimp and Orzo Risotto with Saffron and Lemon

Serves 4

We prefer untreated shrimp—those without added salt or preservatives such as sodium tripolyphosphate.

- 2 tablespoons unsalted butter
- 1 onion, chopped fine
- 2 garlic cloves, minced
- 1½ cups orzo
- 4 cups chicken broth
- 1¾ teaspoons table salt, divided
- ½ teaspoon pepper, divided
- ½ teaspoon saffron threads, crumbled
- 1½ pounds extra-large shrimp (21 to 25 per pound), peeled, deveined, and tails removed
- ¼ cup chopped fresh parsley
- ½ teaspoon grated lemon zest plus 1 tablespoon juice

1. Melt butter in Dutch oven over medium heat. Add onion and garlic and cook until onion is softened, about 4 minutes. Add orzo and cook until lightly toasted, about 3 minutes. Stir in broth, 1¼ teaspoons salt, ¼ teaspoon pepper, and saffron and bring to boil. Reduce heat to medium-low, cover, and simmer, stirring occasionally, until orzo is just tender, about 12 minutes.

2. Pat shrimp dry with paper towels and sprinkle with remaining ½ teaspoon salt and remaining ¼ teaspoon pepper. Stir shrimp into risotto and cook, covered, until shrimp are opaque throughout, about 5 minutes. Off heat, stir in parsley and lemon zest and juice. Serve.

Sausage and White Bean Soup

Serves 4

Serve with grated Parmesan cheese.

- 1 tablespoon extra-virgin olive oil
- 1 pound hot Italian sausage, casings removed
- 1 onion, chopped fine
- 3 garlic cloves, sliced thin
- ¼ teaspoon red pepper flakes
- 4 cups chicken broth
- 1 (15-ounce) can cannellini beans, rinsed
- 1½ cups canned crushed tomatoes
- ½ teaspoon table salt
- ¼ teaspoon pepper
- 3 ounces (3 cups) baby spinach

1. Heat oil in Dutch oven over medium heat until shimmering. Add sausage and cook, breaking up meat with wooden spoon, until no longer pink, about 4 minutes. Add onion, garlic, and pepper flakes and cook until onion is softened, 3 to 5 minutes.

2. Stir in broth, beans, tomatoes, salt, and pepper and bring to boil, scraping up any browned bits. Reduce heat to medium-low, cover, and simmer until flavors have melded, about 15 minutes.

3. Off heat, stir in spinach. Season with salt and pepper to taste. Serve.

Knife Basics

Before you can learn how to dice an onion with the effortless speed and grace of a master (tip of the toque to Jacques Pépin), you need to know which knives to use and how to care for them.

by Scott Kathan

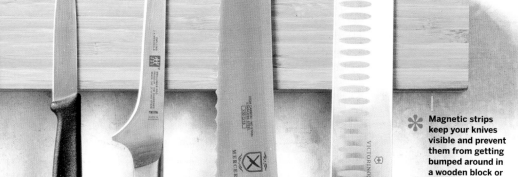

PARING KNIFE For small jobs such as coring apples or trimming radishes, a sharp, agile paring knife is essential.

EF'S KNIFE —
od chef's
e is the most
atile knife in
kitchen and is
t for everyday
oping and slic-
asks.

BONING KNIFE
A flexible boning knife is best for tasks that require the blade to follow the curves of bones and meat.

SERRATED KNIFE —
The teeth of a serrated knife are best for slicing crusty bread or delicate tomatoes.

Magnetic strips keep your knives visible and prevent them from getting bumped around in a wooden block or a drawer.

SLICING KNIFE
A long carving/slicing knife is the proper tool for carving most roasts, a turkey breast, or meats you want to slice thin.

Be Safe and Efficient

Adjust your grip as necessary for the proper balance of control and power; choking up on and pinching the top of the blade between your thumb and forefinger gives the best control. Pay attention to your nonknife hand—it is as instrumental to fast, safe knife work as the hand holding the knife.

For safety, always curl the fingers of your nonknife hand into a "claw." Move your hand and the knife when cutting, never the food.

Making horizontal cuts can be a useful step for efficient dicing. Cut off rounded edges to create a stable base for knife work.

Keep Knives Honed and Sharp (Not the Same Thing)

A honing rod sharpens the cutting edge of a knife. The easiest way to use one is to stand the rod straight on its tip and run the full blade of the knife along it, from heel to tip, at a 15-degree angle, alternating sides with every swipe.

But if your knife is truly dull even when properly honed, you'll need to shave metal off the blade—otherwise known as sharpening. You can send your knives out to be sharpened or use a whetstone (which takes practice), but we prefer to use a manual or electric sharpener.

15°

Wash Knives Correctly

Hand-wash your knives in hot, soapy water; if you have a carbon-steel knife, it's important that you thoroughly dry and (occasionally) oil it, too. Keep your knives out of the dishwasher, since the jets of water can jostle the knives and knock them against racks and other items that can damage or dull the blades. Harsh soaps can also damage the blade and the handle. Knives are easier to clean when you wash them right away, before the gunk has a chance to set up.

For fine paring-knife work, sometimes it's easier to lift the food off the board and carefully work with the food in your hand.

Web subscribers can read the results of our testing of chef's knives at **CooksCountry.com/knifetest**.

BRIOCHE
Buns and More

One simple dough, three perfect uses.

by Cecelia Jenkins

BRIOCHE, THE CLASSIC French bread enriched with plenty of butter and eggs, is perfect as a hamburger bun, dinner roll, or sandwich bread. Its paper-thin, amber crust; dairy-sweet flavor; impossibly soft interior; and buttery aroma make it the gold standard in bread, no matter the format. I wanted to achieve this standard by employing a straightforward method that even novice bakers could use to make brioche buns, rolls, or loaves.

I started with buns. Hamburger buns are usually made from a lean sandwich bread dough; I found a recipe for 12 buns that called for just one egg and a little butter. The buns get their structure from kneading in a stand mixer for about 5 minutes—the kneading realigns the strands of gluten in the dough, creating a strong framework that supports the buns as they rise and bake. This also develops the buns' chew.

Brioche is made a bit differently. Since brioche dough has more eggs and lots more butter than sandwich bread dough does, it has a significantly higher ratio of fat to flour. Fat shortens gluten strands, inhibiting their formation, so the butter is kneaded into the dough gradually (1 tablespoon at a time) while the mixer is running so the gluten has enough time to develop between additions. Once the butter is fully incorporated, the dough must be kneaded for a long time to sufficiently develop its structure.

Some brioche recipes call for a full 45 minutes of extra kneading in the stand mixer, but I had a few tricks up my sleeve that I hoped would help minimize the kneading time. The first trick was to use bread flour instead of all-purpose flour. Because bread flour has more protein than all-purpose flour does, it more readily develops

Butter Makes It Better

Brioche owes its richness to eggs and a hefty amount of butter in the dough. With all that extra fat, many brioche recipes (including ours) call for high-protein bread flour, which creates more gluten than all-purpose flour and thus builds extra structure to support the heavy fat. (All-purpose flour will work here, but the brioche won't stand quite as tall.)

gluten, which I needed here due to all the fat in the dough. The second trick was a power nap. Let me explain.

With 3½ cups of bread flour and a full tablespoon of yeast in the mixer bowl (this dough required more than one packet of yeast—usually 2¼ teaspoons—to help it rise under the weight of all that fat), I mixed in water and eggs until a dough formed. I then stopped the mixer and let the dough sit before adding the sugar, salt, and butter. This resting time, known as autolyse, allowed the flour to fully hydrate, a necessary step for gluten formation. Both sugar and salt slow hydration, so withholding them for a bit helped the flour better absorb the liquid and thus promoted gluten development.

Now for the butter. Softened butter incorporated into the dough more easily than cold butter did; I found that 13 tablespoons was just enough to give the brioche a rich, buttery flavor while still keeping the texture light and airy. After 10 minutes of kneading, the dough was silky, supple, and elastic. It was ready to rise.

After the dough had risen for an hour on the counter, it was time to shape it into buns. I found that simply cupping and rolling each portion of dough against the counter pulled it into a taut ball. I then flattened each ball with the bottom of a dry measuring cup so it would bake up into the perfect bun shape.

The silky, fluffy, feather-light chew of these burger buns was sturdy enough to hold up to a meaty, juicy burger without crumbling or sogging out. What's more, the versatile dough proved easy to shape into a pair of loaves (great for morning toast) or a big batch of dinner rolls. Choose your own baking adventure!

BRIOCHE HAMBURGER BUNS

Makes 12 buns

All-purpose flour can be substituted for the bread flour, but the buns won't be as tall; use the same amount of all-purpose flour by weight, not by volume.

- 3/3 cups (20⅛ ounces) bread flour
- 1 tablespoon instant or rapid-rise yeast
- 1¼ cups (10 ounces) water, room temperature
- 2 large eggs, plus 1 large egg, lightly beaten
- ¼ cup (1¾ ounces) sugar
- 1½ teaspoons table salt
- 13 tablespoons unsalted butter, cut into 13 pieces and softened
- 1½ teaspoons sesame seeds (optional)

1. Whisk flour and yeast together in bowl of stand mixer, then add room-temperature water and 2 eggs. Fit mixer with dough hook and mix on low speed until dough comes together and no dry flour remains, about 2 minutes, scraping down bowl and dough hook frequently. Turn off mixer, cover bowl with dish towel or plastic wrap, and let dough stand for 15 minutes.

2. Add sugar and salt to dough and knead on medium-low speed until incorporated, about 30 seconds. Increase speed to medium and, with mixer running, add butter 1 piece at a time, allowing each piece to incorporate before adding next, about 3 minutes total, scraping down bowl and dough hook as needed. Continue to knead on medium speed until dough is elastic and pulls away cleanly from sides of bowl, about 10 minutes longer. Transfer dough to greased large bowl. Cover tightly with plastic and let rise at room temperature until doubled in size, about 1 hour.

3. Line 2 rimmed baking sheets with parchment paper. Turn out dough onto counter and divide dough into twelve 3-ounce portions; divide any remaining dough evenly among portions. Working with 1 dough portion at a time, cup dough with your palm and roll against counter into smooth, tight ball. Evenly space 6 dough balls on each prepared sheet. Using greased bottom of dry measuring cup, press dough balls to 3-inch diameter, about ¾ inch thick. Poke any air bubbles in dough balls with tip of paring knife.

4. Cover loosely with plastic and let rise at room temperature until doubled in size, about 1 hour. Adjust oven racks to upper-middle and lower-middle positions and heat oven to 350 degrees.

5. Discard plastic and brush tops and sides of dough balls with beaten egg (you do not need to use all of it). Sprinkle tops of dough balls with sesame seeds, if using.

6. Bake until buns are deep golden brown and register 205 to 210 degrees in center, 18 to 20 minutes, switching and rotating sheets halfway through baking. Transfer sheets to wire racks and let cool completely, about 30 minutes. Serve. (Buns can be stored in zipper-lock bags at room temperature for up to 2 days or frozen for up to 1 month.)

TO MAKE AHEAD (BUNS)
At end of step 4, cover sheets with plastic wrap and refrigerate for up to 24 hours. Let dough balls sit at room temperature for 1 hour before proceeding with recipe.

BRIOCHE DINNER ROLLS
Omit sesame seeds. After first rise, divide dough into twenty-four 1½-ounce portions, dividing any remaining dough evenly among portions. Cup each dough portion with your palm and roll against counter into smooth, tight ball. Place in greased 13 by 9-inch baking pan in 6 rows of 4. Cover with plastic wrap and let rise until doubled in size, about 1 hour. Adjust oven rack to middle position and heat oven to 350 degrees. Brush dough balls with beaten egg. Increase baking time to 25 minutes. Let rolls cool in pan for 15 minutes, then transfer to wire rack and brush with 1 tablespoon softened unsalted butter.

BRIOCHE SANDWICH LOAVES
Omit sesame seeds. After first rise, divide dough into 2 equal pieces. Press each piece of dough into 8 by 5-inch rectangle with long side parallel to counter edge. Working with 1 piece of dough at a time, fold top edge of rectangle down to midline, pressing to seal. Fold bottom edge of rectangle up to midline and pinch to seal. Flip dough seam side down and gently push on ends to shape into 7 by 3-inch rectangle. Transfer loaves, seam side down, to two greased 8½ by 4½-inch loaf pans and pat gently to fill pans. Cover with plastic wrap and let rise until doubled in size, about 1 hour. Adjust oven rack to middle position and heat oven to 350 degrees. Brush loaves with beaten egg. Increase baking time to 32 minutes, switching and rotating pans halfway through baking. Let loaves cool in pans for 15 minutes. Remove loaves from pans and let cool completely on wire rack, about 1 hour.

TO MAKE AHEAD (ROLLS AND LOAVES)
Before second rise, cover with plastic wrap and refrigerate for up to 24 hours. Let dough sit at room temperature for 2 hours before baking. Increase baking time by 5 minutes.

Preparing the Dough

As the last of the butter is added to the mixer, the dough will look loose and thin. Don't worry; it will come together and tighten up to a smooth consistency (above) with continued kneading.

FIRST RISE
Let the dough rise until doubled in size, about 1 hour.

Shaping Buns and Rolls

1. Use bench scraper to cut dough, then use scale to portion it.

2. Cup each portion with your palm and move in circles to make smooth balls.

FULLY RISEN
Buns (top) and rolls (bottom)

Shaping Loaves

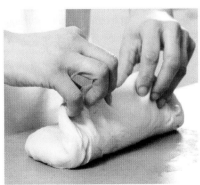

1. Press dough into rectangle, then fold top edge down to middle and press to seal.

2. Fold bottom edge up to middle, pinch to seal, and place seam side down in pan.

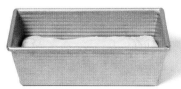

BEFORE AND AFTER
The loaf below is ready to be baked.

Hot Buttered Lobster Rolls

Hold the mayo—and the celery. For lobster lovers, a buttered lobster roll doesn't need 'em.

by Alli Berkey

THERE ARE MANY ways to make a lobster roll—and I love them all. Where I live near Boston, the cold mayonnaise and celery version is the most popular. But since butter and lobster make such a great match, I wanted to take a deep dive into the style of lobster roll that uses melted butter in place of the mayo and celery. I set out to make the best version of the buttered style, one that would be easily achievable for the home cook.

Fresh, live lobster is plentiful (and often relatively inexpensive) where I live; the New England coast is the epicenter of the country's lobster industry. But for the sake of readers in other parts of the country, I knew I needed to look into other options. So in addition to using the meat from live local lobsters that I boiled and shelled myself, I made hot buttered lobster rolls using the meat from frozen lobster tails (which are sold raw and in the shells), canned chunk lobster meat, and a canister of preshelled meat from my fishmonger.

The canned chunk meat was mushy and lacking in flavor, and the preshelled meat was too chewy (likely as a result of overcooking). The lesson: Whether you buy live lobsters (our first choice) or frozen tails (our second choice), it's important to cook them yourself for the best-tasting, most tender meat.

Since neither chewy, stringy meat nor raw lobster would do, I knew that a foolproof cooking method would be key to this recipe's success. Knowing that I'd use the meat from the tails and claws of fresh lobsters (there are lots of tasty morsels in the body, too, but they are smaller and take a bit of work to get to), I determined that I'd need three 1½-pound lobsters to make four rolls. Using three lobsters meant that I couldn't cook them in a

The lobster is bathed in melted butter as it finishes cooking in the skillet.

standard Dutch oven; I'd need a larger stockpot to fit them. I tried poaching, boiling, simmering, and steaming the lobsters. Poaching took too long, and steaming resulted in uneven cooking. Simmering in plenty of salted water (for seasoning) was the way to go; in about 12 minutes, the lobster meat was perfectly cooked and—after a 10-minute rest—easy to remove from the shells.

As for the butter, my plan was to follow other recipes and toss the chopped shelled meat in melted butter in the same skillet I'd use to toast the hot dog buns. After a bit of testing, I landed on toasting the buns first,

removing them from the skillet, and then adding 6 tablespoons of unsalted butter. Once the butter had melted, I tossed in the lobster meat and heated it through for a few minutes before scooping the sweet, glistening morsels into the buns. A minced shallot added to the butter provided another layer of sweet, savory flavor without overcomplicating things or overshadowing the lobster's sweetness.

But I ran into a problem. Since lobster meat is very delicate and prone to overcooking (and becoming rubbery and chewy), fully cooking the lobsters before warming the meat through in the skillet was causing the meat to

overcook. I found that it was best to slightly undercook the lobsters during their initial simmer; after 10 minutes the meat was cooked almost all the way through and still came out of the shell easily. To finish, a sprinkling of minced chives along with lemon wedges on the side brought these lobster rolls over the top.

My colleagues were smitten with these buttery lobster rolls, so much so that a few claimed they were swearing off the cold, mayo-based version forever. While I'm not ready to make that leap, these hot buttered lobster rolls are definitely going into my summer cooking rotation.

HOT BUTTERED LOBSTER ROLLS

Serves 4

For the best results, use live lobsters. If you cannot find live lobsters, eight 4- to 5-ounce frozen lobster tails can be substituted; reduce the cooking time in step 1 to 4 minutes, or cook until the meat registers 135 degrees. If New England–style hot dog buns, also known as "split-top" buns, are unavailable, you can substitute regular hot dog buns or, in a pinch, hamburger buns.

- 3 (1½-pound) live lobsters
- ¼ teaspoon table salt, plus salt for cooking lobsters
- 2 tablespoons unsalted butter, softened, plus 6 tablespoons cut into 6 pieces
- 4 New England–style hot dog buns
- 1 small shallot, minced (optional)
- 2 teaspoons minced fresh chives Lemon wedges

 Web subscribers can read the results of our unsalted butter tasting at **CooksCountry.com/butter**.

1. Bring 6 quarts water to boil in large stockpot over high heat. Add lobsters and 3 tablespoons salt, making sure lobsters are completely submerged. Reduce heat to medium-low, cover, and cook for 10 minutes. Transfer lobsters to rimmed baking sheet and let cool for 10 minutes.

2. Remove lobster meat from claws and tails. Cut meat into rough ¾-inch pieces; set aside. Spread softened butter evenly on outer cut sides of buns. Toast outside of buns in 12-inch skillet over medium heat. Transfer buns to serving platter.

3. Melt remaining 6 tablespoons butter in now-empty skillet over medium-low heat. Stir in shallot, if using; lobster; and salt and cook until lobster is heated through, about 2 minutes.

4. Using slotted spoon, divide lobster mixture among buns. Sprinkle lobster rolls with chives and drizzle with any remaining butter from skillet, if desired. Serve with lemon wedges.

How to Remove Meat from a Cooked Lobster

This is wet, messy work: Hold the lobster using clean dish towels to ensure a secure grip and protect yourself from cuts since the shells are sharp.

CLAWS

1. Twist to remove.
2. Separate claw pieces and knuckles.
3. Crack shells and dig out meat.

BODY

There are tasty morsels within the lobster's body, but they take a bit of work to get to. The small side legs are great for snacking on—some say their fine shreds of meat are the sweetest.

TAIL

1. Twist to separate from body.
2. Pull off small flippers.
3. Use shears to cut through underside of shell, or use your fingers to push meat out through larger (body side) opening.

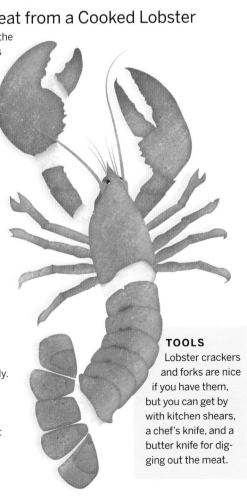

TOOLS
Lobster crackers and forks are nice if you have them, but you can get by with kitchen shears, a chef's knife, and a butter knife for digging out the meat.

Corn Salsa

Chiles and char elevate sweet summer corn.

by Natalie Estrada

I MAKE CORN salsa frequently in the summer by simply throwing corn and whatever else I have on hand on the grill and then buzzing everything in a food processor. Some versions definitely come out better than others. I wanted to create a foolproof recipe that would deliver every time. And since I wanted this recipe to work even on a rainy day or when corn isn't at its peak, I decided to develop it using the broiler instead of the grill.

To start, I added two ears of corn, an onion sliced into rounds, and a few jalapeños to a rimmed baking sheet; slid the sheet under the broiler; and let the heat do its thing. When the vegetables were nicely charred, I chopped them up, squeezed in some lime juice, seasoned with salt and pepper, and had a taste. Yowza! The salsa was too spicy—you couldn't taste the corn through the burn. It was much better, I found, to use a rich poblano chile for flavor and just a single jalapeño for heat and brightness.

There were a few more details to work through. I found that not turning the corn under the broiler resulted in deep, caramelized flavor on the kernels sitting right below the broiler element and crunchy, sweet pops of corn from the unexposed side of the cob. Adding a few garlic cloves brought extra depth to the salsa. And a few meaty plum tomatoes, halved lengthwise and broiled skin side up, tied the elements together without making the salsa read as tomatoey. Fresh cilantro gave the salsa a fragrant blast. Here was summer corn at its finest.

ROASTED CORN SALSA

Serves 10 to 12 (Makes about 3½ cups)

This salsa can be served with chips or as an accompaniment to pork, chicken, or fish. For a spicier salsa, add more cayenne. To get a variety of textures and flavors in the salsa, we do not rotate the corn while we broil it.

- 1 pound plum tomatoes, cored and halved lengthwise
- 2 ears corn, husks and silk removed, halved crosswise
- 1 small onion, sliced into ½-inch-thick rounds
- 1 poblano chile, stemmed, halved, and seeded
- 1 jalapeño chile, stemmed, halved, and seeded
- 1 tablespoon vegetable oil
- 2 garlic cloves, peeled
- 1 teaspoon table salt, divided
- 2 tablespoons lime juice
- ⅛ teaspoon cayenne pepper, plus extra for seasoning
- ½ cup chopped fresh cilantro leaves and stems

1. Adjust oven rack 6 inches from broiler element and heat broiler. Toss tomatoes, corn, onion, poblano, jalapeño, oil, garlic, and ½ teaspoon salt together on rimmed baking sheet. Flip tomatoes and chiles skin side up. Broil until vegetables are well charred, 12 to 14 minutes. Let vegetables cool on sheet for 10 minutes.

2. Cut kernels off cobs and transfer to large bowl. Pulse onion, poblano, and jalapeño in food processor until pieces are no larger than ½ inch, 8 to 10 pulses, scraping down sides of bowl as needed. Add to bowl with corn.

3. Process lime juice, cayenne, tomatoes, garlic, and remaining ½ teaspoon salt in now-empty processor until smooth, about 30 seconds. Stir tomato mixture and cilantro into corn mixture until fully incorporated. Let sit for 1 hour at room temperature. Season with salt and extra cayenne to taste. Serve. (Salsa can be refrigerated for up to 3 days.)

Pineapple Upside-Down Cake

This beautiful retro cake deserved an update—and kicking the can(ned pineapple) was just the start.

by Matthew Fairman

WITH GLISTENING RINGS of sweet-tart pineapple and ruby pops of maraschino cherries adorning a buttery, tender yellow cake, the pineapple upside-down cake is one of America's most iconic desserts. At its most basic, the dessert is a stir-together yellow cake baked atop butter, brown sugar, canned pineapple rings, and jarred cherries and then inverted once baked so the fruit is on top.

My colleagues and I sampled five recipes for this cake, and we were surprised to find that while the cakes looked great, they simply weren't as delicious or as special as they should have been. To start, the cakes themselves didn't have pineapple flavor, and the toppings had metallic notes from the canned fruit. The versions we tried with chunks of fresh pineapple were better, but we all missed the retro beauty of the rings. Plus, all the cakes we tried looked a little dull and lacked a glossy caramel sheen.

We decided it was time for an update. I wanted my version to have loads of fresh pineapple flavor; a moist, buttery, simple-to-make yellow cake with pineapple flavor of its own; and a stunning, glossy look that amplified the iconic appeal of the rings.

I began by cutting a fresh pineapple into ½-inch-thick slices. Then I used round cutters to punch out clean circles and remove the tough core. I set the rings in a greased 9-inch round cake pan with generous amounts of melted butter and brown sugar (which would cook into a caramel). I then poured a simple yellow cake batter on top and popped the pan into the oven. Yes, the flavor of the pineapple rings was much fresher, but the fruit was still a little tough and the moisture it exuded made the cake soggy and mushy. And the cake still didn't look glossy or have its own pineapple flavor.

In my next test I tried to solve the sogginess problem while also doubling down on pineapple flavor. I grabbed a 12-inch skillet and cooked the amped-out fresh pineapple rings in a mixture of 1 cup of pineapple juice and an increased amount of brown sugar. This tenderized the fruit and cooked off some of its juice; I hoped it would also give me more caramel to leave the cake with a gooey, glossy shine.

Once I'd transferred the rings to the cake pan, I concentrated and caramelized the mixture of juice and sugar in the pan by simmering it until it was sticky and syrupy; I then added butter to create a pineapple-flavored caramel sauce. Half the sauce went into the cake pan with the pineapple. While the cake baked, I thinned out the remainder of the pineapple caramel with some dark rum—to cut the sweetness and add aromatic complexity—and a bit more fresh pineapple juice for vibrancy. Then, while the cake cooled, I poked holes all over it with a toothpick and brushed most of my pineapple-rum caramel on top to let it soak in. I reserved just a little bit of the caramel to brush on right before serving.

As I turned out this new, juiced-up version of my cake, I was delighted to find that it looked positively stunning. There was just enough extra pineapple caramel to leave a few drips on the platter and create the right gooey consistency and glossy shine, but not so much as to make the cake soggy.

The real revelation came when we all dug in. The rings were tender, juicy, and vibrant. The cake was ultra-buttery and balanced by the complex, heady pineapple-rum caramel soak. The essence of sunshiny pineapple carried through the entire experience, from top to bottom. This was a pineapple upside-down cake fit for a special occasion.

PINEAPPLE UPSIDE-DOWN CAKE
Serves 8
You will need a 3¼-inch round cutter and a 1¼-inch round cutter or apple corer to make the pineapple rings. If you prefer, you can substitute 2 additional tablespoons of pineapple juice for the rum in step 5.

- 1 pineapple, peeled
- 1½ cups packed (10½ ounces) light brown sugar
- 1 cup plus 2 tablespoons pineapple juice, divided
- 7 maraschino cherries, stemmed and patted dry
- 12 tablespoons unsalted butter, cut into 12 pieces, plus 8 tablespoons melted
- 1 teaspoon table salt, divided
- 2 tablespoons dark rum
- 1½ cups (7½ ounces) all-purpose flour
- 1 teaspoon baking powder
- 1 cup (7 ounces) granulated sugar
- ½ cup whole milk
- 2 large eggs
- 1 teaspoon vanilla extract

1. Adjust oven rack to middle position and heat oven to 350 degrees. Grease 9-inch round cake pan, line with parchment paper, and grease parchment.
2. Cut seven ½-inch-thick crosswise slices from pineapple. (Reserve remaining pineapple for another use.) Using 3¼-inch round cutter, cut slices into neat rounds; discard trimmings. Using 1¼-inch round cutter or apple corer, remove core from pineapple slices to create rings; discard core pieces.
3. Combine brown sugar and 1 cup pineapple juice in 12-inch skillet. Add pineapple rings to skillet in single layer. Bring to boil over medium-high heat and cook until rings have softened, about 10 minutes, flipping rings halfway through cooking. Transfer rings to prepared pan, placing 1 ring in center of pan and arranging remaining 6 rings around circumference of pan (rings will fit snugly in pan without overlapping). Place cherries in centers of rings.
4. Return brown sugar mixture to boil over medium-high heat and cook, stirring frequently, until rubber spatula dragged across bottom of skillet leaves trail that fills in slowly, bubbles increase in size, and mixture registers 260 degrees, 3 to 6 minutes. Carefully stir in 12 tablespoons butter and ½ teaspoon salt until butter is melted (caramel may look separated at first). Return mixture to boil and cook until frothy and uniform in texture, about 1 minute. Let caramel cool off heat for 5 minutes.
5. Transfer caramel to 4-cup liquid measuring cup. Pour ¾ cup caramel evenly over pineapple rings, gently shaking pan to distribute. Whisk rum and remaining 2 tablespoons pineapple juice into remaining caramel; set aside.
6. Whisk flour, baking powder, and remaining ½ teaspoon salt together in bowl. Whisk granulated sugar, milk, eggs, and vanilla in large bowl until smooth, about 1 minute. Whisk 8 tablespoons melted butter into milk mixture until combined. Whisk flour mixture into milk mixture until no dry flour remains.
7. Transfer batter to prepared pan and smooth top with rubber spatula. Bake until light golden brown and toothpick inserted in center comes out clean, 50 minutes to 1 hour.
8. Transfer pan to wire rack. Immediately run paring knife between cake and sides of pan. Using toothpick, poke about 80 holes evenly over cake. Microwave reserved caramel mixture until warm, about 1 minute. Brush cake with ½ cup reserved caramel mixture. Let cake cool in pan for 25 minutes. Carefully invert cake onto serving plate. Brush top of cake with remaining reserved caramel mixture as desired. Serve warm or at room temperature, passing any remaining caramel mixture separately.

BACKSTORY

It's hard to overstate just how glamorous pineapples were in Renaissance Europe. After Christopher Columbus presented a pineapple to King Ferdinand II of Aragon in 1496 following his second voyage to the Caribbean, the fruit became a culinary status symbol. It was so closely associated with European aristocracy that by the start of the English Civil War in 1642, it was a reviled symbol of excess. But the fruit bounced back, becoming a motif of luxury carved into mahogany bedposts, painted into portraits, and etched into ivory boxes. People who'd never tasted one had images of them on their wallpaper.

It wasn't until the late 19th century that pineapple cultivation truly took hold in Hawaii. By 1930, the islands led the world in pineapple production. Today, the top three pineapple producers are Costa Rica, Brazil, and the Philippines.

Key Steps

Use fresh fruit Top and tail a fresh pineapple, and then cut off the rind.

Create rings Use round cutters to remove the tough core from the slices.

Cook rings in syrup Simmer the rings in pineapple juice and brown sugar.

Reduce syrup Remove the cooked rings and boil the syrup down to a rich caramel.

Husk-Grilled Corn
by Matthew Fairman

A simple two-step grilling process produces the best grilled corn you've ever eaten.

BOILED CORN ON the cob slathered with butter is an American summertime tradition. We love corn prepared this way—its clean, sweet flavor shines bright. But corn is capable of expressing itself in deeper, more flavorful ways. When grilled, it picks up tasty browning and intensifies in flavor, and melted butter adds a finishing touch. If you've never tried grilling corn, this is the recipe to get you started.

HUSK-GRILLED CORN WITH SEASONED BUTTER
Serves 6

Look for ears of corn with green husks and golden-brown (not dark-brown) silk protruding from the tops. Also look for ears of similar size so they cook at the same rate. The seasoned butter can be made ahead and refrigerated, but let it come to room temperature before using. Set up a cutting board and knife next to your grill to avoid traveling back and forth between the kitchen and grill.

- 6 ears corn, unshucked
- 6 tablespoons unsalted butter, softened
- ½ teaspoon table salt
- ½ teaspoon pepper

1. Cut and remove silk protruding from top of each ear of corn. Combine butter, salt, and pepper in bowl. Transfer 3 tablespoons butter mixture to large plate. Set aside remaining butter mixture.

2A. FOR A CHARCOAL GRILL: Open bottom vent completely. Light large chimney starter mounded with charcoal briquettes (7 quarts). When top coals are partially covered with ash, pour evenly over half of grill. Set cooking grate in place, cover, and open lid vent completely. Heat grill until hot, about 5 minutes.

2B. FOR A GAS GRILL: Turn all burners to high, cover, and heat grill until hot, about 15 minutes. Leave all burners on high.

3. Place corn on grill (on hotter side if using charcoal, with stem ends facing cooler side). Cover and cook, turning corn every 3 minutes, until husks are blackened all over, 12 to 15 minutes. Transfer corn to cutting board. Using chef's knife, cut stem end off each ear of corn. Holding 1 ear at a time with dish towel, use tongs to peel away and discard husks and silk.

4. Roll each ear in butter mixture on plate to coat lightly, letting excess butter mixture drip back onto plate. Return corn to grill (on hotter side if using charcoal). Cook, uncovered, turning corn as needed to char lightly on each side, about 5 minutes. Remove corn from grill and roll each ear in remaining butter mixture on plate. Transfer corn to platter. Serve, passing reserved butter mixture separately.

 Want to take a deep dive into corn? Web subscribers can read our "Getting to Know" feature on this staple at **CooksCountry.com/gtkcorn**.

Step by Step

1. Cut and remove silk
Use a chef's knife to slice off the silk at the end of each ear.
Why? If left on, the silk would burn and smolder.

2. Make seasoned butter
Combine the softened butter, salt, and pepper in a bowl.
Why? Softening the butter helps the salt and pepper incorporate evenly; it also means the butter will more readily adhere to the hot corn later.

3. Light grill
If using charcoal, light a full chimney of briquettes; when the coals are ready, pour them into an even pile over half the grill. If using gas, turn all the burners to high.
Why? We want a very hot fire for this recipe.

4. Grill corn in husk
Cook the corn on the hotter part of the grill, turning it every 3 minutes, until the husks are blackened all over.
Why? The husk traps the corn's natural moisture to create steam that cooks the corn through.

5. Cut off stem end of corn
Holding the corn with a dish towel or tongs, use a chef's knife to cut off the stem end of each ear.
Why? Removing the stem end makes removing the husk and silk easier.

s: Choose ears that heavy for their size

Husks: Look for deep green husks

Silk: Look for dry, golden-brown silk

THE AMERICAN TABLE

In 1950, archaeologist Paul Sidney Martin was on a field trip to the Tularosa River in New Mexico, hoping to find artifacts related to the ancestral Pueblo (Anasazi) people. But among the artifacts he found were thousands of cobs of dried corn, or maize, in a cave in a bluff over the river. Thanks to radiocarbon dating, researchers found that some of the cobs were 2,500 years old, predating the Pueblo by centuries, which suggested that this crop had been developed and cultivated thousands of years earlier than previously assumed. The discovery further deepened corn's roots in American food history.

Shop Talk

Markets sell different varieties of corn (Butter and Sugar, Buttergold, Sunglow, etc.), but in our experience there's not a lot of difference in flavor or sweetness. The best advice is to buy locally grown corn when you can.

Essential Gear: Grill Tongs

A good pair of grill tongs should be able to handle anything you throw onto your grill—from delicate asparagus spears to floppy, unruly racks of ribs. Our winning tongs are agile but also sturdy and durable, with just the right amount of spring-loaded tension. And at 16 inches, they are just long enough to keep your hands away from the heat but short enough to give great leverage and control. They truly are best in show.

TEST KITCHEN FAVORITE
OXO Good Grips 16" Locking Tongs, $15

Our Hybrid Grilling Method

Shucked corn that's grilled often picks up nice char but doesn't cook through. Corn that's grilled unshucked will steam to tenderness but will lack flavorful char. Our method provides the best aspects of both methods—tender kernels with flavorful char (and lots of butter).

Flavor-Packed Butters for Husk-Grilled Corn

BROWN SUGAR–CAYENNE BUTTER
Stir 2 tablespoons packed brown sugar and ¼ teaspoon cayenne pepper into butter mixture in step 1.

CILANTRO-LIME BUTTER
Stir ¼ cup minced fresh cilantro leaves, 2 teaspoons lime zest plus 1 tablespoon juice, and 1 minced small garlic clove into butter mixture in step 1.

ROSEMARY-PEPPER BUTTER
Increase pepper to 1 teaspoon and stir 1 tablespoon minced fresh rosemary and 1 minced small garlic clove into butter mixture in step 1.

MUSTARD-PAPRIKA BUTTER
Stir 2 tablespoons spicy brown mustard and 1 teaspoon smoked paprika into butter mixture in step 1.

6. Remove husk and silk
Hold one ear at a time with a clean dish towel and use tongs to remove the husk and silk.
Why? The corn is hot, and the towel and tongs protect your fingers. The husk comes off more easily once grilled, too.

7. Butter corn
Use your hands to roll each husked ear in the seasoned butter, letting the excess drip off.
Why? The heat from the corn warms the butter and encourages full coverage. Letting excess butter drip off helps reduce flare-ups when the corn returns to the grill.

8. Grill buttered corn
Return the husked, buttered corn to the hotter part of the grill and cook, turning the ears as needed, until charred, about 5 minutes.
Why? The butter encourages flavorful browning and char on the corn.

9. Roll in butter again
Spin each ear in the seasoned butter a second time to add flavor to the now-charred kernels.
Why? We want lots of flavorful butter on the corn.

10. Serve, passing extra butter
This corn tastes best warm from the grill, with extra butter passed at the table.
Why? Because butter and corn are a perfect match.

Pasta Salad

Brightly seasoned chicken, pasta, cheese, and vegetables—all cooked in one pot for easy cleanup.

by Cecelia Jenkins

PASTA SALAD IS a summertime staple. It's perfect for those blistering days and sticky nights when you need a quick, cool meal that is light but satisfying. I wanted to make a hearty, tasty version that functioned as a complete meal, but it had to be easy—both to make and to clean up.

For many of us, a meal isn't complete without a protein, and quick-cooking chicken breasts made sense here. I started by gently poaching three boneless, skinless breasts in water in a Dutch oven; when the chicken was just cooked through, I transferred it to a plate to cool. Shallow-poaching the chicken in just 2 cups of water (flipping it halfway through) saved time and cooked it quickly yet gently. I then tried cooking the pasta in the poaching water, but the chicken had made the water a little cloudy and funky and it just didn't look right. So I dumped that idea (and the murky poaching water) and cooked 2 cups of fusilli in fresh water that I salted as usual to season the pasta.

One important step was to overcook the pasta. I know what you're thinking: Overcook it on purpose? Yes, because cooked pasta firms up and dries out when it cools. Overcooking it ensures that its texture will be just right once it's cool (see "Yes, Overcook It").

Knowing that I wanted a nice variety of vegetables in the dish—it's a salad, after all—I threw some fresh green beans into the pot with the pasta for the last 5 minutes of cooking. In addition to the perfectly crisp-tender green beans, I tossed a few handfuls of peppery arugula and a heap of halved grape tomatoes into the mix once the pasta had cooled, providing a burst of fresh, summery flavor and bright color.

Now I needed a punchy dressing to add deep seasoning and tie all the elements together. Using extra-virgin olive oil as a base, I tested various vinegars; my tasters preferred the bold, clear tang of red wine vinegar.

A happy jumble of potent ingredients makes this hearty salad sing.

Red pepper flakes turned up the heat, and fresh garlic and minced anchovies provided depth and complexity. A personal favorite ingredient—pickled hot Italian peppers, chopped fine so they'd integrate seamlessly—added another level of liveliness and interest.

The salad was tasting pretty good, but I wanted something with salty punch to take it over the top. "Feta," suggested one colleague. "Olives," lobbied another. Why not both? Delicious. A few final details: So that the recipe would come together quickly, I made the dressing while the chicken was cooling and the pasta was cooking. Seeing an opportunity to deepen the flavors, I tossed the halved grape tomatoes, olives, and pepperoncini right into the dressing to marinate while the pasta cooked.

This spicy, savory, and bright pasta salad has it all. Plus, it's a fast and easy enough meal for even the hottest summer night.

Yes, Overcook It

If you cook pasta according to the package directions—only until it is al dente—the resulting chilled pasta salad will be tough and rubbery. This is because as pasta cools, it goes through a process called retrogradation, in which the water in the pasta becomes bound up in starch crystals, making the pasta firm and dry. To combat this, we boil the pasta for an extra 3 minutes or so, until it's supersoft; during cooling, the retrogradation tightens up the pasta to the proper soft, but pleasantly chewy, texture.

ONE-POT PASTA SALAD WITH CHICKEN
Serves 4 to 6

Poaching the chicken in a very small amount of water reduces the cooking time and yields better chicken flavor. The pasta firms as it cools; overcooking it ensures the proper texture. If the salad is not being eaten right away, don't add the arugula until right before serving.

- Table salt for cooking chicken and pasta
- 3 (6- to 8-ounce) boneless, skinless chicken breasts, trimmed
- 5 tablespoons extra-virgin olive oil
- ¼ cup red wine vinegar
- 2 anchovy fillets, minced
- 1 garlic clove, minced
- ¼ teaspoon red pepper flakes
- 10 ounces grape tomatoes or 12 ounces cherry tomatoes, halved
- ½ cup pitted kalamata olives, halved
- ½ cup finely chopped pepperoncini
- 6 ounces (2 cups) fusilli
- 8 ounces green beans, trimmed and cut into 2-inch lengths
- 2 ounces (2 cups) baby arugula
- 4 ounces feta cheese, crumbled (1 cup)

1. Bring 2 cups water to boil in Dutch oven. Stir in 2 tablespoons salt. Add chicken, reduce heat to medium, cover and simmer until chicken registers 160 degrees, 12 to 15 minutes, flipping chicken halfway through cooking. Transfer chicken to platter and tent with aluminum foil. Discard cooking water. Bring 4 quarts water to boil in now-empty pot.

2. Meanwhile, whisk oil, vinegar, anchovies, garlic, and pepper flakes together in large bowl. Add tomatoes, olives, and pepperoncini to dressing and toss to combine; set aside.

3. Add pasta and 1 tablespoon salt to boiling water and cook, stirring occasionally, until pasta is tender, about 12 minutes (do not drain). Add green beans to boiling pasta and continue to cook until pasta is very soft and green beans are bright green and just tender, about 5 minutes longer. Drain pasta and green beans in colander and rinse under cold water until chilled. Drain well and transfer to bowl with dressing mixture.

4. Cut chicken into 1-inch cubes. Add chicken, arugula, and feta to pasta mixture and toss to combine. Season with salt and pepper to taste. Serve.

TO MAKE AHEAD

Salad can be made without arugula and refrigerated for up to 2 days. Add arugula and toss just before serving.

Chicken Jardinière

*One pot. One chicken.
One hour. One darn
fine dinner.* **by Alli Berkey**

The clean, fresh flavors of this hearty stew make it suitable for any season.

"GARDENER'S STEW" DOESN'T quite cut it in English. But when you borrow a word from the French, chicken jardinière sounds just as elegant as good versions of this dish taste. It's a light braise of bone-in chicken parts, carrots, potatoes, peas, and mushrooms flavored with garlic, herbs, wine, and often cured pork such as pancetta or bacon. It's light but satisfying—equally comforting and refined.

Many recipes for this dish require a lot of work, starting with breaking down a chicken, making stock, and cooking the vegetables separately before combining them at the end. What person, gardener or not, has time for that?

To simplify the process, I started with a bird's worth of bone-in, skin-on chicken parts. I seasoned the chicken parts with salt and pepper, seared them in a little oil, and then transferred them to a plate while I built the stew's flavor base. I started with pancetta (it won out over bacon and salt pork), which I cut into small pieces. I sautéed it with chopped onion, garlic, carrots, mushrooms, and thyme and then stirred in a little flour for thickening. When the flour had cooked just enough to lose its raw taste, it was time to add the liquid.

Traditional recipes call for homemade stock, but I went with store-bought chicken broth (for convenience) combined with some dry white wine; it's a French stew, after all. Then I added the potatoes and the browned (but not fully cooked) chicken parts. After about 40 minutes of gentle, covered simmering on the stove, the chicken thighs (which require more cooking than breasts) had reached

175 degrees. I took the pot off the heat and called my colleagues to taste.

Good, but not great. The white meat was overcooked and dry, and the vegetables lacked a certain je ne sais quoi. For the chicken, I simply started the dark meat 20 minutes earlier than the white meat; this ensured that all the chicken parts were done at the same time. But what about the vegetables?

I've always sautéed vegetables such as carrots and mushrooms along with the onions when making stews and braises. But a coworker prodded me to explore whether that was necessary here. It turns out that withholding

the carrots and mushrooms from the sautéing phase and adding them to the broth-wine mixture with the potatoes was the answer.

To finish the stew, I added frozen peas (right from the freezer, no thawing) at the end of cooking and then sprinkled on a bit of chopped tarragon—licorice-y and bright—before serving.

With whole chicken pieces and hearty chunks of vegetables in a deeply flavorful broth, my Chicken Jardinière doesn't exactly look fancy. But with one taste, you'll understand how it transforms a typical weeknight meal into something rarified and delicious.

ONE-POT CHICKEN JARDINIÈRE
Serves 4 to 6

Buy a 4-ounce hunk of pancetta from the deli counter. Try to buy potatoes with a 1-inch diameter. If you can find only slightly larger potatoes, up to 2 inches in diameter, cut them in half. Do not substitute russet potatoes for Yukon Gold potatoes. Note that the dark and white meat are added to the pot at different times in step 3.

- 3 pounds bone-in chicken pieces (split breasts cut in half, drumsticks, and/or thighs), trimmed
- ¾ teaspoon table salt, divided
- ¾ teaspoon pepper, divided
- 1 teaspoon vegetable oil
- 4 ounces pancetta, cut into ½-inch pieces
- 1 onion, chopped fine
- 3 garlic cloves, minced
- 2 teaspoons minced fresh thyme
- 3 tablespoons all-purpose flour
- 2 cups chicken broth
- ¾ cup dry white wine
- 12 ounces small Yukon Gold potatoes, unpeeled
- 8 ounces small white mushrooms, trimmed and halved
- 4 carrots, cut into 1-inch chunks
- ½ cup frozen peas
- 1 tablespoon chopped fresh tarragon or parsley
  Lemon wedges

1. Pat chicken dry with paper towels and sprinkle with ¼ teaspoon salt and ¼ teaspoon pepper. Heat oil in Dutch oven over medium-high heat until shimmering. Add chicken, skin side down, and cook until well browned on both sides, about 3 minutes per side. Transfer chicken to plate.

2. Reduce heat to medium. Add pancetta, onion, garlic, thyme, and remaining ½ teaspoon salt to now-empty pot and cook until onion just begins to soften, about 4 minutes. Stir in flour and cook for 1 minute. Slowly whisk in broth and wine. Stir in potatoes, mushrooms, carrots, chicken drumsticks and thighs, and remaining ½ teaspoon pepper and bring to simmer. Cover and simmer for 25 minutes.

3. Uncover and stir. Add chicken breasts and any accumulated juices to pot; return to simmer. Cover and continue to cook until breasts register 160 degrees and drumsticks/thighs register at least 175 degrees, about 20 minutes longer. Off heat, stir in peas and let sit uncovered for 5 minutes. Stir in tarragon and season with salt and pepper to taste. Serve with lemon wedges.

Building the Braise Is a Simple Process

1. Brown all chicken pieces and remove from pot.

2. Add pancetta, onion, garlic, and thyme to pot and sauté until starting to soften.

3. Add flour, broth, wine, vegetables, and chicken and simmer before adding peas.

Ultimate Hamburgers

These big, bold, special-occasion burgers are worth the work. **by Alli Berkey**

I LOVE A casual burger as much as (maybe more than) the next person. But burgers can be special-occasion food, too—why not eat burgers by candlelight? Or, since we're cooking for two, why not whip up a couple of burgers for date night?

The first thing to do is let go of the notion of buying ground meat at the supermarket; for the best burgers, you need to grind your own. Don't worry, it's easy to do in the food processor as long as you cube and briefly freeze the pieces of meat first—20 pulses and you're done. But which cut of beef works best for burgers? I tested chuck, sirloin, strip steak, short ribs, and even brisket, and my tasters all favored the burgers made with rich, well-marbled short ribs. It's easiest to buy them boneless, but if all you can find are bone-in English short ribs, you can easily remove the meat from the bone at home.

A couple of tips on shaping the burgers: First, make sure to pick through the ground meat to remove any especially stringy or fatty bits. Second, be gentle when you pick up the meat and shape the patties in your hands; overworking the raw patties can make for tough cooked burgers.

These burgers are big, so I took care to cook them perfectly. That entailed searing one side in a hot skillet for 3 minutes, flipping the patties, and then searing the second side for

2 minutes. Then I pulled the skillet from the burner, covered it, and let the burgers finish cooking gently off the heat (2 minutes more for medium-rare, longer for medium and well-done). I tried a variety of cheeses but ultimately decided to skip the cheese and add a sauce instead.

I tested mushroom sauces, wine reductions, and even homemade ketchup, but none was up to snuff. Since meaty, savory flavor is the name of the burger game, I turned to a super-savory ingredient: white miso. This Japanese soup base is salty, bright, and packed with umami flavor. After a bit of experimentation, I ended up with a quick stir-together sauce of white miso, mayonnaise, scallion, rice vinegar, and pepper. It was perfect—acidic enough to cut through the richness of the short rib burgers while upping the ante on savoriness. Let's eat.

SHORT RIB BURGERS FOR TWO
Bone-in English-style beef short ribs can be used if boneless are unavailable. You will need to purchase 1½ pounds; be sure to remove all silverskin and excess fat next to the bone. While we prefer short ribs, 12 ounces of sirloin steak tips or chuck-eye roast can be substituted. (We use less of those cuts to start because there is less fat and gristle to discard.) If you'd like to top your burgers with cheese, do so right before covering the skillet in step 5.

DIY: Grinding Your Own Meat

1. Trim the meat of excess fat so the burgers won't be greasy or chewy.

2. Cut the meat into small cubes to help them process more efficiently.

3. Briefly freeze the cubes on a plate; this flash-freezing is key to even grinding.

4. Pulse the meat in a food processor in two batches until ground; discard any long strands of gristle.

Secret Ingredient: White Miso

This complex fermented soybean paste adds deeply savory, nutty, sweet, and salty flavors to our burger sauce. A little goes a long way.

Organic Miso
White Miso

JRGER

- 1 pound boneless beef short ribs, trimmed and cut into ½-inch cubes
- ½ teaspoon table salt
- ½ teaspoon pepper
- 1 teaspoon vegetable oil
- 2 hamburger buns, toasted and buttered

UCE

- ¼ cup mayonnaise
- 1 scallion, minced
- 1 tablespoon white miso
- 1 teaspoon rice vinegar
- ¾ teaspoon pepper

FOR THE BURGER: Distrib-
e beef in even layer on large plate.
reeze until very firm and starting to
rden around edges but still pliable,
to 35 minutes.

FOR THE SAUCE: Whisk all
gredients together in bowl.

Pulse half of beef in food proces-
r until ground into 1/16-inch pieces,
out 20 pulses. Return ground beef to
ate. Repeat with remaining beef. Pick
rough ground beef and discard any
ng strands of gristle or large chunks
fat (for short ribs, typically about
ounces).

Divide beef in half and gently form
to 2 patties, ¾ inch thick and about
inches in diameter. Patties should
eigh roughly 6 ounces each. Sprinkle
tties on both sides with salt and pep-
r, using spatula to flip patties.

Heat oil in 12-inch nonstick skillet
ver high heat until just smoking.
sing spatula, transfer patties to skil-
t and cook, without moving them,
r 3 minutes. Gently flip patties and
ntinue to cook until well browned
second side, about 2 minutes
nger. Off heat, cover and let sit
til meat registers 125 degrees (for
edium-rare), about 2 minutes. (For
edium, let sit for 3 minutes to reach
0 to 135 degrees; for medium-well,
t sit for 4 minutes to reach 140 to
5 degrees.) Transfer burgers to
ate, tent with aluminum foil, and let
st for 5 minutes.

Transfer burgers to bun bottoms, add
uce, and cap with bun tops. Serve.

Lemon Chicken

The easiest slow-cooker recipe we've ever published? Maybe. The best lemon chicken you've ever tasted? Definitely.

by Matthew Fairman

WHEN I FIRST set out to develop a recipe for slow-cooker lemon chicken, I thought there'd be nothing to it. What could be simpler? Toss some chicken thighs into the cooker—dark meat is the perfect match for this style of low-and-slow cooking—with some chicken broth and lemon juice and come back a few hours later to a rich, vibrant meal of tender, lemony chicken. In hindsight, I was overcon-fident. My first attempts to make the recipe proved that it wasn't going to be that easy.

The problem? The dish was turning out greasy and with way too much liquid. And the lemon flavor lacked freshness and pop. To fashion a simple recipe that would infuse my chicken with lemon flavor that actu-ally appealed, I knew I'd need to do some work.

My first move was to ditch the broth; the chicken gave up enough of its own tasty juices to make a sauce. As for the greasiness, I knew that bone-in chicken thighs stay juicy in the slow cooker longer than boneless thighs, but they have a lot of fat. To deal with it, I removed and discarded the skin (and with it all the subcutane-ous fat) and thoroughly trimmed the rest of the fat from around the meat. Then I tossed the thighs in the slow cooker with a simple mix of fruity, peppery extra-virgin olive oil and lemon juice.

This time, the results were more promising. Without its fatty, rubbery skin, the chicken was now succulent, with a balanced richness. But the result-ing sauce still lacked the bright lemon punch I was after. I tried whisking a little finely grated lemon zest into the sauce just before serving. It did the trick, adding a bright freshness and lemon aroma that the dish needed.

Now my dish was brighter, but my tasters complained that the sauce was "monotonously lemony." The

lemon's acidity needed other flavors to balance it. To round out the flavor profile, I started my next test by seasoning the chicken with a pantry-friendly mix of black pep-per, paprika, dried oregano, and granulated garlic. Once that was in the cooker, I nestled in 10 herby thyme sprigs.

Hours later, I returned to my slow cooker hungry and hopeful, enticed by the aromas of lemon, garlic, and herbs. I was immediately encouraged by the lovely ruddy color the paprika had given both the chicken and the sauce. The olive oil, lemon, herbs, and spices had combined with the chicken juices in just the way I'd hoped. They made a lovely sauce that we all sopped up with crusty bread once the tender chicken was all gone. As it turns out, making good slow-cooker lemon chicken really is that easy—at least once you've got the right recipe.

USE WHOLE SPRIGS
And save yourself arduous picking.

SLOW-COOKER LEMON CHICKEN
Serves 6
Serve with white rice.

- 8 (5- to 7-ounce) bone-in chicken thighs, skin removed, trimmed
- ¼ cup extra-virgin olive oil
- 2 teaspoons table salt
- 1 teaspoon pepper
- 1 teaspoon paprika
- 1 teaspoon dried oregano
- ¾ teaspoon granulated garlic
- 10 sprigs fresh thyme
- 1 teaspoon finely grated lemon zest plus ¼ cup juice (2 lemons)
- 2 tablespoons coarsely chopped fresh parsley

1. Add chicken, oil, salt, pepper, pa-prika, oregano, and granulated garlic to slow cooker and toss until chicken is well coated with spices. Nestle thyme sprigs into chicken mixture. Add lemon juice, taking care not to wash spices from top of chicken. Cover and cook until chicken is tender, 4 to 6 hours on low.

2. Discard thyme sprigs. Transfer chicken to shallow serving dish. Stir parsley and lemon zest into sauce in slow cooker, then spoon sauce over chicken. Serve.

8-Inch Square Baking Pans

Four key traits set our winning pan apart from all the others. **by Emily Phares**

KEY **Good** ★★★ **Fair** ★★ **Poor**

8 Pans 4 Tests

- Bake brownies and cut cooled brownies in pans into 16 squares
- Bake yellow cake and cut cooled cakes in pans into 16 squares
- Line winning pan with aluminum foil sling and bake brownies
- Wash pans 5 times according to manufacturers' instructions

SQUARE BAKING PANS are handy for making cakes and brownies, but that's not all. We also use them for recipes such as Chocolate Fudge, Honey Cornbread, and Nanaimo Bars. But which of the many pans on the market is best? We chose eight models, ranging in price from about $10 to about $36: five metal (four of which had nonstick coatings), one glass, one silicone, and one stoneware. To test them, we made yellow cake and brownies in each, sliced the cooled baked goods in the pans with a knife, and then washed the pans repeatedly to evaluate durability.

The first thing we noted was the slight differences in baking times. Because metal is generally a better conductor of heat than glass or stoneware is, the nonmetal pans required more time in the oven to finish baking—5 to 8 minutes longer for yellow cake and about 5 minutes longer for brownies. Even with these differences, the baking times with all the pans fell within acceptable ranges.

Regardless of material, all eight pans produced appetizing brownies and cakes with golden-brown tops. Two of the cakes had slightly darker exteriors than the others, likely because they baked in darker-colored pans, but they were still perfectly acceptable. And all the baked goods released easily from their respective pans, even the cakes and brownies baked in pans without nonstick coatings. Our recipes called for either greasing or greasing plus flouring the pans, which was sufficient to prevent sticking. All the pans performed well, but there were other factors to consider.

After turning the cakes out onto wire racks to cool, we examined their shapes. Two of the eight cakes stood out because of their slightly sloped sides. The pans that produced these cakes

had tapered sides, meaning they were wider at the top than at the bottom. We much preferred the appearances of the cakes baked in the remaining six pans; they were appealingly square and had well-defined edges.

We also looked at how easy the pans were to maneuver. Four models in our lineup featured rolled edges with narrow lips that were sometimes tricky to hold securely, especially when removing the pans from a hot oven or greasing and flouring them. The rest of the pans featured defined handles; these pans were easier to grab and lift.

To test the durability of the pans, we used a sharp paring knife to repeatedly slice cake and brownies in each, checking to see if any scratched easily. All five metal pans showed faint nicks, but nothing that would affect their performance. One pan, however, was a total letdown. While slicing brownies in the silicone pan, we inadvertently sliced right through the side, leaving a ¾-inch gash and rendering the pan unusable.

To see how easy the pans were to clean, we washed each pan five times according to the manufacturer's instructions. Six of the pans we tested were dishwasher-safe, but two weren't, so we washed those by hand. A few of the pans were harder to clean than others.

The interiors of the glass, stoneware, and silicone pans were all smooth and seamless and therefore easy to clean. Most of the metal models, though, had seams as a result of the way they were constructed. One metal pan was molded, meaning that a hot sheet of metal was pressed into a mold. The others were folded, meaning that a metal sheet was folded into the shape of a pan, creating seams. The seams of folded pans sometimes trapped food and required extra attention to clean. It wasn't a deal breaker, but it wasn't ideal either.

Our new winner, the Fat Daddio's ProSeries Square Cake Pan, was the only molded-metal pan in our lineup. Its seamless interior didn't trap food and was easy to clean (even though it could be washed only by hand). It produced nicely shaped baked goods and was easy to hold and maneuver. This 8-inch square baking pan excelled at producing aesthetically pleasing baked goods and boasted a low-maintenance design.

 Web subscribers can see the complete results chart at CooksCountry.com/bake8.

HIGHLY RECOMMENDED

CRITERIA

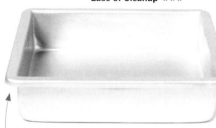

Fat Daddio's
ProSeries Square Cake Pan
Model: PSQ-882
Price: $13.48
Material: Anodized aluminum
Construction: Molded
Dishwasher-Safe: No
Comments: This pan's straight sides produced cakes with well-defined edges, and its ½-inch lip made it easy to hold. It was also easy to clean. We saw faint scratches on the bottom of the pan after repeated passes with a paring knife.

Baked Good Appearance ★★★
Durability ★★½
Ease of Cleanup ★★★

WINNING TRAITS
- Straight sides and well-defined edges
- Flattened lip that's easy to hold
- Smooth, seamless interior
- Durable, exhibiting little to no damage

RECOMMENDED

Williams Sonoma
Goldtouch Nonstick Square Cake Pan, 8"
Model: 1983741
Price: $26.95
Materials: Aluminized steel, Goldtouch ceramic-based coating
Construction: Folded
Dishwasher-Safe: Yes

Baked Good Appearance ★★★
Durability ★★½
Ease of Cleanup ★★½

Comments: Our previous winner still performed well. Its folded design made it a little harder to clean than our winner. It produced beautiful cakes and brownies.

USA Pan
8 Inch Square Cake Pan
Model: 1120BW
Price: $14.99
Materials: Aluminized steel with silicone coating
Construction: Folded
Dishwasher-Safe: No

Baked Good Appearance ★★★
Durability ★★½
Ease of Cleanup ★★½

Comments: This pan features a ridged bottom and sides, which left some faint marks on the finished baked goods but nothing egregious. Overall, it was solid.

KitchenAid
Professional-Grade Nonstick Square Cake Pan, 8" x 8"
Model: KB2NSO08SQWT
Price: $15.00
Materials: Aluminized steel, multilayer nonstick coating
Construction: Folded
Dishwasher-Safe: Yes

Baked Good Appearance ★★★
Durability ★★½
Ease of Cleanup ★★½

Comments: Another model that turned out nicely browned baked goods, this pan had nearly 90-degree sides that made for cakes with straight sides.

RECOMMENDED WITH RESERVATIONS

Staub Stoneware Square Baker, 8" x 8"
Model: 7396010
Price: $36.00
Materials: Stoneware with glass porcelain enamel finish
Construction: Molded
Dishwasher-Safe: Yes

Pyrex Easy Grab 8" Square Baking Dish
Model: 1090950
Price: $9.76
Material: Glass
Construction: Molded
Dishwasher-Safe: Yes

Calphalon Signature Nonstick Bakeware 8" Cake Pan
Model: 2000607
Price: $32.95
Materials: Aluminized steel with hybrid ceramic nonstick coating
Construction: Folded
Dishwasher-Safe: Yes

Sour Cream

ust how sour should sour cream be? **by Riddley Gemperlein-Schirm**

OUR CREAM ISN'T just a topping
r baked potatoes. It's equally at home
hen dolloped on nachos, chili, latkes,
nd all sorts of soups. It's an essential
se for dips, creating a creamy texture
at's the perfect consistency for scoop-
g. It's also used in baking: Some of
r cookie, pound cake, and coffee cake
cipes rely on the pleasant, flavorful
ng of sour cream.

But which sour cream is best? To
d out, we rounded up four nation-
ly available products and tasted them
ain, in Sour Cream Drop Biscuits, and
Caramelized Onion Dip.

Our tasters generally preferred the
oducts they perceived as milder; they
ked milky sweetness with just a hint of
ng. Tart sour creams received lower
arks, especially when tasted plain.

Most of the companies would not
sclose their fermentation processes,
t Kimberlee Burrington, a dairy ex-
ert at the Center for Dairy Research at
e University of Wisconsin–Madison,
plained that the tangier sour creams
ere likely fermented longer or used
rains of bacterial cultures known to
ntribute a more tangy flavor. "The
ngier flavor of a sour cream could be
ecause the pH is lower (probably from
longer, but not a warmer, fermenta-
on period) or different cultures were
sed," Burrington said. "Usually a
ltured product that is tangier is also
wer in pH." A sour cream with a
wer pH would be more acidic and
erefore more sour. A sour cream with
ss fat could also taste more sour, as
t has a way of "rounding out flavors,"
urrington said. However, when we
oked at the nutrition labels, we were
rprised to see that all the samples had
elatively similar amounts of fat, regard-
ss of whether they contained cream,
ilk, or a combination of the two—so
t content wasn't a factor in their flavor
far as we could tell.

Fortunately, the ultratart flavor of
me products was lessened when we
ied them in Sour Cream Drop Biscuits
nd Caramelized Onion Dip, where
her ingredients masked the tanginess.
ur tasters deemed all the biscuits and
ps perfectly acceptable: Biscuits were
l "rich" and "delicious," and every dip
as plenty "creamy" and subtly "tangy."

All the products in our lineup
ontained just dairy (cream and/or
ilk), bacterial cultures, and enzymes,
dairy flavor was front and center for
r tasters. Our top-rated sour cream

RECOMMENDED

Our Favorite
Daisy
Sour Cream
Price: $2.79 for 16 oz ($0.17 per oz)
Comments: The national best seller offered "creamy texture" and "clean dairy flavor." It made "light and fluffy" dip and very "buttery" biscuits.

Horizon
Organic Cultured Sour Cream
Price: $3.79 for 16 oz ($0.24 per oz)
Comments: This sour cream was a bit thinner than our winner. Dip made with it had a "nice kick of flavor," and biscuits were "assertively tangy."

Organic Valley
Sour Cream
Price: $4.19 for 16 oz ($0.26 per oz)
Comments: Tasters were split on this sour cream's texture, which some described as "watery" and "loose." A few said it had an "almost cheesy" flavor.

Breakstone's
All Natural Sour Cream
Price: $2.99 for 16 oz ($0.19 per oz)
Comments: When eaten plain, this product was a bit "too sour" and had a slightly "grainy texture." Biscuits made with it had a "nice buttery tang."

was described as having a "clean dairy flavor" and being almost "buttery." Tasters thought that two lower-ranking sour creams, both made with organic milk, had subtle notes of "barnyard flavor" that were a bit distracting when eaten plain. Burrington explained that this flavor could be attributed to several factors, including what the cows were fed, the quality of the dairy, and how long the dairy was stored prior to being made into sour cream. While some tasters liked the "cheesy" complexity of these sour creams, we generally preferred more neutral products when tasting them plain. As with tangy flavor, the proprietary bacterial cultures manufacturers use to ferment and thicken the sour creams—much like they do when making yogurt—could also have been a factor in the flavor.

Our preferred sour cream texture was thick but still spoonable. To understand the differences in consistency, we first looked at the type of dairy used to make each sour cream. Our two favorite products were made using just cream, whereas the two lowest-ranked sour creams were made with a combination of milk and cream. The sour creams made with just cream were described as "thick and luscious," while the sour creams made with milk and cream were "runny" and "watery."

Burrington explained that the type of dairy used to make sour cream is only partially responsible for the product's

thickness. Manufacturers start the process by homogenizing the dairy—using pressure to break down and evenly distribute dairy's fat globules—to keep the fat and liquid in the dairy emulsified. Burrington said that the amount of pressure used during homogenization determines how small or large the fat globules end up. Higher pressure results in smaller globules, which typically create the thicker, firmer sour creams our tasters loved.

 Web subscribers can read the complete tasting results at **CooksCountry.com/tangy**.

We can recommend all four of the sour creams we tasted, especially for baking or incorporating into a recipe. However, for spooning onto nachos or garnishing soup, our favorite is Daisy Sour Cream. Tasters described it as "creamy and smooth, with the perfect consistency for dolloping."

Cultured Dairy in the Kitchen
Cultured dairy is cream and/or milk with friendly live bacteria (cultures) added. The bacteria convert lactose, or milk sugar, into lactic acid, making these products thick and tangy.

SOUR CREAM
Sour cream is made from cultured light cream (approximately 18 to 20 percent butterfat) and sometimes milk. When we're stirring it into stews or sauces, we always do so off the heat to keep the sour cream from separating.

CRÈME FRAÎCHE
Crème fraîche is made from heavy (not light) cream, which means it contains between 30 and 40 percent fat. It's rich and creamy (no kidding!) and has a subtle nutty flavor. We like a dollop in certain soups and with fruit desserts.

YOGURT
Yogurt is made by adding bacterial cultures to warm milk and letting it ferment and produce lactic acid. We add whole-milk yogurt to sauces, soups, and dressings and use whole-milk and low-fat yogurts to make especially moist cakes.

Peach-Orange Preserves

On the Western Slope of Colorado, peach season can be hit or miss. But in off years we still make these preserves, which are great even if the peaches aren't perfect.

—CYNDI PEARSON,
Grand Junction, CO

PEACH-ORANGE PRESERVES
Serves 32 (Makes 4 cups)
Do not peel the peaches or orange for this recipe.

- 2 **pounds ripe peaches, halved, pitted, and cut into 1-inch pieces**
- 3 **cups (21 ounces) sugar**
- 2½ **cups water**
- 1 **orange, unpeeled, cut into ½-inch pieces**
- ⅛ **teaspoon table salt**
- 2 **teaspoons lemon juice**

1. Combine peaches, sugar, water, orange, and salt in Dutch oven and bring to boil over medium-high heat, stirring occasionally. Reduce heat to medium-low and simmer, stirring frequently and scraping bottom of pot to prevent scorching, until fruit has broken down and mixture registers 220 to 222 degrees, about 30 minutes. (Mixture will be fluid but will thicken as it cools.)
2. Off heat, stir in lemon juice. Let cool for 1½ hours. Transfer to airtight container(s) and refrigerate until ready to serve. (Preserves can be refrigerated for up to 2 months.)

We're looking for recipes that you treasure—the ones that have been handed down in your family for a generation or more, that always come out for the holidays, and that have earned a place at your table and in your heart through many years of meals. Send us the recipes that spell home to you. Visit CooksCountry.com/recipe_submission (or write to Heirloom Recipes, Cook's Country, 21 Drydock Avenue, Suite 210E, Boston, MA 02210) and tell us a little about the recipe. Include your name and address. If we print your recipe, you'll receive a free one-year subscription to Cook's Country.

COMING NEXT ISSUE

The next issue of Cook's Country has a host of fresh ideas for your Thanksgiving table, from our over-the-top **Louisiana-Style Cornbread Dressing** *to our surprising* **Sweet Potato Crunch** *casserole to a heaping helping of* **Turkey Tacos**. *And for dessert, we've got* **Chocolate Pecan Pie with Bourbon Whipped Cream**. *Talk about ending the holiday on a high note. Join us, won't you?*

RC=Recipe Card

FIND THE ROOSTER!

A tiny version of this rooster has been hidden in a photo in the pages of this issue. Write to us with its location and we'll enter you in a random drawing. The first correct entry drawn will win our favorite 8-inch square baking dish, and each of the next five will receive a free one-year subscription to Cook's Country. To enter, visit CooksCountry.com/rooster by August 31, 2019, or write to Rooster AS1 Cook's Country, 21 Drydock Avenue, Suite 210E, Boston, MA 02210. Include your name and address. Sarell Cohen of Glenview, Illinois, found the rooster in the April/May 2019 issue on page 7 and won our favorite inexpensive blender.

WEB EXTRAS

Free for four months online at
CooksCountry.com/sept19

Basic Brownie Batter

READ US ON IPAD

Download the Cook's Country app for iPad and start a free trial subscription or purchase a single issue of the magazine; issues are enhanced with Cooking Mode slide shows that provide step-by-step instructions for completing recipes, plus expanded reviews and ratings. Go to CooksCountry.com/iPad to download our app through iTunes.

"Fried" Ice Cream Cake

Inspired by a beloved midcentury dessert, this cake combines chocolate, cinnamon, and fun. **by Sarah Ewald**

TO MAKE THIS CAKE, YOU WILL NEED:

- 1 **recipe Basic Brownie Batter***
- 3 **pints vanilla ice cream, softened**
- 1⅓ **cups Heath Toffee Bits**
- 1 **teaspoon ground cinnamon**
- 1 **cup (2 ounces) Cinnamon Toast Crunch cereal**
- 1 **tablespoon unsalted butter**
- ½ **cup heavy cream**
- ½ **cup chocolate syrup**
- 1 **maraschino cherry**

FOR THE BROWNIE LAYER:

Adjust oven rack to middle position and heat oven to 350 degrees. Grease 8-inch round cake pan, line with parchment paper, grease parchment, and flour pan. Transfer brownie batter to prepared pan and smooth top with rubber spatula. Bake until toothpick inserted halfway between edge and center of brownie comes out clean, 22 to 27 minutes, rotating pan halfway through baking. Let brownie cool in pan on wire rack for 1 hour. Use paring knife to loosen brownie from sides of pan, then invert onto wire rack; discard parchment. Reinvert brownie and let cool completely on wire rack, about 1½ hours.

TO ASSEMBLE:

Grease 9-inch springform pan, line bottom with parchment, and grease parchment. Place brownie in center of prepared pan. Stir ice cream, toffee bits, and cinnamon in large bowl until combined. Pour ice cream mixture into pan and smooth top with offset spatula. Cover with plastic wrap and freeze until very firm, at least 4 hours.

Process cereal in food processor until finely ground, about 15 seconds. Melt butter in 10-inch skillet over medium heat and cook, swirling skillet and stirring constantly with rubber spatula, until butter is golden brown and has nutty aroma, 2 to 3 minutes. Add cereal and cook, stirring often, until light golden, about 1 minute. Transfer cereal to plate and let cool completely. Using stand mixer fitted with whisk attachment, whip cream on medium-low speed until foamy, about 1 minute. Increase speed to high and whip until stiff peaks form, about 1 minute.

Remove side and bottom of pan. Transfer cake to platter or pedestal, discarding parchment. Smooth sides of cake with offset spatula. Press cereal onto sides of cake. Pour chocolate syrup in center of cake and spread evenly over top with offset spatula, leaving ½-inch border. Fill pastry bag fitted with closed star tip with whipped cream. Pipe swirl around edge of cake to fill in border. Place cherry in center of cake. Serve.

*Our recipe for Basic Brownie Batter is available for free for four months at **CooksCountry.com/browniebatter**.

INSIDE THIS ISSUE

Cook's Country

APPLE CIDER DOUGHNUTS

Sweeten up the season
with these easy
homemade treats.

PAGE 13

Turkey 101
All About the Bird

Stuffed Sopaipillas
New Mexico Special

No-Boil Mac and Cheese
So Simple, So Creamy

Louisiana-Style
Cornbread Dressing
Showstopping Holiday Side

Slow-Roasted Salmon
Never Overcooked

Homemade Butter
Easier Than You Think

**DINNER
TONIGHT**
New Ideas for
Weekday
Meals

OCTOBER/NOVEMBER 2019
$6.95 U.S./$7.95 CANADA

0 71486 02742 3

DISPLAY UNTIL
NOVEMBER 5, 2019

H ERE IN THE *Cook's Country* test kitchen, we celebrate Thanksgiving at least three times a year.

The first celebration happens in the kitchen as the team develops recipes for Thanksgiving appetizers, sides, and more. The second comes around when the photo team prepares and shoots the finished dishes in the studio. And the third, of course, is on Thanksgiving Day itself.

We're not the only ones who celebrate more than once. Many people have multiple Thanksgiving dinners—one for family, perhaps, and then one (or more) for friends. When I was young, we called our second celebration "Thanksmas," because it usually happened between Thanksgiving and Christmas. Today, many people call it "Friendsgiving."

I love the idea of a bonus holiday. It gives you a chance to create a lighter, less austere atmosphere that's still brimming with gratitude—and shake up the menu, too. I recommend our vibrant Braised Turkey Tacos (page 18) followed by our unexpected Chocolate Pecan Pie (page 22). Both are absolutely perfect for a celebratory gathering of friends.

Between celebrations, we've been hard at work to bring you a new department: "How to Make" (page 27). We'll focus on recipes for commonly store-bought items that are surprisingly easy to make at home and impressive enough to merit the extra effort. In this issue, we tackle homemade butter. Our simple recipe yields a creamy, flavorful result that will earn you major bragging rights. You'll tell your friends, "I made this!" and they'll be amazed. That's something to be thankful for.

TUCKER SHAW

Editor in Chief

Illustration: Ross MacDonald

Cook's Country

Chief Executive Officer David Nussbaum
Chief Creative Officer Jack Bishop
Editor in Chief Tucker Shaw
Executive Managing Editor Todd Meier
Executive Food Editor Bryan Roof
Deputy Editor Scott Kathan
Deputy Food Editor Morgan Bolling
Senior Editor Cecelia Jenkins
Associate Editors Alli Berkey, Matthew Fairman
Associate Editor, Web Ashley Delma
Photo Team/Special Events Manager Tim McQuinn
Test Cooks Natalie Estrada, Jessica Rudolph
Assistant Test Cooks, Photo Team Sarah Ewald, Hannah Fe
   Jacqueline Gochenouer, Eric Haessler
Copy Editors Christine Campbell, April Poole, Rachel Schow
Contributing Editor Eva Katz
Senior Science Research Editor Paul Adams
Hosts & Executive Editors, Television Bridget Lancaster,
   Julia Collin Davison

Executive Editors, Tastings & Testings Hannah Crowley,
   Lisa McManus
Senior Editors, Tastings & Testings Lauren Savoie, Kate Sh
Associate Editor, Tastings & Testings Miye Bromberg
Assistant Editors, Tastings & Testings
   Riddley Gemperlein-Schirm, Carolyn Grillo, Emily Phares

Creative Director John Torres
Photography Director Julie Cote
Art Director Susan Levin
Associate Art Director Maggie Edgar
Senior Staff Photographers Steve Klise, Daniel J. van Acker
Staff Photographer Kevin White
Photography Producer Meredith Mulcahy

Senior Director, Creative Operations Alice Carpenter
Senior Editor, Special Projects Christie Morrison
Senior Manager, Publishing Operations Taylor Argenzio
Imaging Manager Lauren Robbins
Production & Imaging Specialists Dennis Noble,
   Jessica Voas, Amanda Yong
Deputy Editor, Editorial Operations Megan Ginsberg
Editorial Assistants, Editorial Operations Tess Berger,
   Sara Zatopek
Test Kitchen Director Erin McMurrer
Assistant Test Kitchen Director Alexxa Benson
Test Kitchen Manager Meridith Lippard
Senior Kitchen Assistant Receiver Heather Tolmie
Kitchen Assistants Gladis Campos, Blanca Castanza,
   Amarilys Merced, Michelle Somoza

Chief Financial Officer Jackie McCauley Ford
Senior Manager, Customer Support Tim Quinn
Customer Support Specialist Mitchell Axelson
Event Coordinator Michaela Hughes

Chief Digital Officer Fran Middleton
VP, Marketing Natalie Vinard
Director, Audience Acquisition & Partnerships Evan Steine
Director, Social Media Marketing Kathryn Przybyla
Social Media Coordinators Charlotte Errity, Sarah Sandler,
   Norma Tentori

Chief Revenue Officer Sara Domville

Director, Public Relations & Communications Brian Frankl
Public Relations Coordinator Madeleine Cohen

**Senior VP, Human Resources & Organizational
   Development** Colleen Zelina
Human Resources Manager Jason Lynott

Photography Keller + Keller
Food Styling Catrine Kelty

Circulation Services ProCirc

On the cover: Apple Cider Doughnuts

THE MOST USEFUL POT YOU OWN

Cook It in Your Dutch Oven

You can prepare dishes of all kinds in this multitasker, thanks to its cast-iron construction and heavy lid. Plus, the broad surface browns foods like a dream. This book contains 150 foolproof recipes tailor-made for your kitchen's most versatile pot. It will have you reaching for your Dutch oven again and again. Order your copy at AmericasTestKitchen.com/dutchoven.

Find us on **Facebook**
facebook.com/CooksCountry

Find us on **Instagram**
instagram.com/CooksCountry

Follow us on **Pinterest**
pinterest.com/TestKitchen

Follow us on **Twitter**
twitter.com/TestKitchen

AMERICA'S TEST KITCHEN

America's Test Kitchen is a real test kitchen located in Boston. It is the home of more than 60 test cooks, editors, and cookware specialists. Our mission is to test recipes until we understand exactly how and why they work and eventually arrive at the very best version. We also test kitchen equipment and supermarket ingredients in search of products that offer the best value and performance. You can watch us work by tuning in to *America's Test Kitchen* (AmericasTestKitchen.com) and *Cook's Country* (CooksCountry.com) on public television, and you can listen to our weekly segments on *The Splendid Table* on public radio. You can also follow us on Facebook, Twitter, Pinterest, and Instagram.

Cook's Country magazine (ISSN 1552-1990), number 89, is published bimonthly by America's Test Kitchen Limited Partnership, 21 Drydock Avenue, Suite 210E, Boston, MA 02210. Copyright 2019 America's Test Kitchen Limited Partnership. Periodicals postage paid at Boston, MA, and additional mailing offices, USPS #023453. Publications Mail Agreement No. 40020778. Return undeliverable Canadian addresses to P.O. Box 875, Station A, Windsor, ON N9A 6P2. POSTMASTER: Send address changes to *Cook's Country*, PO Box 6018, Harlan, IA 51593-1518. For subscription and gift subscription orders, subscription inquiries, or change of address notices, visit AmericasTestKitchen.com/support, call 800-526-8447 in the U.S. or 515-237-3663 from outside the U.S., or write to us at *Cook's Country*, P.O. Box 6018, Harlan, IA 51593-1518. PRINTED IN THE USA.

by Cecelia Jenkins and Morgan Bolling

Easy Onion Dicing

Cooking shows make dicing onions seem easy, but I feel unsafe cutting horizontally into the side of a halved onion. Is there an easier/safer way?

–Kristin Morse, Portland, Maine

We often dice onions according to the method you described: Halve and peel the onion, slice each onion half horizontally, slice downward north to south, and then slice downward again east to west. But there are two other methods that you might feel more comfortable with.

Method 1: Halve the onion through the root end, trim and discard the stem end of each half, peel the halves, and then make a series of radial cuts, stopping just short of the root end. Slice across the radial cuts to create even-size pieces.

Method 2: Halve the onion through the root end, trim and discard the stem end of each half, and peel the halves. Cut onion into quarters through root end. Working with one quarter at a time, set it on one flat side and make a series of parallel cuts, stopping short of root. Flip the quarter on its second flat side and make another series of parallel cuts. Turn quarter and slice perpendicular to parallel cuts to create even-size pieces.

THE BOTTOM LINE: There are many ways to dice an onion; here are two easy options.

Method 1: Working with Onion Halves

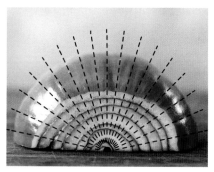

1. Halve onion through root end, trim stem end, and peel. Make series of radial cuts.

2. Slice across radial cuts to create even-size pieces.

Method 2: Working with Onion Quarters

1. Halve onion through root end, trim stem end, and peel. Cut onion into quarters.

2. Set 1 quarter on flat side and make series of parallel cuts, stopping short of root end.

3. Flip quarter onto other flat side and make another series of parallel cuts.

4. Slice onion perpendicular to parallel cuts to get even-size pieces.

A Honey of a Fruit

What is a persimmon?

–Denise Wheelus, Rye, N.Y.

Persimmons are tree fruits native to Asia that also thrive in California and the southern United States. There are many varieties, but the two types you're most likely to see at the supermarket, typically in the fall,

Fuyu persimmons are soft and sweet.

are Hachiya and Fuyu. Hachiyas are acorn-shaped, while Fuyus are tomato-shaped. Both have red-orange skin, though Hachiyas tend to be redder and Fuyus are often a brighter orange. Ripe persimmons have a soft, custardy texture. Both varieties have similar sweet, "honey-like" flavors that one taster describes as a cross between "a pumpkin and a plum." Hachiyas are astringent, so they must fully ripen—they should be soft and squishy—before they can be eaten or they will dry out your mouth and leave a harsh, bitter taste. Fuyus are nonastringent, so they can be eaten while still firm, though we prefer them a little softer. Both varieties should be ripened at room temperature, and they can be cooked into jams, quick breads, cakes, or persimmon pudding.

THE BOTTOM LINE: Persimmons are sweet fruits with lusciously creamy textures when ripe. They are available in the fall months.

Small-Batch Stock

Can I use a single leftover rotisserie chicken carcass to make stock?

–Chris Deer, Dallas, Texas

Not everyone has the forethought—or freezer space—to save up pounds of raw chicken parts (backs, wingtips, etc.) to make a full-size batch of stock. Having found that an average rotisserie chicken carcass (including the skin and any jellied bits) weighs about 1 pound, we added it to a large saucepan with 5 cups of water, half an onion, and a bay leaf and simmered it for 30 minutes. The resulting quart of stock tasted flavorful and richer than stock we typically make from unroasted chicken parts.

THE BOTTOM LINE: You can make about a quart of flavorful chicken stock from a single chicken carcass. Be sure to taste the stock before adding salt because the rotisserie chicken has already been seasoned.

Name That Spud

Are "gold" and "yellow" potatoes the same as Yukon Gold potatoes?

–Carl Kelton, Bend, Ore.

According to the Potato Association of America, potatoes labeled as "yellow" and "gold" both belong to the broad category of yellow-fleshed potato that encompasses many varieties. Similarly, potatoes labeled as "white" refer to the broad category of potato varieties with white interiors. Potato packaging often specifies only the interior flesh color of the potatoes and not the specific variety.

The Yukon Gold potato, though yellow fleshed, is a cross between a yellow and a white potato and is usually labeled as such. A "yellow" or "gold" potato is not a Yukon Gold potato, but all three potatoes have similar starch contents and flavors and can be used interchangeably in recipes.

THE BOTTOM LINE: Potato labels refer to the color of the potatoes' flesh; potatoes labeled "gold" or "yellow" are not Yukon Gold potatoes, but they can be used in place of Yukon Gold potatoes in recipes.

Keeping Eggs Warm

Don Wilson, St. Augustine, Fla.

Often make soft-cooked eggs for the whole family breakfast. I cook them and then run them under cold water so that they're not too hot to peel. Problem is, by the time I've peeled all 10 eggs, they're cold. To keep them warm as I peel, I fill the pot back up with hot water from the tap and place the peeled eggs in the water as I go. They're warm and ready to serve with toast all at once.

Mess-Free Meat Pounding

—Mateo Sandoval, Longmont, Colo.

The classic method for pounding meat thin for cutlets is to place it between two sheets of plastic wrap, but I've always found that a zipper-lock bag works much better. The thin plastic wrap is too fragile and hard to work with; meat juices leak out the sides and onto my cutting board, and the plastic breaks or bunches up on itself. The zipper-lock bag is durable and contains the mess.

Chip Clip Tip

—Ingrid Bloch, Needham, Mass.

I was making a recipe from one of your cookbooks, and the pages wouldn't stay open since the recipe was situated in the first part of the book. I don't have a cookbook stand, so I grabbed a chip clip that was sitting on the counter. It was the perfect inexpensive tool for holding the book open.

Which Canned Green Chiles Are Best?

by Emily Phares

PRODUCT TASTING

CANNED GREEN CHILES are an inexpensive and convenient way to add a burst of flavor to foods, which makes them a pantry staple for some folks. We like to use this versatile ingredient in all kinds of dishes: chilis, stews, dips, biscuits, and more.

To find our favorite, we rounded up six nationally available products and tasted each plain and in Green Chile and Cilantro White Bean Dip. While canned green chiles are available whole and diced, we selected diced (one product was labeled "chopped") because that's what we most frequently call for in recipes. When brands offered both "mild" and "hot" chiles, we selected "mild" because "hot" varieties had added "natural flavor" and we wanted to focus on the flavor of the chiles themselves. And even though some products were labeled "mild," heat levels didn't always correspond—which ended up being a great thing.

The heat levels among the chiles varied widely. We liked the milder products, too, but our top-rated chiles had an assertive fieriness that came through even when mixed with the other ingredients in the dip.

Texture was also key. The best products were pleasantly tender but maintained their structure. All our highly rated chiles were roasted and peeled; tasters noted that the one product that wasn't roasted was rough and fibrous with unpleasant "bits of skin."

Our favorite chiles, from Goya, were soft and maintained their structure, and they had a gentle kick of heat. And at less than $1 a can, they were the least expensive chiles in our lineup.

Web subscribers can read the full testing and see the complete chart at CooksCountry.com/nov19.

RECOMMENDED

Our Favorite
Goya Diced Green Chiles Fire Roasted "Full-flavored peppery taste" and excellent texture

"A good amount of heat" that "kicks in nicely at the finish"

"Bright" and "slightly sweet," with "decent heat"

"Mild" with a "gentle heat on the finish"

"Delicate" heat level but with a "smoky," "sweet," "complex" flavor

RECOMMENDED WITH RESERVATIONS

"Bitter" taste and "mild" heat with "fibrous, uneven texture"

The products are arranged from left to right in descending order of preference.

Chile Roulette

All the canned green chiles we tasted listed either "green chiles" or "green chile peppers" as the primary ingredient. We asked companies if they would further specify chile type, and while most did not, two said they use Anaheim peppers—a variety of the *Capsicum annuum* 'New Mexico No. 9' cultivar with a low to moderate heat level that ranges from 500 to 2,500 Scoville Heat Units.

However, Danise Coon, senior research specialist at New Mexico State University's Chile Breeding Program and Chile Pepper Institute, explained that the cultivar name 'Anaheim' can be used to describe many different green chile cultivars. "Unfortunately in the food packing industry, all green chile cultivars and varieties have been given the moniker 'Anaheim,' whether it is actually an 'Anaheim' or a 'Big Jim,' 'Sandia,' '6-4,' or 'AZ20.'" So there may be differences among products in the exact variety of green chile used, which will translate into differences in flavor and heat levels.

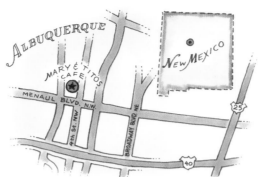

TITO GONZALEZ WAS a firefighter until he retired in the 1960s. According to his grandson Travis Knight (above), Tito got bored about two weeks later. "He was in charge of cooking at the firehouse," Travis says. "His natural progression was a restaurant, I guess." Tito opened Mary & Tito's Cafe soon thereafter. Today, his daughter Antoinette Knight owns and operates the restaurant; Travis and his brother Jordan serve as acting managers. "My grandparents never advertised.

The whole idea was: You do something right and people will find out. It was a word of mouth thing."

Mary & Tito's Cafe is housed in a simple building in an industrial area of Albuquerque, New Mexico. Outside, the gravel parking lot kicks up dust. Inside, you're greeted with warm smiles: It feels like a home kitchen. The vinyl booths spring back like a trampoline when you sit, and picture windows let you watch the traffic hum by.

Tito was the cook during the early years, and he was meticulous about the food—especially the green and red chile sauces that are staples of New Mexican cuisine. He personally sourced the raw chiles from Hatch, New Mexico, 200 miles to the south,

meeting with farmers until he found a product he liked. Those relationships have endured throughout the years. "The biggest compliment we get is, 'Man, I haven't had chile like that since my grandma died,'" Travis says.

I ask Travis if the recipes have changed at all over the years. "Well, there technically aren't recipes. It's all done by eye and feel. Nothing is written down. The amount of garlic that goes in is based on the size of the pot."

Tito passed away when Travis was 7 or 8. "Mom quit her day job and

came in to help Grandma. Everyone helped the family business." As a resu[lt] Travis and his brothers grew up in th[e] restaurant. "We have customers who['ve] been eating here longer than I've bee[n] alive," he says. "We literally had a playpen in the corner. Customers com[e] in and tell me, 'I remember when you[r] mom was changing your diapers here.[']

Over the years, the restaurant expanded to the building next door. "What the kitchen could muster," as Travis puts it, but the atmosphere, food, and sense of family remain unchanged. "We lucked out," Travis say[s] "My grandpa put in the hard work. I don't know if I could do what he di[d]

CHILE
dreams

Text by Bryan Roof; photos by Steve Klise

Mary & Tito's
CAFE
Since 1963
AUTHENTIC
NEW MEXICAN CUISINE
344-6266

Patricio Arguello (top right) has been on staff at Mary & Tito's Cafe for more than 40 years. According to Travis Knight (top left), Arguello is "as close as family can be without being actual blood. We regard [our staff] as un[n]cles and aunts. We keep it real close to the heart here.[']

Stuffed, Smothered Sopaipillas

These chile-drenched sopaipillas bring the heat (along with the beans and cheese).

by Morgan Bolling and Bryan Roof

We stuff our sopaipillas with beans and cheese and top them with green chile sauce.

THE GOLDEN, STUFFED sopaipillas at Mary & Tito's Cafe in Albuquerque, New Mexico (see "Chile Dreams") come smothered in a lightly spicy, smoky green chile sauce that coats every bite. We knew that re-creating this local favorite at home would be a project, so we aimed to keep each element as simple as possible.

The stuffed sopaipillas at Mary & Tito's Cafe are made with a flour tortilla dough that puffs and browns when fried in oil. So we started our own version with a tried-and-true *Cook's Country* recipe for flour tortillas. Adding baking powder helped the dough puff a bit when it hit the hot oil, and while shortening made for a fine and tender dough, lard gave the sopaipillas a much better flavor (see our lard tasting on page 31).

We also used lard to make a batch of quick, savory refried beans—first sautéing some onion in the flavorful melted lard and then adding two cans of drained pinto beans and mashing them right in the skillet with a potato masher.

Before frying our sopaipillas in two batches of four, we rolled portions of the dough into modest 7-inch circles and packed each with ¼ cup of beans and ¼ cup of cheddar cheese before folding them into half-moons. Sealing the dough with water and twisting the sealed edge kept the filling from oozing out. A small steam hole poked on top gave extra insurance against blowouts.

Recipes for green chile sauce vary widely, but we wanted a smoky, spicy version reminiscent of the one at Mary & Tito's. Instead of using hard-to-find New Mexican chiles, we substituted a combination of two widely available chiles: Anaheim and jalapeño. Broiling the chiles added smokiness while intensifying their sweetness. Chopped and cooked with aromatics, flour, and savory chicken broth, they created a flavorful, invigorating sauce.

For more photos from our trip to Albuquerque, visit **CooksCountry.com/newmexican19**.

BEAN AND CHEESE SOPAIPILLAS WITH GREEN CHILE SAUCE *Serves 8*

Use a Dutch oven that holds 6 quarts or more for this recipe. We developed this recipe using John Morrell Snow Cap Lard. You can substitute vegetable shortening for the lard, if desired.

DOUGH

- 2¾ cups (13¾ ounces) all-purpose flour
- 1½ teaspoons table salt
- ½ teaspoon baking powder
- 6 tablespoons lard, cut into ½-inch pieces

REFRIED BEANS

- 4 tablespoons lard
- 1 cup finely chopped onion
- 2 (15-ounce) cans pinto beans, rinsed
- 1 cup chicken broth
- 1 teaspoon table salt

GREEN CHILE SAUCE

- 2 pounds Anaheim chiles
- 1 jalapeño chile
- 2 tablespoons lard
- 1 cup finely chopped onion
- 3 garlic cloves, minced
- 1 tablespoon all-purpose flour
- 1 cup chicken broth
- 1 teaspoon table salt

- 8 ounces mild cheddar cheese, shredded (2 cups)
- 2 quarts peanut or vegetable oil, for frying

1. FOR THE DOUGH: Whisk flour, salt, and baking powder together in large bowl. Rub lard into flour mixture with your fingers until mixture resembles coarse meal. Stir in ¾ cup plus 2 tablespoons water until combined. Turn out dough onto clean counter and knead briefly to form cohesive ball, 6 to 8 turns. Divide dough into 8 equal portions, about 2¾ ounces each (scant ⅓ cup), then roll into balls. Transfer dough balls to plate, cover with plastic wrap, and refrigerate until firm, at least 30 minutes or up to 2 days.

2. FOR THE REFRIED BEANS: Heat lard in 12-inch skillet over medium heat until shimmering. Add onion and cook until softened, about 4 minutes. Stir in beans, broth, and salt. Cook, mashing beans with potato masher, until finely mashed and mixture is thickened, about 8 minutes. Season with salt to taste. Set aside and let cool completely.

3. FOR THE GREEN CHILE SAUCE: Adjust oven rack 6 inches from broiler element and heat broiler. Line rimmed baking sheet with aluminum foil. Arrange Anaheims and jalapeño in single layer on prepared sheet. Broil until chiles are soft and mostly blackened, about 5 minutes per side, rotating sheet halfway through broiling. Transfer chiles to bowl and cover with plastic; let cool for 10 minutes.

4. Remove skins from chiles with spoon. Stem and seed Anaheims, then chop into ¼-inch pieces. Stem (but do not seed) jalapeño; chop into ¼-inch pieces.

5. Heat lard in large saucepan over medium heat until shimmering. Add onion and cook until softened, about 3 minutes. Stir in garlic and cook until fragrant, about 30 seconds. Stir in flour and cook for 1 minute. Stir in broth, salt, Anaheims, and jalapeño and bring to simmer. Simmer until slightly thickened, about 6 minutes. Season with salt to taste; cover and set aside.

6. Keeping other dough balls covered with damp dish towel, roll 1 dough ball into 7-inch circle on lightly floured counter. Lightly squeeze ¼ cup cheese in your palm to form ball. Place cheese in center of dough round, followed by ¼ cup refried beans. Moisten edges of dough round with water. Fold dough round in half, creating half-moon shape to enclose filling, and press to seal.

7. Moisten top of sealed edge with water. Starting at 1 end, fold, slightly twist, and pinch dough diagonally across sealed edge between your thumb and index finger. Continue pinching and twisting dough around seam to create decorative rope edge. Transfer to parchment paper–lined baking sheet. Repeat with remaining dough balls, cheese, and refried beans (reserve any remaining beans for another use). Using paring knife, poke ½-inch hole in center of each sopaipilla. (Filled sopaipillas can be covered and refrigerated for up to 24 hours.)

8. Line baking sheet with triple layer of paper towels. Add oil to large Dutch oven until it measures about 1½ inches deep and heat over medium-high heat to 375 degrees. Add 4 sopaipillas to oil and fry until golden brown, about 3 minutes per side. Adjust burner as needed to maintain oil temperature between 350 and 375 degrees. Transfer fried sopaipillas to prepared sheet. Return oil to 375 degrees and repeat with remaining 4 sopaipillas.

9. Reheat green chile sauce over medium-high heat until hot. Serve sopaipillas topped with chile sauce.

Chicken Provençal

For a rustic yet elegant weeknight meal, look to the flavors of southeast France. **by Alli Berkey**

WEEKNIGHT
EASY

We use common ingredients to turn chicken into a sophisticated weeknight supper.

"CHICKEN PROVENÇAL" SOUNDS fancy, doesn't it? But it's just chicken cooked with the signature flavors and ingredients of Provence, the region of southeast France that borders Italy and the Mediterranean Sea. We're talking herbs, wine, olives, tomatoes, and olive oil—ingredients that are just as common in the United States as they are in Europe. Having long seen recipes for this dish in cookbooks and cooking magazines, I set out to create a weeknight version that used common ingredients to elevate chicken to a new level of deliciousness.

For a dish with such a clear geographic origin, the recipes I found for it were surprisingly all over the map. I had quite a few choices ahead of me: Should I opt for a whole chicken or chicken parts? Red wine or white? Dried herbs or fresh? My first decision was to use bone-in, skin-on chicken thighs; their dark meat is moist and flavorful, and they cook in much less time than a whole chicken. I'd sear the thighs in olive oil, remove them from the skillet, and then build a base of aromatic vegetables and tomatoes that I could use to finish cooking the chicken—basic braising technique.

I started the sauce by sautéing sweet, thinly sliced shallots. Garlic and anchovies—minced so they'd disappear into the sauce—were no-brainers as the next stir-ins, but now I had to figure out how to handle the tomato component. Canned tomato products tasted good but brought the dish too close to stew territory; my tasters preferred a version made with a heap of halved cherry tomatoes, which wrinkled and released their juice in the hot skillet. Red wine was a little too distinct (in flavor and color) here, and while white wine was good, we preferred the more complex flavor of dry vermouth in the sauce.

Many recipes with "provençal" in the name call for herbes de Provence, the region's signature herb blend that typically includes rosemary, thyme, oregano, and savory. Most versions sold in the United States also contain lavender, which my tasters didn't care for in this dish: "Great for soap, but not for chicken." After a bit of experimenting, I found that fresh thyme sprigs provided plenty of heady herbal presence.

With the sauce built, I returned the browned, parcooked thighs to the skillet. I arranged the thighs skin side up so they peeked above the sauce; this would help keep the skin nice and crisp. Then I popped the skillet in a 400-degree oven so the chicken could cook through. This version was pretty good, but the tomatoes had released so much juice that the sauce was too thin. The solution? Dredging the raw thighs in flour before browning them and adding another teaspoon of flour to the sauce ingredients. The flour thickened the fragrant sauce just enough so that it was spoonable but not runny. This dish was now ready for the table—and to take a place in my weeknight rotation.

CHICKEN PROVENÇAL
Serves 4 to 6

You can substitute four 10- to 12-ounce bone-in split chicken breasts for the thighs, if desired. Simply extend the cooking time in step 4 to 30 minutes or until the chicken registers 160 degrees. You can substitute any dry white wine for the vermouth, if desired.

- 8 (5- to 7-ounce) bone-in chicken thighs, trimmed
- ½ teaspoon table salt, divided
- ½ teaspoon pepper, divided
- ½ cup all-purpose flour
- 3 tablespoons extra-virgin olive oil
- 2 shallots, halved and sliced thin
- 3 garlic cloves, minced
- 3 sprigs fresh thyme
- 2 anchovy fillets, rinsed and minced
- ¼ teaspoon red pepper flakes
- 12 ounces cherry tomatoes, halved
- ½ cup pitted kalamata olives, halved
- ½ cup dry vermouth
- ½ cup fresh parsley leaves

1. Adjust oven rack to middle position and heat oven to 400 degrees. Pat chicken dry with paper towels. Sprinkle chicken all over with ¼ teaspoon salt and ¼ teaspoon pepper. Place flour in shallow dish. Dredge chicken in flour, 1 piece at a time, turning to coat all sides. Shake to remove any excess flour, then transfer chicken to large plate. Reserve 1 teaspoon flour; discard remaining flour.

2. Heat oil in 12-inch ovensafe skillet over medium-high heat until just smoking. Add chicken and cook until golden brown on both sides, about 3 minutes per side. Return chicken to plate, skin side up. Carefully pour off all but 2 tablespoons fat from skillet.

3. Return skillet to medium heat. Add shallots to fat left in skillet and cook until softened, about 2 minutes. Stir in garlic, thyme sprigs, anchovies, pepper flakes, and reserved flour and cook until fragrant, about 30 seconds. Stir in tomatoes, olives, vermouth, remaining ¼ teaspoon salt, and remaining ¼ teaspoon pepper, scraping up any browned bits.

4. Return chicken to skillet, skin side up, and bring sauce to boil. Transfer skillet to oven and cook until chicken registers 175 degrees, about 25 minutes. Sprinkle with parsley and serve.

BACKSTORY

Vermouth is simply wine that's been bolstered with extra alcohol and botanical flavorings. It's best known stateside as an ingredient in martinis,

Liquor cabinet powerhouse

but in the kitchen it adds a complex flavor and mild acidity to many dishes. Fortified wines such as vermouth have been around for thousands of years, and some varieties can be traced back to ancient China and Greece.

In the 16th century, German and Italian manufacturers began creating and selling a wine primarily flavored with wormwood (right), a shrubby plant with a strong herbal flavor. The German term for wormwood is *wermwut*; as this drink crossed into France it took on the name "vermouth," and by the time the drink was popularized in England, the name had stuck. Today, wormwood is banned in many countries for its mild (some say mythic) narcotic qualities, so contemporary vermouth makers use a wide array of herbs and plants for flavor.

Sausage with Lentils

Herby, sweet pork sausage and earthy lentils make a perfect pair. **by Alli Berkey**

FRANKS AND BEANS. Cassoulet. Sausage with lentils. These classic combinations prove that legumes and pork are a match made in heaven. But I like the last one best, with the savory, herby sausage elevating the earthy flavor of the tender lentils. This combination is both refined and homey—exactly what I'm looking for in a home-cooked meal. I set out to make a flavorful version of sausage and lentils that could be on the table in less than an hour.

Before I could immerse myself in the nitty-gritty of the recipe development, I had to determine which type of sausage and which type of lentils I wanted to use. I love cooking with *lentilles du Puy* at home, but their thicker skins mean that they take longer to cook than other lentils, and it's tricky to cook them just right. Brown lentils were a much better choice because they cook faster and are more forgiving. I decided on sweet Italian sausage since it is flavor-packed and readily available, but hot Italian sausage could easily be substituted for a spicier dish.

Many recipes for sausage with lentils call first for sautéing chopped onion, carrot, and celery; a few quick tests showed that I could skip the celery without missing much. A few cloves of garlic, fresh rosemary, a bay leaf, and tomato paste rounded out the supporting flavors.

I found that browning the sausage up front didn't add much in terms of flavor or texture. Instead, I started the process by crisping a little cubed pancetta in the skillet before the vegetables went in; the pancetta added a salty, savory flavor that permeated the dish. One cup of lentils, 3 cups of broth, and a pound of sausage rewarded me with a full skillet and plenty of food for four hungry diners. A little fresh parsley stirred in at the end added a bright flavor and a burst of color to this simple, savory meal.

SAUSAGE WITH LENTILS
Serves 4

You can substitute hot Italian sausage for the sweet sausage and fresh basil for the parsley, if desired. Buy a 2-ounce hunk of pancetta from the deli counter, not the presliced variety.

- 2 ounces pancetta, cut into ½-inch pieces
- 1 small onion, chopped fine
- 2 carrots, peeled and chopped fine
- 3 garlic cloves, sliced thin
- 1 tablespoon minced fresh rosemary
- 1 tablespoon tomato paste
- 3 cups chicken broth
- 1 cup dried brown lentils, picked over and rinsed
- 1 bay leaf
- 1 pound sweet Italian sausage
- ½ cup fresh parsley leaves

1. Cook pancetta in 12-inch skillet over medium heat until fat is rendered and pancetta is crispy, about 6 minutes. Add onion, carrots, garlic, and rosemary and continue to cook until vegetables have softened, about 4 minutes longer. Stir in tomato paste and cook for 30 seconds.

2. Stir in broth, lentils, and bay leaf, scraping up any browned bits. Nestle sausage into lentils and bring to boil. Reduce heat to medium-low, cover, and simmer until lentils are tender and sausage registers at least 160 degrees, about 35 minutes.

3. Remove skillet from heat. Transfer sausage to carving board. Discard bay leaf. Stir parsley into lentils and season with salt and pepper to taste. Slice sausage on bias 1 inch thick and place on top of lentils. Serve.

The lentils soak up meaty flavor from the pancetta and sausage.

Stages of Cooking to Build Layers of Flavor

1. Start with pancetta for a savory base.

2. Add the vegetables and aromatics.

3. Add the broth, lentils, and sausage.

HAVING WORKED IN professional kitchens for many years, I offer this advice for cooking salmon: Slow down, and go big. Let me explain.

I've learned the hard way that it's easy to overcook a fillet of salmon—or any fish, for that matter—especially if you are trying to cook several pieces at once. Better to cook one big piece gently at a low temperature. The method is easy and foolproof: The window of optimal doneness is wider and the fish is harder to overcook. Plus, salmon flesh takes on a silky, buttery texture when cooked gently. And finally, there's less splattery mess and fishy smell when you slow-roast salmon in the oven. That's a lot of benefit for a little extra time.

Knowing I wanted to work with a 2½-pound piece of fish that would feed about six people, I tested roasting temperatures ranging from 170 to 350 degrees. Not surprisingly, I found that lower temperatures produced salmon that was moister, silkier, and more evenly cooked. That said, I didn't want to wait 2 hours (or longer) for the fish to cook. I found that the happy medium of temperature and time was 250 degrees for 1 hour.

The texture of the salmon was amazing, and I wanted to bump up the flavor to match it. Many of our recipes for grilled or smoked salmon call for rubbing the flesh with a mixture of salt and sugar and then letting it sit for an hour or more before cooking; as the salmon sits, the salt-sugar mixture lightly cures it, drawing out excess moisture and deeply seasoning the fish. But I didn't want to wait, so I tried sprinkling the salmon with sugar and salt and immediately popping it in the low oven. My tasters loved the sweetness the sugar provided, but they wanted a bit more complexity. A switch to brown sugar did the trick and, as a bonus, gave the cooked salmon a lovely rusty hue.

For a final flourish, I decided to whisk together a simple lemony vinaigrette—just olive oil, lemon zest and juice, and sliced chives—to pour over the fish as soon as it came out of the oven. This dressing mingled with the juices in the baking dish to create a light, bright, savory sauce that perfectly accented the richness of the salmon. This method proved so successful that I made a variation with cayenne and parsley, as well as a version with garlic, mustard, and dill. A worthy mantra for cooking salmon, and for life: Slow down, and go big.

Slow-Roasted Salmon

The secret ingredient for supermoist, perfectly cooked salmon? Time.

by Alli Berkey

Success Starts at the Market

This recipe calls for a 2½-pound center-cut salmon fillet. If the thin belly portion on the side is still attached, remove it and reserve it for another use before cooking. We developed this recipe with farm-raised salmon. You can substitute wild salmon, but be sure to adjust the cooking time to 45 to 50 minutes.

Remove and reserve the thin belly portion for another use.

Pull Out the Pin Bones

To remove the pin bones from a salmon fillet, drape the fillet on an overturned bowl skin side down and remove the protruding bones with tweezers or needle-nose pliers

SLOW-ROASTED SALMON WITH CHIVES AND LEMON *Serves 6*

You can substitute granulated sugar for the brown sugar, if desired. If a 2½-pound salmon fillet is unavailable, you can use six 6- to 8-ounce skinless salmon fillets instead. In step 1, sprinkle both sides of the fillets evenly with the sugar mixture and arrange them side by side in the baking dish so they are touching. The cooking time remains the same. We prefer farm-raised salmon here; if using wild salmon, reduce the cooking time to 45 to 50 minutes, or until the salmon registers 120 degrees. If you're using table salt, use ¾ teaspoon (½ teaspoon in step 1 and ¼ teaspoon in step 3).

- 1 tablespoon packed brown sugar
- 1½ teaspoons kosher salt, divided
- ½ teaspoon pepper
- 1 (2½-pound) skinless center-cut salmon fillet, about 1½ inches thick
- ¼ cup extra-virgin olive oil
- 2 tablespoons sliced fresh chives
- 2 teaspoons grated lemon zest plus 1½ tablespoons juice

1. Adjust oven rack to middle position and heat oven to 250 degrees. Combine sugar, 1 teaspoon salt, and pepper in small bowl. Sprinkle salmon all over with sugar mixture.
2. Place salmon, flesh side up, in 13 by 9-inch baking dish. Roast until center is still translucent when checked with tip of paring knife and registers 125 degrees (for medium-rare), 55 to 60 minutes.
3. Meanwhile, combine oil, chives, lemon zest and juice, and remaining ½ teaspoon salt in bowl.
4. Remove dish from oven and immediately pour oil mixture evenly over salmon. Let rest for 5 minutes. Using spatula and spoon, portion salmon and sauce onto serving platter. Stir together any juices left in dish and spoon over salmon. Serve.

SLOW-ROASTED SALMON WITH DILL AND GARLIC

Substitute 1 teaspoon dry mustard for pepper. Add 1 teaspoon granulated garlic to sugar mixture. Substitute chopped fresh dill for chives.

SLOW-ROASTED SALMON WITH PARSLEY AND CAYENNE

Substitute cayenne pepper for pepper and chopped fresh parsley for chives.

Sautéed Baby Bok Choy

How do you get the most flavor out of this quick-cooking vegetable? Brown it.

by Natalie Estrada

BOK CHOY, A member of the cabbage family, has been cultivated in Asia for thousands of years. Supermarkets sell both large heads of mature bok choy, which can measure over a foot long, and smaller heads of baby bok choy, which are more tender, milder in flavor, and typically measure about 5 inches long. I wanted to create a simple weeknight recipe for the quicker-cooking baby variety.

Many recipes for this vegetable fail because the tender leaves cook much faster than the crisp white stalks. So instead of trying to cook the bok choy whole or halved, I began by removing the leaves from the spoon-shaped stalks before submerging them in water to clean them. Next, I snapped the stalks off the bases and thoroughly washed those, too (bok choy can be very sandy).

After drying the stalks and leaves, I heated some vegetable oil until it was almost smoking and then added the bok choy stalks to the pan. Since I was looking to add flavorful browning to this mild vegetable, I had to be patient and not stir for about 5 minutes. Once the stalks were lightly browned, I added the quick-cooking leaves along with some nutty sesame oil, garlic, and red pepper flakes. Just 1 minute later, the bright, light, flavorful dish was done. Easy, simple, and ready in a flash.

Buy the Little Guys

The stalks of large bok choy heads won't cook through in the amount of time called for here. Be sure to use small heads of baby bok choy (about 5 inches long).

5 inches

SAUTÉED BABY BOK CHOY WITH SESAME OIL AND GARLIC *Serves 4*

Bok choy can sometimes be sandy near the inner base of the head. Look for this sand when you're separating the stalks and make sure to remove it during rinsing. Look for heads of bok choy that weigh 4 to 6 ounces each.

- 1½ pounds baby bok choy
- 2 teaspoons toasted sesame oil
- 1 garlic clove, minced
- ¼ teaspoon red pepper flakes
- 1 tablespoon vegetable oil
- ½ teaspoon table salt

1. Cut dark green leaves from bok choy stalks. Chop leaves coarse. Place leaves in large bowl and cover with water; swish around to remove sand. Remove leaves from water, transfer to salad spinner, and spin dry; transfer leaves to clean bowl and set aside.
2. Cut off bottom ¼ inch of bok choy base and discard. Pull bok choy stalks downward to snap off at base until you reach core; discard core. Repeat washing and spinning with stalks. Pat stalks dry with paper towels if still wet.
3. Combine sesame oil, garlic, and red pepper flakes in small bowl. Heat vegetable oil in 12-inch nonstick skillet over medium-high heat until just smoking. Add stalks, sprinkle with salt, and cook, without stirring, until beginning to brown on bottom,

about 5 minutes. Stir and continue to cook until stalks are just tender, about 1 minute longer.
4. Add leaves and sesame oil mixture and cook, turning constantly with tongs, until leaves are wilted, about 1 minute. Remove skillet from heat and season bok choy with salt to taste. Transfer to platter and serve.

SAUTÉED BABY BOK CHOY WITH HONEY AND ORANGE

Substitute 1 thinly sliced scallion, 2 teaspoons honey, and 2 teaspoons grated orange zest for sesame oil, garlic, and pepper flakes.

Cleaning 1, 2, 3 . . .

1. Snap stalks from core

2. Wash sand from stalks

3. Spin stalks dry

Japanese Steakhouse Dinner

Our recipe delivers all the savory-sweet appeal of this restaurant favorite— no knife juggling or flaming onion volcano required.

by Matthew Fairman

I'M TURNING 12 and I'm out for my birthday dinner. Across the counter from me is a wisecracking daredevil with a hip holster full of knives. He's juggling squeeze bottles and conjuring fireballs on a ripping-hot flat-top grill—and then he makes a flaming volcano out of a sliced onion. At some point, he hits my mom in the arm with a shrimp. I laugh until I cry, and then he serves me a plate of savory, buttery steak; caramelized stir-fried vegetables; zippy white sauce; and fried rice. Decades later, the taste of a "hibachi" dinner ("teppanyaki" would be a more accurate term) can still return me to that revelatory moment from my childhood.

With their knives and spatulas whirling, the pros use the broad cooking surface of the flattop to cook everything at once—steak, vegetables, and fried rice. But I knew I'd need to make some adjustments for my homemade version. To mimic the powerful heat of the flattop, I'd cook in a large cast-iron skillet. I'd also need to split the cooking into stages: steaks first and then the vegetables. As a bonus, this plan would allow the meat to rest while the vegetables cooked. At the restaurant we visited, they chop the steak right on the

Could I re-create the components of this dazzling meal at home? I made and tasted all the copycat recipes I could find, without much satisfaction. Undaunted, I talked my editor into joining me for lunch at the local Japanese steakhouse, where we tried to sleuth out just how the experts did it. The chef used a squeeze bottle filled with sake to conjure the famous fireballs, and then he picked up a bottle of seasoned soy sauce to squirt on pretty much everything. A mound of garlic butter also made its way into most dishes on the flattop. The flavors of garlic, soy sauce, butter, and sake permeated the meal.

flattop and then add a good squirt of seasoned soy sauce and a knob of garlic butter on top, but I decided to make an all-in-one condiment by mixing together soy sauce, garlic, and melted butter. I cooked my steaks whole (tasters preferred rich, beefy rib eye to sirloin and filet), sliced them, and then drizzled on this magic condiment. Delicious.

For the vegetables, I chose the usual suspects: shiitake caps, onions, and zucchini, cut so that they would all be cooked through at the same time. For a superflavorful start, I added them to the drippings my rib eyes had left in the still-hot cast-iron skillet, and to ensure nice browning, I patted them into a single layer and resisted the urge to stir for a few minutes. After a stir and another pause for more browning, I added more soy-garlic butter and a splash of mirin—a sweetened rice wine—for the familiar finishing touch.

The results? Juicy slices of perfectly seared rib eye and beautifully browned and glazed veggies that were just as good as those I'd had so many years ago. When served with the accompanying sauces and my recipe for simple fried rice, the meal was spot-on!

JAPANESE STEAKHOUSE STEAK AND VEGETABLES *Serves 4*
Strip steaks can be substituted for the rib eyes, if desired. Mirin can be found in your supermarket's Asian foods section. We like to serve the steak and vegetables with Simple Hibachi-Style Fried Rice, Spicy Mayonnaise (Yum-Yum Sauce), White Mustard Sauce, and Sweet Ginger Sauce (recipes follow). If using a nonstick skillet, heat the oil in the skillet over medium-high heat until just smoking before adding the steaks in step 2.

- **3 tablespoons unsalted butter, melted**
- **2 tablespoons soy sauce**
- **2 garlic cloves, minced**
- **2 (1-pound) boneless rib-eye steaks, 1½ to 1¾ inches thick, trimmed**
- **1¼ teaspoons white pepper, divided**
- **1 teaspoon table salt, divided**
- **1 tablespoon vegetable oil**
- **2 zucchini (8 ounces each), halved lengthwise and sliced ¾ inch thick**
- **2 onions, cut into ¾-inch pieces**
- **6 ounces shiitake mushrooms, stemmed and halved if small or quartered if large**
- **2 tablespoons mirin**

SIMPLE HIBACHI-STYLE FRIED RICE *Serves 4*

Mirin can be found in your supermarket's Asian foods section. Black pepper can be substituted for the white pepper, if desired.

- 1½ cups long-grain white rice
- 3 large eggs
- 1 teaspoon toasted sesame oil
- ¼ teaspoon table salt
- ¼ teaspoon white pepper
- 1 tablespoon unsalted butter, softened
- 1 garlic clove, minced
- 1 tablespoon vegetable oil
- 4 scallions, sliced ¼ inch thick
- 1½ tablespoons soy sauce
- 1½ tablespoons mirin

1. Bring 3 quarts water to boil in large saucepan over high heat. Add rice and cook, stirring occasionally, until just cooked through, about 12 minutes. Drain rice in fine-mesh strainer or colander. Whisk eggs, sesame oil, salt, and white pepper together in bowl; set aside. Combine butter and garlic in second bowl; set aside.

2. Heat vegetable oil in 12-inch nonstick skillet over medium-high heat until shimmering. Add egg mixture and stir with rubber spatula until set but still wet, about 15 seconds.

3. Add scallions and rice and cook until sizzling and popping loudly, about 3 minutes. Add soy sauce and mirin and cook, stirring constantly, until thoroughly combined, about 2 minutes. Stir in garlic butter until incorporated. Serve.

THE AMERICAN TABLE

Hiroaki "Rocky" Aoki, a Tokyo native, came to the United States in the early 1960s on a wrestling scholarship, earned a restaurant management degree, and began to pursue his dream of opening a Japanese restaurant in New York. Aoki's father agreed to help bankroll the project under one condition: It needed to provide entertainment. When his first Benihana opened in 1964, customers loved the showy "performance" cooking that included sleight-of-hand egg-cracking tricks and onion volcanoes. By 1972, there were six Benihana locations across the country, and Aoki's success continued to grow. He encountered extreme highs and lows along the way, living lavishly but also coming under scrutiny for insider trading and nearly dying in a powerboat race under the Golden Gate Bridge. Aoki died in 2008, leaving behind dozens of restaurants.

. Combine melted
utter, soy sauce, and
arlic in bowl; set aside. Pat
teaks dry with paper towels
nd sprinkle with 1 teaspoon
white pepper and ¾ teaspoon salt.

2. Heat 12-inch cast-iron skillet over
medium-high heat for 5 minutes. Add
il to skillet and swirl to coat. Add steaks
nd cook, flipping steaks every 2 minutes,
ntil well browned and meat registers
120 to 125 degrees (for medium-rare),
0 to 13 minutes. Transfer steaks to carving
oard, tent with aluminum foil, and let rest.

3. While steaks rest, add zucchini, onions,
mushrooms, remaining ¼ teaspoon white
pepper, and remaining ¼ teaspoon salt to
fat left in skillet and stir to combine. Pat
vegetables into even layer and cook over
medium-high heat, without stirring, until
beginning to brown, about 3 minutes. Stir
and continue to cook 2 minutes longer. Add
mirin and 2 tablespoons soy-garlic butter to
skillet and continue to cook until liquid has
evaporated and vegetables are well browned,
about 2 minutes longer.

4. Transfer vegetables to serving platter.
Slice steaks ¼ inch thick and transfer to
platter with vegetables. Drizzle steaks with
remaining soy-garlic butter. Serve.

SPICY MAYONNAISE (YUM-YUM SAUCE)

Serves 4 to 6 (Makes about ¾ cup)
White miso can be substituted for the red miso, if desired.

- ½ cup mayonnaise
- 2 tablespoons water
- 1 tablespoon unsalted butter, melted
- 1 tablespoon red miso
- 1 teaspoon tomato paste
- ¼ teaspoon cayenne pepper
- ¼ teaspoon paprika
- ¼ teaspoon table salt

Whisk all ingredients together in bowl.

WHITE MUSTARD SAUCE

Serves 4 to 6 (Makes about ⅔ cup)
Be sure to use toasted sesame oil here. If you prefer a spicier sauce, add more dry mustard.

- ½ cup heavy cream
- 2 tablespoons soy sauce
- 1½ teaspoons dry mustard
- 1½ teaspoons toasted sesame oil
- 1 teaspoon sugar

Vigorously whisk all ingredients in bowl until combined and slightly thickened.

SWEET GINGER SAUCE

Serves 4 to 6 (Makes about ¾ cup)
Be sure to use unseasoned rice vinegar here.

- ½ cup chopped onion
- 3 tablespoons sugar
- 3 tablespoons rice vinegar
- 3 tablespoons soy sauce
- 1 (¾-inch) piece ginger, peeled and chopped

Process all ingredients in blender until smooth, about 15 seconds, scraping down sides of blender jar as needed.

TIMING IT RIGHT **1.** Put on the water for the rice. **2.** Make the sauces. **3.** Boil and drain the rice; prepare the steak and vegetables while the rice cooks. **4.** Make the fried rice and cover to keep warm. **5.** Cook the steaks. **6.** While the steaks rest, cook the vegetables. **7.** Serve and enjoy!

Sheet-Pan Hash Browns

It took 138 pounds of potatoes and more than 40 tests, but we found a better way to make homemade hash browns. **by Cecelia Jenkins**

These tasty spuds are crispy and brown on the outside but tender within.

ORDER UP! HASH browns! Practiced short order cooks keep a mound of these crispy shredded spuds cooking on their flat-top griddles all through the breakfast rush. But a home cook has two options: using frozen supermarket hash browns (convenient but not very good) or shredding potatoes and cooking them in a skillet. Skillet hash browns are great, but you need to cook multiple batches to serve more than two people—not ideal. Could I find a way to make enough hash browns to feed four to six people in a single batch at home?

In most home kitchens, a rimmed baking sheet is the closest thing in size to a flat-top griddle, so that's what I decided to use. This meant I'd bake my hash browns in the oven. But my first tests weren't very promising. They variously yielded starchy, clumpy tangles; anemic browning and a leathery texture; burnt edges; and undercooked interiors. I wanted hash browns that were deep golden brown on both sides, with a satisfying mix of crispy and creamy textures.

There's no getting around shredding potatoes for hash browns, but luckily the food processor makes it easier. But you still have to peel the potatoes—or do you? A side-by-side test showed that the skins aren't a problem here as long as you wash the potatoes prior to grating. My tasters preferred Yukon Gold potatoes to starchier russets, and 3 pounds proved the right amount. I did find that a little pretreatment of the potatoes was necessary for the best results; first you need to soak the shredded potatoes in water to remove some excess surface starch (so the shreds don't fry up gummy), and then you need to wring out the raw shreds in a dish towel to remove excess moisture that would inhibit browning.

Tossing the potato shreds in a little fat kept them from drying out in the oven; I chose oil over butter because butter contains water, which I'd already worked to minimize. Greasing the baking sheet lightly with vegetable oil spray ensured that no stubborn bits of potato stuck to the sheet. And lightly distributing the mass of shreds into an even layer ensured even cooking.

As for the oven temperature, my tests showed that I needed enough heat to crisp the hash browns, but too much heat caused deep browning on the top and bottom before the interior cooked through. It turned out that 450 degrees on the middle rack was perfect; after about 30 minutes, I removed the hot sheet and used a spatula to flip the hash browns in segments. Then I popped the sheet back into the oven for about 8 minutes to finish cooking the potatoes and to crisp the top. Order up!

SHEET-PAN HASH BROWNS
Serves 4 to 6

We prefer to use the shredding disk of a food processor to shred the potatoes, but you can also use the large holes of a box grater. These hash browns are great topped with sliced American cheese, chopped ham, and sautéed onions and peppers.

    3   pounds Yukon Gold potatoes,
        unpeeled
    6   tablespoons extra-virgin olive oil
    1   teaspoon table salt
    ¼   teaspoon pepper

1. Adjust oven rack to middle position and heat oven to 450 degrees. Fit food processor with shredding disk. Halve or quarter potatoes as needed to fit through processor hopper, then shred potatoes. Transfer potatoes to large bowl and cover with cold water. Let sit for 5 minutes.

2. One handful at a time, lift potatoes out of water and transfer to colander; discard water. Rinse and dry bowl.

3. Place one-quarter of shredded potatoes in center of clean dish towel. Gather ends of towel and twist tightly to wring out excess moisture from potatoes. Transfer dried potatoes to now-empty bowl. Repeat 3 more times with remaining potatoes.

4. Add oil, salt, and pepper to potatoes and toss to combine. Lightly spray 16 by 11-inch rimmed baking sheet with vegetable oil spray. Distribute potatoes in even layer on sheet, but do not pack down. Bake until top of potatoes is spotty brown, 32 to 35 minutes.

5. Remove sheet from oven. Flip hash browns with metal spatula. Return sheet to oven and continue to bake until deep golden brown on top, 6 to 8 minutes longer. Season with salt and pepper to taste. Serve.

Keys to Diner-Quality Hash Browns at Home

1. Shred wedges of unpeeled Yukon Gold potatoes in a food processor.

2. Soak the shreds in cold water, and then squeeze them dry in a dish towel.

Apple Cider Doughnuts

Could the answer to ramping up apple flavor be ditching the cider? **by Alli Berkey**

THE AIR GETS sweeter as you walk through the dirt lot toward the apple orchards in fall. It's the aroma of hot apple cider doughnuts straight from the fryer: warm and spicy. But these treats can be a bait and switch, promising apple flavor but rarely delivering it. I challenged myself to make a home version that packed in a ton of apple flavor. Believe it or not, it can be done!

After researching existing recipes, I gathered the basics: flour, sugar, eggs, butter, and milk. I needed a formula that would yield doughnuts with a rich flavor, tender interior, and lightly crunchy exterior. I settled on 2½ cups of flour, one egg, and ¾ cup of milk for richness and moisture. Four tablespoons of melted, cooled butter gave me plenty of butter flavor and a workable dough.

Leavening came next. I started with both baking powder and baking soda, a combination we've found makes for fluffy doughnuts in other recipes. However, without any acid to activate the baking soda, my doughnuts never puffed up while they cooked. Swapping acidic buttermilk for the milk unleashed the power of the baking soda while also adding a bit of tang.

I had light, tender doughnuts, but I still needed apple flavor. I tried adding store-bought apple cider, boiled cider (reduced for strong flavor), and even shredded apple, but my tasters were disappointed. I needed a new idea.

That was when a colleague mentioned apple juice concentrate. It provided intense apple flavor—no cooking required. I replaced some of the buttermilk with thawed apple juice concentrate to balance the wet and dry ratios, and crossed my fingers.

A quick run through with my round cutters and my doughnuts were ready to fry. When the doughnuts were deep golden brown, I removed them from the oil and tossed them in cinnamon sugar. The sweet apple flavor came through in every bite.

APPLE CIDER DOUGHNUTS

Serves 12 (Makes 12 doughnuts and 12 doughnut holes)

Use a Dutch oven that holds 6 quarts or more for this recipe.

COATING
- ½ cup (3½ ounces) sugar
- ⅛ teaspoon ground cinnamon
- Pinch table salt

DOUGHNUTS
- 2½ cups (12½ ounces) all-purpose flour
- 1 teaspoon baking powder
- ½ teaspoon baking soda
- ½ teaspoon ground cinnamon
- ¼ teaspoon ground nutmeg
- ¼ teaspoon table salt
- ½ cup thawed apple juice concentrate
- ⅓ cup (2⅓ ounces) sugar
- ¼ cup buttermilk
- 4 tablespoons unsalted butter, melted and cooled
- 1 large egg
- 2 quarts vegetable oil, for frying

1. FOR THE COATING: Whisk sugar, cinnamon, and salt together in medium bowl; set aside.

2. FOR THE DOUGHNUTS: Whisk flour, baking powder, baking soda, cinnamon, nutmeg, and salt together in bowl. Whisk apple juice concentrate, sugar, buttermilk, melted butter, and egg together in large bowl. Whisk half of flour mixture into apple juice concentrate mixture until smooth. Add remaining flour mixture; using rubber spatula, use folding motion to mix and press dough until all flour is hydrated and no dry bits remain. (Dough can be covered with plastic wrap and refrigerated for up to 24 hours.)

3. Dust counter heavily with flour. Turn out dough onto floured counter, then dust top of dough with additional flour. Using your floured hands, gently pat dough into ⅓-inch-thick round, 10 to 11 inches in diameter. Using floured 3-inch round cutter, cut out 9 to 10 doughnut rounds. Using 1-inch round cutter, cut hole in center of each round.

4. Lightly dust rimmed baking sheet with flour. Transfer doughnut rounds and holes to prepared sheet. Combine dough scraps, then knead into cohesive ball and pat into ⅓-inch-thick round. Cut out 2 or 3 more doughnut rounds and holes (you should have 12 of each). Transfer to sheet and refrigerate while heating oil.

5. Set wire rack in second rimmed baking sheet and line half of rack with triple layer of paper towels. Add oil to large Dutch oven until it measures about 1½ inches deep and heat over medium-high heat to 350 degrees. Add 6 doughnut rounds and cook, flipping every 30 seconds, until deep golden brown, about 2 minutes. Adjust burner as needed to maintain oil temperature between 325 and 350 degrees.

6. Using spider skimmer or slotted spoon, transfer doughnuts to paper towel–lined side of prepared rack and let sit while frying remaining doughnut rounds. Return oil to 350 degrees and repeat with remaining doughnut rounds.

7. Return oil to 350 degrees and, using spider skimmer or slotted spoon, carefully add doughnut holes to hot oil. Cook, stirring often, until deep golden brown, about 2 minutes. Transfer to paper towel–lined side of wire rack. Lightly toss doughnuts and doughnut holes in coating and transfer to unlined side of wire rack. Serve.

Dust, Pat, and Stamp
Follow the steps below to shape the dough and cut the doughnut rounds and holes.

1. Dust dough with flour, then use your hands to pat dough into round.

2. Use large and small round cutters to stamp out doughnut rounds and holes.

Cook Jhonny Sanchez (above) can make hundreds of chopped cheese sandwiches on a busy day. Most are for locals and regulars, but tourists come from around the globe to taste his handiwork. Efficiency is essential; sandwiches need to come together quickly so they're hot on delivery. Sanchez's process requires sharp focus, fast hands, and steady nerves when the orders come rolling in.

A BODEGA CLASSIC

Text by Bryan Roof; photos by Steve Klise

Could we re-create this bodega classic at home?

by Morgan Bolling and Bryan Roof

Chopped Cheese Sandwiches

IT'S A HOT afternoon in East Harlem. The broad streets are free of the usual New York hustle, but the drumbeats of a salsa festival pop from a few blocks away. I arrive at the corner of 110th Street and First Avenue and step into Blue Sky Deli, known locally as Hajji's. The clerk at the counter hollers out, asking if I want to place an order. Hajji's is part convenience store, part take-out deli. He asks, "Chopped with everything?" I nod.

Tourists from as far away as Australia and Japan make their way here just to order this famed sandwich, which Hajji's claims to have invented. I make my way toward the back of the store where cook Jhonny Sanchez methodically works the griddle. His kitchen is sectioned off by a 5-foot wall. As I settle in to watch, he sends another chopped cheese out the door.

The combination of the temperature outside and the heat radiating from the griddle makes the work space nearly unbearable. But Sanchez moves quickly and wears an earnest smile, proud to be the guy who makes the sandwich everyone talks about. "Snoop Dogg was here last week," he tells me. He estimates he'll make 500 sandwiches on this particular Saturday and chuckles as the number leaves his lips.

He slaps a few ground beef patties onto the griddle, dusts them with two mystery commercial seasoning blends, and scatters a handful of paper-thin onion over the top. He grabs two metal spatulas and begins chopping the beef and onion together with the intensity of a Tito Puente drum solo. The rhythm echoes through the small shop—the music of bodega cuisine.

He divides the meat into long piles the same length as the toasted sub rolls, which he dresses with mayo and ketchup. American cheese is layered on top of the meat, followed by tomato slices so thin they're nearly transparent. With a scoop of the spatula, he slides the meat onto the bread. Shredded iceberg lettuce finishes it off before it's folded and wrapped in paper. As Sanchez hands me my sandwich, the clerk calls out for three more "chopped with everything."

For more photos of our trip to East Harlem, visit **CooksCountry.com/hajji19**.

THERE'S NOTHING LIKE a real bodega chopped cheese sandwich straight off a flat-top griddle in East Harlem. But once you've had one of these local favorites—ground beef, seasonings, and cheese piled atop a soft sub roll along with ketchup, mayonnaise, lettuce, and tomato—the cravings can be relentless. So we set out to create a recipe that would allow home cooks everywhere to enjoy this landmark sandwich.

We started with a pound of ground beef to ensure we'd have enough filling for four hearty sandwiches. Early tests proved that 90 percent lean ground beef was too dry and 80 percent lean was just a tad too greasy; 85 percent lean was just right.

In NYC bodegas, line cooks use the high heat of flat-top griddles to cook big batches of ground beef for dozens of sandwiches every day. We found that a nonstick skillet was a fine substitute for a smaller batch. A wooden spoon made breaking up the meat a breeze.

The bodega cooks in New York sprinkled two mystery seasoning blends on the meat while searing it. After some experimentation, we found a close approximation with a mix of Lawry's Seasoned Salt and Goya Adobo All Purpose Seasoning. The Lawry's seasoning gave the beef a salty, peppery, oniony flavor while the Goya seasoning added more salt, garlic, and oregano. Together, they packed tons of flavor.

To prep our split sub rolls, we spread them with ketchup and mayonnaise, added the seasoned beef, and layered American cheese slices on top. We wanted our sandwiches to have melty cheese and warm condiments, so we transferred them to the oven and baked them until they were lightly toasted.

These sandwiches are a wonderful mess to eat, but if you're unwilling to put your shirt in danger, wrap them tightly in parchment paper and cut them in half before digging in. Your experience will be just a touch neater, and the swaddle helps meld the cheese and the beef.

Deeply seasoned beef, melty cheese, ketchup, mayo, lettuce, and tomato. The perfect sandwich.

CHOPPED CHEESE SANDWICHES
Serves 4

The Goya seasoning can be found in the spice or international section of your grocery store; Lawry's Seasoned Salt is usually stocked with other salt blends in the spice section. You can wrap the sandwiches in butcher paper instead of parchment paper, if desired.

- 1 pound 85 percent lean ground beef
- 1 onion, chopped fine
- 1 teaspoon Goya Adobo All Purpose Seasoning
- 1 teaspoon Lawry's Seasoned Salt
- 4 (8-inch) sub rolls, split
- ⅓ cup mayonnaise
- 2 tablespoons ketchup
- 8 slices yellow American cheese (8 ounces)
- 12 thin tomato slices (2 tomatoes)
- 2 cups shredded iceberg lettuce

1. Adjust oven rack to middle position and heat oven to 400 degrees. Combine beef, onion, all-purpose seasoning, and seasoned salt in 12-inch nonstick skillet. Cook over medium-high heat, constantly breaking up meat into small pieces with wooden spoon, until cooked through and excess moisture is driven off, about 8 minutes.

2. Arrange sub rolls on baking sheet and spread mayonnaise and ketchup evenly on cut sides of rolls. Divide beef mixture evenly among rolls. Layer 2 slices American cheese over beef on each roll. Bake until bread is warmed through and cheese is melted, about 5 minutes.

3. Layer tomatoes and lettuce over cheese. Close 1 sandwich, using spatula as needed to keep ingredients contained within roll (sandwich will be very full). Starting from corner of 16 by 12-inch sheet of parchment paper, immediately wrap sandwich tightly. Repeat closing and wrapping with remaining 3 sandwiches. To serve, cut sandwiches in half through parchment paper and unwrap as you eat.

Spinach-Artichoke Dip

In most versions of this creamy party dip, the artichoke flavor gets lost. We set out to find it. **by Jessica Rudolph**

SPINACH-ARTICHOKE DIP IS an economical comfort food that easily feeds a crowd, making it an ideal holiday appetizer. But all too often, it's overly cheesy and the spinach and artichokes get lost in the mix. I set out to create a more balanced version.

I started by making seven existing recipes. The finished dips ran the gamut from thin to stodgy to grassy to overwhelmingly cheesy. To achieve what I sought—a smooth, creamy dip that showcased bright spinach and nutty artichokes—I'd have to make some adjustments.

I began with some common ingredients: frozen spinach, canned artichokes, Parmesan cheese, melty Monterey Jack, a cream cheese/sour cream/mayonnaise binder, and garlic. I mixed everything together and baked it. The resulting dip looked the part, but the flavor fell flat. The biggest problem was the fibrous and muddy-tasting frozen spinach. For my next batch, I coarsely chopped some fresh baby spinach and sautéed it until it wilted. The resulting dip had a cleaner spinach flavor, and the leaves kept a distinct but soft texture.

Canned artichokes had tough, squeaky leaves and an overpoweringly tangy and briny flavor. Frozen artichokes were dull, with mushy hearts and leathery leaves, but jarred marinated artichokes were tender and had a subtle nutty flavor accented by their bright marinade, which we loved.

The hefty dose of Parmesan I was using supplied the salty, savory backbone the dip needed, so it stayed. And while Monterey Jack seemed like a good choice to provide supple, melty texture, it seized and became stringy as it sat. The cheese turned my dip so stiff that the chips I dipped in it felt as if they were in danger of breaking. After exploring several options, I settled on an unlikely choice: gouda. This cheese melted even more smoothly, stayed creamy after it cooled, and had a toasty sweetness that accentuated the artichokes' nuttiness.

Sour cream proved unnecessary; using equal parts cream cheese and mayonnaise provided the perfect balance of tart and creamy. The garlic added a welcome punch. Lastly, black pepper and cayenne added a kick to offset the heavy richness.

My resulting dip was irresistibly creamy and cheesy, with a prominent spinach and artichoke presence. I knew that the dip would be gracing my holiday table, but I worried about pulling it together on a busy Thanksgiving morning. I tried mixing the dip together and refrigerating it overnight; thankfully, it still tasted great when heated the next day. Now the only worry I'll have on Thanksgiving is whether my guests will save room for the turkey.

SPINACH-ARTICHOKE DIP
Serves 10 to 12

You will need one 12-ounce jar of marinated artichoke hearts to yield the 1⅓ cups called for here. You can substitute canned artichoke hearts if you can't find marinated. If you can find only 5-ounce packages of baby spinach, there's no need to buy a third package to make up the extra ounce; just make the dip with 10 ounces. Use the large holes of a box grater to shred the gouda and a rasp-style grater to grate the Parmesan. Serve with tortilla chips, crusty bread, pita chips, or vegetables.

- 1 tablespoon extra-virgin olive oil
- 3 garlic cloves, minced
- 11 ounces (11 cups) baby spinach, chopped coarse
- 8 ounces cream cheese, softened
- 6 ounces gouda cheese, shredded (1½ cups)
- 3 ounces Parmesan cheese, grated (1½ cups)
- 1⅓ cups marinated artichoke hearts, chopped
- 1 cup mayonnaise
- ¼ teaspoon pepper
- ⅛ teaspoon cayenne pepper

1. Adjust oven rack to middle position and heat oven to 400 degrees. Heat oil in 12-inch skillet over medium-high heat until shimmering. Add garlic and cook until fragrant, about 30 seconds. Add spinach, 1 handful at a time, allowing each to wilt slightly before adding next; cook until wilted and liquid has evaporated, about 4 minutes.
2. Off heat, add cream cheese and stir until melted and combined, about 1 minute. Stir in gouda, Parmesan, artichokes, mayonnaise, pepper, and cayenne until combined. Transfer to 2-quart baking dish and smooth top with rubber spatula.
3. Bake until spotty golden brown and bubbling around edges, about 22 minutes. Let cool for 10 minutes. Serve.

TO MAKE AHEAD

At end of step 2, let dip cool completely, wrap in plastic wrap, and refrigerate for up to 2 days. When ready to serve, continue with step 3, increasing baking time by 10 minutes.

Marinated Artichokes

Avoid artichoke hearts that are canned, jarred and packed in water, or frozen. For the best results, use jarred marinated artichoke hearts, which are packed in oil.

Butternut Squash and Red Pepper Soup

30-MINUTE SUPPER

Cod Baked in Foil with Potatoes, Zucchini, and Sun-Dried Tomatoes

30-MINUTE SUPPER

Quick Pulled Chicken Sandwiches with Red Cabbage Slaw

30-MINUTE SUPPER

Spice-Crusted Pork Tenderloin with Pan-Roasted Vegetables

30-MINUTE SUPPER

Cod Baked in Foil with Potatoes, Zucchini, and Sun-Dried Tomatoes

Serves 4

Use extra-small Yukon Gold potatoes measuring 1 inch or less in diameter. If you can find only larger potatoes, cut them in half.

- 1 pound extra-small Yukon Gold potatoes
- 3 tablespoons sun-dried tomato oil, divided, plus ½ cup minced oil-packed sun-dried tomatoes
- ¾ teaspoon table salt, divided
- ½ teaspoon pepper, divided
- 2 zucchini, sliced into ½-inch-thick rounds
- 1 shallot, halved and sliced thin
- ½ cup frozen peas
- 4 (6-ounce) skinless cod fillets, 1 to 1½ inches thick
- 2 tablespoons chopped fresh basil
  Lemon wedges

1. Adjust oven rack to lowest position and heat oven to 450 degrees. Line rimmed baking sheet with aluminum foil. Toss potatoes, 1 tablespoon oil, ¼ teaspoon salt, and ¼ teaspoon pepper together on prepared sheet and arrange around perimeter of sheet. Roast until potatoes start to brown, about 10 minutes.

2. While potatoes roast, cut eight 12-inch squares of foil. Place 4 squares on counter. Divide zucchini, shallot, and peas evenly among centers of squares, leaving 2½-inch border. Sprinkle cod with remaining ½ teaspoon salt and remaining ¼ teaspoon pepper. Place fillets on top of vegetables. Top fillets with tomatoes and drizzle with remaining 2 tablespoons oil.

3. Place remaining 4 squares of foil on top of each fillet. Pinch and fold top and bottom edges of foil together to create sealed packet. Transfer packets to center of sheet with potatoes. Bake until fish flakes apart when gently prodded with paring knife and registers 140 degrees, about 15 minutes. Sprinkle cod and vegetables with basil and serve with lemon wedges.

Spice-Crusted Pork Tenderloin with Pan-Roasted Vegetables

Serves 4

Use carrots measuring 1 to 1¼ inches in diameter.

- 4 large carrots, peeled and halved lengthwise
- 2 fennel bulbs, stalks discarded, bulbs halved and cut into 1-inch wedges through root end
- ¼ cup extra-virgin olive oil, divided
- 1 tablespoon kosher salt, divided
- 1 teaspoon pepper, divided
- 1 tablespoon chopped fresh rosemary
- 1½ teaspoons grated lemon zest
- 1 teaspoon ground coriander
- 1 teaspoon dry mustard
- 2 (1-pound) pork tenderloins, trimmed
- 2 tablespoons chopped fresh parsley

1. Adjust oven rack to lowest position and heat oven to 450 degrees. Toss carrots, fennel, 2 tablespoons oil, 1 teaspoon salt, and ½ teaspoon pepper together on rimmed baking sheet. Arrange carrots cut side down in middle of sheet, surrounded by fennel. Roast for 13 minutes.

2. Meanwhile, combine rosemary, lemon zest, coriander, mustard, remaining 2 teaspoons salt, and remaining ½ teaspoon pepper in bowl. Sprinkle pork with spice mixture, pressing to adhere. Heat remaining 2 tablespoons oil in 12-inch nonstick skillet over medium-high heat until just smoking. Add pork and cook, turning gently with tongs, until well browned on all sides, about 8 minutes.

3. Place pork in middle of sheet on top of vegetables. Roast until meat registers 140 degrees and vegetables are well browned, about 12 minutes. Transfer pork to carving board and let rest for 5 minutes. Sprinkle parsley over vegetables. Slice pork and serve with vegetables.

Butternut Squash and Red Pepper Soup

Serves 4

Buy a 4-ounce hunk of pancetta from the deli counter, not the presliced variety.

- 4 ounces pancetta, cut into ½-inch pieces
- 2 pounds butternut squash, peeled, seeded, and cut into 1-inch pieces (6 cups)
- 1 red bell pepper, stemmed, seeded, and chopped
- 1 onion, chopped fine
- 3 garlic cloves, minced
- 1 teaspoon dried thyme
- 1 teaspoon table salt
- ½ teaspoon pepper
- 4 cups chicken broth
- 1 tablespoon sherry vinegar
- 2 tablespoons chopped fresh chives

1. Cook pancetta in Dutch oven over medium heat until browned and crispy, about 7 minutes. Using slotted spoon, transfer pancetta to paper towel–lined plate.

2. Add squash, bell pepper, onion, garlic, thyme, salt, and pepper to fat left in pot and cook over medium-high heat until onion is softened, about 5 minutes, stirring occasionally. Stir in broth and bring to boil, scraping up any browned bits. Cook, covered, until squash is tender, about 15 minutes. Remove pot from heat.

3. Working with 2 cups at a time, process soup in blender until smooth, about 1 minute. Transfer pureed soup to saucepan. Stir in vinegar. Season with salt and pepper to taste. Serve, sprinkling individual portions with chives and pancetta.

Quick Pulled Chicken Sandwiches with Red Cabbage Slaw

Serves 4

Coleslaw mix can be used in place of the red cabbage, if desired.

- 2 cups thinly sliced red cabbage
- ½ cup sour cream
- 2 tablespoons bread-and-butter pickle juice, plus ¼ cup bread-and-butter pickles
- 1 teaspoon table salt, divided
- ½ teaspoon pepper
- 1 cup cider vinegar
- ½ cup water
- ¼ cup sugar
- 1 teaspoon red pepper flakes
- 1 (2½-pound) rotisserie chicken, skin and bones discarded, meat shredded into bite-size pieces (3 cups)
- 4 hamburger buns

1. Combine cabbage, sour cream, pickle juice, ½ teaspoon salt, and pepper in bowl; set aside.

2. Bring vinegar, water, sugar, pepper flakes, and remaining ½ teaspoon salt to boil in medium saucepan over high heat. Cook until reduced by half, 8 to 10 minutes. Stir in chicken and cook until warmed through, about 1 minute. Remove saucepan from heat.

3. Divide chicken evenly among bun bottoms. Top with ½ cup cabbage mixture, then divide pickles evenly over cabbage. Cover with bun tops. Serve.

Pan-Seared Pork Chops with Blistered Brussels Sprouts and Pomegranate

30-MINUTE SUPPER

Sautéed Chicken Breasts with Wilted Salad

30-MINUTE SUPPER

Steak Tips with Red Wine–Shallot Sauce and Broccoli Rabe

30-MINUTE SUPPER

Lamb Ragu with Pappardelle

30-MINUTE SUPPER

Sautéed Chicken Breasts with Wilted Salad

Serves 4

Dried cherries can be substituted for the cranberries, if desired.

- 5 tablespoons extra-virgin olive oil, divided
- 2 tablespoons whole-grain mustard
- 1 tablespoon red wine vinegar
- ¾ teaspoon table salt, divided
- ½ teaspoon sugar
- 1 small head green leaf lettuce (8 ounces), cut into 1-inch pieces
- 1 head frisée (6 ounces), cut into 1-inch pieces
- ½ cup dried cranberries
- 4 (6- to 8-ounce) boneless, skinless chicken breasts, trimmed
- ¼ teaspoon pepper
- 2 ounces Pecorino Romano cheese, shaved with vegetable peeler

1. Whisk 3 tablespoons oil, mustard, vinegar, ¼ teaspoon salt, and sugar together in large bowl. Add lettuce, frisée, and cranberries and toss to combine; set aside.

2. Pat chicken dry with paper towels and sprinkle with pepper and remaining ½ teaspoon salt. Heat remaining 2 tablespoons oil in 12-inch nonstick skillet over medium-high heat until just smoking. Add chicken and cook until golden brown and registering 160 degrees, about 5 minutes per side. Transfer chicken to carving board and tent with aluminum foil.

3. Off heat, add lettuce mixture to now-empty skillet and toss until slightly wilted, about 30 seconds. Divide salad among 4 plates and top each with Pecorino. Slice chicken on bias ½ inch thick and serve with salad.

Pan-Seared Pork Chops with Blistered Brussels Sprouts and Pomegranate *Serves 4*

For spicier pork chops, increase the cayenne to ¾ teaspoon.

- 4 (8- to 10-ounce) bone-in pork rib chops, ¾ to 1 inch thick, trimmed
- 1¼ teaspoons table salt, divided
- ½ teaspoon pepper, divided
- ¼ teaspoon cayenne pepper
- 2 tablespoons vegetable oil
- 1½ pounds Brussels sprouts, trimmed and halved
- ¼ cup water
- 2 tablespoons balsamic vinegar
- 2 teaspoons lemon juice
- 2 tablespoons pistachios, toasted and chopped
- 2 tablespoons pomegranate seeds

1. Pat chops dry with paper towels and sprinkle with ½ teaspoon salt, ¼ teaspoon pepper, and cayenne. Heat oil in 12-inch nonstick skillet over medium-high heat until just smoking. Cook chops, flipping every 2 minutes, until browned on both sides and meat registers 140 degrees, 10 to 12 minutes. Transfer chops to platter and tent with aluminum foil.

2. Pour off all but 2 tablespoons fat from skillet. Add Brussels sprouts, cut side down; water; and remaining ¾ teaspoon salt to skillet. Reduce heat to medium, cover, and cook until sprouts are bright green and water has evaporated, about 4 minutes. Uncover and continue to cook until Brussels sprouts are well browned on cut side, about 5 minutes longer.

3. Off heat, stir in vinegar and remaining ¼ teaspoon pepper. Sprinkle Brussels sprouts with lemon juice, pistachios, and pomegranate seeds. Serve with chops.

Lamb Ragu with Pappardelle

Serves 4

Serve with grated Parmesan cheese. You can substitute tagliatelle for the pappardelle, if desired.

- 1 pound ground lamb
- 1 onion, chopped fine
- 2 carrots, peeled and chopped fine
- 4 garlic cloves, sliced thin
- 1½ teaspoons ground fennel
- 1 teaspoon dried oregano
- ½ teaspoon table salt, plus salt for cooking pasta
- ½ teaspoon pepper
- 1 (28-ounce) can crushed tomatoes
- 1 pound pappardelle
- ½ cup torn fresh basil

1. Combine lamb, onion, carrots, garlic, fennel, oregano, salt, and pepper in 12-inch nonstick skillet. Cook over medium-high heat, breaking up meat with wooden spoon, until meat is cooked through and carrots are tender, about 8 minutes. Stir in tomatoes and reduce heat to medium. Cook, covered, until sauce has thickened slightly, about 15 minutes.

2. Meanwhile, bring 4 quarts water to boil in large pot. Add pasta and 1 tablespoon salt and cook, stirring often, until al dente. Reserve 1 cup cooking water, then drain pasta and return it to pot.

3. Add sauce and ¼ cup reserved cooking water to pasta and toss to combine. Adjust consistency with remaining reserved cooking water as needed. Stir in basil and season with salt and pepper to taste. Serve.

Steak Tips with Red Wine–Shallot Sauce and Broccoli Rabe *Serves 4*

Flap meat is often sold as sirloin steak tips; it's best to buy a single steak and cut it yourself.

- 1½ pounds broccoli rabe, trimmed
- ¼ cup vegetable oil, divided
- 1 teaspoon table salt, divided
- ½ teaspoon pepper, divided
- 2 pounds flap meat, trimmed and cut with grain into 4 equal strips
- 1 shallot, minced
- 1 tablespoon tomato paste
- ¼ cup red wine
- ½ cup beef broth
- 2 teaspoons Worcestershire sauce
- 2 tablespoons unsalted butter, cut into ½-inch pieces

1. Adjust oven rack to lowest position and heat oven to 450 degrees. Toss broccoli rabe, 2 tablespoons oil, ½ teaspoon salt, and ¼ teaspoon pepper together on rimmed baking sheet. Roast until tender, about 10 minutes.

2. Meanwhile, pat beef dry with paper towels and sprinkle with remaining ½ teaspoon salt and remaining ¼ teaspoon pepper. Heat remaining 2 tablespoons oil in 12-inch skillet over medium-high heat until just smoking. Add beef and cook until browned all over and meat registers 125 degrees (for medium-rare), about 12 minutes. Transfer beef to carving board and tent with aluminum foil. Let rest for 5 minutes.

3. Reduce heat to medium and add shallot and tomato paste to now-empty skillet. Cook until tomato paste is rust-colored and fragrant, about 1 minute. Whisk in wine and cook until nearly evaporated, about 1 minute. Add broth and Worcestershire and simmer until reduced to ⅓ cup, about 3 minutes. Off heat, whisk in butter until incorporated. Slice beef against grain ¼ inch thick. Serve with broccoli rabe and sauce.

Turkey

The success of any turkey recipe hinges on two things: proper seasoning and getting the white and dark meat perfectly done at the same time. **by Scott Kathan**

At the Store

There are three main types of turkeys for sale in supermarkets; which kind you buy is a matter of personal preference.

SELF-BASTING/ PREBRINED	KOSHER	NATURAL/ UNTREATED
These birds have been injected with a salt solution, so they don't need to be brined or salted in advance.	Kosher birds are salted and processed in accordance to strict Jewish practices; they don't need to be salted or brined.	These birds are minimally processed, so we recommend brining or salting them.

Keys to the Best Bird

Season with Salt
Natural turkeys should be brined or salted in advance of cooking. Salt deeply seasons the meat and encourages it to hold on to more of its natural moisture during cooking. Kosher and self-basting birds come presalted and ready to cook.

Cook Meat to Correct Temperature
This can be a challenge because the dark meat is done at 175 degrees, while the white meat (which is prone to drying out when overcooked) is done at 160 degrees. Our recipes employ various techniques—elevating the bird on a rack, adjusting the oven temperature during cooking, using an oven bag, and even braising—to help the dark and white meat be ready at the same time.

Rest Before Carving
Once out of the oven, all roasted meats should be left undisturbed for a period of time (at least 30 minutes for a big turkey) before carving. Why? Roasting drives the meat's juices toward the center, and a rest allows those juices to redistribute throughout the meat for juicier, more tender results.

Forget the Old Ways

DON'T BASTE
For generations, cooks basted turkey frequently to keep the meat moist and promote crispy skin. It turns out that basting does neither, and in fact it leads to chewier skin and longer roasting times because of how frequently the oven door is opened. Skip the basting.

DON'T STUFF
Stuffing the turkey makes it harder to cook it evenly and introduces potential food safety issues. It's better to cook the stuffing outside of the bird in a baking dish; you can even buy extra wings to place on top so the stuffing will be flavored by the drippings.

THERMOMETER
Ditch the pop-up indicator and instead use a digital instant-read thermometer to gauge doneness (cook thighs/drumsticks to 175 degrees and breasts to 160 degrees). Our favorite is the fast, intuitive **Thermoworks Thermapen Mk4** (about $99).

ROASTING PAN WITH RACK
A good roasting pan should be sturdy, with a roomy rack and handles that are easy to grab. Our winner is the **Calphalon Contemporary Stainless Roasting Pan with Rack** (about $140).

DEFROSTING
It's safest to defrost a frozen turkey in the refrigerator; plan on one day for every 4 pounds of turkey (so for a 16-pound turkey, start defrosting four days out). If this isn't possible, use our "emergency" method: Fill a large bucket with cold water and submerge the turkey in the water for 30 minutes per pound, changing the water every 30 minutes to guard against bacteria.

FIND OUR RECIPES AT COOKSCOUNTRY.COM
Our website features 15 years' worth of great turkey recipes. The following three recipes will be free for four months:
- **Boneless Turkey Breast with Gravy**—for white-meat lovers
- **Turkey and Gravy for a Crowd**—uses an oven bag for efficient, even cooking
- **Easy Herb-Roasted Turkey with Gravy**—an herb butter seasons the meat and drippings

Braised Turkey Tacos

Roasting isn't the only way to prepare this versatile bird.

by Natalie Estrada

Mexican flavors and a refreshing hit of citrus take turkey in an unexpectedly delicious direction.

AMERICANS CONSUME ABOUT 222 million pounds of turkey each Thanksgiving. But the classic method of cooking a turkey—roasting—is just one way to prepare it. I wanted to create a recipe that would employ an alternate cooking method and highlight the versatility of this inexpensive ingredient by using it in a crowd favorite: tacos.

I started my research south of the border in Mexico's Yucatán Peninsula, where domesticated turkey has been eaten for centuries. It's added to soups, folded into tacos, and drenched in mole sauce, but one specific recipe, *pavo en escabeche* (turkey marinated in vinegar), caught my eye.

This dish calls for marinating turkey in vinegar and then braising it in a mixture of onions, warm spices, and broth. The flavors sounded promising. I decided I wanted to braise dark meat from the thighs (dark meat takes well to braising and creates soft, juicy shreds) with a similar mix of flavors.

Early research suggested that marinating in vinegar produced a too-pungent result, so I set the vinegar aside for now. (I'd circle back to it later, making quick-pickled onion as an accompaniment to the tacos.)

Instead I focused on the other ingredients. I started by marinating 4 pounds of turkey thighs with oregano, garlic, cumin, and cinnamon. But when I went to brown the marinated thighs to create a flavorful fond (a step common in many classic braises for developing meatier, more savory flavors), the garlic and oregano burned. I knew I wanted those ingredients in the mix, but the browning step was making it tough.

Could the solution be just seasoning the turkey with salt and pepper, quickly blooming the spices in a Dutch oven, and then adding the rest of the ingredients to braise without browning the turkey at all? I was skeptical at first, but a side-by-side test quelled my doubts.

My tasters preferred the sample that broke with tradition; the browning step just wasn't adding enough flavor. This unorthodox solution was a surprise to me, but I was elated to learn that I could skip the browning and streamline the recipe.

This dish had a great flavor, but something was missing: acidity. Nixing the vinegar earlier in the process had created this shortcoming. I decided to add orange and lime juices for brightness. These two citruses gave the braising liquid a hint of sweetness and piquancy without the abrasiveness of vinegar. What's more, I tried the recipe with chicken thighs (in case the supermarket's out of turkey thighs) and it worked just as well.

What is the benchmark of success in the test kitchen? When the entire team can't speak because our mouths are too full. These turkey tacos were a success.

BRAISED TURKEY TACOS
Serves 6 to 8

We developed this recipe using an enameled cast-iron Dutch oven. If you are using a stainless-steel Dutch oven, the liquid will take up to 15 minutes to reduce in step 4. Use the visual cues in the recipe as your guide. Serve with Pickled Onion (recipe follows), if desired.

- 4 (14- to 16-ounce) bone-in turkey thighs, trimmed
- 2 teaspoons table salt
- 1 teaspoon pepper
- 1 tablespoon extra-virgin olive oil
- 1 onion, chopped fine
- 5 garlic cloves, minced
- 2 teaspoons dried oregano
- 1½ teaspoons ground cumin
- ½ teaspoon red pepper flakes
- ¼ teaspoon ground cinnamon
- 3 tablespoons tomato paste
- 2 cups chicken broth
- ⅓ cup orange juice
- 3 tablespoons lime juice (2 limes), plus lime wedges for serving
- 12 (6-inch) corn tortillas, warmed
- Thinly sliced radishes
- Fresh cilantro leaves

1. Adjust oven rack to middle position and heat oven to 350 degrees. Sprinkle turkey with salt and pepper. Heat oil in Dutch oven over medium-high heat until shimmering. Add onion and garlic and cook until softened, 4 to 6 minutes. Add oregano, cumin, pepper flakes, and cinnamon and cook until fragrant, about 30 seconds.

2. Add tomato paste and cook until fragrant and darkened in color, about 1 minute. Stir in broth, orange juice, and lime juice, scraping up any browned bits. Nestle turkey into liquid and bring to simmer. Cover, transfer to oven, and cook until turkey is fork-tender, 1 hour 45 minutes to 2 hours.

3. Transfer turkey to plate and let cool, about 15 minutes (reserve liquid in pot). Shred meat into bite-size pieces using 2 forks; discard skin and bones. Return meat to pot.

4. Bring turkey mixture to simmer over medium-high heat, reduce heat to medium-low, and cook until liquid is slightly thickened and just coats turkey, 3 to 5 minutes for enameled cast-iron pot or up to 15 minutes for stainless-steel pot. Serve with tortillas, radishes, cilantro, and lime wedges.

PICKLED ONION
Serves 6 to 8 (Makes about 1½ cups)
For more spice, add 1 thinly sliced jalapeño chile to the onion before pouring over the vinegar mixture.

- 1 small onion, halved and sliced thin
- 1 cup white wine vinegar
- 5 teaspoons sugar
- 1 teaspoon dried oregano
- 1 teaspoon table salt

Place onion in medium bowl. Bring vinegar, sugar, oregano, and salt to simmer in small saucepan over medium-high heat. Simmer, stirring occasionally, until sugar is dissolved. Pour vinegar mixture over onion, cover loosely, and let cool completely, about 30 minutes.

Louisiana-Style Cornbread Dressing

Meet your new favorite Thanksgiving side dish. **by Matthew Fairman**

SOUTHERN CORNBREAD DRESSING has a crisp, buttery top and a moist, almost creamy interior. My wife's family in Louisiana makes one studded with smoky andouille sausage and bacon; it balances a Cajun-style spicy kick with sweet corn flavor. I set out to test my way to a no-fuss recipe for this flavorful side.

To start, I knew that store-bought cornbread was out. Too inconsistent. Instead, I made my own, combining equal parts cornmeal and flour, a touch of sugar, melted butter, eggs, and milk. While some Southerners might scoff at the inclusion of flour, it adds a needed sturdiness to cornbread dressing. Some dressing recipes call for letting the cornbread go stale for the best results, but side-by-side tests showed that staling wasn't necessary.

To build a rich Louisiana flavor profile, I diced up a big link of bold andouille sausage and four slices of bacon. I added the meat to a skillet, along with an ample amount of onion, celery, and green bell pepper. Once the vegetables had softened, I bloomed a tablespoon of Creole seasoning in the rendered pork fat.

As soon as my cornbread was ready, I turned it out onto a baking sheet and broke it up with two forks. I then tossed it with the sausage and vegetables, fresh parsley, 3 cups of savory chicken broth, 1 cup of milk, and three beaten eggs. This ratio of milk and eggs to broth was just right to ensure a cohesive, set dressing that didn't become soggy. I put everything back into the casserole dish I used to bake my cornbread and, just before baking, I brushed the top with melted butter and used a spatula to create ridges on the surface. This resulted in a buttery, craggy top that added toasty flavor and crunchy texture. Delicious.

The Missing Link

Our favorite andouille sausage is easily mail-ordered from Louisiana.

JACOB'S WORLD FAMOUS
Our winning andouille

LOUISIANA-STYLE CORNBREAD DRESSING
Serves 10 to 12
We developed this recipe using Quaker Yellow Cornmeal.

CORNBREAD
- 1½ cups (7½ ounces) all-purpose flour
- 1½ cups (7½ ounces) cornmeal
- 3 tablespoons sugar
- 1 tablespoon baking powder
- 1 teaspoon table salt
- 1¾ cups whole milk
- 3 large eggs
- 6 tablespoons unsalted butter, melted

DRESSING
- 2 tablespoons unsalted butter, plus 4 tablespoons unsalted butter, melted
- 12 ounces andouille sausage, cut into ¼-inch pieces
- 2 onions, chopped
- 2 green bell peppers, stemmed, seeded, and chopped
- 2 celery ribs, chopped
- 4 slices bacon, cut into ¼-inch pieces
- 1 tablespoon Tony Chachere's Original Creole Seasoning
- 2 garlic cloves, minced
- 3 cups chicken broth
- 1 cup whole milk
- 3 large eggs, lightly beaten
- ¾ cup chopped fresh parsley
- ½ teaspoon pepper

1. FOR THE CORNBREAD: Adjust oven rack to middle position and heat oven to 425 degrees. Spray 13 by 9-inch baking dish with vegetable oil spray.
2. Whisk flour, cornmeal, sugar, baking powder, and salt together in large bowl. Whisk milk, eggs, and melted butter together in second bowl. Whisk milk mixture into flour mixture until just combined. Transfer batter to prepared dish. Bake until cornbread is golden brown and toothpick inserted in center comes out clean, about 20 minutes.
3. FOR THE DRESSING: While cornbread bakes, melt 2 tablespoons butter in 12-inch nonstick skillet over medium-high heat. Add andouille, onions, bell peppers, celery, and bacon to skillet and cook until vegetables are softened, about 8 minutes. Add Creole seasoning and garlic and cook until fragrant, about 1 minute. Transfer sausage mixture to large bowl.
4. Turn out hot cornbread onto rimmed baking sheet and break into small pieces with two forks. (Cooled, crumbled cornbread can be transferred to zipper-lock bag and stored at room temperature for up to 24 hours.)
5. Transfer crumbled cornbread to bowl with sausage mixture. Add broth, milk, eggs, parsley, and pepper and stir to combine. Transfer dressing to now-empty dish and spread into even layer (do not pack down). Using side of rubber spatula or wooden spoon, create ridges about ½ inch apart on top of dressing.
6. Brush top of dressing with remaining 4 tablespoons melted butter. Bake until browned and crisped on top and heated through, about 35 minutes. Let cool for 10 minutes and serve.

TO MAKE AHEAD

At end of step 5, let dressing cool completely (if using hot cornbread). Cover baking dish with plastic wrap and refrigerate for up to 24 hours or wrap in additional layer of aluminum foil and freeze for up to 1 month. To serve, thaw overnight in refrigerator if frozen. Proceed with step 6, extending baking time by 15 minutes and covering with foil for final 10 minutes of cooking if top begins to get too dark.

SAUSAGE-HERB CORNBREAD DRESSING

Substitute 1 pound sweet Italian sausage, casings removed, for andouille and bacon, breaking up sausage in skillet with wooden spoon. Substitute poultry seasoning for Creole seasoning. Add 1 teaspoon table salt and 1 teaspoon cayenne pepper with poultry seasoning.

For a craggy top with extra crunch, we create ridges with a spatula before baking.

Macaroni and Cheese Casserole

This delicious casserole is so easy to make that you don't even have to boil the pasta.

by Morgan Bolling

I GREW UP head over heels in love with my mom's macaroni and cheese. Her version featured cooked elbow macaroni that was evenly coated with a creamy cheese sauce enriched with eggs and then baked until set. This sliceable casserole was sturdy enough that it wouldn't run into other things on your plate—a far cry from the runny boxed version. The only thing I don't love about my mom's mac and cheese is the work required to make it. Between boiling pasta, making a cheese sauce, assembling, and baking, it often takes hours to put together. I wanted to see if I could get the same sturdy, rich mac with less work.

There is a class of easy macaroni and cheese recipes that call for adding uncooked macaroni to a baking dish, pouring over a no-cook sauce, and baking, so I made a handful of these recipes to get my bearings. The problems were many: unevenly cooked pasta, greasy sauces, scrambled eggs in the casserole, and flat flavor. I knew I could do better.

Working with a baseline of 8 ounces of uncooked macaroni in an 8-inch square baking dish, I first had to figure out the sauce ingredients. After lots of testing with all kinds of dairy (including milk, cream, and cream cheese),

The Creamiest

No cheese melts better than American, which is why we use it here. Sharp cheddar adds a tangy kick.

I landed on a combination of 1 cup of heavy cream, 2 cups of water, two beaten eggs, and a little cornstarch; the water provided enough liquid to help the pasta cook evenly, and the cornstarch contributed thickening power. Sharp cheddar was a must for flavor, while shredded American cheese kept the sauce creamy and silky (American cheese has stabilizers that help hold sauces together). Tossing the shredded cheese with a little more cornstarch helped the sauce stay thick and further discouraged separation. To bump up the flavor, I added three powerhouse ingredients: Dijon mustard, Worcestershire sauce, and hot sauce.

My macaroni and cheese casserole tasted great, but it was prone to overcooking. I developed a fail-safe process: Bake the casserole covered for 30 minutes at 400 degrees, remove the foil and stir, add extra cheese on top, bake it for another 15 minutes, and then blast it under the broiler to melt and brown the cheese on top. A full 25-minute rest before serving gave the casserole a chance to set up.

It took a lot of work to get the recipe just right, but I finally had a macaroni and cheese casserole that was fast and easy enough for a weeknight.

This simple bake makes for an easy supper or crowd-pleasing Thanksgiving side dish.

EASY MACARONI AND CHEESE CASSEROLE *Serves 4 to 6*

Note that the macaroni has not been cooked when it's combined with the cheeses and cornstarch in step 1 of the recipe. For the best results, ask for a 4-ounce block of American cheese at the deli counter and shred it on the large holes of a box grater yourself. We developed this recipe using a ceramic baking dish. If you choose to use a metal baking pan, reduce the cooking time in step 2 to 25 minutes.

- **8** ounces sharp cheddar cheese, shredded (2 cups), divided
- **4** ounces American cheese, shredded (1 cup)
- **4** teaspoons cornstarch, divided
- **8** ounces (2 cups) elbow macaroni
- **1** cup heavy cream
- **2** cups water
- **2** large eggs
- **2** teaspoons Dijon mustard
- **2** teaspoons hot sauce
- **2** teaspoons Worcestershire sauce
- **½** teaspoon table salt
- **½** teaspoon pepper

1. Adjust oven rack 6 inches from broiler element and heat oven to 400 degrees. Toss 4 ounces cheddar, American cheese, and 2 teaspoons cornstarch together in bowl. Add macaroni, toss to combine, and transfer mixture to broiler-safe 8-inch square baking dish.

2. Whisk cream and remaining 2 teaspoons cornstarch together in now-empty bowl until cornstarch is dissolved. Whisk in water, eggs, mustard, hot sauce, Worcestershire, salt, and pepper until fully combined. Pour cream mixture over macaroni mixture in dish. Cover with aluminum foil and bake for 30 minutes.

3. Remove dish from oven and discard foil. Stir to redistribute macaroni. Sprinkle with remaining 4 ounces cheddar. Return dish to oven and continue to bake until edges are bubbling and just set and center registers 150 to 160 degrees, about 15 minutes.

4. Broil until top of casserole is spotty brown, about 2 minutes. Let rest on wire rack for 25 minutes. Serve.

Three Key Steps to Macaroni and Cheese Casserole

1. Start with uncooked pasta
Toss uncooked macaroni with cheese and cornstarch.

2. Add liquid
Pour cream mixture over macaroni in baking dish, cover, and bake for 30 minutes.

3. Bake to 150 to 160 degrees
Bake uncovered for 15 minutes. Take temperature to ensure tender, set casserole.

Sweet Potato Crunch

Women in my family have been making this Thanksgiving side for generations. Now it's my turn. **by Morgan Bolling**

I'M ALWAYS THANKFUL for my mom's sweet potatoes. She roasts the orange spuds in their jackets until they wrinkle and start to ooze a sort of natural sweet potato caramel, and then she removes the peels and whips the soft flesh in a stand mixer with a splash of orange liqueur for a citrusy kick. There's no marshmallow topping here; instead my mother crowns the whipped potatoes with a mixture of crushed oatmeal cookies and melted butter. It may sound a little odd—and it is—but the result is a full-flavored, salty-sweet dish that is always in high demand at our holiday table.

My mom, who got the recipe from her mom, has tweaked the recipe to fit her tastes over the years, and I think it's nearly perfect as is. But just because there's one great version doesn't mean there can't be another. In the spirit of my mom's creativity, I wanted to create a recipe inspired by her version but with my own personal twist.

I started with 4 pounds of sweet potatoes (enough for a Thanksgiving crowd) and a package of oatmeal cookies. For the sake of due diligence, I tried boiling and steaming the sweet potatoes, but roasting was by far the best method; it produced concentrated—not diluted—sweet potato flavor. I also loved how the roasting sweet potatoes made the whole test kitchen smell like Thanksgiving.

As for the whipping, did I really need to haul out the stand mixer? In a word, no: A good romp with a potato masher gave the potatoes a silky texture without the need for a mixer. My tasters loved the orange liqueur, especially when I added grated orange zest and a little brown sugar to enhance it. The cookie topping was great, but when I tested it with different brands of oatmeal cookies, the results were wildly different—and inconsistency just won't do in the test kitchen.

Baking my own cookies to crumble was an option but seemed like too much work here. Instead, I pivoted to another sweet, crunchy topping: a simple stir-together streusel made with flour, brown sugar, and melted butter. The streusel tasted great and provided a proper contrasting crunch on top of the creamy sweet potatoes. A pinch of cayenne added to this topping carried a hint of heat and a reminder that this sweet dish had savory roots, too.

Since my mom reads this magazine, it's important for me to come out and say I know that no sweet potatoes will ever be as good as the ones she makes for me. So, to differentiate our two recipes, I decided to give my version another name: Sweet Potato Crunch. I'm thankful for the many things I've learned from my mom—including how to make some truly amazing sweet potatoes.

Sweet Potatoes versus Yams

In the United States, sweet potatoes are often confused with yams. Although they are similar in shape, these two tubers are not closely related botanically. Yams, which are a staple food in parts of Asia, Africa, Central America, South America, and the West Indies, belong to the genus *Dioscorea* and typically have white flesh and sometimes a rough, shaggy exterior. Sweet potatoes, which are popular in the United States, belong to the genus *Ipomoea* and usually have smoother skins and orange flesh.

SWEET POTATO

YAM

SWEET POTATO CRUNCH
Serves 8

Buy potatoes of similar size and shape, no more than 1 pound each, so they cook at the same rate. Orange juice can be substituted for the Grand Marnier, if you prefer.

SWEET POTATOES
- 4   pounds sweet potatoes, unpeeled
- 4   tablespoons unsalted butter, melted
- 2   tablespoons Grand Marnier
- 1   tablespoon packed light brown sugar
- 1¼ teaspoons table salt
- 1   teaspoon grated orange zest

TOPPING
- ⅔   cup all-purpose flour
- ⅓   cup packed light brown sugar
- ¼   teaspoon table salt
- ⅛   teaspoon cayenne pepper
- 4   tablespoons unsalted butter, melted

1. FOR THE SWEET POTATOES: Adjust oven rack to upper-middle position and heat oven to 400 degrees. Line rimmed baking sheet with aluminum foil. Poke potatoes several times with paring knife and space evenly on prepared sheet. Bake until potatoes are very tender and can be easily squeezed with tongs, 1¼ to 1½ hours. Let potatoes sit until cool enough to handle, at least 20 minutes.

2. Remove and discard potato peels. Transfer potato flesh to large bowl and mash with potato masher until smooth. Stir in melted butter, Grand Marnier, sugar, salt, and orange zest. Transfer potato mixture to 8-inch square baking dish and spread into even layer with rubber spatula.

3. FOR THE TOPPING: Whisk flour, brown sugar, salt, and cayenne together in bowl until fully combined. Stir in melted butter until mixture forms clumps. Break into pea-size pieces and distribute evenly over sweet potato mixture.

4. Bake until topping is fragrant and darkened slightly in color and potatoes are hot, 25 to 30 minutes. Let cool for 25 minutes before serving.

TO MAKE AHEAD

At end of step 2, let sweet potato mixture cool completely. Cover dish with aluminum foil and refrigerate for up to 24 hours. When ready to serve, bake, covered, for 15 minutes. Remove from oven, uncover, and continue with step 3.

Chocolate Pecan Pie

We love pecan pie, but we were looking for something more. **by Cecelia Jenkins**

CHOCOLATE PECAN PIE is a welcome shake-up to your usual pecan pie—still traditional but with a fun twist. It's not a complicated idea: Put some chocolate and pecans into a pie crust (usually prebaked); pour in a filling of eggs, brown sugar, and corn syrup; and bake. The nuts float to the surface to create a crunchy top layer while the filling (a translucent custard) firms up into a silky, sliceable texture.

After making several recipes for this pie, the challenges were clear. Most fillings were much too sweet. Some contained only a sprinkling of nuts; others didn't fully lean into the chocolate and had a just few chips thrown into the filling. A few became disappointing puddles of syrup, while others were too fudgy, like a brownie pie with nuts. I wanted a creamy, balanced chocolate filling that held its shape plus a crisp and buttery crust and crunchy pecans for satisfying textural contrast.

Luckily for me, I had a great starting point: Our recipe for an easy all-butter pie crust is a cinch to work with and tastes amazing. A gentle parbaking ensured that the crust would stay crisp once filled.

For the filling, I knew I had to keep the sweetness level in check. To do so, I looked at the amounts of brown sugar and corn syrup in most pecan

pies—often at least 1 cup of each—and dropped them down to ¾ cup of each. I also turned to unsweetened chocolate to showcase complex, slightly bitter, rich chocolate notes and balance the filling's flavor. Just 2 ounces of unsweetened chocolate melted with butter (for additional richness) made a luxurious, cohesive chocolate filling when combined with the base of eggs and sugar. Chopping the pecans made it easier to cut nice slices, and toasting the nuts maximized their flavor and kept them from becoming spongy in the filling.

If you've ever made a cheesecake, regular pecan pie, or a custard pie, you know that these pies can be difficult to bake—just how jiggly is "jiggly in the center," anyway? After several days and dozens of pies, I found that the pie was perfectly done after just over an hour on the bottom rack of a 325-degree oven. At this point, the center is still a little jiggly, but there are more concrete cues to doneness: The top layer will crack a bit and the filling will register 185 to 190 degrees on an instant-read thermometer. No more guesswork on when to pull the pie for a perfectly smooth and silky filling.

Could this pie be any more irresistible? Yes. A quick bourbon-infused whipped cream dolloped on each slice took it over the top.

CHOCOLATE PECAN PIE

Serves 8

Chilling the pie dough for 2 hours is important; even if you plan to freeze the dough for later use, do not skip this step. Toast the pecans on a rimmed baking sheet in a 300-degree oven for 7 to 10 minutes, stirring occasionally. You can substitute other pie weights for the sugar, if desired. This pie needs to cool for at least 4 hours to set the filling.

CRUST

- 1½ cups (7½ ounces) all-purpose flour
- 1 tablespoon granulated sugar, plus sugar to use as pie weight
- ½ teaspoon table salt
- 12 tablespoons unsalted butter, cut into ½-inch pieces and chilled
- 6 tablespoons ice water

FILLING

- 6 tablespoons unsalted butter
- 2 ounces unsweetened chocolate, chopped fine
- ¾ cup light corn syrup
- ¾ cup packed (5¼ ounces) brown sugar
- 3 large eggs
- 1 tablespoon vanilla extract
- ½ teaspoon table salt
- 2 cups pecans, toasted and chopped coarse

WHIPPED CREAM

- 1 cup heavy cream, chilled
- 3 tablespoons packed brown sugar
- 1-2 tablespoons bourbon
- ½ teaspoon vanilla extract
- Pinch table salt

1. FOR THE CRUST: Process flour, sugar, and salt in food processor until combined, about 3 seconds. Scatter butter over top and pulse until irregular large chunks of butter form with some small pieces throughout, about 5 pulses. Add ice water and process until little balls of butter form and almost no dry flour remains, about 10 seconds, scraping down sides of bowl after 5 seconds.

2. Turn out dough onto clean counter and gather into ball. Sprinkle dough and counter generously with flour and shape dough into 6-inch disk, pressing any cracked edges back together. Roll dough into 13-inch circle, reflouring counter and dough as needed.

3. Loosely roll dough around rolling pin and gently unroll it onto 9-inch pie plate, leaving at least 1-inch overhang around edge. Ease dough into plate by gently lifting edge of dough with your hand while pressing into plate bottom with your other hand. Trim overhang to ½ inch beyond lip of plate.

4. Tuck overhang under itself; folded edge should be flush with edge of plate. Crimp dough evenly around edge of plate using your knuckles. Push protruding crimped edge so it slightly overhangs edge of plate. Pierce bottom and sides of dough all over with fork, about 40 times. Wrap dough-lined plate loosely in plastic wrap and refrigerate until dough is very firm, at least 2 hours or up to 2 days. (After being refrigerated for 2 hours, dough-lined plate can be wrapped tightly in plastic and frozen for up to 1 month. Let dough thaw at room temperature for 25 minutes before using.)

5. Adjust oven rack to lowest position and heat oven to 375 degrees. Line chilled pie shell with aluminum foil and, while pressing into plate bottom with 1 hand to keep foil flush with bottom of plate, work foil around crimped edge with your other hand. Fill foil to lip of plate with sugar. Transfer plate to wire rack set in rimmed baking sheet. Bake until edges are dry and pale, about 45 minutes. Remove foil and sugar, rotate sheet, and continue to bake until center of crust is light golden brown, 20 to 25 minutes longer. Remove sheet from oven, keeping pie shell on wire rack in sheet. Lower oven temperature to 325 degrees. (Pie shell needn't cool completely before proceeding.)

6. FOR THE FILLING: Melt butter and chocolate in bowl at 50 percent power, stirring halfway through microwaving, until melted, about 2 minutes. Add corn syrup, sugar, eggs, vanilla, and salt to chocolate mixture and whisk until combined. Stir in pecans.

7. Place pie shell on rimmed baking sheet. Pour filling into shell and distribute evenly with rubber spatula. Bake until pecan layer that forms on top begins to crack and filling in center of pie registers 185 to 190 degrees (filling will jiggle slightly when pie is shaken), 1 hour to 1 hour 5 minutes, rotating sheet halfway through baking. Let pie cool on wire rack until set, at least 4 hours.

8. FOR THE WHIPPED CREAM: Using stand mixer fitted with whisk attachment, whip cream, sugar, 1 tablespoon bourbon, vanilla, and salt on medium-low speed until foamy, about 1 minute. Increase speed to high and whip until soft peaks form, 1 to 3 minutes. Add remaining 1 tablespoon bourbon to taste. (Whipped cream can be refrigerated in airtight container for up to 24 hours.)

9. Serve pie with whipped cream.

TO MAKE AHEAD

At end of step 7, pie can be wrapped tightly in plastic wrap, then in aluminum foil, and frozen for up to 1 week. To serve, unwrap pie completely and let thaw at room temperature for 5 hours. Make whipped cream while pie thaws.

For a Perfectly Baked Pie Crust, Use the Best Pie Weights.

by Carolyn Grillo

EQUIPMENT REVIEW

MANY OF OUR pie recipes call for blind baking—baking the crust either partially or completely before adding the filling. But without a filling to hold the raw dough in place, the bottom can puff up or the sides can slump during baking, resulting in misshapen pie shells with less room for filling. To prevent this, the test kitchen uses pie weights to hold the crust in place as it bakes. While bakers can use dried beans, raw rice, and granulated sugar as pie weights, we wanted to find the best product designed specifically for the job. We tested four models of pie weights: a set of ceramic balls, a set of aluminum beans, a 6-foot-long stainless-steel chain, and a steel disk ringed with soft silicone flaps.

We had high hopes for the chain and the disk, which promised easier use and storage than traditional loose pie weights. It was a breeze to position them in the dough-lined pie plate and extract them once the dough was baked, but the dough puffed up between gaps in the chain no matter how we arranged it, and neither model sufficiently supported the sides of the dough, which allowed them to slump and shrink.

Although it was a little more time-consuming to layer aluminum foil over the chilled dough before pouring in the ceramic and aluminum weights and baking, these weights produced crusts that were evenly cooked with tall sides. However, neither model came with enough pieces in a single package to completely fill our pie shells, which is critical to preventing a slumped crust. Since we would need to buy multiple packages of pie weights, we zeroed in on the less expensive option, Mrs. Anderson's Baking Ceramic Pie Weights. At about $24 for four packages (a total of 4 cups of pie weights), it was a winner.

 Web subscribers can read the full testing and see the complete results chart at CooksCountry.com/nov19.

A Weighty Matter

Our Chocolate Pecan Pie recipe calls for using granulated sugar to keep the dough in place as it bakes. In a pinch, you can even use raw rice or dried beans. But if you bake a lot of pies, dedicated pie weights are handy to have around, since they are arguably easier to maneuver and store than sugar. Plus, unlike make-shift pie weights such as sugar, rice, and beans, they are infinitely reusable.

KEY   **Good** ★★★   **Fair** ★★   **Poor** ★

RECOMMENDED

Mrs. Anderson's Baking
Ceramic Pie Weights
Model: 108
Price: $5.99 ($23.96 for set of four, our recommended amount)
Material: Ceramic stoneware

Ease of Use ★★½
Performance ★★★
Comments: Four cups of these ceramic balls gave us crisp, flaky, and golden-brown crusts with sides that stood tall.

Matfer Bourgeat
Baking Beans
Model: 340001
Price: $56.02
Material: Aluminum

Ease of Use ★★½
Performance ★★
Comments: It takes two sets of these beans (so more than $100) to fill a pie shell—that's an expensive pie. But they work well.

NOT RECOMMENDED

Chicago Metallic
Pie Weight
Model: CMB164
Price: $13.38
Materials: Silicone and steel

Ease of Use ★★★
Performance ★
Comments: This perforated metal disk with silicone flaps performed inconsistently and didn't work with softer doughs.

Mrs. Anderson's Baking
Pie Weight Chain
Model: 43611
Price: $9.24
Material: Stainless steel

Ease of Use ★★★
Performance ★
Comments: Positioning this chain in unbaked dough was easy. But once baked, our crusts were slumped, uneven, and unusable.

Homemade Corn Tortillas

Fresh homemade tortillas burst with corn flavor and are worlds better than store-bought.

by Matthew Fairman

CORN TORTILLAS

Makes 18 tortillas

Using a clear pie plate to press the ball of dough into a 5½-inch circle in step 3 makes it easy to see the size of the circle as it expands. You can also use a tortilla press or a flat-bottomed skillet. You can find masa harina at your grocery store in the international aisle or near the flour. We recommend stacking the cooked tortillas in a damp dish towel and microwaving them, still wrapped, for 2 minutes before serving. You can also store them in a tortilla warmer (see "Tortilla Gear").

    3 cups (12 ounces) masa harina
    2 teaspoons table salt
2–2½ cups warm water
    2 tablespoons plus 1 teaspoon
       vegetable oil, divided

1. Whisk masa harina and salt together in medium bowl. Stir in 2 cups warm water and 2 tablespoons oil with rubber spatula until combined. Using your hands, knead dough in bowl until it is soft and tacky and has texture of Play-Doh. If necessary, add up to ½ cup more warm water, 1 tablespoon at a time, until proper texture is achieved. (You can test for proper hydration by gently flattening a golf ball–size piece of dough with your hands. If many large cracks form around edges, it is too dry.)

2. Divide dough into 18 equal portions, about a scant 3 tablespoons (1½ ounces) each. Roll each portion into smooth ball between your hands. Transfer dough balls to plate and keep covered with damp paper towel. Cut open seams along sides of 1-gallon zipper-lock bag, leaving bottom seam intact. Spray inside of bag lightly with vegetable oil spray; wipe excess oil spray from bag with paper towel.

3. Heat remaining 1 teaspoon oil in 12-inch nonstick skillet over medium heat until just smoking. Using tongs, wipe skillet with paper towels. Place 1 dough ball in center of prepared bag. Fold top layer of plastic over ball. Using clear pie plate, press dough flat into thin 5½-inch circle.

4. Peel top layer of plastic away from tortilla. Using plastic to lift tortilla from bottom, place exposed side of tortilla in palm of your hand and invert tortilla. Peel away plastic. Carefully flip tortilla into skillet and cook until bottom begins to brown at edges, about 1 minute.

5. Using thin spatula, flip tortilla and cook until second side is browned at edges, about 45 seconds. Flip tortilla again and press center and edges firmly with spatula so tortilla puffs, about 15 seconds.

6. Transfer cooked tortilla to tortilla warmer or wrap in damp dish towel. Repeat with remaining dough balls, lightly spraying bag with oil spray and wiping off excess as needed to keep tortillas from sticking. Serve. (If storing tortillas in damp dish towel, microwave for 2 minutes to rewarm before serving.)

Go to **CooksCountry.com/tacos** for a collection of taco recipes that call for corn tortillas.

Step by Step

1. Mix and knead dough
Stir masa harina, salt, warm water, and oil together with a rubber spatula, then knead the dough until it is the texture of Play-Doh.
Why? To create a workable dough, everything needs to be fully incorporated.

2. Test hydration
Pinch off a golf ball–size piece of dough, roll it into a ball, and gently press it flat. A properly hydrated dough will not crack significantly when flattened.
Why? Proper hydration yields tender, pliable tortillas.

3. Portion dough
Divide and roll dough into 18 equal balls, keeping dough covered with damp dish towel.
Why? Equal portions yield uniform tortillas that cook in the same amount of time. Keeping the dough covered prevents it from drying out.

4. Prep bag
Cut sides from 1-gallon zipper-lock bag, spray inside lightly with oil spray, and wipe off excess.
Why? The greased bag provides a tidy nonstick surface for pressing the dough flat.

5. Press dough
Use a clear pie plate (or a tortilla press) to press each round into a flat 5½-inch circle.
Why? The clear plate lets you see the tortillas as they're pressed, allowing you to make any necessary adjustments to ensure an even size and thickness.

...warming Tortillas

...esh corn tortillas are best eaten within ...ew hours of making them, but we un-...rstand that that's not always possible. ...u can wrap stacks of tortillas in plastic ...d refrigerate them for a few days; to re-...at, quickly dip each tortilla in a bowl of ...ter and reheat it over medium heat in a ...y nonstick skillet for about 30 seconds ...r side.

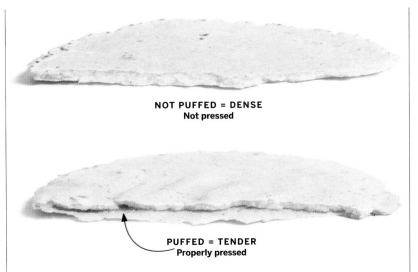

NOT PUFFED = DENSE
Not pressed

PUFFED = TENDER
Properly pressed

Press to Puff

Toward the end of cooking each tortilla, we press on it with a spatula; this pressing releases steam in the tortilla and causes it to puff in the middle, which makes for a fluffier, less dense finished tortilla with a layered interior.

How Much Water Is Enough Water?

Our recipe calls for a range of water: 2 to 2½ cups. So how do you know how much to use? First, add 2 cups of water to 3 cups of masa harina and hand-knead the dough until it's the texture of Play-Doh. Then, test the dough by flattening a golf ball–size piece; if a lot of cracks form along the edges, the dough needs more water.

TOO DRY

PERFECT DOUGH

Tortilla Gear

Tortilla Warmer

Eating your tortillas fresh from the skillet sounds great, but it's not always practical. In fact, we found that the tortillas were much more tender and pliable if they were allowed to steam together in a tortilla warmer while we finished cooking the rest of the batch. Stacking the tortillas wrapped in a damp dish towel and then microwaving the stack for 2 minutes proved to be a suitable substitute for the tortilla warmer, but our favorite warmer—the **Imusa 12" Cloth Tortilla Warmer** (about $14)—worked best, keeping the tortillas warm and pliable for more than an hour.

KEEP 'EM WARM
Our winning tortilla warmer

Tortilla Press

Our recipe is written so you don't need a special tortilla press—it calls for using a clear pie plate to press out the dough. But if you have a tortilla press, by all means use it. Our favorite affordable tortilla press is the **Norpro Cast Aluminum Tortilla Press** (about $12); our testers liked its compact, easy-to-store shape and light weight. Since it's not as heavy as other presses (many of which are cast iron), it does require a little trial and error to get the pressing motion just right, but our testers got the hang of it after a few tries.

IM-PRESSIVE
Our Best Buy tortilla press

... Remove tortilla
...eel top layer of plastic away from ...rtilla. Lift tortilla from under ...ttom layer of plastic and gently ...vert onto your palm.
...hy? Raw tortillas are very ...agile; this is the gentlest way to ...andle them.

7. Cook on first side
Carefully flip tortilla into preheated skillet and cook until edges begin to dry out and bottom begins to brown on edges, about 1 minute.
Why? For the best texture, the first side should be set and just beginning to brown, but not dry.

8. Cook on second side
Flip tortilla and cook until second side begins to brown at edges, about 45 seconds.
Why? If not fully cooked, the inside of the tortillas will be dense and wet. If overcooked, it can be dry and leathery. We're shooting for the sweet spot.

9. Press to puff
Flip again and press with spatula on center and edges of tortilla; this causes the tortilla to puff.
Why? Puffing gives the finished tortillas a tender, light texture. Tortillas that don't puff are dense in comparison.

10. Keep warm
Wrap cooked tortillas in damp dish towel or place in tortilla warmer until ready to use.
Why? These tortillas are much more tender and pliable if they are kept in a steamy environment after cooking.

Curried Roast Chicken and Vegetables

This inspired one-pan dinner couldn't be easier.

by Cecelia Jenkins

I LOVE INDIAN food, but I don't cook many Indian-inspired dishes at home. So to expand my repertoire, I looked to an icon of Indian cuisine, Madhur Jaffrey—and specifically to her recipe for Durban-style roast chicken. My goal was to take some seasoning cues from her recipe (she calls for coating a whole bird with a puree of garlic, ginger, lemon juice, and spices) but add a starch and vegetables for a flavorful one-pan dinner.

While Jaffrey's recipe calls for a whole chicken, I chose bone-in chicken pieces for ease (no carving!) and a quicker roasting time. Knowing that chicken parts take about 45 minutes to cook in the oven, I started looking for a vegetable and a starch that would cook at roughly the same rate. I chose potatoes and cauliflower, both cut into bite-size pieces, thinking I'd lay the vegetables in a 13 by 9-inch baking dish and then throw the seasoned chicken pieces on top and roast it all together. Since a lot of curries that use those two vegetables also add chickpeas to the mix, I decided to follow suit and tossed in a can of drained chickpeas.

For the spice puree, I followed Jaffrey's cues and tossed fresh garlic and ginger into the blender along with the juice from two lemons. Wanting a simpler approach to the spices, I opted for ½ teaspoon each of sweet curry powder and garam masala; together these blends provided a deeply complex hit of fragrant spice and seasoning. You would not believe how good the test kitchen smelled as this was cooking.

But there were a few problems. For one, the chicken pieces tasted great, but the vegetables (which I'd seasoned only with salt and pepper) were a little bland. No problem; I'd simply reserve half the potent spice puree to toss with the vegetables and keep half for the chicken pieces. Since the potatoes and cauliflower were a smidge too firm after 45 minutes, I popped the dish with the vegetables back into the oven for 10 minutes once I'd removed the perfectly cooked chicken. Problems solved, and dinner served.

ONE-PAN CURRIED ROAST CHICKEN WITH CAULIFLOWER, POTATOES, AND CHICKPEAS
Serves 4

We developed this recipe using Penzeys Sweet Curry Powder, a mail-order curry powder, which is neither too sweet nor too hot. We call for garam masala in this recipe, but you can omit it and increase the amount of curry powder to 1 teaspoon, if desired. This dish is great served with Raita Sauce (recipe follows).

- ¼ cup lemon juice (2 lemons)
- 2 tablespoons extra-virgin olive oil
- 1 (2-inch) piece ginger, peeled and chopped coarse
- 3 garlic cloves, peeled
- 1¾ teaspoons table salt
- 1 teaspoon pepper
- ½ teaspoon curry powder
- ½ teaspoon garam masala
- 1 small head cauliflower (1½ pounds), cored and cut into 1-inch florets
- 1 pound Yukon Gold potatoes, peeled and cut into ½-inch pieces
- 1 (15-ounce) can chickpeas, rinsed
- 3 pounds bone-in chicken pieces (2 split breasts cut in half crosswise, 2 drumsticks, and 2 thighs), trimmed
- 1 tablespoon chopped fresh cilantro

Two Indian spice blends, curry powder and garam masala, add flavor.

1. Adjust oven rack to middle position and heat oven to 425 degrees. Process lemon juice, oil, ginger, garlic, salt, pepper, curry powder, and garam masala in blender until smooth, about 30 seconds. Toss cauliflower, potatoes, chickpeas, and ¼ cup spice puree together in medium bowl. Transfer cauliflower mixture to 13 by 9-inch baking dish.

2. Pat chicken dry with paper towels and transfer to now-empty bowl. Add remaining spice puree to chicken and toss until chicken is evenly coated. Place chicken, skin side up, on top of vegetables in dish. Roast until breasts register 160 degrees and drumsticks/thighs register 175 degrees, 45 to 48 minutes.

3. Transfer chicken to serving platter and tent with aluminum foil. Stir vegetables in dish and return dish to oven. Continue to roast until fork inserted into potatoes and cauliflower meets no resistance, about 10 minutes longer.

4. Transfer vegetables to platter with chicken. Sprinkle with cilantro. Serve.

RAITA SAUCE
Serves 4 (Makes about 1 cup)
Do not use nonfat yogurt here.

- 1 cup plain whole-milk yogurt
- 2 tablespoons chopped fresh cilantro
- 2 teaspoons lemon juice
- 1 small garlic clove, minced
- ½ teaspoon table salt
- Pinch cayenne pepper

Whisk all ingredients together in bowl. Season with salt to taste. Serve.

Nailing the Timing for Tender Chicken and Vegetables

We cooked the chicken atop a mix of cauliflower, potatoes, and chickpeas.

We removed the chicken and roasted the vegetables for 10 more minutes.

Salted Butter

Transform heavy cream into bread-ready butter in four simple steps.

by Matthew Fairman

IN THE PAST, home cooks didn't have the luxury of buying their butter in sticks at the supermarket; for many, making butter was a tedious and labor-intensive household chore. Today, transforming cream into butter can be as easy as it is satisfying: The food processor removes the drudgery of churning and leaves only the fun parts of the process behind. In total, it takes about 10 minutes, and your butter will be as delicious and creamy as any you've ever had. What's more, in that span of time you'll learn loads about the dairy products that we tend to take for granted.

When you blitz the heavy cream in the food processor, you'll witness a multistep metamorphosis: First the cream puffs up into stiff whipped cream, and then it tightens further into a texture approaching whipped cream cheese. Just when you think all is lost, the cream starts to look grainy at the center. Suddenly, the whole thing deflates and breaks into a thousand tiny lumps of butter splashing in a white sea of buttermilk.

To separate out the buttermilk, you pour everything into a fine-mesh strainer (catching the buttermilk in a bowl below) and then press the little bits of butter together into one solid hunk. Kneading this mass of butter in your hands over that bowl will extract the rest of the buttermilk. (Have a bowl of ice water ready to firm up the butter if it starts to melt in your warm hands.) Near the end of kneading, you'll work in some salt for flavor.

The buttermilk that you collect while making this butter is nothing like the cultured stuff you buy at the market. It's sweet—not sour—and it tastes like a richer version of low-fat milk. I finally understand the stories my dad used to tell me about drinking buttermilk as a kid on his family's farm. Now, I pour this buttermilk on my breakfast cereal.

All that's left to do is spread your homemade salted butter—with its fresh, milky flavor—in gobs all over warm biscuits, wedges of cornbread, and stacks of hot pancakes.

1. Process the cream in a food processor until it looks grainy and small lumps start to form.

2. Transfer the butter solids and buttermilk to a fine-mesh strainer set over a bowl and let the buttermilk drain.

3. Knead the butter with your hands to extract any excess liquid, dipping the butter periodically in a bowl of ice water to chill.

4. Sprinkle the butter evenly with salt, then knead in the salt until it is thoroughly incorporated.

SALTED BUTTER

Serves 26 (Makes 1⅔ cups)

In step 1, the cream will increase in volume, thicken into a stiff whipped cream, and then turn grainy and decrease in volume before it separates into butter solids and buttermilk. This recipe will work with both pasteurized and ultra-pasteurized heavy cream. Pasteurized cream will turn to butter more quickly than ultra-pasteurized cream. The buttermilk from this recipe is much more like low-fat milk than cultured buttermilk, which has a tangy, almost sour flavor. You can use this milk as you would any low-fat milk.

   4   cups heavy cream, chilled
   ½   teaspoon table salt

1. Process cream in food processor until mixture transforms from grainy whipped cream to lumps of butter solids surrounded by cloudy buttermilk, 2 to 6 minutes.

2. Fill large bowl halfway with ice and water. Transfer contents of processor to fine-mesh strainer set over medium bowl. Using rubber spatula, press and turn butter solids gently in strainer to extract as much liquid as possible, about 2 minutes.

3. Using your hands, press butter solids together into ball. Knead ball over strainer to squeeze out excess liquid, about 30 seconds. Transfer buttermilk collected in bowl to airtight container and reserve in refrigerator for another use. Wipe bowl clean with paper towels; set aside. Return butter to fine-mesh strainer and place strainer in ice bath (strainer will shield butter from ice) until butter has cooled and firmed up slightly, about 1 minute. Repeat process of kneading and dipping butter in ice bath until very little liquid can be squeezed out of butter, 2 to 3 times (knead butter over ice bath).

4. Transfer butter to now-empty medium bowl. Sprinkle salt evenly over butter, then knead butter until salt is thoroughly incorporated, about 30 seconds.

5. Transfer butter to butter dish or airtight container and refrigerate until ready to use. (Butter can be refrigerated for up to 2 weeks.)

Chicken and Corn Chowder

Layering the ingredients is key for this creamy slow-cooker chowder.

by Natalie Estrada

The corn adds subtle sweetness to this creamy, savory chowder.

I LOVE CHOWDERS of all kinds, whether they're brimming with briny clams or studded with sweet corn kernels. But what *is* a chowder, anyway? As it turns out, a chowder is simply a thick soup enriched with dairy that usually contains potatoes and onions. Chowders typically include a pork product for flavor and are often thickened with a roux. I thought I was familiar with every kind of chowder until I heard a colleague reminisce about a corn and chicken version she grew up eating. It sounded great—and perfect for making in a slow cooker.

My colleague's mom made her version of the chowder with chicken pieces, but after a few tests, I decided to go with boneless, skinless thighs instead. The dark-meat thighs had lots of flavor and could handle a long cooking time without drying out. As for the corn, fresh is great if you have it, but I decided to develop this recipe using frozen corn (which we prefer to canned) so you can make it year-round. For aromatics, I tested leek, onion, and shallot; the shallot won out for its gentle sweetness. Minced celery and garlic bolstered the flavor base of the soup.

While testing potatoes, I found that russets broke down too easily over the long cooking time, and red potatoes left their sloughed-off skins floating in the soup. Yukon Gold potatoes were perfect; they were creamy and soft but didn't disintegrate. For the pork, we preferred savory salt pork to bacon, since the bacon's smokiness overpowered the sweetness of the corn.

Now, how to thicken the chowder? I tried making a roux of butter and flour on the stovetop, adding broth, and dumping it all into the slow cooker, but the resulting chowder turned out grainy and lumpy. Cornstarch made for a chowder that felt a little slippery. It was better, I found, to pull out some of the chowder at the end of cooking, puree it in a blender, and return it to the soup. The puree, along with a good pour of heavy cream, thickened the soup and gave it a velvety consistency. This method left plenty of hunks of potatoes and corn kernels intact, ensuring a nice range of textures in the finished chowder.

For most slow-cooker recipes, it doesn't matter how the ingredients are added to the cooker. But it was important to the success of my chowder to place the potatoes and aromatics on the bottom of the slow cooker, nestle the chicken on top of them, scatter on the corn, and then pour the broth over everything. In this arrangement, the chicken weighed down the potatoes, keeping them submerged and ensuring that they cooked evenly. Perfect.

SLOW-COOKER CHICKEN AND CORN CHOWDER

Serves 6 to 8

It's important to layer the ingredients in the order listed to ensure that the potatoes fully cook and the chicken doesn't dry out. If you can't find salt pork, you can use 2 slices of bacon. You can substitute fresh corn kernels for the frozen corn, if desired.

- 1½ pounds boneless, skinless chicken thighs, trimmed
- ½ teaspoon table salt
- 1½ pounds Yukon Gold potatoes, peeled and cut into ½-inch pieces
- 4 ounces salt pork, cut into 4 pieces
- ¼ cup minced celery
- 1 shallot, minced
- 3 garlic cloves, minced
- 1 teaspoon sugar
- ½ teaspoon pepper
- 1 bay leaf
- 3 cups frozen corn
- 3 cups chicken broth
- ¾ cup heavy cream
- 3 tablespoons chopped fresh chives

1. Pat chicken dry with paper towels and sprinkle with salt. Toss potatoes, salt pork, celery, shallot, garlic, sugar, pepper, and bay leaf together in slow cooker; spread into even layer. Layer chicken over top of potato mixture to cover. Scatter corn over chicken. Add chicken broth; do not stir contents of slow cooker. Cover and cook until chicken is tender, 4 to 5 hours on high or 7 to 8 hours on low.

2. Discard bay leaf and salt pork. Transfer chicken to cutting board and shred into bite-size pieces with 2 forks; set aside.

3. Transfer 2 cups chowder to blender and process until smooth, 1 to 2 minutes. Return blended chowder to slow cooker.

4. Stir cream and chicken into chowder. Season with salt and pepper to taste. Serve, sprinkled with chives.

Order of Operations

For even cooking, it's essential to layer the ingredients as shown below.

Corn on the top; broth poured over

Chicken thighs in the middle

Potato–salt pork mixture on the bottom

Beef Chili

Making small-batch chili shouldn't require any sacrifices—except maybe the long cooking time. **by Jessica Rudolph**

WHEN MOST PEOPLE think of chili, they think of a large pot of rich, saucy meat and (sometimes) beans simmering for hours on the back of the stove. It's quintessential weekend food: easy to prepare, feeds an army, and makes great leftovers. While a big batch of chili is the norm, sometimes I want a faster, more contained option that is doable on a weeknight—a small pot of chili for two. But here's the catch: I wanted my chili with chunks of beef, not ground meat. Could I still make it weeknight friendly?

While we love the beefy flavor and silky texture of well-marbled chuck-eye roast, I didn't want to buy a giant hunk of meat for just two servings of chili. I chose beef blade steaks instead, which are also cut from the chuck—and thus have a similar big, beefy flavor—but are readily available in smaller portions.

I stuck with a simple, pantry-friendly flavor profile of chili powder, cumin, oregano, canned chipotle in adobo sauce, and garlic, which together delivered earthy, smoky spice but didn't overpower the beef. As for the beans, we favored pintos for their creamy texture and small size. Onion and canned diced tomatoes rounded out the flavors, providing aromatic sweetness and acidity. A tablespoon of brown sugar added complexity and depth.

I built a batch of my working chili in a medium saucepan and simmered until the beef was tender, about 1½ hours (an improvement over the 2 to 3 hours required for larger batches), but with less simmering the canned tomatoes stayed too firm. I tried tomato sauce instead, which conveniently came in a smaller 8-ounce can.

The chili was delicious, but I wondered if I could further streamline the process. A coworker suggested throwing the whole shebang in the oven instead of simmering it on the stovetop; I gave it a go and it worked great, eliminating the need for frequent stirring and monitoring. What's more, I could comfortably cook the chili at a higher temperature (and therefore faster) without the threat of scorched chili on the bottom of the pan. My cooking time was now down to an hour and change, with most of that being hands-off. The result? A Tuesday-night chili for two with an all-day-Sunday taste.

This rich and meaty chili comes together easily.

Two-Part Cooking Method

Start on the Stovetop
For clear visibility and high heat when browning the beef

Finish in the Oven
To eliminate the risk of the bottom scorching

A Cut Above

We tried every beef cut in the book for this chili before landing on blade steak. This cut, which comes from the chuck, has a big, beefy flavor and, unlike some fattier cuts that require several hours of cooking, gets nice and tender with just about an hour of simmering (most of which is done hands-off in the oven).

BEEF CHILI FOR TWO

You will need a medium ovensafe saucepan for this recipe. Before using the blade steaks, trim and discard their interior line of gristle. You can substitute sirloin steak tips (also known as flap meat) for the blade steaks, if desired. Serve with your favorite chili garnishes.

- 1 **pound beef blade steaks, trimmed and cut into 1-inch pieces**
- ¼ **teaspoon table salt**
- ¼ **teaspoon pepper**
- 1 **tablespoon vegetable oil**
- 1 **small onion, chopped**
- 1 **tablespoon chili powder**
- 2 **teaspoons ground cumin**
- 2 **teaspoons minced canned chipotle chile in adobo sauce**
- 1 **garlic clove, minced**
- ½ **teaspoon dried oregano**
- 1 **(8-ounce) can tomato sauce**
- 1 **cup water**
- 1 **(15-ounce) can pinto beans, rinsed**
- 1 **tablespoon packed brown sugar**

1. Adjust oven rack to middle position and heat oven to 325 degrees. Pat beef dry with paper towels and sprinkle with salt and pepper. Heat oil in ovensafe medium saucepan over medium-high heat until just smoking. Brown beef on all sides, about 8 minutes.

2. Reduce heat to medium, stir in onion, and cook until softened, about 5 minutes. Stir in chili powder, cumin, chipotle, garlic, and oregano and cook until fragrant, about 30 seconds. Stir in tomato sauce and water, scraping up any browned bits. Stir in beans and sugar and bring to boil over high heat. Cover, transfer to oven, and cook until beef is tender, about 1 hour.

3. Let chili sit, uncovered, for 10 minutes. Season with salt and pepper to taste. Serve.

Broiler-Safe Baking Dishes

We set out to find a 13 by 9-inch dish that was easy to use and could handle the broiler's heat.

by Emily Phares

7 Dishes 5 Tests

- Bake yellow cake and cut into 24 squares with paring knife
- Make Classic Macaroni and Cheese and portion and remove from baking dish with metal spatula
- Make One-Pan Salmon with Broccoli and Shiitake Mushrooms and portion and remove from baking dish with metal spatula
- Wash each dish 5 times according to manufacturer's instructions
- Move dishes in and out of oven, using both dish towels and oven mitts

Our favorite dishes were roomy enough to accommodate all our recipes.

Broiling is a direct-heat cooking method that can subject baking dishes to temperatures exceeding 550 degrees, which is too hot for our favorite glass baking dish as well as our winning 13 by 9-inch nonstick metal baking pan. Rather than give up broiling foods, we needed to find an alternative dish that could withstand the heat.

We purchased seven widely available broiler-safe baking dishes that measured roughly 13 inches by 9 inches. All were made of materials that are capable of withstanding the extreme heat of the broiler. We made yellow cake, Classic Macaroni and Cheese, and One-Pan Salmon with Broccoli and Shiitake Mushrooms in each dish.

All the dishes performed well and were fairly easy to clean. But two key factors separated the winner from the rest: handle design and capacity.

The dishes offered two types of handles: loops or tabs. The models with tab handles were problematic. We didn't struggle much when putting the dishes into the oven, but these handles were challenging when rotating the dishes midbake and when removing them from the oven. We couldn't easily or securely grab the tabs, especially while wearing thick oven mitts or while trying to grip them with slippery dish towels. One model's tabs stuck out just 0.75 inches, which didn't give us much room to grip. On two other models, the tabs slanted upward at about a 45-degree angle, giving us much less leverage when lifting.

The dishes with looped handles were much easier to maneuver and carry because they offered a more secure grip, even when our hands were protected by oven mitts or a dish towel. It was also easier to rotate these dishes in the oven. Our favorite baking dish had looped handles that offered plenty of room for us to wrap our fingers around them, which is crucial given how heavy these dishes can be when filled with food.

Next we took a look at capacity by filling the baking dishes with water and measuring the volume of that water. The capacities ranged from 12 cups to a hefty 19.38 cups. Although the lengths and widths of the baking dishes didn't vary much, the depths of the dishes ranged from 2.38 inches to 3.88 inches—a substantial difference that helped explain the varying capacities.

We occasionally found it harder to arrange food in the dishes with smaller capacities (12 to 13 cups). Food also sat higher in these dishes, so when we sprinkled bread crumbs on top of mac and cheese, some of the bread crumbs fell onto the counter instead of being neatly contained in the dish. The dish with the largest capacity posed its own challenges, producing thinner cakes and macaroni and cheese that looked "a little sad" because it sat lower in this dish than it did in others.

Our favorite dishes were roomy but not too big: Our winner, from Mrs. Anderson's Baking, has a 14.25-cup capacity, which was large enough to accommodate all our recipes with no crowding yet small enough that every recipe looked aesthetically pleasing.

 Web subscribers can read the full tasting and see the complete chart at **CooksCountry.com/bkdish**.

KEY **Good** ★★★ **Fair** ★★ **Poor** ★

HIGHLY RECOMMENDED   CRITERIA

Mrs. Anderson's Baking Lasagna Pan with Handle (Rose)
Model: 98048RS
Price: $36.96
Weight: 5 lb, 2.6 oz
Capacity: 14.25 cups
Dishwasher-Safe: Yes

Handles ★★★
Capacity ★★★
Performance ★★★
Comments: This dish's looped handles were ea[sy] to grab, and its 14.25-c[up] capacity easily accommodated all foods.

RECOMMENDED

Staub 13x9 Rectangular Baking Dish, Dark Blue
Model: 40508-594
Price: $69.95
Weight: 5 lb, 11.4 oz
Capacity: 16.25 cups
Dishwasher-Safe: Yes

Handles ★★★
Capacity ★★½
Performance ★★★
Comments: This relatively large dish felt easy to maneuver, and we liked its looped handles.

Belle Cuisine Rectangular Baking Dish 13.5 x 9.75
Model: 5571
Price: $100.00
Weight: 5 lb, 7.5 oz
Capacity: 16.25 cups
Dishwasher-Safe: Yes

Handles ★★★
Capacity ★★½
Performance ★★★
Comments: Foods looked slightly wider and flatter in this model, but it wasn't egr[e]gious, and we appreciated the looped handles.

HIC Lasagna Pan with Handles
Model: 98048
Price: $54.99
Weight: 4 lb, 6.6 oz
Capacity: 12.75 cups
Dishwasher-Safe: Yes

Handles ★★★
Capacity ★★
Performance ★★★
Comments: This dish had helpful handles, but it sometimes felt a wee bit small compared to the other dishes.

RECOMMENDED WITH RESERVATIONS

Le Creuset Heritage Covered Rectangular Casserole
Model: PG07053A-33
Price: $109.95
Weight: 5 lb, 0.7 oz
Capacity: 13 cups
Dishwasher-Safe: Yes

Handles ★★
Capacity ★★
Performance ★★★
Comments: This model performed fairly well, but we downgraded it for its hard-to-grip handles and small capacity.

Pillivuyt Large Deep Rectangular Eared Roaster
Model: 220238BL
Price: $108.50
Weight: 3 lb, 10.5 oz
Capacity: 12 cups
Dishwasher-Safe: Yes

Handles ★½
Capacity ★★
Performance ★★★
Comments: This dainty dish was the smallest in the lineup. The tab-style handle[s] weren't easy to grip.

NOT RECOMMENDED

Emile Henry Modern Classics Large Rectangular Baker, Rouge
Model: 369626
Price: $49.99
Weight: 5 lb, 8.4 oz
Capacity: 19.38 cups
Dishwasher-Safe: Yes

Handles ★
Capacity ★½
Performance ★★★
Comments: This model's capacity was too big, and poorly designed handles made this dish hard to maneuver.

Lard

This creamy, white pork fat used to be America's mainstream choice for baking and frying.
Is it time to bring lard back? **by Lisa McManus**

nce America's everyday choice for fry-
g and baking, lard went out of fashion
the 20th century. Crisco arrived in
11, and it found success with the help
health reports—now mostly discred-
d—about the evils of animal fat. But a
thful few kept lard as a secret weapon
r making extra-flaky pie crusts and
scuits, fried chicken, and dishes such
tamales and carnitas.

To survey the lard landscape, we
ught seven products, three from
permarkets and four online, to try in
nd tastings. First, we swapped lard for
tter in biscuits and pie crust. Then we
epared pork carnitas, for which the
eat simmers in lard until it is melt-
gly tender. We scored each food for
vor, texture, and overall appeal.

We first noticed flavor differences.
me lards made biscuits and pie crusts
at tasted "very neutral, almost but-
ry." Other lards with a pronounced
rky flavor excelled in the carnitas,
hancing the rich flavor of the meat.
ill, we wanted an all-purpose lard to
e in both sweet and savory recipes.

Because lard has a higher melt-
g point than butter, it remains solid
nger in the oven's heat. This promotes
kiness in baked goods because it gives
ore time for air pockets to form in the
ugh. Lard also helps with tenderness
cause it lacks the water necessary to
courage gluten development: Butter
n contain up to 20 percent water,
hile lard is 100 percent fat. But tasters
so noticed textural differences in the
ked goods—some baked up sandy,
hile others were flaky.

To probe these differences, we asked
dependent labs to measure the lards'
elting points and fatty acids. While
tter melts between 90 and 95 degrees,
r lards had melting points rang-
g from 98 to 116 degrees. Our two
wer-ranking lards had the lowest melt-
g points, which might explain why they
eated less-flaky baked goods. They also
d the highest iodine values (a measure
double-bond fatty acids), a sign of
fter fat and lower melting points.

Depending on the speed and tem-
erature of its processing, lard forms
fferent types of fat crystals as it cools.
ow cooling creates bigger, more stable
ystals with a higher melting point,
they yield flakier pastry. Rapidly
oled lards form smaller, more delicate
ystals with a lower melting point,
sulting in crumbly pastries.

Three Things to Know

· **Most supermarket lards are fully
or partially hydrogenated.** This
process of saturating the fat with
hydrogen atoms makes its texture
firmer and helps it resist spoilage.
The process can create trans fats,
so some people seek lard that isn't
hydrogenated for health reasons.

· **Shopping for lard can be tricky.**
Because hydrogenation makes lard
shelf-stable without refrigeration,
some supermarkets stock it on
the shelf with oils and shortenings,
while others put it in the refrigerated section with butter or even in
the meat section sometimes.

· **Store lard in the refrigerator
anyway.** If you're going to bake
with lard, chilling keeps it firm so
your baked goods come out light
and flaky.

We also looked at product labels.
While our top-rated lard, a small-batch
artisan product, is processed without
hydrogenation, our favorite supermarket product is partially hydrogenated,
which helps lard maintain a firm texture
and resist oxidation. Hydrogenation
makes lard "creamier," confirmed Jason
Apple, professor of animal science at the
University of Arkansas. "Hydrogenation
changes the mouthfeel; it's more of a
firmer fat. It doesn't melt as quick." So
even though our supermarket favorite
wasn't a simply processed artisan lard, it
behaved like one. Because of the health
risks associated with hydrogenated fats,
we were pleased that our top two lards
were not made using this process.

Our top lard was made by U.S.
Dreams, an Ohio company that renders
the fat from local non-GMO grain- and
grass-fed pigs at a "low-and-slow" temperature; the resulting lard makes flaky
baked goods without additional ingredients or hydrogenation. Creamy, white,
firm, and nearly odorless, this lard
performed well across the board, giving
us "clean"-tasting, flaky pastry; light and
fluffy biscuits; and savory carnitas. Our
top supermarket favorite, John Morrell
Snow Cap Lard, performed almost as
well in every application.

Web subscribers can read the full
testing and see the complete results
chart at **CooksCountry.com/lard.**

RECOMMENDED · TASTERS' COMMENTS

Our Favorite

U.S. Dreams Lard
Price: $11.99 for 1 lb ($0.75 per oz)
Source: Online
Ingredients: 100% pork lard
Melting Point: 110°F
Hydrogenated: No
Iodine Value: 55.5
(Iodine value = g iodine per 100 g fat)

Biscuits and pie crust made
using this preservative-free,
nonhydrogenated lard came out
"beautifully crisp and tender,"
with "clean rich flavor" that was
"devoid of any fatty funk." It made
"lovely" carnitas, too.

Tenderflake Lard
Price: $10.98 for 1 lb ($0.69 per oz)
Source: Online
Ingredients: Lard, BHA, BHT, citric acid
Melting Point: 102.1°F
Hydrogenated: No
Iodine Value: 60.7

This Canadian lard nearly tied
for first place. Biscuits came out
"notably rich, crisp, and tender."
Carnitas were "very tender,"
"rich and decadent." And tasters
deemed pie crust made with this
lard "delicious," with a "great
flaky structure."

Supermarket Favorite

John Morrell Snow Cap Lard
Price: $1.69 for 1 lb ($0.11 per oz)
Source: Supermarket
Ingredients: Partially hydrogenated
lard, BHT and BHA added to help
protect flavor
Melting Point: 105°F
Hydrogenated: Partially
Iodine Value: 62.5

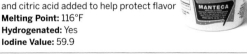

With a "soft," "flaky," "moist"
texture, biscuits made with this
widely available lard were a hit
with tasters. Partial hydrogenation helped ensure the firmness
of this fat, so pie crust came out
"flaky," and "very, very tender." Its
flavor was "neutral" and "mellow."

Armour Lard
Price: $3.99 for 1 lb ($0.25 per oz)
Source: Supermarket
Ingredients: Lard, BHA, propyl gallate
and citric acid added to protect flavor
Melting Point: 115°F
Hydrogenated: Yes
Iodine Value: 58.5

Tasters enjoyed biscuits from
this supermarket lard, calling
them "salty, clean, savory," with
a "crisp" exterior. Pie crust had
"neutral" flavor, with "not much
character" but "good flakiness";
"definitely acceptable." Carnitas
struck us as "rich, creamy,
smooth, and meaty."

Goya Lard
Price: $2.28 for 1 lb ($0.14 per oz)
Source: Supermarket
Ingredients: Refined lard and
hydrogenated lard, BHA, propyl gallate,
and citric acid added to help protect flavor
Melting Point: 116°F
Hydrogenated: Yes
Iodine Value: 59.9

This supermarket lard gave
biscuits a "savory," "lightly porky
taste." Pie crust was also "a bit on
the pork-flavored side," though it
was flaky. It stood out in carnitas:
"Incredible almost-fried crispy
exterior and meltingly tender,
juicy, moist interior."

Fatworks Pasture Raised Pork Lard
Price: $22.49 for 14 oz ($1.61 per oz)
Source: Online
Ingredients: Pasture raised pork fat,
organic rosemary extract
Melting Point: 98.3°F
Hydrogenated: No
Iodine Value: 71

Tasters called this pricey artisan
lard "quite porky," "savory and
lardy" in biscuits and pie crust,
where it had a texture "like shortbread," with "more crumb than
flake." It had the lowest melting
point of the lineup. In carnitas, it
had a "gamy, porky richness."

RECOMMENDED WITH RESERVATIONS

Armour Premium All Natural Lard
Price: $10.95 for 1 lb ($0.68 per oz)
Source: Online
Ingredients: Lard
Melting Point: 101.9°F
Hydrogenated: No
Iodine Value: 66.9

This preservative-free, nonhydrogenated lard gave us carnitas
that were "meaty" and full of
"piggy goodness." It wasn't a
hit in biscuits: "Oof, way too
piggy," "heavy and porky in an
unpleasant way." "Not for sweet
applications."

Pumpkin-Chocolate Chip Snack Cake

When my sisters and I were little, my mom would make this snack cake; we got excited about the chocolate chips! When we got older, she would send us off to college every fall with a few pieces in a wax paper bag.

—CECELIA JENKINS,
Senior Editor

PUMPKIN-CHOCOLATE CHIP SNACK CAKE *Serves 16*
We prefer mini chocolate chips here, but you can substitute standard-size semisweet chocolate chips, if desired.

- 1 cup (5 ounces) all-purpose flour
- 1 tablespoon pumpkin pie spice
- 1 teaspoon baking powder
- ½ teaspoon baking soda
- ¼ teaspoon table salt
- 1 cup canned unsweetened pumpkin puree
- 1 cup (7 ounces) sugar
- ½ cup vegetable oil
- 2 large eggs
- ½ cup (3 ounces) mini semisweet chocolate chips

1. Adjust oven rack to middle position and heat oven to 350 degrees. Grease and flour 8-inch square baking pan. Whisk flour, pumpkin pie spice, baking powder, baking soda, and salt together in large bowl. Whisk pumpkin, sugar, oil, and eggs together in second bowl.
2. Stir pumpkin mixture into flour mixture until just combined. Stir in chocolate chips until just incorporated. Transfer batter to prepared pan and smooth top with rubber spatula. Bake until paring knife inserted in center comes out clean, about 35 minutes.
3. Let cake cool in pan on wire rack for 20 minutes. Remove cake from pan and let cool completely on rack, about 1 hour. Serve. (Cooled cake can be wrapped in plastic wrap and stored at room temperature for up to 2 days.)

We're looking for recipes that you treasure—the ones that have been handed down in your family for a generation or more, that always come out for the holidays, and that have earned a place at your table and in your heart through many years of meals. Send us the recipes that spell home to you. Visit CooksCountry.com/recipe_submission (or write to Heirloom Recipes, Cook's Country, 21 Drydock Avenue, Suite 210E, Boston, MA 02210) and tell us a little about the recipe. Include your name and address. If we print your recipe, you'll receive a free one-year subscription to Cook's Country.

COMING NEXT ISSUE

Winter is coming, but don't worry: We'll keep you warm with **Slow-Cooker Smothered Pork Chops**, **One-Pan Pasta with Sausage and Mushrooms**, superflavorful **Greek-Style Meatballs**, an everyday **Spiced Roasted Chicken**, and plenty of festive cookies for the holidays. Plus, we make visits to Coney Island and Santa Fe to learn about local favorites from the folks who make them. Come along for the ride!

RECIPE INDEX

FIND THE ROOSTER!

A tiny version of this rooster has been hidden in a photo in the pages of this issu Write to us with its location and we'll ente you in a random drawing. The first correc entry drawn will win our favorite broiler-sa baking dish, and each of the next five will ceive a free one-year subscription to Coo Country. To enter, visit CooksCountry.com rooster by October 31, 2019, or write to Rooster ON19, Cook's Country, 21 Drydo Avenue, Suite 210E, Boston, MA 02210. Ir clude your name and address. Daniel Hic of Goodlettsville, Tenn., found the rooster in the June/July 2019 issue on page 20 ar won our favorite can opener.

WEB EXTRAS

Free for four months online at
CooksCountry.com/nov19

Boneless Turkey Breast with Gravy
Chocolate Cake Batter
Easy Herb-Roasted Turkey with Gravy
Faux Swiss Meringue Frosting
Turkey and Gravy for a Crowd

READ US ON IPAD

Download the Cook's Country app for iPad and start a free trial subscription or purchase a single issue of the magazine. issues are enhanced with Cooking Mode slide shows that provide step-by-step instructions for completing recipes, plus expanded reviews and ratings. Go to CooksCountry.com/iPad to download o app through iTunes.

Candy Corn Cake

For a frighteningly delicious treat with no trick, we concocted this bewitching cake inspired by an iconic Halloween candy.

by Sarah Ewald

TO MAKE THIS CAKE, YOU WILL NEED:

- ½ teaspoon black gel food coloring
- 1 recipe Chocolate Cake Batter*
- 1 recipe Faux Swiss Meringue Frosting*
- 4 teaspoons orange gel food coloring
- ¼ teaspoon red gel food coloring
- 2¼ teaspoons yellow gel food coloring
- 45–50 pieces candy corn

FOR THE CAKE:

Adjust oven rack to middle position and heat oven to 350 degrees. Grease three 8-inch round cake pans, line with parchment paper, grease parchment, and flour pans. Whisk black food coloring into cake batter until fully combined. Divide batter evenly among prepared pans and smooth tops with rubber spatula. Bake until toothpick inserted in center comes out clean, about 20 minutes. Let cakes cool in pans on wire rack for 5 minutes. Run knife around edges of pans. Remove cakes from pans, discarding parchment, and let cool completely on rack, at least 1 hour.

FOR THE FROSTING:

Transfer 1⅓ cups frosting to each of 2 small bowls. Add orange and red food coloring to first bowl and yellow food coloring to second bowl, stirring well to combine. Set aside remaining white frosting.

TO ASSEMBLE:

Place 1 cake layer on cake turntable. Spread 1 cup yellow frosting evenly over top, right to edge of cake. Top with second cake layer, press lightly to adhere, then spread 1 cup orange frosting evenly over top, right to edge of cake. Top with remaining cake layer, pressing lightly to adhere. Spread 1½ cups white frosting evenly over top and sides of cake. Refrigerate cake for 30 minutes.

Using offset spatula, spread remaining ⅓ cup yellow frosting over bottom third of sides of cake. Spread remaining ⅓ cup orange frosting over middle third of sides of cake. Spread ⅓ cup white frosting over top third of sides of cake. While spinning cake turntable, run edge of offset spatula around cake to blend colors and smooth sides of cake.

Arrange candy corn around top edge of cake, alternating orientation of white side and yellow side. Fill pastry bag fitted with ½-inch-wide straight tip with remaining 1¼ cups white frosting and pipe dots inside ring of candy corn. Refrigerate until frosting is firm, at least 30 minutes. Serve.

*Our recipes for Chocolate Cake Batter and Faux Swiss Meringue Frosting are available for free for four months at **CooksCountry.com/candycorncake.**

INSIDE THIS ISSUE

Cook's Country

CELEBRATE THE SEASON

LET'S BAKE

Fully Loaded Turtle Bars

Chocolate Brownie Cookies

Cinnamon Biscochitos

Tuscan Tomato Soup
Simple, Cozy, Quick

Spice-Cabinet Roast Chicken
Turned-Up Weeknight Flavor

Tasting Milk Chocolate
Our Favorite Is Smooth and Sweet

Georgian-Style Cheese Bread
Brooklyn Boardwalk Fave

Pork Cordon Bleu
Turn a Classic on Its Head

DECEMBER/JANUARY 2020
$6.95 U.S. / $7.95 CANADA

01>

7 1486 02742 3

DISPLAY UNTIL
JANUARY 6, 2020

AMERICA'S
TEST KITCHEN

LETTER FROM THE EDITOR

Illustration: Ross MacDonald

THE MAJOR HOLIDAYS are so much fun. Music, laughter, big meals, celebration, happy times.

But I think a lot about the days just before and after the big dates, the ones we tend to overlook. That Wednesday night before Thanksgiving, with the breeze of anticipation (or is it anxiety?) in the air. Or that afternoon the day after Christmas, when you still don't want to get out of your pj's but you might scream if you see another cookie.

I think those are the days when cooking really shows its power. The glamour shots are always of the tableful of pies you baked or beautiful centerpiece roast you prepared, but think of the beauty in that simple dish you'll make on a holiday season "off" night. Something warm, restorative, and thoughtful for yourself and your nearest. I recommend our dead-easy One-Pot Pasta with Sausage, Mushrooms, and Peas (page 27). Or maybe our Spice-Roasted Chicken with Chili and Oregano (page 11), our Chicken Biryani (page 10), or any of the recipe cards you'll find in the middle of this issue.

I wish you the happiest of times during the marquee moments this season, but let's hear it for the downtime, too. The kitchen's quieter then; hop in there and revel in its peace. Cook something special.

TUCKER SHAW

Editor in Chief

YOUNG CHEFS' CLUB!

Get monthly themed boxes filled with kid-tested, kid-approved recipes; engaging hands-on activities; STEAM-focused experiments; and more! All these items plus our digital library come together to inspire fun, experimentation, learning, and community in the kitchen for kids. Go to **ATKkids.com/CC** to join the club today!

 Find us on **Facebook**
facebook.com/CooksCountry

 Find us on **Instagram**
instagram.com/CooksCountry

 Follow us on **Pinterest**
pinterest.com/TestKitchen

 Follow us on **Twitter**
twitter.com/TestKitchen

Cook's Country

Chief Executive Officer David Nussbaum
Chief Creative Officer Jack Bishop
Editor in Chief Tucker Shaw
Executive Managing Editor Todd Meier
Executive Food Editor Bryan Roof
Deputy Editor Scott Kathan
Deputy Food Editor Morgan Bolling
Senior Editor Cecelia Jenkins
Associate Editors Alli Berkey, Matthew Fairman
Associate Editor, Web Ashley Delma
Photo Team/Special Events Manager Tim McQuinn
Test Cooks Natalie Estrada, Jessica Rudolph
Lead Test Cook, Photo Team Eric Haessler
Assistant Test Cooks, Photo Team Hannah Fenton, Jacqueline Gochenouer, Christa West
Copy Editors Christine Campbell, April Poole, Rachel Schowalter
Contributing Editor Eva Katz
Senior Science Research Editor Paul Adams
Hosts & Executive Editors, Television Bridget Lancaster, Julia Collin Davison

Executive Editors, Tastings & Testings Hannah Crowley, Lisa McManus
Senior Editors, Tastings & Testings Lauren Savoie, Kate Shan
Associate Editor, Tastings & Testings Miye Bromberg
Assistant Editors, Tastings & Testings Riddley Gemperlein-Schirm, Carolyn Grillo, Emily Phares

Creative Director John Torres
Photography Director Julie Cote
Art Director Susan Levin
Associate Art Director Maggie Edgar
Art Director, Tastings & Testings Marissa Angelone
Senior Staff Photographers Steve Klise, Daniel J. van Ackere
Staff Photographer Kevin White
Photography Producer Meredith Mulcahy

Senior Director, Creative Operations Alice Carpenter
Senior Editor, Special Projects Christie Morrison
Senior Manager, Publishing Operations Taylor Argenzio
Imaging Manager Lauren Robbins
Production & Imaging Specialists Tricia Neumyer, Dennis No, Amanda Yong
Deputy Editor, Editorial Operations Megan Ginsberg
Editorial Assistants, Editorial Operations Tess Berger, Sara Zatopek
Test Kitchen Director Erin McMurrer
Assistant Test Kitchen Director Alexxa Benson
Test Kitchen Manager Meridith Lippard
Test Kitchen Facilities Manager Kayce Vanpelt
Senior Kitchen Assistant Receiver Heather Tolmie
Senior Kitchen Assistant Shopper Avery Lowe
Kitchen Assistants Gladis Campos, Blanca Castanza, Amarilys Merced, Michelle Somoza

Chief Financial Officer Jackie McCauley Ford
Senior Manager, Customer Support Tim Quinn
Customer Support Specialist Mitchell Axelson
Event Coordinator Michaela Hughes

Chief Digital Officer Fran Middleton
VP, Marketing Natalie Vinard
Director, Audience Acquisition & Partnerships Evan Steiner
Director, Social Media Marketing Kathryn Przybyla
Social Media Coordinators Charlotte Errity, Sarah Sandler, Norma Tentori

Chief Revenue Officer Sara Domville

Director, Public Relations & Communications Brian Franklin
Public Relations Coordinator Madeleine Cohen

Senior VP, Human Resources & Organizational Development Colleen Zelina
Human Resources Manager Jason Lynott

Food Styling Catrine Kelty, Ashley Moore

Circulation Services ProCirc

AMERICA'S TEST KITCHEN ®

America's Test Kitchen is a real test kitchen located in Boston. It is the home of more than 60 test cooks, editors, and cookware specialists. Our mission is to test recipes until we understand exactly how and why they work and eventually arrive at the very best version. We also test kitchen equipment and supermarket ingredients in search of products that offer the best value and performance. You can watch us work by tuning in to *America's Test Kitchen* (AmericasTestKitchen.com) and *Cook's Country* (CooksCountry.com) on public television, and you can listen to our weekly segments on *The Splendid Table* on public radio. You can also follow us on Facebook, Twitter, Pinterest, and Instagram.

33

Cook's Country magazine (ISSN 1552-1990), number 90, is published bimonthly by America's Test Kitchen Limited Partnership, 21 Drydock Avenue, Suite 210E, Boston, MA 02210. Copyright 2019 America's Test Kitchen Limited Partnership. Periodicals postage paid at Boston, MA, and additional mailing offices, USPS #023453. Publications Mail Agreement No. 40020778. Return undeliverable Canadian addresses to P.O. Box 875, Station A, Windsor, ON N9A 6P2. POSTMASTER: Send address changes to *Cook's Country*, P.O. Box 6018, Harlan, IA 51593-1518. For subscription and gift subscription orders, subscription inquiries, or change of address notices, visit AmericasTestKitchen.com/support, call 800-526-8447 in the U.S. or 515-237-3663 from outside the U.S., or write to us at *Cook's Country*, P.O. Box 6018, Harlan, IA 51593-1518. PRINTED IN THE USA.

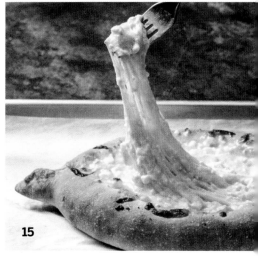
15

*by Cecelia Jenkins
and Morgan Bolling*

Mailing Cookies

I want to mail cookies to friends as holiday gifts. Do you have any packing tips that will ensure their safe arrival?
–*Donna Sayers, Marietta, Ga.*

To test the best way to mail holiday cookies, we made batches of our New Mexico Biscochitos, Turtle Bars, and Chocolate Brownie Cookies (page 20) and experimented with different methods of packing and mailing to send them off to lucky friends around the country. The recipients then reported back on how the cookies held up through transit.

Our hefty Turtle Bars held up the best, followed by the biscochitos. While the Chocolate Brownie Cookies were the most prone to breaking, almost any cookies can be successfully mailed with some care.

For delicate cookies and hefty, sticky bar cookies, we recommend making stacks of three or four with small pieces of parchment paper between the cookies and then wrapping

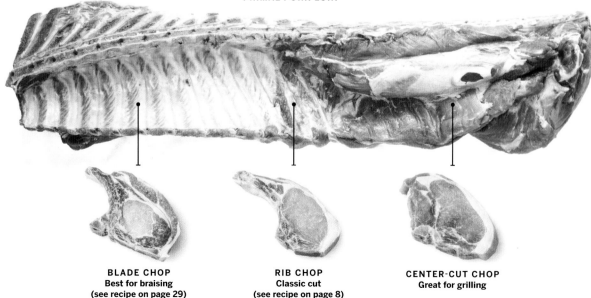

Use Plenty of Padding

Stack for Fewer Broken Cookies

the stacks in a tight double layer of plastic wrap. For sturdy cookies, simply seal them in a zipper-lock bag. You can mail different cookies in the same box, but don't wrap different cookies together, since their flavors can transfer. Pad the box generously with at least 3 inches of bubble wrap, recycled packing peanuts, crumpled newspaper, or air-popped popcorn.

And finally, spend the extra money to mail them faster so the cookies arrive fresher; USPS two-day Priority Mail is a good choice.

THE BOTTOM LINE: Thoughtful wrapping (zipper-lock bags or plastic wrap) and a good amount of padding (popcorn, packing peanuts, or crumpled newspaper) ensure successful cookie shipping.

Stay Sharp

My favorite chef's knife has a plastic handle, but the care instructions caution against putting the knife in the dishwasher. Why?
–*Mick Bornhurst, Oklahoma City, Okla.*

Although most plastic handles are dishwasher-safe (wooden handles aren't), sharp knives won't stay sharp if they go through the dishwasher. Water in the wash cycle can jostle knives, which can cause the blade to bump against the rack or other objects, significantly dulling or chipping the blade. Also, dishwasher detergent can dull and discolor chef's knives.

But the biggest reason to avoid the dishwasher is safety: No matter how you load knives—flat on a rack or standing in the basket—they can shift around, become hidden under other objects, or end up at awkward angles that make them dangerous to unload.

THE BOTTOM LINE: Hand-wash your chef's knives so that you stay safe and your knives remain in tip-top shape.

Pork Chop Primer

There are many cuts of pork chops at the market; how do they differ?
–*Kerry Agnew, Port Jefferson, N.Y.*

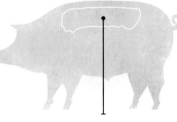

PRIMAL PORK LOIN
This section runs along the back from behind the shoulder to the hind legs. It is where pork chops are cut from.

Pork chops are typically cut from the primal loin, the long stretch of muscles (and bones) in the center of the hog's back between the shoulder and the hind legs. How you cook pork chops depends in part on which muscles they're cut from and how much fat they contain.

The portion of the loin closest to the head is known as the blade end because it abuts the blade, or shoulder; blade chops contain parts of several different muscles, lots of dark meat, and/or some connective tissue. They have a bit of fat and a ton of flavor and often require extended cooking to become tender.

Next up are rib chops, which contain a large "eye" of loin with some fat around it—they look like classic chops. They are flavorful, and the fat surrounding the lean eye of loin meat helps keep the meat moist.

Moving down the loin, the next chops are center-cut chops; these resemble mini T-bone steaks with loin meat on one side of the bone and lean tenderloin meat on the other. Since tenderloin cooks faster than loin, center-cut chops can be a challenge to cook evenly, but they are flavorful and can be especially great on the grill (the bone prevents them from lying flat in a skillet).

Finally, cuts from the back end of the loin, closest to the tail, contain some meat from the sirloin as well as the loin and sometimes the tenderloin and the hip; these chops are labeled sirloin chops or sirloin-end chops and are not commonly found in the supermarket (and are not shown at left). They are a challenge to cook evenly.

As for what this all means in the kitchen (or on the grill): Lean cuts from the center of the loin are naturally tender and should be cooked quickly so they don't dry out; those from the blade or the sirloin end usually need a bit more cooking to melt the additional fat and connective tissue and to make sure that the different muscles all cook through.

THE BOTTOM LINE: There are different types of pork chops; blade chops and sirloin chops contain dark meat, different muscles, more connective tissue, and more fat, so they need more cooking than leaner rib or center-cut loin chops.

PRIMAL PORK LOIN

BLADE CHOP
Best for braising
(see recipe on page 29)

RIB CHOP
Classic cut
(see recipe on page 8)

CENTER-CUT CHOP
Great for grilling

Easy, Not Greasy
–Molly Ball, Lake Waccamaw, N.C.

I used to hate poking around with a spoon to skim the excess grease off sauces, stocks, and soups, until a friend of mine shared a trick he learned in culinary school. If you set just one side of a pot over the burner on a flat-top stove, the simmering bubbles will push the slick of fat to the other side of the pot, making it easier to spoon off.

Better Butter Cutting
–Lindsay Hayes, Tacoma, Wash.

I've always found cutting cold butter into flour for pie crust and biscuits difficult to do without it melting and becoming mangled. But a while back, I thought of an easy solution that I now use each time I cut butter. I sprinkle some of my measured flour—flour that's already going into the recipe, not extra flour—onto the butter on the counter to keep the pieces from sticking to each other as I cut them with my bench scraper. I cut the butter into large pieces and toss them with a little flour. The flour keeps the pieces from sticking together as I continue to cut the butter into smaller pieces. I then use my bench scraper to scrape up all the flour and butter pieces from the counter, making sure it all gets included in the finished product.

Boil It Clean
John Fante, Tucson, Ariz.

Here's a simple trick I picked up from my mom: Whenever I have a skillet with a lot of dark bits cooked onto it, I pour in some water and bring to a boil on the stovetop. The boiling action loosens all the gunk and makes cleaning the pan with soap and a scrubber a breeze. This technique works great with both stainless-steel and cast-iron pans.

Searching for the Best Spread
by Emily Phares

Our previous favorite strawberry spread was discontinued, so it was time to find a new one. Strawberry is the nation's most popular flavor of jams, jellies, and preserves, and this was evident in the number of products we found on the market. Some companies offered multiple options, so we conducted a pretasting of 14 products to narrow down our lineup to one jam, two preserves, and three spreads. We then tasted each of these products plain, in peanut butter and jelly sandwiches, and in Jam Thumbprint Cookies.

PRODUCT TASTING

We found that even if two products had the same name (e.g., preserves), they might have very different flavors and consistencies. Strawberry flavors ranged from subtle to vibrant, and consistencies ran the gamut from "syrupy" and "runny" to "stiff" and "thick." The runny sample was problematic, making for "messy," "oozy" sandwiches.

A few products had muted fruit flavor, while one had "strong strawberry flavor" that some tasters found to be artificial. The amounts of sugar in each product also varied, from 7 grams to 13 grams per tablespoon serving.

Our Favorite Smucker's Strawberry Preserves	Welch's Natural Strawberry Spread	Crofter's Organic Strawberry Just Fruit Spread	Crofter's Organic Strawberry Premium Spread	Bonne Maman Strawberry Preserves	Stonewall Kitchen Strawberry Jam
Price: $3.89 for 18 oz ($0.22 per oz) **Sugar:** 12 g **Comments:** Our winner's "deep berry flavor" was sweet but "not too sweet" and most likely tempered by its high acidity level.	**Price:** $3.00 for 27 oz ($0.11 per oz) **Sugar:** 10 g **Comments:** This spread had a "strong strawberry flavor" and a balance of "chunky and smooth" textures.	**Price:** $3.79 for 10 oz ($0.38 per oz) **Sugar:** 8 g **Comments:** We appreciated this sample's muted sweetness, with one taster noting it "tastes like it's healthy." In the sandwich, it tasted "fresh," but its texture was "thin."	**Price:** $4.99 for 16.5 oz ($0.30 per oz) **Sugar:** 8 g **Comments:** This spread had a lower sugar content that imparted a mellow sweetness and a "light strawberry flavor" that was "clean."	**Price:** $5.19 for 13 oz ($0.40 per oz) **Sugar:** 13 g **Comments:** With the highest sugar content in the lineup, this product had an "intense sweetness" and a "syrupy" consistency that was "messy" and "oozy" in the sandwich.	**Price:** $7.99 for 13 oz ($0.61 per oz) **Sugar:** 7 g **Comments:** This "subtle" jam, with the lowest sugar level in the lineup, didn't have a strong berry flavor, nor was it overly sweet. We liked it plain, but it really excelled in sandwiches.

— **RECOMMENDED** —

Three products on the lower end of this range were deemed "subtle" and "not overly sweet." By contrast, products on the opposite end of the spectrum were described as "a little too sweet." Interestingly, our favorite product had 12 grams of sugar per serving yet did not taste cloyingly sweet, likely thanks to its higher acidity, which muted the perception of sweetness.

Our favorite, Smucker's Strawberry Preserves, was "potent," with a natural, "classic" flavor that reminded tasters of a "truly ripe strawberry." It was also spreadable but not too thin, with a moderate and pleasing amount of chunky fruit pieces. We liked it plain and in peanut butter and jelly sandwiches, and it baked up well in the thumbprint cookies, too, making it an exceptionally vibrant, versatile spread.

Holiday Roast Beef on the Cheap

Christmas is a great time to splurge. But do you need to?

by Morgan Bolling

DON'T GET ME wrong; I love beef tenderloins and standing rib roasts as much as the next person. But sometimes you need a less expensive option. I wanted to see if I could create a celebration-worthy beef roast using one of my favorite affordable cuts: chuck-eye roast. Chuck eye has a big, beefy flavor and is easy to find—and it typically rings in at about a third of the cost of beef tenderloin.

Chuck-eye roast is cut from the shoulder of the cow—the chuck—so the muscles are hardworking and can be chewy when cooked too quickly. Cooking the meat low and slow helps it become tender. So to start my testing, I seasoned a 5-pound boneless beef chuck-eye roast with salt and pepper and cooked it in a 275-degree oven. I removed it when the center was medium-rare (120 degrees), as I would for tenderloin, and let it rest for 30 minutes before slicing. But this meat wasn't tender—it was chewy. Was my target temperature the problem?

To find out, I cooked half a dozen roasts, cooking each of them to a different final temperature. I landed on a sweet spot between 145 and 150 degrees in the center (which we usually call medium to medium-well). This meat was juicy and light rosy pink inside. As an added bonus, since the roast took about 3½ hours to cook, the exterior developed nice color without a searing step. Letting the cooked meat rest a full 45 minutes before slicing allowed its internal juices to redistribute, resulting in the moistest meat (try saying that ten times fast). Plus, the resting time made it easier to slice the beef thin—an important step with this cut—so it was nice and tender.

Unfortunately, my tasters were put off by the strip of unrendered fat in the center of the chuck-eye roast. So for my next test, I took the raw roast and pulled it apart into two pieces right through this line of fat and then cut away (and discarded) the fat. I tried roasting these two small pieces, but the end results didn't look the part of a grand holiday roast. Instead, I seasoned each piece and tied them back together with twine to make one evenly shaped, impressive-looking hunk of meat. Allowing the salted-and-tied roast to sit overnight improved both the flavor and texture.

For a flavorful condiment, I auditioned both a creamy horseradish sauce and a fresh parsley sauce. My tasters couldn't decide between the two, so I meshed them into one spicy, herby condiment to serve with the beef. I finally had a roast worthy of the holiday table, and I didn't have to break the bank to get there.

ROASTED BEEF CHUCK ROAST WITH HORSERADISH-PARSLEY SAUCE
Serves 8 to 10

Plan ahead: The roast must be seasoned at least 18 hours before cooking. If using table salt, cut the amount in half. Buy refrigerated prepared horseradish, not the shelf-stable kind, which contains preservatives and additives. The horseradish-parsley sauce can be refrigerated for up to two days; let come to room temperature before serving.

BEEF
- **1 (5-pound) boneless beef chuck-eye roast, trimmed**
- **2 tablespoons kosher salt**
- **2 teaspoons pepper**
- **2 tablespoons extra-virgin olive oil**

SAUCE
- **1 cup fresh parsley leaves**
- **¼ cup prepared horseradish**
- **1 shallot, chopped**
- **2 tablespoons capers, rinsed**
- **1 tablespoon lemon juice**
- **1 garlic clove, minced**
- **½ teaspoon kosher salt**
- **¾ cup extra-virgin olive oil**

1. FOR THE BEEF: Pull roast into 2 pieces at major seam delineated by line of white fat, cutting with boning knife as needed. Using knife, remove large knobs of fat from each piece.

2. Sprinkle roast pieces all over with salt and pepper. Place pieces back together along major seam. Tie together with kitchen twine at 1-inch intervals to create 1 evenly shaped roast. Wrap tightly in plastic wrap and refrigerate for 18 to 24 hours.

3. Adjust oven rack to lower-middle position and heat oven to 275 degrees. Set

huck-Eye Prep

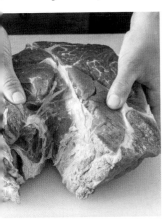

parate and Trim
sect the roast along its natural
am (using a knife if necessary) and
en trim and discard any excess fat
d connective tissue.

eassemble and Tie
se kitchen twine to tie the two
immed pieces together into one
g roast.

ire rack in rimmed baking sheet.
Jnwrap roast and rub all over
vith oil. Place roast on prepared
vire rack. Transfer sheet to oven
nd roast until meat registers
45 to 150 degrees, 3¼ to
¾ hours. Transfer roast to carv-
ng board, tent with aluminum
oil, and let rest for 45 minutes.
. FOR THE SAUCE: Mean-
vhile, pulse parsley, horseradish,
hallot, capers, lemon juice, garlic,
nd salt in food processor until
arsley is finely chopped, 6 to
pulses, scraping down sides of
owl as needed. Transfer to bowl
nd stir in oil until combined. Sea-
on with salt to taste; set aside.
. Slice roast thin, removing twine
s you go so roast stays intact.
erve, passing sauce separately.

Roasted Butternut Squash and Apple

What does squash need to go from good to great? Plenty of browning and a surprising dressing.

by Natalie Estrada

LET'S BE HONEST: Does anyone get excited to see butternut squash in the grocery store? I think the reason for the lukewarm reception is that most recipes don't do the squash's earthy flavor justice. Instead of covering it up with creamy sauces or too many spices, I wanted to highlight its inherent sweetness by deeply caramelizing the squash in a hot oven.

After peeling the squash, I tested roasting cubes, chunks, and even halves. I settled on cutting a halved squash crosswise into 1-inch pieces; this gave me large-ish pieces that were easy to manage on the plate and had the perfect ratio of flavorful browned exterior to creamy, soft interior. For intense caramelization, I set the oven to 450 degrees and adjusted the oven rack to the lowest position, nearest to the heat source.

To enhance the squash's mild sweetness, I wanted to make a simple vinaigrette to spoon over the roasted squash. I started with minced shallot for its gentle flavor and then added red wine vinegar for fruity tang. Some sugar provided balance, red pepper flakes brought kick, and parsley added freshness.

But the dish needed one more element to make it truly shine. The answer was right next to the squash in the supermarket: apples. Their mix of sweet and tart flavors accented the squash's sweetness without overpowering the dish. I cut one Gala apple (Fuji and Braeburn work great, too) into wedges and added them to the rimmed baking sheet with the squash, but they came out mushy. It was better, I found, to add the apples partway through the squash's cooking time. This way, they stayed relatively firm and provided plenty of complementary flavor. Now I'm excited for squash season.

  Our recipe for Roasted Butternut Squash with Goat Cheese and Pepitas is available for free for four months at **CooksCountry.com/squash**.

ROASTED BUTTERNUT SQUASH WITH APPLE
Serves 4 to 6
When peeling the squash, be sure to also remove the fibrous yellow flesh just beneath the skin.

VINAIGRETTE
- 3 tablespoons red wine vinegar
- 1 tablespoon sugar
- ⅛ teaspoon table salt
- 3 tablespoons minced shallot
- 2 tablespoons chopped fresh parsley
- 2 tablespoons extra-virgin olive oil
- ¼ teaspoon red pepper flakes

SQUASH AND APPLE
- 1 (2¼- to 2¾-pound) butternut squash
- 3 tablespoons extra-virgin olive oil, divided
- 1 teaspoon table salt
- 1 Gala, Fuji, or Braeburn apple, unpeeled, cored, halved, and cut into ½-inch-thick wedges

1. FOR THE VINAIGRETTE: Stir vinegar, sugar, and salt in small bowl until sugar is dissolved. Stir in shallot, parsley, oil, and pepper flakes; set aside.
2. FOR THE SQUASH AND APPLE: Adjust oven rack to lowest position and heat oven to 450 degrees. Trim ends from squash and peel squash. Halve squash lengthwise and scrape out seeds. Place squash cut side down on cutting board and slice crosswise 1 inch thick.
3. Toss squash, 2 tablespoons oil, and salt together in bowl. Spread squash in even layer on rimmed baking sheet, cut side down. Roast until squash is tender and bottoms are beginning to brown, 14 to 16 minutes.
4. Toss apple and remaining 1 tablespoon oil together in now-empty bowl. Remove sheet from oven. Place apple between squash on sheet, cut side down. (Do not flip squash.) Return sheet to oven and continue to roast until apple is tender and squash is fully browned on bottoms (tops of squash will not be browned), about 8 minutes longer.
5. Using spatula, transfer squash and apple to shallow platter and spread into even layer. Drizzle vinaigrette over top. Serve warm or at room temperature.

ROASTED BUTTERNUT SQUASH WITH PEAR AND PANCETTA
Reduce salt for squash to ½ teaspoon. Substitute 1 teaspoon minced fresh thyme for parsley and 1 Bosc pear for apple. Add 3 ounces pancetta, cut into ½-inch pieces, to sheet with pears in step 4.

Our blue cheese variation—shown here—has a pleasantly funky, salty kick.

POTATO TAR

A RUSTIC TART can serve as an eye-catching holiday dessert, but with the right filling, a tart can also be a handsomely nontraditional savory side dish. I wanted to create a recipe for a tart packed with potatoes and nutty Parmesan cheese.

The good news was that the test kitchen has a fantastic recipe for a buttery, crisp, easy-to-work-with tart dough that I could use as a reliable starting point. So I began my testing by filling batches of that dough with different kinds of potatoes (russet, Yukon Gold, and red) in different cuts (chunks, wedges, and thin rounds). I tossed the spuds with grated Parmesan and baked the tarts for a taste test.

My tasters liked the texture of russets sliced into thin rounds the best. When stacked up inside the dough, the sliced russets compacted into a pleasantly cohesive layer that cooked through evenly with no dry or underdone spots (problems that plagued the potatoes cut into chunks and wedges).

But something was missing. The Parmesan provided nice background flavor, but the tart needed a creamy element for richness and cohesion. I tried adding a little cream to the raw potatoes, but the filling became too liquid-y and made the dough soggy.

If I wanted something creamy and cheesy, why not try cream cheese? Plain cream cheese was a little, well, plain. I tried gussying it up and landed on a combination of an egg yolk for stability and richness, Parmesan cheese for nuttiness, Dijon mustard for its sharp tang, rosemary for its piney punch, and sliced shallot for a savory-sweet base flavor. By tossing the sliced potatoes with this potent, creamy mixture, I ensured that every bite was packed with flavor. A sprinkling of more Parmesan around the pastry's edge was the final flourish that took this rustic tart over the top.

Tarts aren't just for dessert. This beautiful savory side dish proves the point. **by Alli Berkey**

asier Tart Construction

1. Add ice water to dry ingredients and utter in processor bowl.

2. Roll chilled dough square into 14 by 11-inch rectangle.

3. Add sliced potatoes and shallot to cream cheese mixture and stir to coat.

4. Transfer filling to center of dough, leaving 2-inch border on all sides.

Sprinkle Parmesan and remaining osemary over filling.

6. Fold 1 long side of dough 1½ inches over filling; repeat with opposing long side.

7. Fold in short sides and press gently on edges to seal.

8. Brush dough with egg white and sprinkle with Parmesan before baking.

OTATO AND PARMESAN TART
erves 6 to 8

mandoline makes quick work of venly slicing the potatoes. We use usset potatoes for their starchiness ere, but you can substitute Yukon old potatoes, if desired.

1½ cups (7½ ounces) all-purpose flour
  1 teaspoon table salt, divided
 10 tablespoons unsalted butter,
    cut into ½-inch pieces and chilled
 –7 tablespoons ice water
  4 ounces cream cheese
  2 ounces Parmesan cheese,
    grated (1 cup), divided
  2 tablespoons extra-virgin olive oil
  2 teaspoons Dijon mustard
1½ teaspoons minced fresh rosemary,
    divided
  ¼ teaspoon pepper
  1 large egg, separated
  1 pound russet potatoes,
    peeled and sliced ⅛ inch thick
  1 shallot, sliced thin

. Process flour and ½ teaspoon salt in ood processor until combined, about seconds. Scatter butter over top and ulse until mixture resembles coarse rumbs, about 10 pulses. Add 6 table-poons ice water and process until

almost no dry flour remains, about 10 seconds, scraping down sides of bowl after 5 seconds. Add up to 1 additional tablespoon ice water if dough doesn't come together.
2. Turn out dough onto lightly floured counter, form into 4-inch square, wrap tightly in plastic wrap, and refrigerate for 1 hour. (Wrapped dough can be refrigerated for up to 2 days or frozen for up to 1 month.)
3. Adjust oven rack to lower-middle position and heat oven to 375 degrees. Line rimmed baking sheet with parchment paper. Let chilled dough sit on counter to soften slightly before rolling, about 10 minutes. Roll dough into 14 by 11-inch rectangle on lightly floured counter, then transfer to prepared sheet.
4. Microwave cream cheese in large bowl until softened, 20 to 30 seconds. Whisk in ½ cup Parmesan, oil, mustard, 1 teaspoon rosemary, pepper, and remaining ½ teaspoon salt until combined, about 20 seconds. Whisk in egg yolk. Add potatoes and shallot to cream cheese mixture and stir to thoroughly coat potatoes.
5. Transfer filling to center of dough. Press filling into even layer, leaving 2-inch border on all sides. Sprinkle

6 tablespoons Parmesan and remaining ½ teaspoon rosemary over filling.
6. Grasp 1 long side of dough and fold about 1½ inches over filling. Repeat with opposing long side. Fold in short sides of dough, overlapping corners of dough to secure. Lightly beat egg white and brush over folded crust (you won't need it all). Sprinkle remaining 2 tablespoons Parmesan over crust.
7. Bake until crust and filling are golden brown and potatoes meet little resistance when poked with fork, about 45 minutes. Transfer sheet to wire rack and let tart cool for 10 minutes. Using metal spatula, loosen tart from parchment and carefully slide onto wire rack; let cool until just warm, about 20 minutes. Cut into slices and serve warm.

POTATO AND BLUE CHEESE TART
Reduce Parmesan to ½ cup. Use ¼ cup in cream cheese mixture in step 4, 2 tablespoons to sprinkle over potatoes in step 5, and 2 tablespoons to sprinkle over folded crust in step 6. Add ¼ cup crumbled blue cheese to cream cheese mixture in step 4. Sprinkle additional ¼ cup crumbled blue cheese over potato mixture in step 5.

The Slice Is Right
If you're not used to using one, a mandoline can feel intimidating. But with a little common sense and care, these gadgets can do a lot to elevate your cooking. Here are a few tips for using a mandoline.
- **Always use the hand guard.** And don't feel like you have to get every last slice out of your vegetables.
- **Expand your horizons.** Apples, pears, kiwi, citrus, carrots, zucchini, onions, fennel, cucumbers, cabbage, beets, and hard cheeses are easy to slice perfectly with a mandoline.
- **Store your slicer in a plastic container or wrap it in a dish towel.** This ensures safety and keeps the blades sharp. Our favorite model is equipped with a storage caddy.

OUR WINNING MANDOLINE
Swissmar Börner Original V-Slicer Plus
Mandoline (about $50)

Indoor Barbecue Pork Chops

Why should summer get all the fun? These chops deliver all the flavor of an outdoor barbecue from the comfort of your kitchen.

by Jessica Rudolph

IN THE SUMMERTIME, barbecue pork chops are about as straightforward as you can get: Throw some chops on the grill, slather them with your favorite sauce (bottled or homemade), and you've got a satisfying meal of smoky, sweet pork in no time. But what happens when it's not summertime or you don't have easy access to a grill? I set out to create an easy indoor recipe for "barbecue" pork chops that had all the flavor and appeal of the outdoor version.

I started off easy by searing 1-inch-thick pork rib chops in oil in a skillet and brushing them with our favorite store-bought barbecue sauce. The results were not good. The meat was bland and dry, and the sauce tasted one-note and too sweet. Both brining and salting the chops ahead of time gave me juicier and better-seasoned results but took more work and time than I wanted for an easy weeknight meal.

A potent dry rub of paprika, cayenne, kosher salt, and plenty of black pepper gave me a better-tasting and more barbecue-like exterior, but those flavors didn't penetrate the inside of the chops at all. Ultimately, thinner ½-inch chops were the answer: They gave me a higher ratio of flavorful spiced and sauced crust to mild meat; plus, they cooked more evenly and twice as fast (which meant less chance of drying out).

The downside of thinner chops was that they had less opportunity to develop flavorful browning since they spent less time in the skillet. It took a two-pronged approach—adding both brown sugar and cornstarch to the dry rub—to fix the problem. The brown sugar encouraged caramelization while

the cornstarch absorbed excess moisture on the meat's exterior for a drier surface and thus more even browning.

Sauce time. I knew I wanted a tangy, brightly spiced sauce and nothing too dark or cloying that might clobber the naturally sweet, mild flavor of the pork chops. Ketchup and cider vinegar were a must, and to keep things simple I added the same spice blend I used to season the chops, along with extra brown sugar. A touch of liquid smoke gave straight-off-the-grill flavor. For a finishing touch of richness, butter was just the ticket; it smoothed out any of the sauce's rough edges, added depth, and gave the sauce body and an appealing sheen.

In the end, I was able to get tender, juicy chops with all the barbecue flavor I sought in less time than it takes to fire up the grill. Barbecue pork chops just became a year-round dish.

Turning the chops in the sauce before serving ensures a thick coating and plenty of flavor.

What's in a Word?

Some renegade etymologists still point to French roots for the word "barbecue" (*barbe a queue*, meaning "beard to tail"), but the most likely origin story can be traced back to the Taino, an indigenous population in and around the Caribbean, who built structures called *barbacoas* to smoke fish.

Today, purists hold to the idea that "barbecue" refers specifically to low-and-slow cooking, but in practice, it signifies a whole range of culinary ideas and flavors—from the pulled pork dished up at a roadside shack to the grilled hot dogs and chicken wings served at a backyard party to the commercial potato chip flavor. What "barbecue" means depends on history, region, and context.

INDOOR BARBECUE PORK CHOPS
Serves 4 to 6

Be sure to use kosher salt and unsalted butter in this recipe or the dish will be too salty. Thinner pork chops, such as the ½-inch-thick chops we call for here, can buckle during cooking, which will cause them to cook unevenly. To prevent this, we use kitchen shears to snip the fat surrounding the loin portion of each chop. We recommend using a liquid smoke product that contains just water and smoke, such as Wright's Liquid Smoke.

- 3 tablespoons packed brown sugar, divided
- 1 tablespoon paprika
- 1 tablespoon kosher salt
- 1 teaspoon pepper
- ½ teaspoon cayenne pepper
- 1 tablespoon cornstarch
- 8 (5- to 7-ounce) bone-in pork rib chops, ½ inch thick, trimmed
- 1 tablespoon vegetable oil
- 4 tablespoons unsalted butter
- ½ cup ketchup
- 1 tablespoon cider vinegar
- 1 teaspoon liquid smoke

1. Combine 1 tablespoon sugar, paprika, salt, pepper, and cayenne in bowl. Transfer 2 tablespoons spice mixture to second bowl and stir in cornstarch; reserve remaining spice mixture for sauce. Using kitchen shears, snip through fat surrounding loin muscle of each chop in 2 places, about 2 inches apart. Pat chops dry with paper towels and sprinkle all over with cornstarch mixture.

2. Heat oil in 12-inch nonstick skillet over medium-high heat until just smoking. Add 4 chops to skillet and cook until browned and meat registers 140 degrees, about 2 minutes per side. Transfer chops to rimmed baking sheet and tent with aluminum foil. Repeat with remaining 4 chops.

3. Add butter to now-empty skillet and melt over medium heat. Add reserved spice mixture and cook until fragrant, about 30 seconds. Carefully whisk in ketchup, vinegar, liquid smoke, and remaining 2 tablespoons sugar; bring to simmer; and remove from heat. Return chops to skillet one at a time, turn to coat with sauce, and transfer to platter. Stir any accumulated juices from sheet into remaining sauce. Serve chops, passing remaining sauce separately.

Pork Cordon Bleu

Construction counts: Layering, not stuffing, was the key to updating this classic dish. **by Natalie Estrada**

CHICKEN CORDON BLEU, or "blue ribbon" chicken, features a boneless breast that's stuffed with (or rolled around) a ham and cheese filling, coated in bread crumbs, and baked or fried. It's a well-loved dish but, in my opinion, it's one that could use a bit of a refresh (maybe because I've had it at so many weddings). What's more, I wanted to swap out chicken breast in favor of tender, mildly sweet pork tenderloin. And I wanted it to be fast and easy enough for a weeknight.

Classic cordon bleu calls for Black Forest ham, and it was the best option here too, for its consistently robust flavor and wide availability. After experimenting with several different cheeses, I settled on Gruyère for its unbeatable combination of nutty flavor and smooth meltability.

As for the construction, many cordon bleu recipes call for cutting a pocket into the side of a chicken or pork cutlet and then stuffing the pocket with cheese and ham, but I wanted an easier method. I tried pounding pieces of the tenderloin into cutlets, rolling them around the filling, and tying the bundles with twine, but it wasn't easy.

My next thought was to sandwich the ham and cheese between two cutlets, but the assembled mass was too thick to cook through before the bread crumbs on the exterior burned. In the end, the solution was to create a simple stack.

I started by cutting a pork tenderloin into four equal pieces, standing the pieces on end (cut side up), and pounding them out into cutlets. Covering the pork pieces with plastic wrap while pounding helped contain any mess (see "Pork Prep"). From there I breaded and pan-fried the cutlets and then topped each with ham and cheese and slid the stacks under the broiler to bubble and brown.

How about a sauce? I stirred together potent Dijon mustard, sour cream, chives, and a bit of salt and pepper for a creamy, tangy sauce that balanced the rich meat and cheese. Rather than using the sauce just as a garnish, I spread a tablespoon right on top of the fried cutlets before adding the ham and cheese and broiling them. This dish was definitely worthy of a blue ribbon.

WEEKNIGHT EASY

Our layered Pork Cordon Bleu is perfectly crunchy and easy to assemble.

Pork Prep: How to Make the Cutlets

Cut tenderloin into 4 equal pieces.

Stand each piece cut side up, cover with plastic wrap, and pound.

PORK CORDON BLEU
Serves 4
For the best results, be sure to purchase a tenderloin that weighs no more than 1 pound. We like to serve these cutlets with a green salad.

MUSTARD SAUCE
- ¾ cup sour cream
- ¼ cup Dijon mustard
- 2 tablespoons minced fresh chives
- ⅛ teaspoon table salt
- ⅛ teaspoon pepper

PORK
- ¼ cup all-purpose flour
- 2 large eggs
- 1 tablespoon Dijon mustard
- 1½ cups panko bread crumbs
- 1 (14- to 16-ounce) pork tenderloin, trimmed
- ¼ teaspoon table salt
- ¼ teaspoon pepper
- ½ cup vegetable oil for frying
- 8 thin slices deli Black Forest ham (8 ounces)
- 4 ounces Gruyère cheese, shredded (1 cup)

1. FOR THE MUSTARD SAUCE: Combine all ingredients in bowl; set aside.
2. FOR THE PORK: Adjust oven rack 6 inches from broiler element and heat broiler. Place flour in shallow dish. Lightly beat eggs and mustard together in second shallow dish. Place panko in third shallow dish.
3. Cut tenderloin crosswise into 4 equal pieces. Working with 1 piece at a time, arrange tenderloin pieces cut side up on cutting board. Cover with plastic wrap and pound to even ¼-inch thickness with meat pounder. Pat cutlets dry with paper towels and sprinkle with salt and pepper.
4. Dredge cutlets in flour, shaking off excess; dip in egg mixture, allowing excess to drip off; then coat with panko, pressing to adhere. Transfer cutlets to plate.
5. Set wire rack in rimmed baking sheet. Heat oil in 12-inch nonstick skillet over medium-high heat to 350 degrees. Place 2 cutlets in skillet and cook until golden brown on first side, about 3 minutes.
6. Using 2 spatulas, gently flip cutlets and continue to cook until golden brown on second side and just cooked through, about 3 minutes longer. Transfer to prepared rack. Return oil to 350 degrees and repeat with remaining 2 cutlets.
7. Spread 2 tablespoons mustard sauce over top of each cutlet, leaving ¼-inch border. Place 2 slices ham on each cutlet, folding ham as needed to keep from overhanging cutlet. Sprinkle ¼ cup Gruyère over ham on each cutlet.
8. Broil until Gruyère is melted and lightly browned in spots, 2 to 3 minutes. Serve cutlets with remaining mustard sauce.

Chicken Biryani

Could we streamline this complex, aromatic dish for the home cook? **by Matthew Fairman**

IN A CLASSIC chicken biryani, richly spiced and perfectly fluffy basmati rice is lavished with butter and studded with dried fruit and nuts. The rice—a confetti of vermillion saffron and white grains—is layered with sauced chicken pieces and topped with fried onions and a shower of fresh herbs. It is a celebration of the delicious complexity of Indian cooking and a staple of Indian American restaurants.

But chicken biryani takes a lot of time, effort, and dishes to make, as I found when I prepared a few existing recipes. For each one, I toasted and ground myriad whole spices. I cut up a chicken and marinated it for up to 48 hours before browning it. I soaked, rinsed, and parcooked the rice in spice-infused water and sliced and deep-fried a heap of onions. Finally, I layered the rice and chicken into a casserole dish, covered it tightly, and steamed everything in the oven. The biryanis were delicious, but I wondered if there was a faster path to a similarly tasty payoff.

I made some important timesaving discoveries in my early testing. First, I learned that I could still end up with flavorful, juicy chicken by using chunks of boneless chicken thighs and skipping the lengthy marinating in favor of cooking the chunks in the marinade ingredients. (Plus, the pieces of boneless thighs were easier to eat.) Second, I found that I could prepare the whole recipe on the stovetop, thankfully eliminating the need for the oven.

I also learned that I could sauté the onion in butter instead of deep-frying it and then brown the chicken in the same large skillet, saving a pan. Finally, rather than partially cooking the rice up front and steaming it to doneness later—which made it hard to get perfectly cooked rice—I could cook the rice through (in spiced water) and then steam it just briefly with the chicken at the end. Now I just had to prune the ingredient list.

For the whole spices to season the rice, my tasters loved the simple combo of a cinnamon stick, cumin seeds, and heady, floral saffron. To season the chicken, garam masala delivered a ton of complexity without my having to buy, toast, and grind a litany of spices. I simply browned the chicken chunks and then stirred in the garam masala, ginger, garlic, and chile, followed by

some creamy, tangy whole-milk yogurt to add moisture to the chicken layer.

I stirred a fistful of dried currants into the cooked rice and, taking a cue from a recipe I found in my research, poured over the butter I'd used to sauté the onion. I spooned the flavorful rice on top of the chicken in the pan, added the bright-orange saffron (bloomed in a little warm water), and then covered and steamed it all for 5 minutes to bring the flavors together. With my tasters assembled, I lifted the lid off my biryani and invited them to lean closer and breathe in the incredible aroma. With garnishes of fried onion, fresh mint and cilantro, and an easy, herby yogurt sauce, this streamlined biryani looked and tasted every bit as good as it smelled.

CHICKEN BIRYANI
Serves 6

To make this dish spicier, reserve and add the jalapeño seeds to the biryani as desired. You can substitute long-grain white rice for the basmati, if you like; it will be less fluffy and will need to cook for about 12 minutes in step 3.

GARNISH AND SAUCE
- ½ teaspoon saffron threads, crumbled
- 3 tablespoons warm water
- 1 cup plain whole-milk yogurt
- 2 tablespoons chopped fresh cilantro
- 2 tablespoons chopped fresh mint
- 1 garlic clove, minced
- ¼ teaspoon table salt
- ¼ teaspoon pepper

BIRYANI
- 6 tablespoons unsalted butter
- 2 cups thinly sliced onion
- 1¼ teaspoons table salt, divided, plus salt for cooking rice
- 1 cinnamon stick
- 2 teaspoons cumin seeds
- 2 cups basmati rice
- ⅓ cup dried currants
- 2 pounds boneless, skinless chicken thighs, trimmed and cut into 1½-inch chunks
- ½ teaspoon pepper
- 1 jalapeño chile, stemmed, seeded, and minced
- 1 tablespoon grated fresh ginger
- 1 tablespoon garam masala
- 3 garlic cloves, minced
- ½ cup plain whole-milk yogurt
- 2 tablespoons chopped fresh mint
- 2 tablespoons chopped fresh cilantro

Spiced rice, deeply seasoned chicken, and a host of flavorful accents make this biryani sing.

1. FOR THE GARNISH AND SAUCE: Combine saffron and water in bowl and set aside. Combine yogurt, cilantro, mint, garlic, salt, and pepper in second bowl and set aside.

2. FOR THE BIRYANI: Set fine-mesh strainer in medium bowl. Melt butter in 12-inch nonstick skillet over medium heat. Add onion and cook, stirring often, until dark brown, 11 to 14 minutes. Transfer onion to prepared strainer and press with spatula to squeeze out excess butter (reserve butter). Spread onion on small plate and sprinkle with ¼ teaspoon salt. Set aside onion and butter (do not wash skillet).

3. Meanwhile, bring 12 cups water, cinnamon stick, and cumin seeds to boil in large saucepan over high heat. Add rice and 1 tablespoon salt and cook, stirring occasionally, until tender, about 10 minutes. Drain rice in fine-mesh strainer. Return rice to saucepan and stir in currants, reserved butter, and ¼ teaspoon salt; cover and set aside.

4. Combine chicken, pepper, and remaining ¾ teaspoon salt in now-empty skillet and cook over medium-high heat until browned and cooked through,

about 10 minutes. Stir in jalapeño, ginger, garam masala, and garlic and cook until fragrant, about 1 minute. Off heat stir in yogurt until combined.

5. Spoon rice over chicken mixture and spread into even layer. Drizzle saffron mixture evenly over rice, spiraling in from edge of skillet to center. Cover skillet, return to medium heat, and cook until heated through and steam escapes from under lid, about 5 minutes. Off heat, sprinkle biryani with reserved fried onion, mint, and cilantro. Serve with yogurt sauce.

This Is Dark Brown
To get the sliced onion to express all its depth and sweetness, you need to cook it past the "golden brown" stage to fully dark brown (below). Be patient.

Spice-Cabinet Roast Chicken

Roast chicken is a great weeknight dinner. Raiding your spice cabinet can make it even better.

By Alli Berkey

ROASTING A CHICKEN shouldn't be hard. But some recipes make it seem so, calling for brines, marinades, advance salting, fancy butchering, and multistep cooking procedures. Not today. I set out to create a simple, stress-free recipe for juicy, perfectly browned, and surprisingly flavorful roast chicken you can make any night of the week.

First off, I decided to roast in a 12-inch skillet because it's the perfect size and always at the ready. I knew from experience that the average 3½- to 4-pound chicken cooks through in about an hour in a 400-degree oven. To enhance its browning, I rubbed the uncooked chicken all over with olive oil.

Turning my attention to flavor, I considered easy ways to season the chicken. Fresh herbs can taste steamed when sprinkled over a bird that's roasted, and most cooks avoid using lots of dried spices or dried herbs for fear they'll burn. But will they? After rubbing the chicken with oil (which also helps the spices stick), I sprinkled on a Mexican-inspired combination of chili powder, cumin, coriander, granulated garlic, and dried oregano and popped it into a preheated oven. The chicken emerged beautifully bronzed—not burnt—and superflavorful, if a little unfocused. Score one for the dried herbs and spices.

To refine the seasoning, I went through jars and jars of spices and dried herbs to find the best combinations. I wanted big, surprising flavors that would make you think about roast chicken in new ways. For my master recipe, I cut out the cumin and coriander and went with chili powder, granulated garlic, and dried oregano; the spice flavor was bright, clear, and potent. A second version was powered by dried dill and garlic. And finally, a third version boasted a fragrant, floral combination of fennel seeds, ground coriander, and lemon zest.

There were flavorful drippings in the bottom of the skillet with all three variations. To make use of them, I skimmed a little of the excess fat and then thickened the drippings with a simple slurry of water and cornstarch. A spritz of bright, refreshing lemon juice was the perfect finishing touch. This is roast chicken as it was meant to be: juicy, flavorful, and—best of all—easy.

SPICE-ROASTED CHICKEN WITH CHILI AND OREGANO *Serves 4*

We used a stainless-steel skillet when developing this recipe, but you can also use a 12-inch cast-iron skillet. If using table salt, reduce the amount to 1 teaspoon.

- 1 tablespoon chili powder
- 1 tablespoon dried oregano
- 2 teaspoons kosher salt
- 1 teaspoon granulated garlic
- 1 teaspoon pepper
- 1 (3½- to 4-pound) whole chicken, giblets discarded
- 2 tablespoons extra-virgin olive oil, divided
- 1 teaspoon cornstarch
- ½ cup water
- 2 teaspoons lemon juice

1. Adjust oven rack to middle position and heat oven to 400 degrees. Combine chili powder, oregano, salt, granulated garlic, and pepper in bowl. Pat chicken dry with paper towels. Transfer chicken, breast side down, to 12-inch oven-safe skillet and rub exposed side with 1 tablespoon oil. Sprinkle with half of spice mixture. Flip chicken breast side up and rub exposed side with remaining 1 tablespoon oil and sprinkle with remaining spice mixture.

2. Transfer skillet to oven and roast until breast registers 160 degrees and drumsticks/thighs register 175 degrees, about 1 hour. Transfer chicken to carving board and let rest for 20 minutes. Reserve drippings in skillet.

3. While chicken rests, dissolve cornstarch in water. Carefully skim as much fat as possible from drippings and discard. Add cornstarch mixture to drippings and place over medium-high heat, whisking to scrape up any browned bits. Cook until mixture is boiling and slightly thickened, about 2 minutes. Off heat, whisk in lemon juice. Carve chicken and serve, passing sauce separately.

SPICE-ROASTED CHICKEN WITH DILL AND GARLIC

Substitute 1 tablespoon dried dill weed for chili powder and oregano.

SPICE-ROASTED CHICKEN WITH FENNEL, CORIANDER, AND LEMON

Substitute 1 tablespoon fennel seeds, 1 tablespoon ground coriander, and 1 tablespoon lemon zest for chili powder and oregano.

The flavor and color of the spice mixture intensifies in the heat of the oven.

Finessing the Sauce

Use a spoon to remove the fat from the tasty drippings.

After adding the cornstarch slurry, whisk to deglaze the skillet.

Tuscan Tomato and Bread Soup

This hearty, thrifty soup delivers rich flavor. Fast.

by Alli Berkey

White bread thickens the soup and also adds gentle sweetness.

WHAT IMPRESSES ME most about Italian cuisine is how a dish based on something as humble as stale bread can still be unbelievably delicious. So it goes with *pappa al pomodoro*, the fantastic Tuscan bread and tomato soup perfumed with garlic and olive oil: A few key ingredients come together to make a bright, silky, ultraflavorful soup. I challenged myself to make a streamlined version from supermarket staples.

I tried several varieties of fresh tomatoes—globe, vine-ripened, plum, and even cherry—in a basic tomato soup, but peeling them was a pain and their quality was inconsistent; some were red, juicy, and ripe, while others were hard, pink, and virtually flavorless. Canned tomatoes would make my recipe easy and consistent throughout the year. My two finalists were canned whole peeled tomatoes and canned crushed tomatoes; I went with crushed to save myself the effort of crushing them by hand.

Next up was the bread. Did it really have to be Italian? I tested ciabatta, baguette, sourdough, sandwich bread, and supermarket Italian loaves. My tasters were emphatic in their belief that the bread should be only a supporting player, so anything too strong in flavor was out. Dense and crusty loaves didn't soften into the soup, so they were out, too. Soft, mild, and slightly sweet was the ideal bread profile here, and white sandwich bread fit the bill. Its sweetness nicely balanced out the acidity of the tomatoes, and the bread broke down quickly. Fresh or stale, white sandwich bread worked perfectly.

Working through the rest of the process was easy. I lightly browned some garlic in olive oil (with a pinch of red pepper flakes for kick) and then added a can of crushed tomatoes, the cubed sandwich bread, broth, and a sprig of fresh basil. I brought the soup to a simmer and cooked it for 15 minutes, at which point the bread was mostly broken down. A minute of brisk whisking helped the bread fully dissolve and incorporate, and a finishing dusting of Parmesan cheese, a splash of nice olive oil, and a light sprinkling of chopped basil brought the dish home.

TUSCAN TOMATO AND BREAD SOUP
Serves 4

Good-quality olive oil makes a difference here. Depending on the brand of sandwich bread that you buy, 4 ounces can range from two and a half to four slices. It's best to use weight as your guide; if you don't have a scale, defer to the volume measurement.

- ¼ cup extra-virgin olive oil, plus extra for serving
- 3 garlic cloves, sliced thin
- ¼ teaspoon red pepper flakes
- 1 (28-ounce) can crushed tomatoes
- 4 ounces hearty white sandwich bread, cut into ½-inch cubes (3 cups)
- 2 cups chicken broth
- 1 sprig fresh basil plus 2 tablespoons chopped
- ½ teaspoon table salt
- ¼ teaspoon pepper
  Grated Parmesan cheese

1. Combine oil, garlic, and pepper flakes in large saucepan and cook over medium heat until garlic is lightly browned, about 4 minutes.
2. Stir in tomatoes, bread, broth, basil sprig, salt, and pepper and bring to boil over high heat. Reduce heat to medium, cover, and simmer vigorously until bread has softened completely and soup has thickened slightly, about 15 minutes, stirring occasionally.
3. Off heat, discard basil sprig. Whisk soup until bread has fully broken down and soup has thickened further, about 1 minute. Sprinkle with Parmesan and chopped basil, drizzle with extra oil, and serve.

Which Size Dutch Oven Is Best for You?
by Riddley Gemperlein-Schirm

EQUIPMENT REVIEW

A LARGE ENAMELLED cast-iron Dutch oven with a capacity of at least 7 quarts is good for nearly any task, from deep frying to baking bread. However, these pots take up a lot of cabinet space and can weigh more than 16 pounds. Our two highest-rated pots, from Le Creuset and Cuisinart, are each available in two smaller sizes, and we wondered if these lighter pots would perform just as well as the full-size pots. To find out, we used each to cook rice, brown meatballs, fry french fries, and braise short ribs. In the medium pots, we also baked bread,

and in the small pots, we also made pear crisp and a half batch of bread.

While we still prefer the large Dutch ovens, especially for deep frying, we think that the medium-size pots are great options if you rarely cook for a crowd and don't do much frying. The small Dutch ovens were more limited in their uses—they're too small for braises and deep frying—but they were the perfect size for cooking grains, making recipes that serve just two people, and reheating leftovers. They function much like a 3-quart saucepan. Plus, both models weighed about 8 pounds. For relatively lighter pots for smaller cooking tasks, we can recommend all four.

Cuisinart Chef's Classic Enameled Cast Iron Round Covered Casseroles

3 qt $67 7.7 lb   5 qt $80 12.4 lb   7 qt $76 16.7 lb

SMALL
Good for grains, reheating soup and leftovers

MEDIUM
Good for bread, smaller braises, soups, stews

LARGE
Good for braising, deep frying, bread, soups, stews, double batches

3.5 qt $240 8.2 lb   5.5 qt $340 11.2 lb   7.25 qt $370 13.7 lb

Le Creuset Round Dutch Ovens

The medium and small sizes of our top two Dutch ovens, from Le Creuset and Cuisinart, performed just as well as their full-size versions but had more limited uses.

Southern-Style Collard Greens

Celebrate the New Year in style with collard greens and plenty of (pot) liquor.

by Morgan Bolling

SOUTHERN TRADITION SAYS eating collard greens on January 1st will bring good luck and prosperity in the New Year. While I can't prove this is true, why risk it?

Slowly braised collard greens are an emblematic Southern recipe; the greens are braised with a salty smoked pork product until they turn silky and ultratender. Over this long cooking time, the pork and greens intermingle and transform the cooking water into a supersavory pot liquor (or "pot likker") to sip on the side. Some consider the pot liquor the best part of the dish.

I started my testing by making half a dozen recipes for collard greens from respected Southern chefs. I learned that as long as I trimmed the thick woody stems from the leaves, there was no need to separate the collard leaves from the ribs, which became tender over the long simmering time. The amount of water I started with was critical: too much and the pot liquor was bland, but too little and there wasn't enough left at the end of cooking.

For my working recipe, I started by cutting 2 pounds of collard greens, enough to serve a crowd of six to eight, into roughly bite-size pieces. I added the collards to a Dutch oven with 6 cups of water, two smoked ham hocks, 2 teaspoons of sugar to take the edge off the collard greens' bitterness, and a good pinch of red pepper flakes. I covered the pot and simmered the collard greens until they were soft and the hocks were fully tender, about 1½ hours.

I loved these greens simmered with smoky ham hocks, but due diligence dictated testing hocks against bacon, salt pork, and ham steaks. While the greens themselves tasted great in all the batches, we preferred the more robust body of the pot liquor made from the batch with the hocks. Once the hocks were braised until tender (and cooled), it was easy to pull the savory little chunks of meat off them to add back to the greens. A sautéed onion and some smashed garlic added background savory flavor. One final move made the recipe foolproof: Switching from the stovetop to the oven for the long simmer meant that I didn't have to watch the pot as closely.

Another Southern New Year's Day tradition is to eat pan-fried cornbread, which symbolizes gold. So I stirred together a batter for some quick cornmeal cakes. I cooked these in bacon fat to serve alongside, or crumbled into, the pot liquor. It doesn't matter if my bank account grows in the New Year—with these collard greens I'm rich with good eating.

SOUTHERN-STYLE COLLARD GREENS
Serves 6 to 8

If you can't find ham hocks, you can substitute 6 slices of bacon and 3 ounces of ham steak cut into ½-inch pieces. Be sure to remove the rind from the ham before cutting it into pieces. Add the bacon and ham in place of the ham hocks in step 2, but discard the bacon before serving. Do not drain off the cooking liquid before serving. This flavorful, savory pot liquor should be sipped while eating the collards. Any leftover pot liquor can be used as a soup base. Serve with Cornmeal Cakes (recipe follows), if desired.

- 2 pounds collard greens
- 2 tablespoons unsalted butter
- 1 onion, chopped
- 6 cups water
- 2 (12-ounce) smoked ham hocks
- 3 garlic cloves, smashed and peeled
- 2¼ teaspoons table salt
- 2 teaspoons sugar
- ⅛ teaspoon red pepper flakes
  Hot sauce

1. Adjust oven rack to lower-middle position and heat oven to 300 degrees. Trim collard stems to base of leaves; discard trimmings. Cut leaves into roughly 2-inch pieces. Place collard greens in large bowl and cover with water. Swish with your hand to remove grit. Repeat with fresh water, as needed, until grit no longer appears in bottom of bowl. Remove collard greens from water and set aside (you needn't dry them).

2. Melt butter in large Dutch oven over medium heat. Add onion and cook until lightly browned, 6 to 8 minutes. Add water, ham hocks, garlic, salt, sugar, and pepper flakes and bring to boil over high heat. Add collard greens (pot may be full) and stir until collard greens wilt slightly, about 1 minute. Cover, transfer to oven, and cook until collard greens are very tender, about 1½ hours.

3. Transfer ham hocks to cutting board and let cool for 10 minutes. Remove meat from ham hocks, chop, and return to pot; discard skin and bones. Season collard greens with salt to taste. Serve with hot sauce.

CORNMEAL CAKES
Serves 6 to 8 (Makes 12 cornmeal cakes)

We prefer the flavor bacon fat adds to these cornmeal cakes, but you can substitute vegetable oil for the bacon fat, if desired. The batter will thicken slightly after sitting in step 1.

- 1½ cups (7½ ounces) cornmeal
- ½ cup (2½ ounces) all-purpose flour
- 2¼ teaspoons baking powder
- 1 teaspoon table salt
- 1½ cups whole milk
- 3 tablespoons bacon fat, divided

1. Set wire rack in rimmed baking sheet. Whisk cornmeal, flour, baking powder, and salt together in large bowl. Whisk in milk until no lumps remain. Let sit for 5 minutes.

2. Heat 1 tablespoon bacon fat in 12-inch nonstick skillet over medium-high heat until shimmering. Using ¼-cup dry measuring cup, portion 4 evenly spaced scant ¼-cup scoops of batter in skillet.

3. Cook until edges of cakes are set and first side is deep golden brown, about 1½ minutes. Flip and continue to cook until second side is golden brown, about 1 minute longer. Transfer cornmeal cakes to prepared rack. Repeat with remaining bacon fat and batter in 2 batches. Serve.

Rich, smoky, silky greens and lightly sweet cornmeal cakes make a perfect pair.

Breaking Bread in Brooklyn

Text by Bryan Roof; photos by Steve Klise

The Coney Island boardwalk, above, attracts crowds in every season for its fresh air, amusements, and nearby food. The area has a high concentration of Russian and eastern European immigrants, including Gocha Lomidze, (left). Lomidze demonstrates his take on *adjaruli khachapuri* at Toné Cafe.

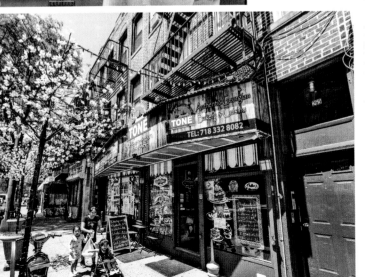

GROWING UP, I spent summers in Coney Island, a beachfront neighborhood in Brooklyn, New York. My grandparents had a comfortable two-bedroom apartment in a high-rise next to the subway and across from the fire department on West Eighth Street, close enough to the shore to smell the salt air. On the weekends, the Q, F, and D trains deposited beachgoers, aquarium visitors, and amusement park junkies at the foot of their building. My brother and I would sit on their 10th-floor terrace and watch the Cyclone, a rickety wooden roller coaster, "click-click" up the ascent and then descend in a great racket. The roar of that coaster and the screams of its riders were the soundtrack to those summers.

As we got older, my mother would take us on boardwalk expeditions. We would start in Coney Island and walk the mile or so down to Brighton Beach. We'd stop to watch guys get into heated matches at the handball courts, listen to the honk of the walrus carrying from the aquarium, and just take in some of the best people watching to be found anywhere. When we reached the end of the boardwalk, we'd walk back home through the streets and neighborhoods, smelling the smells, browsing the buffet selections, and stopping for lunch at any number of eastern European groceries, restaurants, and bakeries.

These days, I tend to hurry off the boardwalk and head straight to the restaurants. I might stop at Toné Cafe for the *adjaruli khachapuri*, the chewy Georgian bread filled with cheese and a cracked egg; or hit up Georgian House for *shkmeruli*, a garlicky dish of chicken cooked in milk; or dine on grilled lamb shashlik (kebabs) at Cafe Kashkar. Just like when I was young, days spent walking and eating and taking in the sights in that densely populated corner of Brooklyn are still my best days.

Adjaruli Khachapuri

Crusty bread filled with gooey cheese?
Sounds like a party to us. **by Jessica Rudolph**

ADJARULI KHACHAPURI, ORIGINALLY from the country of Georgia in the Caucasus region of Asia, is more common stateside than ever. It's showing up on restaurant tables, on social media, and on trend lists. It's not hard to see why: Khachapuri—essentially bread filled with melty cheese—is like a cross between deep-dish pizza and cheese fondue. And then some.

There are several distinct styles; the shape I chose to work with is similar to a flattened football. When filled with a pool of molten cheese and topped with an egg and butter, which are stirred in before serving, the result is like a cheesy bread bowl. Diners tear off chunks of the crusty bread to dunk into the gooey cheese inside—perfect party food for a group of good friends.

I started with a simple pizza dough, knowing that it would be easy to shape, provide structure to contain the oozy cheese, and have a satisfyingly chewy texture and mild flavor. I whipped together a batch in the food processor and let it rise for a couple of hours. I then shaped it by rolling it first into a circle, nudging the edges into a football shape, and pinching the ends closed.

Georgian cheeses such as *sulguni* and *imeruli*—both semisoft, mozzarella-like cheeses—are most traditional, providing a sharp flavor and epic meltness. I wanted to replicate their flavor and texture with supermarket cheeses. I found that a mixture of mozzarella and feta approximated the briny, salty tang and stringy texture found in the Georgian cheeses. I piled equal parts of my two cheeses high in my dough boat, popped it in the oven, and watched as the dough puffed and browned while the cheeses bubbled.

As soon as the bread was out of the oven, I added a raw egg yolk (the white gave it a sulfurous flavor) and a pat of butter to the filling. Both additions are standard and necessary: The lecithin in the egg yolk emulsifies any broken cheese to make a cohesive filling, and the butter provides richness. I stirred everything together with a fork until the cheese was smooth and stretchy. The only task remaining was persuading my tasters to let it cool slightly before diving in—I failed every time.

Go to CooksCountry.com/brooklyn to see more photos from our trip to Coney Island, New York.

ADJARULI KHACHAPURI
Serves 6

Using cold water to make the dough keeps it from overheating in the food processor. Use block mozzarella, not fresh, here.

- 1¾ cups (8¾ ounces) all-purpose flour
- 1½ teaspoons sugar
- 1 teaspoon instant or rapid-rise yeast
- ¾ teaspoon table salt
- ½ cup plus 2 tablespoons cold water
- 1 tablespoon extra-virgin olive oil
- 6 ounces whole-milk mozzarella cheese, shredded (1½ cups)
- 6 ounces feta cheese, crumbled (1½ cups)
- 1 large egg yolk
- 1 tablespoon unsalted butter

1. Process flour, sugar, yeast, and salt in food processor until combined, about 3 seconds. With processor running, slowly add cold water and oil and process until dough forms sticky ball that clears sides of bowl, 30 to 60 seconds.

2. Transfer dough to counter and knead until smooth, about 1 minute. Shape dough into tight ball and place in greased bowl. Cover bowl with plastic wrap and let dough rise at room temperature until almost doubled in size, 2 to 2½ hours. (Alternatively, dough can rise in refrigerator until doubled in size, about 24 hours. Let come to room temperature, about 2 hours, before proceeding.)

3. Turn out dough onto lightly floured 16 by 12-inch sheet of parchment paper and coat lightly with flour. Flatten into 8-inch disk using your hands. Using rolling pin, roll dough into 12-inch circle, dusting dough lightly with flour as needed.

4. Roll bottom edge of dough 2½ inches in toward center. Rotate parchment 180 degrees and roll bottom edge of dough (directly opposite first rolled side) 2½ inches toward center. (Opposing edges of rolled sides should be 7 inches apart.)

5. Roll ends of rolled sides toward centerline and pinch firmly together to form football shape about 12 inches long and about 7 inches across at its widest point. Transfer parchment with dough to rimmed baking sheet. Cover loosely with plastic and let rise until puffy, 30 minutes to 1 hour. Adjust oven rack to middle position and heat oven to 450 degrees.

Stages of beauty and bliss: stirring the butter and egg yolk into the molten cheese (top), which is a bit chunky at first; picture-perfect gooey cheese pull (middle); and dipping torn crust into the melted filling (right).

6. Combine mozzarella and feta in bowl. Fill dough with cheese mixture, lightly compacting and mounding in center (cheese will be piled higher than edge of dough). Bake until crust is well browned and cheese is bubbly and beginning to brown in spots, 15 to 17 minutes. Transfer sheet to wire rack. Add egg yolk and butter to cheese filling and stir with fork until fully incorporated and cheese is smooth and stretchy. Lift parchment off sheet and slide bread onto serving dish. Serve immediately.

Rudy Lieu seasons his egg foo yong with a mix of spices that he keeps secret, but fans know when it's right.

St. Paul Sandwich

ON THE ROAD

This crispy egg foo yong sandwich—actually a St. Louis specialty—tastes great in any city.

Text by Bryan Roof; photos by Steve Klise

RUDY LIEU FIRST ate egg foo yong at the age of 15 on a visit to his uncle's Chinese restaurant in St. Louis. It was a new concept for a kid from Los Angeles: a deep-fried omelet filled with bean sprouts, onions, and meat smothered in a savory brown gravy. He hurried home to share this new dish with his friends and family. "People just thought I was crazy," says Rudy. "They asked, 'Why are you frying an omelet?'"

On the same fateful trip, Rudy tried St. Louis's famous St. Paul sandwich: an egg foo yong patty nestled between two slices of white bread with iceberg lettuce, tomatoes, pickles, and mayonnaise. "When you have it for the first time, it's like, Whoa! This is interesting."

In the early 1980s, Rudy's uncle, Anthony Lieu, worked for a man named Stephen Yuen at his restaurant Park Chop Suey. Rudy refers to Yuen as a "pioneer" of the Chinese restaurant

scene at that time. Yuen had moved to St. Louis from St. Paul, Minnesota, a city he loved, so he invented the St. Paul sandwich as an homage. It became well-known in St. Louis but remained virtually unheard of in St. Paul. "It started selling like hotcakes. Everyone [in St. Louis] started making St. Paul sandwiches," says Rudy.

Today, Rudy invites me into the kitchen at Fortune Express to watch him make a St. Paul sandwich. He stirs mung bean sprouts and onion together with eggs, chopping the sprouts into smaller pieces as he goes. Next come slivers of chicken (or ham or shrimp)

followed by a few tablespoons of hot oil, which he says "loosens up" the mixture. He cranks the heat beneath an oil-filled wok and then carefully adds a ladle of the egg mixture. Once it's deeply browned, he lifts the egg foo yong from the oil and presses it hard between his utensils to shape it and force out the excess oil. He builds the sandwich on white bread, layering on lettuce, tomato, pickles, mayonnaise, and a sprinkle of a homemade spice mixture. All he'll tell me is that there's garlic powder and "other stuff" in it. He smiles and says, "In St. Louis, nobody doesn't know what a St. Paul sandwich is."

ST. PAUL SANDWICH *Serves 4*
Be sure to pat the ham steak dry with paper towels before adding it to the skillet in step 1; this will keep it from splattering as it cooks.

- 4 large eggs
- ½ teaspoon table salt
- ½ teaspoon white pepper
- ½ teaspoon granulated garlic
- 2 ounces (1 cup) mung bean sprouts, coarsely chopped
- 1 cup chopped onion
- 5 ounces ham steak, patted dry and cut into ½-inch pieces
- ½ cup vegetable oil for frying
- 4 tablespoons mayonnaise
- 8 slices hearty white sandwich bread
- 2 cups shredded iceberg lettuce
- 8 thin tomato slices
- 16 dill pickle chips

1. Beat eggs, salt, white pepper, and granulated garlic together in medium bowl. Stir in bean sprouts, onion, and ham until thoroughly combined.
2. Heat oil in 12-inch nonstick skillet over medium heat until just smoking. Using ½-cup dry measuring cup, portion 4 evenly spaced scoops of egg mixture in skillet. (Eggs may run together; this is OK.) Cover and cook, without stirring, until bottoms of egg foo yong patties are browned and tops are set, about 5 minutes.
3. Using spatula, cut and separate egg foo yong patties in skillet. Flip each patty and continue to cook, covered, until browned on second side, about 3 minutes longer. Transfer egg foo yong patties to paper towel–lined plate and let drain for 1 minute.
4. Spread mayonnaise on 1 side of each piece of bread. Top each of 4 slices of bread with ½ cup lettuce, 1 egg foo yong patty, 2 tomato slices, 4 pickles, and 1 slice of bread. Serve.

To see more photos from our trip to Missouri, go to **CooksCountry.com/saintlouis.**

Spicy Corn and Tomato Soup

30-MINUTE SUPPER

Filets Mignons with Sage-Buttered Mushrooms and Black Pepper Polenta

30-MINUTE SUPPER

Pan-Seared Chicken Breasts with Artichokes and Spinach

30-MINUTE SUPPER

Chorizo and Bell Pepper Tacos with Salsa Verde

30-MINUTE SUPPER

Filets Mignons with Sage-Buttered Mushrooms and Black Pepper Polenta
Serves 4
You can substitute white mushrooms for the cremini, if you like.

- 3 **cups water**
- 2 **teaspoons pepper, divided**
- ¾ **cup instant polenta**
- 2 **ounces Parmesan cheese, grated (1 cup)**
- 6 **tablespoons unsalted butter, divided**
- 1¼ **teaspoons table salt, divided**
- 4 **(6- to 8-ounce) center-cut filets mignons**
- 1 **pound cremini mushrooms, trimmed and sliced thin**
- 1 **tablespoon minced fresh sage**
- 2 **garlic cloves, minced**

1. Bring water and 1½ teaspoons pepper to boil in large saucepan over high heat. Whisk in polenta, reduce heat to medium-low, and cook until thickened, about 3 minutes. Off heat, stir in Parmesan, 2 tablespoons butter, and ½ teaspoon salt. Cover to keep warm.
2. Meanwhile, pat steaks dry with paper towels and sprinkle with ½ teaspoon salt and remaining ½ teaspoon pepper. Melt 1 tablespoon butter in 12-inch nonstick skillet over medium-high heat. Add steaks and cook, flipping every 2 minutes, until meat registers 125 degrees (for medium-rare), 10 to 12 minutes. Transfer to plate and tent with aluminum foil.
3. Melt 2 tablespoons butter in now-empty skillet. Add mushrooms and remaining ¼ teaspoon salt and cook until mushrooms are well browned, about 6 minutes. Off heat, stir in sage, garlic, and remaining 1 tablespoon butter until mushrooms are well coated. Serve steaks with polenta and mushrooms.

Spicy Corn and Tomato Soup
Serves 4
Serve this soup with thinly sliced radishes and diced avocado.

- 1 **(28-ounce) can whole peeled tomatoes**
- 2 **tablespoons unsalted butter**
- 1 **onion, chopped fine**
- 2 **garlic cloves, minced**
- 1½ **teaspoons ground cumin**
- 1 **teaspoon table salt, divided**
- ½ **teaspoon pepper**
- 4 **cups vegetable broth**
- 2½ **cups frozen corn**
- 2 **teaspoons minced canned chipotle chile in adobo sauce**
- 2 **ounces cotija cheese, crumbled (½ cup)**

1. Drain tomatoes in fine-mesh strainer set over bowl; reserve juice. Chop tomatoes coarse. Melt butter in Dutch oven over medium heat. Add onion, garlic, cumin, ½ teaspoon salt, and pepper and cook until onion is soft, about 4 minutes.
2. Increase heat to medium-high. Stir in broth, corn, chipotle, tomatoes and reserved juice, and remaining ½ teaspoon salt and bring to boil, scraping up any browned bits. Reduce heat to medium-low, cover, and simmer until flavors have melded, about 20 minutes.
3. Season with salt and pepper to taste. Serve, sprinkled with cotija.

Chorizo and Bell Pepper Tacos with Salsa Verde *Serves 4*
Use fresh Mexican chorizo here, not the dry-cured Spanish version. We like to serve these tacos with thinly sliced onions.

- ¼ **cup sour cream**
- 1 **tablespoon water**
- 1 **tablespoon lime juice, plus lime wedges for serving**
- ½ **teaspoon table salt, divided**
- 1 **pound Mexican-style chorizo sausage, casings removed**
- 1 **red bell pepper, stemmed, seeded, and sliced thin**
- 1 **teaspoon ground cumin**
- ⅛ **teaspoon pepper**
- ½ **cup jarred green salsa, plus extra for serving**
- 8 **(6-inch) corn tortillas, warmed**
- ½ **cup fresh cilantro leaves**

1. Combine sour cream, water, lime juice, and ¼ teaspoon salt in bowl; set aside.
2. Cook chorizo in 12-inch nonstick skillet over medium-high heat, breaking up meat with wooden spoon, until no longer pink, about 4 minutes. Stir in bell pepper, cumin, pepper, and remaining ¼ teaspoon salt. Continue to cook until bell pepper is just softened and meat is cooked through, about 4 minutes longer. Stir in salsa and cook until heated through, about 1 minute.
3. Divide filling among tortillas. Top with sour cream mixture, cilantro, and extra salsa. Serve with lime wedges.

Pan-Seared Chicken Breasts with Artichokes and Spinach *Serves 4*
If you can't find crème fraîche, you can substitute sour cream.

- 4 **(6- to 8-ounce) boneless, skinless chicken breasts, trimmed**
- 2 **teaspoons minced fresh thyme**
- 1 **teaspoon table salt, divided**
- ¾ **teaspoon pepper, divided**
- 3 **tablespoons unsalted butter, divided**
- 2 **cups jarred baby artichoke hearts packed in water, patted dry**
- 3 **garlic cloves, sliced thin**
- ¼ **cup white wine**
- 1 **tablespoon grated lemon zest**
- 10 **ounces (10 cups) baby spinach**
- ½ **cup crème fraîche**

1. Pat chicken dry with paper towels and sprinkle with thyme, ½ teaspoon salt, and ½ teaspoon pepper. Melt 2 tablespoons butter in 12-inch nonstick skillet over medium-high heat. Cook until chicken is golden brown and registers 160 degrees, about 6 minutes per side. Transfer chicken to plate and tent with aluminum foil.
2. Melt remaining 1 tablespoon butter in now-empty skillet over medium-high heat. Add artichokes and garlic and cook until lightly browned, about 2 minutes. Stir in wine and lemon zest and cook until fragrant, about 30 seconds. Stir in spinach, 1 handful at a time, until wilted, about 3 minutes.
3. Stir in crème fraîche, remaining ½ teaspoon salt, and remaining ¼ teaspoon pepper and cook until sauce is slightly thickened and vegetables are well coated with sauce, about 1 minute. Serve chicken with vegetables.

Sirloin Steak with Arugula-Couscous Salad

30-MINUTE SUPPER

Poached Halibut with Leek Compote and Red Potatoes

30-MINUTE SUPPER

Roasted Chicken Thighs with Harissa and Cannellini Beans

30-MINUTE SUPPER

Honey-Mustard Pork Tenderloin with Buttered Egg Noodles

30-MINUTE SUPPER

Poached Halibut with Leek Compote and Red Potatoes *Serves 4*

Leeks can be sandy, so be sure to wash them thoroughly after slicing.

1½   pounds Red Bliss potatoes, unpeeled, halved
2   tablespoons unsalted butter, melted, plus 3 tablespoons unsalted butter
1¼   teaspoons table salt, divided
3   tablespoons chopped fresh parsley, divided
2   teaspoons grated lemon zest plus 2 teaspoons juice
4   (6-ounce) skinless halibut fillets, 1 inch thick
¼   teaspoon cayenne pepper, plus extra for seasoning
2   pounds leeks, white and light green parts only, halved lengthwise, sliced thin, and washed thoroughly (4½ cups)
2   garlic cloves, minced
¼   cup white wine
1   cup chicken broth

1. Adjust oven rack to lowest position and heat oven to 425 degrees. Toss potatoes, melted butter, and ½ teaspoon salt together in bowl. Place potatoes on rimmed baking sheet, cut side down. Roast until potatoes are tender, about 25 minutes.

2. While potatoes roast, combine 1 tablespoon parsley and lemon zest in bowl; set aside. Sprinkle halibut with cayenne and ½ teaspoon salt. Melt remaining 3 tablespoons butter in 12-inch skillet over medium-high heat. Add leeks, garlic, and remaining ¼ teaspoon salt and cook until leeks have wilted, about 5 minutes. Add wine and cook until nearly evaporated, about 1 minute. Add broth and bring to simmer.

3. Reduce heat to medium-low. Place halibut on top of leek mixture and cook, covered, until fish registers 140 degrees, 13 to 15 minutes. Using spatula, transfer halibut to large plate and tent with aluminum foil. Stir lemon juice and remaining 2 tablespoons parsley into leek mixture. Season with salt and extra cayenne to taste. Sprinkle halibut with lemon zest mixture and serve with potatoes and leek compote.

Honey-Mustard Pork Tenderloin with Buttered Egg Noodles *Serves 4*

We like to serve this dish with a side salad.

¼   cup whole-grain mustard
2   tablespoons honey
1   teaspoon grated lemon zest, plus 1 tablespoon juice, divided
2   (14- to 16-ounce) pork tenderloins, trimmed
1½   teaspoons table salt, plus salt for cooking pasta
½   teaspoon pepper
3   tablespoons unsalted butter, divided
12   ounces (6 cups) egg noodles
½   cup chicken broth
1   shallot, minced
2   tablespoons chopped fresh dill

1. Adjust oven rack to middle position and heat oven to 375 degrees. Combine mustard, honey, and 1 teaspoon lemon juice in bowl; set aside. Pat pork dry with paper towels and sprinkle with salt and pepper. Melt 1 tablespoon butter in 12-inch skillet over medium-high heat. Cook pork until browned on all sides, 5 to 7 minutes. Off heat, brush mustard mixture evenly over top of pork. Transfer skillet to oven and roast until meat registers 135 degrees, 10 to 14 minutes. Transfer pork to carving board, tent with aluminum foil, and let rest for 5 minutes. Do not wash skillet.

2. Meanwhile, bring 4 quarts water to boil in large pot. Add noodles and 1 tablespoon salt and cook, stirring occasionally, until al dente. Drain noodles and return them to pot.

3. Add broth and shallot to now-empty skillet. Bring to simmer over medium heat and cook until slightly thickened, about 2 minutes, scraping up any browned bits. Off heat, stir in dill, lemon zest, remaining 2 tablespoons butter, and remaining 2 teaspoons lemon juice. Add sauce to noodles and toss to coat. Slice pork ½ inch thick and serve over noodles.

Sirloin Steak with Arugula-Couscous Salad
Serves 4

Flap meat is often sold as sirloin steak tips. Toasted slivered almonds can be substituted for the pine nuts, if desired.

½   cup water
5   tablespoons extra-virgin olive oil, divided
1½   teaspoons table salt, divided
½   cup couscous
1½   teaspoons orange zest, divided, plus 1 large orange, quartered and sliced
1½   pounds flap meat, cut with grain into 3 equal pieces, trimmed
¾   teaspoon pepper, divided
2   tablespoons lemon juice
5   ounces (5 cups) baby arugula
2   ounces Parmesan cheese, shaved with vegetable peeler
¼   cup pine nuts, toasted

1. Bring water, 1 tablespoon oil, and ½ teaspoon salt to boil in small saucepan over high heat. Remove from heat, stir in couscous, cover, and let sit for 5 minutes. Add 1 teaspoon orange zest and fluff with fork. Set aside and let cool uncovered.

2. Sprinkle beef with ½ teaspoon salt and ½ teaspoon pepper. Heat 1 tablespoon oil in 12-inch nonstick skillet over medium-high heat until just smoking. Add beef and cook until browned on all sides and meat registers 125 degrees (for medium-rare), 8 to 10 minutes. Transfer beef to carving board and tent with aluminum foil.

3. Whisk lemon juice, remaining 3 tablespoons oil, remaining ½ teaspoon orange zest, remaining ½ teaspoon salt, and remaining ¼ teaspoon pepper together in large bowl. Add arugula, Parmesan, pine nuts, couscous, and orange slices and toss to combine. Slice steak thin against grain. Serve steak with salad.

Roasted Chicken Thighs with Harissa and Cannellini Beans *Serves 4*

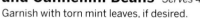

Garnish with torn mint leaves, if desired.

8   (5- to 7-ounce) bone-in chicken thighs, trimmed
1¼   teaspoons table salt, divided
1   tablespoon extra-virgin olive oil
1   tablespoon harissa
1   onion, chopped fine
4   garlic cloves, sliced thin
2   (15-ounce) cans cannellini beans, rinsed
1   cup chicken broth
1   cup jarred roasted red peppers, rinsed, patted dry, and chopped coarse
½   cup pitted green olives, chopped coarse

1. Adjust oven rack to middle position and heat oven to 400 degrees. Pat chicken dry with paper towels and sprinkle with 1 teaspoon salt. Heat oil in 12-inch nonstick skillet over medium-high heat until just smoking. Add chicken, skin side down, and cook until well browned, about 7 minutes. Transfer chicken, skin side up, to wire rack set in rimmed baking sheet (leave fat in skillet). Brush harissa evenly over chicken skin and roast until chicken registers 175 degrees, about 15 minutes.

2. While chicken roasts, pour off all but 1 tablespoon fat from now-empty skillet. Add onion and garlic to skillet and cook over medium-high heat until onion has softened, about 4 minutes. Add beans, broth, red peppers, olives, and remaining ¼ teaspoon salt and bring to simmer. Cook until liquid has reduced slightly and flavors have melded, about 8 minutes. Serve chicken with beans.

Browning

There's some truth to the old saying "we eat with our eyes first"—most browned food looks better than pale food, but it tastes better, too. Here's what you need to know about how and why to brown foods.

by Scott Kathan

Light Golden Brown Chicken Thigh

Golden Brown Chicken Thigh

Dark Golden Brown Chicken Thigh

Maillard Reaction

The Maillard reaction occurs when sugars and the amino acids that make up proteins are heated and undergo a series of chemical transformations that result in browning and the creation of many different flavor molecules. The Maillard reaction usually happens in conjunction with caramelization; in most scenarios, the Maillard reaction happens before caramelization kicks in at slightly higher temperatures.

This reaction was named for Louis Camille Maillard, the French chemist and physician who first documented it.

EXAMPLES:
Bread crusts, roasted coffee beans, seared meats

Caramelization

Caramelization happens when sugar (whether added or naturally occurring in the food) is heated to the point where its molecules break apart and generate hundreds of new flavor, color, and aroma compounds that add depth and roundness.

EXAMPLES:
Caramel, crème brûlée, browned onions

Four Keys to Deeper Browning

HIGH HEAT
Turn the burner up to 10, position your oven rack close to the broiler and set the broiler to high, or pile those briquettes into a mound.

ADD FAT
Butter, oil, beaten egg, and meat's natural fat all accelerate browning.

DRY THE FOOD
For the best browning, dry your steaks—whether they are beef, tofu, or cauliflower—by patting them with paper towels before cooking.

ADD SUGAR
That could mean barbecue sauce, hoisin sauce, honey in the glaze, brown sugar in the spice rub, or apple juice in the marinade. Any form of sugar aids in browning.

MYTH BUSTING

MYTH
You can't achieve deep browning on a gas grill.

REALITY
It all depends on the grill and weather conditions, but with proper preheating and a little brush of oil on the food, most gas grills will brown foods just fine. If your grill struggles with browning, double down on patting foods dry before grilling and consider adding a sugary element.

MYTH
You shouldn't sear foods in olive oil.

REALITY
While it's true that extra-virgin olive oil will lose some flavor nuance when heated to high temperatures, it typically doesn't taste bad when this happens. Extra-virgin olive oil is fine for most cooking, but it's more expensive than neutral oils such as canola, vegetable, and peanut.

MYTH
Nonstick pans aren't good for searing food.

REALITY
This can be true because not all cooks are comfortable preheating their nonstick skillets over high heat (remember to add some oil). But in terms of browning, you can sometimes get more of it in nonstick pans since less of the browned matter sticks to the pan—leaving more of it on the food.

MYTH
Searing meat creates a crust that retains moisture.

REALITY
This is simply not true—you can still cook the moisture out of well-seared and crusted meats. That's why it's always best to use a digital instant-read thermometer to protect against overcooking.

Browning in the Oven

Whether you're baking snickerdoodles or roasting a chicken, there is one oven variable (aside from temperature) that greatly affects browning: oven rack position. If you want the bottom of your food to brown (as with, say, the cauliflower florets shown at left), position the rack closer to the bottom of the oven, where the heating element is; if you want the top of the food to brown, position the rack closer to the top of the oven, since the heat rises to the top and reflects off the oven ceiling.

Extra-Crunchy Onion Rings

To make 'em nice, bread 'em twice. **by Matthew Fairman**

SWEET, TENDER ONIONS encased in a beautifully browned, crunchy coating—why would you ever choose fries when onion rings are in play? But onion rings can be a challenge to make at home—the recipes I tried used a ridiculous number of dishes and called for jumping through a lot of hoops, all for mediocre (or worse) results.

The most promising recipe called for dipping sliced onions into tangy buttermilk and then dredging them in seasoned flour; the resulting rings had a coating reminiscent of great fried chicken. But I had to bread them twice (dunk in buttermilk, dredge in flour, re-dunk, and re-dredge) before frying in a single layer in a Dutch oven, which meant frying almost 10 batches! Double-breading was clearly the key to great rings, but I was determined to find an easier way to do it. I sliced a mountain of onions, wiped away the tears, and got cooking.

Two things I discovered early in my testing were that adding both cornstarch and a little baking powder to the flour gave the fried rings extra lightness and crunch. And for the frying, I found that with the right amount of oil (3 quarts), I could fry 2 pounds of sliced onions in just three batches. But what about simplifying the breading process?

A colleague gave me a great idea: He wondered if I could use the "shake and bake" paper bag method, which is how some people bread chicken pieces for frying. Eager to try it out, I grabbed a large mixing bowl and poured in a quart of buttermilk, and then doubled up two large paper grocery bags to make sure there was no risk of a bag blowout. I dumped in my flour mix, gave my rings a quick dip in the buttermilk, plopped them all into the bag, and gave the whole thing a vigorous shake. I returned the rings to the buttermilk and then to the bag again to build a thick coating. These rings fried up incredibly crunchy. They're great plain, but they're even better dipped in a flavorful stir-together horseradish sauce.

ULTIMATE EXTRA-CRUNCHY ONION RINGS *Serves 6 to 8*

Look for large onions (about 1 pound each) for this recipe. Be sure to use a double-bagged large paper shopping bag in step 2. Note that the onions are double-breaded, so don't discard the flour bag after the first shake. Buy refrigerated prepared horseradish, not the shelf-stable kind, which contains preservatives and additives.

SAUCE

- ½ cup mayonnaise
- 2 tablespoons prepared horseradish
- 2 tablespoons Dijon mustard
- ¼ teaspoon cayenne pepper
- ¼ teaspoon pepper

ONION RINGS

- 4 cups buttermilk
- 4 cups all-purpose flour
- ½ cup cornstarch
- 2 tablespoons Lawry's Seasoned Salt
- 2 tablespoons baking powder
- 2 teaspoons pepper
- ½ teaspoon table salt
- 2 large onions (1 pound each), peeled
- 3 quarts peanut or vegetable oil for frying

1. FOR THE SAUCE: Whisk all ingredients together in bowl; set aside.

2. FOR THE ONION RINGS: Adjust oven rack to middle position and heat oven to 200 degrees. Add buttermilk to large bowl. Combine flour, cornstarch, seasoned salt, baking powder, pepper, and salt in second large bowl. Transfer flour mixture to double-bagged large paper shopping bag. Slice onions crosswise into ½-inch-thick rounds. Reserve onion slices smaller than 2 inches in diameter for another use.

3. Separate remaining onion rounds into rings. Toss one-third of onion rings in buttermilk to thoroughly coat. Shake off excess buttermilk and transfer onion rings to flour mixture in bag. Repeat with remaining onion rings in 2 batches. Roll top of bag to seal and shake vigorously to coat onion rings in flour mixture. Remove onion rings from bag, shaking off excess flour mixture, and transfer to rimmed baking sheet.

4. Transfer one-third of onion rings back to buttermilk and toss to thoroughly coat. Shake off excess buttermilk and transfer onion rings back to flour mixture in bag. Repeat with remaining onion rings in 2 batches. Roll top of bag to seal and shake vigorously to coat onion rings in flour mixture. Pour contents of bag onto sheet. Separate any onion rings that stick together.

5. Line second rimmed baking sheet with triple layer of paper towels. Add oil to large Dutch oven until it measures about 2 inches deep and heat over medium-high heat to 375 degrees.

6. Add one-third of onion rings to hot oil and fry, without stirring, until breading is just set, 30 to 60 seconds. Stir gently with tongs or spider skimmer and continue to fry until dark golden brown, 3 to 5 minutes longer, flipping onion rings occasionally and separating any that stick together. Adjust burner, if necessary, to maintain oil temperature between 325 and 375 degrees. Transfer fried onion rings to paper towel-lined sheet and place in oven to keep warm.

7. Return oil to 375 degrees and repeat with remaining onion rings in 2 batches. Serve onion rings with sauce.

Bread Them in a Bag

Breading the onion rings twice is essential to getting the big crunch we want. But it can get messy—unless you do it in a bag, as we do here.

Double-breading leads to big crunch.

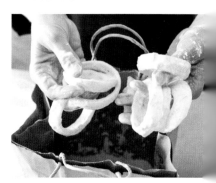

These tasty morsels pop with the flavors of aromatic spices, lemon, garlic, and mint.

Greek Meatballs

Our aim: tender party snacks with flavors inspired by Greece—by way of Alabama. **by Cecelia Jenkins**

GREEK MEATBALLS
Serves 8 to 10
You can substitute ground beef for the ground lamb, if desired.

MEATBALLS

20	square saltines
½	cup milk
½	cup chopped fresh mint, plus leaves for sprinkling
6	scallions, minced
2	tablespoons dried oregano
5	garlic cloves, minced
1	tablespoon grated lemon zest
2	teaspoons ground cumin
2	teaspoons ground coriander
1½	teaspoons pepper
1¼	teaspoons table salt
2	pounds ground lamb

SAUCE

1	cup plain whole-milk yogurt
½	cup tahini
¼	cup lemon juice (2 lemons)
1	teaspoon table salt
½	teaspoon pepper

1. FOR THE MEATBALLS: Adjust oven rack to upper-middle position and heat oven to 450 degrees. Set wire rack in aluminum foil–lined rimmed baking sheet.
2. Place saltines in large zipper-lock bag, seal bag, and crush fine with rolling pin (you should end up with 1 scant cup crushed saltines). Combine saltines and milk in large bowl, mashing with rubber spatula until paste forms, about 1 minute.
3. Add chopped mint, scallions, oregano, garlic, lemon zest, cumin, coriander, pepper, and salt to saltine mixture and mash until thoroughly combined. Add lamb and mix with your hands until thoroughly combined.
4. Divide mixture into 40 portions (1 heaping tablespoon each). Roll portions between your wet hands to form 1½-inch meatballs and evenly space on prepared wire rack. Roast until meatballs are lightly browned, about 20 minutes.
5. FOR THE SAUCE: While meatballs roast, whisk all ingredients together in bowl; set aside.
6. Using tongs, transfer meatballs to serving platter. Serve with sauce and sprinkle with mint leaves.

TO MAKE AHEAD
Uncooked meatballs can be frozen for up to 2 months. After shaping meatballs in step 4, transfer to greased plate and freeze until completely frozen, at least 2 hours. Transfer frozen meatballs to 1-gallon zipper-lock freezer bag. To serve, cook from frozen and increase roasting time to 25 minutes.

1. FREEZE ON PLATE

E-Z Freeze
These delicious meatballs are practically made to be frozen. Simply freeze the raw meatballs on a plate, transfer to a zipper-lock bag, and freeze them for up to two months. You can cook the frozen meatballs on a wire rack set in a rimmed baking sheet whenever company unexpectedly stops by.

2. BAG AND KEEP IN FREEZER

3. COOK FROM FROZEN ON WIRE RACK

T JOHNNY'S RESTAURANT in Homewood, Alabama, you won't find he meatballs on top of spaghetti, ll covered with cheese. At Johnny's, hey're a reflection of owner Tim Hontzas's Greek heritage and Southern upbringing, made with lamb and ull of bright herb flavor and warm pices. Inspired, I hit the kitchen to reate my own version.

Existing recipes for Greek meat-alls (aka *keftedes*) gave me mixed esults. Some versions were perfect ut required more work than I wanted o invest. Other versions were unbal-nced: too heavy on the cinnamon, or example, or too light on the herbs. My goal was to create a tender, juicy neatball with a Greek twist that had old yet balanced garlic and herb fla-or and was perfectly perfumed with pices and lemony brightness. Just ight for the holidays.

I started with ground lamb, a core ngredient in Greek cuisine. Tasters greed that fresh mint and scallions, as well as dried oregano with its licorice undertones, provided the best mix. Garlic and lemon zest added pungency and brightness, and citrusy coriander and earthy cumin provided fragrant complexity and depth.

A panade—a mixture of liquid and starch—can help keep meatballs tender and juicy. After experimenting with panko and regular dried bread crumbs (too gummy) and fresh bread crumbs (too sweet), I chose crushed saltines and milk. Just right.

I prefer roasting meatballs in the oven to searing them on the stovetop because it means hands-off browning and no splatter. For these party-size meatballs, about an inch and a half in diameter, I found that 450 degrees for about 20 minutes did the trick: The meatballs were cooked through with flavorful browning on top. A quick tahini and yogurt dip was just perfect for these Greek-inspired snacks.

Now these were meatballs worth singing about.

COOKIES COOKIES COOKIES

It's baking season. Actually, every season is baking season as far as we're concerned. But with the holidays ahead, it's time to kick your kitchen (and your sweet tooth) into high gear.

Your first step is a visit to the grocery store to stock up on butter, sugar, flour, and other baking essentials. Then, block off an afternoon and call in the troops to help. Start with one of these three new cookie recipes and visit **CooksCountry.com/holidaycookies** for even more sweet ideas.

TIPS TO GET YOU STARTED

BAKING IN BATCHES	SOFTENING BUTTER	CHOCOLATE
When baking in batches, make sure the baking sheets have cooled before adding the next round of dough. Our winning baking sheet is the **Nordic Ware Baker's Half Sheet**.	If a recipe calls for softened butter, it should be 67 degrees; be sure to take it out of the refrigerator about 30 minutes before using.	Choose your chocolate wisely. Our favorite dark chocolate is **Ghirardelli 60% Cacao Bittersweet Chocolate Premium Baking Bar**. Our favorite cocoa is **Droste Cacao**.
PARCHMENT PAPER	USE A SCALE	OVEN TEMPERATURE
Use parchment paper to keep the cookies from sticking to the baking sheets. We like **King Arthur Flour Parchment Paper 100 Half-Sheets**.	It is more precise to measure baking ingredients by weight than by volume. Our favorite scale is the **OXO Good Grips 11 lb Food Scale with Pull Out Display**.	Position the oven racks before heating the oven. Use an oven thermometer to make sure your temperature settings are accurate. Our favorite is the **CDN Pro Accurate Oven Thermometer**.

SEND COOKIES AS HOLIDAY GIFTS!

Follow our packing tips in "Ask Cook's Country" on page 2.

ADDING CHIPS

Let the chocolate chips sit atop the caramel layer for 5 minutes to soften before swirling.

Turtle Bars

Three layers of fun. **by Jessica Rudolph**

Walk into any candy shop and you'll find chocolate turtles nestled among the truffles and nougats. These seductive clusters of pecans, caramel, and chocolate got their name in 1918 when a candy dipper in Chicago noted that their rounded shape resembled a turtle.

I used chocolate turtles as inspiration for layered bar cookies for the holidays. After making a sturdy chocolate shortbread base, I created a caramel layer by cooking down dulce de leche, butter, brown sugar, cream, and corn syrup; stirring in some toasted pecans; and spreading this mixture over the shortbread. Some chocolate chips swirled into the still-warm caramel melted beautifully, and a sprinkle of flake sea salt was the perfect finish.

TURTLE BARS

Makes 24 bars

Dulce de leche, a thick, caramel-like sauce, can be found in the international or baking aisle of most supermarkets. If you can't find it, you can substitute one 14-ounce can of sweetened condensed milk, but the topping's caramel flavor won't be as strong. For a caramel topping with the right texture, monitor the temperature with an instant-read thermometer as it cooks; it is essential to bring the mixture to between 235 and 240 degrees in step 4 for the caramel to set up properly. If you're using an electric stove, the mixture will likely take longer than 11 minutes to reach 235 degrees once it starts to boil. Using a large heavy-bottomed saucepan and stirring frequently will help ensure that the caramel doesn't scorch.

CRUST

- 1²/₃ cups (8¹/₃ ounces) all-purpose flour
- ½ cup (3½ ounces) granulated sugar
- ⅓ cup (1 ounce) unsweetened cocoa powder
- ¾ teaspoon table salt
- 12 tablespoons unsalted butter, melted

TOPPING

- 1 (13.4-ounce) can dulce de leche
- 1 cup packed (7 ounces) light brown sugar
- ½ cup heavy cream
- ½ cup light corn syrup
- 8 tablespoons unsalted butter
- ½ teaspoon table salt
- 2 cups coarsely chopped pecans, toasted, divided
- 1 cup (6 ounces) semisweet chocolate chips
- ½ teaspoon flake sea salt

1. Adjust oven rack to middle position and heat oven to 350 degrees. Make foil sling for 13 by 9-inch baking pan by folding 2 long sheets of aluminum foil; first sheet should be 13 inches wide and second sheet should be 9 inches wide. Lay sheets of foil in pan perpendicular to each other, with extra foil hanging over edges of pan. Push foil into corners and up sides of pan, smoothing foil flush to pan. Spray foil with vegetable oil spray.

2. FOR THE CRUST: Combine flour, sugar, cocoa, and salt in bowl. Add melted butter and stir with rubber spatula until evenly moistened. Crumble dough over bottom of prepared pan. Press dough to even thickness using bottom of dry measuring cup. Using fork, poke dough all over, about 20 times. Bake until crust is fragrant and looks dry, 18 to 20 minutes. Transfer pan to wire rack. (Crust needn't cool completely before adding topping.)

3. FOR THE TOPPING: Combine dulce de leche, sugar, cream, corn syrup, butter, and table salt in large heavy-bottomed saucepan. Bring to boil over medium heat, 7 to 9 minutes, stirring frequently with rubber spatula.

4. Once boiling, continue to cook, stirring frequently to prevent scorching, until mixture registers between 235 and 240 degrees in several places, 9 to 11 minutes longer. (Mixture will be thick and bubbling vigorously.)

Off heat, stir in 1½ cups pecans. Pour caramel mixture over crust and spread to even thickness. Sprinkle with chocolate chips and let sit until chocolate chips have softened, about 5 minutes.

5. Swirl softened chocolate chips through caramel mixture using butter knife. Sprinkle with remaining ½ cup pecans and flake sea salt. Let bars sit at room temperature until chocolate is set, at least 3 hours.

6. Using foil overhang, lift bars out of pan. (Caramel may stick to foil. Use paring knife to separate, if necessary.) Cut into 24 pieces (5 cuts by 3 cuts) and serve. (Bars can be stored in airtight container at room temperature for up to 5 days.)

LAYERED CRUNCH

Tossing some nuts with the dulce de leche adds crunch to the middle layer, too.

TOASTING NUTS

Toast the nuts in a 350-degree oven for 5 to 7 minutes, stirring often. They should be light brown all the way through.

EASY MELTING

Microwave method: Chop chocolate and nuke at 50 percent power, stirring often, until no chunks remain.

COOLING TIM

These cookies wil look underbaked when you remove them from the oven. They'll firm up as they cool on the sheet for 30 minutes.

Chocolate Brownie Cookies

Chewy, crinkly, and superchocolaty. **by Matthew Fairman**

The best brownies balance their sweetness with deep chocolate flavor accented with a bit of salt to bring out the chocolate's complexity. They're rich and chewy with a pleasant, dense fudginess and a crackly, shiny top. So why not make a brownie in cookie form?

To maximize the chocolate's complexity, I used both melted bittersweet chocolate and cocoa powder plus a good dose of salt, which helped intensify the chocolate flavor. The key to chewiness was a mix of butter and vegetable oil, and using both baking soda and powder ensured that my cookies would spread just enough and crackle on top.

STICKY BATTER?

Grease your portioning measure (a 1-tablespoon measure or #30 scoop) so the batter doesn't stick.

CHOCOLATE BROWNIE COOKIES
Makes 20 cookies

We developed this recipe using Ghirardelli 60% Cacao Bittersweet Chocolate Premium Baking Bar and Droste Cacao Dutch-processed cocoa powder.

- 1 cup (5 ounces) all-purpose flour
- ¼ cup (¾ ounce) Dutch-processed cocoa powder
- 1 teaspoon baking powder
- ¼ teaspoon baking soda
- ¾ teaspoon table salt
- 10 ounces bittersweet chocolate, chopped, divided
- 3 tablespoons vegetable oil
- 1 tablespoon unsalted butter
- 2 tablespoons whole milk
- 1 cup (7 ounces) sugar
- 2 large eggs

1. Adjust oven racks to upper-middle and lower-middle positions and heat oven to 300 degrees. Line 2 rimmed baking sheets with parchment paper. Whisk flour, cocoa, baking powder, baking soda, and salt together in bowl; set aside.

2. Microwave 6 ounces chocolate, oil, and butter in medium bowl at 50 percent power, stirring halfway through microwaving, until melted, about 3 minutes. Whisk milk into chocolate mixture until combined.

3. Using stand mixer fitted with whisk attachment, whip sugar and eggs on medium-high speed until very thick and pale, about 4 minutes. Remove bowl from mixer. Add melted chocolate mixture and whisk by hand until uniform. Fold in flour mixture with rubber spatula until thoroughly combined and no dry pockets remain. Fold in remaining 4 ounces chocolate.

4. Using 1-tablespoon measure or #30 scoop, scoop 10 heaping-tablespoon portions of batter onto each prepared sheet (you should have 20 cookies total). (Use soupspoon to help scrape batter from tablespoon, if necessary.) Bake until cookies are puffed and covered with large cracks (cookies will look raw between cracks and seem underdone), about 16 minutes, switching and rotating sheets halfway through baking.

5. Let cookies cool completely on sheets, about 30 minutes. Slide thin spatula under cookies to remove from sheets. Serve. (Cookies can be stored in airtight container at room temperature for up to 3 days.)

TWO FATS

Vegetable oil and butter combine for the right mix of saturated and unsaturated fats to create the perfect chew.

Biscochitos

southwestern holiday favorite.

Morgan Bolling

Many home cooks in New Mexico use butter or shortening to make simple cinnamon-and-anise-flavored biscochito cookies, but old-school purists such as Angie Delgado (see "On The Road") use lard (aka rendered pork fat) to give them a faint savory note. Together with sweet sugar, floral vanilla, festive cinnamon, and the heady licorice flavor of crushed anise seeds, this choice of fat helps balance the cookie.

To be fair, when I experimented with butter and shortening, these also produced lovely holiday treats. Tossed in cinnamon sugar after they come out of the oven, they're just perfect with a cup of coffee or glass of bubbles.

NEW MEXICO BISCOCHITOS

Makes about 48 cookies

We developed this recipe using John Morrell Snow Cap Lard. We prefer the flavor and texture lard gives these cookies, but ⅔ cup of softened unsalted butter or vegetable shortening can be substituted, if desired.

- ¾ cups (8¾ ounces) all-purpose flour
- ¼ teaspoon baking powder
- ¼ teaspoon plus pinch table salt, divided
- ½ teaspoons anise seeds
- ⅔ cup (4⅔ ounces) lard
- ¾ cup (5¼ ounces) sugar, divided
- 1 large egg
- ½ teaspoon vanilla extract
- ¼ teaspoon ground cinnamon

Whisk flour, baking powder, and teaspoon salt together in bowl; set aside. Place anise seeds in zipper-lock bag, seal bag, and crush seeds coarse with rolling pin or meat pounder.

2. Using stand mixer fitted with paddle, beat lard, ½ cup sugar, and crushed anise seeds on medium-high speed until light and fluffy, about 3 minutes. Add egg and vanilla and beat until combined, scraping down bowl as needed. Reduce speed to low, slowly add flour mixture, and mix until just combined.

3. Turn out dough onto counter. Divide dough in half (about 9 ounces per half) and roll each half into 6-inch log. Wrap dough logs tightly in plastic wrap, roll against counter to form tight cylinder, and refrigerate until firm, at least 3 hours or up to 3 days.

4. Adjust oven rack to middle position and heat oven to 350 degrees. Line 2 baking sheets with parchment paper. Slice dough logs into ¼-inch-thick rounds, rolling logs as you cut to keep circular shape of dough. Evenly space cookies on prepared sheets (about 24 cookies per sheet). Bake cookies, 1 sheet at a time, until edges are lightly browned, 13 to 15 minutes, rotating sheet halfway through baking. Let cookies cool on sheets for at least 5 minutes.

5. Combine cinnamon, remaining pinch salt, and remaining ¼ cup sugar in shallow dish. Gently toss cookies, a few at a time, in cinnamon sugar. Transfer to wire rack and let cookies cool completely, at least 30 minutes, before serving. (Cookies can be stored in airtight container for up to 3 days.)

CINNAMON SUGAR

Toss slightly warm cookies in cinnamon sugar for a final sweet, spicy flourish.

ON THE ROAD

Baking Biscochitos with the Queen

Angie Delgado pulls a 1-pound block of lard from her shopping bag; it's the most important ingredient in her biscochitos. For her, butter just won't do if you're after the real thing. She's arrived with all her ingredients premeasured and portioned, along with a sturdy white cookie press that looks like a caulking gun, her preferred method for shaping biscochitos. The recipe was passed down to her from her great-grandmother, and she puts tremendous value on preserving that legacy. "Although," she whispers to me, "I don't follow all the directions."

Angie is the former First Lady of Santa Fe and a past Fiesta Queen of the Fiesta de Santa Fe. She's eaten these cookies all her life. They've shown up at every birthday, wedding, baptism, holiday, and family gathering for generations. Of the ingredients laid before us on the counter, I inquire about a small vial of whiskey. She giggles and tells me that while she prefers Jack Daniels, wine is a suitable substitute. "But I'm happy when Jack's in the house," she says as her smile widens and her laugh fills the colorfully tiled kitchen. Time to make cookies.

Boiled Eggs

Boiling eggs was already easy, but we made it foolproof.

by Matthew Fairman

BOILED EGGS

Makes 8 eggs
Start timing after adding the last egg to the boiling water. This recipe works equally well with as few as two eggs; however, the timing changes when more than eight eggs are cooked at once.

8 large eggs

1. Bring 12 cups water to boil in large saucepan over high heat. Fill large bowl halfway with ice and water.

2. Using spider skimmer or slotted spoon, gently lower eggs into boiling water and cook for 7 minutes for soft-cooked eggs or 13 minutes for hard-cooked eggs. Transfer eggs to ice bath and let cool for 5 minutes.

3. To peel, gently tap 1 egg on counter to crack shell all over. Begin peeling off shell at wider end of egg, making sure to break membrane between shell and egg white. Under gently running water, carefully peel membrane and shell off egg. Repeat with remaining 7 eggs. Serve.

With our simple method and timetable, it's easy to make boiled eggs however hard or soft you like them.

Web subscribers can access the results of our kitchen timers testing at **CooksCountry.com/timers**.

Step by Step

1. Measure water
Use a liquid measuring cup to measure out 12 cups of water for cooking the eggs.
Why? Using a measured amount of water ensures dependable results; cooking the same number of eggs in more or less water would change the cooking time.

2. Boil water
Bring the water to a boil over high heat in a large saucepan.
Why? Adding eggs to boiling water sets the edge of the egg white quickly, causing it to pull away from the membrane, which makes peeling easier.

3. Set up ice bath
Fill a large bowl halfway with ice and cold water.
Why? The ice bath needs to be set up and ready to use as soon as the eggs are done cooking.

4. Lower eggs into water
Use a spider skimmer or slotted spoon to gently lower the eggs into the boiling water. Work quickly and avoid splashing.
Why? The raw eggs are fragile. Gently setting them on the bottom of the pot helps prevent them from cracking.

5. Set timer and cook
Cook the eggs for exactly 7 minutes for soft-cooked eggs or 13 minutes for hard-cooked eggs.
Why? With a precise amount of boiling water, these times result in boiled eggs perfectly cooked to your preference.

DEVILED EGG SALAD
Serves 4

A pastry cutter makes easy work of chopping the eggs and blending the salad. If you don't have one, simply chop the eggs with a knife before stirring them together with the remaining ingredients.

- 8 hard-cooked large eggs
- ⅓ cup mayonnaise
- 2 tablespoons Dijon mustard
- 2 teaspoons Tabasco sauce
- ½ teaspoon table salt
- ½ teaspoon pepper
- ¼ cup minced celery
- ¼ cup chopped dill pickles

Using pastry cutter, chop eggs, mayonnaise, mustard, Tabasco, salt, and pepper in bowl until combined and egg whites are cut into rough ¼-inch pieces. Stir in celery and pickles. Serve.

Egg Storage

Does your refrigerator have an egg holder built into the door? If so, don't use it (at least not for eggs). We recommend storing eggs in their carton on a shelf. Why? The door is usually the warmest place in a refrigerator, and it's better to store eggs in a colder environment on the shelf. The carton helps the eggs retain their natural moisture and keeps the eggs from absorbing smells and flavors from potent ingredients nearby.

Gear

TIMER

Sure, you can use the timer built into your stove or mobile phone, but our favorite, the **OXO Good Grips Triple Timer ($20)**, can time three projects at once. This squat, sturdy triple timer is simple and intuitive, with a dedicated "clear" button and a full 0-to-9 keypad. It displays all its timers at once, so you can check everything at a glance, and its stainless-steel face is easy to clean.

SPIDER SKIMMER

Spider skimmers are great for removing large pasta (such as ravioli), dumplings, gnocchi, or boiled vegetables from boiling water. Our favorite, the **Rösle Wire Skimmer ($35)**, has a basket made from a single smooth spiral of thick wire. This beautiful, long-handled, well-balanced spider skimmer is easy to maneuver and clean and capable of handling fragile foods with care.

6-MINUTE EGG
Yolk still a little too runny and undercooked

7-MINUTE EGG
Perfectly soft-cooked, runny yolk
Our Favorite Soft-Cooked

8-MINUTE EGG
Between soft- and medium-cooked

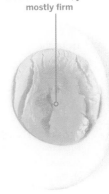
9-MINUTE EGG
Medium-cooked; center of yolk still very soft

10-MINUTE EGG
Medium-cooked; yolk solid but gooey

11-MINUTE EGG
Medium-cooked; yolk mostly firm

12-MINUTE EGG
Mostly hard-cooked; some soft yolk

13-MINUTE EGG
Perfectly hard-cooked
Our Favorite Hard-Cooked

14-MINUTE EGG
A shade overcooked; yolk a little chalky

6. Shock eggs
Use your spider skimmer or spoon to remove the eggs and place them in the ice bath. **Why?** Shocking the eggs in ice water halts their cooking, ensuring that they don't overcook. It also cools them quickly, decreasing the waiting time before peeling.

7. Crack shells
Gently crack the shells all over by tapping the eggs on the counter. **Why?** Cracking the entire shell makes for the most efficient peeling.

8. Begin peeling
Use your fingers to start peeling from the wider end of the egg. **Why?** Eggs have an air pocket between the egg white and the shell at the wider end. It's easiest to begin peeling here.

9. Grab shell and membrane
Pinch both the shell and the thin membrane and pull to remove together. **Why?** Grabbing both the shell and membrane allows you to peel larger, flexible sheets away from the egg white and keep the egg white unblemished.

10. Finish peeling
Continue to peel the eggs under gently running water. **Why?** The water will further facilitate the membrane and shell coming off together. This results in less damage to the egg white.

Chicken Fricassee

A surprise ingredient—apple—brings fricassee into the modern age.

by Jessica Rudolph

CHICKEN FRICASSEE IS a traditional country-style chicken dish in which chicken pieces are seasoned and dredged in flour, lightly browned, braised with broth and onions, and then served with a creamy sauce made from the braising liquid. The dish has been around for ages, and it can sometimes taste that way—many old recipes yield bland chicken covered in a gloppy sauce.

A few years ago, though, we developed a recipe that breathed new life into chicken fricassee by adding apples—their sweet, fruity acidity cuts through the rich cream sauce and adds complexity and interest. That recipe is much beloved in the test kitchen (and beyond), but I wanted to further streamline it into an even faster weeknight dinner for two.

Our previous recipe called for browning thin slices of apple in butter, removing them from the pan, and later stirring them back into the cream sauce before serving. I hoped to cut down on time and effort by leaving the apple slices in the skillet through the whole process instead.

I started with a trimmed-down version of our existing recipe, which used boneless chicken breasts instead of bone-in pieces. I dredged two boneless, skinless chicken breasts in flour and then browned them in melted butter in a nonstick skillet. After removing the chicken, I browned apple slices and kept them in the pan while I built the braising liquid with chopped onion, apple cider, chicken broth, and whole sprigs of thyme. I added the chicken back in and simmered it, covered, until the meat was cooked through, and then removed it from the skillet and reduced the sauce with some cream, finishing it with a touch of cider vinegar. I put the chicken, apple, and sauce on a platter and sprinkled it all with minced chives before serving.

The resulting dish had winning flavor, but the apple was (perhaps predictably) mushy from the extended cooking time. Cutting the apple into thicker 1-inch wedges solved that

Wedges of fresh apple, plus cider and cider vinegar, give our modernized fricassee extra spark.

problem. Since the thicker apple wedges were taking up less space in the skillet, I tried browning the chicken and apple together instead of in batches to shave off even more time. Success; this version came together in a snap and left me with barely any dishes to clean. The one complaint my tasters had was that the apple flavor was too subtle. Doubling the amount of cider I added to my braising liquid—and omitting the chicken broth entirely—did the trick. The sauce was fruity and gently sweet but still savory and nicely balanced.

The final version of my recipe clocked in at about 20 minutes total cooking time—half the cooking time and serving size of the original, but with every bit as much flavor.

A Tight Fit

Don't worry if the skillet seems too full. The chicken, apple, and onion will all brown evenly if you follow the recipe.

CHICKEN FRICASSEE WITH APPLE FOR TWO

If you use chicken breasts that weigh more than 8 ounces, your cooking times will be different and you run the risk of overreducing the apple cider. You can substitute apple juice if apple cider is unavailable, though the resulting sauce will be less rich.

- 2 (6- to 8-ounce) boneless, skinless chicken breasts, trimmed
- ¾ teaspoon table salt, divided
- ½ teaspoon pepper, divided
- 2 tablespoons all-purpose flour
- 2 tablespoons unsalted butter
- 1 Fuji, Gala, or Braeburn apple, unpeeled, cored and cut into 1-inch-thick wedges
- ¾ cup chopped onion
- ½ cup apple cider
- 2 sprigs fresh thyme
- ¼ cup heavy cream
- 1 teaspoon cider vinegar
- 1½ teaspoons minced fresh chives

1. Pat chicken dry with paper towels and sprinkle with ½ teaspoon salt and ¼ teaspoon pepper. Spread flour in shallow dish.

2. Melt butter in 12-inch nonstick skillet over medium-high heat. Dredge chicken in flour to coat, shake to remove excess, and add to skillet. Place apple cut side down in skillet around chicken. Cook, flipping apple as needed, until evenly browned on cut sides and chicken is golden brown on bottom, about 5 minutes.

3. Flip chicken. Leaving chicken and apple in skillet, add onion, remaining ¼ teaspoon salt, and remaining ¼ teaspoon pepper and cook, stirring occasionally, until onion is softened and browned, about 4 minutes.

4. Add cider and thyme sprigs to skillet and bring to boil. Reduce heat to medium-low, cover, and simmer until chicken registers 160 degrees, 6 to 8 minutes.

5. Transfer chicken to platter. Add cream to skillet, increase heat to medium-high, and bring to boil. Cook until sauce has thickened slightly, about 2 minutes. Stir in vinegar and any accumulated chicken juices. Discard thyme sprigs and season with salt and pepper to taste. Spoon sauce and apple over chicken and sprinkle with chives. Serve.

Pasta with Sausage, Mushrooms, and Peas

Lively lemon zest, bright peas, and summery basil help chase away the winter doldrums in this refreshing one-pot pasta. **by Cecelia Jenkins**

THE BEST WAY to pull off a one-pot pasta dinner is to forgo the standard approach of boiling, draining, and saucing the pasta. Instead, the test kitchen often calls for cooking the pasta in a carefully controlled amount of liquid that reduces into a flavorful sauce. With this technique in mind, I set out to combine pasta, meat, and vegetables into a satisfying, light, and lively winter dish.

For a flavorful base, I started by taking a few links of sweet Italian sausage out of their casings and browning the crumbles in a Dutch oven with sliced cremini mushrooms. I then deglazed the pot with dry white wine.

I looked at existing test kitchen recipes and determined that 4 cups of liquid was needed to cook 12 ounces of pasta—plenty for four people—and reduce into a sauce with just the right texture. As for the pasta shape, small shells perfectly cradled the bits of sausage and mushrooms. In a test of water versus chicken broth for the liquid, my tasters liked the cleaner flavor of water.

How about something green? I considered adding spinach or broccoli, but neither was as easy nor as bright as frozen peas, which I could add without thawing. Inspired by the springy, fresh turn the dish had taken, I added a handful of fresh basil to lighten the feel of the meaty mushrooms and sausage. A good amount of grated lemon zest added another bright boost.

One final step remained: stirring it all vigorously for 1 minute. Agitating it this way knocked starch from the pasta into the small amount of cooking liquid, transforming it into a sauce that lightly cloaked each shell.

ONE-POT PASTA WITH SAUSAGE, MUSHROOMS, AND PEAS
Serves 4

You can substitute white mushrooms for the cremini and 12 ounces (3⅓ cups) of orecchiette for the medium pasta shells, if desired. The pasta will not absorb all the cooking liquid in step 2; stirring vigorously in step 3 helps thicken the sauce so it will coat the pasta. For a nonalcoholic version, substitute ½ cup of water for the wine in step 2 and stir in 1 tablespoon of lemon juice with the lemon zest in step 3. There is no need to thaw the peas.

- 1 pound cremini mushrooms, trimmed and sliced thin
- 1 pound sweet Italian sausage, casings removed
- 2 shallots, chopped
- 1¼ teaspoons table salt
- 1 teaspoon pepper
- ¼ teaspoon red pepper flakes
- ½ cup dry white wine
- 12 ounces (4½ cups) medium pasta shells
- 4 cups water
- 2 cups frozen peas
- 1 cup fresh basil leaves, chopped
- 1 ounce Parmesan cheese, grated (½ cup), plus extra for serving
- 2 teaspoons grated lemon zest, plus lemon wedges for serving

1. In large Dutch oven set over high heat, cook mushrooms, sausage, shallots, salt, pepper, and pepper flakes, stirring mixture frequently and breaking up meat with wooden spoon, until liquid has evaporated and browned bits have formed on bottom of pot, about 15 minutes.

2. Add wine and cook, scraping up any browned bits, until liquid has evaporated, about 2 minutes.

3. Stir in pasta and water and bring to boil. Reduce heat to medium-low, cover, and simmer, stirring occasionally, until pasta is al dente, about 10 minutes (some liquid will remain in bottom of pot).

4. Off heat, add peas, basil, Parmesan, and lemon zest. Stir vigorously for 1 minute, until sauce has thickened. Serve, passing lemon wedges and extra Parmesan separately.

Three Stages of Cooking

1. Build a base Brown mushrooms, sausage, and shallots in Dutch oven.

2. Cook pasta After deglazing pot, add pasta and water and cook for 10 minutes.

3. Finish Add peas, basil, Parmesan, and zest and stir vigorously to emulsify sauce.

Easy Homemade Hot Sauce

For an all-purpose hit of heat and peppery flavor, we turn to an age-old method. **by Matthew Fairman**

MAKING HOT SAUCE from fermented chiles delivers exceptional results (most supermarket hot sauces are fermented), but to understand why you'd ever want to do it yourself, it might help to step back and talk about what fermentation is and what it does.

Think of the difference between milk and Parmigiano-Reggiano, or between grapes and a prized French Burgundy. Fermentation preserves raw foods and infuses them with an array of new aromas and flavors. With a few days of fermentation, the chiles for hot sauce go from raw and aggressive to tart and fruity with an overarching savory complexity. So why do it yourself, instead of just leaving it to the pros? Well, not only is it easy and completely safe, but it gives you the ability to customize the heat, acidity, and saltiness for a sauce that is specific to your preferences.

The process starts simply: Just submerge your raw chiles in salted water and wait. After various tests, we settled on four days for the best results. The briny environment inhibits the growth of mold and pathogens and encourages the growth of a friendly family of lactic acid bacteria that transforms the chiles in delicious ways and creates the kind of acidic environment that ensures your food remains safe to eat (see "Preservation Through Fermentation").

Our favorite chiles to use for a well-rounded, dynamic hot sauce are fruity, fiery Fresnos. Sweet red bell pepper and a little bit of sugar balance the heat of the Fresnos and yield a brilliant-red sauce that has just enough heat but doesn't overwhelm the palate. Further tailoring the spice level to individual taste is as simple as leaving out some or all of the Fresnos' seeds. A bit of olive oil adds sheen and mild richness.

With just a few ingredients and a little bit of patience to let fermentation work its magic, this hot sauce rewards you with flavors that will have you trying countless new ways to incorporate it into your meals. Whether it's slathered on an egg sandwich, splashed onto a fish taco, stirred into a bowl of noodles, or drizzled all over a slice of pizza, I think you'll agree that it's worth the wait.

EASY HOMEMADE HOT SAUCE
Makes about 1 cup

This recipe makes a medium-spicy hot sauce. For a spicier sauce, include all the Fresno chile seeds. For a milder sauce, remove the seeds from the chiles. We recommend wearing rubber gloves when handling the chiles. If you can't find Fresno chiles, you can substitute red jalapeño chiles. The leftover brine can be used in marinades, dressings, cocktails, and on its own as a condiment to spice up soups or braised greens.

- 2 tablespoons kosher salt for brining
- 8 ounces Fresno chiles, stemmed and halved lengthwise
- 4 ounces (1 cup) coarsely chopped red bell pepper
- 1 tablespoon sugar
- 1 teaspoon kosher salt
- 2 tablespoons extra-virgin olive oil

1. Whisk 2 cups water and 2 tablespoons salt together in 4-cup liquid measuring cup until salt is dissolved. Remove seeds from half of Fresnos. Place Fresnos and bell pepper in 1-quart Mason jar, pressing peppers firmly into bottom of jar.

2. Pour brine into jar with peppers, making sure liquid covers peppers. Fill 1-quart zipper-lock bag with ⅓ cup water, press out air, and seal bag. Place bag of water on top of peppers in jar to keep submerged in brine. Affix jar lid but only partially tighten, leaving lid loose enough to allow air to escape as mixture ferments.

3. Let jar sit at room temperature away from direct sunlight for 4 days. Check container daily, skimming residue from surface and ensuring that peppers remain submerged. (After 2 or 3 days, brine will become cloudy and bubbles will rise to surface when jar is moved.)

4. Drain peppers in fine-mesh strainer, reserving brine for another use, if desired. Process peppers, sugar, and salt in food processor until coarsely pureed, about 1 minute, scraping down sides of bowl as needed. Add oil and pulse until combined, about 2 pulses. Refrigerate hot sauce in airtight container until ready to use. (Hot sauce can be refrigerated for up to 3 months.)

You can adjust the heat level of this tasty hot sauce by altering the amount of chile seeds.

Preservation Through Fermentation

If you're not an experienced fermenter, this recipe might seem a little weird. Is it safe to store the peppers and brine outside the refrigerator for days on end? Have no fear: The salt water creates a selective environment in which the growth of harmful bacteria and molds is severely limited and the conversion of sugar to lactic acid—a natural preservative—is encouraged. Fermentation has been used as a method of food preservation and flavor enhancement for millennia. Pass the hot sauce!

FRESNO CHILE

DAY 1 **DAY 2** **DAY 3** **DAY 4**

Southern-Style Smothered Pork Chops

For the best version, you need to choose the right chops—and season them well. **by Natalie Estrada**

I AM A huge fan of rich, meaty southern-style smothered pork chops. They're the epitome of simple, satisfying comfort food: Just heavily season the chops, sear them, and then simmer them in a roux-based onion gravy until they're perfectly tender.

Unfortunately, many versions of smothered pork chops disappoint—especially the handful of existing slow-cooker recipes I prepared for my colleagues in the test kitchen. Their comments ranged from "really tough meat" to "bland and boring" to "resembles horrible diner food."

I set out to create a slow-cooker recipe for smothered pork chops that lived up to its full potential. My first step toward that goal was choosing the right chops. The chops in my initial tests were tough because they were too lean—and lean cuts dry out when they are overcooked. So I turned to bone-in blade chops. Blade chops contain a good bit of fat and connective tissue that can be chewy if the chops are cooked quickly, but when they are cooked slowly and gently, that fat and connective tissue breaks down and melts away. After about 5 hours on low in the slow cooker, the blade chops were meaty and tender.

But how to season them? Many southern recipes call for Lawry's Seasoned Salt, and my tasters gave it an enthusiastic thumbs-up here. Sweet paprika, savory onion powder, granulated garlic, and lots of potent black pepper amplified the seasoning. A side-by-side test of chops seared on the stovetop and chops placed in the slow cooker raw resulted in a draw, so I chose to put them in raw to save myself a step. On to the gravy.

I started by sautéing sliced onions in plenty of oil, stirring in some flour, and finally whisking in broth. I found it easier to soften the onions and then simply scatter them over the raw chops in the slow cooker instead of keeping them in the skillet while I built my roux (which is necessary to create a properly thick gravy here). So after transferring the onions to the slow cooker, I added more oil to the skillet, stirred in some flour, and added the broth. Another test proved that there was enough flavor in my seasoning mix for plain water to work just as well

A splash of cider vinegar adds a final pop of freshness to these soft, savory chops.

as broth. Blooming some reserved seasoning mix in the roux brought out its flavors even more.

Two final steps brought this recipe home: Skimming the fat from the surface of the sauce at the end of cooking (so the gravy wasn't too greasy) and adding a glug of cider vinegar before serving to provide a spark of brightness.

No Lawry's? No Problem!

If you don't have any Lawry's Seasoned Salt on hand, you can mix your own. Simply stir together the ingredients listed below. (If you are making the Slow-Cooker Smothered Pork Chops, you'll have an extra teaspoon of our homemade blend; it's great sprinkled on eggs or sandwiches.)

CORNSTARCH
1/4 teaspoon

PAPRIKA
1 teaspoon

ONION POWDER
1/4 teaspoon

SUGAR
1/2 teaspoon

TABLE SALT
1 tablespoon

GRANULATED GARLIC
1 teaspoon

SLOW-COOKER SMOTHERED PORK CHOPS *Serves 6*

Bottled preground pepper is bland and dusty, so for the best results, grind your own peppercorns. Be sure to use blade-cut pork chops in this recipe; they have enough fat to keep them from drying out over the prolonged cooking time. Serve the chops and gravy with steamed white rice or egg noodles. Garnish with sliced scallions, if desired.

- 1 tablespoon plus 2 teaspoons Lawry's Seasoned Salt
- 2 teaspoons paprika
- 1½ teaspoons onion powder
- 1½ teaspoons pepper
- 1 teaspoon granulated garlic
- 6 (8- to 10-ounce) bone-in blade-cut pork chops, ¾ to 1 inch thick, trimmed
- ½ cup vegetable oil, divided
- 3 cups thinly sliced onions
- ½ cup all-purpose flour
- 2½ cups water
- 1½ teaspoons cider vinegar

1. Combine seasoned salt, paprika, onion powder, pepper, and granulated garlic in bowl. Pat chops dry with paper towels and sprinkle all over with 2 tablespoons spice mixture. Transfer chops to slow cooker.

2. Heat 2 tablespoons oil in 12-inch skillet over medium-high heat until shimmering. Add onions and cook until softened, 5 to 7 minutes. Scatter onions evenly over chops in slow cooker.

3. Whisk flour and remaining 6 tablespoons oil together in now-empty skillet. Cook over medium heat, whisking constantly, until roux is color of peanut butter, 3 to 5 minutes. Whisk in remaining spice mixture and cook until fragrant, about 30 seconds.

4. Slowly whisk water into roux mixture until gravy is smooth and free of lumps. Bring to boil, then pour gravy over chops and onions in slow cooker. Cover and cook until chops are tender, about 5 hours on low.

5. Carefully transfer chops to platter (chops will be delicate and may fall apart). Using wide spoon, skim fat from surface of gravy. Stir vinegar into gravy and season with salt and pepper to taste. Pour gravy over chops on platter. Serve.

Milk Chocolate

Candy for kids? Not anymore—we found milk chocolate bars for even the pickiest chocolate connoisseur. **by Lauren Savoie**

IN 2018, THE Specialty Food Association noted that more manufacturers than ever are making "dark milk" chocolates—products that feature higher cacao percentages but still contain enough milk for a smooth, creamy texture and nuanced flavor. These products are meant to appeal to those looking for something more robust than classic milk chocolate but not quite as bitter as some dark chocolates.

When we last tasted milk chocolate, we named Dove Silky Smooth Milk Chocolate as our winner. But with so many new products pushing the boundaries of milk chocolate, it was time to take another look. We gathered 10 nationally available products, priced from about $0.40 to about $1.30 per ounce, and sampled them plain and in Milk Chocolate Pots de Crème.

Our top two milk chocolates had cacao percentages higher than 40 percent, and the winning chocolate had the highest cacao percentage of all: 48 percent. Milk chocolates with lower cacao percentages had more sugar than those with higher cacao percentages. Our winning product contains 35 percent sugar, while lower-ranked products contain as much as 58 percent sugar. While not unpleasant, products that contained more sugar were described by tasters as "one-note" and "ultrasweet." For the most robust chocolate flavor, we recommend purchasing a product that lists chocolate as the first ingredient over products that list milk or sugar first.

Products with a higher cacao percentage made thick, luscious pots de crème. A higher cacao percentage means that the chocolate contains more cocoa solids, a feature that helps puddings set up thicker. By contrast, products with lower cacao percentages made runny and drippy pots de crème. Although we ultimately chose not to factor the pots de crème test into our final rankings, it's important to use a milk chocolate with a high cacao percentage if you're making a recipe that relies heavily on the chocolate for its texture.

We can recommend all the products we tasted, especially for eating plain. In both the plain and pots de crème tastings, we preferred milk chocolates that had balanced sweetness, prominent cocoa notes, and a hint of bitterness. Our favorite milk chocolate bar is Endangered Species Chocolate Smooth + Creamy Milk Chocolate, which we loved for its nuanced chocolate flavor and balanced sweetness.

Go to **CooksCountry.com/milkchocolate** to read the full testing and see the complete results chart.

---

❶ Our Favorite
Endangered Species Chocolate
Smooth + Creamy Milk Chocolate
48% **cacao**

RECOMMENDED

❷ *41%* **cacao**

"Deeply cocoa"-flavored, "on the border of milk and dark chocolate." Vanilla beans add complexity.

"Rich" and "caramel-y"; not just one-note sweetness. "Smooth" and "slick" texture.

❸ *31%* **cacao**

"Sweet," "almost syrupy," with a "classic" milk chocolate creaminess and smooth texture.

❹

❻ This British chocolate, now being made and sold in the United States by Hershey's, was "creamy," "sweet," and "ultramilky." Tasters liked its "tender," "melt-in-your-mouth" texture.

❺ *31%* **cacao**

❼ "Soft," almost "melty," with "ultrasweet," prominent "caramel" notes.

"Soft" and "creamy," with a prominent "milkiness" and a slight "malted" taste.

❾ "Ultrasweet," "comforting," and "familiar" flavor was deemed "one-note" by some.

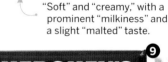

❽ *27-32%* **cacao**

"Sweet" and "milky," with trace notes of vanilla. "Classic" and "simple" milk chocolate.

❿ *45%* **cacao**

"Complex," "robust" flavor; a bit "funky" for milk chocolate.

Color = Complexity

There's an inverse relationship between the proportion of sugar or milk to the amount of cocoa solids and cocoa butter (cacao percentage) in the milk chocolates we tasted. The darker the milk chocolate, the higher its cacao percentage, which translates into a more complex flavor.

← more cacao - less sugar   more sugar - less cacao →

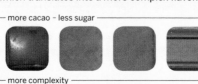

← more complexity   less complexity →

Not all manufacturers would disclose their cacao percentages.

Inexpensive Stand Mixers

We tested six models against our previous major-brand winner. Could any stand up to the challenge? **by Lisa McManus**

STAND MIXERS WORK wonders when you want to whip up layer cakes, cookies, meringue, or bread, but if you're only an occasional baker—or just don't have a lot of dough to spend in a stand mixer—do you really need a high-end model? When we last tested stand mixers, we named the KitchenAid KSM75WH Classic Plus Series 4.5-Quart Tilt-Head Stand Mixer our Best Buy. With new contenders available for less than $200, is it still the best? We bought six challengers to find out.

Every mixer came with three standard attachments: a whisk for whipping, a paddle for creaming, and a dough hook for kneading. We whipped heavy cream and egg whites with the whisk attachments, creamed ingredients in cookie dough and cake batter with the paddles, and kneaded stiff dough for bagel bread and sticky dough for ciabatta with the hooks.

While most mixers could perform all these tasks, some models struggled to fully mix the ingredients. When we tried to whip two egg whites, two models flopped—one just spun its whisk above the egg; another left unwhipped egg beneath the whipped portion. It's an unusually small amount of egg white to whip, but our test demonstrated that some mixers couldn't handle small volumes of ingredients. To get to the bottom of the issue, we measured the space between the bowl bottom and each attachment, and the results were revealing: A greater gap between the bowl bottom and the attachment equaled a less efficient mixer. One model's paddle attachment didn't extend far enough around the bowl;

when we made cookies, mixing with the paddle happened only in the center, leaving the bowl walls lined with a thick coating of dry ingredients. You may have to stop and scrape the bowl at least once with most mixers, but this one required it many more times.

Some of the mixers struggled when kneading heavy doughs. They rocked and whined throughout, an indication of motor strain and potential long-term durability issues. Two emitted a burning-oil smell and their casing felt hot.

All the mixers in our lineup were "tilt-head" models: You access the bowl by tilting back the horizontal head of the mixer, usually by pushing a button or lever that unlocks it. We strongly preferred models that offered head-release buttons or latches that were easy to use. A bowl handle wasn't essential, but we prefer to have a large, vertical handle that makes it easy to grip the bowl securely. Finally, we preferred heavier mixers, as we found that they were more stable.

After all the whipping and mixing, we had a (repeat) winner: The KitchenAid KSM75WH Classic Plus Series 4.5-Quart Tilt-Head Stand Mixer. Our previous winner outperformed its competition once again. Its mixing action is highly efficient and powerful; ingredients came together quickly and blended thoroughly; and it handled difficult doughs with ease. While most of the models we tested worked adequately, those mixers took more time and more effort from the cook.

7 Mixers 7 Tests

- Measure total actual bowl capacity using water poured to top of attachment
- Record total weight of machine, with bowl in place
- Whip 1 cup heavy cream to stiff peaks
- Whip 2 egg whites to stiff peaks
- Cream butter and sugar to pale, aerated consistency in sugar cookie recipe
- Reverse-cream flour mixture with pats of butter in cake recipe
- Knead heavy dough for extended session in bagel bread and ciabatta recipes

Go to **CooksCountry.com/mixers** to read the full testing and see the complete results chart.

Key to Efficiency

The best mixers have less space between the bottom of the attachment and the bowl; the worst have more.

MORE SPACE = BAD   **LESS SPACE = GOOD**

HIGHLY RECOMMENDED   CRITERIA

KitchenAid KSM75WH Classic Plus Series 4.5-Quart Tilt-Head Stand Mixer
Model: KSM75WH
Price: $207.99   **Stated Capacity:** 4.5 qt
Actual Capacity: 3 qt   **Weight:** 21.8 lb
Distance from Bowl to Paddle: 5 mm

Whipping ★★★
Creaming ★★★
Kneading ★★★
Ease of Use ★★½
Design ★★½

This old favorite aced every test, whipping, creaming and kneading quickly and thoroughly.

RECOMMENDED

Farberware 6 Speed 4.7-Quart Professional Stand Mixer
Model: SM3481RBG
Price: $99.99 (walmart.com exclusive)
Stated Capacity: 4.7 qt
Actual Capacity: 3.7 qt   **Weight:** 14.7 lb
Distance from Bowl to Paddle: 3 mm

Whipping ★★★
Creaming ★★★
Kneading ★★½
Ease of Use ★★½
Design ★★

This mixer excelled at mixing and creaming, but felt a little underpowered when kneading.

Oster Planetary Stand Mixer
Model: FPSTSMPL1
Price: $199.99   **Stated Capacity:** 4.5 qt
Actual Capacity: 3.3 qt   **Weight:** 12.75 lb
Distance from Bowl to Paddle: 6.3 mm

Whipping ★★★
Creaming ★★½
Kneading ★★½
Ease of Use ★★½
Design ★★★

This compact, lightweight mixer is easy to lift, but it was loud and struggled a bit with heavy jobs.

RECOMMENDED WITH RESERVATIONS

Bosch Compact Tilt-Head Stand Mixer
Model: MUM4405
Price: $159.00   **Stated Capacity:** 4 qt
Actual Capacity: 3 qt   **Weight:** 6.4 lb
Distance from Bowl to Paddle: 5 mm

Whipping ★★½
Creaming ★★½
Kneading ★★★
Ease of Use ★½
Design ★½

This toylike mixer works surprisingly well but slowly. Some of the design features were annoying.

Cuisinart SM-50R Stand Mixer
Model: SM-50R
Price: $154.25   **Stated Capacity:** 5.5 qt
Actual Capacity: 3.6 qt   **Weight:** 16.65 lb
Distance from Bowl to Paddle: 10.4 mm

Whipping ★★½
Creaming ★★
Kneading ★½
Ease of Use ★★
Design ★★★

This sturdy mixer had big gaps between the attachments and bowl, making for inefficient work.

Hamilton Beach Eclectrics All-Metal Stand Mixer
Model: 63232
Price: $199.00   **Stated Capacity:** 4.5 qt
Actual Capacity: 3 qt   **Weight:** 15.85 lb
Distance from Bowl to Paddle: 5 mm

Whipping ★★★
Creaming ★★★
Kneading ★
Ease of Use ★★
Design ★★

This model mixed and creamed like a champ, but it struggled to knead.

NOT RECOMMENDED

Sencor Foodie Stand Mixer
Model: STM43OR
Price: $199.99   **Stated Capacity:** 4.75 qt
Actual Capacity: 3.5 qt   **Weight:** 18.75 lb
Distance from Bowl to Paddle: 18.75 mm

Whipping ★★
Creaming ★★
Kneading ★½
Ease of Use ★★
Design ★★

Kneading was a struggle: The mixer rocked, "walked," and smelled like burning oil.

KEY   **Good** ★★★   **Fair** ★★   **Poor** ★

Coquito

Many families with Latin American heritage have their own treasured version of this recipe. We like our Coquito, which is based on a Puerto Rican version, served over ice—but some folks swear by drinking it chilled, without ice. It's your call!

COQUITO

Serves 8 to 10

We tested this recipe using Coco López brand cream of coconut, which is often found in the soda and drink-mix aisle of the grocery store.

- 1 (15-ounce) can cream of coconut
- 1 (14-ounce) can coconut milk
- 1 (12-ounce) can evaporated milk
- 1¼ cups gold rum
- 1 teaspoon vanilla extract
- ½ teaspoon ground cinnamon
- ¼ teaspoon ground nutmeg, plus extra for serving

1. Whisk all ingredients together in large pitcher until combined. Refrigerate for at least 1 hour or up to 3 days.
2. Just before serving, working in batches, transfer cream of coconut mixture to blender and process until slightly frothy, about 1 minute per batch. Serve over ice, garnished with extra nutmeg.

We're looking for recipes that you treasure—the ones that have been handed down in your family for a generation or more, that always come out for the holidays, and that have earned a place at your table and in your heart through many years of meals. Send us the recipes that spell home to you. Visit CooksCountry.com/recipe_submission (or write to Heirloom Recipes, Cook's Country, 21 Drydock Avenue, Suite 210E, Boston, MA 02210) and tell us a little about the recipe. Include your name and address. If we print your recipe, you'll receive a free one-year subscription to Cook's Country.

FIND THE ROOSTER!

A tiny version of this rooster has been hidden in a photo in the pages of this issue. Write to us with its location and we'll enter you in a random drawing. The first correct entry drawn will win our favorite inexpensive stand mixer, and each of the next five will receive a free one-year subscription to Cook's Country. To enter, visit CooksCountry. com/rooster by December 31, 2019, or write to Rooster DJ20, Cook's Country, 21 Drydock Avenue, Suite 210E, Boston, MA 02210. Include your name and address. Juliana Bolsinger of Northbrook, Illinois, found the rooster in the August/September 2019 issue on page 8 and won our favorite 8-inch square baking dish.

WEB EXTRAS

Free for four months online at **CooksCountry.com**

Cranberry Curd
Easy Vanilla Buttercream
Orange–Olive Oil Layer Cake
Roasted Butternut Squash with Goat Cheese and Pepitas

READ US ON IPAD

Download the Cook's Country app for iPad and start a free trial subscription or purchase a single issue of the magazine. All issues are enhanced with Cooking Mode slide shows that provide step-by-step instructions for completing recipes, plus expanded reviews and ratings. Go to CooksCountry.com/iPad to download our app through iTunes.

U.S. POSTAL SERVICE STATEMENT OF OWNERSHIP, MANAGEMENT AND CIRCULATION

1. Publication Title: *Cook's Country*; 2. Publication No. 1552-1990; 3. Filing date: 10/01/19; 4. Issue frequency: Dec/Jan; Feb/Mar; Apr/May; Jun/Jul; Aug/Sept; Oct/Nov; 5. No. of issues published annually: 6; 6. Annual Subscription Price is $35.70; 7. Complete mailing address of known office of publication: 21 Drydock Avenue, Suite 210E, Boston, MA 02210; 8. Complete mailing address of headquarters or general business office of publisher: 21 Drydock Avenue, Suite 210E, Boston, MA 02210; 9. Full names and complete mailing addresses of publisher, editor, and managing editor. Publisher, David Nussbaum, 21 Drydock Avenue, Suite 210E, Boston, MA 02210, Editor, Tucker Shaw, 21 Drydock Avenue, Suite 210E, Boston, MA 02210, Managing Editor, Todd Meier, 21 Drydock Avenue, Suite 210E, Boston, MA 02210; 10. Owner: America's Test Kitchen LP; 21 Drydock Avenue, Suite 210E, Boston, MA 02210; 11. Known bondholders, mortgages, and other securities: NONE; 12. Tax status: Has Not Changed During Preceding 12 Months; 13. Publication title: *Cook's Country*; 14. Issue date for circulation data below: August/September 2019; 15A. Total number of copies: Average number of copies each issue during the preceding 12 months: 325,294 (Aug/Sep 2019: 338,867); B. Paid circulation: 1. Mailed outside-county paid subscriptions. Average number of copies each issue during the preceding 12 months: 252,881 (Aug/Sep 2019: 262,626); 2. Mailed in-county paid subscriptions. Average number of copies each issue during the preceding 12 months: 0 (Aug/Sep 2019: 0); 3. Sales through dealers and carriers, street vendors and counter sales. Average number of copies each issue during the preceding 12 months: 13,617 (Aug/Sep 2019: 16,748); 4. Paid distribution through other classes mailed through the USPS. Average number of copies each issue during the preceding 12 months: 0 (Aug/Sep 2019: 0); C. Total paid distribution. Average number of copies each issue during preceding 12 months: 266,597 (Aug/Sep 2019: 279,374); D. Free or nominal rate distribution (by mail and outside mail); 1. Free or nominal Outside-County. Average number of copies each issue during the preceding 12 months: 1,274 (Aug/Sep 2019: 1,525); 2. Free or nominal rate in-county copies. Average number of copies each issue during preceding 12 months: 0 (Aug/Sep 2019: 0); 3. Free or nominal rate copies mailed at other Classes through the USPS. Average number of copies each issue during preceding 12 months: 0 (Aug/Sep 2019: 0); 4. Free or nominal rate distribution outside the mail. Average number of copies each issue during preceding 12 months: 725 (Aug/Sep 2019: 725); E. Total free or nominal rate distribution. Average number of copies each issue during preceding 12 months: 1,999 (Aug/Sep 2019: 2,250); F. Total free distribution. Average number of copies each issue during preceding 12 months: 268,596 (Aug/Sep 2019: 281,624); G. Copies not Distributed. Average number of copies each issue during preceding 12 months: 56,698 (Aug/Sep 2019: 57,243); H. Total. Average number of copies each issue during preceding 12 months: 325,294 (Aug/Sep 2019: 338,867); I. Percent paid. Average percent of copies paid for the preceding 12 months: 99.26% (Aug/Sep 2019: 99.20%)

Cranberry-Orange Olive Oil Cake

Bring the magic of snow inside with this dazzling and delightful cake.

by Sarah Ewald

TO MAKE THIS CAKE, YOU WILL NEED:

- **1¾ cups (12¼ ounces) plus 2 tablespoons sugar, divided**
- **2 (3- to 4-inch-long) fresh rosemary sprigs**
- **10 ounces (2½ cups) frozen cranberries**
- **¼ cup Grand Marnier or other orange liqueur**
- **1 recipe Orange–Olive Oil Layer Cake***
- **1 recipe Easy Vanilla Buttercream***
- **1 recipe Cranberry Curd***

FOR THE TOPPING:

Place ¾ cup sugar in shallow dish; set aside. Bring 1 cup sugar and 1 cup water to boil in medium saucepan over high heat; cook, stirring constantly, until sugar dissolves, about 3 minutes. Off heat, dip rosemary sprigs in sugar syrup, then roll in sugar in dish. Transfer to plate.

Stir cranberries into syrup in saucepan and let syrup cool completely, about 30 minutes. (Cranberries in syrup can be refrigerated for up to 24 hours.) Drain cranberries in fine-mesh strainer; discard syrup. Working in 3 batches, roll cranberries in sugar in dish and transfer to large plate. Let stand at room temperature to dry, about 1 hour.

FOR THE GRAND MARNIER SYRUP:

Bring Grand Marnier, ¼ cup water, and remaining 2 tablespoons sugar to boil in small saucepan over medium heat; cook until sugar dissolves, about 3 minutes. Let cool completely, about 30 minutes.

TO ASSEMBLE:

Brush Grand Marnier syrup over top and sides of each cake layer. Fill pastry bag fitted with ½-inch-wide straight tip with 1 cup buttercream. Place 1 cake layer on cake turntable. Using half of buttercream, pipe ½-inch-high ring of buttercream around top perimeter of cake layer. Spread half of cranberry curd (about 1 scant cup) evenly inside buttercream ring. Place second cake layer on top, pressing lightly to adhere. Pipe another ½-inch-high ring of buttercream around top perimeter of cake layer with remaining buttercream in pastry bag. Spread remaining cranberry curd evenly inside buttercream ring. Top with remaining cake layer, pressing lightly to adhere. Refrigerate to allow buttercream to firm up, about 30 minutes.

Spread ¾ cup buttercream evenly over top of cake. Spread remaining buttercream evenly over sides of cake to cover with thin coat of buttercream. Run edge of offset spatula around cake sides to create sheer veil of frosting so cake beneath is visible. Scatter ½ cup cranberries around bottom of cake. Pile remaining cranberries on top of 1 side of cake in half-moon shape. Place rosemary sprigs at base of half-moon shape. Serve.

Our recipes for Orange–Olive Oil Layer Cake, Easy Vanilla Buttercream, and Cranberry Curd are available for free for four months at CooksCountry.com/cranberrycake.

INSIDE THIS ISSUE